1948

1948

Harry Truman's Improbable Victory and the Year That Transformed America's Role in the World

DAVID PIETRUSZA

UNION SQUARE PRESS
New York

UNION SQUARE PRESS
New York

An Imprint of Sterling Publishing
387 Park Avenue South
New York, NY 10016

STERLING and the distinctive Sterling logo are registered trademarks of
Sterling Publishing Co., Inc.

ISBN 978-1-4027-6748-7 (hardcover)
ISBN 978-1-4027-9082-9 (ebook)

Distributed in Canada by Sterling Publishing
^c/o Canadian Manda Group, 165 Dufferin Street
Toronto, Ontario, Canada M6K 3H6
Distributed in the United Kingdom by GMC Distribution Services
Castle Place, 166 High Street, Lewes, East Sussex, England BN7 1XU
Distributed in Australia by Capricorn Link (Australia) Pty. Ltd.
P.O. Box 704, Windsor, NSW 2756, Australia

For information about custom editions, special sales, and premium and corporate purchases,
please contact Sterling Special Sales at 800-805-5489 or specialsales@sterlingpublishing.com.

Manufactured in the United States of America

2 4 6 8 10 9 7 5 3 1

www.sterlingpublishing.com

A. M. D. G.

CONTENTS

CAST OF CHARACTERS

Col. Jacob M. Arvey: Fifty-two-year-old Chicago Democratic leader. A rare non-Irish (Jewish, in fact) big-city boss. Passionately liberal. The five-foot-four-and-a-half-inch Arvey, desperate for victory in 1948, contends that Gen. Dwight D. Eisenhower is "the kind of liberal with whom we could win, both nationally and locally."

Lauren Bacall: Brooklyn-bred twenty-something Hollywood star. The legs on Harry Truman's piano.

C. B. "Beanie" Baldwin: Forty-six-year-old, Virginia-born former executive vice president of Sidney Hillman's Political Action Committee of the Congress of Industrial Organizations (CIO-PAC). Henry Wallace's Progressive Party campaign manager in 1948. A covert Communist.

Tallulah Bankhead: Forty-six-year-old Hollywood and Broadway star. Daughter of the late Speaker of the House, William Bankhead. "Tom Dewey," the Alabama-born Tallulah informs a nationwide radio audience, "is not a real man."

Alben W. Barkley: Seventy-year-old Democratic U.S. senator from Kentucky. Senate minority leader. Barkley's electrifying 1948 convention keynote speech eventually propels him to the vice-presidential nomination. "It will have to come quick," the Kentuckian finally complains, but adds, "I don't want it passed around so long it is like a cold biscuit."

Elliott V. Bell: Forty-six-year-old New York State superintendent of banks. Tom Dewey's hunchbacked Columbia University classmate, speechwriter, and alter ego. "If anyone can be tagged as the architect of the disaster," says one historian of the campaign, "it is Bell."

Elmer A. Benson: Fifty-three-year-old Progressive Party chairman. Defeated by Harold Stassen for reelection as Minnesota governor in 1938.

Andrew J. Biemiller: Forty-two-year-old former Socialist Party member and Milwaukee Democratic congressman. Cosponsor, with Hubert Humphrey, of the liberal civil rights plank adopted at the 1948 Democratic National Convention (DNC). In Harry Truman's opinion, "Crackpot Biemiller."

Leslie L. Biffle: Sixty-eight-year-old secretary to Senate Minority Leader Alben Barkley. Truman suspects "my 'good' friend" Biffle of angling to replace him with Barkley, but by campaign's end, the diminutive Biffle will embark on an undercover personal mission to gauge the embattled Truman's support. One of a handful of political operatives who are convinced Truman will win. "They don't make them any better than Biffle," says Truman publicly, "and you can quote me on that."

Chester Bliss Bowles: Forty-seven-year-old, blue-blooded former New Deal price-controls czar. Democratic candidate for Connecticut governor in 1948. Quintessentially liberal. Aboard, albeit with deep reservations, the July 1948 draft-Ike movement.

David Brinkley: Twenty-eight-year-old, North Carolina–born NBC News White House correspondent.

Herbert Brownell Jr.: Forty-four-year-old Manhattan attorney. Former chairman of the Republican National Committee. Tom Dewey's uneasy campaign manager in 1944 and 1948.

McGeorge Bundy: Twenty-nine-year-old Boston Brahmin. Dewey speechwriter and member of his elite shadow State Department. "There was only one rule," recalled Bundy: "Never write anything the governor hasn't said before."

Warren Earl Burger: Forty-one-year-old St. Paul, Minnesota, attorney. A key player in Harold Stassen's energetic but ill-fated effort.

Whittaker Chambers: Forty-seven-year-old *Time* magazine editor. Onetime Soviet espionage operative. His bombshell charges against former New Dealer Alger Hiss ("the closest friend I ever had in the Communist Party") will fuel the Reds-in-government issue erupting just before Election Day 1948. "I know that I am leaving the winning side for the losing side," Chambers tells the House Un-American Activities Committee (HUAC), "but it is better to die on the losing side than to live under communism."

Clark M. Clifford: Forty-one-year-old special counsel to the president. Truman's most influential adviser. The handsome, wavy-haired Clifford shamelessly assumes credit for James Rowe's startlingly prescient blueprint for the 1948 Democratic victory. "The greatest ambition Harry Truman had," Clifford will recall, "was to get elected in his own right."

T. Eugene "Bull" Connor: Birmingham, Alabama's fifty-one-year-old segregationist public safety commissioner. In May 1948, Connor arrests Progressive Party vice-presidential nominee Glen H. Taylor. Says Connor, "There's not enough room in town for Bull and the Commies." Will he arrest Henry Wallace as well?

Jonathan W. Daniels: Forty-six-year-old Truman campaign aide, on leave from his post as editor of the *Raleigh News & Observer*. Former press secretary to both Truman and FDR.

Jo Davidson: Sixty-five-year-old dean of American portrait sculptors. Honorary president of the Progressive Citizens of America (PCA). Cochairman of the Wallace-for-President Committee.

Thomas Edmund Dewey: New York's forty-six-year-old Republican Governor. Renowned former racket-busting Manhattan district attorney. GOP presidential nominee in 1944 and 1948. Derided by Alice Roosevelt Longworth as "the little man on the wedding cake." "You know that your future is still ahead of you," Dewey blandly tells voters. Dewey's already lies behind him.

William O. Douglas: Fifty-year-old U.S. Supreme Court justice. Former chairman of Franklin D. Roosevelt's Securities and Exchange Commission. Harry Truman wants him on his ticket; Douglas refuses, unwilling to be, as he jibes to a friend, "number two man to a number two man."

W.E.B. Du Bois: Eighty-year-old icon of the civil rights movement. For Wallace in 1948. "No president has spoken fairer on race discrimination than President Truman," contends the skeptical Du Bois, "and few presidents have done less."

Allen W. Dulles: Fifty-five-year-old Wall Street attorney and a key man in the wartime intelligence agency, the Office of Strategic Services (OSS). In 1948, Dewey's gout-ridden key adviser on foreign policy and intelligence issues.

John Foster Dulles: Allen Dulles's sixty-year-old brother. Dewey's foremost foreign policy counselor and his choice for secretary of state. Dulles's passion for a bipartisan foreign policy helps hamstring Dewey's campaign. Alger Hiss's mentor at the Carnegie Endowment for International Peace.

Dwight David "Ike" Eisenhower: Fifty-eight-year-old former supreme commander of Allied forces in Europe. Wildly popular in both parties. The choice of many Democrats to replace the unpopular Truman—but Ike responds, "I am not available for and could not accept nomination to high political office." In 1948, Eisenhower will, nonetheless, be inaugurated president—of Columbia University.

George M. Elsey: Truman's thirty-year-old, Harvard-trained speechwriter. Author of Truman's pivotal 1948 State of the Union address.

James V. Forrestal: Fifty-six-year-old secretary of defense. Staunch cold warrior. Opposed to Truman's recognition of the State of Israel. "You just don't understand," Forrestal lectures Clark Clifford. "Forty million Arabs are going to push 400,000 Jews into the sea. And that's all there is to it. Oil—that is the side we ought to be on."

Dwight H. Green: Fifty-one-year-old Illinois governor. Former Al Capone prosecutor—"The Chicago edition of Thomas Edmund Dewey." GOP Convention keynote speaker and possible vice-presidential nominee.

Frank "I am the Law" Hague: Seventy-two-year-old long-serving Democratic boss (and former mayor) of Jersey City. Anti-Truman. Pro-Ike.

Charles A. Halleck: Forty-eight-year-old Indiana Republican congressman. House majority leader. A conservative—but for Dewey. "Two Cadillac Charlie" thinks he's been promised Dewey's nod for vice president—but he hasn't. Halleck, Herbert Brownell would declare, "should have been grown-up enough to realize he didn't have a promise."

Dashiell Hammett: Fifty-four-year-old detective story writer—and Communist Party (CPUSA) member. Lillian Hellman's longtime lover. Of Henry Wallace, Hammett writes to Hellman, "He'd be better off leaving things alone and cross-breeding himself."

Robert E. "Bob" Hannegan: Forty-five-year-old St. Louis Democratic powerhouse. Former DNC chairman and U.S. postmaster general. In 1940, Hannegan saved Harry Truman's tottering Senate seat. In 1944 he helped deliver the vice presidency—and ultimately the presidency itself—to his Missouri ally.

William Randolph Hearst: Eighty-five-year-old press baron. Decades ago a radical Democrat, now a conservative Republican. Backer of Douglas MacArthur's abortive 1948 bid.

Lillian Hellman: Forty-three-year-old playwright and Communist Party member. Soon to be disillusioned with Henry Wallace. "I understand Henry Wallace," she warns her fellow party members. "When he loses, he will turn on all of you, and you will deserve it."

Alger Hiss: Forty-three-year-old president of the Carnegie Endowment for International Peace. Former assistant secretary of state and secretary-general of the United Nations Conference on International Organization. Hiss will vehemently deny Whittaker Chambers's accusation of being a Communist espionage agent. "They [the Republicans] are using these charges as a red herring," jeers Truman, "to keep them from doing what they ought to do."

Brig. Gen. Herbert C. Holdridge: An eccentric challenger to Harry Truman in 1948. "No more depression," promises the fifty-six-year-old Holdridge, "no more war, and no compromise with capitalism."

Hubert Horatio Humphrey Jr.: Thirty-seven-year-old mayor of Minneapolis. Backs the Ike boomlet. Hopeful of a vice-presidential nomination. In 1948, a candidate for the U.S. Senate. His forceful advocacy of a strong civil rights plank at the 1948 Democratic Convention helps further divide an already dangerously fractious party. "The time has arrived . . . for the Democratic Party to get out of the shadows of state's rights," Humphrey challenges, "and to walk forthrightly into the bright sunshine of human rights."

Harold LeClair Ickes: Acerbic seventy-four-year-old former secretary of the interior. No friend of Truman, "the Old Curmudgeon" ultimately campaigns for him anyway. "I could not but feel," Ickes confides to his diary, "that Truman presented something of a pathetic figure."

Leo Isacson: Thirty-eight-year-old Bronx congressman. His February 1948 election on the pro-Wallace American Labor Party (ALP) ticket shocks the political world.

Edward "Eddie" Jacobson: Fifty-seven-year-old former haberdashery partner of Harry Truman. At a crucial moment, Jacobson begs Truman to meet with the Zionist Chaim Weizmann. "You win," Truman informs his old buddy, "you bald-headed son of a bitch. I will see him."

Lyndon Baines Johnson: Forty-year-old ("old enough to know how and young enough to get the job done") Texas congressman. Once an ardent New Dealer. Now rapidly scurrying rightward, he covets a U.S. Senate seat. "The civil rights program," charges LBJ, "is a farce and a sham—an effort to set up a police state in the guise of liberty."

H. V. Kaltenborn: Seventy-year-old NBC news commentator. His election-night forecasts of a Dewey victory prove, shall we say, unfounded.

Oksana Stepanovna Kasenkina: Fifty-two-year-old Ukrainian-born tutor of natural sciences at the USSR's New York legation. Her dramatic August 1948 three-story leap to freedom brings Cold War realities home to Americans.

Lt. Gen. Curtis Emerson LeMay: Forty-one-year-old commander of the United States Air Force in Europe. Oversees the Berlin Airlift. "If the decision was fight," he will recall, "we would have hit the Russian air with everything we had. . . ."

Walter Lippmann: Fifty-nine-year-old dean of the nation's columnists. Liberalism's intellectual point man. To Lippmann, Harry Truman is "a president who . . . is not performing and gives no evidence of ability to perform."

Clare Boothe Luce: Forty-five-year-old playwright and conservative Republican former congresswoman from Connecticut. Wife of Time-Life publishing mogul, Henry Luce. The people, she informs the Republican National Convention, "understand now why the New Dealers were attracted—and are still attracted—by the Communists, and the Communists are even more attracted to the New Dealers."

Henry R. Luce: Fifty-year-old publisher of *Time, Life,* and *Fortune.* He hopes to be secretary of state under Arthur Vandenberg but settles on Dewey.

Gen. Douglas A. MacArthur: Sixty-eight-year-old supreme commander of the Allied powers in the Southwest Pacific. Darling of the GOP Right. "I do not actively seek or covet any office," MacArthur announces from Tokyo—but he's running anyway.

Norman Mailer: Twenty-five-year-old Sorbonne-educated author of *The Naked and the Dead*. He will stump for Wallace in the fall. "When they put the spotlight on me," Mailer boasts, "I'm going to stand up and say that I'm joining the Communist Party tomorrow."

Vito A. Marcantonio: Forty-five-year-old fellow-traveling East Harlem congressman. New York State chairman of the American Labor Party (ALP). For Wallace.

George Catlett Marshall Jr.: Sixty-seven-year-old U.S. secretary of state. Author of the Marshall Plan. As 1948 unfolds and Truman recognizes Israeli statehood, Marshall rebels. If Truman were to recognize Israel, Marshall angrily warns him, "and in the election I were to vote, I would vote against you."

Edward Martin: Sixty-nine-year-old U.S. senator from Pennsylvania and favorite-son candidate. Former governor. Key to Tom Dewey's nomination.

Joseph W. Martin Jr.: Sixty-three-year-old bachelor and Speaker of the House of Representatives. A rock-solid conservative. Dark-horse candidate for the GOP nomination.

Joseph Raymond "Joe" McCarthy: Thirty-nine-year-old freshman Republican U.S. senator from Wisconsin. An ardent Stassen backer.

J. Howard McGrath: Forty-four-year-old first-term Democratic U.S. senator from Rhode Island. Bob Hannegan's successor as national party chairman. He will alienate white southerners but successfully woo northern black voters.

Henry Louis "H. L." Mencken, "The Sage of Baltimore": Sixty-eight-year-old *Baltimore Sun* columnist. "Everybody named Henry should be put to death," proclaims the iconoclastic Mencken. "If somebody will do it for Henry Wallace, I promise to commit suicide."

William H. "Alfalfa Bill" Murray: Seventy-eight-year-old former Democratic governor of Oklahoma. Now a bedraggled Dixiecrat. "Social or any intimacy, with a Negro and white woman," writes Murray, "is too great a risk to tolerate or condone."

Reinhold Niebuhr: Fifty-six-year-old theologian and anticommunist liberal. Vice-chairman of the Liberal Party in New York. "I would," he says, "support almost any decent man to avoid four years of Republican rule."

Richard Milhous Nixon: Thirty-five-year-old, first-term Southern California congressman. Member of HUAC. Dubious regarding Alger Hiss's innocence. "He was rather insolent to me," Nixon later admits. "Frankly, I didn't like it."

Paul O'Dwyer: Forty-one-year-old Democratic and American Labor Party challenger to incumbent Manhattan congressman Jacob Javits. William O'Dwyer's brother. For Wallace.

William O'Dwyer: Fifty-eight-year-old Tammany mayor of New York City. Looking for an alternative to Truman. O'Dwyer, Truman sneers, is "a bandwagon boy."

Drew Pearson: Fifty-year-old Washington syndicated columnist. He will infuriate Harry Truman, embarrass Strom Thurmond and Henry Wallace, and bring down Congressman Parnell Thomas.

Westbrook Pegler: Vitriolic fifty-four-year-old right-wing Hearst columnist. In March 1948, he lambastes Henry "Galahad" Wallace over Wallace's "Guru letters."

Thomas Joseph "TJ" Pendergast: Now-deceased boss of Kansas City's spectacularly corrupt political machine. Harry Truman's original patron. The unsavory ghost that forever dogs Truman's reputation.

Claude Denson Pepper: Forty-eight-year-old New Deal senator from Florida. For Wallace, then for Truman, then for Ike—then for Pepper. "This is," says Pepper, "no time for politics as usual."

Lee Pressman: Forty-two-year-old architect of the Progressive Party platform. Former New Deal functionary. Fired in February 1948 as Congress of Industrial Organizations (CIO) general counsel. Brooklyn ALP congressional candidate. An underground, but hardly discreet, CPUSA member.

A. Philip Randolph: Fifty-nine-year-old president of the black Brotherhood of Sleeping Car Porters. Former Socialist Party activist. In 1948 Randolph threatens "mass civil disobedience" if Truman fails to integrate the armed services. He means it.

John E. Rankin: Sixty-six-year-old Mississippi congressman. The wizened former chair of HUAC. A rabid anti-Semite, but cosponsor of the Tennessee Valley Authority and a believer in Alger Hiss's innocence.

Samuel Taliaferro "Mr. Sam" Rayburn: Sixty-six-year-old Democratic House minority leader.

Ronald Wilson Reagan: Liberal thirty-seven-year-old Hollywood star. President of the Screen Actors Guild (SAG). Active in forming the Americans for Democratic Action (ADA) in 1948. "We must elect not only President Truman," Reagan informs a radio audience, "but also men like Mayor Hubert Humphrey."

Paul Robeson: Marvelously talented but increasingly controversial fifty-year-old black entertainer and left-wing political activist. Foursquare for Wallace and the Progressives. "Paul," his manager warns him, "in your going around defending labor, fighting for Wallace, you have no more concert career."

Nicholas Roerich: Exiled Russian painter, scientist, explorer, and mystic. Admired by Henry Wallace and the recipient of Wallace's controversial "Guru Letters." Died at age seventy-three in 1947.

Eleanor Roosevelt: FDR's sixty-four-year-old widow. A passionate liberal. She initially declines to endorse Truman and works behind the scenes to jettison her husband's heir. "I haven't actually endorsed Mr. Truman," she privately explains, "because he has been such a weak and vacillating person and made such poor appointments in his Cabinet and entourage."

Elliott Roosevelt: FDR's thirty-eight-year-old son. Eleanor's favorite. For Eisenhower.

Franklin Delano Roosevelt: Harry Truman's late four-term predecessor. The act that no Democrat could hope to follow.

Franklin D. Roosevelt Jr.: FDR's thirty-four-year-old son. Enthusiastic backer of Eisenhower.

James Roosevelt: FDR's forty-year-old son. California state Democratic chairman. Eventually another open backer of Eisenhower. "If your father knew what you are doing to me," Truman informs him, "he would turn over in his grave."

Judge Samuel I. Rosenman: Fifty-two-year-old Truman speechwriter and adviser. One of the few key former New Dealers still on the Truman team.

Charlie Ross: Harry Truman's Pulitzer Prize–winning but gray-haired and cadaverous-looking sixty-two-year-old press secretary.

James H. Rowe Jr.: Thirty-nine-year-old former New Deal insider. Distrusted by Truman but, nonetheless, the unheralded author of "Give 'em Hell" Harry's successful 1948 strategy.

Richard B. Russell Jr.: Fifty-one-year-old Democratic U.S. senator from Georgia. Segregationist. Harry Truman's formal opposition at the 1948 Democratic National Convention. Russell considers Truman's civil rights program "a vicious and unwarranted attack by the President of the United States on our Southern civilization."

Dorothy "Dolly" Schiff: Forty-five-year-old publisher of the liberal *New York Post*. The paper's editor (and her third husband), Theodore "Ted" Thackrey, sticks with Henry Wallace. Disgusted by Truman, Schiff stuns her staff by endorsing the Republican Dewey. Truman, Schiff informs her readers, "has proved himself to be the weakest, worst informed, most opportunistic President ever to hold the highest office in the land."

Arthur M. Schlesinger Jr.: Thirty-one-year-old Harvard associate professor and Pulitzer Prize–winning historian. Vigorously anticommunist, anti-Wallace liberal. Unenthusiastic regarding Truman.

Hugh D. Scott Jr.: Forty-seven-year-old moderate Republican congressman from Philadelphia's Chestnut Hill. Tom Dewey's mustachioed choice to chair the Republican National Committee.

Pete Seeger: Twenty-nine-year-old folk singer. Communist Party member. Progressive Party activist. "We have some people," he tells Henry Wallace, "who may believe that you can talk to God, but we have a great many who say you're just talking to yourself."

John W. Snyder: Fifty-three-year-old Treasury secretary. Harry Truman's crony—the liberals' bête noire.

Harold E. Stassen: Forty-one-year-old former GOP "boy wonder" governor of Minnesota. The internationalist Republican presidential hopeful for "the millions of Republicans who are tired of winning in June and losing in November."

Adlai Ewing Stevenson II: Forty-eight-year-old former New Dealer. Will second Alben Barkley's nomination at the 1948 Democratic National Convention. Dwight Green's erudite underdog opponent for Illinois governor.

Robert Alphonso Taft: Fifty-nine-year-old Republican U.S. senator from Ohio. Son of President William Howard Taft. Forthright but colorless leader ("Taft can't win") of the party's faltering conservative and isolationist wings. "Mr. Conservative" will dig in his heels when Truman convenes a special session of Congress. Says Taft of Truman: "We're not going to give that fellow anything."

Glen Hearst Taylor: Forty-four-year-old Democratic U.S. senator from Idaho. Erstwhile country-and-western singer. Henry Wallace's Progressive Party vice-presidential running mate. Singing cowboy Taylor has literally ridden his horse up the Capitol steps. "I think the pink Communists who believe in changes in our form of government by evolution rather than revolution, will support our party," explains Taylor. "The red Communists will support Mr. Dewey because they hope that the best way to get a revolution is to have another Hoover administration."

J. Parnell Thomas: Fifty-three-year-old Republican chairman of HUAC. High-profile investigator of Hollywood Communists and Alger Hiss. In August 1948, columnist Drew Pearson will expose Thomas's staff kickback schemes.

Norman Thomas: Sixty-three-year-old longtime Socialist Party activist. Former Presbyterian minister. Socialist Party presidential nominee in 1948, making his sixth—and final—run. "I have made almost as many farewell tours for the presidency as Sarah Bernhardt," he tells audiences. "But, ladies and gentlemen, this is your last chance."

J. Strom Thurmond: Forty-five-year-old governor of South Carolina. An ardent segregationist, formerly ardent with a black family servant and the father of her twenty-three-year-old illegitimate daughter. "Candidate by default" of the breakaway State's Rights ("Dixiecrat") Party. "Harry Truman has never been elected president of the United State," vows Thurmond, "and he never will be."

Elizabeth Wallace "Bess" Truman: Harry Truman's sixty-three-year-old First Lady and childhood sweetheart. "The Boss" detests Washington and remains profoundly skeptical of her husband's 1948 chances.

Harry S. Truman (HST): America's accidental chief executive in 1948, having become president upon FDR's April 1945 death. Self-educated, feisty, and intensely partisan. Sixty-four years old. Buffeted by both the right and left wings of his party. Nonetheless, "Give 'em Hell" Harry vows: "Senator Barkley and I will win this election and make those Republicans like it."

Margaret Truman: The Trumans' twenty-four-year-old only child. A star of her father's whistle-stop campaign tour. "Daddy," Miss Margaret warns him, "you shouldn't say 'hell.'"

Rexford Guy Tugwell: Fifty-seven-year-old former Roosevelt brain trust economist. A Progressive in 1948, but increasingly wary of Communist Party influence.

Arthur Hendrick Vandenberg: Sixty-four-year-old Michigan Republican U.S. senator. Pompous isolationist turned pompous internationalist. Dark-horse presidential hopeful. "At least two hundred members of the House—mostly Republican—hate my guts," admits Vandenberg.

George Corley Wallace: Twenty-nine-year-old delegate to the Democratic National Convention. "The South," says the Alabamian, "will not be crucified upon the cross of so-called civil rights."

Henry Agard Wallace: Sixty-year-old former U.S. vice president and secretary of commerce. He will challenge Truman in 1948 as the nominee of the far-left Progressive Party. "I would say," Wallace publicly contends, "that the Communists are the closest thing to the early Christian martyrs."

Earl Warren: Fifty-seven-year-old liberal Republican governor of California. Favorite-son candidate for the GOP presidential nomination. Republican vice-presidential candidate. "Maybe they know what they're doing," Warren confides to a family friend regarding the Dewey brain trust, "but I can tell you I never won any of *my* campaigns this way."

Nina Palmquist Warren: Earl Warren's fifty-five-year-old wife. The campaign will expose her long-buried family secret.

Essie Mae Washington-Williams: Twenty-three-year-old illegitimate daughter of Dixiecrat Strom Thurmond and black Thurmond-family housemaid Carrie Butler. "Well," Thurmond informs Essie Mae, "you look like one of my sisters. You've got those cheekbones like our family."

James A. Wechsler: Thirty-three-year-old *New York Post* Washington correspondent. Former member of the Young Communist League. For Wechsler, the 1948 campaign concludes with a punch in the nose at Henry Wallace's Park Avenue headquarters. "I tried to spell out the obvious facts about the men behind Wallace's campaign," Wechsler would recall, "but as the months passed, Wallace grew increasingly irritable at any reference to facts."

Harry Dexter White: FDR's assistant secretary of the Treasury and Truman's appointee to the International Monetary Fund. Accused by Whittaker Chambers and Elizabeth Bentley of being a Soviet agent, the fifty-six-year-old White will drop dead in August 1948.

Walter F. White: Fifty-five-year-old executive secretary of the National Association for the Advancement of Colored People (NAACP). W.E.B. Du Bois's longtime rival for black leadership. Doggedly pro-Truman. Extremely lightskinned, the mixed-race White will one day write, "I am a Negro. My skin is white, my eyes are blue, my hair is blond. The traits of my race are nowhere visible upon me."

Walter Winchell: Influential fifty-one-year-old *New York Daily Mirror* Broadway gossip columnist. An ardent FDR admirer, grievously disappointed in Harry Truman—"He's not a President."

Fielding L. Wright: Fifty-three-year-old segregationist Democratic governor of Mississippi. Strom Thurmond's Dixiecrat vice-presidential running mate. Wright warns his state's blacks that they would "be much happier in some other state than Mississippi" if they dare prefer integration.

1

"Three sizes too large"

He was barely twenty-three, an unlikely witness to great events, ambling down the aisle to a front-row seat at history's arena. Not originating from any private eastern boarding school or Ivy League campus, he came rather from North Carolina, and—for what it was worth—the best schools the South had to offer. Too bad David Brinkley hadn't graduated from any of them.

Discharged from the Navy for health reasons—not the easiest of accomplishments during a world war—he bounced from Montgomery to Nashville to Charlotte before seeking work in radio at CBS in Washington, D.C.

CBS didn't want him.

"Go to hell," Brinkley responded and walked four blocks to NBC. NBC had decided it needed a White House correspondent, and, as Brinkley himself admitted, he met their basic qualifications: "tall, white, Protestant and neatly dressed." He was not particularly well versed on any of the national and international issues he would need to cover each day, but NBC did not bother asking about such things. And he did not bother telling them.

He trundled nervously to the White House for his first presidential news conference, and found himself stationed but a few feet away from the president of the United States of America, part of a semicircle of jaded reporters, casually flicking cigarette and cigar ashes upon the White House carpeting.

What he saw scared him: the president of the United States—Franklin Delano Roosevelt—all monochrome and weak and fading.

"It was a shock, unnerving," Brinkley remembered. "Here was the most famous face in the world, one . . . seen a thousand times. In carefully edited newspaper and magazine and newsreel pictures it remained the face of a handsome man with strong, well-formed features, displaying a smiling, good-natured manner, chin tilted high, ivory cigarette holder pointed jauntily skyward. Those were the pictures. But here was the reality—a man in his early sixties who looked terribly old and tired. No doubt youth was too quick to notice the effects of age, but this man's face was more gray than pink, his hands shook, his eyes were hazy and wandering, his neck drooped in stringy, sagging folds accentuated by a shirt collar that must have fit at one time but now was two or three sizes too large."

David Brinkley saw it. The men in Roosevelt's Democratic Party—who loved FDR, but loved power more—saw it too. In their more cunning, less sentimental moments, they knew that this sick, gray man could not possibly survive another term. Whoever became the nation's next vice president would also be the nation's next president.

What they did not know was that whatever choice Franklin D. Roosevelt might make regarding a running mate would not only prove crucial for America in 1944, but would detonate their party four years hence, realigning it forever, setting in motion the most unlikely upset in all of American politics.

No, Franklin D. Roosevelt looked not well at all.

2

"You judge. I can't."

Harry Truman was not a haberdasher.

Not really.

Yes, he had *attempted* to be a haberdasher but had failed at it, rather quickly and spectacularly, at that. He was, however, a farmer, a husband and father, a veteran, a Mason, a Democrat, and ultimately—above all—a politician.

Harry was born in Lamar, Barton County, Missouri, on May 8, 1884, to John Anderson and Martha Ellen Young Truman. Hot-tempered John Anderson Truman traded horses and farmed. Both the paternal and maternal halves of Harry's lineage had migrated from Kentucky to rural Missouri, and at various times the Trumans and the Youngs owned substantial amounts of land. While neither family was rich, neither was poor either, though their fortunes might on occasion turn precarious.

Young Harry suffered from unusually poor eyesight ("blind as a mole," as he put it; his first pair of glasses cost ten dollars in 1892). Although bright enough, he did not start school until he was eight-and-a-half. He studied piano, becoming particularly proficient at Paderewski and Chopin—actually meeting Paderewski in 1900.

"To tell the truth," he once revealed, "I was kind of a sissy. If there was any danger of getting into a fight, I always ran."

He read voraciously. "I don't know anybody in the world that ever read as much or as constantly as he did," recalled his cousin Mary Ethel Noland. Most of all, he read history, taking away the lesson that the great men of America had been trained "on the farm, in finance, or in the military."

He also discerned that three things "get a man [destroyed]: No. 1 is power. . . . No. 2 is ambition for high social recognition. That is all tinsel and fake. No. 3 is appetite or inability to exercise physical restraint [i.e., drunkenness and lust]."

His first White House press secretary, Jonathan W. Daniels, sniffed that Truman's reading list was "the kind of history that McGuffey would have put into his [one-room schoolhouse] readers." But that was not such a bad thing. "He had a remarkable education," observed his fourth and final secretary of state, the exceedingly patrician Dean Acheson. "Mr. Truman read every book in the Independence Library, which had about 3,500 to 5,000 volumes, including three encyclopedias, and he read them all the way through. He took in a hell of a lot more . . . than he would listening to all the crap that goes on at Yale and Harvard."

Graduating from high school in 1901, he took work as a timekeeper for a contractor engaged with the Santa Fe Railroad, often sleeping in hobo jungles. His next job contained a modicum more prestige—bookkeeping (top salary sixty dollars a month) for a Kansas City bank. In 1904, on his father's orders, he returned to the family farm. There followed, he recalled, "the happiest days of my life," though the farm itself was not particularly profitable. Neither were his own ill-fated speculations in a zinc mine and oil wells, nor his father's disastrous adventure speculating in grain futures.

He courted Bess Wallace, his former Independence High School classmate. "I thought," he recalled, "she was the most beautiful and the sweetest person on earth." The Wallaces enjoyed a higher social station than the Trumans. But thanks to Bess's father's alcoholism, they now faced severe financial difficulties. Harry's courtship was steady, long, and not always successful. He proposed in June 1911—and she refused. That July 12 he wrote to her:

> You know that you turned me down so easy that I am almost happy anyway. I never was fool enough to think that a girl like you could ever care for a fellow like me but I couldn't help telling you how I felt. I have always wanted you to have some fine, rich, good-looking man, but I knew that if ever I got the chance I'd tell you how I felt even if I didn't even get to say another word to you. What makes me feel real good is that you were good enough to answer me seriously and not make fun of me anyway.

It was not until early 1917 that she accepted, just before he left for wartime France with the American Expeditionary Forces. "Just think of what [the Kaiser would] do to our country and our beautiful women if only he could. That is the reason we go. . . . They have no hearts or souls."

"Sometimes I think," their only child, Margaret, recorded, "he might [otherwise] not have married her until he was forty or fifty, and I might never have got here."

Harry Truman had once applied for admission to West Point; "short sight" caused his rejection. Now, as a captain of the 2nd Missouri Field Artillery, he discovered latent but very real leadership skills. As his Battery D threatened to disintegrate under German fire, he kept his head. Unleashing a barrage of profanity at his men, he prevented a rout, and his company did not lose a single man. "It really doesn't seem possible," he wrote home, "that a common old farmer boy could take a battery in and shoot it such a drive."

Harry returned home to establish both housekeeping with Bess (in Independence with her mother) and a haberdashery in downtown Kansas City. It went bust in 1922. Harry Truman blamed neither his extended inventory nor his limited business sense, but the Republicans in Washington.

In France, Truman had befriended Lt. James M. Pendergast, nephew of Kansas City Democratic boss Thomas Joseph "TJ" Pendergast. In 1922, the Pendergast machine required a candidate for the $3,465-a-year post of county judge (an administrative post, akin to a county commissioner or supervisor) representing Jackson County's rural western district. Jim Pendergast plumped Truman for the nomination. Though Harry had never previously sought public office, there existed a certain logic to his selection. He was a lifelong Democrat from a strong Democratic family. He was a Baptist and an active Mason (the Pendergast machine was top-heavy with Catholics). Within the district he boasted a sizable number of relatives and friends, particularly his fellow Battery D veterans. He was also a hard worker, genuinely enjoyed meeting people, and would emerge as a tireless campaigner.

At one point, however, he enjoyed meeting the white-sheeted brotherhood of the local Ku Klux Klan. Coveting its electoral support, he stood ready to join it, even depositing his ten-dollar initiation fee. They demanded, however, that he support no Catholics in patronage positions (a dangerous promise to make while aligned with the Pendergast clan). He drew away—and demanded his ten dollars back.

He won the five-man primary by 279 votes and triumphed 9,063 to 6,314 in November. But when the party split (and the Klan turned on him as well) in 1924, he was defeated 8,791 to 7,932 by only the second Republican the district ever elected. At liberty, he threw himself into selling Kansas City Automobile Club memberships ("It gave me a substantial income") and into organizing the local Reserve Officers Association. Two years later, he returned to county government, more powerful and prominent than ever, winning election as the county's $6,300-a-year presiding judge.

As presiding judge, he oversaw what one biographer characterized as "a sound, clean, constructive administration," an accomplishment all the more remarkable considering that, in truth, he worked not so much for the people of Jackson County as for the increasingly venal Tom Pendergast. Truman cut spending, halved the county's accumulated debt, reduced interest rates granted to the county for future borrowing, eliminated unnecessary positions (mostly political rivals, it must be admitted), and, most notably, oversaw creation of a $60-million county highway system that rivaled the nation's finest. Jackson County reelected him in 1930 by 58,000 votes.

It was heady stuff for a "farmer boy" and a failed haberdasher, but the cost accompanying accomplishment and glory proved steep: Truman would forever be linked to the Pendergast machine. As the *New York Times* would later note, "The real seat of government in Kansas City, as everyone knew, was [Pendergast's] Jackson Democratic Club at 1908 Main Street."

Bluff, cigar-chomping, pony-playing, exceptionally rotund, syphilitic, and spectacularly corrupt, Tom Pendergast ran a machine that was, to say the least, unsavory. Kansas City suffered not merely unprecedented graft, but also wide-open vice and even mob-style violence. "If you want to see some sin," noted the *Omaha World-Herald*, "forget about Paris and go to Kansas City. With the possible exceptions of such renowned centers as Singapore and Port Said, Kansas City probably has the greatest sin industry in the world."

Harry Truman did not sin—at least, carnally—and he did not steal. ("Am I a fool or an ethical giant? I don't know.") No money stuck to Truman's fingers, for while Pendergast's henchmen cavalierly ran riot in Kansas City itself (even issuing a tire-stealing concession to a local crook named "Fat

Willie"), maintaining power in the remaining sedate, rural portions of Jackson County required a more deft hand. Truman resolved to be as honest as he could, and Tom Pendergast had no great problem with that, provided that he and his allies, nonetheless, still fattened themselves from Truman's multimillion-dollar highway bond issues. And the best way to gain public approval for continued referenda-generated highway borrowing was to keep the graft as relatively modest and circumspect as possible.

Truman was, thus, as honest as one could reasonably be while working for a thief like Pendergast, though he was hardly the principled innocent that history has often chronicled. From December 1930 to May 1934, a conflicted Truman confided his concerns to paper. In secret, holed up in downtown Kansas City's Pickwick Hotel, he poured out his increasingly troubled soul:

> I had to compromise in order to get the voted road system carried out. . . . I had to let a former saloon keeper and murderer[,] a friend of the Big Boss[,] steal about . . . [illegible amount, perhaps $10,000] from the general revenues of the County to satisfy my ideal associate [western district judge Robert Barr] and to keep the crooks from getting a million or more out of the bond issue. Was I right or did I compound a felony? I don't know.

Sometime in the course of 1931, Truman wrote: "At the same time I gave away about a million in general revenue to satisfy the politicians. But if I hadn't done that the crooks would have half the seven million [presumably the amount of the first highway bond issue]."

And again that year: "Am I an administrator or not? Or am I a crook to compromise in order to get the job done? You judge. I can't."

No wonder that he itched to get out—out of county government, but not yet (or ever) fully out of Pendergast's machine. "I am obligated to the Big Boss, a man of his word, though he gives it very seldom and usually on a sure thing. But he's not a trimmer. He in times past owned a bawdy house, a saloon and gambling establishment, was raised in that environment but he's all man. I wonder who is worth more in the sight of the Lord?"

"Truman adored Pendergast and the other Democratic bosses of Missouri," remembered U.S. Supreme Court justice William O. Douglas. "I would often listen to his praises of them and write them off as a form of sophomoric sentimentalism. But when I met those men and saw how vulgar, sleazy, and uncivilized they were, I somewhat revised my ideas of my friend Harry."

Facing a statutory two-term limit as presiding judge, Truman requested Pendergast's support for governor in 1932 and congressman in 1934. "I have," he mused, "the opportunity to be a power in the nation as Congressman." Pendergast turned him down both times. In the latter year, however, Pendergast required a candidate for an open U.S. Senate seat. After every other choice had refused TJ, he tapped Truman.

The year of 1934 proved auspicious for Democrats, but not for Truman. Powerful St. Louis Democrats opposed him. Unwanted publicity arrived in June when Pendergast's Northside henchman, gang lord John "Brother John" Lazia, was spectacularly gunned down while exiting his car.

Truman, nonetheless, stumped tirelessly through rural Missouri, pressing the flesh with the courthouse, veterans, and Masonic contacts he had accumulated through the years, running as the pro–New Deal candidate, speaking wherever and whenever he could ("I just told the people the facts"). He carried those counties. But much more helpful was Pendergast's support within Kansas City. Truman swept the city's first district 17,485 to 49, its second 15,145 to 24, and the third 8,182 to 34.

In November, Harry Truman triumphed by a comfortable quarter-million votes. In Washington, he emerged as a dependable New Dealer, even supporting FDR's ill-fated 1937 Supreme Court packing scheme. Such loyalty, however, garnered him little respect from the White House, which, like virtually everyone else, dismissed him as an inconsequential Pendergast puppet. Truman merely reinforced that reputation when, in February 1938, he waged a lonely war to block Senate confirmation of Pendergast-busting federal prosecutor Maurice M. Milligan. Not a single Senate colleague supported him.

Milligan eventually indicted 278—and convicted 259—Pendergast henchmen on charges of election fraud. Worse, he zeroed in on the Big Boss himself, who was by now obsessed by a growing gambling mania and had grown sloppy with stealing, bookkeeping, and taxpaying. "He was like a man on dope," Pendergast's son once wrote to Margaret Truman. "He needed a fix. A fix for him was each race."

On Good Friday 1939, Milligan indicted Tom Pendergast for income tax evasion, convicting him later that year. His man Truman seemed finished, despondently mulling retirement. "Tell them to go to hell," Truman finally said, "because I've made up my mind that I'm going to run for the Senate."

Maurice Milligan opposed Truman in the 1940 primary, as did his ambitious onetime ally, Missouri governor Lloyd Stark ("a no good son of a bitch"). The Pendergast machine was fast deteriorating; Truman needed new patrons and allies. A. F. Whitney's powerful Brotherhood of Railroad Trainmen union endorsed him. With the race hanging in the balance, fellow Missouri senator Bennett Champ Clark jumped aboard the Truman bandwagon, as did rising St. Louis politico star Robert E. Hannegan, hitherto for Stark.

Harry Truman survived.

Within the Senate, Truman had made few friends among its more liberal elements. Florida's Claude Pepper, the South's most prominent progressive, considered him "pleasant enough, conscientious, and decent" but a "political hack," obviously "among the least likely to ascend to higher office." The bulk of Truman's friendships lay with southern and western conservatives and moderates. Never an orator, he had been a workhorse, busying himself on such mundane matters as licensing transport on interstate highways and drafting legislation creating the Civil Aeronautics Administration. As America prepared for war, however, Truman received disquieting reports of widespread inefficiencies within the war effort regarding defense contracts performance and the construction of military bases. In February 1941, he presented his findings in a well-received, matter-of-fact Senate speech and found himself chairing the newly constituted Senate Special Committee to Investigate the National Defense Program—far better known to history as the "Truman Committee."

His crusade started humbly. The Roosevelt administration viewed it warily. The Senate provided only $15,000 in funding. With minimal staff and resources but maximum energy and resolve, Truman plowed forward. In August 1941, he issued a ninety-eight-page report alleging the "needless waste" of $100 million of the army's $1 billion construction program. Additional findings—made carefully, calmly, and professionally—excoriated business, labor, the bureaucracy, and the military alike. "Republican [committee members Homer] Ferguson of Michigan and [Owen] Brewster of Maine will tell you when it comes to the war," reported syndicated Washington columnist Drew Pearson, "Truman has leaned over backward not to let politics interfere with . . . cleaning up war scandals."

Republicans were pleased. The administration grew less comfortable with Truman with each report. Following Pearl Harbor, Under Secretary of War Robert P. Patterson publicly called for the committee's disbandment. Truman held firm.

The experience transformed the onetime "Senator from Pendergast" into a respected national figure. In 1944, Washington newsmen named Harry Truman as among "the ten most valuable men in Washington in the war"— the only member of Congress so designated.

Such respectability qualified Truman for higher honors, and, in 1944, higher things meant the Democratic vice-presidential nomination. Bronx Democratic boss Edward J. Flynn, a key Roosevelt confidant, recalled:

> We [FDR and I] went over every man in the Senate, and Truman was the only one who fitted. His record [investigating the] National Defense Program was excellent; his labor votes in the Senate were good; on the other hand he seemed to represent to some degree the conservatives in the party, he came from a border state, and he had never made any "racial" remarks. He just dropped into the slot. It was agreed that Truman was the man who would hurt [FDR] least.

The vice presidency's current occupant, the ultraliberal—some said radical—Henry A. Wallace, did hurt FDR. Roosevelt had peevishly forced Wallace upon the party four years previously, but now, with FDR's health precipitously declining, the party hierarchy desperately demanded Wallace's ouster. "You are not nominating a Vice-President of the United States," warned DNC treasurer Ed Pauley in spring 1944, "but a President."

Among Truman's boosters was his old St. Louis ally Bob Hannegan, now (thanks in part to Truman's recommendation) chairman of the DNC. Yet Truman's advancement remained uncertain. Wallace—backed by the party's powerful liberal wing and by Eleanor Roosevelt personally—naturally fought to remain on the ticket. Other powerful Democrats, of far higher profile than Truman, coveted the nod: Senate Majority Leader Alben W. Barkley, for one, as well as former Supreme Court justice James F. Byrnes. Both the Barkley and Byrnes candidacies, however, possessed significant drawbacks. Barkley was sufficiently competent and liberal, but was sixty-six—five years FDR's senior. He seemed too old. The South Carolinian Byrnes, now head of the powerful Office of War Mobilization (OWM), was popularly known as FDR's "Assistant President." Not only was Byrnes too southern and anti-union, he was a fallen-away Catholic. Neither Barkley nor Byrnes would do.

Forty-five-year-old Supreme Court justice William O. Douglas was far more youthful than Barkley, far more liberal than Byrnes, and far more polished than Truman. Unlike his competition, however, Douglas had never competed for elective office, but of this quartet he may have enjoyed FDR's personal favor most.

Complicating the situation, however, was Roosevelt's innate deviousness. "Of course, everybody knows I am for Henry Wallace," FDR informed his administrative assistant Jonathan Daniels in late June 1944, though he would soon publicly undercut his vice president by issuing the most mixed of messages regarding his preference. Finally, Roosevelt handed Bob Hannegan a letter, reading: "Dear Bob: You have written me about Harry Truman and Bill Douglas. I should, of course, be very glad to run with either of them and believe that either of them would bring real strength to the ticket."

But was *Truman* glad? Comfortable in the Senate, he remained wary regarding a position normally considered a worthless sinecure—and exceedingly nervous regarding the possibility of acceding to the presidency. "I'm not going to get into this thing," he complained to a friend, "unless the President wants me to. Do you remember your American history well enough to recall what happened to most Vice-Presidents who succeeded to the Presidency? Usually they were ridiculed in office, had their hearts broken, lost any vestige of respect they had had before. I don't want that to happen to me."

In Chicago, at their party's national convention, Bob Hannegan summoned Truman to his Blackstone Hotel suite. There, not only pasty-faced Hannegan, but jowly postmaster general Frank C. Walker and a trio of the nation's most powerful big-city bosses—New York's Ed Flynn, Mayor Ed Kelly of Chicago, and Jersey City's Frank "I am the Law" Hague—worked at bludgeoning Truman into taking the job. He still resisted. The phone rang.

It was FDR. Truman heard Roosevelt bark to Hannegan, "Well, tell him if he wants to break up the Democratic Party in the middle of a war, that's his responsibility." Truman surrendered. The "second Missouri Compromise" was about to roll.

Not everyone approved. The usually taciturn Frank Walker bounced into a roomful of Wallace supporters to gloat: "Hello, fellows, I just dropped by to tell you it's Truman."

"Goddamn it," secretary of the interior Harold L. Ickes angrily shouted, "I'm a member of this cabinet and they haven't told me yet."

"Well," answered Walker, "I'm telling you now. It's Truman. Remember, Harold, we're all members of a team."

"Goddamn it," Ickes snapped, "so was Pontius Pilate."

Bennett Champ Clark was not angry. He was drunk. It required a prodigious quantity of hot coffee to get him in shape to nominate his Missouri colleague. Wallace led on the first ballot and barely trailed Truman on the second. When Truman won on the third ballot, a shocked and disgusted Los Angeles congressional candidate named Helen Gahagan Douglas fainted. Revived, she informed those around her just what she thought of Missouri's junior senator.

Truman, columnist Tris Coffin noted, "watched the proceedings with the cheerful, wide-eyed wonder of the poor orphan boy who, quite by miracle, gets an electric train for Christmas. He didn't quite understand it. But it was swell."

Others also observed the same gee-whiz, aw-shucks attitude. But was it real? "I missed . . . what seems plain to me now," Jonathan Daniels would eventually conclude. "It is incredible he did not know the plan for him which his man Hannegan had long been developing. I feel certain that he played the role of the reluctant candidate with the skill of a maestro. There was nothing in his action which made him seem a man of indecision. . . . No man ever played 'hard to get' with more conviction than Harry Truman."

Truman's acceptance speech, in its brevity and simplicity, reflected that attitude—as did the fact that he was unexpectedly called to the podium while eating a sandwich. In its entirety it read:

You don't know how much I appreciate the very great honor which has come to the state of Missouri. It is also a great responsibility which I am perfectly willing to assume.

Nine years and five months ago I came to the Senate. I expect to continue the efforts I have made there to help shorten the war and to win the peace under the great leader, Franklin D. Roosevelt.

I don't know what else I can say except I accept this great honor with all humility.

I thank you.

Bennett Clark's nominating speech had included the promise that Truman "met the requirements of possessing all the qualifications necessary and desirable for the presidency." Some, however, merely saw the Truman of old. The fiercely Republican *Chicago Tribune* condemned him as "the grinning skeleton of Truman the bankrupt . . . Truman the yes man and apologist in the Senate for political gangsters." Other reports informed voters of Truman's 1922 flirtation with the Klan, or, conversely and inaccurately, that he was part Jewish—the "S" in his name supposedly standing for "Solomon," his maternal grandfather's name. Republicans revealed how he had placed Bess on the public payroll as his highest-paid Senate staffer, at $4,500 per annum. Connecticut congresswoman Clare Boothe Luce dubbed Mrs. Truman "Payroll Bess." Harry fired back that his beloved spouse was worth "every cent of it. I never write a speech without going over it with her . . . and I never make any decisions unless she is in on them." In fact, Bess had spent little time in Truman's office, and the charges stung.

It was, Truman recalled, "the meanest campaign I can ever remember."

Roosevelt and Truman triumphed that November, but, by then, Truman had personally witnessed the precarious nature of his chief's health, how FDR's hands shook and his clothes hung loose upon him. In early 1945, Truman and his old army buddy Edward D. McKim Jr. visited the White House. "Hey, Bud," McKim said to Truman as they departed the east entrance, "turn around and take a look. You're going to be living in that house before long."

"Eddie," Harry responded, "I'm afraid I am, and it scares the hell out of me."

Two very public events marked Truman's brief vice presidency. Six days following Truman's oath of office, the disgraced Tom Pendergast died. Cautioned to ignore his old patron, Truman instead commandeered an army bomber to transport him to Kansas City and the funeral. "He was always my friend," said Truman, "and I have always been his."

Soon afterward, he attended a luncheon at the National Press Club. He could not help playing the piano, nor seemingly could he avoid it when twenty-year-old Hollywood star Lauren Bacall climbed atop the upright, ostentatiously flashing her curvaceous legs. The new vice president grinned broadly for the cameras, and the photo appeared in newspapers across the country. Mrs. Truman grinned not at all.

In the late afternoon of Tuesday, April 12, 1945, after presiding over a desultory session of the U.S. Senate, Harry S. Truman, vice president of the United States for eighty-two days, adjourned to House Speaker Sam Rayburn's private office for what "Mr. Sam" invariably termed a "libation." A call for Truman from the White House preceded his arrival. He phoned back, and White House appointments secretary Steve Early urged HST to leave for the White House "as quickly and as quietly" as he could.

Truman went white.

Eluding his Secret Service escorts, he arrived at 5:25 PM, to be escorted to the First Family's private quarters, into Eleanor Roosevelt's sitting room. Eleanor stepped forward. She placed her arms upon his shoulder.

"Harry," she said, "the president is dead."

"Is there anything I can do for you?" he answered.

"Is there anything I can do for *you*?" she responded. "For you are the one in trouble now."

"I hope it's the same team again, Henry"

Harry S. Truman was now president of the United States of America.
Henry Agard Wallace was not.

Both hailed from the Midwest. Both were farmers. Both were now Democrats and both had served Franklin Delano Roosevelt as vice president. And that exhausted their list of similarities.

Henry A. Wallace was born on an Iowa farm on October 7, 1888, the eldest of Henry Cantwell "Harry" Wallace's six children and the grandson of yet another Henry Wallace—"Uncle Henry" Wallace. All the Henry Wallaces, whatever their middle initials or lack thereof, counted for something in agriculture. Bearded "Uncle Henry," originally a United Presbyterian minister, had founded *Wallaces' Farmer*, a magazine devoted to "Good Farming. Clear Thinking. Right Living." His redheaded oldest son, Henry Cantwell Wallace, parlayed the magazine into not only his family's massive influence within the agriculture community (George Washington Carver was a protégé) but also a cabinet post under presidents Harding and Coolidge. Secretary of Agriculture Wallace died suddenly in October 1924, but not before acquiring an abiding dislike for his ambitious fellow cabinet member, Secretary of Commerce Herbert Hoover.

Upon earning a degree in agriculture from the Iowa State College at Ames (now Iowa State University) in 1910, Henry Agard Wallace joined *Wallaces' Farmer*, assuming its editorship when his father went to Washington in 1921. Exceptionally proficient in the science of corn breeding, he personally bred several new, hardy, and highly profitable varieties of corn. His Hi-Bred Corn Company eventually earned millions, the company's gross income reaching $4 million by 1944.

The Wallaces had always been Republicans, albeit of the progressive, Theodore Roosevelt stripe. In 1928, however, Henry Agard Wallace—blaming Hoover for his father's ill health and early death—backed Democratic presidential hopeful Al Smith. In 1932, he endorsed FDR ("He is open-minded where Hoover is cold.") and helped carry Iowa for him. Returning the favor, Roosevelt appointed Wallace to his father's former cabinet post. Henry journeyed to Washington, where, as he put it, he would "make the world safe for corn breeders."

The secretaryship of agriculture was then a key position. A quarter of all Americans still remained on the farm. Wallace proved tireless in implementing and proselytizing for the New Deal's revolutionary agricultural policies. "He seems to have impressed his subordinates in those days," noted his eventual critic, Dwight Macdonald, "with his modesty, human decency, competence, energy, and receptivity to new ideas."

"Roosevelt," added New Deal economist John Kenneth Galbraith, "had to deal with quite a large number of people whose enthusiasm far exceeded their competence or their personality. [Wallace was] a solid source of good work and . . . service along with no more than a handful of others . . . a really good servant of FDR. And FDR liked somebody who was a faithful ally."

Roosevelt's backing was crucial. Wallace proved controversial. While city-dwellers remained ill-clad and hungry, Wallace limited farm production to force up farm prices, plowing fewer than ten million acres of cotton and slaughtering six million small pigs. The *Chicago Tribune* dubbed him "The Greatest Butcher in Christendom."

Slaughtering little piggies was, however, the least of Henry Wallace's problems. For he was—well, different.

"There was a medium in Georgetown who conducted séances," recalled Supreme Court justice Bill Douglas. "People would sit holding hands and wait for the spirit to appear in the form of a cloud over the piano. Then questions would be asked and the spirit would reply. The Washington scuttlebutt was that the spirit's answers to Henry's questions determined the price of corn."

Therein lay Henry Wallace's problem. For all his hardheaded agricultural connections, he remained a mystic, more than a bit on the daydreamer side, a teetotaling vegetarian not quite made for the hurly-burly world of Washington politics—and until 1936 not even an enrolled Democrat. Even his hobbies—ambidextrous volleyball, boxing (he once KO'd Louisiana senator Allen Ellender), arm-wrestling aides, piloting an airplane, studying the aerodynamics of boomerangs—seemed a bit strange. According to historian and Democratic Party activist Arthur M. Schlesinger Jr.:

> He remained out of place in the smart apartment at the Wardman Park [Hotel] . . . ill at ease at capital cocktail parties or official dinners; uncomfortable even in his own office, where, unable to get used to buzzing for secretaries, he walked to the door and called them.

> In conference he would sit slumped in his chair, eyes half closed, vest unbuttoned, feet propped on a wastebasket, head resting on hand. Sometimes he disconcerted people by the apparent vacancy of his gaze or by his nervous grin or giggle.

"Henry Wallace," observed author and illustrator Peggy Bacon, "looks as if he were going somewhere on a bus, possibly to the fair, self-conscious, all dressed up and scrubbed, determined to behave, taking it all in and simply thrilled."

Wallace's faith in the perfectibility of man exceeded the mere utopian. "How wonderful it would be," he once exclaimed to his chief campaign speechwriter, Lew Frank Jr., "if we could practice eugenics on people. We could turn out a beautiful golden race."

And yet, this strange man remained in FDR's favor. Roosevelt praised him as "Old Man Common Sense," and, indeed, Henry Wallace possessed enough common sense to be the first cabinet member to endorse an unprecedented, though not unconstitutional, third term for his chief. As early as July 1937, journalist Stanley High would write: "A good many people believe that Henry Wallace is Mr. Roosevelt's heir apparent."

In 1940, FDR, wanting a third term, required a new vice president. His old one, Texan John Nance "Cactus Jack" Garner, increasingly a conservative odd man out in Roosevelt's liberal New Deal, refused to countenance FDR remaining in office. Garner had to go, and when FDR's first choice for vice president, sixty-nine-year-old Secretary of State Cordell Hull, declined the honor, Roosevelt selected Wallace. DNC chairman James A. Farley warned FDR that "you must know the people look on him as a wild-eyed fellow," but such advice now counted for little, as Roosevelt's contrary streak kicked into overdrive.

"Exhibiting the weakness he sometimes displayed for unsuitable appointments," FDR biographer Conrad Black noted, "especially those designed to affront an annoying constituency, Roosevelt settled on the improbable [Wallace]. . . . This was as insane a choice as fascistic defeatist Joseph Kennedy for the London embassy, Stalin-dupe Joseph Davies to Moscow, isolationist [Harry] Woodring in the War Department, anti-allotment, unsuccessful plough-manufacturer George Peek to head the Agricultural Adjustment Administration (AAA), or anti-Semite Breckinridge Long in charge of refugee affairs."

Roosevelt's "annoying constituency" in Wallace's case was their party's vexatious conservative wing. "The conservative resurgence had really taken a hold," observed historian Doris Kearns Goodwin. "In 1940 there was a real sense that liberalism was under attack from a rising conservatism. . . . [W]hen [FDR] chose Wallace he wanted . . . somebody . . . he wasn't going to have to argue with, [who] would be as strong or stronger than he was on those liberal issues, then he could somehow have a weapon against the conservatives. . . . [I]t was a very important choice for him."

The Democratic National Convention of 1940 displayed precious little enthusiasm for a Roosevelt-Wallace ticket—or, at least, for its back end. "Just because the Republicans have nominated an apostate Democrat [Wendell Willkie]," one delegate shouted from the convention floor, "let us not for God's sake nominate an apostate Republican [Wallace]."

"Henry's my second choice," admitted Oklahoma's anti-FDR governor, Leon "Red" Phillips. Asked who his first might be, Phillips growled, "Anyone—red, white, black, or yellow—who can get the nomination."

News of such reluctance soon reached FDR.

"Well, damn it to hell," he fumed to his speechwriters Robert Sherwood and Samuel I. Rosenman. "They will go for Wallace or I won't run and you can jolly well tell them so. I suppose all the conservatives in America are going to bring pressure on the convention to beat Henry. I won't deliver that acceptance speech until we see who they nominate."

Resistance continued. "Something close to mob mentality had taken over Chicago Stadium," noted Wallace biographers John C. Culver and John Hyde. "Every mention of Wallace's name was greeted with boos and hisses."

"I shall never forget Henry Wallace's face as he sat there," recalled Roosevelt's secretary of labor Frances Perkins. "I have never lived through anything worse. . . . He was listening . . . but his eyes were way off. . . . I remember thinking that his face and posture depicted the kind of suffering that a man in the Middle Ages being tried for some heresy which he couldn't understand might show."

Eleanor Roosevelt delivered an unprecedented speech, designed to inspire—or, at least, cajole—delegates to hunker down and do what they had to do. "You cannot treat it as an ordinary nomination in an ordinary time," she hectored delegates, but she dared not mention Wallace by name.

Wallace rolled to an uneasy first-ballot nomination. Insiders like Jimmy Byrnes and FDR confidant Harry Hopkins warned him not to address the hall. "Don't do it, Henry," advised Byrnes. "Don't go out there. You'll ruin the party if you do." Henry Wallace delivered no acceptance speech.

The FDR-Wallace ticket carried Roosevelt to a third term that November, but as it did, a storm cloud materialized. Wendell Willkie carried Iowa 632,370 to 578,800.

As vice president, Wallace proved, in the words of political scientist Michael Barone, "cheerful and loyal," and Roosevelt entrusted to him unprecedented tasks, appointing him chairman of the board of the Board of Economic Warfare (BEW) and dispatching him on significant foreign missions. As his profile soared, so did his rhetoric, now often mixing his religious and mystical persona with an increasing leftward drift. Addressing the Free World Association at Manhattan's Hotel Commodore in May 1942, he issued this warning:

> The march of freedom of the past one hundred and fifty years has been a long-drawn-out people's revolution. In this Great Revolution of the people, there were the American Revolution of 1775, the French Revolution of 1792, the Latin-American revolutions of the Bolivarian era, the German Revolution of 1848, and the Russian Revolution of 1917. Each spoke for the common man in terms of blood on the battlefield. Some went to excess. But the significant thing is that the people groped their way to the light. More of them learned to think and work together. . . .

Some have spoken of the "American Century." I say that the century we are now entering—the century that will come out of this war—can and must be the century of the common man. . . . The people's revolution is on the march, and the devil and all his angels cannot prevail against it. They cannot prevail, for on the side of the people is the Lord.

He spoke of battling not only against fascist tyranny, but idealistically for a better world for all mankind. The words of a skilled orator and accomplished politician might have inspired audiences (as FDR's soaring "Freedom from Want" speech had in 1941), but Wallace's words were often merely silly. In May 1942, he prattled on about telling the wife of Soviet ambassador Maxim Litvinov "half in fun and half seriously" that "[t]he object of this war is to make sure that everybody in the world has the privilege of drinking a quart of milk a day." His critics soon ridiculed him for urging the nation "to give away a quart of milk for every Hottentot."

At Ohio Wesleyan University in March 1943, he seemed to anticipate taking another nation's side against his own:

> We shall decide sometime in 1943 or 1944 whether to plant the seeds for World War No. 3. The war will be certain if we allow Prussia to rearm either materially or psychologically.
>
> That war will be probable in case we double-cross Russia.
>
> That war will be probable if we fail to demonstrate that we can furnish full employment after the war comes to an end and Fascist interests motivated largely by anti-Russian bias get control of our government.
>
> Unless the Western democracies and Russia come to a satisfactory understanding before the war ends, I very much fear that World War No. 3 will be inevitable.

In mid-May 1944, FDR dispatched him as far away as he could—to tour war-ravaged China and Siberia. Describing the operation that ran that infamous gulag-infested region of the Soviet Union as "a combination of TVA [Tennessee Valley Authority] and Hudson's Bay Company," Wallace recounted how he had "gamboled" about the larches with its chief administrator, Lt.

Gen. Ivan Fedorovich Nikishov. At the huge Magadan concentration camp he noticed not its many political prisoners but rather "an extraordinary exhibit of paintings in embroidery . . . made by a group of women who gathered regularly during the severe winter to study needlework."

"In traveling through Siberia," he would write, "we were 'accompanied' by 'old soldiers' with blue tops on their caps. Everybody treated them with great respect. They were members of the NKVD [Secret Police]. . . . I became very fond of their leader, Major Mikhail Cheremisenov."

It might have been the gamboling NKVD commissars. It might have been the Hottentots. Most likely, it was the election returns from Iowa and disquieting thoughts of further diminished returns to come. For whatever reasons, Franklin Roosevelt came to realize Henry Wallace had done precious little to help secure his third term and might seriously jeopardize his anticipated fourth. In June 1944, Jonathan Daniels confided to his diary: "He [Roosevelt] had thought the feeling against Wallace had been largely that of politicians but he was beginning to believe it went down below. Some people told him that it meant forty per cent of the vote in their precincts. He said that if you cut that in half and then half again, it still might mean the loss of a million or two votes."

To renominate such a candidate, "who divides the people so deeply and sharply," columnist Walter Lippmann wrote as the 1944 convention drew near, "would produce a profound, perhaps an unreasonable, sense of anxiety, and a loss of confidence in the conduct of government."

"Wallace had his chance," FDR informed Eleanor, herself still supportive of her husband's embattled running mate, "and if he could not convince the party leaders that he was the right person, I cannot dictate to them twice."

When Wallace returned from Siberia, FDR reassured him, "I hope it's the same team again, Henry," before adding this ominous addendum: "Even though they do beat you out at Chicago, we will have a job for you in world economic affairs."

Worse omens followed. FDR provided Wallace with a letter to bring to the convention. It included these words: "I have been associated with Henry Wallace during the past four years as Vice-President, for eight years earlier while he was Secretary of Agriculture and well before that. I like him and I respect him and he is my personal friend. For these reasons I personally would vote for his nomination if I were a delegate to the convention. Obviously the convention must do the deciding."

Obviously the convention must do the deciding.

"That," summarized Alben Barkley, "was the coup de grace."

FDR, however, continued to exercise caution. Wallace, despite his myriad shortcomings, still retained the support of 64 percent of enrolled Democrats for a second term. At that July's convention, college students sang in support of Wallace to the tune of "Joshua Fit the Battle of Jericho":

You can talk about Senator Barkley.

You can talk about Jimmy Byrnes.

You can talk about Senator Truman.

But the Democratic party has learned that

Wallace fought the battle for the common man,

Common man, common man.

Wallace fought the battle for the common man.

And he'll fight that battle again.

And he would, but not as a vice-presidential nominee. He did, however—loyal FDR man to the end—campaign tirelessly for the man who had dumped him. "A Dewey victory," he warned voters, "no matter how estimable Mr. Dewey himself may be personally, will inevitably give hope to the wrong element in Germany and Japan."

"[Wallace] campaigned for Roosevelt sixteen hours a day through the summer and fall," noted historian Lawrence Lader. "Once he had to catch a crowded day-coach to make his next speech and stood in the aisles from 6 PM to 2 AM. No one offered him a seat or even seemed to recognize him. Associates often tried to argue him out of carrying his heavy suitcase from the station to his distant hotel."

In January 1945, after Henry Wallace had held the Bible on which his successor had been sworn in, he and his wife returned alone to their apartment. FDR speechwriter Samuel Rosenman, a fellow Wardman Park resident, phoned to see if the Wallaces would welcome visitors. They would. Expecting to find the Wallaces surrounded by friends and allies, Sam and Dorothy Rosenman were stunned to discover Henry and Ilo Wallace, abandoned by all their supposed friends and allies, with Henry busy studying Russian-language instructional records.

Roosevelt, however, had not completely thrown Wallace overboard, and offered him his choice (save for secretary of state) of government positions. Wallace selected secretary of commerce.

It was an unfortunate selection. Wallace should not have elected to remain in an administration in which he clearly retained such diminished respect. But beyond that, motivated partially by spite ("poetic justice," Wallace repeatedly termed it to FDR), he had compounded his initial woeful judgment by designating a position that would place him at immediate loggerheads with the current secretary, the powerful Texas conservative Jesse H. Jones.

Wallace had already alienated Jones, having engaged him in turf battles regarding the Board of Economic Warfare, the upshot being FDR's abolition of the BEW. Jones, now burned twice by Wallace, quickly exacted vengeance. His congressional allies stripped the immensely powerful Reconstruction Finance Corporation from Commerce Department control. They nearly torpedoed Wallace's nomination. "Henry was not at all liked in the Senate," recalled Harry Truman, "and I had to break two ties [as vice president] to get the son of a bitch confirmed. I didn't want to do it, but if that's what the old man [FDR] wanted, I did it."

In April 1945, Franklin Roosevelt expired, and Henry Wallace mourned him. He also mourned that it was not he, but high school graduate Harry Truman, who had succeeded him. "The century of the common man," noted John C. Culver and John Hyde, "would be led [not by Henry Wallace] but by one of its own."

Wallace remained in the cabinet. On Thursday night, September 12, 1946, he addressed a Madison Square Garden rally designed to boost New York State Democratic chances and perhaps even to derail Republican Governor Thomas E. Dewey's reelection bid. All of which seemed harmless enough, but, as historian Richard Norton Smith has pointed out, Wallace "was the only secretary of commerce with his own foreign policy," and that policy was now increasingly at odds with Harry Truman's progressively harder line against Moscow. Two days previously, Wallace had traveled to the White House to clear his address with the president, particularly the passage reading, "I want one thing clearly understood. I am neither anti-British nor pro-British, neither anti-Russian nor pro-Russian." Truman assented ("That's right. . . . Yes, that is what I believe"), and Wallace scribbled this addition to his speech: "And just two days ago, when President Truman read these words, he said that they represented the policy of his administration." Truman okayed that as well.

What Truman did not okay was the vociferous, pro-Soviet atmosphere of the nineteen-thousand-person crowd. Nor did he okay it when the program's organizer insisted Wallace excise the more pointed anti-Soviet passages from his speech—and Wallace agreed. Neither could Truman have approved of this passage from Florida senator Claude Pepper's warm-up speech, eviscerating Truman's increasingly "get tough" foreign policy:

> With conservative Democrats and reactionary Republicans making our foreign policy as they are today, it is all we can do to keep foolish people from having us pull a Hitler blitzkrieg and drop our atomic bombs on the Russian people. It is not so far from "get tough" to "get rough." I think we ought to remember, however, that the last two fellows who tried to get rough with the Russians—you may remember them from their first names, Napoleon and Adolf—did not fare so well.
>
> You and I know that today the reason we have got so much Republican unity behind the foreign policy is because there is so much McKinley imperialism in our foreign policy.
>
> What do you expect in a foreign policy which really meets the approval of [Senate Foreign Relations Committee chairman] Senator Vandenberg and [Dewey adviser] John Foster Dulles?

Nor would Truman have approved of this passage from Wallace's final address, a message hardly consistent with being "neither anti-Russian nor pro-Russian":

To prevent war and insure our survival in a stable world, it is essential that we look abroad through our own American eyes and not through the eyes of either the British Foreign Office or a pro-British or anti-Russian press. . . . The tougher we get, the tougher the Russians will get.

The speech led to this not inconsequential story on the front page of the Friday, September 13, 1946, edition of the *Washington Post*:

Henry A. Wallace, in a speech fully endorsed by the President last night proposed division of the world into two main spheres of political influence.

Mr. Wallace put it this way:

On our part, we should recognize that we have no more business in the political affairs of Eastern Europe than Russia has in the political affairs of Latin America, Western Europe and the United States.

And with that, Harry Truman saw wards of Eastern European voters in Chicago, Milwaukee, Buffalo, Detroit, Scranton, and points in between vanishing from the Democratic column in 1948.

Truman's own actions compounded his fears and embarrassment. Just four hours after Wallace's speech, Truman, natty in a double-breasted brown suit with matching tie and handkerchief, hosted a press conference. "In the middle of [Wallace's] speech are these words," the Cowles newspapers' William Mylander prompted: "'When President Truman read these words he said that they represented the policy of his administration.'"

"That is correct," Truman responded.

The *St. Louis Post-Dispatch*'s Raymond Brandt followed up: "[D]oes that apply to just that paragraph, or to the whole speech?"

"I approved the whole speech," Truman cavalierly snapped.

"Mr. President," another reporter would ask, "do you regard Wallace's speech as a departure from [Secretary of State James] Byrnes's policy . . . toward Russia?"

"I do not," Truman responded, further compounding his earlier blunders. "They are exactly in line."

But, of course, they weren't. Senator Vandenberg pointedly warned Truman that "we can only cooperate with one Secretary of State at a time."

James Byrnes threatened to quit. "You and I spent fifteen months building a bipartisan foreign policy," he told Truman. "We did a fine job convincing the world that it was a policy on which the world could rely. Wallace destroyed it in a day."

Soon, Truman was awkwardly backtracking, unconvincingly contending that his remarks had been subject to a "natural misunderstanding" and that he had merely "inten[ded] to express that I approved the right of my Secretary of Commerce to deliver the speech."

Daily, the situation spun further out of control. Truman and Wallace conferred privately. They settled little. Truman angrily recorded his frustrations:

> He [Wallace] is a pacifist. He wants to disband our armed forces, give Russia our atomic secrets and trust a bunch of adventurers in the Kremlin. I do not understand a "dreamer" like that. The German-American Bund under Fritz Kuhn was not half so dangerous. The Reds, Phonies, and the "parlor pinks" seem to be banded together and are becoming a national danger.
>
> I am afraid they are a sabotage front for Uncle Joe Stalin.

A twenty-three-page, single-spaced letter from Wallace to Truman, dated July 23, 1946, leaked to Drew Pearson's syndicated column. It added fuel to the fire, as Wallace, criticizing presidential adviser Bernard M. Baruch's plan on atomic energy, justified a Soviet-dominated "security zone" in Eastern Europe, and intimated that administration officials were plotting a "preventive war" against Russia.

Truman wrote to Wallace, intemperately demanding his departure. But before receiving Wallace's answer, he placed a call. "Henry," he said, "I'm sorry, but I'm asking for your resignation."

He also asked for his letter back. He got both Wallace's resignation and his own offending correspondence. To his mother and sister, Truman wrote, "He was so nice about it I almost backed out."

For his part, Henry Wallace wrote out a two-sentence letter of resignation and went back to a book he was reading about chickens.

And so, thanks to Harry Truman, Henry Agard Wallace was no longer secretary of commerce, just as he was no longer vice president of the United States of America.

But he was still very capable of splitting the Democratic Party wide open.

4

"You men who have nigger children"

Henry Wallace was—now more than ever—willing to split the Democratic Party wide open.

And so, by February 1948, was J. Strom Thurmond.

South Carolina governor James Strom Thurmond was born on December 5, 1902, in Edgefield, South Carolina. Both date and locale possessed significance. The Palmetto State's system of Jim Crow legislation was nearly complete in 1902, the last year any black won election to state office for decades to come. Edgefield County, for its part, was not merely any South Carolina county, but the epicenter of its traditions and politics. As historian Robert Sherrill noted:

> Edgefield [sired] Travis and Bonham, two of the rebels who died at the Alamo; it was also the home of Chancellor Wardlaw, who wrote South Carolina's ordinance of secession; it was the home of Congressman Preston S. Brooks who, to avenge a slur on the name of U.S. Senator A. P. Butler (of Edgefield), caned to the Senate floor Senator Charles Sumner of Massachusetts and thereby helped establish the atmosphere in which reconciliation over the disputes leading to the Civil War was impossible; it was the home of [United States Senator] Ben Tillman, who led the farmers in revolt against a state government controlled by Charleston and Columbia aristocrats with the Luciferian cry, "I had rather follow the majority to hell than these men into heaven."

Eyepatch-wearing Tillman was no plantation-owning conservative. He spoke, in the words of one opposition newspaper, for those who "carry pistols in their hip pockets, who expectorate upon the floors, who have no tooth brushes, and comb their hair with their fingers."

Tillman did not speak for blacks. He hated them. "We have done our level best [to prevent blacks from voting]," "Pitchfork Ben" boasted in February 1900; "we have scratched our heads to find out how we could eliminate the last one of them. We stuffed ballot boxes. We shot them. We are not ashamed of it."

His campaign manager was his Edgefield neighbor, J. William "Will" Thurmond, a burly sharecropper-employing landowner, attorney, state legislator, and circuit solicitor who (thanks to Tillman's intervention with President Woodrow Wilson) ultimately become a federal attorney. Will Thurmond might have advanced yet further, either into the governor's mansion or to join Ben Tillman in the Senate, but for one thing: in March 1897 he had shot and killed a man in front of his Edgefield law office.

Will Thurmond ("He was my idol," Strom would recall; "I tried to imitate him as much as I could") introduced his son both to politics and to the great Pitchfork Ben himself. Driving his buggy to the Tillman farm, Will instructed six-year-old Strom to offer his hand to Pitchfork Ben.

"I want to shake your hand," the small boy informed the fearsome one-eyed giant.

"You said you wanted to shake," Tillman roared. "Why the hell don't you shake?"

"I shook and I shook," Thurmond later recalled, "and I've been shaking ever since."

Will Thurmond insisted that his sons be taught other lessons as well, instructing his wife, Eleanor Gertrude Strom Thurmond: "Stint them until they know the value of money. Encourage them until they have a religious creed. Teach them to rely on themselves. Let them mingle with others to learn human nature and . . . know more about [their professions] than do their competitors."

Young Strom learned about oratory and the power it held over men's hearts and votes. In 1912, Will Thurmond managed South Carolina Supreme Court chief justice Ira B. Jones's campaign for governor against Tillman protégé Coleman "Cole" L. Blease. "You people who want social equality vote for Jones," the frock-coated, string-tie-wearing, race-baiting Blease harangued his audiences. "You men who have nigger children vote for Jones. You who have a nigger wife in your back yard vote for Jones." Strom recalled decades later:

> They put up a platform for them to speak on and brought a big pitcher of water. [Ira] Jones, he made a good talk, a literary talk. But he just didn't stir people. Well, Cole Blease was a fiery kind of fellow and a great orator. You could see people who were not really the thinking people who were carried away by his speech. I could see then the influence that he was going to have over the state for being such a good speaker.

> After hearing him speak, I knew that I was going to run for governor. And I was going to speak, and I would never let a man do me like Blease did Jones that day.

In 1918, Strom graduated high school. At just fifteen he entered Clemson University, quickly becoming an on-campus presence—academically, and what might most delicately be termed "socially."

"This handsome young man," noted Clemson's 1923 yearbook, had emerged as a "ladies man of the 'first water.'" Strom Thurmond, it said, fluttered "so many extra heartbeats among the fairer sex."

The most significant heartbeat was yet to come. Taking up teaching at Edgefield's high school, Strom returned to his father's house, where he also took up with one of the help, teenaged Carrie Butler, who cooked and cleaned and was beautiful—and black. "Love," she would recall, "is blind. It's color-blind. Besides, all that hate talk is just politics."

It was Strom's older brother Will, a medical student, who had first taken a shine to Carrie. "Mister Will, that's what we called him . . . ," said Carrie, "would come home and flirt with me like crazy. And Mr. Strom would see this, and I think he got jealous."

Strom found excuses to be with Carrie, in the kitchen and in the family vegetable garden. "He knew everything about fruits and vegetables," she recalled. "He taught agriculture in the high school and wrote articles in the papers. We'd go out to the orchards and pick peaches, and he'd know exactly when they were ripe and which ones would be the sweetest. One thing led to another.

"It was a big house. These were busy people always out doing something. Love finds a way."

As did the creation of new human life.

On October 12, 1925, in Aiken, South Carolina, twenty miles from Edgefield, Carrie Butler gave birth to a daughter, Essie Mae.

J. Strom Thurmond was the father.

He could not acknowledge the child. Race aside—a very huge aside—he could not do that. He was already on a path toward history. In 1922, at age twenty-four, he had been elected to the Edgefield County Board of Education. In 1928 he became its superintendent of education. A year later—after clerking in his father's office, completing three years of work in one—he won admittance to the South Carolina bar. Elected a state senator in 1933, five years later, he became his state's youngest circuit judge.

Carrie Butler surrendered care of her illegitimate baby to her sister Mary and to Mary's common-law husband, John Washington, who lived up north, thirty-eight miles west of Philadelphia, in a small mill town called Coatesville. Even here, questions of race haunted the family. In the summer of 1938, a young black man, accused of raping a white woman, was nearly dragged from the town jail and lynched. Only memories of an earlier outrage halted his potential murderers: In August 1911, Coatesville witnessed Pennsylvania's first lynching, when Zachariah Walker, a recent black arrival from Virginia, was taken from a local hospital and burned alive after shooting a local steel-mill security guard.

In 1939, Essie Mae Washington discovered her true lineage—or at least part of it—when a stylish and beautiful black woman appeared in Coatesville. This was her real mother. Her supposed mother was merely her aunt.

Mother and daughter later journeyed south to Edgefield to meet the girl's father. Not told whom that man might be, Essie Mae stood dumbstruck as a white man—J. Strom Thurmond—walked through the door. "With all the talk that [my mother] did about him and what a wonderful person he was," Essie Mae would recall, "she never once mentioned that he was a Caucasian."

"Well," Thurmond informed the girl, "you look like one of my sisters. You've got those cheekbones like our family."

Strom allegedly later sent his sister Mary to the Butler family shanty to deliver an envelope stuffed with twenty ten-dollar bills—and to witness for herself the family resemblance. And that, for the time being, would be all the contact father and daughter would have.

When war arrived a few months later, circuit judge Thurmond, nearly thirty-nine years old, enlisted. He flew an 82nd Airborne Division glider into Normandy on D-Day, operating behind enemy lines for two days. Rising to a lieutenant colonelcy, he earned the Bronze Star, the Legion of Merit, the Army Commendation Ribbon, the Purple Heart, the Presidential Distinguished Merit Citation, the Bronze Arrowhead, five battle stars, Belgium's Order of the Crown, France's *Croix de guerre* with *Étoile de Vermeil*, and the Cross of Military Service—the last order awarded by the United Daughters of the Confederacy.

Such derring-do proved no bar to political advancement. Neither did an incident barely preceding Thurmond's enlistment: A mule had gotten loose and kicked a calf to death; the Timmermans owned the mule, and the Logues owned the calf—two Edgefield-area families traditionally on less than cordial terms. When Davis Timmerman refused to compensate Wallace Logue in the amount of $40 (he would go no higher than $20), Logue continued discussions, employing an ax handle as a negotiating tool. Timmerman responded by shooting Logue dead.

In March 1941, the jury said it was self-defense, but Wallace Logue's diminutive widow, Sue, their sharecropper Fred Dorn, and Wallace's brother George said vengeance was theirs. Though no one was ever charged, a black Timmerman sharecropper was later killed by a single rifle shot, and, for $500, Sue Logue and the Dorn brothers engaged the deceased's nephew, Joe Frank Logue, to further dispatch Davis Timmerman. Joe Frank Logue in turn subcontracted his duties to a fellow named Clarence Bagwell. Bagwell emptied his .38 caliber revolver three times into Timmerman—and then proceeded to shoot off his mouth one time too many.

When, in November 1941, Sheriff Wad Allen (a Logue cousin) and Deputy W. L. "Doc" Clark attempted to arrest these feckless homicidal conspirators, Fred Dorn and George Logue responded by wounding Deputy Clark in the arm and shoulder. George Logue shot Sheriff Allen in the face, instantly killing him. Clark shot and killed Dorn before retreating.

A gun-toting crowd of neighbors surrounded the Logue home, and greater mayhem seemed foreordained. Thurmond sped ten miles from his Sunday morning church service to the scene. "Don't come in, Strom," someone shouted from inside the home, "or we'll have to kill you."

To verify he was unarmed, Thurmond stripped off his suit coat and vest and turned his pants pockets inside out, then slowly walked toward the house. The Logue clan motioned him to its rear. There, a family friend ("a cross-eyed fellow") pointed a shotgun at his head. Strom entered. He found Fred Dorn dead and George Logue missing. He promised Sue Logue (who had taught in the local school system when he was superintendent; Wallace Logue's father had been a school trustee) safe passage through the angry mob outside and convinced her to surrender. Exiting, he quickly returned with two recently arrived, out-of-county police officers. Together, they escorted Mrs. Logue through the still heavily armed throng.

"Now," said one witness, "that takes guts."

Such courage inspired eyewitnesses—and voters. On May 15, 1946, Thurmond announced his candidacy for governor, pledging to South Carolinians "a progressive outlook, a progressive program and a progressive leadership."

One Thurmond campaign newspaper ad touted his properly enlightened record:

> As a member of the State Senate, Strom Thurmond supported higher salaries for teachers, longer school terms, and the school attendance law. He [authored] a bill increasing benefits to laborers under the Workmen's Compensation Act; supported measures to provide for tobacco research and other bills vitally affecting farmers. He was a member of the Social Security committee that wrote the first Social Security Bill, which provided assistance for the aged, and benefits for dependent children, the blind and other handicapped people. He was a member of the committee that prepared the Rural Electrification. . . . [He] was chairman of the Public Buildings committee that sponsored the bill that resulted in the erection of the new State Office Building, saving the State over $20,000 annually in rents. And when the General Assembly voted its members extra pay of over $1,000, he refused to accept it.

Thurmond, the *Washington Post* would note, "was known as a liberal by all Southern standards. . . . [He] eschewed all appeal to racial prejudice and was even accused by some of his opponents of being a Communist. In fact, his election was interpreted as confirming a long-felt suspicion that the Southern people are more advanced in their thinking than professional Southern politicians believe."

In the eleven-candidate Democratic primary of 1946, he led the field, receiving 92 percent of the Edgefield vote. In the runoff, he captured 56 percent (136,821 to 106,749), becoming the state's tenth governor from Edgefield County, its first since Pitchfork Ben.

"A half-century later," wrote his biographers Jack Bass and Marilyn Thompson, "his inaugural address stands out as a progressive and realistic assessment of the state's needs, a 15,000-word document of reform that set the direction of South Carolina government for the next four decades." He called for a 25 percent increase in teacher salaries, better roads, a state minimum wage law, and for "more attention given to Negro education." Many saw him as a governor not following Tillman's or Blease's traditions, but rather Franklin Roosevelt's.

He told South Carolina's virtually disenfranchised blacks: "The low standing of South Carolina, educationally, is due primarily to the high rate of illiteracy and lack of education among our Negroes. If we provide better educational facilities for them, not only will much be accomplished in human values, but we shall raise our per capita income as well as the educational standing of the state."

Fate soon put his liberal sentiments to the test. Barely six weeks later, a twenty-four-year-old black epileptic named Willie Earle robbed and stabbed to death Thomas Watson Brown, a forty-eight-year-old white Greenville cabdriver. Police quickly apprehended Earle. It was an open-and-shut case, but Brown's fellow cabdrivers didn't feel like waiting for a trial. Like an army of drawling Travis Bickles, twenty-eight of them (led by the improbably named Roosevelt Carlos Hurd and abetted by three local businessmen) determined to hurry justice. Masked, but arriving at the Pickens County Jail in eight telltale taxicabs, they forced the lone deputy on duty to surrender "the Negro," upon whom they inflicted the most horrifying vengeance.

Reported the black *Pittsburgh Courier:* "Using one or more knives, they carved away most of the lower left face and part of the neck, slashed the left arm and thigh to the bone, cut a five-inch diameter under the heart, and another circle out of the stomach in the region of the solar plexus, hacked a hole in the forehead and then blasted away practically all of his right face with a shotgun."

Cole Blease had vowed to "never order out a militia to shoot down their neighbors and protect a black brute who commits a crime against a white woman." He had promised to defend lynchers pro bono. Strom Thurmond came from a different time and perspective. In Europe, helping to liberate Nazi concentration camps, he witnessed how corrosive the admixture of racism and violence might be. Germans, he informed South Carolina audiences upon his return, must "prove their fitness to assume a position in civilized society before they are accepted by other nations of the world."

And so, it occurred to him, must South Carolinians. Thurmond pledged to employ "every facility at his disposal until this case has been completely solved," declaring the lynching to be beyond "decency, law and the democratic way of living." Ordering the largest manhunt in state history, he even summoned FBI investigators. A hundred police fanned out. A hundred-and-fifty men were interrogated. Thirty-one suspects were arrested. Twenty-six confessed. Thurmond assigned the state's top prosecutor to the case.

Every man was acquitted.

Yet even the state's NAACP applauded Thurmond's actions ("Governor Thurmond has acted with unhesitating vigor"), and the *New York Times* commented, "There seems little doubt here that Governor Thurmond has earned the enmity of the purveyors of race hatred and can expect to receive a certain number of 'resentment votes' in any future primary contest." A Negro corporal wrote to *Life* magazine from Lockbourne Army Air Base that it "was nice to know there were such men as . . . Thurmond."

"I believe," wrote Thurmond to a constituent, "that [my] position will assist in the future in preventing lynchings."

It was, indeed, South Carolina's last lynching.

Thus, Thurmond maintained his reputation as a new style of Southern liberal, even adding to it when, in September 1947, he stunned a visiting regional convention of real-estate agents by dispatching to them a welcome message with the distinctly unwelcoming words: "I will do everything in my power to help rent control until some measure of sanity returns to profiteering real estate owners."

"It is amazing to me," fumed National Association of Real Estate Boards president, Morgan L. Finch, "to find here in the tradition-rich state of South Carolina the Chief Executive making a speech based upon an apparent release from the New York office of the CIO, or the internationalist offices of the Communist Party."

That November, the forty-four-year-old Thurmond garnered more headlines by marrying his beautiful twenty-one-year-old secretary (and former Azalea Festival queen), Jean Crouch. If their age differences did not raise eyebrows, the fitness-obsessed governor's actions just before the ceremony did: stripping to his white gym shorts and performing a headstand for the cameras. *Life* magazine's caption read: "Virile Governor demonstrates his prowess in the mansion yard before wedding." Others preferred: "There's no fool like an old fool."

"To most people, who didn't know about gym shorts," recalled South Carolina congressman William Jennings Bryan Dorn, "it looked like Thurmond had pulled off his pants, left his shoes on, and then stood on his head for the cameras."

It was hardly the way for the father of a twenty-two-year-old daughter to act—particularly when that daughter was now residing in South Carolina.

Thurmond had never forgotten Essie Mae Washington, visiting her in Philadelphia during the war and later when she resided in Harlem. He encouraged her to attend college, particularly a college in South Carolina—the Colored Normal, Industrial, Agricultural and Mechanical College of South Carolina (now South Carolina State University), located at Orangeburg. She started classes in autumn 1946.

It was a risky business. "Among the black people, it [that Thurmond had a black child] was common knowledge," as Essie Mae observed. "They didn't do too much talking to other people," she added. But they talked enough. The rumors spread and never died. Modjeska Simkins, a South Carolina black leader in the late 1960s, said: "He knows that people know about the Negro girl he schooled at Orangeburg. She used to come to the mansion and get shopping money when he was governor. All the Negroes know about that."

"Though apparently without foundation," author Robert Sherrill wrote mistakenly—but not unperceptively—in the 1960s, "it was one of the most widespread political rumors I ever saw wrapped around a state: that Thurmond had a paternal interest in a Negro girl. I never talked with anyone who had ever seen the girl, but she certainly lived in their minds. And the odd part of it, to me, was that instead of crediting Thurmond with good faith for sending this legendary girl to college, many of the Negroes I talked with somehow seemed to hold it that he did not recognize her more authoritatively, although this would of course have been politically fatal."

Yes, it would have. South Carolina was not merely Southern—it was ultra-Southern. Home rule was nonexistent. The state legislature enacted all county legislation (Thurmond lobbied to change that). South Carolina's Democratic primary was (until the Supreme Court ruled otherwise) whites-only. The state's generally superfluous general election featured a one-dollar poll tax (Thurmond urged its repeal). Voting was not secret. Ballots could not be split. All of which added up to a one-party state, unprecedented in American history. In 1924, when Democratic nominee John W. Davis took but 28.8 percent of the national vote, he secured an astounding 96.56 percent in South Carolina.

It would thus take a great deal to induce Strom Thurmond to ever leave the Democratic Party.

But, then again, it would not be the first time South Carolinians had seceded.

5

"I'll be different, not like I used to be"

Strom Thurmond's life contained more than enough of the unlikely stuff of Hollywood screenwriting—the gunplay and steely-eyed physical courage of Clint Eastwood's Dirty Harry leavened with elements of Faulkneresque 1950s tales of sexually dysfunctional Southern families.

Thomas E. Dewey's biography also seemed the heady stuff of cinema, of flashing news photographers' cameras, big-city scandal, blaring police sirens, and strong-jawed, incorruptible heroism. Unfortunately, though the first few reels of the Dewey biopic had indeed commenced spectacularly, by 1948 its plotline had deteriorated into distressing mediocrity: the leaden predictability of second features starring Brian Donlevy or George Brent, of mustachioed leading men not quite good enough even to be Warner Baxter, let alone William Powell or Clark Gable.

Not quite good enough to be president.

Thomas Edmund Dewey, like Harry Truman and Henry Wallace, sprung from the Midwest. Born on March 24, 1902, in small-town Owosso, Michigan, Dewey too was part of a political family. His father, editor of the weekly *Owosso Times*, chaired the county GOP committee. His paternal grandfather, George Martin Dewey, had, in 1854, assisted in the founding of the national party; in 1856, he helped nominate its first presidential candidate, John C. Frémont. Admiral George Dewey, hero of the Spanish-American War's pivotal Battle of Manila Bay, was a third cousin.

Do the paths of life end in unexpected lands? Or merely begin in them? Harry Truman had begun as a bank clerk and farmer, Henry Wallace as an editor; Strom Thurmond as a teacher. Young Tom Dewey, descendant of politicians, craved not public office but public acclaim—in music. He had played bass horn in the Owosso high school band. He possessed a magnificent baritone voice, and earned $7.50 each Sunday at the University of Michigan with an Ann Arbor Methodist church choir. And he attended Chicago Musical College.

Yet, more practical avocations had always beckoned. When Harvard Law School rejected him, he traveled instead to New York City and to Columbia Law School (William O. Douglas and Paul Robeson were classmates), where he completed three years of study in two. All the while, he retained hopes of a musical career, continuing to sing for cash in churches and synagogues. On March 24, 1923—his twenty-first birthday—he scheduled his first solo recital. In attendance was the distinguished music critic, the *New York World*'s Deems Taylor, who might have realigned Tom Dewey's career path once more with a positive review. It was not to be. Laryngitis struck, and Taylor found Dewey's performance lacked emotion. Dewey, even then ever so practical and cautious, concluded that hanging a livelihood upon something as slender and delicate as a pair of vocal chords was mere folly.

He would be a lawyer.

Graduating in 1925, he joined a private firm. In June 1928, he wed. Oklahoma-born Frances Eileen Hutt, a grandniece of Jefferson Davis, was another professional singer, an understudy mezzo-soprano for George White's *Scandals*. She not only married Dewey but also approved of the mustache he grew—on a bet—during a postgraduate European tour.

The law was profitable. The law was safe. But a young man with a young mustache wanted more. And to Tom Dewey, adventure spelled Republican politics and tramping streets for GOP candidates in Manhattan's Greenwich Village. In such humble ways, political contacts are made, and, in 1931, Dewey secured appointment to the office of newly commissioned U.S. attorney for the Southern District of New York, George Z. Medalie.

"I dropped him in the cold water and let him swim out," Medalie later observed of his protégé. "He made a darned good job of it—so good a job that I relieved him of some of the administrative work and turned him loose on the racketeering field."

Medalie resigned following Herbert Hoover's November 1932 defeat. Nine federal judges designated the thirty-one-year-old Dewey, just eight years out of law school, as Medalie's interim successor. Such lame-duck appointments normally count for little. This one, however, allowed Dewey to complete Medalie's headline-generating prosecution of the notorious mobster and bootlegger Irving "Waxey" Gordon. Exhibiting trademark bloodless efficiency, in the course of nine days, Dewey ("Gentlemen, there will be a lot of dead men mentioned during this case") presented 900 pieces of evidence and 131 witnesses. (In 1930 Gordon tendered just $10.76 to the Internal Revenue Service; Dewey demonstrated he had earned $1,427,531.) Fifty-one minutes later, the jury convicted Gordon on all four counts of tax evasion. The judge fined the uncouth Gordon $80,000 and sentenced him to ten years in Atlanta.

The legend of Tom Dewey, Gotham's fearless, incorruptible, racket-busting prosecutor was thus born.

With Democrat FDR in the White House, however, Republican Dewey involuntarily returned to a lucrative private practice. He might have remained there, but for a device seemingly the province only of movie fiction: a runaway Manhattan grand jury. Newly elected Tammany district attorney William Copeland Dodge had ordered an investigation into the numbers racket and bail-bond irregularities. Revolted by Dodge's incompetence and his obfuscation regarding the mob-related racketeering and extortion then infesting the city, grand jury members loudly demanded a new special prosecutor. Public outcry forced Governor Herbert Lehman to promise to appoint one.

But whom? George Medalie and Charles Evans Hughes Jr., son of the current chief justice of the U.S. Supreme Court, both declined. Dewey was considered too young—and too Republican. But William O. Douglas, now chairing FDR's Securities and Exchange Commission, intervened with White House insider Thomas "Tommy the Cork" Corcoran. Corcoran lobbied Lehman, FDR's former lieutenant governor, on behalf of former Douglas classmate Dewey.

Establishing his headquarters on the fourteenth floor of the Woolworth Building, Dewey ran a tight ship, instructing his men that nothing but the highest dedication would suffice. "If you want to have a good time," he pronounced, "go to New Jersey."

Dewey dramatically informed New Yorkers over radio stations WABC, WOR, and WMCA in July 1935:

> Your businesses, your safety, and your daily lives are affected by criminal conditions in this city. There is today scarcely a business in New York which does not somehow pay its tribute to the underworld—a tribute levied by force and collected by fear. . . . In my opinion you can be freed from organized racketeering in this city. Those of you who have knowledge of criminal conditions owe it to yourselves and the people of this city to give this investigation your co-operation. . . .
>
> Truck tires are slashed in the night. Fresh vegetables and fish are soaked with gasoline or stolen. Customers are intimidated, employees are beaten up, plate-glass windows are broken, and often whole stores are completely destroyed. . . . Every shakedown, every threat, every stink-bomb throwing, is a state crime. We will prosecute every crime which is part of an organized racket . . . every crime in the book, from conspiracy and malicious mischief to assault in the first degree, from extortion to perjury, from income tax violations all the way to murder.

The embattled William Copeland Dodge dared not seek reelection in 1937, and Dewey became Manhattan district attorney by a whopping 109,019 votes. In a corrupt, racket-dominated city, his record proved quite amazing. Among his high-profile victims: former New York Stock Exchange head Richard "The Voice of Wall Street" Whitney, West Harlem Tammany leader Jimmy Hines, and vice king Charles "Lucky" Luciano.

So feared was this young crusader that, in August 1939, vicious "Murder, Inc." chieftain Louis "Lepke" Buchalter dramatically surrendered to federal authorities (through an equally dramatic intermediary, Broadway gossip columnist Walter Winchell) rather than face Dewey's wrath.

And so feared that numbers kingpin and former beer baron Arthur "Dutch Schultz" Flegenheimer broke unwritten mob rules and plotted to assassinate Dewey—the plan short-circuited when Schultz's nervous gangland allies prudently rubbed him out instead.

Author Irving Stone, not an uncritical Dewey observer, summarized his gangbusting career thus:

Tom Dewey broke these rackets, broke them by his courage, tenacity, and daring use of new techniques. He freed labor unions from the racketeers that were milking them dry; in conviction after conviction he sent up the bosses and henchmen whose protective societies had been terrorizing nearly every industry in the city. By exposure, by publicity, by giving courage to the oppressed businessman, and by obtaining almost unfailing convictions, Tom Dewey eliminated industrial racketeering from New York.

By this time he was a hero in his own country. Stories, novels, plays and motion pictures were spun about his work. It was almost impossible to pick up a newspaper or magazine without seeing his picture and the story of a new accomplishment. Every class and group in America admired him and gave him full credit for the job he was doing.

Such a hero was clearly destined for greater things—and that was exactly how Thomas E. Dewey saw it. In 1938, barely a year into elective office, he challenged the popular Lehman for the governorship. He fell short by just 64,394 of 4,821,631 votes cast.

This impressive near miss merely emboldened Dewey. When charges against Jimmy Hines had initially been dismissed, Dewey had cockily informed his staff, "Don't worry, boys, there will be another chance and we will win it." Now, he was not merely certain of inevitable political triumph; he raised the stakes to the presidency itself.

Which makes this, perhaps, the optimal point to raise Thomas Edmund Dewey's most noted character trait: his unbridled arrogance. To achieve great fame while still possessing the bulk of one's youth is a dangerous thing. For Tom Dewey it represented a significant peril. He was good—and he knew it, and there was something, a very great something, about his precise, frigid manner that let nearly everyone else also know it. "If a young man," *New York Post* columnist Samuel Grafton wrote in 1940, "is as cold as this at thirty-seven he will reach absolute zero at fifty."

"In public," David Brinkley would later observe, "Dewey came across as pompous and cold. And for good reason. He was both." Others thought it misleading to focus merely upon his public persona. "You really have to know Tom Dewey well," Helen Porter Simpson, wife of Manhattan's doggedly liberal GOP chairman, Kenneth F. Simpson, famously observed, "in order to dislike him."

He craved adulation. While still district attorney he had spent a week vacationing at a Charlottesville, Virginia, country club recommended to him by Bill Douglas. Douglas inquired how his friend had enjoyed his stay. Fine, responded Dewey, save for one thing: "Only one person asked me for my autograph during one whole week."

According to Chicago isolationist Sterling Morton's summary, Dewey was a self-made man who worshipped his creator.

And so, Tom Dewey voluntarily retired from the district attorneyship and embarked upon a new mission: to slay his biggest dragon of all—the very biggest dragon, period. Franklin Delano Roosevelt.

Such a challenge failed to daunt him. "You make me sick," he curtly informed *Daily News* reporter Lowell Limpus. "You're like all the rest of them. Don't you realize that Franklin Roosevelt is the easiest man in the world for me to beat?"

Oddly enough, FDR himself vaguely agreed. "I . . . think it will be Dewey," he advised Jim Farley, "and he will make a formidable opponent. That will make it all the more necessary for you and me to work together."

On Friday, December 1, 1939, the still only thirty-seven-year-old Dewey announced his candidacy. He had, snarled Harold Ickes, "thrown his diaper in the political ring."

Five days later, Dewey embarked upon a nationwide tour, eventually covering twenty-five thousand miles. His polling numbers were good, and Thomas Dewey always believed in polling. That spring, George Gallup's presidential preference poll read:

	January 1940	March 1940	April 1940
Thomas Dewey	60%	53%	67%
Robert Taft	11%	17%	12%
Arthur Vandenberg	16%	19%	14%
Herbert Hoover	5%	5%	2%
Others	8%	6%	5%

Former Massachusetts governor Alvan T. Fuller had declared Dewey to be the "Sir Galahad to lead the Republican Party to victory." Others remained skeptical. At their annual dinner, members of the National Press Club sang:

N'ya, N'ya, N'ya, I'm the wonder boy,

N'ya, N'ya, you can't catch me,

N'ya, N'ya, N'ya, I'm the glamour boy–Infant prodegee.

On each fine speech I work for weeks,

Casting a binding spell;

I want a chance to wear long pants and give the New Deal Hell.

N'ya, N'ya, N'ya, I'm the foxy boy,

N'ya, N'ya, you can't catch me,

N'ya, N'ya, N'ya, I'm the pretty boy,

Where's the White House key?

Oh, Washington needs me!

A storm cloud arose. In early May, Dewey remained at a healthy 67 percent, but suddenly, the hitherto unknown Wendell Willkie ("a simple barefoot Wall Street lawyer," observed Harold Ickes) registered 3 percent. "This department," the *New Yorker* observed, "is prepared to state that Tom Dewey, New York's favorite grandson, will lead on early ballots in Philadelphia, but will never get enough to win." They were right. Within a month, Dewey had plummeted twenty percentage points, and Willkie had skyrocketed to 29 percent. A faltering Dewey led for the first three ballots. As he ruefully quipped, "they were the wrong three."

Undaunted, in 1942 he contested yet again for the governor's mansion, facing not the popular Herbert Lehman but a badly fractured Democratic Party. He won by 647,628 votes, carrying Queens and Staten Island and losing Manhattan by just 19,078 votes.

"For my part," he had told voters, "let me say right now that I shall devote the next four years exclusively to the service of the people of the state of New York."

If he ever meant it, it was difficult to discern. In 1944, with Willkie no longer an irresistible novelty and Senator Robert Taft ensnared in fighting for reelection in Ohio, Dewey enjoyed a relatively clear field toward the Republican presidential nomination. He took advantage of it.

"How can the Republican Party nominate a man who looks like the bridegroom on a wedding cake?" Congresswoman Clare Boothe Luce incredulously inquired of Senator Arthur Vandenberg, but Harold Ickes was no longer so sanguine regarding a Dewey candidacy. In January 1944, he privately wrote to a friend: "I regard Dewey as the strongest candidate and the most likely nominee, I regard him as a miniature fascist, and, therefore, dangerous."

He may not have been a fascist, but he was "calm, neat, painstaking, and deadly efficient," running New York State government and the state's GOP as if they were his own private fiefdoms. "Dewey and his political advisors," charged Helen Porter Simpson, "have succeeded in turning the Republican Party . . . into the most rigid and disciplined machine the State of New York has seen since the days of [Boss] Tom Platt."

He might have become president that year but for one small matter: World War II. Polling revealed that if the war were over by Election Day 1944, Dewey would triumph 51 to 30 percent.

But the war was not over, and Dewey faced an uphill climb.

Also conspiring against him was an attribute hampering him his entire life: a disposition to straddle issues, to switch sides as polling numbers changed. In the 1930s, he had allowed himself to be termed a "New Deal Republican." Now, he vociferously attacked the New Deal. In 1940, he had been isolationist. "If there is one thing upon which we are all agreed," he promised the Women's National Republican Club that January, "it is that we shall send no American to die on the battlefields of Europe." By 1944, he had careened into the internationalist camp, profoundly influenced by such advisers as prominent Wall Street attorney John Foster Dulles. "So far as policies go," the Republican *New York Herald Tribune* wrote in 1944, "Mr. Dewey has yet to give his full specifications. . . . We are confident that he will. For that is the sort of campaign he makes—terse, forceful, clear."

Sometimes, he indeed proved forceful and clear. Sometimes, not. Sometimes, he weakly echoed Democratic policies—"We refuse to be against the Ten Commandments just because the Democrats say they are for all of them."

Sometimes, he could not speak at all.

In September, Dewey's Republican allies—representatives Hugh Scott of Pennsylvania and Clare Boothe Luce of Connecticut and senators Styles Bridges of New Hampshire and John Bricker of Ohio (Dewey's running mate)—spoke out regarding Japan's attack on Pearl Harbor, and what Washington had known preceding it. Republican barbs struck a nerve. The United States, it seemed, had broken the Japanese codes before December 7, 1941, deciphering messages referencing the attack. Army Chief of Staff George C. Marshall dispatched an emissary to Dewey. He admitted that military intelligence had cracked the codes and that the warnings had not been properly relayed. He begged for Dewey's silence, revealing that Japan continued to employ two of the broken codes. Intelligence gleaned from them still remained invaluable to the war effort, in both the Pacific and European theaters.

Dewey privately fumed that "traitor" Roosevelt "ought to be impeached," but he kept his mouth shut. And, following Arthur Vandenberg's advice, he kept his silence regarding postwar Polish-Soviet boundaries.

Republicans also proceeded gingerly regarding FDR's increasingly flagging health. At November 1943's Tehran Conference, he had, in the words of his translator, Charles "Chip" Bohlen, suddenly "turned green and great drops of sweat began to bead off his head." Harry Hopkins thought his boss's subsequent interface with Stalin to be "inept," and his answers to the Soviet leader just plain "wrong."

On the very day of his fourth nomination, FDR ("I don't know if I can make it—I have horrible pains") suffered an excruciating seizure. A *Life* magazine photo of him finally accepting the nomination revealed an eerily hollow-eyed, slack-jawed man—"a sitting ghost," as Harold Ickes fearfully put it. Yet the presidential physician, Vice Adm. Ross T. McIntire, publicly declared that "the President's health is perfectly okay. There are absolutely no organic difficulties at all." *St. Louis Post-Dispatch* syndicated columnist Marquis Childs blasted the rumors as "a wicked business. It is the vilest kind of fear campaign." Dewey again kept silent. Republican National Committee press chief Steve Hanigan quit in disgust.

Dewey remained mute and vague and ever so magisterial, largely upon the advice of those who knew the least about politics—his friends in suburban Dutchess County, his wife, Frances, and his banking superintendent and close friend, the copper-haired, hunchbacked Elliot V. Bell. Savvy New York politician Herbert Brownell, Dewey's choice for chairman of the Republican National Committee, recalled that Dewey "had not learned to avoid or disregard well-meant advice, especially in the Pawling [NY] community where he resided, who reflected their rank amateurism in politics. [They] would have Saturday-night get-togethers . . . freely offering their advice to the candidate. They had sure-fire solutions for Dewey. Such as 'avoid politicians,' 'ignore your opponent,' and 'act statesmanlike.' Many . . . wanted active roles in the campaign."

Dewey—and fellow Republicans—however, proved less shy regarding the circumstances surrounding Harry Truman's vice-presidential nomination. As Henry Wallace's chances fell to ground (and Bill Douglas's never ascended), FDR tossed a sop to his left-wing and union supporters, ordering Bob Hannegan to "Clear it with Sidney" before Harry Truman's nomination could move forward.

"Sidney" was Sidney Hillman, the Lithuanian-born former rabbinical student and former czarist-era revolutionary, who had helped found first the Amalgamated Clothing Workers of America (ACWA) and then the Congress of Industrial Organizations. In 1944, Hillman was busy, successfully organizing the CIO's powerful new political arm, the Political Action Committee (PAC) ("Every worker a voter"). "Sidney Hillman," recalled Henry Wallace, "had a payroll of $65,000 a month and a more powerful organization for getting out the vote than the Democratic National Committee." The CIO-PAC was, said *Time* magazine, generating "the slickest political propaganda produced in the U.S. in a generation."

The anti-Hillman campaign ("It's your country—Why let Sidney Hillman run it?") soon accelerated into an anticommunist campaign, as Dewey excoriated Communist Party support for FDR's fourth term. "Now . . . with the aid of Sidney Hillman," Dewey told a crowd of twenty-four thousand at the Boston Garden, "the Communists are seizing control of the New Deal . . . to control the Government of the United States."

The attack garnered Dewey votes among Boston Irish and in the midwestern hinterlands. It spawned dissension within the campaign itself. Dewey's wife, Frances, hated it. His counsel, Charles D. Breitel (himself Jewish), thought it reeked of anti-Semitism. Editorialists recoiled in horror. Dewey would never again exploit the issue of domestic Communism.

He proved even more sensitive regarding his height. Though he was not *that* short, he reacted as if he were. At Oklahoma City, he had a large book placed behind a podium so that he might perch upon it and seem taller. His sensitivity merely magnified the issue. Trying to defuse it, Dewey's six-foot-four executive secretary, Paul Lockwood, merely exacerbated it. "I've done some research," Lockwood responded to a *Nation* article finding Dewey to be shorter than all of his possible running mates: "I find that Stalin is five feet five, Churchill is five feet seven, and Chiang Kai-shek is five feet three. Governor Dewey, on the other hand, is five feet eight."

While Dewey faltered, FDR jabbed, his most famous moment of the campaign being not one of profound substance, but of sheer, joyous, masterful ridicule: his famous defense of his black Scottish terrier, Fala. Rumors circulated that Fala's master had dispatched a U.S. Navy destroyer to the Aleutians "at a cost to the taxpayers of two or three, or eight or twenty million dollars" to rescue the stranded canine. FDR responded:

> These Republican leaders have not been content with attacks on me, or my wife, or on my sons. No, not content with that, they now include my little dog, Fala. Well, of course, I don't resent attacks, and my family don't [sic] resent attacks, but Fala does resent them. You know, Fala is Scotch, and being a Scottie, as soon as he learned that the Republican fiction writers in Congress and out had concocted a story that I had left him behind on the Aleutian Islands and had sent a destroyer back to find him—at a cost to the taxpayers of two or three, or eight or twenty million dollars—his Scotch soul was furious. He has not been the same dog since.

Nor was Tom Dewey the same dog after that. Perhaps it was Fala, perhaps not, but from that moment on he seemed more energized, more slashing, and a campaign that once seemed as dead as a mackerel ("Dewey," wrote columnist Dorothy Thompson, "seems to think he is running for an office manager's job") assumed signs of life. At Oklahoma City, he thundered:

> Now I had not intended in this campaign to rake over my opponent's sad record of failing to prepare the defenses of this country for war. It has cost countless American lives; it has cost untold misery. . . . In 1940, the year after the war began in Europe, the United States was in such a tragic condition that it couldn't put into the field as a mobile force 75,000 men. The Army was only about 25 percent ready. Now, Mr. Roosevelt, did these statements come from Goebbels? Was that fraud or falsehood? Those are the words of General George C. Marshall, Chief of Staff of the United States Army, under oath.

As Election Day drew near, the Crossley, Elmo Roper, and *Newsweek* polls all projected a slight FDR lead. Gallup even gave Dewey a narrow edge. All, however, hedged their bets. Even the normally ebullient Roosevelt feared a close race.

It wasn't. FDR won 53.8 percent of the vote, triumphing 25,130,113 to 21,615,439. The Electoral College witnessed a 432 to 99 landslide. But Dewey had, nonetheless, fared better against FDR than any other opponent, and had posted the best losing presidential numbers since Charles Evans Hughes's eyelash 1916 defeat. He carried Hyde Park and Independence and shifted two hundred counties to the GOP. Most significantly, a switch of three hundred thousand votes in key states would have given Dewey the Electoral College.

Thomas E. Dewey conceded at 3:45 AM. FDR, who considered this to have been the dirtiest campaign he had yet endured, muttered, "I still think he is a son of a bitch."

Dewey dusted off his homburg and picked himself off the floor yet again. If he had not been successful, he had at least been efficient and frugal: the Republican National Campaign Committee concluded 1944's effort with an unprecedented $350,000 surplus. And in 1946, Dewey ran once more for New York governor, defeating U.S. senator James M. Mead by a record 687,151 votes—the largest-ever majority for governor. He was the first Republican to carry New York City since 1928.

With Republicanism suddenly resurgent, the 1948 Republican presidential nomination was worth having, and Tom Dewey, despite his considerable flaws as a national candidate, wanted it very, very much. Could he change? Could he make himself warm, human, and, above all, electable beyond Albany?

In New York City, reporters in their annual Inner Circle show produced a skit entitled "In a Smoke-filled Room." The journalist portraying Tom Dewey sang:

I'll be different if I'm the nominee,

I'll be different, not like I used to be.

I'll be so real; get sex appeal.

Pleasant and sweet, I'll outdo the new deal.

I'll learn to laugh, but not like Bob Taft, If I'm the nominee.

Thomas Edmund Dewey would have to be different.

6

"To err is Truman"

Harry Truman had to change too.

He had commenced his presidency not with swagger, but almost imprisoned by stunned humility. The afternoon following FDR's passing, he returned to the Capitol to confer with congressional leaders. As he exited, he asked reporters: "Boys, if you ever pray, pray for me now. I don't know if you fellows ever had a load of hay fall on you, but when they told me yesterday what had happened, I felt like the moon, the stars, and all the planets had fallen on me."

He placed upon his desk a simple sign—crafted in an Oklahoma penitentiary—reading, "The buck stops here;" and when the time arrived to decide to drop atomic weapons on Japan, he decided, and ultimately 220,000 people died.

"It was a terrible decision. But I made it," he would declare. "And I'd made it to save 250,000 boys from the United States and I'd make it again under similar circumstances. It stopped the Jap War."

It was a great thing to preside over a nation victorious in war. In May 1945, he recorded the highest presidential approval rating in history: 87 percent. Only 3 percent disapproved.

But then fifteen million men returned home. Defense plants closed or retooled. Couples married—and faced a housing shortage. Prices skyrocketed. Between April 1945 and fall 1946, real wages dropped by 8.5 percent.

The moon, the stars, and all the planets began falling on Harry Truman.

All such postwar events were quite predictable, and, in the very short run, there was nothing any president might have done about them. What Harry Truman—new to the presidency—did about his difficulties was to compound them. Inflation ran rampant. In August 1946, one wire service provided this dismal report:

> Food prices rose 13.3 percent between mid-June and mid-July—the largest monthly change ever recorded. The largest previous monthly increase was 9 percent from March to April 1917. Meats advanced 29.6 percent and dairy products 21.2 percent in the June–July period. Other important foods went up 37 percent. [The Bureau of Labor Statistics] said some of the meat price advance may have occurred between April and June "when the meat shortage was so severe that the bureau could not obtain an adequate number of meat prices."

Truman's response to the problem had traversed the gamut—and not very artfully. At war's end he withdrew price controls on most commodities. Prices, not surprisingly, skyrocketed. In December 1945, he reimposed controls on building materials. Meat prices proved particularly volatile— as did Truman's position on controls. In June 1946, with controls set to expire, he urged their extension, and then vetoed one bill on the subject before signing a particularly ill-conceived measure that reimposed them on August 20, 1946. Meat supplies flooded the market preceding that date— and disappeared following it. On October 14, 1946, he decreed an end to price controls on meat. The price of a pound of round steak soared from 40.6 cents a pound in 1945 to 83.3 cents in 1948. Chuck roast increased from 37.1 cents to 71.7 cents. The exercise left few happy—or impressed.

Labor remained key to Democratic fortunes. The big-city machines, as Harry Truman knew quite well, were helpful, but they had their limits. The South had its charms, but its leaders lay largely somnolent and tentative. The rapidly emerging black vote, fueled by a million-person migration to northern cities, had yet to fully exert its growing power. Labor, on the other hand, buoyed by the New Deal's Wagner Act, wielded real clout, its numbers rising from 7 percent of the work force in 1933 to 15 percent in 1939 to 27 percent in 1944. Organized labor—rich in money, votes, and manpower— could make or break a candidate.

Having been reelected to his Senate seat in 1940, largely thanks to labor's help, Harry Truman now, in 1946, endeavored to break labor.

Labor had often acted less than responsibly during the war. Following V-J Day it seemed to abandon all restraint. As in the post–World War I period, strikes engulfed the economy. 1946 was, by a wide margin, the most strike-ridden year in American history. About 4.6 million workers (10 percent of those employed) walked off the job; 4,956 different work stoppages cost industry 116 million man-days of lost production, virtually as many as in the previous seven years combined. Four hundred thousand of John L. Lewis's coal miners struck. Brownouts affecting streetlights and public buildings were ordered in twenty-one eastern and midwestern states. Coal shipments to freezing, war-torn Europe might soon halt entirely. Three hundred thousand rail workers had struck even before that. Truman threatened that the army would seize the railroads and draft striking railmen.

"Draft men who strike in peacetime, into the armed services?" asked a clearly dumbstruck anonymous columnist of the *New Republic*, "T.R.B." (the *Christian Science Monitor*'s Richard L. Strout). "Is this Russia or Germany?"

"I am not willing to vote for a measure which provides that the President may be a dictator," warned Robert Taft. "It offends not only the Constitution but every basic principle for which the American Republic was established."

The Democratic-controlled Senate crushed Truman's proposal seventy to thirteen. Had they known of the intemperate speech ("the worst I ever saw," said his aide Clark Clifford) that Truman had at one point planned to deliver if the strike were not settled, they might have crushed him as well. Redolent of lynch law, it read in part:

> I am tired of government being flouted, vilified and now I want you men who are my comrades in arms [you men who fought the battles to save the nation just as I did twenty-five years ago] to come along with me and eliminate the [John L.] Lewises, the Whitneys [Brotherhood of Railroad Trainmen president, A. F. Whitney], the [Brotherhood of Locomotive Engineers' Alvanley] Johnstons, the Communist [Harry] Bridges [of the International Longshore and Warehouse Union] and the Russian Senators and Representatives and make this a government of, by and for the people. I think no more of the Wall Street crowd than I do of Lewis and Whitney.

Let us give the country back to the people, hang a few traitors, make our own country safe for democracy, tell Russia where to get off and make the United Nations work. Come on, boys, let's do the job.

The seventy-three-year-old Whitney (not even knowing of Truman's urge to string him up) decried Truman's actions as reeking "of the warp and woof of fascism" and sniffed that "You can't make a President out of a ribbon clerk." In May 1946, he vowed to employ every cent of his $47 million treasury to defeat labor's erstwhile ally in 1948.

Labor comprised but one part of the liberal coalition that the new president tried—but increasingly failed—to hold. In September 1945, he had proposed hiking the minimum wage (from forty to sixty-five cents in one year, and seventy-five cents in two), increasing unemployment insurance benefits to twenty-five dollars a week for fifty-two weeks, instituting a permanent Fair Employment Practices Commission (FEPC), continuing price controls, passing a full-employment bill, and authorizing badly needed public housing. In November, he advocated federal health insurance. Liberals, nonetheless, still shunned him, unable to forget Franklin Roosevelt—nor able to forget that midwestern machine-politician Harry Truman was not Franklin Roosevelt. On radio station WJZ, in January 1947, twenty months after FDR's death, former New York City mayor Fiorello LaGuardia spoke for millions when he mourned:

We cannot think of President Roosevelt as one who is gone. He is here. Every hope, yes, the peace of the world, requires his constant spiritual presence. . . .

How we miss him. Hardly a domestic problem or an international situation today [exists] but what we say "Oh, if F.D.R. were only here."

"Liberal rhetoric and political perceptions were dominated to a remarkable extent by symbol and myth," Truman scholar Alonzo Hamby has noted. "Criticisms of Truman . . . were almost invariably expressed in terms of a comparison with . . . Roosevelt. . . . [I]f Truman 'departed' from a 'Roosevelt policy,' the departure had to be bad. If Truman's style was unlike Roosevelt's, then Truman could not be a liberal leader. . . . Criticism became alienation."

Unlike FDR—and so many of FDR's mourners—Truman did not wear his liberalism on his sleeve. Compounding matters, he had, of course, replaced the sainted Henry Wallace on the ticket—and ultimately in the White House. Within the Senate, he had never warmed to the party's progressive block, aligning himself with men like Jimmy Byrnes and even with staunch Montana isolationist Burton K. Wheeler. It was, in fact, Wheeler who secured for Truman the vitally needed railmen's support in 1940. In 1946, Truman shocked liberals by returning the favor and endorsing Wheeler in that year's Democratic primary. In 1937, Truman had even defied FDR (and, yes, even Pendergast) to support Mississippi conservative Pat Harrison for majority leader over the much more liberal Alben Barkley.

Nor could liberals (or many observers, for that matter) have taken much comfort in Truman's comment, uttered upon 1941's Nazi invasion of Soviet Russia: "If we see that Germany is winning we ought to help Russia, and if we see that Russia is winning we ought to help Germany, and that way let them kill as many as possible."

About labor leaders he fumed intemperately and privately to Chester Bowles, administrator of the Office of Price Administration (OPA), in the early winter of 1945 to 1946: "Those labor leaders, you can't trust 'em. They're wrecking the country. There's only one you can trust and that's John L. Lewis. Aside from him I wouldn't trust any of those labor leaders." Not surprisingly, word got out.

"What line his [Truman's] subordinates follow has yet to be developed," Texas New Deal congressman Lyndon Johnson wrote disgustedly to James H. Rowe Jr., former assistant to "Tommy the Cork" Corcoran, in July 1945. "Most of our old friends are bewildered and I think that is true, generally speaking, of the people who have acquired responsibility and power so quickly. . . . My own course in political affairs is yet to be charted. We are giving serious thought to going back to the Hill Country in Texas and making our contribution to a better world from that spot."

Not only liberals saw Harry Truman detouring rightward from New Deal policies. In October 1944, former ambassador to the United Kingdom Joseph P. Kennedy Sr. confided to his diary (and later to his family) that he had conferred in Boston with both Truman and Bob Hannegan, and that both Democrats "believe Roosevelt won't live long, particularly Hannegan. . . .

They felt that Truman will be President and will kick out all these incompetents and Jews out of Washington and ask fellows like myself and others to come back and run the government. Truman assured me that that is what he would do. He said that he disliked Mrs. Roosevelt very much. . . . I state again—both Truman and Hannegan discussed what they would do when the President died."

Truman remembered the meeting far differently ("If you say another word about Roosevelt, I'm going to throw you out the window"), but whoever spoke the truth about that particular encounter, it reflected Truman's personality. In safe hindsight his combativeness has been praised as picturesque feistiness—almost a compulsion to portray even the commonest interactions as glorious, bare-knuckle battle royals— but it often exhibited itself as mere defensiveness wrapped in hostility and tucked inside a tantrum. The one-time "sissy," the former "Senator from Pendergast," seemed driven to display often inexplicable toughness and independence.

"I have been with the president on occasions," recalled Truman's naval aide, Adm. Robert Dennison, "when he had what appeared to me to be a perfectly normal and amiable conversation with a caller. After the caller left, he would say to me, in effect, 'I certainly set him straight,' or 'I let him have it.'

"The president's remarks seemed to me to have no conceivable relation to the conversation I had just heard."

Commented Alonzo Hamby:

Dennison [described] what had become a common behavioral pattern by the time Truman reached the White House: the smiling, friendly conversation that smoothed over or failed to touch upon some difficulty with another person, then the surging feelings of aggression when that individual was out of range, at times discharged orally to a third party, at other times committed to paper in the form of an angry memorandum or letter that often was filed and forgotten but occasionally made its way to the addressee. Enough such missives, often directed to people with whom Truman had a friendly relationship, have been discovered in his presidential papers to provide the material for a small book.

Within the White House, ensconced in the great Roosevelt's place, surrounded by movers and shakers from the best schools, law and brokerage firms, and country clubs, HST's insecurity could only grow.

"Truman," recalled Bill Douglas, who had graduated from Columbia and taught at Yale, "would give me lectures on the problems of the world, taking me over to the big globe in the Oval Office and explaining the history and present plight of the area I planned to visit at any particular time. I always thanked him, but I always realized his abysmal ignorance of what actually went on in the world."

"What got Truman's goat was that he thought we New Dealers looked down on him," recalled attorney Ernest L. Cuneo, yet another veteran of the FDR White House. "And we did."

It was all very unnerving. "What else can the little guy do?" asked Hearst columnist Westbrook Pegler, regarding the nation's unlikely new president:

Dwarfed by the doubledomes of Harvard law, a humble hick and, undoubtedly an Elk, if not an Eagle or an Owl, Mr. Truman personified the awkward Middle Western culture which had been ridiculed for thirty years by the same proto-communist papers that cultivate him now. He was the kind who would put ginger ale in red liquor and wear a green dinner jacket with a button flower of purple feathers. You saw him at the country club in small Ohio towns and in West Palm Beach, but never at The Breakers across Lake Worth. Ten years ago Harry S. Truman of Kansas City would have been turned off at the door of Bradley's gambling house at Palm Beach as a Babbitt with a sweaty little roll of vacation money who belonged in a sawdust joint.

No, neither liberals nor Washington elites knew what to make of Harry Truman. And their doubts were not always misplaced. In May 1945, he confided to his diary that he regarded a professional liberal as "the lowest form of politician." The following month, convinced of Democratic Party cabals against the new president, Truman crony Maj. Gen. Harry H. Vaughan ordered FBI director J. Edgar Hoover to illegally wiretap former FDR confidant Tommy "The Cork" Corcoran. Corcoran's offense? He had preferred Douglas to Truman in 1944.

Among Corcoran comments reported back to Truman was a complaint Truman might have heard on any street corner: that the new president thought he could "surround himself almost entirely with mediocre Missourians and run the greatest country in the world."

Had he listened carefully, he might have discerned similar unease within the White House itself. "Missourians are most in evidence," noted his aide Eben Ayers, "and there is a feeling of an attempt by the 'gang' to move in."

A California liberal privately commented, regarding the gang popularly known as "Truman's midgets": "You get this stuff every place you turn: Truman is a nice man, but no superman; he is surrounded by a bunch of 'regular' party hacks who are going to drive every decent person out of important administrative positions."

It was not exactly true. There were capable men among the Truman appointees—Gen. George C. Marshall (after Truman sacked the dangerously ambitious Jimmy Byrnes at the State Department), Navy secretary James V. Forrestal, counsel Clark Clifford, and press secretary Charles G. Ross among them. But in those early days, the spectacularly incompetent and the merely run-of-the-mill incompetent seemed most in evidence.

And, yes, many appointees—even Ross, a Pulitzer Prize winner, and Clifford—were Missourians. Old Battery D buddy Eddie McKim became Truman's chief administrative assistant. He lasted six weeks. HST's National Guard comrade, the crass Harry Hood Vaughan, also came aboard. So did St. Louis attorney James K. "J. K." Vardaman (son of the virulently racist, populist, Mississippi U.S. senator James K. "The Great White Chief" Vardaman), who, like McKim, soon exited—improbably being designated a governor of the Federal Reserve System. Vaughan, despite Alonzo Hamby's assessment of him as "a bull in constant search for a new china shop," remained throughout his friend's tenure.

Occupying a far more exalted position than either Vardaman, McKim, or Vaughan, however, was another of Truman's fellow artillerymen, the stocky, waddling John W. Snyder, an individual of not only decidedly few qualifications but (perhaps worse for the New Deal crowd) of profoundly conservative bent.

"I was very fond of both Snyder and Vaughan," noted Bill Douglas, "but if Truman had had the Secret Service pull any two men off Pennsylvania Avenue and send them in, Truman would have received better advice."

One by one, the old FDR men and women departed—Wallace, of course, but also the silver-haired nonentity Edward R. Stettinius Jr. at State, seventy-eight-year-old Republican Henry L. Stimson at War, Henry Morgenthau Jr. (HST considered him a "block head, nut") at Treasury, Frank C. Walker (replaced by Bob Hannegan) in the Post Office, Frances Perkins at Labor (he privately admitted he "did not want any woman in the cabinet"), and the Paris-born Philadelphia patrician Francis Biddle as attorney general. The last was a particularly cruel sacking.

It grew worse and worse. In February 1948, Drew Pearson recorded in his column:

> Democratic leaders on Capitol Hill are just as sore at their old pal, Harry Truman, as they were at Roosevelt—possibly more so. What Alben Barkley and Sam Rayburn say about their chief in the White House can't be printed in a family newspaper.

> They were especially indignant at the way he handled the attempt to fire [Federal Reserve chairman] Marriner Eccles, replacing him with dyed-in-the-wool Republican Tom McCabe. They were also burned up at the way Truman ousted James Landis [a Joe Kennedy protégé] from Civil Aeronautics, after his long service . . . and after Truman had given a categorical commitment to Rayburn that Landis would be reappointed.

"When I became President," Truman justified himself to the unfortunate Landis, "[former DNC chairman] Ed Flynn told me that I'd have to be a son of a bitch half the time. This is one of the times." Other explanations of such controversial actions did little to ameliorate ill feelings, as witnessed by this exchange from the presidential press conference that followed the Eccles dismissal:

> Q. Mr. President, what prompted you to replace Mr. Eccles with this Philadelphia Republican [McCabe]?

> THE PRESIDENT. That is my prerogative. I decided to make the change without anybody's request or influence.

Q. Was it because—

THE PRESIDENT. The President has a right to do that if he wants to do that.

Q. Do you prefer Mr. McCabe's fiscal policies to Mr. Eccles's?

THE PRESIDENT. That question I will not answer.

The Eccles dustup, however, was nothing compared to Interior secretary Harold Ickes's departure. It began when Truman appointed his old patron, hulking California oilman and DNC treasurer Edwin W. Pauley, as assistant Navy secretary. Ickes contended that on the return train ride from FDR's Hyde Park burial, Pauley indicated to him that if Ickes did not file a suit for tidelands oil ownership, hundreds of thousands of dollars in donations would conveniently flow into Democratic Party coffers.

"This is the rawest proposition that has ever been made to me," Ickes recorded shortly thereafter in a private memorandum. "I don't intend to smear my record in oil at this stage of the game."

Was this the Democratic version of the Teapot Dome scandal? The *Nation*'s Freda Kirchwey sniffed "the unsavory odor of oil politics," contending, "the greater intelligence and probity of Mr. Truman does not suffice to wipe out an unhappy resemblance to Mr. [Warren] Harding."

"Mr. Truman, Mr. Hannegan, and Mr. Pauley . . . ," added Walter Lippmann, "have gone back avowedly and unashamedly to the politics of the Tammany-Prendergast [sic] era in its crudest and nakedest form."

In late morning, Wednesday, February 13, 1946, Harold Ickes addressed the largest press conference in Washington history, very publicly announcing his resignation. "I don't care to stay," he told 450 print and radio correspondents, "in an Administration where I am expected to commit perjury for the sake of my party."

Harry Truman didn't care for him to stay either.

Reminders of Truman's Pendergast days remained painfully evident. In August 1946, Truman flew home to assist his old friend Jim Pendergast (now running what remained of the local machine) in a series of primary contests—most prominently to help organization candidate Enos Axtell defeat anti–New Deal, anti-FEPC incumbent congressman Roger C. Slaughter. Vote fraud permeated the primary, so much so that on Thursday, May 27, 1948, a federal grand jury handed down eighty-one indictments. Less than twelve hours later—with Harry Truman sleeping three blocks away at the Hotel Muehlebach—thieves blasted open two steel vault doors in the offices of the Jackson County Board of Elections, departing with three boxes of evidence crucial to the case.

This new president seemed barely able to speak in public. Recalled his appointments secretary, Massachusetts Democrat Matthew J. Connelly, a veteran of the Truman Committee investigations: "He was not a natural public speaker and did not like to make speeches. . . . I doubt if he made more than a half a dozen speeches all the time that he was in the Senate. He was not known as a speaker, and, as a matter [of] fact, in my first association with him he was pretty terrible."

His extemporaneous speaking also seemed askew. Observers marveled at his comment at the 1944 convention, when he placed his arm around his beloved Bess, and cooed, "She looks just like a woman ought to look who's been married twenty-five years."

Even in endorsing Enos Axtell in 1946, he had flubbed his lines, claiming Axtell to be a lifelong friend—and then at a press conference proving unable to provide his first name. The embarrassing sequence went like this:

Q. —have you ever met Mr. Axtell? Are you endorsing him—

THE PRESIDENT. I know him very well. I have known his family. I have known him all his life. He is a neighbor of mine. He lives down home.

Q. What's his first name?

THE PRESIDENT. Ed—or En—or something of that sort. [Laughter] What's his first name? [More laughter] What's his first name? •

Q. Enos—E-n-o-s.

THE PRESIDENT. Enos—E-n-o-s. That's right. [Continued laughter]

Dorothy Thompson blasted Truman as an "intellectual nonentity." Illinois Democratic senator Scott W. Lucas predicted, "He won't get enough votes to wad a shotgun."

And the jokes began:

A reporter at a Truman press conference asked, "What are they doing? Why do we have to wait?"

"They are trying to get his foot out of his mouth," a colleague replied.

"I'm just mild about Harry," voters laughed.

And Robert Taft's wife, Martha, chortled, "To err is Truman."

But such comments soon proved tame compared to others in the avalanche of anti-Truman jibes making the rounds:

"I wonder what Truman would do if he were alive."

"Don't shoot the piano player; he's doing the best he can."

"Who is the power behind the drone?"

Harry Truman's approval ratings never again reached 87 percent. By June 1946, they had dropped to a worrisome 43 percent. By fall, he had hit 32 percent.

The midterm elections of 1946 drew near. Traditionally, the party in power lost congressional seats. In 1942, Democrats had dropped eight Senate and forty-five House seats. In 1938, they had lost six Senate and seventy-two House seats. Yet this year seemed even more perilous. Bob Hannegan, cognizant of Harry Truman's fading popularity and wary of diminishing it even further by tying it to a lost cause, advised him not to campaign in 1946.

Hannegan proved prescient. Aided by unusually low turnout, Republicans swept through the large industrial states, posting net gains of eleven Senate and fifty-five House seats, assuming control of both houses of Congress for the first time since 1928.

In Massachusetts, patrician liberal Henry Cabot Lodge Jr. reclaimed his Senate seat. In Wisconsin, a difficult sort of Republican, thirty-five-year-old ex-Marine and circuit court judge Joseph R. McCarthy entered the Senate. Democrats lost Harry Truman's and Burton Wheeler's old Senate seats. In New York, venerable Herbert Lehman lost a Senate bid. In California's 12th district, thirty-three-year-old attorney and Navy veteran Richard Nixon defeated five-term incumbent Democratic congressman Jerry Voorhis.

Liberal forces—on both sides of the aisle—were in disarray. Sidney Hillman's CIO-PAC endorsed 318 House candidates. Only seventy-three won, leaving the House Democratic caucus largely in conservative Southern hands. Of seventy-seven leftward-leaning House Republicans (as graded by the *New Republic*), only thirty-six lived to fight another day.

Victory has a thousand fathers.

Defeat, in 1946, had one: Harry Truman.

If he appeared ineffectual before Election Day, he seemed outright repulsive after it. Democrats faulted him—and not the effects of sixteen years of their rule—for their debacle. They wanted him out, and they wanted him out *now*.

Freshman Arkansas senator J. William Fulbright demanded that Truman appoint a Republican secretary of state (presumably Michigan's Arthur Vandenberg) and resign, so that with the vice presidency vacant a Republican might assume the White House. Former Birmingham, Alabama, congressman Luther Patrick quickly agreed. The normally Democratic *Chicago Sun* advised Truman to assume a "patriotic and courageous" stance and heed the "unmistakable verdict" of the electorate—and scram. The liberal *New York Post* possessed little confidence Truman could do even that right.

"The *Constitution* does not urge resignation upon Mr. Truman," argued the *Atlanta Constitution*, "but it does suggest that a very serious weighing of Senator Fulbright's proposal be a part of the Democratic strategy within the next few days."

Walter Lippmann concurred:

> How are the affairs of the country to be conducted by a President who not only has lost the support of his party, but is not in command of his own administration . . . [who] is not performing and gives no evidence of ability to perform, the functions of commander in chief. It is a poor conception of the public service which makes it a moral duty for a man to cling to an office, or to be a prisoner in it, if he cannot exercise its functions.

The right to resign is one of the cherished privileges of a free man; the willingness to resign, when principle and the public interest are served, is always present in the public-spirited and the self-respecting. They look upon resigning, not as cowardice and quitting and a personal disaster, but as the ultimate guaranty of their useful influence and of their personal dignity.

Harry Truman might now be lacking in dignity.
He was not, however, lacking in courage.

7

"My very stomach turned"

Harry Truman was a most unlikely candidate for the title of civil rights crusader.

He descended, after all, from Kentucky and Missouri slaveholders. Without any great embarrassment, he said, regarding his family's human chattels, "Most were wedding presents." In 1863, Truman's mother, Martha, then eleven years old, was herded, along with her mother and five siblings, into what might best be called a Union internment camp. Truman called such facilities "concentration camps."

"I thought it was a good thing Lincoln was shot," Martha Truman would tell neighbors. She retained Confederate sympathies until her June 1947 death, triggering the following comment from Alabama governor Chauncey Sparks upon her son's vice-presidential nomination: "The South has won a substantial victory. . . . In the matter of race relations Senator Truman told me he is the son of an unreconstructed rebel mother."

Sparks spoke the truth. Courting his Bess, young Harry once wrote to her this vision of social equality: "I think one man is just as good as another, so long as he's honest and decent and not a nigger or a Chinaman." He went on to explain that his uncle Will Young had told him, "the Lord made a white man of dust, a nigger from mud, then threw up what was left and it came down a Chinaman. He does hate Chinks and Japs. So do I. It is race prejudice I guess. But I am strongly of the opinion that negroes ought to be in Africa, yellow men in Asia, and white men in Europe and America."

In Washington, he still employed the word "nigger," and wrote home about the city's black waiters (an "army of coons") and what he termed a "Nigger picnic day."

In 1940, he bluntly informed the National Colored Democratic Association in Chicago: "I wish to make it clear that I am not appealing for social equality of the Negro. The Negro himself knows better than that, and the highest types of Negro leaders say quite frankly that they prefer the society of their own people. Negroes want justice, not social relations."

His younger sister, Mary Jane, stated it more bluntly still: "Harry isn't any more in favor of nigger equality than I am."

But while he believed in a crude racism, he also favored a crude fairness. Campaigning for reelection in 1940, he informed a largely white Sedalia, Missouri, audience:

> I believe in the brotherhood of man; not merely the brotherhood of white men, but the brotherhood of all men before the law. . . . If any class or race can be permanently set apart from, or pushed below the rest in political and civil rights, so may any other class or race when it shall incur the displeasure of its more powerful associates, and we may say farewell to the principles on which we count our safety. . . .
>
> Negroes have been preyed upon by all types of exploiters, from the installment salesmen of clothing, pianos, and furniture to the vendors of vice. The majority of our Negro people find but cold comfort in shanties and tenements. Surely, as freemen, they are entitled to something better than this.

"This" was the American form of racial separation and discrimination, still largely undented in 1945 after a dozen years of comforting but still vague dollops of New Deal sympathy. In the South, black voters might be scared off by outright intimidation. "I call upon every red-blooded white man to use any means to keep the nigger away from the polls," said Mississippi senator Theodore Bilbo in 1946. "The best way to keep a nigger from voting is to have a little talk with him the night before." Less violently, an intricate pattern of legal barriers—literacy tests (rigged or not), grandfather clauses, poll taxes, and all-white Democratic primaries— largely disenfranchised Southern blacks. As late as 1935, the U.S. Supreme Court (in *Grovey v. Townsend*) had ruled unanimously that primaries (as well as political parties) were essentially private entities, free to determine their own qualifications (race included) for membership. In April 1944, however, in *Smith v. Allwright,* the Court overturned Texas's white primary by an eight to one margin. The foundations of southern white supremacy started shaking. In April 1948, South Carolina's blacks voted in their state's Democratic primary for the first time since 1876.

Segregation, of course, involved more than mere voting rights. Blacks found themselves barred from all manner of public facilities, excluded from large numbers of employment opportunities, and relegated to invariably inferior "separate-but-equal" schools—if admitted to any at all. Not until January 1948 did the U.S. Supreme Court rule in *Sipuel v. Board of Regents of University of Oklahoma* that state-funded law schools must admit all races. All in all, blacks had plentiful reasons for discontent, and, as the 1940s progressed, they finally had opportunities via the ballot box to redress them—not only in the Solid South, but also in the teeming cities of the industrial north.

Since World War I, blacks, bereft of opportunity in the South, had steadily migrated northward where they could not only hope to earn a better living—they could vote. Until the New Deal, blacks tended to be Republican, but since 1932, they had trended Democratic. During World War II another million blacks had migrated northward. Detroit's African-American population grew by 40 percent during the 1940s, San Francisco's by 237 percent. Largely settled in key electoral states—New York, Illinois, Pennsylvania, Michigan, New Jersey, California, and Ohio—2.5 million northern black voters now had to be taken seriously.

Their electoral power had, in a sense, created Harry Truman. Had Bronx boss Ed Flynn not warned FDR in 1944 that Jimmy Byrnes would cost his ticket two hundred thousand black votes in New York State alone, it might have been Roosevelt-Byrnes that November, and President Byrnes—not President Truman—the following April. That same year, fifty thousand black votes in Baltimore provided FDR with his Maryland victory margin. Similar totals in five New Jersey cities gave him New Jersey's electoral votes. Blacks proved crucial (though not entirely pivotal) in strongly Republican Pennsylvania.

Such numbers grew more significant in 1948. In that year, Henry Lee Moon, a black director of the CIO-PAC, published a significant study entitled *Balance of Power: The Negro Vote*, chronicling how African-American voters might swing 277 electoral votes in fifteen northern states into—or out of—the Democratic column.

What if, worried the Democrats, Tom Dewey returned to combat in 1948? In 1942, he carried Harlem. His civil rights record was particularly attractive, including a number of significant black appointments and support for New York State's pioneering anti-discrimination measure, March 1945's Ives-Quinn Act. Accordingly, in June 1945, Eleanor Roosevelt wrote to Bob Hannegan:

> I have been thinking a good deal about the political situation as I view it from New York State. I know that my husband felt very strongly that we have to carry the congressional election in 1946 in order to win in 1948. If Governor Dewey is not defeated the chances are that we will be defeated in 1948, so what happens to him is vitally important.
>
> I notice a number of things. Governor Dewey certainly learned from the last campaign that he could not ignore the colored vote and, at the expense of some of his most conservative support, he is now playing up very strongly to the minority groups in this state and also to the liberals.

That Harry Truman would recognize this danger—and act upon it—was by no means guaranteed. In 1939, Eleanor Roosevelt had famously resigned from the Daughters of the American Revolution (DAR) when its Washington chapter refused its Constitution Hall venue to black contralto Marian Anderson. In October 1945, the DAR similarly barred pianist Hazel Scott, wife of freshman Harlem congressman Adam Clayton Powell. Not only did Bess Truman fail to protest, she meekly attended a subsequent DAR tea party. "From now on there is only one First Lady," Powell declared to a reporter at New York's Columbus Day Parade, "Mrs. Roosevelt; Mrs. Truman is the last."

Truman banned Powell ("That damn nigger preacher") from the White House.

Yet Harry Truman understood the power of the black vote more than most politicians. Missouri boasted an unusually large complement of African-

American votes—130,000—with many of them centered in Democratic strongholds Kansas City and St. Louis. Some said he attributed his 1940 victory to black votes.

In late 1947, high-ranking Democratic strategists (very privately) said: "Unless the Administration makes a determined campaign to help the Negro (and everybody else) on the problems of high prices and housing—and capitalizes politically on its efforts—the Negro vote is already lost. Unless there are new and real efforts (as distinguished from mere political gestures which are today thoroughly understood and strongly resented by sophisticated Negro leaders), the Negro bloc, which certainly in Illinois and probably in New York and Ohio *does* hold the balance of power, will go Republican."

In 1948, however, Truman might face not only Dewey on his left racial flank, but also a far more dangerous foe. Unlike Truman, Henry Wallace had few white southern votes to lose and stood eager to snatch hundreds of thousands of black northern votes from Truman. And if Wallace could not win a general election, he might ensure Truman's loss.

"Negroes and the common people demand [Wallace's] re-nomination," black journalist Frank Marshall Davis had argued in the weekly *Chicago Star* in July 1944. "Wallace is right on the race question. Publicly and fearlessly he has lambasted the silly myths of race differences and inferiority. . . . There is no other known prospective running mate for Roosevelt who can compare with Wallace. None other has the respect of labor and the Negro."

"Mr. Wallace's championship of the underdog," noted Henry Lee Moon, "his demand for an end to racial discrimination, his defiance of the South's segregation pattern, and his call for the Century of the Common Man have enhanced his stature among colored citizens. Nor have they been unduly disturbed by the name-calling to which he has been subjected—Communist, dreamer, dilettante, agitator. Were the impossible to happen, nomination by a major party, undoubtedly an overwhelming majority of Negro voters would cast their ballots for the man who told the poll taxers to their teeth that the 'poll tax must go; equality of opportunity must come.'"

A May 1946 *Negro Digest* poll revealed that black Democrats favored Wallace over Truman 91 to 3 percent. In March 1948, Moon estimated that African-American voters in the Minnesota cities of St. Paul and Duluth preferred Wallace 54 to 22 percent. One Progressive Party operative contended that 85 percent of blacks nationwide favored their man. New York black leaders warned Truman ally Oscar Ewing that 75 percent of their constituents might tilt toward Wallace. A January 1948 Southern Negro Youth Congress (SNYC) poll of four thousand southern black college students placed both Wallace (58 percent) and Dewey (16 percent) ahead of Truman (13 percent).

Politics must have counted for something in Harry Truman's calculations, but so did an innate sense of fairness—and outrage. In September 1946, NAACP executive secretary Walter F. White led a six-person delegation from the National Emergency Committee Against Mob Violence to the White House, demanding action. They told Truman of the twenty-seven-year-old black army sergeant, Isaac Woodard Jr., being beaten and blinded by 210-pound Batesburg, South Carolina, chief of police Linwood Shull, just hours after his discharge. They told him of the murder of a black voter in Georgia and the murder of two black women elsewhere in the state. "My God," Truman exclaimed, "I had no idea it was as terrible as that. We've got to do something!"

In December 1946, Truman, after consulting White on its subsequent membership, signed an executive order creating a fifteen-member President's Committee on Civil Rights. Its October 1947 report, *To Secure These Rights,* contained thirty-five recommendations, including federal antilynching, anti–poll tax, and antidiscrimination measures, desegregation of the armed forces, transportation, and education, plus the creation of a variety of antidiscrimination mechanisms, including a revived Fair Employment Practices Commission, a commission on civil rights, a civil rights division in the Justice Department, and a joint congressional committee on civil rights.

It was, said White, "the most uncompromising and specific pronouncement by a Government agency on the explosive issue of racial and religious bigotry."

It seemed so out of character for Confederate-gray Harry Truman. Yet Southerners—as well as party liberals and intellectuals—should not have been entirely surprised. Twice in the Senate he had voted to end antilynching filibusters. As president, in June 1945, he had written to House Rules Committee chairman Adolph Sabath supporting a permanent FEPC.

Southerners reacted to *To Secure These Rights* with fury. "Be a Southernor [sic]," read one letter reaching the White House in February 1948. "You are one. Stick to your colors. You are a white man. Be one."

To Southern leaders he responded:

> My forebears were Confederates. . . . Every factor and influence in my background—and in my wife's for that matter—would foster the personal belief that you are right.
>
> But my very stomach turned over when I learned that Negro soldiers, just back from overseas, were being dumped out of Army trucks in Mississippi and beaten.
>
> Whatever my inclinations as a native of Missouri might have been, as President I know this is bad. I shall fight to end evils like this.

That Truman felt strongly and genuinely about such matters may be gauged from what he wrote in the midst of his 1948 reelection campaign to an old friend, World War I artillery veteran Ernest W. Roberts. It is quite without fanfare and, indeed, without guile:

> I am going to send you a copy of the report of my Commission on Civil Rights and then if you still have that antebellum proslavery outlook, I'll be thoroughly disappointed in you.
>
> The main difficulty with the South is that they are living eighty years behind the times and the sooner they come out of it the better it will be for the country and themselves. I am not asking for social equality, because no such thing exists, but I am asking for equality of opportunity for all human beings and, as long as I stay here, I am going to continue that fight. When the mob gangs can take four people out and shoot them in the back, and everybody in the country is acquainted with who did the shooting and nothing is done about it, that country is in a pretty bad fix from a law enforcement standpoint.
>
> When a mayor and a city marshal [sic] can take a Negro sergeant off a bus in South Carolina, beat him up and put out one of his eyes, and nothing

is done about it by the state authorities, something is radically wrong with the system.

On the Louisiana and Arkansas Railway when coal-burning locomotives were used, the Negro firemen were the thing because it was a backbreaking job and a dirty one. As soon as they turned to oil as a fuel it became customary for people to take shots at the Negro firemen and a number were murdered because it was thought that this was now a white-collar job and should go to a white man. I can't approve of such goings-on and I shall never approve it, as long as I am here, as I told you before. I am going to try to remedy it and if that ends up in my failure to be reelected, that failure will be in a good cause.

As 1947 drew to a close, however, he might still have drawn back, soft-pedaling his commission's findings. For, despite all his brave words, he had already retreated once on enactment of any FEPC measure. And, as Clark Clifford recalled, "the White House was no equal opportunity employer—there were, for example, no black staff members or black secretaries in the White House."

Furthermore, the nation was *not* clamoring for action. As late as July 1948, a Gallup poll revealed that while a majority supported poll-tax abolition (though not through federal fiat), and a plurality supported federal action on lynching, there remained no consensus at all regarding public accommodations or federal fair employment measures:

At present, state governments deal with most crimes committed in their own states. In the case of a lynching do you think the Federal Government should have the right to step in and deal with the crime—or do you think this should be left entirely to the state government?

	Federal	State	No Opinion
National	48%	41%	11%
South	23%	65%	12%
Outside South	51%	38%	11%

Some Southern states require every voter to pay a poll tax amounting to about a dollar a year before they can vote. Do you think these poll taxes should be abolished?

	Abolish	Retain	No Opinion
National	65%	24%	11%
South	48%	43%	9%
Outside South	67%	21%	12%
Poll Tax State	36%	56%	8%

Do you think Negroes should or should not be required to occupy a separate part of a train or bus when traveling from one state to another?

	Abolish	Retain	No Opinion
National	42%	49%	9%
South	84%	12%	4%
Outside South	36%	54%	10%

How far do you yourself think the Federal Government should go in requiring employers to hire people without regard to race, religion, color or nationality?

	Nation	South	Outside South
All the way	32%	9%	36%
None of the way	45%	69%	42%
Depends on the type of work	7%	3%	7%
Should be left to state government	2%	2%	2%
Don't know	14%	18%	13%

Truman briefly punted during his crucial January 1948 State of the Union address, merely promising to address civil rights at some undefined later moment. That moment occurred on February 2, 1948. His message is today remembered largely for its impact on black civil rights, but it proved remarkably wide-ranging, dealing not only with poll taxes and lynching (Attorney General Tom Clark warned Clark Clifford to keep such measures out of the speech) and the FEPC and the Justice Department, but also proposing self-rule for the District of Columbia, Alaskan and Hawaiian statehood, reform of naturalization laws, and justice for Japanese-Americans shabbily treated during World War II.

His program provided African-Americans with hope. "We hail the important message of the President," editorialized the black *Chicago Defender,* "as a courageous attack upon racism in America and a noble declaration of principles which distinguish our democracy from all other political systems. . . . He is standing on firm ground hallowed by the footprints of Abraham Lincoln and all the great heroes of our democratic liberal leadership and Mr. Truman is giving us that leadership."

But not all black leaders were so pleased. "Truman talks like Abraham Lincoln and acts like Hitler," jeered black New York City councilman Benjamin J. Davis, a Communist Party (CPUSA) member. The venerable black leader (and Henry Wallace backer), W.E.B. Du Bois, the NAACP's eighty-year-old director of special research, was skeptical:

> No president has spoken fairer on race discrimination than President Truman and few presidents have done less to implement their sayings. What Truman said, in his annual message, leaves nothing to be desired. But Truman has said this before, and it is going to cost him nothing to say it again. He knows perfectly well that the main backing of his own party in the South will not stand behind him in legislation, and that the Republicans cannot be expected to take any action. He is therefore, quite free to make a true, even flamboyant, expression, knowing that in all probability he will not be called upon to implement it. It is a characteristic Missouri politician's gesture."

It remained to be seen whether the *Chicago Defender*—or Du Bois—was right.

8

"The South can be considered safely Democratic"

White Southerners respectfully chose to disagree with Professor Du Bois. To them, Harry Truman's words and actions spelled profound trouble. He had already gone too far, far beyond anything the great liberal—but also the great political balancer—Franklin Delano Roosevelt might have dared contemplate.

Advisers assured Truman that his risks were minimal. His top political aide, Clark Clifford, had, after all, strategized in late-1947, "President Truman will be elected if the Administration will successfully concentrate on the traditional Democratic alliance between the South and the West. It is inconceivable that any policies initiated by the Truman Administration no matter how 'liberal' could so alienate the South in the next year that it would revolt. As always, the South can be considered safely Democratic. And in formulating national policy it can be safely ignored."

It seemed like a safe bet. In January 1948, George Gallup forecast Truman safely in the Southern driver's seat, drawing 75 percent of the Dixie vote against Tom Dewey, 76 percent against Senator Taft. Even against Dwight Eisenhower, to whom Truman lost 40 to 47 percent nationally, he carried 69 percent of the South.

But Clark Clifford was wrong.

Southern anger preceded Truman's February 1948 special message to Congress. January 20, 1948, had witnessed another ceremony, normally of no national or even regional consequence, in the deepest portion of the Deep South, in Jackson, Mississippi—the inauguration of Governor Fielding L. Wright. The fifty-two-year-old Wright, despite being a distant relative of

George Washington, seemed an unlikely figure to spark any revolution. The son of a prominent Delta planter and the nondescript former chair of both houses of the state legislature, Wright "wasn't what you'd call a popular man," recalled one Mississippian. "He wasn't a backslapper. [He] was not an affable fellow. . . . He was very stern even in social discussions."

An accidental chief executive, Wright had succeeded to the governorship upon the November 1946 death of Governor Thomas L. Bailey, but it was no accident that the white South's revolt against Truman began in Mississippi, which was 49.2 percent black. Taking office in his own right that January 20, Wright, always an opponent of Mississippi's vociferously racist Theodore Bilbo, nonetheless picked up the late senator's arch-segregationist torch. "Vital principles and eternal truths transcend party lines," Wright charged, "and the day is now at hand when determined action must be taken."

Wright attacked Truman from the right. Six-foot-eight Alabama governor Jim Folsom ("The Little Man's Big Friend") attacked from the left. On January 28, the thirty-nine-year-old, left-wing Folsom (said one Alabama paper, he "worships at the feet of [Henry] Wallace") announced his own favorite-son presidential candidacy. "Who's running our party in Washington?" asked Folsom. "The head of our party is a nice man. But he's not running our party any more. And he's not running our country. He's let himself get hog-tied . . . [by] Monopolists, brass hats, Wall Street lawyers, tea sippers. They're not real Democrats. . . . What have they got in common with the peace loving, God-fearing people of the Cotton Belt?"

"He's been nice to me and I like him," said Folsom of Truman. "But nice wasn't enough." Folsom said he could think of about twenty-five people who would do a better job as the leader of the country and the party than Truman.

In Strom Thurmond's South Carolina, forty-eight General Assembly members angrily informed the state Democratic Party executive committee, "The South's distaste for some acts of the National Party has mounted until it now has reached the point that we should reconsider our position in the National Party."

All this *preceded* Harry Truman's civil rights message to Congress.

Georgia's normally circumspect senator, Richard B. Russell Jr., exploded, charging that Truman was proposing a Soviet-style secret police. Arkansas governor Ben Laney averred to a Little Rock press conference that he would "consider every method possible to prevent the imposition of such legislation. . . . I am ready to help even to extreme measures to bring this about." Russell's fellow Georgian, Rep. Eugene Cox, fumed that "Harlem is wielding more influence with the Administration than the entire white South."

Mississippi senator James O. Eastland proposed a strategy—based on Alabama native Charles Wallace Collins's 1947 book, *Whither Solid South?*— to restore Southern influence. "Give our [127] electoral votes to some other candidate," Eastland informed the Senate. "We can call the turn. We can dictate the party's policies. . . . By withholding her electoral votes the South can defeat in 1948 any Democratic candidate. In fact, no candidate would be nominated [who] would not receive the South's electoral votes. The machines of the North which control the party are not crazy. They will nominate no candidate whose defeat is certain. If the South should support a Southern candidate for President the election this year would in all probability be thrown in the House of Representatives. If this were done, I am confident a Southerner would name the President."

Strom Thurmond, remaining largely a New Deal liberal (and effusively praising Truman as late as October 1947), steered a less emotional course. Initially, he avoided public comment, but within a few days of Truman's message he attended an already scheduled Southern governors' meeting. When Fielding Wright, feverish with a 101-degree temperature, proposed bolting the Democratic Party, he met instant resistance. Georgia governor M. E. Thompson prepared a resolution denouncing his scheme. Even Jim Folsom, so recently critical of Truman, announced: "I am a Democrat. We'll argue it out within the party. I'll always support the Democratic nominee."

Thurmond advocated an opposition based on "dignity, self-respect and restraint" to "all ill-considered proposals . . . dividing our people" and proposed a cooling-off period and negotiations with Washington. Few cooled off in either Mississippi or South Carolina. Wright resented Thurmond's call for caution and refused to serve on the committee that resulted from it. On Thursday, February 12—Lincoln's birthday—1948, four thousand Mississippians ("blood of the Confederacy and of true Jeffersonian Democracy") convened in Jackson to sing "Dixie" and to rally "all true white Jeffersonian Democrats." That same day, South Carolina's

House of Representatives unanimously denounced Truman's "un-American" program.

Thurmond had pleased neither Wright nor South Carolina's blacks. State NAACP president James M. Hinton condemned his actions as "a keen disappointment to the negroes of South Carolina." Previously, Hinton continued, South Carolina blacks had believed that "they had a Chief Executive, free from White Supremacy attitudes and expressions, and one who would hasten the day, when Negroes in South Carolina would enjoy 'EQUALITY OF OPPORTUNITY.'" He warned Thurmond that he would "live to REGRET THE STAND TAKEN."

Meanwhile, Thurmond's administrative assistant, William Lowndes Daniel, cajoled his boss to assume leadership of the growing Southern resistance movement. Daniel wrote to Thurmond on February 19:

> Please do not discount your own ability during this struggle. . . . President Truman would not be in the White House today except for having taken advantage of a similar situation when it occurred[;] if we watch developments carefully, the opportunity may present itself to work wonders with you, also. The difference in these two cases could be that wonders were worked with Truman, who in my opinion just does not have it—you do have it—All you need is the opportunity.

But before Thurmond and his fellow governors—Arkansas's diminutive Laney, Texas's beefy Beauford H. Jester ("the majority of Texas Democrats do not want Truman re-nominated for the Presidency"), and North Carolina's convivial R. Gregg Cherry (said to be the best lawyer in Gastonia when sober, the second best when drunk)—could confer with either Truman or any of his associates, another event intervened: the Democratic Party's annual Jefferson–Jackson Day celebration.

In Little Rock, Harry Truman's voice, broadcast from Washington's Mayflower Hotel, crackled out of the ballroom loudspeakers. Roughly half the crowd of 850 angrily stormed out. At the Mayflower itself, South Carolina senator Olin D. Johnston and his wife, the event's vice-chairwoman, had reserved a full table directly in front of the dais at which Truman would speak. DNC chairman J. Howard McGrath (Bob Hannegan had retired in 1947 due to severe ill health—as well as due to 1946's election returns) had indicated that the dinner would be fully integrated, and Gladys "Happy" Johnston and her New Dealer but ardently segregationist husband announced they would boycott the event "because she might be seated next to a Negro," leaving their entire table conspicuously deserted. To insure it remained vacant, Senator Johnston engaged a professional boxer to patrol said empty table. Among the hundred-dollar seats remaining empty were two for Governor and Mrs. Thurmond. Also absent were Johnston's fellow Southern senators—Fulbright, McClellan, Russell, Ellender, George, and Maybank.

The next day, fifty-two Southern Democratic House members voted to support Thurmond and his fellow Southern governors "to the finish." In Washington, on Monday afternoon, February 23, Thurmond, Laney, Cherry, and Jester (with Maryland governor W. Preston Lane as intermediary) conferred behind closed doors with DNC chairman McGrath. Cherry and Laney were tractable. Thurmond, eschewing small talk, refused to sit, even though repeatedly invited to do so. He honed in on McGrath with a series of six typewritten questions, beginning with: "Do you . . . deny that the proposed anti–poll tax law, the proposed antilynching law, the proposed FEPC law, and Federal laws dealing with the separation of races . . . would be unconstitutional invasions of the field of government belonging to the states under the Bill of Rights in the Constitution?"

McGrath ignored Thurmond's queries as well as his demand that the party reinstate its national convention two-thirds rule. He blandly promised only to oppose any attacks on legitimate states' rights and to support retaining the party's mild 1944 civil rights plank. He denied that Truman's proposed Justice Department civil rights division was aimed at the South ("the farthest thing from the President's mind"), but rather at "hoodlumism" in labor disputes.

Thurmond persisted: "Will you now, at a time when national unity is so vital to the solution of the problem of peace in the world, use your influence as chairman of the Democratic National Committee to have the highly controversial civil-rights legislation, which tends to divide our people, withdrawn from consideration by the Congress?"

McGrath responded with a blunt, flat "No."

Back at the Mayflower Hotel, Thurmond rallied his fellow governors to issue the following statement:

> The Southern states are aroused and the Democratic Party will soon realize that the South is "no longer in the bag."
>
> Each Southern State, under the framework of an overall program, will work out the most effective means of resisting the proposals of the present leadership of the party, but resist them we will.
>
> The time has come for strong and effective action by the Southern States not only to save the Democratic [P]arty but to preserve the rights of the States to govern themselves and Preserve American Democracy.
>
> In this fight we are not only expecting support from the Democrats of the South but support from Democrats everywhere who are opposed to a centralized government invading the rights of the people and the rights of the respective states.

Yet the walls of resistance were crumbling before Thurmond. On April 19, the Supreme Court overturned South Carolina legislation designed to subvert *Smith v. Allwright*. On May 10, following a thirty-one-year NAACP campaign, it unanimously banned restrictive racial and religious deed covenants. Dissension reigned among Thurmond's colleagues. Exiting the McGrath session, North Carolina's Cherry had publicly grumbled at Thurmond, "It wasn't as much of a session as some folks thought it was going to be. There was just a lot of talk, talk, talk. McGrath handled himself pretty well." He added that the governors who attended "with blood in their eyes didn't get exactly what they were after."

The bloodiest eye of all, however, belonged to Fielding Wright. Having scheduled another states' rights meeting in Jackson for Monday, May 10, he warned Mississippi blacks, via a statewide radio hookup, on the previous morning: "It is fitting and proper on this Sabbath day of peace and quiet, of meditation and of prayer, for me to discuss with you . . . one of the gravest threats to our tranquility and our happiness. . . . The stirring up of prejudices is unfortunate for both races in the South, but more particularly for yours. If you cast your lot with those who are your friends . . . you will reap the benefits. If you prefer to follow the leadership of the other element, I am sorry—but you will find that you will be much happier in some other state than in Mississippi."

That Monday, fifteen hundred delegates and two thousand spectators gathered in the stifling heat of the Jackson Municipal Auditorium to sing "Dixie" (and, for good measure, to hear an original composition entitled "Let's Send Harry Back to the Farm") and, of course, to forge a path of resistance. Again, harmony proved elusive. Tennessee Democratic chieftain "Boss Ed" Crump and Texas governor Jester merely sent their regards. At least, it *appeared* that Jester sent his regards—three separate individuals arrived claiming to be his emissary. Only three governors—Laney (chosen as the group's permanent chair), Wright, and Thurmond—actually bothered to come. From afar, Georgia governor Thompson reiterated his longstanding opposition. "Kissin' Jim" Folsom, who had promised to attend, didn't.

Thurmond began his keynote address by downplaying racial themes and expressing sympathy toward blacks. No region of the nation, he contended, had . . .

> . . . suffered from such vicious propaganda. No effort was spared to make it appear that we fought to perpetuate human slavery, and thereby obscure the fundamental constitutional and economic issues which brought on that unhappy conflict. . . .
>
> [T]he American people are [now] being propagandized to believe that Southerners have been mistreating the Negroes in our midst, and that we are unfit for local self-government. . . . We hear not a word of the tremendous efforts which have been made through the years to give both races in the South the opportunity to improve and progress. We hear not a word of recognition of the progress which the Negro has made since slavery days as a result of the efforts of the Southern people.

But such talk was mere prelude, easily discarded as Thurmond progressed to a dissection of Harry Truman's despised civil rights program, and what he—and everyone else—knew their gathering really centered on—integration. Thurmond raged:

These big city bosses and their puppets in office, as well as those who think everything can be done by law from Washington, should once and for all realize that on the question of social intermingling of the races our people draw the line. No decent and self-respecting Negro would ask for a law to force people to accept him where he is not wanted. They themselves do not want social intermingling. They are entitled to equality of opportunity, and they will get it through our efforts. But all the laws of Washington and all the bayonets of the army cannot force the Negro into our homes, our schools, our churches, and our places of recreation and amusement. . . .

There's not enough troops in the Army to force the Southern people to break down segregation and admit the Negro race into our theaters, into our swimming pools, into schools and into our homes.

Yet, for all Thurmond's rhetoric and for all the stars-and-bars flags festooning Jackson's boulevards, this group—now christened "Dixiecrats"—once more elected to bide its time, agreeing only to reconvene in Birmingham on Saturday, July 17, immediately following their national party's Philadelphia convention. Again, their avowed goal remained vague but threatening (to take "all necessary and appropriate actions"), but of one thing they were sure: "Harry Truman," vowed Strom Thurmond, in the one line of his speech which pleased him most, "has never been elected president of the United States and he never will be."

9

"No one laughs at Harold Stassen"

With so many people upset with Harry Truman, the Republican field had grown a bit crowded.

Thomas E. Dewey had competition.

No man was ever born to be president of the United States of America more than U.S. senator Robert Alphonso Taft—or less.

Born on September 8, 1889, to future president William Howard Taft and his ambitious wife, Nellie, Robert Taft advanced steadily, if unspectacularly, first through Ohio and then through national Republican ranks. First in his class at Yale, he also finished first in the Ohio bar exams. Exempt from World War I conscription because of extreme nearsightedness (as a senator, he hesitated to greet oncomers, as he had trouble recognizing them), he instead enlisted as an assistant counsel with Herbert Hoover's U.S. Food Administration, assisting in ensuring a stable wartime national food supply. Following Armistice Day, Taft similarly assisted Hoover's successful European and Middle Eastern food relief efforts.

In 1921, he won election to the Ohio House of Representatives, rising to GOP house leader in 1925 and speaker in 1926. In 1936 Ohio Republicans designated him as their favorite-son presidential candidate. Two years later, he graduated to the U.S. Senate, defeating a boss-supported candidate in the primary by 75,000 votes, and then trouncing Democratic incumbent, Robert J. Bulkley (a former FDR Harvard classmate), by 170,597 votes. By 1940, he was a legitimate candidate for the GOP presidential nomination. In 1944, however, facing reelection to the Senate, Taft supported his fellow conservative, Ohio governor John W. Bricker, for the White House. That year, the GOP's gubernatorial candidate lost by 112,359 votes, and Dewey and Bricker carried Ohio by only 11,530 votes. Taft, facing unrelenting opposition from the state American Federation of Labor (AFL) and Congress of Industrial Organizations, triumphed by 17,740 votes.

And yet Bob Taft was among the least likely of candidates for *any* political office. He was, to say the least, not the glad-hander. His father, William Howard Taft, may have been the jolly fat man, but while Bob Taft may have been somewhat paunchy (though never approaching his father's great bulk), he could never be described as jolly, gregarious, or even particularly compelling. *Time* magazine pronounced him "dull, prosy, colorless, with not a tithe of Franklin Roosevelt's great charm and personal magnetism." Taft, *Time* mocked, was the "Dagwood Bumstead of American Politics."

He remained, observed David Brinkley, "all blue suits, white shirts, bare scalp, rimless glasses, vest and gold watch chain. And it was said he looked like 'a composite picture of sixteen million Republicans.' . . . [I]f Dewey's speaking voice sounded like a cello quartet, Taft's was rusty hinges on a henhouse door."

But henhouse doors have a purpose. So did Robert Taft. "Impatient with nonsense," noted journalist and historian (and active Democrat) Booth Mooney, Taft "was not a man to suffer fools gladly and often he would not suffer them at all. But, as his fellow senators, both Republicans and Democrats, knew, he was by no means the cold, unapproachable person he was generally pictured as being. He had a dry, friendly wit, liked a moderate drink of Scotch in the company of friends, and enjoyed a special rapport with certain senior southern members of the Senate establishment."

He was, above all, solid. Said his biographer, the *New York Times*'s William S. White, "There is no instance known to me in all his days in the Senate where Taft let down an associate in any agreed enterprise, no matter how sticky the going might have become."

His "informed intelligence and massive sincerity of purpose," concluded journalist Richard Rovere, "make him seem, alongside the *papier-mâché* statesmen of the period, almost a figure of granite."

"To my surprise," noted arch-liberal Arthur Schlesinger Jr., "I found that I liked him."

What charisma Robert Taft lacked, his intelligent, outspoken, and aggressive Bryn Mawr- and Sorbonne-educated wife, Martha Wheaton Bowers Taft, did not. During her husband's 1938 Senate primary campaign, Ohio GOP boss Ed Schorr had ordered her to remain out of it. Storming from Schorr's office, she instead beelined for an opposition rally held in a local black church. She also bluntly informed a group of coal miners, "My husband is not a simple man. He did not start from humble beginnings. My husband is a brilliant man. He had a fine education. . . . He has been trained well for the job. Isn't that what you want when you pick a man to work for you?" For her—and for him—the argument worked.

Taft remained conservative by reputation, yet he often deviated from conventional laissez-faire constructs, most notably in proposing a half million units of federally funded public housing (1948's $1 billion Taft-Ellender-Wagner bill). "Probably you think I have been somewhat too liberal with government money in the positions I have taken," he explained to Delaware fiscal watchdog Senator John Williams, "but I was most anxious to maintain a unified party during this period in order that we might reach the one essential goal of ousting the present gang from control."

"Taft [was an] enormously capable man," Richard Nixon recalled decades later, "an intellectual giant and a giant in terms of just sheer character and belief and not a reactionary. As a matter of fact, Taft was a progressive. . . . [H]e had very progressive, advanced views on aid to education, on health care, and on housing. In fact, some of the conservatives . . . only stuck with him because they thought he was more, shall we say, isolationist, and [that] held them in line. They didn't agree with his domestic views."

With Republicans controlling the Senate after 1946, Taft emerged as his conference's unofficial leader (Maine's septuagenarian liberal, Wallace H. White Jr., held the official title, but as author John Gunther pointed out, "Everybody likes White; few people pay much attention to him"). As 1948 neared, Taft seemed a logical contender for the nomination. Questions, however, remained, not merely regarding his tart personality, but also regarding his aforementioned prewar (and even postwar) isolationism, and his efforts to reign in often-destructive labor union power. Following 1935's Wagner Act, the balance of power had swung markedly in favor of unions. As labor's influence increased, its sense of responsibility shrank, culminating not only in a wave of strikes that crippled the economy—and so infuriated Harry Truman in 1946—but also in widespread violence and corruption.

Taft's efforts resulted both in 1947's landmark Taft-Hartley Act and in massive labor union animus toward its Senate sponsor. Numerous observers wrote off his chances for 1948. Harry Truman and Bob Hannegan disagreed. "Don't make the mistake of underestimating Taft," argued Hannegan. "Many people think he'd be easy to beat. But that's because they see in his nomination the simple matter of a clear division between the parties. The fact is that Taft is a fighter and will make a terrific fight for what he represents."

"They think he would be easy to defeat because he doesn't have labor support," said Truman. "Well, he has. He has plenty of labor support when he runs and wins in Ohio for the Senate. He would be a very much tougher opponent for me than Governor Dewey."

Sheer hate greeted the July 1947 announcement of Taft's candidacy. CIO pickets surrounded his son's June 1947 wedding. In September 1947, when Senator and Mrs. Taft tested the waters in California, Oregon, Washington, Idaho, and Wyoming, Santa Cruz union protesters chanted: "Robert A. Taft—R. A. T." In San Francisco, fifteen hundred picketed. In Los Angeles, their signs read: TAFT'S CREED: MEIN KAMPF and TAFT IS A SCHNOOK: HE BORROWED A LEAF FROM HITLER'S STORY BOOK. In Seattle, "an egg or a tomato or something" was tossed onto his car, and a nervous chauffeur slammed a car door on his hand. "You goddamned son of a bitch!" an angry demonstrator screamed into the pain-stricken senator's face. Taft was in agony, but his "self-control amazed his aides," wrote his biographer James T. Patterson. "He turned away, demanded stitches for his hand, and carried out his schedule without interruption. One can only wonder at the determination that carried him stoically through such demonstrations of the hatred and rhetoric of public life in the 1940s."

In San Francisco, however, he merely compounded his difficulties. Asked how consumers should respond to rising food prices, he bluntly responded, "Eat less meat and eat less extravagantly."

His opponents again pronounced him heartless—and finished. "That didn't bother us," Martha Taft calmly informed a Seattle audience. "He'd been through it so many times before."

Internationalist Senator Arthur Hendrick Vandenberg was running distinctly behind Robert Taft, though the veteran Michigan Republican's pace was more like a gentle lope at best; at worst, a coy invitation to a coronation march.

In 1906, Vandenberg, then the *New York Herald's* twenty-two-year-old City Hall reporter, assumed editorship of the *Grand Rapids Herald*. He quickly achieved eminence within Michigan's Republican Party—and as an Alexander Hamilton scholar, publishing two somewhat gushing studies on his boyhood hero. Richard Rovere viewed the highly egotistical Vandenberg as "gassy and pompous," though in an amiable sort of way. It was widely observed that Vandenberg, like the arrogant Dewey, "could strut sitting down."

In 1928, he won his Senate seat "with the largest plurality ever given any Michigan candidate," thanks in part, no doubt, to having his original Democratic opponent, incumbent senator Woodbridge N. Ferris, drop dead. Reelected in 1934's GOP bloodbath (the *only* large-state Republican senator reelected that year), he found himself within the party's top national circle. Some, however, sneered that it was "by the simple expedient of being the only man in it."

He was, nonetheless, sharp. "His head and large eyes gave him an owlish appearance," recalled Bill Douglas. "His rapierlike mind never missed a point." But he was a trimmer. One observer noted in 1940: "Vandenberg has stood squarely on both sides of every issue of the past ten years." Alternately liberal and conservative, his oratory carefully masked his often meandering convictions. "You can't find out what makes him go," complained the *Nation* in May 1940. "Dewey and Taft have cores; you may not like them, but they're there. . . . Vandenberg doesn't add up to anything. He cancels out."

He was mentioned for the 1936 presidential nomination, and was offered, but declined, the vice-presidential nod. To *Chicago Tribune* publisher Col. Robert "Bertie" McCormick, he tartly responded, "Let me ask you one question. How would *you* like to be vice president of anything?" In 1940, DNC chairman Jim Farley proclaimed, "Senator Vandenberg is the Republican to defeat." At that year's convention, Dewey, desperate to block Wendell Willkie, offered Vandenberg the vice presidency. Vandenberg remained uninterested.

"I'll make [Dewey] a sporting proposition," he jested. "I'll meet him at eleven o'clock and flip a coin to see which end of the ticket we each take."

Vandenberg was then a staunch isolationist. In January 1934, he was one of only two Foreign Relations Committee members opposing the appointment of an ambassador to Moscow. He served on the famed Nye Committee that lacerated the armaments industry; supported the decade's various Neutrality Acts; and opposed both FDR's Lend-Lease program and September 1940's Burke-Wadsworth Act, creating peacetime conscription. "Say what you please," he noted in August 1940, "something precious goes out of the American way of life and something sinister takes its place under conscription." At one point, he even considered himself an ally ("It certainly is comforting to have you in my corner") of the similarly isolationist, but also vehemently anti-Semitic, rabble-rouser Gerald L. K. Smith.

Vandenberg, however, remained capable of flexibility. In January 1945, he delivered a momentous (though still windy) speech announcing his conversion to internationalism—and the birth of a new era of bipartisan foreign policy. Assuming command of the Senate Foreign Relations Committee in 1947, much to Robert Taft's chagrin, he championed the new bipartisan coalition supporting Harry Truman's emerging Cold War policies. He was, observed the *New York Times's* Arthur Krock, "a statesman, yet a very good politician. He is a powerful orator and a clear thinker. He has shown the courage to change his mind on major issues and announce it. He is the candidate the Democrats fear most—those Democrats, that is, who really want Mr. Truman elected."

Richard Rovere thought, however, that Vandenberg's role was far more modest: "Vandenberg contributed only his large and amiable presence. He never really did anything. When he went to [international conferences] his function was to prove to allies and adversaries that we had something approaching national unity in this country. He was a kind of property eagle. He could fulfill his function without opening his mouth—though he generally opened it quite a bit. Still, many things might have been different, and worse, if we had not had him."

In 1944, still the isolationist, Vandenberg had supported Douglas MacArthur's abortive candidacy. By 1948, his own ambitions seemed resuscitated. Walter Lippmann preferred him. Bill Douglas regarded him as "the most realistic of all senators when it came to world affairs." But several factors necessitated caution, the first being a long-standing heart ailment, and to friends he stated rather bluntly that he possessed no desire to die in the White House. Beyond that, his egotism and sudden lurch to the internationalist camp, plus the concomitant praise he now drew from liberal pundits and activists, only fueled Republican resentment. "At least two hundred members of the House—mostly Republican—hate my guts," he once admitted.

Yes, Arthur Hendrick Vandenberg was indeed realistic.

Henry Lewis "H. L." Mencken dismissed Harold Stassen as a "cow country messiah."

But Richard Nixon disagreed. Toward the end of his life, Nixon recalled:

> Stassen was the most interesting candidate. He was also one who could relate to World War II people because he had been a veteran in World War II.
>
> He was young, he was charismatic. Many people think since that time [that] he was dull, but he really wasn't at that time. And he was smart, very, very smart. . . .
>
> I would say that of the lot that we had there at the convention, Stassen, if he could have been nominated, would have been the strongest candidate. I think he would have won.

Harold Stassen had wasted no time as he moved up the political ladder. Born on April 13, 1907, to a Norwegian-German-Czech Minnesota farm family, he graduated from high school at fifteen. At the University of Minnesota, the strapping six-foot-three Stassen supported himself as a grocery clerk, Pullman car conductor, and grease boy in a bakery. Graduating from the university's law school in 1929, he won the Dakota County district attorneyship the following year—at just twenty-three—and won reelection four years later.

In 1938, Stassen challenged Minnesota's incumbent governor, the radical Farmer-Labor Party standard-bearer Elmer A. Benson. Elected with

58 percent of the vote in 1936, Benson had soon frittered away his mandate, mixing "truculence and impatience" with a "tolerance of Communists in the Farmer-Labor organization." Stassen campaigned furiously, holding every speech to twenty minutes, sprinting from the platform as he finished to plant himself at the doorway between each voter and the exit. Walloping Benson with 59 percent of the vote, he became not only Minnesota's youngest governor ever, but the youngest ever anywhere.

He was also, as journalist Booth Mooney observed, "not a man afflicted with self-doubt."

At thirty-one, he looked like he could go anywhere. "As Governor," *Christian Science Monitor* Washington bureau chief Roscoe Drummond noted in *Life* magazine, "he replaced a socialistic, class-conscious Farmer-Labor administration with a progressive, solvent, and humane Republican administration which ultimately won even the support of labor leaders." Reelected in 1940 and 1942 (despite vowing in the latter campaign to resign within four months to enter the service), he keynoted 1940's Republican National Convention. Resigning as promised from the governorship, in April 1943 he enlisted as an aide and flag secretary to South Pacific commander Adm. William F. "Bull" Halsey. Repeatedly under Japanese fire, he won the Legion of Merit. On leave from the Navy in 1945, he was named by Franklin Roosevelt as one of the delegates (alongside Arthur Vandenberg) to the San Francisco Conference that established the United Nations (UN).

In December 1946, holding no political office and still barely thirty-nine, he startled most observers by announcing his candidacy for the presidency. No one had ever announced so early. With no great links to any party power structure, he constructed his own—touring Europe for nine weeks (and interviewing Joseph Stalin in the bargain), covering forty thousand miles domestically by August 1947, and penning his political philosophy, *Where I Stand!* Not everyone approved. "If Mr. Stassen were going to expose himself to the political perils of book-writing," Arthur Schlesinger Jr. sniped in the *New York Times*, "he made a mistake in not taking the job more seriously."

He was, nonetheless, the very essence of a modern presidential candidate, pioneering in eschewing traditional train travel for planes. Reporters wrote admiringly of Stassen's "revolutionizing campaign methods with his plane-borne duplicating machine and an efficient organization that not only keeps him abreast of all that's going on but takes care of every demand of a much-demanding press corps."

"If I traveled by train from Chicago to Denver without stopping in Iowa and Nebraska," Stassen explained, "somebody's feelings would be hurt. But nobody thinks anything about it if I fly over his state without stopping. Sometimes it is politically desirable to visit that state at a later date. Flying is an ideal solution."

He preached a reborn Republicanism, staunchly internationalist abroad, a hybrid of liberalism and conservatism at home, proposing massive public housing, substantial decreases in marginal tax rates, and wobbling all over the place on Taft-Hartley. "I may do him an injustice," Robert Taft wrote to a friend, "but I think he is a complete opportunist but basically a New Dealer and an internationalist." Regarding Stassen's internationalism, Taft (he thought Stassen "sophomoric") had not exaggerated. In March 1945, Stassen had publicly declared, "we are willing to delegate a limited portion of our sovereignty to our United Nations organization."

Others shared Taft's hostility. "Certain of the party bosses," reported columnist Drew Pearson in June 1948, "would almost cut off their left arm before they would let [Stassen] get the nomination."

Yet by August 1947 he had forced himself into contention, running behind Dewey, at least at pace with Taft, and far ahead of Washington insider Vandenberg.

"Among the rank and file of politicians, the boys who know the ropes," wrote *Time* magazine (itself in Vandenberg's corner), "no one laughs at Harold Stassen."

10

"Maybe Masaryk had cancer"

In the grand scheme of things, Republican rivals and price controls—even the vexing question of civil rights—may have been among the lesser of Harry Truman's problems.

A cold war—threatening to erupt into world war—loomed.

It was not entirely unexpected, though its rapid onset certainly was. Until August 1945, the United States and Soviet Russia had cooperated as wartime allies, contributing blood and materiel toward Hitler's defeat. Despite an acrimonious first meeting with Soviet foreign minister Vyacheslav Molotov in April 1945 at Potsdam, Harry Truman—thinking Stalin to be some sort of Eastern European version of Tom Pendergast—recorded in his diary that July: "I can deal with Stalin. He is honest—but smart as hell." But by January 1946, infuriated by the failure of Jimmy Byrnes's recent Moscow conference of foreign ministers, he fumed, "I'm tired of babying the Soviets."

The nub of the matter was Stalin's increasingly evident designs on Eastern, Southern, and even Western Europe. The USSR had already annexed Latvia, Lithuania, and Estonia, as well as eastern Polish, Finnish, and Romanian territory gained by the Hitler-Stalin pact of August 1939. Communist governments sprang up in Poland, Romania, Hungary, Yugoslavia, Albania, and Bulgaria. Red Army units remained in Czechoslovakia, Germany, and Austria. Through outright landgrabs or its new puppet regimes, Moscow had added 390,000 square miles and ninety million persons to its domain. A Moscow-backed insurgency threatened Greece. Growing Soviet pressure on Turkey seemed equally ominous. Powerful native French and Italian communist parties stood poised for triumph at the ballot box—or, at least, positioned to prevent functional governments from arising in those key war-torn nations.

Beyond Europe, Soviet troops remained in northern Iran, where, in 1945, pro-Moscow elements had established the People's Republic of Azerbaijan and the Kurdish People's Republic. In China, Mao Tse-tung's People's Liberation Army and Generalissimo Chiang Kai-shek's Kuomintang renewed their seemingly endless civil war. In colonial Indochina, a onetime Harlem and Boston resident and Comintern agent now calling himself Ho Chi Minh challenged the French for independence. North of Korea's 38th parallel, Stalinist Kim Il-sung established yet another Soviet-style regime.

By March 1946, Winston Churchill, unceremoniously and ungratefully dumped from power in Britain, had traveled with Harry Truman to central Missouri to provide Americans "my true and faithful counsel in these anxious and baffling times": From Stettin in the Baltic to Trieste in the Adriatic, an iron curtain has descended across the continent. Behind that line lie all the capitals of the ancient states of Central and Eastern Europe. Warsaw, Berlin, Prague, Vienna, Budapest, Belgrade, Bucharest, and Sofia. All these famous cities and the populations around them lie in what I must call the Soviet sphere, and all are subject in one form or another, not only to Soviet influence but to a very high and, in many cases, increasing measure of control from Moscow.

It required nearly a solid year, however, for Truman to act. In March 1947, with a virtually bankrupt Britain no longer capable of bankrolling Greek and Turkish resistance, Truman addressed a joint session of Congress, proposing $400 million in Greek-Turkish military aid. "The very existence of the Greek state," he bluntly announced, "is today threatened by the terrorist activities of several thousand armed men, led by Communists."

He also proposed a far bolder strategy, to confront "totalitarian" aggression wherever it existed. Presaging John Kennedy's summons to "pay any price, bear any burden," Truman announced:

I believe that it must be the policy of the United States to support free peoples who are resisting attempted subjugation by armed minorities or by outside pressures.

I believe that we must assist free peoples to work out their own destinies in their own way.

I believe that our help should be primarily through economic and financial aid which is essential to economic stability and orderly political processes.

It was the unveiling of the Truman Doctrine—and the birth of the Cold War.

Rexford Guy Tugwell, Henry Wallace's former undersecretary of agriculture, and one of the very few New Deal higher-ups to have joined Wallace's crusade, summarized outraged Progressive reaction to Truman's policy of containment. Tugwell viewed Truman's actions not as a response to potential totalitarian aggression but rather as evidence of the military's control over a lightweight, jingoistic president. The Pentagon, wrote Tugwell, "chose a line running from the Balkans east to Turkey and in effect said to Russia that it might go so far, but she must not come farther. It was exactly like a tough adolescent bully daring a weaker boy to cross a line and risk a thrashing."

At Harvard University's commencement that July, Jimmy Byrnes's successor at the State Department, Gen. George C. Marshall, raised the stakes, unveiling the multibillion-dollar European Recovery Program (ERP), better known to history as the Marshall Plan, designed to revitalize the entire European continent. "Our policy," Marshall announced, "is directed not against any country or doctrine but against hunger, poverty, desperation, and chaos. Its purpose should be the revival of a working economy in the world so as to permit the emergence of political and social conditions in which free institutions can exist."

Though in dire need of aid, the Soviet Union quickly rejected participation in the plan, denouncing Marshall's ERP as an imperialist tool. In July 1947, Moscow pressured Czechoslovakia (not yet a Red puppet, but teetering on the brink) to also cold-shoulder American assistance.

In February 1948, a bloodless Communist-backed coup ousted democratically elected Czech President Eduard Beneš. On March 10, Czech Foreign Minister Jan Masaryk, son of the nation's first president, Tomáš Masaryk, plunged to his death from a Prague bathroom window. Many said he was murdered. Czechoslovakia's demise excited a particularly sensitive western nerve. The nation possessed a real, though admittedly brief, democratic tradition. Mention of Czechoslovakia inevitably conjured up memories of the Munich Pact, prewar appeasement, and a road of least resistance that culminated in world war sooner rather than later.

Even before Masaryk's death, U.S. military governor Gen. Lucius D. Clay telegraphed from Berlin:

> For many months, based on logical analysis, I have felt and held that war was unlikely for at least ten years. Within the last few weeks, I have felt a subtle change in Soviet attitude which I cannot define but which now gives me a feeling that it may come with dramatic suddenness. I cannot support this change in my own thinking with any data or outword [sic] evidence in relationships other than to describe it as a feeling of a new tenseness in every Soviet individual with whom we have official relations. I am unable to submit any official report in the absence of supporting data but my feeling is real. You may advise the chief of staff of this for whatever it may be worth if you feel it advisable.

"Papers this morning full of rumors and portents of war," defense secretary James V. Forrestal grimly noted in his diary on March 16, simultaneously inquiring of Atomic Energy Commission chairman David E. Lilienthal how expeditiously nuclear weapons might be moved "to, say, the Mediterranean." Stewart and Joseph Alsop nervously began their March 17 syndicated column thus: "The atmosphere in Washington today is no longer postwar. It is, to put it bluntly, a prewar atmosphere."

On Wednesday, March 15, Truman had decided on a clarion call to worldwide action—improbably to be issued two evenings hence at a St. Patrick's Day dinner in Times Square. General Marshall persuaded him that a joint session of Congress might be a more appropriate venue than a joint full of Irishmen. On March 17, in droning monotone, Truman (wearing a green carnation in his buttonhole), delivered one of the most significant foreign policy addresses of his—or any—presidential career, pointedly identifying the Soviets as a "growing menace":

> It is [their] ruthless course of action, and the clear design to extend it to the remaining free nations of Europe, that have brought about the critical situation in Europe today. . . . I believe that we have reached a point at

which the position of the United States should be made unmistakably clear. . . . There are times in world history when it is far wiser to act than to hesitate.

He advocated "prompt passage" of George Marshall's ERP and the "temporary reenactment of selective service legislation"—reversing his March 1947 recommendation of "no extension of Selective Service at this time." Most radically of all, he advocated the "prompt enactment of universal training." Marshall had, in fact, advocated "universal *military* training" since 1947. Politician Truman refused to use that term.

Truman now flew to New York to deal with foes not foreign but domestic: the Henry Wallace movement.

Two hundred detectives and five hundred uniformed police guarded him as he reviewed eighty thousand St. Patrick's Day marchers along Fifth Avenue. Fifty motorcycle police escorted him to the Hotel Astor ballroom podium, to address 2,600 members and guests of the Friendly Sons of St. Patrick. His prepared text included nothing more than a reiteration of his earlier Cold War rhetoric. Suddenly, he veered into the realm of the extemporaneous— and for Harry Truman, the extemporaneous often proved more interesting than for just about anyone else. "I do not want and will not accept," he told this Catholic, anticommunist crowd, "the political support of Henry Wallace and his Communists. If joining them or permitting them to join me is the price of victory, I recommend defeat. These are days of high prices for everything. But any price for Wallace and his Communists is too high for me to pay. I'm not buying now."

Twelve nights later, at Washington's Statler Hotel, he addressed the Greek-American fraternal Order of AHEPA. New York State Liberal Party leader Dean Alfange had preceded Truman. He suggested that Wallace repair to the Rocky Mountains to fight a guerilla war as communist insurgents had done in Greece. Truman, with 269 members of Congress before him, went the Greek-American Alfange a step further. "If [they] want to see [this country's] liberties subverted," he said of Wallace and his followers, "I suggest that they go not to the Rocky Mountains—that's fine country out there. He ought to go to the country he loves so well and help them against his own country if that's the way he feels."

Truman's moves—aimed at both Moscow and his former commerce secretary—made perfect political sense. Following Armistice Day 1918, Americans had recoiled from foreign entanglements, but the rise of fascism and inevitable involvement in an even bloodier conflict made post–V-J Day voters wary of renewed isolationism. An October 1947 poll, for example, with the Truman Doctrine already enunciated and Greek-Turkish aid in the pipeline, indicated that 62 percent of Americans considered the nation's actions "too soft" vis-à-vis the Soviets, while 24 percent thought them "about right." A mere 6 percent believed the administration was "too tough." By early 1948, a full 73 percent thought the United States "too soft" on Moscow.

Henry Wallace was among that 6 percent minority, and while it might prove a crucial 6 percent in the November election, it was still a political fringe. Departing the Commerce Department, Wallace had accepted an offer from former FDR speechwriter (and covert NKVD agent; codename: NIGEL) Michael Straight to edit the then-leftish journal the *New Republic*. From his new post, Wallace intensified his opposition to Truman's foreign policy initiatives, passionately arguing for reconciliation with Moscow. Opposing Greek-Turkish aid, he warned that propping up authoritarian regimes abroad would make America "the most hated nation in the world."

"Greek children still cry for milk," he wrote, "while the American-trained Greek army parades the severed heads of Greek guerillas through the streets. The peoples of the world must see that there is another America than the Truman-led, Wall Street–dominated, military-backed group that is blackening the name of American democracy."

Originally, Wallace had supported the Marshall Plan, praising it as working "toward an overall program which is what I have been advocating all along." When Moscow opposed it, however, he opposed it.

In the spring of 1947, he compounded the controversy by embarking for Europe to assail Truman's emerging foreign policy. In Britain, he attacked Greek and Turkish aid. In Paris, he consorted with French Communist Party leaders Marcel Cachin and Jacques Duclos. Some demanded that he be prosecuted under the Logan Act, a long-standing (but never enforced) federal law forbidding unauthorized private citizens to negotiate with foreign governments. In his diary, Defense Secretary Forrestal wrote: "I inquired why we had not denied Wallace a passport and why we should not do so now. The President felt that to deny an ex-Vice President and an ex-Cabinet member the right of travel abroad would expose us to severe criticism. I said I would prefer to take the criticism than permit Wallace to interfere with American policy. The Attorney General [Tom Clark] suggested that it might be even better to weigh carefully the reentry of the gentleman in question into the United States."

Yet Wallace still retained significant support. On his departure for Europe, 125 supporters had signed a "scroll of greeting" to their English brethren, touting Wallace for embodying "the spirit and faith of the democratic tradition of our two countries." Signatories included Fiorello LaGuardia; Rexford Guy Tugwell; U.S. senators Claude Pepper, Glen H. Taylor, Harley Kilgore, James E. Murray, and Elbert Thomas; Representatives Helen Gahagan Douglas and Adolph Sabath; rail union head A. F. Whitney; Helen Keller; Pulitzer Prize–winning composer Aaron Copland; actors Fredric March and Gene Kelly; authors Thomas Mann and Donald Ogden Stewart; playwrights Arthur Miller and Lillian Hellman; and even FDR's son Elliott.

Returning stateside, Wallace appeared before huge crowds. Fifty-five hundred students greeted him in Ann Arbor, six thousand in Minneapolis, eight thousand in Detroit. Twenty-thousand paid to see him at Chicago Stadium, with another five to ten thousand listening outside via loudspeaker. Another ten thousand heard him on the streets of Berkeley. Pointedly refusing to distance himself from Communist support, before twenty thousand at Los Angeles's Gilmore Stadium on May 19, he announced: "I am not afraid of Communism. If I fail to cry out that I am anti-Communist, it is not because I am friendly to Communism, but because at this time of growing intolerance I refuse to join even the outer circle of that band of men who stir the steaming cauldron of hate and fear."

Such rhetoric garnered attention—and, in the view of Truman's inner circle, ominously growing support. In January 1947, even Frank Sinatra publicly petitioned Wallace to seek the presidency. "Take up the fight we like to think of as ours," Sinatra exhorted, "the fight for tolerance, which is the basis for any peace." In early May 1947, self-styled Wallaceite Charles R. Savage ("I am not a Communist") defeated a "Truman Democrat" in a special House primary in Olympia, Washington. November 1947 witnessed a remarkable show of Wallace strength in Cook County. Running for Illinois's superior court, Progressive Homer F. Carey, a fifty-three-year-old Northwestern University Law School professor, polled 313,848 votes—40 percent of the vote. Early reports indicated Wallace might carry three urban Missouri congressional districts.

In June, DNC executive director Gael E. Sullivan warned Clark Clifford, "There is no question that Wallace has captured the imagination of a strong segment of the American public."

Wallace, Sullivan said bluntly, is "hotter than a busted blow torch."

On Monday, December 29, 1947, Wallace flew from New York to Chicago. At the latter city's Knickerbocker Hotel, with the press excluded, he privately addressed a thousand supporters. A tearful Paul Robeson serenaded him and his followers, reducing Wallace as well to tears. That evening, from Chicago's Tribune Tower, Wallace announced his candidacy for the presidency of the United States. Over a nationwide Mutual Network radio hookup, he attacked the Democratic Party as it was now organized (a party of "war and depression"), the high cost of living, segregation, "lukewarm liberals," corporate profits, the draft, universal military training ("the first decisive step on the road to fascism"), "military adventures," the Marshall Plan ("Those whom we buy politically with food will soon desert us"), and the Truman Doctrine ("we want to hem Russia in"). He concluded:

> Thousands of people all over the United States have asked me to engage in this great fight. The people are on the march. I hope that you who are listening to me tonight will lead the forces in peace, progress and prosperity throughout your communities and throughout our country. Will you let me know that you have come out fighting against the powers of evil?
>
> We have assembled a Gideon's Army, small in number, powerful in conviction, ready for action. We have said with Gideon, "Let those who

are fearful and trembling depart." For every fearful one who leaves, there will be a thousand to take his place. A just cause is worth a hundred armies. We face the future unfettered—unfettered by any principle but the general welfare. We owe no allegiance to any group which does not serve that welfare. By God's grace, the people's peace will usher in the century of the common man.

In Washington, D.C., Helen Gahagan Douglas, now representing California's fourteenth congressional district, heard the news. She despaired for her friend and the great mistake she feared he was making. On Sunday evenings, Douglas and Wallace had the habit of dining with their fellow liberals at Washington's elite Cosmos Club. "I think," he had mused, "I'll try for the nomination." His associates, including Douglas and her fellow Southern California congressman, Chet Holifield, were aghast at this, and even more aghast when Wallace broached the idea of a third party. "They said good night pleasantly to Henry," recalled Douglas of her friends, "and piled out of the door as if fleeing a bad odor." Holifield and Douglas remained behind, however, attempting to warn Wallace of what little support he would enjoy even from his friends—even, indeed, from them. Wallace merely looked hurt.

Later Douglas happened upon her friend (some said her lover), Texas congressman Lyndon Baines Johnson. LBJ was ebullient, confiding how Truman's forces planned to rip Wallace apart by painting him as a Communist dupe.

Lyndon was looking forward to it.

Wallace quit editing the *New Republic* and cobbled together a new party, at first known as just that—the New Party—and eventually as the Progressives. He established its proletarian national headquarters in a forty-room, marble-fireplaced Park Avenue mansion built by a nineteenth-century railroad baron. He ordered corn planted on its tiny grounds—nourished, so the *New Yorker* reported, by a half ton of manure. Estimates of his popularity fluctuated wildly. Some said he would garner only a half million votes. Others said five million. Jim Farley said seven million. Maverick Oregon Republican Wayne Morse and Wallace's own close supporter, CIO general counsel Lee Pressman, both forecast eleven million votes. In April 1948, the *New Republic* noted, "The new party has raised its sights. Ten million votes seem so clearly in view to the Wallaceites that they have decided to try for twenty million."

Despite a year of solidly counterintuitive public relations, Wallace seemed to have succeeded, if not as a winner, at least as a potential spoiler. One February poll found him at 11.5 percent. Depending on who Truman's GOP opposition might be, a January Gallup poll revealed Wallace to be garnering between 15 and 18 percent of New York State's vote. In California, he ran at 11 percent.

These latter two numbers were perhaps most crucial of all. Save for Woodrow Wilson's eyelash 1916 victory, no Democratic president since James Buchanan in 1856 had won without carrying New York. The Empire State served as epicenter of the Wallace movement. There he enjoyed the advantage of an endorsement from its local, increasingly Communist-dominated American Labor Party. In February 1948, an underdog, pro-Wallace ALP candidate, thirty-seven-year-old former assemblyman Leo Isacson, had won a landslide victory in a special House election in a rundown section of the Bronx, triggering shock waves in national Democratic circles. "The Communist menace in this country," said Bronx Democratic boss Ed Flynn, "is much greater than people thought."

"The people have spoken—," contended the *Daily Worker*–backed Isacson, "for Henry A. Wallace, the trustee of the Roosevelt program."

New York controlled forty-seven electoral votes, by far the largest haul, and with New Yorker Tom Dewey looming as Truman's Republican opposition, Truman's situation assumed even greater peril.

The noncommunist left adjourned from its normal fretting over Harry Truman and viewed Wallace with alarm. By early 1948, Communist Party influence within Wallace's movement had become painfully obvious. Many of Wallace's mainstream, liberal admirers—including the CIO's Philip Murray, the railway brotherhood's A. F. Whitney, and journalist A. J. Liebling—had accordingly jumped ship from Wallace's umbrella organization, the Progressive Citizens of America. "Who asked Henry Wallace to run?" former PCA cochair Frank Kingdon pointedly asked in his *New York Post* column. "The call to Wallace came from the Communist party and the only progressive organization admitting Communists to its membership [the PCA]."

In January 1947, prominent liberals—Eleanor Roosevelt and Franklin D. Roosevelt Jr.; theologians Reinhold Niebuhr and Methodist Episcopal Bishop G. Bromley Oxnam; labor leaders David Dubinsky and Walter P. Reuther; the NAACP's Walter White; journalists Marquis Childs, Stewart Alsop, and James Wechsler; broadcaster Elmer Davis; academics Arthur M. Schlesinger Jr. and John Kenneth Galbraith; former New Deal functionaries Leon Henderson, Chester Bowles, and Wilson Wyatt; now former congressman Jerry Voorhis, and Minneapolis's thirty-six-year-old rising-star mayor, Hubert H. Humphrey—gathered in Washington to found a counterweight to the pro-Wallace PCA. Eleanor Roosevelt volunteered the first contribution—a hundred dollars. The newly established Americans for Democratic Action (ADA) announced:

> Within the general framework of present American foreign policy, steps must be taken to raise standards of living and support civil and political freedoms everywhere. These policies are in the great democratic tradition of Jefferson, Jackson, Lincoln, Wilson and Franklin D. Roosevelt. We reject any association with Communists or sympathizers with communism in the United States as completely as we reject any association with Fascists or their sympathizers. Both are hostile to the principles of freedom and democracy on which this Republic has grown great.

To Progressives, the ADA seemed merely paranoid. "From everything we can gather," *New Republic* editor (and Wallace's temporary roommate at Michael Straight's East Ninety-second Street family townhouse), Penn T. Kimball, bluntly informed Arthur Schlesinger, the "ADA is obsessed with the Communist problem to the neglect of all the great fascist and war-making forces which are the real enemies of liberals."

"We believe," added Kimball's fellow *New Republic* staffer, the thirty-two-year-old Theodore H. White, "that the present U.S. policy toward the U.S.S.R. menaces the U.S.S.R. more and is more provocative than the present U.S.S.R. policy toward the U.S." White would soon discover, however, that "there was less freedom to deviate from the line at the *New Republic*" than at White's old gig at Republican Henry Luce's *Time*. The real Henry Wallace, White painfully learned, was "a bitter man; eccentric, ambitious and self-righteous," surrounded by "an unpleasant breed of [Communist] neurotics." Kimball merely found Wallace to be an "enigma" who "couldn't write" and the *New Republic* to be a "madhouse." He quit after five months.

"Wallace," White eventually concluded, "was susceptible to flattery; the Communists flattered him, burned incense in his nostrils, inflated his opinion of himself, wasted his name and honors, and left him beached years later in history as an eccentric, a hissing word in American politics."

Or, as journalist William Harlan Hale noted, by mid-1947, Wallace "was seeing more and more of fewer and fewer people."

The debate continued. The Wallace bandwagon rattled on. From his Gramercy Park home, perennial Socialist Party candidate Norman Thomas observed:

> I originally predicted 3,000,000 to 5,000,000 votes for Wallace, but I have been revising my estimate upward.
>
> Wallace has developed real popular support and his organization shows that it has a very considerable amount of money behind it, at least compared to Socialist funds.
>
> There is a profound, widespread dissatisfaction with the two big parties. Many people cannot accept the Republican policy and yet feel President Truman is not strong enough. It is a state of feeling, not of reason. Wallace is using Franklin Roosevelt's name. He has some personality at a time when we are weak on personalities. His campaign is emotion with very clever manipulation underneath. Many very decent people are turning to Wallace. I am sorry to see it.
>
> Wallace is not a Communist. A great many of his supporters are not. But the group who are manipulating his campaign, pulling the strings, are Communists or Communist sympathizers. Communist support is not to be despised from a practical standpoint because the Communists have learned through hard experience to conduct a disciplined, effective campaign.

In March 1948, as worldwide tensions escalated, Wallace startled many by providing bland excuses for the Czechoslovak coup. At his Park Avenue headquarters, he argued to skeptical reporters that it was the American ambassador's presence in that nation that had somehow compelled Soviet force. Unfortunately, Ambassador Laurence A. Steinhardt did not arrive until two days *after* the coup. Wallace also parroted the *Daily Worker* line that Masaryk had been depressed after being diagnosed with cancer: "I live in the house that John G. Winant [late U.S. ambassador to Britain] lived in and I've heard rumors why he committed suicide. Maybe Winant had cancer. Maybe Masaryk had cancer. Maybe Winant was unhappy about the fate of the world. Who knows?"

To Truman's March 17 calls against Communism and Wallacism, Wallace responded: "It is a shameful call for world remobilization, a complete admission of the failure of the Truman Doctrine and a call for an American police state to which I shall pay my complete respects."

Wallace spoke with passion on this topic:

> Yesterday, we heard a call for universal military training. Tonight I plead the case for universal peace. Mothers and sons rightfully believe a draft and compulsory military training are not the way to preserve freedom at home or to guarantee democracy abroad.
>
> . . . [T]he men who are running our government fear the power of the common men and women the world over.
>
> They have recognized that the peoples of the world are on the march. They know that the people of France, Italy, Czechoslovakia—yes, and the people of China and Greece—want to try a new approach.
>
> They are afraid of this demand for change and they are standing against it. They are using our resources, our science, our productive facilities—and soon they hope to use the bodies of our young men—to stop the demands of the people everywhere.

But it was not merely in China and Greece that young men were dying. The winds of war had also visited a corner of the world called Palestine.

11

"The Bronx is not cheering"

Trouble had been building in the Holy Land for decades. Europe's Jews had fled Russian pogroms and later Hitler's Zyklon B–shrouded wrath, swelling Palestine's population, transforming a once overwhelmingly Muslim Arab land into one that by 1945 was a full third Jewish. During World War I, Britain issued the Balfour Declaration supporting "establishment in Palestine of a national home for the Jewish people," a sentiment the United States Congress endorsed in September 1922. At World War II's conclusion, Palestine's Jews were ready for their own state. Palestine's Arabs stood equally ready to oppose them.

All of which translated into major problems for the Truman administration, now having to juggle priorities in yet one more segment of a fractious globe, not merely between Jews and Arabs, but also between competing British, Soviet, and oil interests.

Palestine was complicated enough, without being a major factor in the election—or nonelection—of a still-unelected Harry Truman.

America's 5.6 million Jews comprised a key component of the now-shaky New Deal–Fair Deal coalition. In ordinary times, the Jewish vote might be considered as safely Democratic as, say, the white South. FDR had, after all, captured 92 percent of the Jewish vote in 1944. But 1948 was not an ordinary time.

The strategically placed Jewish vote was up for grabs.

Two-and-a-half million Jews resided in New York, and Tom Dewey had done sufficiently well with them to carry even New York City just two years previously. Dewey, however, remained the lesser of Harry Truman's Jewish electoral problems, as many New York Jews stood poised to abandon the Democratic ship to board Henry Wallace's. Polls gave Wallace up to

18 percent of New York State's vote and presumably a far higher percentage in the city itself.

Truman and his advisers viewed the situation with growing unease. Sixty-five percent of all American Jews lived in three key states—New York, Pennsylvania, and Illinois—accounting for 110 electoral votes. Add in Ohio, with 23 electoral votes, and with 266 needed to win, Harry Truman could retain the Jewish vote and squeak by to win, or alienate it and lose in a landslide.

Leo Isacson's February 1948 special election reflected Truman's peril. Fifty-five percent of Isacson's overwhelmingly Democratic congressional district was Jewish, yet not even Eleanor Roosevelt's campaigning for Isacson's Democratic opponent could stem the tide.

Isacson's 24th district was left-leaning, a natural breeding ground for a pro-Wallace insurgency. But compounding the situation was the Truman administration's wobbling regarding the new Jewish state. "Truman talks Jewish," declared Henry Wallace, while campaigning for Isacson, "but acts Arab."

Others shared Wallace's skepticism. Following Isacson's victory, the *Hartford Courant* editorialized regarding Truman's Middle Eastern and civil rights policies:

> Both moves have backfired. If Mr. Truman's previous record showed him to be either a liberal or a President whose decisions were not strongly motivated by partisan considerations, it would be possible to place a kindlier interpretation on his actions. But his record is shot through with partisan decisions. Hence it is impossible to conclude that in either his civil-rights program or his original policy on Palestine partition he was motivated by more than political advantage. He has not regained the so-called liberal vote from Mr. Wallace for the first, and he seems to have alienated a large number of voters in New York and elsewhere for his about-face on the second. No wonder the Bronx is not cheering except in its own inimitable way.

Harry Truman had indeed issued mixed messages. Trapped between the realities of domestic politics, his own sympathy for a hideously persecuted and nearly exterminated people ("the Jews have no place to go"), and the demands of international politics (facing potentially greater dangers on the European continent), Truman had—like FDR before him—artlessly equivocated for much of his first three years in office on two separate issues: Jewish immigration to the Holy Land and Palestinian partition.

In May 1939, bowing to Arab pressure, the United Kingdom limited Jewish immigration to the Holy Land to a mere 75,000 persons over the next five years. In April 1945, Britain terminated it completely. Following V-E Day, however, hundreds of thousands of surviving European Jews desperately sought new lives in Palestine. Jewish groups lobbied Downing Street—and the Truman administration—to allow 100,000 additional immigrants. Britain, still facing Arab opposition, resisted, and in June 1946 Britain's foreign secretary, the beefy former truck driver Ernest Bevin, rather bluntly and publicly informed the annual conference of the Labour Party: "Regarding the agitation in the United States, and particularly in New York, for 100,000 to be put into Palestine, I hope it will not be misunderstood in America if I say, with the purest of motives, that that was because they do not want too many of them in New York."

Truman's earliest inclinations were to accede to Jewish demands, although his motives were not always born of idealism. "I am sorry, gentlemen," he lectured a delegation of four American diplomats in 1945, "but I have to answer to hundreds of thousands who are anxious for the success of Zionism: I do not have hundreds of thousands of Arabs among my constituents."

Britain, however, remained adamant, and the incessant Jewish domestic pressure for action—Truman received 100,000 letters on the subject in 1947 alone—often exasperated the rarely sanguine HST. In August 1946, he wrote to Ed Flynn:

> Of course, the British control Palestine and there is no way of getting One Hundred Thousand Jews in there unless they want them in.
>
> I have done my best to get them in but I don't believe there is any possible way of pleasing our Jewish friends.

"Jesus Christ," he fumed to his cabinet in July 1946, "couldn't please them [the Jews] when He was here on earth, so how could anyone expect that I would have any luck?"

It was not his only such outburst. As each became public, his difficulties with the Jewish community only worsened. In January 1948, he exploded to *New York Post* editor Ted Thackrey (married to the Jewish Dorothy Schiff), "Those New York Jews! They're disloyal to their country. Disloyal."

"Would you mind explaining that a little further, Mr. President?" Thackrey demanded. "When you speak of New York Jews are you referring to such people as Bernard Baruch? Or are you referring to such New York Jews as my wife?"

Truman cut the conversation short. Reported soon enough in Drew Pearson's syndicated column, it led to this testy exchange at a March 1948 press conference:

THE PRESIDENT. First, I want to pay attention to a vicious statement that was made by a columnist in a New York gossip paper, in which he said I had made the statement to an editor of a New York paper here that the Jews in New York were disloyal. I had thought I wouldn't have to add another liar's star to that fellow's crown, but I will have to do it. That is just a lie out of the whole cloth. That is as emphatic as I can put it. Now I am ready for questions.

Q. May we quote you on that, sir?

THE PRESIDENT. Verbatim, if you like.

Q. All Jews? The Jews?

THE PRESIDENT. Jews. Jews in New York are disloyal, which is a lie out of the whole cloth. It makes good reading in a political year.

Such intemperate incidents were not unique—neither regarding Drew Pearson (a Quaker) nor to Jews. In July 1948, Pearson reported that Bob Hannegan, retired from the cabinet and the DNC after repeated battles with Truman confidant and Treasury secretary John Snyder, believed Truman unelectable. Hannegan penned a quick denial to Truman. "Whenever I get my information from Pearson," Truman responded, "I hope somebody will have my head examined—I'll need it. Articles like that are merely an attempt to upset the 'apple cart' and Pearson and your friend [Broadway columnist and radio commentator Walter] Winchell are the 'sphere heads' for that purpose. If either one of them ever tells the truth, it is by accident and not intentional."

Truman trod on dangerous ground by challenging the powerful—and hitherto loyally Democratic—Winchell. Seeking to restore peace, he invited Winchell to the White House, but only exacerbated matters with yet another racially tinged attack on Dorothy Schiff. "Truman made a remark," recalled Winchell radio producer Paul Scheffels. "I don't remember it word for word, but something about that 'damn kike,' and of course you call anybody a 'kike,' and he'll go after you hammer and tongs. . . . That was the beginning."

Said Winchell on returning to New York: "He's not a President."

Symptomatic of Truman's hesitancy on Palestinian affairs were White House efforts preceding the 1946 midterm elections. On October 4, 1946 (Yom Kippur), Truman released a statement on the Palestinian question (in his memoirs he claims the document to be a mere holiday greeting), noting that "the Jewish Agency proposed a solution of the Palestine problem by means of the creation of a viable Jewish state in control of its own immigration and economic policies in an adequate area of Palestine instead of in the whole of Palestine. It proposed . . . certificates for 100,000 Jewish immigrants. . . . [I]t is my belief that a solution along these lines would command the support of public opinion in the United States."

Foreign Secretary Bevin had begged Secretary of State Byrnes for Truman not to reference the hundred thousand settlers, arguing that such a statement would only undermine Britain's negotiating position vis-à-vis Jewish and Arab elements in Palestine. Nonetheless, a call for increased Jewish immigration was established American policy. The "creation of a Jewish state" was not.

Arabs felt betrayed. From Jerusalem, Dr. Hussein el Khalidi, secretary of the Arab Higher Committee, threatened:

If [Truman] . . . puts his aggressive policy into effect, we shall ask the Arab League . . . to sever all economic, cultural and diplomatic relations with the United States, boycott all American colleges and institutions and close down those in Arab countries and revoke all oil and other concessions and politely ask every American in our midst to leave us in peace. President Truman will thus become responsible for any and all repercussions which might result from his aggressive policy.

The British proved only moderately less infuriated. Their very public response only reinforced domestic suspicions that Truman had acted from political motives. "A few days later Governor Dewey said that several hundred thousand should be admitted," Truman would ruefully recall, "and Bevin now told the British House of Commons that I had made my statement to forestall Dewey's, in other words, I had taken my position for political reasons only."

The year of 1947 witnessed escalating violence in the Holy Land, most tragically at Gush Etzion, Deir Yassin, and Kfar Etzion. Pressure mounted on Truman not only to support increased Jewish immigration, but also to lift the arms embargo on Zionists already there.

In July 1947, British authorities had seized the Mossad Le'Aliyah Bet-operated refugee craft *Exodus 1947* (the incident upon which Otto Preminger's 1960 film, *Exodus*, was based), transporting 4,554 Holocaust survivors to Haifa. On July 21, former Treasury secretary Henry Morgenthau conferred with Truman regarding the incident. Frustrated, Truman wrote in his diary:

Had ten minutes conversation with Henry Morgenthau about a Jewish ship to Palistine [sic]. . . . He'd no business, whatever to call me. The Jews have no sense of proportion nor do they have any judgment on world affairs.

Henry brought a thousand Jews to New York on a supposedly temporary basis and they stayed. When the country went backward and Republican in the election of 1946, this incident loomed large on the Displaced Persons program.

The Jews I find are very, very selfish. They care not how many Estonians, Latvians, Finns, Poles, Yugoslavs or Greeks get murdered or mistreated as Displaced Persons as long as the Jews get special treatment. Yet when they have power, physical, financial or political neither Hitler nor Stalin has anything on them for cruelty or mistreatment to the underdog. Put an underdog on top and it makes no difference whether his name is Russian, Jewish, Negro, Management, Labor, Mormon, Baptist[,] he goes haywire. I've found very, very few who remember their past condition when prosperity comes.

To the now indefatigably Zionist Eleanor Roosevelt, Truman similarly wrote on August 27, 1947, concerning Zionist efforts to break the British arms blockade:

[T]hese ships . . . started to Palestine with American funds and American backing—they were loaded knowing that they were trying to do an illegal act.

The action of some United States Zionists will eventually prejudice everyone against what they are trying to get done. I fear very much that the Jews are like all underdogs—when they get on top they are just as intolerant and cruel as people were to them when they were underneath. I regret this situation very much because my sympathy has always been on their side.

American Jewry wearied of Truman's mixed messages (and his unmixed message opposing American arms shipments to Jewish settlers) and reciprocated his growing testiness. In late 1947, he received a letter accusing him of "preferring fascist and Arab elements to the democracy-loving Jewish people of Palestine." Truman forwarded the offending document to White House minorities adviser, the Jewish David K. Niles, adding, "It is such drivels [sic] as this that makes Anti-Semites. I thought you had best answer it because I might tell him what's good for him."

In October 1948, Truman conferred with his old friend, former Montana Democratic senator Burton K. Wheeler. The isolationist Wheeler advised Truman to back the Zionist position. Truman demurred, arguing he had plenty of Jewish support. Wheeler countered that Truman required Jewish backing in 1948. "I don't know about that," Truman responded. "I think that a candidate on an anti-Semitic platform might sweep the country."

Nonetheless, despite all his cranky sputtering (a very Trumanesque sputtering to those who knew him), Truman's commitment to a Jewish state remained remarkably constant. "I don't care about the oil," he contended, "I want to do what's right." On November 29, 1947, the United States spearheaded adoption of UN General Assembly Resolution 181, dividing Palestine into Arab and Jewish states. The vote stood thirty-three in favor, including the U.S., the USSR (which had been supplying arms to Zionist forces through Czechoslovakia), most of Europe, and the British Commonwealth. Ten Muslim states plus India, Greece, and Cuba voted against. Britain and nine other nations abstained.

Republican pressure added to Truman's discomfort. Both Tom Dewey and Robert Taft (a close associate of Cleveland's particularly vexatious Zionist leader, Rabbi Abba Hillel Silver) advocated a strong Zionist position. If they criticized Truman at all for his Palestinian policy, it was to term him insufficiently pro-Zionist.

Secretary of Defense James Forrestal, however, along with the bulk of high-level State Department personnel (George Marshall; Under Secretary of State Robert Lovett; Lovett's predecessor, Dean Acheson; director of the division of Near Eastern and African affairs, Loy Henderson; chief of the policy planning staff, George Kennan; department counsel Charles "Chip" Bohlen; and United Nations section head Dean Rusk), argued strenuously against tilting toward Palestine's Jewish settlers and provoking British and Arab backlashes. In the course of December 1947's annual Gridiron Club dinner, Forrestal, supposedly with Truman's knowledge, approached both Dewey and Arthur Vandenberg, endeavoring to have Palestine removed from the political spotlight. Forrestal got nowhere.

If the anti-Zionist Forrestal felt frustration, so did American Zionist leaders.

Termination of the British mandate drew near. Truman refused even to meet with Zionist leader Chaim Weizmann. Zionist leaders approached Truman's closest Jewish friend, his former business partner Eddie Jacobson, for assistance, but Truman rebuffed even Jacobson's intercession. On

Saturday, March 13, 1948, Jacobson—sans appointment; he was that close to Truman—walked into the White House to talk with Truman. Administration Appointments secretary Matt Connelly warned Jacobson not to mention Palestine. Jacobson did anyway. Truman's harsh response stunned him. He might have expected it. The embattled Truman faced nearly unbearable pressures on all fronts. Three days previously, Jan Masaryk had fallen to his death. War might erupt momentarily. In two days Truman would announce he would address Congress to lobby for the Marshall Plan, call for universal training, and reintroduce the draft. In four days he would denounce "Henry Wallace and his Communists."

Harry Truman had more than enough on his plate without Palestine. His body stiffened. His face became taut, and he poured out his frustration and resentment, deriding the criticism he had already faced from Jews regarding Palestine as "disrespectful and mean."

"My dear friend, the President of the United States," Jacobson recalled, "was at that moment as close to being an anti-Semite as a man could possibly be."

Jacobson began once more. He got nowhere. Tears ran down his cheeks. His voice betrayed his frayed nerves. He plodded on:

Harry, all your life you have had a hero. . . . I too have a hero, a man I never met, but who is, I think, the greatest Jew who ever lived. . . . I am talking about Chaim Weizmann. He is a very sick man, almost broken in health, but he traveled thousands of miles just to see you and plead the cause of my people. Now you refuse to see him just because you are insulted by some of our American Jewish leaders, even though you know that Weizmann had absolutely nothing to do with these insults and would be the last man to be party to them. It doesn't sound like you, Harry, because I thought you could take this stuff they have been handing out.

Truman drummed his fingers on his great desk. Swiveling round, he stared out toward the White House gardens, his back turned against his friend. His silence continued. Jacobson's unease grew excruciating. Truman swung back. Staring Jacobson square in the eye, he answered: "You win, you bald-headed son of a bitch. I will see him."

At 12:15 PM on Thursday, March 18, 1948, the seventy-three-year-old Weizmann secretly passed through the White House's little-used East Gate to meet with Truman. The session went well. Truman, recalled the Jewish Agency's Washington representative Eliahu Elath, "informed Weizmann that no change occurred in his support for partition, which still remained the basis for American policy on Palestine."

That was Thursday. On Friday, March 19, United States UN representative Warren Austin, a seventy-year-old former Republican senator from Vermont, informed the Security Council:

> my government believes that a temporary trusteeship for Palestine should be established . . . to maintain the peace and to afford the Jews and Arabs of Palestine further opportunity to reach an agreement regarding [its] future government. . . . Such a United Nations trusteeship would, of course, be without prejudice to the character of the eventual political settlement, which we hope can be achieved without long delay.

The United States had completely reversed the position Truman had enunciated to Weizmann the previous day.

Reaction was violent. "Shift on Palestine a Shock to Capitol: Some Hold U.S. Plan 'Sellout'" headlined the *New York Times*. It editorialized that the "land of milk and honey now flows with oil, and the homeland of three great religions is having its fate decided by expediency without a sign of . . . spiritual and ethical considerations." Truman's action, the *Times* charged, culminated a "series of moves which has seldom been matched for ineptness in the handling of any international issue by an American administration."

Addressing a Jewish women's group at Washington's Mayflower Hotel, freshman Manhattan Republican congressman Jacob K. Javits (filling in for Claude Pepper) excoriated Truman's "double cross" and proclaimed that "the Jews must depend on themselves. . . . We'll fight to the death and make a Jewish state in Palestine if it's the last thing we do." Democratic Lower East Side congressman Arthur G. Klein, an Orthodox Jew and ardent Zionist, condemned the situation as "the most terrible sellout of the common people since Munich. This is not alone a betrayal of the hopes of the Jewish people. It is a betrayal of all the peoples everywhere who believe in peace and justice.

Repeal the American embargo against shipping of arms to Palestine and the Jewish people themselves will enforce partition in their own blood."

Fumed Rabbi Louis I. Newman of West 83rd Street's Congregation Rodeph Sholom:

> With sorrow, every American citizen regrets that the President of the United States seems to be talking out of both sides of his mouth with respect to Palestine.
>
> Formerly, we were told that the Jews could not press for a homeland in Palestine because the Arabs had to be kept contented when the Second World War was in progress. Now another excuse is being given to sell the Jews down the river again.

"The UN security council," charged Robert Taft, "will have to send an armed force to Palestine to support the UN trusteeship." Eleanor Roosevelt, now a member of the United States UN delegation, nearly resigned in protest. "The Jews, bearing the wounds of Hitler's decade upon their bodies and souls have been again grievously wounded," wrote Reinhold Niebuhr.

"There wasn't one human being in Kansas City or anywhere else," mourned Eddie Jacobson, "during those terrible days who expressed faith and confidence in the words of the president of the United States."

Truman played the innocent, claiming to have been double-crossed by pro-Arab, career State Department bureaucrats. In his diary, he wrote:

> The State Dept. pulled the rug from under me today. . . . This morning I find that the State Dept. has reversed my Palestine policy. The first I know about it is what I see in the papers! Isn't that hell! I am now in the position of a liar and a double-crosser. . . .
>
> There are people on the third and fourth levels of the State Dept., who have always wanted to cut my throat. They've succeeded in doing so. . . .

He was *not* innocent. On March 6, 1948, Truman had reviewed a draft of Warren Austin's address. Two days later, following a meeting with Marshall and Robert Lovett, he again signaled assent. "There is absolutely no question but that the president approved it," Lovett recalled. "There was a definite clearance there."

"As I quickly learned in delving into the record and querying White House and State staff," admitted Truman speechwriter George M. Elsey, "Truman had personally read and approved . . . the Austin speech. . . . He hadn't remembered? Or he hadn't understood? Whichever, it was another example of Truman's trying to juggle too many problems all by himself without allowing his staff to help."

At a March 25, 1948, news conference, Truman, while reiterating support for partition, nonetheless continued support for trusteeship. "It has become clear," he carefully equivocated, "that the [UN Palestine] partition plan cannot be carried out at this time by peaceful means. . . . Trusteeship is not proposed as a substitution for the partition plan but as an effort to fill the vacuum soon to be created by the termination of the mandate."

As Henry Wallace had discovered, Harry Truman might approve many things—and then disown them. At day's end, however, Truman—supported by aides Clark Clifford and David K. Niles—held firm for partition. "The choice for our people . . . ," Weizmann had written to Truman, "is between Statehood and extermination. History and providence have placed this issue in your hands, and I am confident that you will yet decide it in the spirit of the moral law."

That is how Truman saw it.

James Forrestal, however, argued to the indefatigably pro-statehood Clark Clifford, "You just don't understand. Forty million Arabs are going to push 400,000 Jews into the sea. And that's all there is to it. Oil—that is the side we ought to be on."

"Jim," Clifford responded, "the President knows just as well as you do what the numbers are, but he doesn't consider this to be a question of numbers. He has always supported the right of the Jews to have their own homeland from the moment he became President. He considers this to be a question about . . . moral and ethical considerations. . . . He is sympathetic to their needs and their desires, and I assure you he is going to continue to lend our country's support to . . . a Jewish state."

The clock wound down on Britain's partition. On April 20, 1948, UN ambassador Austin (with Truman's approval) indicated that "a limited number of police" might participate in a "temporary trusteeship." With Europe in continuing crisis, however, there was little chance the United States might commit sizable forces to the Middle East.

On April 23, FDR and Truman speechwriter Sam Rosenman informed Weizmann that Truman would recognize the Jewish state as soon as it was proclaimed. If Weizmann proved wary of such a promise, he had justification—and not merely from past experience. The State Department continued to resist recognition. On Wednesday, May 12, 1948, Truman summoned Marshall, Lovett, Clifford ("Marshall did not like me"), and David Niles to confer regarding recognition of this yet-to-be proclaimed, still nameless Jewish state.

"I don't even know why Clifford is here," Marshall fumed. "He is a domestic adviser, and this is a foreign policy matter."

"Well, General," Truman responded, relying on chain-of-command-style reasoning, "he's here because I asked him to be here."

"These considerations," the usually unemotional Marshall sputtered, "have nothing to do with the issue. I fear that the only reason Clifford is here is that he is pressing a political consideration with regard to this issue. I don't think politics should play any part in this."

"He said it . . . ," remembered the infuriated Clifford, "in a righteous God-damned Baptist tone."

Robert Lovett hoped, at least, to delay events. "Mr. President," he argued, "to recognize the Jewish state prematurely would be buying a pig in a poke." There would be no delay.

"If you follow Clifford's advice," Marshall icily warned Truman, "and in the election I were to vote, I would vote against you."

Harry Truman would have tolerated—let alone admired—few men after such an outburst. But George Catlett Marshall was one of them. Beyond that, what if Marshall *did* resign? The resultant shock waves might crash not only Truman's Palestine policy, but also his European policy, and, most likely, capsize what little chance he possessed that November. Truman dispatched Clifford to confer privately with Lovett. His mission: Keep Marshall on board.

"Be careful," Truman advised, "I can't afford to lose General Marshall."

Over bourbon and sherry that evening, in Lovett's home library, came the words that Clifford—and Truman—had dreaded might come. "I'm afraid," said Lovett, "that Marshall could resign."

Marshall, however, retained his sense of duty. Lovett did indeed dissuade him. "One did not resign," Marshall reminded associates, "because the President, who had a constitutional right to make a decision, had made one."

At 6 PM on Thursday, May 14, 1948, Chaim Weizmann proclaimed the independence of his new Jewish state. Only then, over shortwave radio from Tel Aviv, did the world learn the name of this new nation: Israel. Eleven minutes later, despite Lovett's continued pleading against "indecent haste," the United States became the first nation to extend recognition.

It was a short statement—two paragraphs, forty words, and not a bit of oratory in it:

> THIS GOVERNMENT has been informed that a Jewish state has been proclaimed in Palestine, and recognition has been requested by the provisional government thereof. The United States recognizes the provisional government as the de facto authority of the new State of Israel.

In Manhattan, Jews danced the hora and prayed, "Blessed art Thou, O Lord, King of the Universe, that Thou hast maintained and preserved us to witness this day." At the United Nations' temporary headquarters at Lake Success, New York, the U.S. delegation (Eleanor Roosevelt included), taken once more by surprise, felt betrayed. At the State Department, George Marshall ordered Dean Rusk to "get up to New York right away to keep our UN delegation from resigning en masse." In Cairo, Sheikh Mohamed Mamoun el-Shennawy, chief of the Moslem Theological Institute, proclaimed, "The hour for jihad has struck."

And that night, at Washington's Mayflower Hotel, a jubilant Harry Truman informed Howard McGrath, a ballroom full of Young Democrats, and a nationwide radio hookup: "I want to say to you that for the next four years there will be a Democrat in the White House, and you are looking at him!"

12

"A lost ball in high grass"

Exactly why, on May 14, 1948, Harry Truman thought he would occupy the White House "for the next four years" was, to say the least, baffling.

True, he had picked himself off the ground following 1946's electoral bloodletting, and, by July 1947, had bounced back to lead comfortably in the polls. But trouble was brewing—and Truman knew it. "The family are going to spend Christmas at the White House this year," he wrote to a friend in late November 1947, "because it probably will be the last chance for such a performance."

Truman's personal approval rating had rebounded to 57 percent in June 1947, and held at 55 percent as late as October. A late-summer 1947 *Fortune* magazine poll showed Dewey and Truman neck and neck. In December 1947, *Look* magazine polled fifty-seven Washington correspondents. Only five thought Truman would win election. In April 1948, the Roper poll reported a 47 to 39 percent Dewey advantage, and Gallup contended that every Republican but Taft led Truman. That same month, Truman's personal approval rating had skidded to a worrisome 36 percent. In June 1948, Roper projected Dewey (44 to 32 percent), Stassen and Vandenberg (42 to 32 percent), and MacArthur (43 to 33 percent) vanquishing Truman. Drew Pearson forecast Truman would lose every state south of the Mason-Dixon line—and every state *above* it.

Labor remained leery of the chief executive who threatened to draft strikers. New Dealers saw Truman as an inadequate substitute for the jaunty aristocrat who had led them through depression and war. Republicans thought the New Deal had gone on long enough, and didn't appreciate Harry Truman's prolonging it. Northern blacks and southern whites—for obviously contradictory motives—threatened defection from Democratic ranks. Farmers complained about low prices. Consumers complained about high prices and a lack of housing. Most Americans worried about Communism's advance in Europe and the Far East. Left-wingers fretted about anti-Communism and flocked to Henry Wallace.

All the while, Harry Truman bumbled and alienated common folks and Washington insiders alike.

In 1947, the center of Harry Truman's White House political operation was no longer staunch New Dealer Bob Hannegan, beset by increasing blood pressure and decreasing favor. Nor was it cabinet members such as Marshall or Forrestal, or even the jealous and ambitious John Snyder. Nor was it any other of Truman's Missouri cronies.

It *was*, however, someone from Missouri.

Clark Clifford was just thirty-nine when he became White House counsel in 1946. Before Pearl Harbor, uninterested in politics, he had practiced law in St. Louis, where he had made the acquaintance of fellow opera aficionado, J. K. "Jake" Vardaman. During the war, Clifford and Vardaman went their separate ways, both separate ways leading to the Navy. When Truman appointed the largely unqualified Vardaman as his naval aide, Vardaman almost instantly ran afoul of then naval secretary James Forrestal. Requiring allies, he selected Clifford as his assistant. Vardaman soon wore out his White House welcome. Clifford did not.

"He was like a Greek god—way over six feet, and handsome," recalled another White House aide of Clifford's. But beyond being handsome, Clifford was good. "He was energetic and highly capable," observed Harvard-educated Truman speechwriter George Elsey, pointedly adding, "which could not be said of several of Truman's early appointees."

Clifford and Elsey shared both a predilection for natty wardrobes and strongly pessimistic views regarding their president's diminishing prospects. Elsey calculated that Truman's upcoming State of the Union address must be, even by Washington standards, a political document. It must, Elsey argued, "be controversial as hell, must state the issues of the election, must draw the line sharply between Republicans and Democrats. The Democratic platform will stem from it, and the election will be fought on the issues it presents."

Clifford, meanwhile, toiled on another document, a broad overview of where the president stood and what he must do to remain president.

Elsewhere in Washington, so did thirty-six-year-old James H. Rowe Jr., former aide to "Tommy the Cork" Corcoran. Truman, however, despised Corcoran—so much so, of course, that he had Corcoran's phone tapped. Thus, any advice Rowe tendered would be speedily ignored—if it were read at all—once it reached the presidential desk. Accordingly, Clifford largely adopted Rowe's work as his own. In a town bristling with egos, Rowe didn't seem to mind.

Though hardly infallible, Rowe's document proved remarkably practical, prescient, and, above all, workable. It pinpointed Tom Dewey and Henry Wallace as Truman's ultimate opponents, and advised dispatching only "prominent liberals and progressives—*and no one else*—to move publicly into the fray [against Wallace]. They must point out that the core of the Wallace backing is made up of Communists and the fellow-travelers. At the same time some lines should be kept out so that if the unpredictable Henry finally sees the light and can be talked into supporting the Administration, he will have handy rope to climb back on the bandwagon—if he is wanted."

It enumerated a Democratic coalition of liberals, farmers, unions, Southerners, Catholics, Jews, Italians, and immigrants. Not every group counted equally in the Rowe equation. Though Rowe identified Italians as "volatile," he failed to propose any measures to hold their vote. Catholics fared little better, though they might be mollified by healthy doses of anti-Communism.

Southerners fared worst of all. "It is inconceivable," Rowe advised, "that any policy initiated by the Truman Administration no matter how 'liberal' could so alienate the South in the next year that it would revolt. As always, the South can be considered safely Democratic. And in formulating national policy, it can be safely ignored."

History's selective memory has focused largely on the attention that liberals, labor, African-Americans, and Jews would now receive from the Truman campaign team, but Rowe's document expends substantial time advocating the wooing of the farm vote. Geographically, it focused not on the teeming immigrants, Catholics, Jews, and union members of the East, but, rather, upon wide-open western vistas, where votes were up for grabs. Rowe wrote:

In the land of Electoral Votes, the West is the "Number one Priority" for the Democrats. Its people are more liberal because they need the economic help of government and in the years of the New Deal have come to understand how it functions. Even the Chambers of Commerce of the West rarely prate of governmental economy; they learned better long ago.

There is no need for an extended discussion here about what should be done politically for the Western States. They know their needs—less discrimination in freight rates, reclamation projects and lots of them, better roads (their road system suffered from lack of maintenance in the war years), public power, help in the development and protection of their resources, and so forth. Their needs are not hard to understand. The Administration, which in the last year or two has at least budget wise not shown much sympathy (although far more than Republicans), must display a constant and increasing interest in these Western needs.

At this time, most (if not all) dispassionate observers would have downplayed employing Truman as a campaign asset. The Rowe-Clifford memo, however, pointed out:

The public has a tremendous interest in its Chief Executive and is invariably hungry for news about him. . . . The press must print news of the President—so he controls his publicity by his own whim. One or two non-political personages a week should be the target. The technique of a summons to the White House has the added virtue, besides publicity, of building good will. . . .

So a President who is also a candidate must resort to subterfuge—for he cannot sit silent. He must be in the limelight. He . . . must also resort to the kind of trip which Roosevelt made famous in the 1940 campaign— the "inspection tour." No matter how much the opposition and the press pointed out the political overtones of those trips, the people paid little attention because what they saw was the Head of State performing his duties.

Before Clifford could fully unveil this new strategy, Truman would have to deliver Elsey's "Democratic platform" State of the Union address. On Wednesday afternoon, January 7, 1948, in his trademark uninspiring monotone, Truman unveiled the most comprehensive package of liberal initiatives ever proposed: public housing, federal health insurance, increased aid to education, a higher minimum wage, greater farm supports, new conservation and reclamation efforts, a ten-point anti-inflation package, $3.2 billion more in corporate taxes, a $40 tax rebate for each taxpayer—and a powerful hint of action on civil rights.

Prior to Truman's address, congressmen and senators enthusiastically cheered Gen. Marshall's entrance. Their fervor noticeably declined as Truman entered. Michigan congressman Clare E. Hoffman didn't bother standing. Seven times during his address Truman paused for applause, only to be greeted by stony silence.

"The extraordinary chilly reception . . . ," noted the *New York Times*'s James Reston, "created the impression that . . . Mr. Truman was long on rags and tatters and short on pattern, that he did not clarify the central issues but confused them, that he did not provide a priority list for the new year's problems but merely lumped them all together."

Harold Ickes, in a decidedly biblical mood, harrumphed in his nationally syndicated newspaper column that the presidential "performance was a rather shabby dramatization of the return of the Prodigal Son. His eleventh-hour confessions of error will not atone for his acts. . . . To term Truman's political harangue a State-of-the-Union Message is akin to slander. . . . The words purported to be that of the Roosevelt New Deal, but the voice was the voice of Esau. . . . The sudden conversion of the wandering Harry probably came as a surprise to Henry [Wallace]. Henry should know, and probably does, that a Billy Sunday cannot pick his converts. Neither can he be sure whether returning prodigals are insincerely repentant, or only thinking of a fatted calf."

From the right, another former New Dealer, Dr. Raymond Moley, concurred. "The Wallace issues are to be grabbed before he has a chance to have a convention," Moley noted. "The infant is stolen from the delivery room."

If such critiques inflamed Truman's sensibilities, for once he didn't display his irritation. Returning to the Oval Office, he gathered his staff about him, broke open bottles of scotch and bourbon, and toasted to "Success in '48!" As the celebration subsided, he pulled George Elsey aside to offer his appreciation. "I was astounded," recorded Elsey; "such comments from him were rare. It just wasn't his nature."

Truman now had a theme, but needed to sell it. Even Elsey conceded that Truman had delivered his State of the Union address in a "flat, emotionless manner"—and there, in a nutshell, lay a great problem. Franklin D. Roosevelt had rarely developed his own material, but he possessed a rare gift: a great actor's flair for delivery. In FDR's hands, "a day that will live in infamy" rallied a nation to victory; in Harry Truman's, the same rhetoric might have fallen as flat as a Missouri landscape.

Truman simply could not read from a text, which was ironic for a man who loved reading. His eyesight remained so limited and his glasses so thick that he struggled to read the words before him, and struggled even harder to speak them at the same time. His vision, noted aide Ken Hechler, was "so bad that when he leaned over to read his manuscript more closely, all you could see was the top of his head."

Yet, even had Harry Truman possessed perfect vision, his delivery would never have approached his predecessor's. It is one thing to be a gentleman farmer, another to be a midwestern dirt farmer. Accordingly, Truman rarely delivered prepared speeches in the Senate. Being president mandated being a speechmaker, though he remained horrible at it.

From Washington's Statler Hotel on Saturday night, April 17, 1948, Truman addressed the American Society of Newspaper Editors. His fifteen-minute prepared remarks left their recipients wondering when the bar would reopen. Having concluded, however, he decided on speaking off the cuff, and the results proved quite remarkable. Former FDR and Truman press secretary Jonathan Daniels, now editor the *Raleigh News & Observer*, recorded: "He began . . . in his own vocabulary, out of his own humor and his own heart. . . . He made the story of his own problems seem one told in earnestness and almost intimacy with each man in the hall. He was suddenly a very interesting man of great candor who discussed the problems of American leadership with men as neighbors. He spoke the language of them all out of traditions common to them all."

Even the pro-Wallace *New Republic* nodded approval. The staunchly conservative syndicated columnist David Lawrence publicly marveled: "It [created] an impression of naturalness and simplicity. Many an editor said afterward that if Mr. Truman would only discard formal speeches and talk in the same earnest and matter-of-fact way to all audiences he would be revealed as almost an entirely different personality.

"What the President said wasn't in itself new, [the editors present] added—but there was a ring of sincerity and persuasiveness in his voice and manner that carried conviction."

Everyone seemed pleased with the result. A policy of presidential ad-libbing, however, still seemed fraught with peril, particularly a policy of Truman ad-libbing. Nonetheless, when Truman extemporized once more—this time before the National Health Assembly—the tactic succeeded once more. In his diary, Truman wrote: "Seemed to go over big. . . . Suppose I am in for a lot of work now getting my head full of facts before each public appearance. If it must be done, I will have to do it. Comes of poor ability to read a speech and put feeling into it."

On Thursday afternoon, May 6, Truman went extemporaneous over a live national radio hookup. Again, he succeeded. In the course of thirteen-and-a-half minutes, Truman's audience laughed or applauded eight times. He had come a long way from the State of the Union address.

Yet few in his party noticed—or cared. In early March, Alabama U.S. senator John Sparkman, by no means a conservative, announced: "There is only one way this controversy can be settled and only one way to avoid defeat for the Democratic Party in November—that is for Mr. Truman to withdraw. . . . There is no use hiding our heads in the sand. People in the South . . . will never accept him as the nominee. I wish very much that he would sense the situation and would withdraw."

Or as Alabama state senator Tully A. Goodwin wrote to a friend, "President Truman is out of the picture, he is a lost ball in high grass of discord and unrest."

Truman's woes transcended region. In March 1948, only three of thirteen Democratic candidates for the Senate (Montana's James E. Murray, Rhode Island's venerable Theodore F. Green, and New Mexico's Clinton P. Anderson—Truman's former agriculture secretary) would admit to running as Truman Democrats. The following month, Truman's personal popularity imploded to a mere 36 percent. When he vetoed a Republican-sponsored $4.8-billion income tax reduction, Congress stampeded to oppose him, voting to override in just four hours. Only eighty-eight Democratic congressmen and ten senators voted to sustain Truman.

The *New York Times*'s Arthur Krock observed in early May: "The Democratic Party is imperiling the President's effectiveness as no major party in this country has done since the Republican radicals impeached Andrew Johnson. . . . A President whose defeat at the next poll is generally prophesied faces difficulties in performing his office that could conceivably bring disaster. . . . [His] influence is weaker than any President's has been in modern history."

Pundits and party leadership wrote Truman off. Yet the party rank and file did not. In fact, its support grew steadily. In December 1946, only 48 percent of Democrats supported Truman's nomination. By July 1947, his Democratic support soared to 71 percent; in June 1948 to an all-time high 76 percent.

Jim Rowe had written that the West was the Democrats' "Number one Priority." Clark Clifford had argued that Truman must "resort" to "an inspection tour" to reach the people. An opportunity arose to combine both strategies when the University of California at Berkeley invited Truman to address its June 1948 commencement and receive an honorary degree (his thirteenth). At 11:05 PM, Thursday, June 3, 1948, Truman departed Washington's Union Station for the West Coast. Along Pennsylvania Avenue, banners mocked him, reading: "Democrats Dump Truman" and "America Needs William Douglas."

"If I felt any better," he informed well-wishers, "I couldn't stand it."

Logistically, the trip had been made easier, even comfortable, by a wartime bequest that the Association of American Railroads had tendered to Franklin Roosevelt. Sold to the federal government for one dollar, the steel-and concrete-reinforced, 285,000-pound railroad car, the Ferdinand Magellan, would be Truman's home for what would turn out to be a 9,505-mile, eighteen-state journey.

The Ferdinand Magellan provided a marvelous venue. Its blue-curtained and presidential-seal-bedecked rear platform boasted not only a lectern, but also three roof-mounted loudspeakers to amplify the president's words throughout whatever crowds might greet him. Sixteen other cars accompanied it, jammed with 125 persons—wife Bess and daughter Margaret, eighteen White House staffers (including Clifford; the president's personal physician, Wallace Graham; and the hapless Harry Hood Vaughan), various Secret Service men, Signal Corps personnel, and, of course, reporters (fifty-nine of them, including one British, one French, and two Chinese). Absent were any representatives of the Democratic National Committee. The White House's gossamer official story held that this voyage was a "non-political" trip.

It didn't, however, take Truman long to disabuse anyone of that notion. At noon the next day, to a thousand locals in tiny Crestline, Ohio, he introduced Democratic gubernatorial candidate Frank Lausche as "the next Governor of Ohio."

"On this nonpartisan, bipartisan trip that we are taking here," he chortled, "I understand there are a whole lot of Democrats present, too."

Soon Truman found little excuse for laughter. Chicago saw more pickets bearing signs supporting Douglas and Dwight Eisenhower. To twenty-five thousand Swedish-Americans at Chicago Stadium that night, he delivered a stiff, lifeless speech that left his audience largely nonplussed. The poet Carl Sandburg fell asleep.

Of his Chicago speech, a supremely frustrated Richard L. Strout (the *New Republic*'s "TRB") complained that Truman's material "was rousing stuff in type. He read his speech through thick lenses, hardly looking at [the] audience, and with never a gesture. Even so it was generally agreed among the sixty-five news and radio men aboard that for Truman he said it pretty well. Some of us, listening to him, have to restrain ourselves all the time. This columnist found himself stressing words that Truman elided, pounding the press table at climaxes he missed. . . . It was like listening to a well-meaning amateur church organist trying to play Chopin."

At Chicago Stadium, people at least showed up. At Omaha, they didn't. Truman should have seen it coming.

Even before his tour had departed Union Station, columnist Drew Pearson had reported, "Nebraska Democrats are hopping mad at President Truman for assigning his old pal, insurance executive Ed McKim, to handle the presidential visit in Nebraska next week. McKim, who won Truman more enemies than friends while in Washington, now is doing the same thing among Nebraska Democrats."

Pearson proved uncomfortably correct. On Saturday night, June 5, at Omaha's ten-thousand-seat Ak-Sar-Ben (Nebraska spelled backward) Coliseum, Truman delivered a major farm policy address to a largely empty auditorium, with *Life* magazine gleefully publishing a half-page photo of "acres of empty seats." Nebraska Democratic chairman William Ritchie publicly blasted Truman's "cronies," complaining that local Democrats "were given the bum's rush." Concluded the disgusted Ritchie, "the Democratic party needs a new nominee for President."

Truman dismissed the Ak-Sar-Ben fiasco as a mere sideshow; he was, he claimed, concentrating on the nationwide broadcast audience he reached that night. "I am making a speech on the radio to the farmers," he reassured McKim. "They won't be there—they'll be home listening to that radio. They're the ones I'm going to talk to." Beyond that, crowds greeting him on Republican Omaha's streets—as on Democratic Chicago's—had been huge: 160,000 Omaha residents had cheered him before his evening speech.

In Missoula, Montana, Truman appeared on the Magellan platform in his pajamas. "I understand it was announced I would speak here," he explained. "I am sorry that I had gone to bed. But I thought I would let you see what I look like, even if I didn't have on any clothes." Montana's Democratic chairman, Lester Loble, expressed overall disgust. The "treatment accorded your committee," Loble wired his Nebraska counterpart, "is same we are receiving."

In Idaho, Truman's party relaxed at former Commerce Secretary W. Averell Harriman's sumptuous Sun Valley resort. The mayor of nearby Ketchum desired Truman's assistance in dedicating the local airport. White House press secretary Charlie Ross, still hungover from imbibing with reporters the previous evening, delegated the assignment to the Secret Service and to Harry Hood Vaughan. Truman roared off toward Ketchum. Incorrectly briefed, and eyeing the many veterans present, he extemporaneously expounded upon the fine young man, "Wilmer" Coates—"one of the great heroes of the last war"—for whom the airport was being named. The crowd buzzed. The deceased's mother whispered in the president's ear: "It's a girl"—*Wilma* Coates. Undaunted, Truman pronounced himself even "more honored to dedicate the airport to the young woman who bravely gave her life for her country."

"No," he was now informed, "our Wilma was killed right here." Wilma Coates was, indeed, no war heroine. She was a sixteen-year-old prom queen, killed while joyriding in an airplane piloted by her twenty-four-year-old boyfriend.

Idaho was a minefield. At Pocatello, at 7:45 AM, June 7, Truman told five hundred Idahoans, "I have been in politics a long time, and it makes no difference what they say about you, if it isn't so. If they can prove it on you, you are in a bad fix indeed. They have never been able to prove it on me."

To cynical reporters, familiar with his Pendergast connections, the remark seemed all too revealing.

In Eugene, Oregon, on Saturday, June 12, he provided listeners ("in the chatty tone of a man passing the time of day with neighbors at the corner drug store") his thoughts regarding Joseph Stalin. "I like old Joe," Truman gushed. "He's a decent fellow but he's a prisoner of the Politburo. He can't do what he wants to. He makes agreements, and if he could he would keep them. But the people who run the government are very specific in saying he can't keep them."

The State Department was aghast. From Washington, career diplomat Chip Bohlen phoned, pleading, "Isn't there some way to stop the president from his careless remarks about Stalin and the Soviet Union?"

"Well," Truman apologized to Clark Clifford and Charlie Ross, "I guess I goofed."

In Davis, California, he burbled, "I am going down here to Berkeley to get me a degree." Freshly minted syndicated columnist Thomas L. Stokes took pen to hand. To the tune of "Oh, Susanna," Stokes gleefully sang, "They can't prove nothing. / They ain't got a thing on me. / I'm going down to Berkeley / fur to get me a degree."

In Berkeley, however, Truman delivered what historian David McCullough has characterized as "one of the finest, most thoughtful speeches of his presidency," addressing a crowd of 55,000 at Berkeley's 80,000-seat Memorial Stadium, clad in academic cap and gown, the California sun in his eyes occasionally causing him to stumble.

Harry Truman had not traveled west to discuss foreign policy. He went to see and be seen by the American people, and in this he succeeded. In the fourteen days, thirteen hours, and thirty-nine minutes of his tour, he delivered seventy-three speeches and literally dozens more informal talks. Two-and-a-half to three million persons—a million in Los Angeles alone—had seen their president. He had not, however, extemporized every word. In fact, his brain trust had concluded that between late spring and Election Day, they would need to compose between two and three hundred speeches for him. He might provide the schmaltz and the vitriol, but others would have to supply him with an astonishing array of facts, on both the issues and the scores of localities he would visit.

The Democratic National Committee had assembled a secret team of experts to supply Truman with such data. Headquartered in stifling and noisy quarters on Dupont Circle, its research division consisted of failed Philadelphia congressional candidate William L. Batt Jr.; Batt's friend, ADA organizer Dr. Johannes Hoeber; liberal veterans activist Kenneth M. Birkhead; Oregon-born natural resources expert Philip Dreyer; the ADA's Harvard-educated research director David D. Lloyd; former *Kansas City Star* reporter and budding novelist Frank K. Kelly; and twenty-nine-year-old Senate Banking and Currency Committee staffer John E. Barriere. "We won't be peddling any baloney," Truman had told them. "Facts—that's what people want, and that's what we'll give them." The original plan had been for various government agencies to compose Truman's whistle-stop addresses, but the results were dreadful, dry, lifeless statistical litanies. Soon enough, the research division became the speechwriting division.

Recalled research division chief Bill Batt:

> We [provided our local data] through the WPA Guide, which was our secret weapon, and we got a complete set out of the Library of Congress. The WPA Guides are a gold mine about every community of any size in the United States as you know. Also the President himself from his Truman Committee travels had a vast compendium of odd, assorted knowledge. He was a bug on history anyway, and on many of these communities themselves. Between the WPA Guides and Harry Truman, there was an amazing collection of local background, so when he went into James Whitcomb Riley's hometown, he was quoting from Riley's poetry about the old swimming hole. I remember talking to newspaper men later who traveled on both the Republican and Democratic trains and were impressed by the fact that the President had something to say in each place and also had taken some trouble to brief himself on each area, while Dewey's speeches all came out alike.

That spring, Truman attempted to ingratiate himself to the people of an often-neglected western half of the nation—and, more than that, to drive a wedge between them and his opposition. "You know," he told Los Angelenos, "Daniel Webster, when the United States was trying to build the Pacific Railroad, made the statement that the West wasn't any good . . . and there are a lot of Republicans now ready to believe like old Daniel Webster did."

He established a theme. From very early on—from that noontime in Crestline, Ohio—he had lambasted the Republican Eightieth Congress. For if his ratings were tenuous, theirs were worse. In late 1947, only 22 percent rated the Congress as excellent or good. "Two-thirds of you stayed home in 1946," he excoriated listeners, "and look what a Congress we got! That is your fault. . . . [I]f you people want to continue the policies of the Eightieth Congress, that will be your funeral."

In Gary he informed listeners, "Your dollar now in purchase of food is worth only sixty cents of what your dollar was in 1946, when the government was controlling prices in favor of the consumer. . . . The Eightieth Congress, I am afraid, will adjourn without doing anything about it."

He warned his audience at Butte's Naranche Memorial Stadium:

> [T]his Congress is going to adjourn, and some of this Congress is going to Philadelphia [to the GOP Convention] to try to fool the people into making them believe they have done something for them in this Congress.

> Let's wait and see. If this Congress goes away without passing a housing bill, without doing something about prices—this Congress has not done anything for this country.

> They should stay there until they get these things done.

For good measure, before leaving Butte, he laced into Robert Taft: "I guess he would let you starve, I don't know."

In Washington state, he struck deeper. At Bremerton (before "about two acres of people" by his estimate) he charged, "They're going to Philadelphia to tell you what a great Congress they have been. If you believe that you are a bigger sucker than I think you are."

Twenty-four-year-old Spokane *Spokesman-Review* cub reporter Rhea "Ray" Felknor attempted to interview him at that city's Northern Pacific depot. Truman acidly responded, "The *Chicago Tribune* and this paper are the worst in the United States. You've got just what you ought to have. You've got the worst Congress in the United States you've ever had. And the papers, this paper, are responsible for it."

His attacks infuriated congressional Republicans. Ohio's Cliff Clevenger took to the House floor to deride Truman as "a Missouri jackass" and "nasty little gamin." At Philadelphia's posh Union League Club, Senator Taft accused Truman of "blackguarding the Congress at whistle-stops all across the country."

It was an unfortunate choice of words. The Democratic National Committee leapt at Taft's use of the term "whistle-stop" to imply that he had insulted the various towns comprising Truman's itinerary. "Very poor taste," sniffed Gary, Indiana, mayor Eugene Swartz. "Must have the wrong city," said Eugene mayor Earl McNutt. "The term hardly applies," commented Los Angeles mayor Fletcher Bowron.

Truman's trip had been undignified, unprecedented, and unpresidential. But such qualities were of mere gossamer significance. Harry Truman, stripping for battle, was relearning something he already knew: Americans love a fighter—and they love a show.

Most observers thought that Truman had simply dug himself an even deeper hole, but columnist Thomas Stokes dissented:

> His easy air of informality and confidence has developed gradually during the trip. After a few days, he had acquired a style where it was not at all as if he were making a speech, but as if he were leaning over the back platform chatting in man-to-man fashion. His language, at first reserved, took on a saltiness. . . .
>
> This trip has been a rehearsal for the campaign to come. . . . The technique of the road show has been polished, and now is about ready for the "big time" after tryouts in the tank towns. At the start it was rough and uneven, both technically and as regards the roles and performances of the principal characters and managers. The miscues, the uncertain gestures, the ill-timed entrances and exits have been duly recorded by the corps of dramatic critics who accompanied the president. These reviews have been noted by the stage managers, while the president simultaneously was making caustic cracks about the critics.

Yes, Stokes concluded, politics was a sideshow—and awkward Harry Truman had emerged, quite improbably, "the best barker for his own show."

He might have added that Harry Truman was very, very lucky that his Republican critics were hardly their own best pitchmen.

13

"We have a lot of Communists in New York"

For all the noisy, pessimistic, even desperate disarray in Democratic ranks, at least they had a candidate.

Republicans did not. At least, not yet.

In 1948, the path to both major nominations lay not so much in state primaries, but in state conventions and back rooms and the courting of numerous important and self-important favorite sons. In winks and nods and promises kept and promises broken.

The presidential primary process lay in disarray. In the Progressive Era, twenty-six states had featured primary contests. Since then, the number had been in decline. In 1940, Tom Dewey captured six of only seven contested primaries. Bob Taft took the other. But Dewey still lost at the convention to Wendell Willkie, who had not bothered to enter a single primary. By 1948, only five true primaries remained—New Hampshire, Wisconsin, Nebraska, Ohio, and Oregon. Only Oregon was winner-take-all.

Front-runner Thomas Dewey might still have ignored the process, but even now it would have been at his peril. In 1944, then-front-runner Wendell Willkie stumbled in Wisconsin and saw his chances instantly implode. As 1948 progressed, Dewey faced little primary competition from Robert Taft's decidedly antipopulist message or Arthur Vandenberg's stealth candidacy. He did, however, have much to fear from a new kind of candidate, even more youthful and liberal than Dewey and nearly as brash as Harry Truman— Harold Stassen. Stassen possessed virtually no Republican organizational support, but more than compensated for that deficiency with his galvanizing "modern Republican" message, his unlimited energy and ambition, and the assistance of armies of enthusiastic volunteers—his "Paul Revere Riders," coordinated by forty-year-old, $60,000-a-year St. Paul attorney Warren E. Burger.

Harold Stassen spelled true danger for Tom Dewey.

Stassen refused to play by the rules. In October 1947, Stassen conferred with Taft during an Iowa Republican Party luncheon, sparking rumors of a nascent anti-Dewey alliance. Yes, they differed, Taft admitted, "but not on the fundamental principles." Stassen praised Taft's "integrity, sincerity and ability." In January 1948, he nonetheless informed Taft that he would challenge him in his home state Ohio's primary. Taft, shocked at such effrontery, warned the upstart that he was committing a "grave mistake."

Preceding Ohio's primary, however, was New Hampshire's. Taft conceded the Granite State to Dewey. Stassen did not. Dewey enjoyed powerful local backing, including that of Governor Charles M. Dale. Low-key and confident, Dewey made but a single "non-political" trip to the state (visiting the Lebanon cemetery—"Old cemeteries fascinate me"), while his supporters distributed 125,000 copies of a slick but vapid four-page tabloid, *Republican Good News Pre-Convention Edition,* featuring such headlines as TOM DEWEY LEADS IN NATIONAL POLLS. Underdog Stassen, meanwhile, swept through the state. At Dartmouth, he informed fifteen hundred students that he waged "an uphill battle to liberalize the Republican Party."

In 1940, Dewey had captured only two New Hampshire delegates. In 1944, he received none. In 1948, he predicted he'd secure five of the eight but privately hoped for even more. He won six, but his triumph had been narrow. The switch of only a few hundred votes would have given Stassen five delegates—and the victory. Stassen would fight on.

In Wisconsin, a major new contestant entered the fray: Gen. Douglas MacArthur.

Briefly touted for the presidency in 1944, MacArthur now ruled postwar occupied Japan. Washington, Grant, and Andrew Jackson had ridden military careers to the presidency, but they at least resided in the country, not across the Pacific as proconsul of a defeated empire. Neither were they sixty-nine years old when they entered the White House, as MacArthur had become on January 26, 1948.

Nonetheless, if MacArthur could return victoriously to the Philippines in 1944, some reasoned he might also ultimately return stateside to become commander in chief. A March 1947 Gallup poll revealed him to be the person Americans admired most (followed by Ike, Churchill, Truman, Marshall, Eleanor Roosevelt, Jimmy Byrnes, Pope Pius XII, the anti-polio therapist "Sister" Elizabeth Kenny, and, only then, Tom Dewey). In March 1948, eighty-four-year-old press lord William Randolph Hearst wrote to Hearst Corporation president Richard Berlin:

> I think we are going to have war with Russia. I think MacArthur is the only President who could avert war with Russia and, if it could not be averted, I think MacArthur would be the only President who could win [it]. You see, therefore, my advocacy . . . is not a matter of political expediency. It is a matter upon which the safety of our Country might depend. I am going to advocate MacArthur to the last moment and, if necessary, go down with flags flying.

The boom was off and running. On Monday, March 1, 1948, Hearst's papers endorsed their absent candidate: "We must DRAFT General MacArthur for the Presidency. . . . Beyond any rivalry and any partisanship . . . Douglas MacArthur is the MAN OF THE HOUR." Two days later, Wisconsin supporters filed petitions for him to contest Dewey and Stassen in their state's April 6 primary. The following day, three New England Democrats—scandal-plagued seventy-three-year-old Boston mayor James Michael Curley, former Massachusetts governor Joseph B. Ely (an old FDR foe), and former New Hampshire governor Francis P. Murphy—endorsed MacArthur for *their* party's nomination. "The man in the White House," said Governor Murphy, "is gone beyond recall." On March 5, MacArthur-for-President offices opened in Washington.

Missing, however, was an actual candidate. On January 26, MacArthur vowed he would not leave Tokyo until Japan's reconstruction was complete—or unless summoned home by some "extraordinary occurrence." On March 8 (the same day Truman finally declared his own candidacy), however, MacArthur announced:

I have been informed that petitions have been filed in Madison. . . . I am deeply grateful for this spontaneous display of friendly confidence. No man could fail to be profoundly stirred by such a public movement in this hour of momentous import, national and international, temporal and spiritual.

While it seems unnecessary for me to repeat that I do not actively seek or covet any office and have no plans for leaving my post in Japan, I can say, and with due humility, that I would be recreant to all my concepts of good citizenship were I to shrink because of the hazards and responsibilities involved from accepting any public duty to which I might be called by the American people.

In Japan, shopkeepers hung signs in their windows reading, "We Japanese Want MacArthur for President" and "Pray for Gen. MacArthur's Success in the Presidential Election." Stateside, Dewey, Stassen, and Taft now faced serious competition. The March 15 Gallup poll had placed MacArthur fifth (12 percent), behind Dewey (37 percent), Stassen (15 percent), Taft (14 percent), and Vandenberg (13 percent). Two weeks later, MacArthur scored 19 percent, still trailing Dewey (34 percent), but leading Stassen (15 percent), Vandenberg (13 percent), and Taft (12 percent).

MacArthur seemed particularly potent in Wisconsin. Not only was it his official stateside residence, but his paternal grandfather, a pre–Civil War Democrat, had very briefly (for five days) served as Wisconsin governor. Stassen's hopes hinged on an upset victory in the Badger State. Dewey, in turn, feared being sidetracked there, as he himself had upended Willkie in 1944.

Internal Wisconsin GOP politics, riven by Progressive and old-guard factions, proved crucial in the April 6 contest. Logically, local Progressives, led by the once-powerful LaFollette family, should have supported the liberal Stassen. Old-guard Republicans should have backed the profoundly conservative MacArthur. Foreign policy, however, intruded. The waning LaFollette dynasty was long isolationist. Abhorring Stassen's atomic-age internationalism, they backed MacArthur.

The revitalized old guard, meanwhile, featured a distinctive new face: thirty-nine-year-old U.S. senator Joseph R. McCarthy. With Harold Stassen's

Franklin D. Roosevelt with his vice president, Henry Wallace (right), at his side during Wallace's happier days. (Franklin D. Roosevelt Library)

Progressive Party candidate Henry A. Wallace, photographed when he was still vice president of the United States. (Collection of the Author)

Going down? Then–Vice President Henry A. Wallace (center) with Secretary of the Treasury Henry Morgenthau Jr. (Library of Congress)

POLITICAL ADVERTISEMENT

RALLY TO ROLL UP THE VOTE FOR WALLACE, TAYLOR, AND PEACE

A NEW KIND OF POLITICAL RALLY!

WITH Henry Wallace
VITO MARCANTONIO · LEO ISACSON
PAUL ROBESON
ALBERT J. FITZGERALD O. JOHN ROGGE

Great singing rally—exciting parade of candidates. Special participation by New York Trade Unionists. Final city-wide election meeting.

Madison Square Garden, Tues.
OCTOBER 26 · 7:30 p.m

Tickets 60¢ thru 3.60
available at 39 Park Ave., MU 6-5313;
Y. Labor Committee for Wallace,
570 7th Ave., LO 5-1206;
Bookfair, 133 W. 44 St.;
al ALP and Wallace Clubs.

Sponsored by American Labor Party

Massive rallies remained in vogue for political campaigns, and Henry Wallace attracted some of the biggest crowds of all. (Collection of the Author)

Left-wing East Harlem congressman Vito Marcantonio was one of Henry Wallace's few congressional supporters. (Collection of the Author)

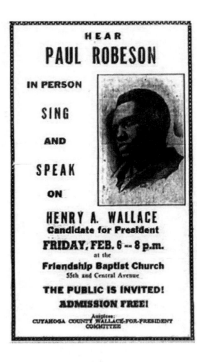

Controversial entertainer Paul Robeson was among the many supporters Henry Wallace attracted from the entertainment world and the fine arts. (Collection of the Author)

September 5, 1941: Young Tom Dewey, not yet a governor, on the stump before local Republicans in Schenectady, New York. (Collection of the Author)

Thomas Edmund Dewey took his duties as governor of the state of New York—and himself—very seriously. (Collection of the Author)

Tom Dewey's hunchbacked Columbia University classmate, speechwriter, and alter-ego, Elliott V. Bell. "If anyone can be tagged as the architect of the disaster," says one historian of the campaign, "it is Bell." (Collection of the Author)

Prominent Wall Street attorney John Foster Dulles, grandson of one secretary of state and nephew of another, helped shape Thomas E. Dewey's foreign policy. (Collection of the Author)

Tom Dewey's
executive secretary,
Paul Lockwood,
advocated a
dignified, play-
it safe campaign.
(Collection of the
Author)

Progressive
Republican
governor Earl
Warren, a favorite-
son candidate in
1948 and ultimately
Tom Dewey's
reluctant running
mate. (Collection of
the Author)

A Dewey ad in the *New York Amsterdam News*. Dewey's campaign hoped to capture a sizable portion of the growing African-American vote but lost ground following the introduction of Truman's groundbreaking 1948 civil rights program. (Collection of the Author)

Governor Dewey's executive assistant, Lillian Rosse. An incident involving her in Beaucoup, Illinois, helps define Dewey's ill-fated campaign. (Collection of the Author)

Dewey press secretary James Hagerty. (Collection of the Author)

Thomas E. Dewey, looking very much like the next president of the United States of America in Philippe Halsman's portrait. (The Library of Congress)

Tom Dewey campaigning from his Victory Special train at Springfield, Missouri, in October 1948. (Courtesy of the Harry S. Truman Library & Museum)

IT HAS BEEN WISELY SAID THAT

"BUT A SINGLE HEARTBEAT SEPARATES THE VICE-PRESIDENT FROM THE PRESIDENCY OF THIS COUNTRY"...

declared California's Governor Earl Warren in his speech at Columbus, Ohio, October 4, 1944

WHO IS THIS MAN

WHO

"Boss" Ed Kelly of Chicago, raising the hand of "Boss" Pendergast's choice for the U.S Senator in 1934 and the "Clear Everything with Sidney" choice for the Democratic Vice Presidential nominee in 1944— Harry S. Truman.

MAY BE PRESIDENT?

How important is the VICE PRESIDENT of the United States? He is the SECOND most important man in the United States because he is the man that may become President at any SECOND.

Yes, only a single heartbeat stands between the VICE PRESIDENT and the highest office on earth—THE PRESIDENCY OF THE UNITED STATES.

Under Roosevelt, we have HARRY TRUMAN! Who is Harry Truman? Why, he's the man who was "made" a Senator by Boss Pendergast, the Kansas City (Missouri) convicted political boss who was recently released from the Federal penitentiary at Leavenworth.

Truman was the choice of the bosses at the "CLEAR EVERYTHING WITH SIDNEY" Democratic Convention in Chicago—he was the choice of Hannegan, Hague, Hillman—and Browder, the Communist.

Contrast Roosevelt and Truman with the strong, vigorous, successful administrators chosen by the Republican Convention — GOVERNOR THOMAS E. DEWEY and GOVERNOR JOHN W. BRICKER.

Corrupt "Boss" Tom Pendergast of Kansas City, Mo., told a newspaperman "that he could name his 'office boy' to the U.S. Senate." Harry S. Truman (above), whose political career started under the Pendergast reign, today is a member of the U.S. Senate and the New Deal candidate for the vice-presidency. Pendergast's portrait hangs on the wall.

"THINK BEFORE YOU VOTE"

SPONSORED BY
The Sikeston Dewey-for-President Club

In 1944, Republicans pointed to Harry Truman's Kansas City–machine connections in an attempt to dissuade voters from voting for the Roosevelt-Truman ticket. (Collection of the Author) help, he had defeated Robert M. "Young Bob" LaFollette Jr. in the 1946 GOP primary. That same year, Stassen highlighted McCarthy as one of five GOP congressional candidates who were especially "wholesome and constructive and progressive."

McCarthy, enjoying solid backing from state GOP chairman Tom Coleman's organization, held Wisconsin together for Stassen. Through 1947 and 1948, he stumped for Stassen, attacking Dewey's "refusal to discuss the issues." Dewey responded with typical blandness in this prepared statement: "The Governor never criticizes other members of his party publicly and he does not answer criticisms of other members who follow this practice."

On March 15, 1948, McCarthy wrote to state voters, subtly skewering MacArthur's age and checkered marital situation:

Dear Folks:

Governor Stassen is in the prime of life. He will be the same age as Teddy Roosevelt was when as President he handled the Panama Canal and Alaskan situation without getting our country into trouble.

General MacArthur has been a great General. But he is now ready for retirement, he would be 72 years old before his term as President ended. Twice before we have had Presidents [Wilson and FDR] who became physically weakened during their term of office, and both times it has had very sad results for our country. . . .

General MacArthur would be much older than either of these two men. . . .

It has been 50 years since he commenced his Army career, and has not been in the United States for 10 years. This is why I believe that we should give the General his well-deserved hero's retirement when his job is done and not try to have him undergo the strain of years as President of our country in this difficult time.

On returning to Wisconsin, I notice that hundreds of big campaign billboards tell the people to support the General because he is a native son of Wisconsin. The Hearst papers, which are booming the General's candidacy, refer to him as the "Wisconsin-born General." This is not true.

The general was born in Little Rock, Arkansas, on January 26, 1880, and not in Wisconsin. He is not listed on any poll list as a voter of Wisconsin. Neither his first nor second marriage, nor his divorce, took place in Wisconsin. He was first married in Florida to Mrs. Walter Brooks of Baltimore, who now lives in Washington, D.C. After she divorced him in Reno, Nevada, he was remarried in New York City. Neither wife ever resided or voted in Wisconsin. . . .

Sincerely,

Joe McCarthy

McCarthy was hardly Stassen's only advantage. Even before New Hampshire's primary, Stassen had boosted his profile by testifying before Congress regarding grain speculation by the Truman administration "insiders," including the ubiquitous Ed Pauley and Truman's personal physician, Dr. Wallace Graham. In Wisconsin, the Minnesotan Stassen enjoyed a clear geographical advantage. Ten times he visited the state. In a single week, Warren Burger flooded Wisconsin with 340 carloads of Stassen's "Paul Revere Riders," who strenuously leafleted a thousand towns.

Dewey remained nearly as absent as MacArthur. Having pledged not to leave Albany as long as the legislature remained in session, he found himself ensnared in a prolonged and contentious debate over local school aid as well as a rare revolt from assembly Republicans. Finally arriving in Wisconsin a mere five days before the primary, he campaigned there for just forty-eight hours. The race, however, remained between vigorous elder statesman MacArthur and aging boy wonder Stassen, with MacArthur enjoying a distinct edge. Privately, Dewey fretted, "I will probably be lucky if the result is not worse than this: MacArthur 19, Stassen 6, Dewey 2. In the popular vote, I expect the vote to be much closer and in the following order: MacArthur, Dewey, Stassen."

He was not lucky. Stassen drubbed MacArthur nineteen delegates to eight. Dewey received none.

From New York, Dewey tried putting a game face on disastrous events. "Now we have lost one primary and won one primary," he contended. "On the total yesterday was a pretty good day. We gained ninety delegates in New York, which was four times the number any other candidate acquired."

Technically, Dewey was correct. On paper, he *had* enjoyed a good day, officially gaining ninety delegates from his handpicked New York State convention. Overall, he remained well in the lead—Dewey, 108 delegates; Stassen, 46; Vandenberg, 41 (all from Michigan); and MacArthur, 8. Meanwhile, 102 delegates remained uninstructed.

Others viewed Dewey's situation less sanguinely. "Mr. Stassen has emerged as a giant killer," contended Arthur Krock. The New York governor, jeered former Hudson Valley congressman Hamilton Fish (a longtime Dewey foe), "should follow the example of Wendell Willkie [in 1944] by withdrawing from the campaign. Dewey's nonveteran feet of clay collapsed when he tried to keep up with real war veterans such as Stassen and MacArthur in the march across Wisconsin."

MacArthur was, however, no longer on the march. His unexpected Wisconsin defeat essentially knocked him out of the race. On April 9, he wrote to his Nebraska chairman, Mrs. Mary E. Kenny: "My statement of March 9, that I was available for any public duty to which I might be called by the American people, was not limited to any particular political test. That was a restatement of the responsibility of citizenship on which I then stood, I now stand, and I shall continue to stand until I die." Mrs. Kenny viewed such words as a sign that the general was fighting on. She was wrong.

With MacArthur essentially finished, Robert Taft hoped to seize some badly needed momentum in Nebraska's April 13 nonbinding beauty contest. Nebraska law required no permission to enter a candidate's name and provided no mechanism for a candidate to withdraw it once entered. Accordingly, forty-three-year-old *Nebraska State Journal* editor Raymond A. McConnell Jr., scheming to generate national attention for an otherwise humdrum contest, formed a committee to enter the whole lot of GOP hopefuls—Dewey, Stassen, Taft, MacArthur, Vandenberg, California governor Earl Warren, House Speaker Joe Martin—whether they desired ballot position or feared it.

Taft enjoyed local organization support, including the support of U.S. senators Hugh Butler and Kenneth "The Merry Mortician" Wherry. But Stassen had won the state's 1944 contest and again benefited from massive volunteer efforts ("dramatic and extravagant circus tactics of the Minnesota carpetbaggers," as Senator Butler phrased it). Exacerbating Taft's problems was a speech he delivered in Omaha that February critiquing farm supports. Stassen crushed Taft, who finished an exceedingly poor third. Dewey, despite a rather lackluster effort, far exceeded expectations. Nebraska's final results: Stassen, 43 percent; Dewey, 35 percent; Taft, 11 percent; Vandenberg, 5 percent; MacArthur, 4 percent; Warren, 1 percent; and Joe Martin, 0.5 percent.

Stassen's brace of midwestern triumphs propelled him into a slim nationwide lead (his first) over Dewey. On April 25, 1948, George Gallup projected these preferences:

Stassen	31%
Dewey	29%
MacArthur	16%
Vandenberg	10%
Taft	9%
Warren	2%
Martin	1%
No choice	2%

Republican competition now shifted east, and still the Stassen bandwagon gathered steam. On April 20, some 405,000 Republicans voted in New Jersey's largely perfunctory GOP primary, designed to ratify Governor Alfred E. Driscoll's selection as the state's favorite son. Yet 1,411 wrote in Stassen and just 1,064 wrote in Dewey. On April 27, in Pennsylvania's purely write-in beauty contest, 74,000 Pennsylvania Republicans penciled in Stassen, 68,161 penciled in Dewey, and just 41,764 penciled in favorite-son U.S. senator Edward Martin. Four years previously, Dewey had run first with 146,706 write-ins, while Stassen had finished seventh with only 1,052.

May 4 finally witnessed Ohio's Taft-Stassen showdown. Stassen had not proven fully reckless. He had not challenged every local Taft slate. Selectively, he concentrated on heavily unionized areas such as Akron, Cleveland, Dayton, and Youngstown. Results proved strangely inconclusive. Stassen projected that he would win twelve delegates. He secured just nine, finally blunting his momentum. Yet Taft also failed to secure the triumph that his sputtering, nonstarting campaign so badly needed. Ohio's battlefield left both armies vanquished.

The Stassen bubble, however, had not quite burst. *Business Week's* April 17 issue forecast: "Your Next President: Harold Stassen. Two months before Philadelphia, six months before Election Day it looks as if you can say that." On May 9, George Gallup reported Stassen crushing Truman 56 to 33 percent, even defeating him 42 to 41 percent in the South—the first instance in Gallup polling history that a Republican fared so well in Dixie. The *New York Times* and the *Nation* reported rumblings of a Taft-Dewey Stop-Stassen coalition.

One real contest remained: Oregon.

Dewey's position was now desperate. Some already wrote his political obituary. "Although [Dewey] is not a popular figure," said the *Nation*, "there is an element of tragedy in his collapse as a leading contender. He has a good mind and considerable administrative talent. But he has pursued such a cautious course and been so clearly motivated by ambition that he stands for nothing and has no real friends."

On April 21, Dewey himself confided to intimates that it was "win or else." The following day, Dewey's New York headquarters wired $1,000 to Oregon to jumpstart his flagging effort. An additional $3,000 followed on May 6. Within another week, $71,000 had arrived. Billboards (126 of them) were contracted for, radio attack ads were launched, and newspaper ads appeared by the carload—five per day in the *Portland Oregonian* alone. Betting money flowed westward to prop up the sagging odds on a Dewey victory. Thousands of personalized letters and phone calls went out to local interest groups—farmers, bankers, doctors, realtors, rail workers, Michigan alumni, dentists, lawyers, osteopaths, blacks. Harold Stassen was about to learn what Waxey Gordon, Lucky Luciano, and Wendell Willkie had learned the hard way: Thomas Edmund Dewey was not to be trifled with.

Yet Tom Dewey always found it easier to dispatch cash and organization into the breach than his own enthusiasm. A Dewey campaign tour invariably proceeded with clockwork sangfroid. That would not do in Oregon. Stassen not only led, he led big. For three weeks, the usually reserved Tom Dewey campaigned furiously ("some good old campaigning, which I love"), delivering ninety-two speeches. He met fishermen and loggers and dairy farmers. He donned a ten-gallon hat and an Indian headdress. He had his arm pricked to enroll in blood with the Coos Bay Pirates club, and cavorted indecorously with fur-bedecked, bone-wielding Grants Pass "cavemen."

Dewey forces attacked on every front. His Oregon chairman, John C. Higgins, skewered Joe McCarthy—who was now running Stassen's Oregon campaign—for senatorial absenteeism:

> Senator McCarthy was recorded absent when the Great Waterways bill was voted upon . . . involving $640,000,000, much of which is for the vitally needed McNary Dam, for other water power and for the development in the Great Northwest.
>
> Governor Dewey's close friend, [New York] Senator [Irving] Ives, was on the job, supporting Governor Dewey's petition for increased appropriations and working Oregon's Senators, [Guy] Cordon and [Wayne] Morse.
>
> Mr. Stassen's friend and campaign manager, Senator McCarthy, was absent. Here is the difference between the men—one performs and the other merely promises.

Dewey spent a reported $250,000. He covered two thousand miles, delivering two hundred speeches to a hundred thousand persons. Still he trailed, and as he shifted to high gear, Stassen more than kept pace. In the campaign's final nine days, Stassen's campaign bus logged 2,465 miles. Dewey's campaign bus ran over a cocker spaniel. A logging truck transporting Stassen demolished a lamppost. But as the primary drew near, one issue— unlikely as it seemed in comparison to inflation, housing, universal military training, or Taft-Hartley—emerged as the touchstone of the Oregon contest: outlawing the Communist Party.

It was Stassen's issue. Perhaps he meant to compensate for his too-often un-Republican liberal positions. Perhaps it was nascent subversion-hunter Joe McCarthy's influence or a holdover from his 1938 race against Red-friendly incumbent governor Elmer Benson. Perhaps it was to tweak his rival for hailing from New York City, the epicenter of domestic Stalinism.

Stassen had first raised the issue ("one of the keys toward stopping World

War III") in Milwaukee on Thursday evening, April 1, directly challenging Dewey on the issue:

> The Communist Party organization has been clearly shown to be a subversive arm of the foreign policy of the Soviet Union and as such I think it should be outlawed in the United States and all freedom-loving countries.
>
> We should not permit a treasonable form of organization to use the cloak of legality and by deceitful underground organization to murder world freedom.

Dewey consistently opposed the idea—in Wisconsin, Nebraska, and in Oregon. DEWEY IN OREGON LASHES AT STASSEN, headlined the *New York Times*. "He Starts 3-Week Campaign with Thrust at Proposal to Outlaw Communist Party."

"The proper understanding of that issue . . . go[es] to the very root of the qualifications of men to hold high public office," proclaimed Dewey as he landed in Portland, "I shall discuss it entirely without personalities, but I shall discuss it bluntly and with all the force of my command." Americans, Dewey continued, "know how to deal with termites and, if we keep our heads and do not follow hysterical suggestions, we need have no fear of the outcome."

"Staring into the abyss of defeat seems to have focused Dewey's mind," observed campaign historian Zachary Karabell. "His letters and speeches conveyed clarity and passion, and for the first time, there was fire in his eyes and emotion in his words. He believed in something unequivocally, and he stated it unequivocally."

In mid-April, Tom Swafford, the recently hired program director of Portland radio station KPOJ, proposed a Dewey-Stassen debate under the auspices of that city's Reed College, to be broadcast nationwide by radio's Mutual Broadcasting System. Stassen had already unsuccessfully challenged Dewey to debate in New Hampshire, and both Dewey and MacArthur in Wisconsin. Confident of his debating skills, Stassen instantly agreed to face "the little son of a bitch." Dewey—despite his current underdog position—refused.

"With Stassen having accepted," Swafford argued to Dewey aide Paul Lockwood, "how does that make Governor Dewey look?"

"I think you can take the guy to pieces," said Lockwood to Dewey.

"All right," answered Dewey, "God damn it, let's do it!"

Dewey, however, demanded certain conditions. The debate would examine but one issue—outlawing the Communist Party. It would be sponsored not by Reed College but rather by the Multnomah County Republican Central Committee. Stassen, however, balked at one final demand of Dewey's: shifting the debate venue from the five-thousand-seat Portland Civic Auditorium to the audience-free studios of Portland ABC affiliate KEX.

The diminutive Dewey did not want the six-foot-three, 230-pound Stassen hulking over him. But, more importantly, he knew that his rival invariably generated his heartiest applause from his anticommunist appeal. Stassen refused to budge. Finally, Swafford argued, "Governor, if you can beat Dewey in a debate, does it [matter] whether you do it in front of a live audience? There'll be millions of people listening. They'll know you beat him. Isn't that what will count, the voters?" Stassen relented. The debate was on.

At 6 PM Pacific Standard Time (10 PM in the East) on Monday, May 17, somewhere between forty and eighty million persons heard Dewey and Stassen square off on roughly nine hundred Mutual, NBC, and ABC stations nationwide. Twenty-minute opening statements were to be followed by eight-minute rebuttals. Stassen led off, reading his prepared message in uninspiring fashion. He hung his argument upon one key point: that the proposed Mundt-Nixon Bill, establishing a Subversive Activities Control Board, also called for outlawing the CPUSA.

> It does not add up to me, to say that loyal, patriotic young Americans must of necessity be drafted, that their liberties must be taken away in order to make America strong in the face of the menace to peace caused by communist organizations of the Soviet Union, but that none of the privileges and blessings of legality should be taken away from the communist organizations themselves, which in fact are causing the menace that makes the drafting necessary.

Stassen fumbled on virtually every level. Proceeding first, he provided accomplished prosecutor Dewey with the opportunity to flay his case to ribbons. Stassen read his remarks. Dewey spoke extemporaneously, allowing him to project more sincerity—much more warmth—and to connect much more with his nationwide radio audience. But most importantly, Stassen was dead wrong, spectacularly wrong. The Mundt-Nixon Bill did not outlaw the Communist Party; it merely mandated registration of its organizations and members. Stassen quoted only one source to buttress his argument—the Communist Party itself—in contending that the bill would outlaw the CPUSA. Calmly, almost serenely, Dewey flayed Stassen ("my distinguished confrere"), demolishing his arguments at every turn and deriding the veracity of the Communist Party as a source. Casually he leafed through documents to quote Rep. Karl Mundt (R-SD) and the Republican-controlled House Committee on Un-American Activities to the contrary.

Stassen collapsed. "In rebuttal the Minnesotan was a different man," KPOJ's Swafford recalled, "wearing the kind of half smile a boxer puts on after taking a damaging blow when he wants the judges to think it didn't hurt. The radio audience couldn't see that, of course, but it could hear the uncertain, diffident delivery that had replaced the earlier booming confidence."

"Now," Stassen balefully asked, "if Governor Dewey will support unequivocally the Mundt-Nixon bill, we may go forward to the other issues facing this nation."

"Why is it," he continued, "that New York, with 9 percent of the nation's population, has 80 percent of the Communists in America? New York is the capital, [the] Communist center in America."

Dewey responded almost gleefully. "I gather from Mr. Stassen's remarks that he has completely surrendered. The Mundt bill obviously doesn't outlaw the Communist party. Mr. Stassen has covered the country from New Jersey to Oregon contending the Communist Party should be outlawed. If Mr. Stassen says all he wanted is my support for the Mundt bill, then he has completely surrendered. For he admits he didn't mean it when he stumped from one end of the country to the other."

Dewey continued:

I am unalterably, wholeheartedly, and unswervingly against any scheme to write laws outlawing people because of their religious, political, social, or economic ideas. I am against it because it is a violation of the Constitution of the United States and of the Bill of Rights, and clearly so. I am against it because it is immoral and nothing but totalitarianism itself. I am against it because I know from a great many years experience in the enforcement of the law that the proposal wouldn't work, and instead it would rapidly advance the cause of Communism. . . . Stripped to its naked essentials, this is nothing but the method of Hitler and Stalin. It is thought control, borrowed from the Japanese war leadership. It is an attempt to beat down ideas with a club. It is a surrender of everything we believe in. . . .

Now, we have a lot of Communists in New York—we have a great many of them—and they cause us great troubles. But we lick them. The number in the country is down from 100,000 two years ago to 70,000 last year to 68,000 this year. In New York their influence is at the lowest ebb in its history. They ganged up with the Democrats, the American Labor Party, the mislabeled "Liberal Party," and the PAC, to beat us. Two years ago, the Communists labeled me as their Public Enemy Number 1, and we licked them by the biggest majority in history. Why? Because we kept them out in the open; because we everlastingly believe in the Bill of Rights; because we know that if, in this country, we will always keep every idea that is bad out in the open, we will lick it. It will never get any place in the United States.

Dewey had been gaining on Stassen even before the debate. On its eve, Dewey's campaign manager even predicted a 7,500-vote victory. Another Dewey functionary later calculated the margin at 12,000. In any case, the debate seemed to crush Stassen not merely in Oregon but nationwide. On Primary Day, Dewey captured 53 percent of the vote—111,657 to Stassen's 101,419—securing all twelve Oregon delegates.

Was Oregon Dewey's splendid triumph? Or merely the first installment of Harold Stassen's lifelong pratfall? "Dewey's substantial victory . . . demonstrated that there is no continental demand among Republicans for Harold E. Stassen," observed an unimpressed Arthur Krock, "just as earlier primaries established the same fact about Senator Robert A. Taft and Mr. Dewey himself."

Dewey's delegate vote now stood at roughly three hundred—far more than any other contender. Yet many still questioned his chances.

For as one critic had sniped regarding Dewey's chances for a second national nomination: "You can't make a soufflé rise twice."

14

"Professors who scratch their waffles"

---

he public seemed less than enamored of Thomas E. Dewey . . . and of Harold Stassen . . . and of Robert Taft . . . and of Harry Truman . . . And certainly now of Henry Wallace.

Wallace's trend had been steadily downward. In December 1946, 24 percent of Democrats preferred him over Harry Truman. In June 1947, 13 percent of all voters favored Wallace. By January 1948, however, that figure had dipped to 7 percent. By June 1948, it lingered at 6 percent, in part because of another Gallup set of numbers: 51 percent believed the new party was Communist-dominated; only 21 percent disagreed.

The Communist Party had eagerly hopped on board Wallace's once-accelerating bandwagon. The CPUSA, its general secretary Eugene Dennis wrote in 1946, must "lay the foundation now to establish in time for the 1948 elections a national third party—a broad people's antimonopoly, anti-imperialist party. . . . [S]teps toward forming a third party should be taken early in 1947."

Addressing thirteen thousand persons at Madison Square Garden in September 1947—three months before Wallace announced his candidacy—Dennis had pledged party support for "the building of the foundation of a strong, independent people's party closely connected with the pro–Roosevelt-Wallace program and movement." In January 1948, CPUSA chairman William Z. Foster, at a rally marking the twenty-fourth anniversary of Lenin's death, reiterated party support for "the Wallace movement [as] the one movement that [can put a] halt to this drive toward a new war."

Two key Wallace movement staffers, both former New Deal agricultural policy aides, provoked particular suspicion regarding Communist Party involvement: forty-two-year-old Progressive Party platform committee chair Lee Pressman and forty-four-year-old party general counsel John J. Abt.

The Lower East Side–born Pressman had served in Wallace's New Deal Agricultural Adjustment Administration (AAA), but was originally as ignorant of agriculture as Wallace was knowledgeable. Once, while conferring with macaroni producers, he famously asked, "What will this code do for the macaroni growers?" He knew far more, however, about labor, and quickly moved on to become CIO general counsel and, as columnist Murray Kempton noted, "a symbol of the Communist influence" in that fast-growing organization.

Pressman denied his Communist Party membership until 1950. Abt rarely bothered to camouflage his. In December 1946, when Wallace campaign manager C. B. "Beanie" Baldwin asked the mustachioed Abt, then chief counsel to the Amalgamated Clothing Workers of America, to assume his new party's general counsel slot, Abt first proved reluctant. After clearing the request with his Communist Party superiors, he still attempted to dissuade Wallace himself from the appointment. "I told him," Abt revealed in his memoirs, *Advocate and Activist: Memoirs of an American Communist Lawyer,* "that I'd recently been subpoenaed before the [New York] federal grand jury [investigating the Communist Party]; I told him that I'd been married to Jessica [Smith Ware—widow of Soviet agent Harold Ware], the editor of *Soviet Russia Today;* and that my sister, Marion [Bachrach], was public relations director for the Communist Party. Wallace was no more alarmed than he would have been had I informed him of my admittance to the Illinois Bar. He brushed aside my concerns and said, 'Well, let them shell that position if they want to.' Then he urged me to become general counsel."

Other hard-line leftists accompanied Abt and Pressman. Bespectacled Wallace speechwriter Charles Kramer (a former aide to Claude Pepper) had been an NKVD agent. Official party filmmaker Carl Aldo Marzani (KGB codename: Kollega), former head of the CPUSA's forty-branch, three-thousand-member Lower East Side section, was appealing his conviction for perjury for concealing his continued party membership on becoming an Office of Strategic Services (OSS) officer. CPUSA legislative director Arnold Johnson and California CPUSA chairman William Schneiderman augmented that state's faltering Progressive Party petition drive. National Lawyers Guild executive secretary (and "Hollywood Ten" defense attorney) Martin Popper came aboard to help develop the party platform. The now Communist-dominated splinter American Labor Party—a powerful force within New York City, and even statewide, politics—provided crucial Empire State ballot position.

And though it was not generally known, perhaps most significantly of all, the forty-five-year-old, Virginia-born Wallace campaign manager, C. B. "Beanie" Baldwin himself, was a covert Communist Party operative. In the words of CPUSA national committeeman John Gates, Baldwin was "the chief agent of [Eugene] Dennis and [Albert] Blumberg [the head of the Communist Party in Maryland and Washington, D.C.] in influencing Wallace."

On the party's celebrity front, PCA honorary chairman, the renowned sculptor Jo Davidson, publicly crowed, "Our efforts are nothing until you're called Communist. When you're called a Communist then you know you're doing something." In its headiest early days, the Progressive Citizens of America attracted an impressive range of entertainment industry support, including such non-Communists as Gregory Peck, Katharine Hepburn, Lena Horne, Gene Kelly, Edward G. Robinson, José Ferrer, Nina Foch, Uta Hagen, Norman Corwin, and Richard Conte; it also attracted such CPUSA members as John Garfield, Larry Parks, Howard Da Silva, and Lee J. Cobb. As Wallace's campaign lurched grimly leftward, however, its celebrity ranks narrowed to such hard-line, card-carrying types as Cobb, singer Paul Robeson, comedian Zero Mostel, and folksinger Pete Seeger.

Not every activist cherished the Wallace candidacy. Author (and CPUSA member) Lillian Hellman enlisted early on. "If someone with imagination could break out of the fetish," she posited, "I would think a third party would go." Her erstwhile lover (and still close friend), Dashiell Hammett, remained skeptical. "I love him as much as you do, but you simply can't make a politician out of him," Hammett warned her in early 1946. Hammett remained unconvinced, ultimately concluding, "He'd be better off leaving things alone, and cross-breeding himself."

Wallace remained studiously blasé regarding his new associates. Screenwriter Budd Schulberg, a former Communist Party activist, hosted a Bucks County fundraiser for Wallace. "I'm very upset because I know you're not a Communist," Schulberg told the candidate. "But are you aware that you are actually in the hands of the Party?" Wallace sloughed him off. "He was naïve and trusting," concluded Schulberg, "and didn't want to believe it." Wallace's special assistant Philip Hauser tried the same tack. Wallace merely shook his head and sadly sighed, "Phil, now you've become a red-baiter, too." Naïveté was only part of the answer. A normal politician's susceptibility to flattery was another. "Wallace was plainly not a Communist," Arthur Schlesinger explained, but "[t]his well-intentioned, woolly-minded, increasingly embittered man was made to order for Communist exploitation; his own sense of martyrdom was swiftly generalized to embrace all friends of Soviet totalitarianism."

Bitterness and martyrdom.

Here were the keys to the Wallace effort. Henry Wallace would not be human if he were not devastated by the thought that he—FDR's true heir—had advanced so near to the presidency only to see it swept from him by the likes of Harry Truman. And devastated further by being ingloriously dismissed even from the cabinet by that same interloper. In December 1947, on the verge of Wallace's announcement, a supporter, Pittsfield, Massachusetts, newspaper distributor Leon Mohill, inquired of Wallace as to why he ran. The usual stock answers poured forth. Mohill persisted. Finally, Henry Wallace provided what might have been his truest motive. "Harry Truman," he blurted, "is a son-of-a-bitch."

Not all in Henry Wallace's diminishing band of true believers were Reds, or even crypto-Reds, though once the process of contraction began, it increasingly fed upon itself, spiraling into patterns of greater Communist support and diminishing appeal for non-Reds. "If there had been a flood of Progressives [to the party]—energetic, determined, dedicated—where would the Communists, about whom we hear so much, have been?" complained Rexford Guy Tugwell. "They would have been lost as they were always lost when they tried to claim President Roosevelt. . . . The reason Communist workers were so prominent to the Wallace campaign was that the Progressives were . . . sitting it out; wringing their hands; and wailing."

Standing at their distance were the Eleanor Roosevelts and the Arthur

Schlesingers, the Hubert Humphreys and the Chester Bowleses. "We are not prepared," said Humphrey, "to see the century of the common man become the century of the Comintern." Remaining were the flotsam and jetsam of the unelectable (save in New York's environs) Left.

Wallace, observed columnist Tristram Coffin,

> will appeal mightily to that class of men and women whose thought processes are such, that in their wills they leave the bulk of their money to a favorite cat or a faithful canary. There are many such people in this broad land of ours and Wallace is almost certain to get most of their votes. No candidate has ever completely brought out the absent-minded professor vote—you know the professors who scratch their waffles and pour syrup down their backs and hold their overshoes over their heads and wear their umbrellas. Wallace undoubtedly has a strong hold on these dreamy minded souls.

Opposition to Wallace's crusade accelerated. In upstate New York, in March 1948, ALP state committeeman, artist, and dairyman Rockwell Kent circulated Wallace leaflets. A third of his three hundred milk-route customers cancelled their accounts. In Evansville, Indiana, in April, picketers broke through an auditorium door and slugged Beanie Baldwin and two other Wallace aides. Evansville College fired religion and philosophy professor George Parker, who had presided over the meeting. Protesters egged Wallace at a Des Moines city park. In Indianapolis, a hotel cancelled reservations for a joint Wallace–Paul Robeson address. Fistfights followed a May Madison Square Garden rally, when Wallace supporters picketing an anticommunist film (an instrument of "the militarists") clashed with members of the Catholic War Veterans. Newspapers in Pennsylvania, Ohio, Tennessee, Alabama, New Hampshire, and Massachusetts printed the addresses of Wallace petition signatories. In Charleston, South Carolina, in May, twenty-eight-year-old Wallace supporter Robert W. New Jr. (a "nigger lover") was murdered by inebriated fellow worker Rudolpho Serreo. "At the trial," Serreo's defense attorney, former Charleston mayor Thomas P. Stoney, vowed, "I will prosecute Bob New for raising unrest among the colored people of the South. I will prosecute him also as the chairman of the Wallace Committee and as [one of] the despicable, slimy Communists prowling the waterfront."

In Detroit, at 9:55 PM, Tuesday, April 20, 1948, the United Automobile Workers' (UAW) Walter Reuther went into his kitchen for a bowl of peaches. A shotgun blast exploded through a window, ripping into his arm. Had Reuther not just turned to speak to his wife, the blast would have torn square through his chest and into his heart. "Help me!" Reuther pleaded. "Get me to a hospital. They've shot off my arm."

"Those dirty bastards!" he gasped. "They have to shoot a man in the back. They won't come out in the open and fight." Reuther survived. The crime was never solved. Reuther theorized its perpetrators to be "management, Communists or a screwball."

Among those jumping Henry Wallace's ship was Florida's left-wing senator, Claude Pepper—Wallace's initial preference for vice president. Pepper more than shared Wallace's worldview. In New York, in November 1946, he had observed that the USSR was achieving progress "that many who decry it might well imitate and emulate rather than despair."

Yet Pepper drew back, and not just from sharing Henry Wallace's ticket, but from the entire Wallace candidacy. He even briefly fancied delusions of a Truman-Pepper ticket. Harold Ickes might have also provided Wallace with liberal firepower—but he could stand neither Wallace nor his new acolytes. "I have felt for some time," the vain, intriguing, and jealous Ickes wrote to Arthur Schlesinger Jr. in January 1947, "that Henry Wallace should not be permitted to range all over the universe plucking and sticking, in halo-like form, the bright flowers that he preferred and which he seemed to think adorned him in particular."

Wallace's remaining vice-presidential alternatives were scant: East Harlem ("the poorest and most crime-ridden Little Italy in all the world") congressman Vito Marcantonio, a kindred spirit—and the ultimate fellow traveler—might do. But Marcantonio might have been even too left-wing for Wallace. The *Daily Worker* had after all once gushed, "His voting record is perfect." In any case, residing in New York State—now also Wallace's residence—Marcantonio was constitutionally barred from the position. In Washington State, Charles R. Savage's House candidacy had fallen to November 1946's Republican onslaught.

Former California attorney general Robert W. Kenny, not long previously an ardent PCA supporter, displayed little inclination to abandon the Democratic Party.

Which left Idaho's Glen Hearst Taylor, not only an unlikely vice-presidential candidate, but also among the more unlikely of individuals ever to grace the U.S. Senate.

Born in Portland, Oregon, on April 12, 1904—the twelfth of the Rev. Pleasant John Taylor's (once the youngest-ever Texas Ranger) thirteen children—Glen Taylor, at age thirteen, abandoned school to herd sheep in Idaho's Bitterroot Mountains. A stint managing two ramshackle silent-movie houses followed, before his brother Fern recruited the still-teenaged Glen to portray villains in his itinerant dramatic stock company, the Taylor Players. Glen continued in low-level show business, forming his own troupe, the Slade Musical Comedy Company. Competition from talking pictures—and then the Great Depression—hit him hard.

"I began to see all the misery," he remembered. "Kids didn't have proper clothes in winter. People came up to us, half-starving and miserable, and offered us chickens in exchange for tickets. We still had a truck, and we kept moving from town to town every day, provided we took in enough at the box office to buy gas. . . . Finally, we went bust. And when folks were sick with hunger in the towns, we saw either fields still producing food or potatoes lying out to rot. I began to brood over how things could go so wrong."

He studied economics, reading voraciously, influenced most particularly by Stuart Chase's 1932 volume, *A New Deal*, and disposable-razor inventor King C. Gillette's 1924 socialist-oriented tome, *The People's Corporation*. Taylor's troupe dwindled to the four-person Glendora Ranch Gang, with Taylor billed as "The Crooning Cowboy." He ran for Congress in 1937 and for the U.S. Senate in 1938 and 1940.

He took work in a San Francisco defense plant. In 1944, with just seventy-five dollars in his campaign war chest, he competed once more for the Senate. "We were so broke," he recalled, "we lived on peaches and oatmeal cookies." The improbable happened. Campaigning in support of a postwar peacekeeping organization and a TVA-style Columbia Valley Authority, the forty-year-old Taylor defeated isolationist ("We have needlessly insulted Japan in the Pacific") incumbent D. Worth Clark in the

Democratic primary and former governor Clarence A. Bottolfsen 107,096 to 102,373 that November.

In November 1947, the white-sombrero-sporting Taylor embarked on a cross-country "Ride for Peace." He concluded by riding his sorrel horse, Nugget, up the Capitol steps, an exercise heralding a progressive mindset that, in its more exuberant moments, made Henry Wallace seem like Robert Taft. Deriding Greek-Turkish aid as "not a relief plan but an oil grab," he vowed to "get rid of the militarists" in the War and State departments, entities he lumped together as "the State of War Department."

"It isn't a question of bigness," he charged. "It's a question of the smallness of the President of the United States." The administration, said Taylor, was leading the nation "down the road Hitler took the Germans. We have moved into Hitler's shoes, [determined to] exploit the world." For good measure, Taylor damned Secretary of Defense Forrestal as "the most dangerous man in America today—he is a potential Hitler."

Not surprisingly, Taylor gathered little praise. Critics labeled him "rhetorically self-intoxicated" and "the least effective member of the Senate." H. L. Mencken excoriated him as "a third-rate mountebank from the great open spaces. . . . Soak a radio clown for ten days and nights in the rectified juices of all the cow-state Messiahs ever heard of and you have him to the life."

Yet he possessed his talents. "Taylor's style in the Senate is exactly what one would not expect," observed author John Gunther. "The man is undoubtedly an actor, but he doesn't talk like one. His manner is quiet, his language excellent, his approach candid, his mood beguiling. There are few men who speak with a more subtle combination of formality and charm."

His first speech on the Senate floor was in behalf of Henry Wallace, but choosing to be his running mate was another matter entirely. Wallace enjoyed his hybrid corn patents, his millions, and his suburban New York estate. Glen Taylor possessed nothing more than his Senate seat. Enlisting in Wallace's foredoomed mission, he would almost certainly forfeit reelection, leaving his family with little save bitterness over what he had so carelessly tossed away. His wife, Dora, he recalled, "pleaded with me for weeks not to join Wallace. She had such high hopes that our sons would be afforded an opportunity to attend college and, as she pointed out, this would almost certainly be the end of my political career. There was little or no prospect that I could carve out a new career for myself at my age. When I finally made my decision . . . she wept."

Still, he might have drawn back. But Truman's shabby firing of Civil Aeronautics Board chairman James Landis incensed Taylor and convinced him that Truman could not be trusted. On Thursday, February 12, 1948, with rumors floating of Taylor's move, he and Truman conferred at the White House. Taylor somehow nursed hope that Truman might offer him a place on his own ticket. Instead, Truman asked, "What's this I hear about you thinking of running with that nut?" Taylor tried discussing the Soviets. "All the Russians understand," Truman answered, "is force."

"He repeated the popular cliché at least three times during our conversation," Taylor recalled. "I got the impression that he had heard the phrase and liked it, and his repetitious use of it reminded me of a parrot."

Three days later, Leo Isacson won his special election in the Bronx. Eight days after that, as Strom Thurmond met across town with Howard McGrath, Taylor announced his candidacy. "This," he proclaimed, "is the most glorious moment in man's long climb from the caves of savagery and ignorance."

"I am not leaving the Democratic Party," Taylor concluded, "It left me. Wall Street and the military have taken over."

On Saturday evening, May 1, in Birmingham, Alabama, Taylor addressed the Southern Negro Youth Congress (SNYC). Or, at least, Taylor was *scheduled* to address them, for as Birmingham public safety commissioner Eugene "Bull" Connor had publicly indicated, "There's not enough room in town for Bull and the Commies." Five weeks earlier, attorney general Tom Clark had included the SNYC on his list of subversive organizations.

Taylor's audience would, by local law, be segregated: 150 blacks at the rear of their church—the Alliance Gospel Tabernacle—twenty whites in the front; blacks would enter through the front door, whites through the side. Arriving by taxicab, Taylor attempted to enter the Tabernacle's main entrance. Earlier, two white men, a twenty-five-year-old white woman from New York, and Tabernacle pastor H. Douglas Oliver had been arrested for violating city segregation ordinances and for disobeying police. The *New York Times* reported that Patrolman W. W. Casey ("really a huge man. Six feet two at least, I'd say, and he probably weighed two-twenty or -thirty, if he weighed a pound") advised Taylor, "This is the colored entrance. The white entrance is on the side."

Taylor responded, "I'll go in here anyway." He pushed forward. Four city detectives restrained him. The result was chaos, with Taylor (and perhaps everyone else) tripping over a wire fence (he said he was shoved) and being jammed into a waiting patrol car to be taken to the local jail. There, he was fingerprinted, locked in the holding area, and freed a few minutes later on $100 bail. Released, Taylor went forward with a scheduled, though understandably delayed, address on a local radio station. In the interim, Dora Taylor waited fearfully in her hotel room, unsure of her husband's whereabouts or even his safety.

Two days later, Taylor provided the Senate with a lurid account of his captivity, and of being driven along a remote country road. "It was obvious," he said, "they had taken a detour, just hoping I would provoke something." Taylor claimed he was "not sure I would be here today" if he had made any moves of resistance. "In fact, I am not sure I would be alive today. . . . I was locked up in the bullpen, I didn't get a private cell befitting a United States senator."

"I expected that when I had finished," recalled Taylor, "every senator, at least those from above the Mason-Dixon line, would express indignation and outrage at the physical mistreatment I had endured and the indignities which had been heaped upon a colleague. . . . Not one senator opened his mouth."

The following evening, Taylor was convicted of "breach of the peace," fined fifty dollars, and sentenced to 180 days in the city jail, the jail sentence suspended in lieu of sixty days of probation.

In New York, a group of doubly outraged anticommunist intellectuals—including Mary McCarthy, Philip Rahv, Alfred Kazin, Sidney Hook, and Dwight Macdonald—dispatched a telegram to Bull Connor. Their wire read:

> Please accept our congratulations on the help you have just given to the Wallace third-party movement and Soviet foreign policy. Your disgraceful arrest of Senator Taylor forces opponents of Wallace like ourselves to support Taylor 100 per cent in his challenge to your city's barbarous and unjust racial practices, although we know that he is exploiting this issue for political aims we find abhorrent. If Senator Taylor becomes Vice President (God forbid), it will be largely because of such episodes as his arrest in Birmingham on the charge of passing through a doorway consecrated to persons of another color.

And that was about as much sympathy as Glen Taylor got.

15

"Why can't a simple soldier be left alone . . . ?"

While the public evinced its skepticism of Dewey, Stassen, Taft, Truman, and Wallace, it exhibited few doubts regarding Dwight David Eisenhower.

Born in Denison, Texas, on October 14, 1890, he was raised in Abilene, Kansas. The future commander of Allied armies in Europe ironically hailed from strongly pacifist roots, his family (originally the more Germanic "Eisenhauer") at one time adhering to the antiwar River Brethren Mennonite sect. When Dwight was five, the family converted to the equally pacifistic Watchtower Society, later and better known as the Jehovah's Witnesses. The family's religious affiliations, however, proved no barrier to Eisenhower's enrolling at West Point in June 1911. There, "Ike" distinguished himself more upon the gridiron than in the classroom.

Commissioned to the infantry in 1915, he nonetheless failed to see combat in World War I. His postwar military career proved largely uninteresting, until he was assigned as an aide to Douglas MacArthur, first in Washington, when MacArthur served as army chief of staff, and later in the Philippines, where MacArthur commanded the fledgling Philippine Army. "I studied dramatics under him for seven years!" remembered Ike. For his part, MacArthur regarded the decidedly less flamboyant Eisenhower as "the best clerk I ever had."

Eisenhower's hitherto nondescript career—he made non-brevet lieutenant colonel only in 1938—accelerated following Pearl Harbor, when George C. Marshall's general staff tasked him with creating war plans for both the European and Pacific campaigns. In 1942, Marshall appointed him commanding officer of the European Theater of Operations. Overseeing the Allied invasions of both North Africa and Normandy, Eisenhower defeated Hitler's Germany and established himself as a national hero, his popularity overtaking that of either Marshall or MacArthur.

Even then, Ike's name was being bruited about for high office. In August 1943, his older brother Arthur (coincidentally Harry Truman's fellow boarder in a Kansas City rooming house in 1905) wrote to Ike regarding increasing speculation of an Eisenhower White House boom—including then-Senator Truman's recommendation to Arthur that Ike immediately short-circuit such talk. The following month, however, Kansas's seventy-eight-year-old Republican senator Arthur Capper, an isolationist-minded progressive, wrote to Eisenhower, soliciting his candidacy.

That October, DNC secretary George E. Allen mailed to Ike a *Washington Post* clipping reporting that the New York City Tank Corps American Legion Post had passed a resolution in support of an Eisenhower candidacy. "Baloney!" Ike scribbled back. "Why can't a simple soldier be left alone to carry out his orders?"

In June 1945, the victorious Ike returned stateside. Four million people lined city avenues to cheer him in New York. By 1947, with a majority of the public clamoring for, or at least sympathetic to, an Eisenhower presidency, Ike's acolytes had been joined by a most unlikely recruit—Harry S. Truman.

Before Truman grew fully accustomed to the presidency, he toyed with the idea of stepping down in 1948. "General," he informed Ike, as they rode together with Gen. Omar Bradley during July 1945's Potsdam Conference, "there is nothing that you may want that I won't try to help you get. That definitely includes the presidency in 1948."

In 1947, Truman conferred again with Eisenhower. In his diary, on Friday, July 25, 1947, he confided:

At 3:30 today had a very interesting conversation with Gen[eral] Eisenhower. . . . Ike & I think MacArthur expects to make a Roman Triumphal return to the U.S. a short time before the Republican Convention meets in Philadelphia. I told Ike that if he did that that he (Ike) should announce for the nomination for President on the Democratic ticket and that I'd be glad to be in second place, or Vice President. I like the Senate anyway. Ike & I could be elected and my family & myself would be happy outside this great white jail, known as the White House.

Ike won't quot [sic] me & I won't quote him.

That fall, Secretary of the Army Kenneth C. Royall, very much impressed by his subordinate Eisenhower, revealed to Truman that if Ike were to challenge Truman, Royall would not oppose him—and offered to resign. Truman not only urged Royall to remain, he requested a favor: Would he approach Ike with the same bargain Truman had previously extended personally to Ike? Again, Eisenhower declined.

"Was Truman serious?" wondered his biographer Alonzo Hamby. "Did he expect Eisenhower to be a figurehead president who would let the second-in-command run things? Did he simply want to escape back to the familiar setting of the Senate? Or did he expect Eisenhower to decline and thereby remove himself from the race at an early date?"

Hamby never provided an answer to his questions, and we may never provide one either. We do know, however, that Harry Truman tendered his offers in private and spent the rest of his life denying ever having extended them. Ike "said I offered him the Presidency," Truman informed author Merle Miller, "which I didn't. In the first place it wasn't mine to offer. What happened [was] . . . we had a talk, and again he assured me he had no political intentions whatsoever of going into politics. I told him that was the right decision. And it was."

Harry Truman's diary, of course, argues otherwise. So does testimony from such witnesses as Kenneth Royall, Sam Rosenman, and International News Service (INS) reporter Robert G. Nixon, to all of whom Truman confided his actions.

It remains far easier to speculate about why Truman would never admit his offers to Eisenhower than about why he made them. They do not fit into the narrative of the spunky, never-say-die scrapper history now remembers, an image he did so much to foster. For all his real courage and feistiness, there were times when "Give 'em Hell" Harry did falter, did despair of his chances, did ponder surrender.

And the above instances were but three of them.

Truman, of course, had reason to lose heart, to calculate what deal he might negotiate with Eisenhower. Not only was Truman's own position increasingly vulnerable, Eisenhower loomed as unstoppable. The public might not know if Ike were a Republican or a Democrat (in August 1947, 22 percent thought him a Republican, 20 percent a Democrat, and 58 percent were unsure), but neither did it seem to care. A September 1947 Gallup poll showed Ike crushing Truman 55 to 45 percent. By January 1948, as Truman recovered enough popularity to edge Dewey, MacArthur, and Stassen and to demolish Robert Taft, he trailed Eisenhower 40 to 47 percent, losing every region save the South.

In August 1947, Tom Dewey had shared a dais with Ike, and Eisenhower had asked for advice on what he might say when called on to speak. "He gave the best speech I ever heard," recalled Dewey, his worries only accelerating from that point on. In October 1947, Dewey dined with James Forrestal, who recorded in his diary:

> He is obviously concerned about General Eisenhower's candidacy, and certain that he, Eisenhower, could dispose of it very quickly if he wished to. . . . He said Ike was obviously campaigning. He thought, however, that Eisenhower's boom had been launched too early and that the general did not realize how complicated his position would become the longer the boom is permitted to continue. Politics look very simple to the outsider whether he is a businessman or a soldier—it is only when you get into it that all the angles and hard work become apparent.

Soon Dewey commissioned an advertising campaign to marshal "every sound and cogent reason" in opposition to a military man's assuming the presidency. "We had," he warned advisers, "better batten down the hatches."

In October 1947, rumors circulated that Henry Wallace had privately attempted to persuade Ike to challenge Truman for the nomination. "Not only is the entire story fantastic," Ike fumed to his younger brother, Milton, "but the implication that I had even countenanced people talking to me about a subject like this while I am still in the Army is very close to challenging a soldier's loyalty."

Whether Ike cared for Wallace's politics or not (an unlikely notion), the announcement of Wallace's candidacy in December 1947 brought Ike immeasurable relief. Displaying unusual perspicacity for a supposed political neophyte, he wrote to his brother Milton, "Wallace's third party has completely taken me off the spot. He has increased the confidence of the Republicans that anyone can win for them."

Meanwhile, Eisenhower remained U.S. Army chief of staff. In June 1947, however, he announced that he would leave the service the following year to assume the presidency of Columbia University. Privately, he expected the move to provide "some shelter from the constant political darts that are launched in my direction by well-meaning, but I fear shortsighted, friends."

Yet he could never forsake the notion that if his nation once again required his services, he could not decline. "I do not believe," he wrote to his friend Gen. Walter Bedell "Beetle" Smith (now ambassador to Moscow) in mid-September 1947, "that you or I or anyone else has the right to state categorically, that he will not perform any duty that his country might demand of him. . . . There is no question in my mind that Nathan Hale accepted the order to serve as a spy with extreme reluctance and distaste. Nevertheless, he did so serve. [To refuse the nomination] would be almost the same thing as a soldier refusing to carry out the desires of his commander."

Eisenhower, long bathed in public adulation, would soon discover how glaring the limelight might be. At Washington's elegant and exclusive F Street Club, on Friday, December 5, 1947, he attended a dinner hosted by Bethlehem Steel executive John M. Gross, honoring the recently elected Pennsylvania congressman, Franklin H. Lichtenwalter. Also present were Taft, Vandenberg, columnists Arthur Krock and Frank Kent, and a variety of Pennsylvania Republican politicians, including Governor James H. Duff, Senator Edward Martin, former United States senator and state GOP boss Joseph R. Grundy, national committeeman G. Mason Owlett, and Sun Oil president Joseph Newton Pew Jr.

As the evening progressed, the supposedly non-political Eisenhower grew quite voluble concerning current events. His less cogent comments were soon leaked to conservative Mutual Broadcasting System commentator Fulton Lewis Jr., who informed his radio audience that:

General Eisenhower . . . pronounced his views on how to cure the domestic inflation threat, and his proposal was that the government call in the big industrial leaders of the nation and put the pressure on them to agree to reduce all prices for a period of two or three years, so as to eliminate all profits whatsoever. . . . When it was suggested that maybe the idea would not appeal to them, the General is reported to have suggested that the solution, then, would be for Congress to enact a 100 percent tax on corporation profits, and use the proceeds for a program of subsidies, to bring the prices down by force of government.

Lewis's exclusive was a bombshell. "Political observers here," reported the *Washington Post*'s Carl Levin, "were startled by this report, which they considered obvious political suicide if true."

Privately, Arthur Vandenberg professed sympathy, writing to Ike, "I would advise you . . . to take no notice. . . . Should you, however, decide to . . . clear up the matter, I would regard it as a real privilege if you would permit me to make a public statement, detailing not only what you did or did not say, but also who was responsible for the story."

Publicly, however, Vandenberg ducked the issue, snapping to a Hearst reporter, "There is only one person who can clear that up—the general." Neither he nor Taft, he said, wanted to "get into that."

Ike ruefully admitted to Arthur Krock:

On such occasions as the dinner the other night, I normally succeed in keeping my mouth closed about matters concerning which soldiers are not expected to have opinions. It happened that something suddenly touched upon one of my deep-seated convictions and I was guilty of very warm advocacy of a particular idea. Possibly I was stupid in not realizing that the dinner was not the completely private social affair that I had supposed. Anyway, you have seen in the press how badly my simple little idea was distorted and misrepresented. But I still believe that some big man in the industrial world has an opportunity, or at least a chance, by sincere, even dramatic action, to help halt the inflationary spiral.

As 1947 became 1948, Eisenhower could no longer seek shelter behind silence or polite denials. "Draft Eisenhower" clubs sprang up from coast to coast. Hollywood's Jack Warner, a longtime Democrat, signed on for one. A New York advertising agency developed "I Like Ike" buttons. Editorials urged him on. On January 10, 1948, Leonard V. Finder—publisher of New Hampshire's *Manchester Evening-Leader* and half-owner of the *Manchester Union* ("My partner runs the Republican paper and I run the independent paper. Fifty-fifty and no interference")—dispatched an open letter to Eisenhower, entreating him to enter his state's March primary: "While we appreciate that you are not anxious for political aspirations, we are equally confident that you will not resist or resent a genuine grass-roots movement. That is exactly what we have here in New Hampshire. . . . All that we are attempting is to have the will of the people made so clear that it cannot be obviated by the usual politicians assembled in convention."

In his diary on January 15, 1948, Ike wrote:

> The tossing about of my name in the political whirlwind is becoming embarrassing. Much as I've hated to say more than "I don't want a political office," I've decided I must. Too many people are taking the columnists' interpretation of my intentions as fact. How to say anything without violating my own sense of propriety—how to decline something that has not been offered me, how to answer those, like Finder, who honestly believe I have a "duty"—all this cannot be done in the words of Sherman. What a mess! But I've come to the conclusion I must face up to it . . . it's criminal to allow people to waste their votes.

Eisenhower sequestered himself for three days at his Fort Myer, Virginia, home, painfully drafting his reply on a yellow legal pad.

The decision tortured Eisenhower. Hours before releasing his response he shared its contents with James Forrestal, who (as he wrote in his diary):

> [R]emarked to General Eisenhower that the language of his letter was conclusive and meant that he was definitely out of politics. He agreed and said that was his intention.

He added that he had spent a great deal of time in the composition of the letter and that his only misgiving had been that a construction could be put upon it of its constituting a refusal to respond to a duty, around which, he said, his entire life had been built. He remarked that there were many youngsters in the country who, whether with reason or not, had made him more or less a symbol of the duties and obligations, as well as the opportunities, open to American youth, and he was truly worried about . . . in effect, telling them that there was a limit to any man's conception of his obligation to respond to the call of duty. . . .

There is no question in my mind as to his complete sincerity or that his letter reflects the outcome of a genuine moral struggle with himself.

On Friday, January 23, Ike released his statement, contending that:

my failure to convince thoughtful and earnest men . . . proves that I must make some amplification. I am not available and could not accept nomination to high political office [even though I do not desire to] violate that concept of duty to country which calls upon every good citizen to place no limitations upon his readiness to serve in any designated capacity. . . . My decision to remove myself completely from the political scene is definite and positive [and] I could not accept nomination even under the remote circumstances that it were tendered me. . . . The necessary and wise subordination of the military to civil power will best be sustained . . . when lifelong professional soldiers . . . abstain from seeking high political office.

To his boyhood friend Everett E. "Swede" Hazlett, Ike wrote three days later:

Several of my warm friends—men whose judgment I completely respect—differed from me sharply as to the wisdom of issuing such a statement. In fact, I had only two real supporters, among all my friends, in my belief that I must do so. There were many factors other than those mentioned . . . that had some influence with me but . . . personal desire and convenience were not predominating among them. Now that it is done, I can at least devote my mind unreservedly to a number of other important things and will not feel like I am constantly on the "witness stand."

Only days after Eisenhower demurred, columnist Walter Winchell conspired to undo his disclaimer. At 9 PM on Sunday, February 1, 1948, Winchell, perhaps settling old scores with Harry Truman, appealed to his weekly ABC radio audience to bombard Ike with postcards indicating whether they wanted him to run or not. Within a week, Eisenhower received twenty thousand pieces of mail. Two months later, Winchell repeated, "If General Eisenhower really wants to do something for the students of Columbia, he'll take that job in Washington." By June, twelve million responses had reached Winchell, overwhelmingly urging Ike's candidacy.

Finder, for his part, quickly tossed his support to Dewey. But while Eisenhower's response stilled a Republican boomlet, it only seemed to fuel Democratic interest. On March 26, 1948, two of FDR's sons—FDR Jr. and Elliott—issued separate statements supporting Eisenhower's nomination. "I believe the Democratic Party has failed to provide the leadership that was needed in the winning of the peace," said Elliott from Hyde Park. "That peace can still be won."

James Forrestal caught wind of the Roosevelts' upcoming statements and warned Eisenhower. Ike contacted FDR Jr., urging him to desist. FDR Jr. ignored him.

The Roosevelt brothers' action, noted *New York Herald Tribune* columnists Joseph and Stewart Alsop (themselves grandsons of Theodore Roosevelt's younger sister, Corinne), "brings things into the open with a vengeance. They openly reflect the northern leaders' discontent . . . which is almost as strong as [that] of the South."

Publicly, Eleanor Roosevelt declined comment. Privately, she wrote to Truman:

There is without any question among the younger Democrats a feeling that the party as at present constituted is going down to serious defeat and may not be able to survive as the liberal party. Whether they are right or wrong, I do not know. I made up my mind long ago that working on the United Nations meant, as far as possible, putting aside partisan political activity and I would not presume to dictate to my children or to any one else what their actions should be. I have not and I do not intend to have any part in pre-convention activities.

It was not exactly a vote of confidence for Harry Truman.

The situation proved unusually frustrating for an administration scrambling to forge an increasingly (even unprecedentedly) progressive record. Recalled Clark Clifford:

> Here was President Truman, who had met every liberal test . . . He had fought for the people economically, . . . for housing, . . . civil rights, and . . . labor. It was one of the finest liberal records that a President had and here was supposedly the professional liberal organization who demonstrated their true colors. They weren't interested in a liberal candidate; they were interested in the candidate who they thought could win. And obviously, they knew nothing about what General Eisenhower's political opinions were. Before General Eisenhower left the military service, I think I remember him telling me one time that he had never voted. He had never become a member of a political party.

The Roosevelt brothers had ignited a firestorm of resistance to the increasingly embattled Truman. On March 29, the Liberal Party of New York State (which had delivered 329,235 votes to Roosevelt in 1944) convened in a Times Square hotel. Ignoring yet another Eisenhower disclaimer, it endorsed Ike as "a candidate of the democratic and liberal forces [who] could unite the greatest number of Americans at this time."

In April, the seventy-person Americans for Democratic Action board of directors (which in February had pointedly failed to endorse Truman) met in Pittsburgh and endorsed an Eisenhower-Douglas ticket. "We are sunk now," Reinhold Niebuhr mourned, "and Eisenhower is the only possible candidate who could defeat the Republicans. I would support almost any decent man to avoid four years of Republican rule."

According to the ADA's James Loeb, Eisenhower might indeed have run, had circumstances proven different in Republican ranks. But with such liberal internationalists as Dewey, Stassen, and Vandenberg holding sway, Ike saw little rationale for entering the fray. "Eisenhower for a whole year was *clearly* available," Loeb revealed in 1970. "Everybody who saw him agreed on this, and he would see almost anybody . . . ; he saw Chester Bowles; he saw Leon Henderson; he saw all sorts of people. He was extremely receptive. . . . If Robert Taft had been the Republican nominee as an isolationist, I have no question . . . Eisenhower would have been available . . . on the Democratic ticket."

The Alsops had been correct that the "northern leaders" (a.k.a. the big-city bosses), nervous about forfeiting their own power in a Truman debacle, were joining the cabal. In Chicago, Cook County boss Col. Jacob M. Arvey praised Ike as "the kind of liberal with whom we could win, both nationally and locally." The *New Republic* headlined, AS A CANDIDATE FOR PRESIDENT, TRUMAN SHOULD QUIT. And on the labor union front, Louis Hollander, anti-Wallace leader of New York State's CIO-PAC, urged Democrats to drop their putative leader.

Numerous labor leaders shared Hollander's infatuation with Eisenhower. In fact, ADA support for Ike had been triggered by the labor movement's national leadership. Recalled James Loeb:

> The Eisenhower thing came in a very peculiar way. . . . [T]he first person to be impressed with Eisenhower from . . . the liberal-labor side, was Sidney Hillman, who met him [in] Germany and was impressed. And it was through Sidney Hillman that Eisenhower was then invited to speak by Philip Murray to the CIO convention . . . in Atlantic City in [November 1946]. . . . [S]omebody had written a very good speech for General Eisenhower . . . a kind of a pro-labor speech. Phil Murray got to know him and fell in love with him. He obviously was a very charming man, and from that point . . . the question was whether Eisenhower could be persuaded to run on the Democratic ticket. . . . [W]e were persuaded in the ADA by the CIO, which preferred that somebody else do the main work rather than do it as a labor organization.

Adding his usual insult to injury, Harold Ickes, on March 27, dispatched a blistering open letter to Truman. "You have the choice of retiring voluntarily and with dignity," Harold advised Harry, "or of being driven out of office by a disillusioned and indignant citizenry. Have you ever seen the ice on a pond suddenly break in every conceivable direction under the rays of the warming spring sun? That is what has happened to the Democratic Party under you, except that your party has not responded to bright sunlight. It has broken up spontaneously."

The non-Dixiecrat South chimed in. Alabama's two relatively liberal U.S. senators, Lister Hill and John Sparkman, now openly endorsed Eisenhower. "There cannot be," said Sparkman, "Democratic Party unity with President Truman as the nominee." Further rightward, Georgia's junior U.S. senator, Richard B. Russell Jr., announced that he would "be happy to see Truman step out and . . . Eisenhower step in. . . . That would be indeed an excellent exchange. However, if Eisenhower would support the [Truman] civil rights program . . . we would not vote for him either." In Alabama's third congressional district, twenty-eight-year-old state representative George Corley Wallace won election as a national convention alternate, after pledging to be "unalterably opposed to nominating Harry S. Truman and the so-called civil rights program." The *New York Times* reported "speculation [that Truman] would fail to win the Democratic nomination," losing, if not to Eisenhower, then to Secretary of State Marshall.

Ike could not escape being aware of the tumult. In April 1948, he wrote again to Walter Bedell Smith, this time confiding that "the Democrats have taken the attitude that Mr. Truman cannot be reelected, therefore they do not want to renominate him. In this situation they are turning desperately to anyone that might give them a chance of winning, and they have the cockeyed notion that I might be tempted to make the effort. I don't know why they cannot accept [it], but I think most of them know that my position was taken as a matter of conviction [and] that I expect to stand on it."

Everywhere there were Roosevelts. In April 1947, the North Dakota State Democratic Committee endorsed Eleanor for vice president, and before long there were whispers of her assuming the presidency itself. More worrisome to Truman than any Eleanor boomlet, however, was the Roosevelt clan's increased flirtation with the nascent Eisenhower coup. At New York's Town Hall, Elliott Roosevelt appeared alongside Leonard Finder to tout Eisenhower's candidacy. Elliott predicted that if Harry Truman remained the Democratic standard-bearer, Henry Wallace would outpoll him. Worse still, word had reached Truman that a third Roosevelt brother, James (California's state Democratic chairman), despite his public pledges of "sticking with Mr. Truman," had also enlisted in the burgeoning Dump-HST movement, delivering a noticeably pro-Eisenhower address at an April 12 Jackson Day Dinner in Los Angeles. Two years earlier, James had similarly flirted with the party's Wallace wing, serving as $25,000-a-year national director of the pro-Wallace, often pro-Communist, Independent Citizens Committee of the Arts, Sciences and Professions (ICCASP). James had initially defended his organization's refusal to exclude Communists, but quickly exhibited second thoughts. In July 1946, he abruptly resigned.

On Monday afternoon, June 14, 1948, as Harry Truman whistle-stopped through the West, he addressed the Greater Los Angeles Press Club at that city's Ambassador Hotel. His task completed, at 4 PM he journeyed upstairs to his presidential suite. Awaiting Truman was James Roosevelt, who had led his forty-person delegation up a back stairway to Truman's quarters. Much to Roosevelt's displeasure, his arrival had been preceded by that of his hated state Democratic rival, Ed Pauley—the same Ed Pauley who had precipitated Harold Ickes's heated cabinet exit. Pauley and his associates (including Tom Scully, whom Roosevelt had defeated for the chairmanship) seemed altogether too at ease in Truman's quarters.

On Truman's arrival, James extended his hand, ready for a friendly, or at least superficially cordial, conversation with the president of the United States of America. Truman took him aside, into a sitting room. There, he jabbed his right forefinger into Roosevelt's chest. "Your father asked me to take this job," he challenged the much taller, much younger man. "I didn't want it. I was happy in the Senate. But your father asked me to take it and I took it. And if your father knew what you are doing to me, he would turn over in his grave. But get this straight: Whether you like it or not, I am going to be the next president of the United States. That will be all. Good day." And with that, Harry S. Truman turned and stalked out of the room.

Newsmen soon cornered Roosevelt. Unaware of his discomfort, they inquired if he and Truman had finally smoked a peace pipe.

"No smoke," James answered grimly, and though he added that California's delegates remained committed to the president on the first ballot, the savvier of his listeners picked up on the fact that he had said nothing about any second ballot.

Nothing at all.

16

"It's such outrageous sport, really"

om Dewey was not yet a sure thing.

Oregon had left Harold Stassen bleeding and virtually finished, but Dewey had not closed the deal. With 548 convention votes needed for nomination, he remained stalled at roughly 300. True, no one commanded more, but with his demonstrated lack of intraparty popularity, Dewey might, as in 1940, fall short. Yes, Stassen's engine seemed finally to have run out of gas, and Taft had never succeeded in even starting his, but there always remained the chance of a deadlocked convention and a dramatic triumph by a favorite son or dark horse.

Most prominent—and most ambitious—among such dark horses were two Republicans residing at both geographic and ideological antipodes: sixty-three-year-old House Speaker Joseph W. Martin of Massachusetts and fifty-seven-year-old California governor Earl Warren.

Martin was a lifelong bachelor and the son of a blacksmith. His father had been a Grover Cleveland Democrat until the party abandoned both Cleveland and the gold standard. Joe eventually became publisher of the North Attleborough *Evening Chronicle,* and had served in the House since 1924, generally opposing FDR's measures. In 1940, FDR had memorialized Martin as part of a reactionary triumvirate of "Martin, Barton, and Fish." Baptized a Catholic, he never practiced his mother's faith—and, though sympathetic to Christianity, claimed no denomination. Past childhood, he had never attended church. Nonsmoking, nondrinking, nonmarrying, the rumpled, stocky Martin did not look like much, but he was, as even his Democratic rival Sam Rayburn admitted, "a friend of mankind, a man of unquestioned integrity, of demonstrated ability, with a great, fine heart." To Democratic House Minority Whip John W. McCormack,

Truman privately declared Martin to be a "a great Speaker . . . courteous and kind."

His life was politics—Republican politics. "We are not reformers," Martin once argued, "not do-gooders, not theorists, not the advocates of any alien philosophies or political dipsy-doo. We are just practical Americans trying to do a practical job to reach practical goals. We do not belong to that school of political thought which has for so many years pursued the fallacious proposition that if a little bit is good for us—ten times as much is wonderful."

In August 1947, he had undertaken a five-week national speaking tour. Ostensibly to support continued GOP control of the House, it looked suspiciously like a presidential campaign jaunt, launched as it was with brass bands, an air show, and even kind words from thirty-year-old freshman Boston Democratic congressman John F. Kennedy. As the convention approached, Texas national committeeman H. J. Porter attempted to ignite the flame-resistant Martin boomlet. Porter "was insistent," Martin recalled. "He not only took an option on a ballroom to be used as a headquarters if I became a serious contender, but as a sort of interim headquarters he also rented the rooms of the Harvard Club in [Philadelphia's] Bellevue-Stratford Hotel and kept them so full of turkey sandwiches that one could hardly move about."

But Massachusetts's first-ballot delegates remained pledged to the state's senior U.S. senator, fifty-five-year-old, lantern-jawed patrician liberal Leverett Saltonstall. And neither Martin nor Saltonstall quite controlled Henry Cabot Lodge Jr., the forty-six-year-old junior senator from Massachusetts. Himself a vice-presidential possibility, Lodge stood foursquare for Vandenberg.

Far to Martin's left resided Earl Warren, "by long odds the most progressive of all the Republicans of national stature," in the studied words of the Alsop brothers. As Warren himself once admitted, "I was a Republican simply because California [had been] an overwhelmingly Republican state." In 1912, he had supported Democrat Woodrow Wilson; in 1924, third-party Progressive Robert LaFollette Sr.

Born in Los Angeles on March 19, 1891, the Norwegian-Swedish Warren grew up in dusty, small-town Bakersfield. Steadily climbing California's political ladder, Berkeley Law School graduate Warren ascended from clerk of the state senate judiciary committee to deputy Oakland city attorney, to Alameda County deputy district attorney, to three-term district attorney, before winning the attorney generalship in 1938 on not only the Republican, but also the Democratic and Progressive party lines. The victory was tarnished, however, by his seventy-three-year-old father's mysterious death by bludgeoning back home that May. In 1942, Warren challenged incumbent governor Culbert L. Olson (a Mormon-turned-atheist who refused to say "so help me God" at his inauguration), who derided Warren as a "political eunuch, political hypocrite, puppet pretender not fit or competent to be governor." Warren countered with an aggressive nonpartisan pitch. His slogan: "Leadership, not politics."

Aided by future Richard Nixon operative Murray Chotiner and a former army buddy, the Mexican-American character actor Leo Carrillo, Warren barnstormed the state. Nearly vanquishing Olson in the Democratic primary, in the general election Warren carried fifty-seven of fifty-eight counties. "Earl Warren," Olson ultimately mourned, "is the slickest politician I ever met."

"Warren," noted columnist Marquis Childs, "has liberal views which he expresses sometimes fuzzily, sometimes with forthrightness and courage. Rich Tories mutter that he is a dangerous radical."

Or as author John Gunther put it: "Warren's dominant note is, to sum up, decency, stability, sincerity, and lack of genuine intellectual distinction."

In 1945, Warren proposed a controversial, and ill-fated, statewide mandatory medical insurance program (funded by a 3 percent payroll tax). He claimed it was a "state's rights" effort to preempt any possible federal action. His opponents excoriated it as "socialized medicine." Despite his progressive leanings, Warren also oversaw FDR's wartime internment of the state's sizable Japanese Nisei population. Warren's actions should not, however, have emerged as a total surprise. His hero, the progressive California U.S. senator Hiram Johnson, had vociferously opposed Oriental immigration and liberties. In Warren's 1942 campaign, Leo Carrillo had informed voters—with no contradiction from Warren—that "there's no such thing as a Japanese-American. . . . If we ever permit those termites to stick their filthy fingers into the sacred soul of our state again, we don't deserve to live here ourselves."

Warren proved to be a skilled, efficient administrator, and was smart enough to recognize the publicity value of his photogenic, pure-Scandinavian family—his attractive wife, Nina, and their three sons (one a California tennis star) and three daughters. "Earl Warren embodied the middle-class California dream of the 1940s and 1950s: the family, the lawn, the dog, the middle class success," observed California historian Kevin Starr. "Before the Kennedys, Warren understood the power of family and family values in political values."

In 1944, Warren keynoted that year's Republican National Convention, and Tom Dewey offered him the vice-presidential nomination. Warren said no.

Four years later, with California's favorite-son delegates in his pocket, Warren sought a higher office than the vice presidency. To casual observers, it wasn't much of a candidacy, really nothing more than a favorite-son placeholder, through which delegates might be squirreled safely away on early ballots, to be thrown into the balance when circumstances warranted. He even returned campaign donations—"I wouldn't know what to do with the money." In actuality, Warren followed a relaxed California version of Warren Harding's successful 1920 nominating strategy. Seeking votes in no other state and lying low on early ballots, he would alienate none of his rivals and emerge as an acceptable second, third, or even fourth or fifth choice in the event of an extended deadlock. He calculated that delegate breakthroughs might first occur as Michigan (for Vandenberg) and Connecticut (for U.S. senator Raymond Baldwin) folded their own favorite-son tents and hopefully tossed their support westward.

Less transparent, though perhaps more ambitious, was Arthur Vandenberg. Throughout the spring, he continued playing his hand in exceedingly coy fashion. On June 15, 1948, however, *U.S. News & World Report* released a poll of 815 daily newspaper editors, four-fifths of whom were Republican. They preferred Vandenberg 271 to 143 over Stassen, with 141 for Taft, 121 for Dewey, 26 for Warren, and 10 for Martin. Polled on whom they thought the GOP would ultimately nominate, Vandenberg galloped away with it: Vandenberg, 417; Dewey, 195; Taft, 45; Stassen, 33; and Warren and Martin, 7 each.

Perhaps such support—or perhaps merely the rapidly depleting sands of time—finally generated activity in the Vandenberg camp. From Philadelphia's Benjamin Franklin Hotel, on Saturday, June 19 (just two days prior to the convention's start), Michigan governor Kim "Hollywood Kim" Sigler pronounced that Vandenberg's "unselfish devotion to his country makes him available . . . should that be the demand of the people. I feel this convention will demonstrate that demand."

Queried if he might be speaking out of turn, the natty Sigler snapped, "I wouldn't be doing what I am doing if I didn't know what I was doing." Vandenberg had in fact already averred to Marquis Childs that if by any chance he should yield to a genuine draft, he would eschew any barnstorming style of campaigning and limit himself to a single term.

While Sigler boomed Vandenberg, however, anonymous forces aimed to tear him apart. "Several pamphlets," noted the *New York Times*, "in the hands of delegates reflect on [his] private life. . . . They have been circulated chiefly among rural delegates, and in one state the chairman had to hold a conference to whip his wavering followers into line."

Harold Stassen, meanwhile, was reduced to predicting his nomination on the ninth ballot, and Earl Warren was informing reporters, "I have never had any interest in the Vice Presidency, and I have none now."

Douglas MacArthur, still Tokyo-bound, but clinging to his eight Wisconsin delegates, issued marching orders to Gen. Jonathan M. Wainwright, who had arrived in Philadelphia to second his old commander's nomination. MacArthur diehards and political pundits interpreted this to mean that MacArthur remained in the hunt. Medal of Honor–winner Wainwright was far less specific in his prediction than Stassen: "It may be the sixth or the twenty-fifth ballot."

At a mercifully air-conditioned press conference, Earl Warren piously professed that he would "make no deal with anyone in a smoke-filled room."

"Do you mean," came a loud shout, "that no one can smoke in the room where you make a deal?"

Dewey and Warren opened their respective headquarters at the Bellevue-Stratford. Dewey commandeered the hotel's $1,000-a-day grand ballroom—stage and balcony included. Warren's center of operations was on the ninth floor, but, hamstrung by jammed elevators, it soon closed. Taft's command center was on the seventh floor of the Benjamin Franklin. Stassen boasted three headquarters, including the $500-a-day Bellevue-Stratford ballroom, "usually reserved for weddings" but now featuring a neon-illuminated "Stassen Hdqs." entrance sign. A "working headquarters" was situated in a nearby office building, a press office at the Warwick.

Stassen's Bellevue-Stratford digs offered coffee, doughnuts, cheese, "dainty wafers," iced tea with lemon, and iced coffee. Nine hundred pounds—

four-and-a-half wheels—of Wisconsin cheese was mistakenly delivered for forty dollars COD (collect on delivery) to Dewey's headquarters. "Cheese at Stassen's very good," commented the correspondent from the *New Yorker.*

"We thought of giving away whisky all day," confided one Stassen worker. "But we were afraid we'd attract nothing but barflies."

Wayward cheese aside, Dewey's hospitality suite provided the most elaborate giveaways. Pepsi-Cola supplied soft drinks. Upstate New York's Beech-Nut Co. furnished five thousand packages of Life Savers. Other New York State merchants donated a wide array of souvenirs visitors might haul away: stockings, cosmetics, silver cigarette cases, dresses, comb cases, even silk lingerie. Two young women stationed at the entrance and armed with automatic counters tabulated every visitor. Every hundredth entrant received a special door prize; every thousandth, a grand door prize. "It's such outrageous sport, really," gushed one GOP dowager, who confessed to twenty-five visits. By week's end, fifty thousand persons had visited the Dewey operation.

At Earl Warren's ill-fated Bellevue-Stratford suite, a Spanish-garbed young woman presented visitors with orange juice. Taft's suite distributed the convention's largest campaign buttons (blue and orange and three inches in diameter) plus ten thousand copies of *This Week in Philadelphia* magazine—unfortunately with rival Tom Dewey gracing that issue's cover. Taft also boasted the largest (and only) actual elephant, a five-hundred-pound baby pachyderm flown in from Columbus, Ohio, and temporarily named Miss Eva Tfat—*Taft* spelled backward. A placard festooned upon her proclaimed, "Renounce Obstinate Bureaucracy, End Roguish Tactics, and Tally Americanism, Freedom, Truth" (forming the acronym: R-O-B-E-R-T A. T-A-F-T).

Both the Stassen and Dewey headquarters featured organ music and television sets, though Dewey boasted four sets and, each evening, an eleven-piece orchestra. Taft provided a fifteen-piece brass band. Its repertoire included a "Taft Victory Song" that went:

We're looking over a four leaf clover,

That we overlooked before;

One leaf is courage, the second is fight,

Third is our party, that always is right;

No need explainin' the one remainin',

Taft is the one we're for;

Let's put Taft over—the four leaf clover

That we'll overlook no more.

No one, however, could overlook the Taft faction's ineptitude. Some of it stemmed from the fact that Taft and his 350-pound campaign manager (only 150 pounds lighter than Eva Tfat and the proud author of the four-leaf-clover jingle), Ohio congressman Clarence Brown, had been tied up in the barely concluded congressional session. Not until Sunday morning, June 20, did Congress adjourn, having been in session for forty-three consecutive hours and having just enacted the Marshall Plan. Only then did the sleep-deprived Taft pack Martha and himself into his small Plymouth sedan to personally drive the 158 miles to the Ben Franklin.

The weary Taft entered the hotel's Crystal Room to address reporters, with Brown lounging on a pink sofa behind him. Behind them both, workmen were mounting two large portraits of Taft. One crashed down on Brown, the other upon Taft's bald head.

Further indignities awaited him.

"Shake his trunk," one cameraman demanded of Taft, regarding Eva Tfat. Taft unenthusiastically complied.

"Shake it again. It's your baby."

Neither the recently arrived Taft nor the recently air-transported elephant seemed all too comfortable in the poorly ventilated room. Noted perennial Socialist Party candidate Norman Thomas, now reporting for the *Denver Post*: "The elephant was maneuvered out of the room like a docile Republican voter. Once, however—and in my immediate vicinity—he started to walk backwards with a determination that seemed to me prophetic."

Taft's elephantine Clarence Brown was never a match for Dewey's highly organized triumvirate of Herbert Brownell, Ed Jaeckle, and J. Russell

Sprague. "There is more cussing of Clarence Brown," one reporter observed, "than there has been heard in any political ruckus in recent times. . . . [His] vast bulk . . . has blocked every road to effective action."

Present for the festivities was sixty-eight-year-old *Baltimore Sun* correspondent H. L. Mencken, who derided national conventions as "All bla-a-ah." But something about their chaos, crudity, and bunkum nonetheless appealed to the curmudgeonly Sage of Baltimore. "Shortly after Taft announced his candidacy," recalled twenty-six-year-old *Sun* reporter William Manchester, "he showed up . . . wearing an enormous button bearing the legend 'Taft for President,' which, under close inspection, turned out to be a souvenir of the convention of 1908."

Bow-tied ABC radio comedian Henry Morgan arrived with two damsels attired in "tight, pull-over shirts and cotton shorts that reached barely to their thighs," touting him as a non-presidential, "un-conventional" candidate. There was a fashion show for the more fashionable among the Dewey partisans. The *New Yorker* correspondent reported that the candidate "[w]as escorted [into it] by four young ladies wearing Warren buttons. . . . Mrs. Dewey, in bottle green, entered [a] box overlooking [the] stage, accompanied by Mrs. Worthington Scranton, Mrs. Randolph Wilkes-Barre, and Mrs. Herbert Harrisburg."

And there was television.

The medium had been a long time coming, rattling around since the 1920s, functioning at first in vague, experimental ways, broadcasting from a handful of studios to a barely larger number of receiving sets. Television might have caught on sooner but for two items—the Great Depression and World War II. But once America had those inconveniences out of the way, it was ready for TV.

And politicians—some of them, at least—were ready for TV too. Even before FDR's "fireside chats" over the radio, politicians had seen television's possibilities. Cathode-ray tubes transported politicians into millions of homes, making them part of the family, in a way that radio and newsreels never could.

It was a politician's dream—and it sure beat going door-to-door.

In April 1939, NBC inaugurated its regular broadcast schedule by telecasting FDR dedicating RCA's exhibition at Flushing Meadows' World's Fair to set-owners within a fifty-mile radius. In 1940, viewers witnessed the Republican Convention broadcast from Philadelphia—but again only in New York.

Television, still largely a Northeastern phenomenon, returned to the conventions in 1948, though folks were working on ways to extend its signals farther west. Stratovision, for example, involved the beaming of signals received from Baltimore and Washington stations to a plane circling Pittsburgh and then back down to stations within a 250-mile radius of the Steel City. Stratovision programming included not only Republican convention coverage but also 1948's Joe Louis v. Jersey Joe Walcott heavyweight fight.

That year also witnessed the emergence of commercial television broadcasting. Two shows that would help define the new media debuted during 1948. Ed Sullivan's variety show, *Toast of the Town*—showcasing Dean Martin and Jerry Lewis (they earned a combined two hundred dollars), Rodgers and Hammerstein, a collection of singing New York City firemen, and six dancing "Toastettes"—launched on June 20. NBC inaugurated Milton Berle's *Texaco Star Theater* that September.

Audiences had grown but slowly—only two thousand homes owned sets worldwide in 1936, fourteen thousand nationwide in 1947. But, in 1948, the boom began. Sets could be had for as little as $149.50 (the twenty-two-tube, walnut-encased Tele-Tone model), but the nation's average manufacturing wage amounted to just $51.89 per week (farm workers earned $99 per *month*). The Tele-Tone's black-and-white picture tube spanned just seven inches.

By June, thirty-seven stations provided programming to 314,000 home receivers. Another forty thousand sets in bars and other public places attracted huge numbers of viewers. Philadelphia seemed inundated with coverage. Gimbel Brothers department store placed sets in all of its twenty display windows. WCAU-TV installed sets atop jeeps parked strategically around town. The six-thousand-seat Commercial Museum, adjacent to the convention itself, was jammed with curious viewers due to the presence of a hundred sets.

"Thanks to TV," *Time* magazine estimated, "about ten million spectators along the Eastern seaboard actually saw the [1948 GOP] convention in action. In scattered communities across the U.S., five million others saw telefilm versions while the news was still warm—three to 24 hours after it happened."

Life magazine combined its print coverage with NBC television's, with John Cameron Swayze (soon to host the network's ten-minute *Camel Newsreel Theatre*), Ben Grauer, and Bob Stanton supplying commentary. At CBS, it was Douglas Edwards, with Charles Collingwood providing backup from the floor. Though the *Baltimore Sun*-owned television station WMAR, H. L. Mencken fussed, "I hate to see a good newspaperman wasted on [TV's] puerilities. As soon as a television or any kind of radio enterprise gets into a newspaper an enormous number of men including some of the best become radio crooners, not newspapermen. . . . They get stage-struck, in brief. It shows in the newspaper instantly. The way for newspapers to meet the competition of radio and television is simply to get out better newspapers."

There were nearly as many networks present as stations broadcasting the event, and very nearly as many networks as there were cameras—four networks (NBC, CBS, ABC, and the short-lived and invariably short-funded DuMont) pooling coverage and sharing five cameras, to beam live coverage to seventeen stations between Boston and Richmond. Viewers beyond the northeast corridor settled for day-old kinescopes.

The old newsreel cameras still cranked away, filming GOP convention keynoter Dwight Green and national chairman B. Carroll Reece a day before their actual performances, but the accoutrements of the new media were now assuming precedence. Newsreel spotlights seemed balmy compared to television's. At Philadelphia's Convention Hall, ten 10,000-watt bulbs beamed down upon the speaker's podium. Down below, ten 5,000-watt bulbs shone upward. Two glass-enclosed TV control rooms flanked the podium. "In a few minutes I began to wilt and go blind," confessed Mencken, a casualty of 115-degree heat, "so the rest of my observations had to be made from a distance and through a brown beer bottle."

GOP officials pointedly advised delegates to "keep your clothes neat," "don't take off your shoes," and "take the toothpick out of your mouth."

And of course there was makeup.

Silver-maned Dwight Green prepared for his close-up with a session under the ultraviolet sunlamps. No pasty-faced, proto–Dick Nixon look for him. Tom Dewey sat still while technicians applied No. 25 natural flesh tinge to his pores. "I look just awful," he worried. He still needed a shave.

"No politician yet has refused face make-up," revealed the *New York Times*, "which may or may not be further indication that the political male is going flabby in the current generation."

That would remain to be seen.

17

"It might have been worse"

With or without cosmetic enhancement, 1948's Republican National Convention officially commenced at 11:00 AM, Monday, June 21. It did not really pick up steam, however, until the 9:05 PM evening session, when Dwight Green's keynote address lambasted all things Trumanesque, including the "bosses, boodle, buncombe, and blarney" that marked the Democratic administration, "the motley collection of embittered failures, back-alley revolutionaries, and parlor anarchists with which the New Deal has disgraced the party of Jefferson and Jackson."

"The cold war we face today," Green—perspiration staining his hard collar—continued, "is the lusty child of the New Deal's rendezvous with Communism. And I say to you tonight that rendezvous began with recognition of the Soviets in 1933. It continued with the socialistic compromises with Communism preached by Henry Wallace and the vote-catching compromises engineered by Harry Hopkins. It reached its tragic climax in those years when we supinely suffered Communism to master half of Europe."

For a full five minutes, the crowd cheered every swipe at Truman and cheered for Green, who, as a U.S. attorney, had helped jail Al Capone (*Time* dubbed him Dewey's "Chicago edition"). More ominously, it sat upon its hands as he praised congressional Republicans. All in all, Green had delivered the goods. Yet, speeches aside, he was not enjoying a good convention.

Chicago Tribune publisher Col. Robert Rutherford "Bertie" McCormick wielded immense sway over his party's national conservative and isolationist wings. He virtually owned the Illinois GOP. In 1940, McCormick, grandson of inventor Cyrus McCormick and one form ahead of FDR at Groton School, had enthusiastically supported Dewey's presidential ambitions. For 1948, however, he flirted with MacArthur, even conferring with him in Tokyo in

November 1947. But when his longtime rival William Randolph Hearst endorsed the general, the colonel settled not only upon Robert Taft, but also, oddly, upon the party's premier internationalist, Harold Stassen.

McCormick announced on Monday, June 21:

> I am for Taft and I have no second choice. Vandenberg can't even carry Michigan. . . . Dewey [in 1944] ran 250,000 votes behind the ticket in Illinois and dragged a great many state and county candidates down with him. . . . I don't think he can carry more than 12 states again this year.
>
> Stassen is strong with young people but mature people think he lacks maturity. In 1900, McKinley was nominated for his prestige and Theodore Roosevelt for his personal popularity. Therefore, it seems reasonable to nominate Taft and Stassen for the same reasons.

Dwight Green possessed other ideas. Pondering vice-presidential possibilities, the increasingly confident Dewey team now gave Green, an early Dewey supporter in 1944, increasing consideration. "I was convinced that [Green] personally favored Dewey's stand in foreign affairs," Dewey strategist Herbert Brownell recalled, "and [might] be able to swing the Illinois delegation." How great a factor Green might prove in swinging his home state in the general election was, in fact, debatable. His 237,000-vote victory margin in 1940 had shrunk to a precarious 72,000 in 1944.

Green, nonetheless, angled mightily to please the Dewey camp, originally crafting a vaguely internationalist keynote address. But both Harold Stassen and Illinois's passionately isolationist U.S. senator, Wayland "Curly" Brooks (no friend of Green, and, in Drew Pearson's estimation, "wholly controlled by the *Chicago Tribune*" and "almost proud of it"), had tipped off McCormick regarding Green's negotiations with Dewey. To further curry McCormick's favor, Brooks implicated *Tribune* city editor Don Maxwell in the Green-Dewey cabal.

Catching wind of events, *Tribune* Washington correspondent Walter Trohan rushed to McCormick's Warwick Hotel suite to vouch for Maxwell's innocence. In McCormick's absence, Trohan pleaded his fellow employee's case to McCormick's negligee-clad, fifty-one-year-old second wife, Maryland.

"What in the hell are you and my wife up to?" demanded the irate, six-foot-four McCormick, when he had returned. Trohan fled, but Maxwell kept his job.

Meanwhile, Green had run his keynote address text past McCormick. The colonel angrily gutted anything even mildly internationalist, and Green, in the end, pleased neither McCormick nor Dewey.

"Green's chances for the nomination," noted Brownell, "vanished quickly."

Former Connecticut congresswoman Clare Boothe Luce followed Green to the convention podium—"a sight to see," reported columnist Dorothy Kilgallen, "as she stood on tiptoe in her black suede flatties." At 1944's national gathering, her address ("a brilliantly vicious speech," marveled one historian) had skewered "the unheroic Roosevelt decade: a decade of confusion and conflict that ended in war."

This evening, noted the *New York Times*'s Meyer Berger, she "launched into her speech, and her voice was magic. Fans slowed, handkerchiefs were at rest. A few incisive thrusts, and the crowd was hers."

Luce argued that "Democratic Presidents are always troubadours of trouble, crooners of catastrophe; they cannot win elections except in the climate of crisis. So the party by its composition has a vested interest in depression at home and war abroad."

"Let us waste no time measuring the unfortunate man in the White House against our specifications," she jeered, to prolonged laughter and applause. "Mr. Truman's time is short; his situation is hopeless. Frankly, he is a gone goose."

Gone as well, it seemed, was Arthur Vandenberg. Mrs. Luce's address had evoked the Michigan senator's name to decent applause—the most heartfelt applause of the convention so far, actually. But just preceding the evening session's opening gavel, white-linen-suit-clad Vandenberg himself had entered the hall, hoping to trigger a response enthusiastic enough to ultimately propel him to a nomination. It did not happen.

Columnist Tris Coffin noted:

Reporters jumped up, and crowded around [Vandenberg]. Cameramen appeared as if by magic. This was supposed to be the beginning of a mass demonstration. Governor Kim Sigler . . . grabbed the Michigan standard and led a file of shouting delegates from his state down the center aisle. While the professional politicians sat on the edges of their seats and held their breath, the delegates on the floor and the visitors in the gallery seemed unaware of what was happening. There was no answering roar of cheers from the hall—just the feeble yelling of the loyal men from Michigan.

"Vandenberg," wrote Washington observers Robert Allen and James Shannon, "was like a man who had stumbled into a deep-freeze by mistake; he crawled out of the hall all covered with hoarfrost and carrying his nomination chances like wilted posies in his limp hand."

Senator Vandenberg never did formally declare his candidacy, instead continuing his pious mouthings of a noncandidate candidacy. But following his April 1951 death, discovered among his documents was one very private paper ("Probably it will be misunderstood as being some sort of proof that I was not sincere") of one very pronounced non-candidate: Arthur Hendrick Vandenberg's acceptance speech for the 1948 Republican presidential nomination.

"It was said, half in jest but with something resembling the literal truth," noted the *New York Times*'s William S. White, "that the Dewey organization could give a fairly accurate report on the whereabouts of a single one among the thousand-odd delegates at any hour of day or night. The Taft organization did not know where even most of the Taft people were, at any time."

Indicative of that ineptitude was the largely unnecessary and avoidable setback it endured on Tuesday, June 22, 1948, when the credentials committee ruled on the composition of the contested Georgia, Mississippi, South Carolina, and Alaska delegations. Dewey's forces offered to split Georgia's sixteen contested delegates down the middle, but with Taft's man Carroll Reece still GOP national chairman, Taft calculated he might win them all. Instead, it was Dewey who swept Georgia, as committee members from such Taft- and Stassen-controlled states as Illinois, Tennessee, and Mississippi jumped ship. In retribution, the frustrated Reece vowed to block pro-Dewey Michigan committeewoman Mrs. Dudley C. Hay's reelection as national committeewoman. "Don't worry, Mr. Reece," Mrs. Hay calmly responded; "when this convention is over you won't be national chairman."

Rumors flew that Dewey had dangled federal judgeships before key credentials committee members. Particularly galling was Mississippi's defection. Through Mississippi national committeeman Perry Howard, whose son worked in the Senate post office, Robert Taft controlled Mississippi's votes, but Dewey's aide, shrewd-eyed Erie County boss Ed Jaeckle, cajoled Mississippi's credentials committee representative into supporting Dewey's Georgia slate. The defecting Mississippi delegate died rushing to catch a train home, reputedly with $1,500 in cash—the price of his betrayal—found upon his person.

A story—perhaps apocryphal, perhaps not—made the rounds. A reporter asked a Southern delegate whom he was for. "Well," came the response, "some of us is for Dewey and some of us is for Taft, and all of us is for sale."

Far more crucial than Georgia was Pennsylvania.

"If I was Taft," the GOP's futile 1936 nominee Alf Landon observed, following his party's 1946 landslide, "I would give Martin of Pennsylvania . . . a lot of attention."

Landon meant U.S. senator Edward Martin: six-foot-four, booming-voiced son of a Presbyterian clergyman, sixty-nine years old on Election Day, 1948, fifteen times a candidate—and never a loser.

Before 1946, Senator Martin had been Governor Martin. He had met Dewey at various national gubernatorial conferences and considered their friendship "one of the very finest things in my public life." Martin, however, represented but one wing of the powerful, yet exceedingly fractured, Keystone State GOP. A small group led by Philadelphia banker Jay Cooke IV supported Stassen. Martin's gubernatorial successor, James Henderson Duff, a Teddy Roosevelt Progressive Party elector in the 1912 election, stood on the party's left. "Uncle Joe" Grundy and Mason Owlett (who despised Duff) stood on its right. In 1946, Martin, Grundy, and Duff ("a strapping redhead with the comfortable girth of an archbishop and the piercing eyes of an evangelist") had all been aligned, but upon assuming the governorship, "Big Red" Duff quickly tossed his old allies overboard, barring their organizations from state patronage mills.

Regarding presidential competition, these factions reacted counterintuitively. The liberal Duff despised Dewey. He had first favored Eisenhower, but now, partially thanks to promises of favorable coverage in *Time* and *Life* from the pro-Vandenberg Henry Luce, he backed Vandenberg.

Meanwhile, impeccable conservatives Grundy and Owlett remained oddly leery of Robert Taft. Two days before the convention opened, the eighty-five-year-old and stone-deaf Grundy pronounced Taft a "socialist."

Thus, save for Martin, all factions opposed Dewey and found it in their interest to slow his advancing juggernaut. An early-1948 attempt to compromise on Massachusetts's Joe Martin had failed. Duff, lurching wildly about, at one point threw his support to Taft, prompting a frantic response from Clare Boothe Luce. Eventually, the warring Duff-Pew and Grundy-Owlett factions agreed upon Ed Martin as a favorite son—but only for the first ballot. Duff's people would then shift to Vandenberg, the Grundy-Owlett bloc to Dewey.

But very quickly, Martin was conferring with Herbert Brownell and the square-shouldered, invariably tanned J. Russell Sprague in Room 807 of Dewey's Bellevue-Stratford headquarters. A second meeting brought Dewey and Martin directly together. A grinning Brownell, with his arms extended, was soon promising reporters "a story that big." Just before 3:00 PM, Ed Martin stunned everyone. He was abandoning his favorite-son status, throwing his support to Dewey, and even placing Dewey's name in nomination that evening.

At a televised news conference (history's first ever), a beaming Dewey blandly swore, "There has been no understanding, arrangement, bargains or deals for anything of any kind or character—for Vice President, for Cabinet offices, jobs or patronage. Is that clear?"

The stampede to Dewey was proceeding.

Dewey's foes struggled to place a stubborn, brave face on events. Stassen termed it a "Grundy-Dewey" deal—"a desperate admission of weakness." Dewey, fussed Taft kingpin Clarence Brown, "must now be nominated on the first ballot or not at all." Kim Sigler derided the move as "a deal in a smoke-filled room," and desperately portrayed it as "a great break" for Vandenberg.

But it was Herbert Brownell who had it right. Perched upon a tabletop in the jubilant Dewey headquarters, he pronounced that Martin's shift possessed "the force of a new, improved atomic bomb."

Another key favorite-son state was Indiana, where ambitious House majority leader Charles "Two Cadillac Charlie" Halleck—generally considered a Dewey man—controlled a substantial portion of state delegates. He was generally not admired. Tris Coffin regarded him as "a familiar American type, the well-to-do, small-town smart aleck." Authors Robert S. Allen and William V. Shannon were harsher still, dismissing him as "one of the most thoroughly unattractive men in Washington."

Nonetheless, on Wednesday morning, the convention's third, Dewey operatives Sprague, Brownell, Jaeckle, and veteran Nassau County congressman Leonard W. Hall conferred with Halleck at Dewey's suite, regarding a possible deal. Dewey remained discreetly beyond earshot, as Sprague, speaking for the group, asked, "Charlie, do you believe that if we promise something we can deliver?" The stubby, bulbous-nosed Halleck nodded yes, and Sprague continued. "Well, you look to us like the Vice-Presidential nominee." Halleck, not the total fool, asked what was involved.

"You will have to deliver the Indiana delegation," Sprague answered.

"I think that I can deliver most of it," countered Halleck, "but I'm not sure of some [of it]."

"No, no, Charlie," Sprague insisted, "part won't be enough. It must be all."

Two hours later, Halleck delivered Indiana, lock, stock, and barrel.

Taft and Stassen were in deep trouble—and knew it.

They conferred at former national chairman John Hamilton's Drake Hotel penthouse apartment. Delayed after being stuck in the elevator, Taft bluntly suggested that Stassen throw his support to him. Stassen countered that they should unite behind Vandenberg. Taft contended that his Ohio delegates would sooner bolt to his chum John Bricker. Colonel McCormick fumed that he would rather "give Illinois to Dewey." At 2:00 AM, all departed, having accomplished nothing.

"Neither Stassen nor Taft hated Dewey enough to withdraw," summarized

Taft biographer James Patterson, "and neither man thought he could get his delegates to follow if he did."

On Wednesday, Taft, Stassen, and James Duff conferred twice more. Earl Warren, with rumors swirling that he might ultimately emerge as the stop-Dewey candidate, pointedly absented himself. Taft struggled to project equanimity. Dewey, he claimed, would not receive more than four hundred votes on the second ballot and had "to be nominated on the second ballot or not at all."

"There is no semblance of a deal. I believe there is no chance for one," argued Stassen floor manager Joe McCarthy, contending that Dewey might reach as high as 470 votes on the second ballot, but not much beyond that.

The maneuvering continued. Dwight Green committed his second-ballot favorite-son votes to Taft. Governors Alfred Driscoll of New Jersey and Robert F. Bradford of Massachusetts, along with the white-haired, staunchly conservative U.S. senator James P. Kem of Missouri, tossed their support to Dewey. "I could not support Robert Taft," Kem informed Kim Sigler after the convention. "He is too socialistic."

Stassen campaign manager Warren E. Burger took pencil to paper and jotted down his estimate of how the first ballot would shake out: Warren, 55; Vandenberg, 56; Stassen, 155; Taft, 209; and Dewey, 448. It was not looking good for Harold Stassen.

The GOP secured advice regarding their platform from an unlikely source. From New York, on June 16, 1948, Eleanor Roosevelt observed, "I am particularly interested in the platform of the two major parties, because from past experience I should expect both platforms to come out of the mill fairly similar. The Republicans, obliged to write theirs first, will certainly attempt to say as little as possible. They will bear in mind that they must give their opponents as few points as possible on which to attack them, and generalities are always safer than specific stands."

The GOP had reason for caution, tottering as it was along a dangerous internal fault line, largely that of old, prewar, isolationist-internationalist debates. As Joseph and Stewart Alsop warned, "The stage is set at Philadelphia for the final struggle between isolationists and men of the Vandenberg school, between backward looking and modern-minded Republicans."

The battle raged on several fronts, between Vandenberg himself and Dewey's foremost foreign policy adviser, the slightly less internationalist John Foster Dulles. And it raged less civilly on the 104-member platform committee, where Massachusetts senator Henry Cabot Lodge Jr.—another repentant isolationist—pitted himself against unrepentant isolationist "Curly" Brooks of Illinois. The result was a mushily worded plank, avoiding any mention of Yalta, Potsdam, or even any Republican credit for the Marshall Plan. It merely pledged support for the plan "within the prudent limits of our own economic welfare," more or less supported the United Nations as "the world's best hope" for peace, and hedgingly supported recognizing the State of Israel, "subject to the letter and spirit of the United Nations Charter."

"*My* platform," chortled Arthur Vandenberg in his diary, "was adopted by the Convention *unanimously*—which means that the Chicago Colonel [McCormick] and many of my bitter Congressional foes who were delegates must have voted for it. Life *does* have its amusing consolations."

All in all, it was a platform that quoted Lincoln without being Lincolnesque. The convention itself, more preoccupied with choosing a candidate than choosing sides, adopted it without opposition.

On Wednesday evening, June 23, delegates heard seven names placed in nomination. Senator Edward Martin, presenting Dewey (he "towers above all others"), proceeded first. "We have known him a long time," said Martin. "Through all that time he has grown in the confidence of the party and the people. Today we have reason to be thankful that he started so young on the national scene, and that he has already led us in a great national campaign. He emerges today in a robust majority, ripened by years of high responsibility—still a young man in the prime of vitality—fit to lead a nation that is still young, still expanding, still going places." From the gallery, angry Stassenites jeered.

John Bricker nominated Taft, who seemed to generate the most genuine affection. At 12:32 AM University of California president Dr. Robert Gordon Sproul nominated Earl Warren, whom he pronounced to be "calm, logical, and judicial." Warren's name, vowed Sproul, would not be found "on the sucker lists with which the Communists entrap the unwary." Hollywood's

Irene Dunne upstaged the perspiring Sproul by taking the platform as he began. Resplendent in upswept hairdo, black jersey blouse, India-print skirt, and pearl choker, she seconded Warren, as did a Georgia delegate who rated the California governor's integrity equal to "that of the South's favorite son, Robert E. Lee." Film industry personalities George Murphy, Hedda Hopper, and Harold Lloyd (an alternate delegate filling in for Robert Montgomery) joined in the twenty-two-minute floor demonstration that followed.

Minnesota congressman Walter H. Judd, speaking, he said, for "the millions of Republicans who are tired of winning in June and losing in November," nominated Harold Stassen. A twenty-five-minute demonstration followed, featuring flags, balloons, Marines carrying a canoe, Sioux Indian chief William Spotted Crow (escorted to the podium by Minnesota governor Luther Youngdahl and a sweat-drenched Joe McCarthy), banners, noise upon noise, and remarkable enthusiasm. The *New York Times* termed the spectacle "unprecedented in the history of political conventions. For sound, for sheer theatre, for variety it had never been matched."

Connecticut secretary of state Frances Burke Redick placed Senator Raymond Baldwin in nomination. Kim Sigler nominated Arthur Vandenberg. And, to a virtually empty hall, at 3:30 AM, the blind Harlan W. Kelley, district attorney of Sauk County, Wisconsin, expended twenty two minutes nominating Gen. MacArthur.

Dewey's forces remained skittish. "It was the only convention in which I was active," recalled Herbert Brownell, "that I could not predict the outcome until the final roll call." Brownell feared a stampede and had his reasons. Wisconsin's Joe McCarthy and Tom Coleman were reported to be in contact with draft-Vandenberg forces. Earl Warren ally Sen. William F. Knowland conspired with Vandenberg's man, Henry Cabot Lodge Jr. Yale-educated Kentucky Senator John Sherman Cooper announced his first-ballot support for his Michigan colleague.

Balloting commenced on Thursday afternoon, June 24, with temperatures climbing above the hundred-degree mark and the humidity equally unbearable. Stassen watched events from the platform. His rivals, absenting themselves according to tradition, monitored events via television from air-conditioned hotel suites. Before convention chairman Joe Martin could poll the first delegation, a jolt of severe back pain nearly threw the exhausted Herbert Brownell to the floor. "I decided that if this was the way I was to go, so be it," recalled Brownell. "What better way for a Republican loyalist than at his party's convention?"

Few surprises marked the first-ballot voting. Michigan held for Vandenberg. Oklahoma cast its eighteen votes for "its favorite son-in-law" Dewey. When it was over, the New Yorker held a substantial, though hardly invincible, lead. All depended upon the second round, whether he gained or lost delegates, whether Taft or Stassen or Vandenberg, or even Warren, exhibited unexpected strength. With a substantial number of favorite-son votes still being cast, significant movement remained possible. The first-ballot tally:

Thomas E. Dewey	434
Robert A. Taft	224
Harold Stassen	157
Arthur Vandenberg	62
Earl Warren	59
Dwight Green	56
Alfred E. Driscoll	35
Raymond Baldwin	19
Joseph Martin	18
B. Carroll Reece	15
Douglas MacArthur	11
Everett M. Dirksen	1

As promised, Dwight Green ceded his second-ballot votes to Taft. Harold Stassen declined by eight votes. He was finished. Dewey gained ground in Iowa, Kansas, Kentucky, Maryland, Massachusetts, Missouri, Montana, Nebraska, and New Jersey, even acquiring a solitary Ohio delegate. He had added eighty-one votes to his total and stood a slim thirty-three votes short of nomination. The second-ballot tally:

Thomas E. Dewey	517
Robert A. Taft	274
Harold Stassen	149
Arthur Vandenberg	62
Earl Warren	57
Raymond Baldwin	19

Joseph Martin	10
Douglas MacArthur	7
B. Carroll Reece	1

Anti-Dewey forces teetered on the brink of disaster. Desperate to buy time, "Big Red" Duff moved to recess. Senator Knowland and Congressman Brown seconded his motion. Joe Martin called for a voice vote. It *sounded* like the "no" votes had it, but with the gallery joining in, who could tell? Martin proceeded to call the roll.

Textbook strategy mandated that Dewey oppose any recess and press for a quick third ballot to wrap things up immediately. Herbert Brownell reasoned differently. Dewey stood near enough to victory—with Connecticut, Michigan, and Arizona all poised to board his bandwagon—that his nomination was inevitable *unless* he lost on Duff's motion to recess. If that happened—and it might very well occur—Dewey's momentum, surging forward with each step since Oregon, might finally be broken and never recover. Without consulting Dewey, Brownell decided against opposing adjournment.

"The New York delegation," blared the Empire State's chairman, the canny former Westchester County executive, William F. Bleakley, "has no objection to a recess."

At 4:55 PM the convention recessed. For the next two-and-a-half hours the maneuvering proceeded. But it was far too late in the day. Harold Stassen, increasingly obsessed with halting the Dewey juggernaut (but never obsessed enough to back Taft), offered to support Vandenberg. Vandenberg wasn't interested. With Henry Cabot Lodge Jr. in tow, Stassen then tried phoning Dwight Eisenhower at Columbia University to derail Dewey. "I believe the General would have accepted *if* the track could have been cleared for him," Arthur Vandenberg recorded in his diary. "But it could not be cleared for *anybody.*"

Disconsolate, Stassen poured out his soul to Carroll Reece. "Harold," Reece could only respond, "you have no idea of the pressure put on me. That Dewey machine is like a row of tanks."

"Carroll," Stassen answered, his brow pouring sweat, his eyes blazing anger, even hatred, "we mustn't let them get away with it. That Grundy machine and the big-city New York machine will destroy public confidence in the Republican Party."

At Earl Warren's sixteenth-floor Warwick Hotel suite, Warren conferred with advisers and then phoned Dewey with congratulations.

Emerging from his own suite, an inexplicably calm Robert Taft informed reporters, "I think it is wide open. He [Dewey] is close so I might be right and I might be wrong."

"I don't know," Clarence Brown sputtered. "I'm just so damned tired I don't know."

The convention reconvened, and Warren released his state's fifty-three delegates—but failed to endorse Dewey.

Anticipating California's move, however, Taft soon conceded. "I have a statement, which I have been authorized to present . . . on behalf of Senator Taft," John Bricker informed the convention. "These are his words as he dictated them to me: 'A careful analysis of the situation shows that a majority of the delegates will support Governor Dewey on the third ballot. I therefore release my delegates and ask them to vote for Governor Dewey with all of their force and enthusiasm.'" Knowland and Sigler—and even Stassen—scurried to follow Bricker's lead.

"I saw [Joe McCarthy]," recalled Richard Nixon, "I can remember vividly, at the entrance to the auditorium. Particularly—it's funny the things you remember. The sweat was just pouring down his cheeks and so forth, and his shirt was wet, and he was saying, 'Well, fellas, we've had it. There's no way that Stassen can make it, and now let's go out and work for Dewey.'"

Thunderstorms erupted outside the hall. The convention nominated Dewey unanimously—1,904 to 0—only because Col. McCormick, intractably opposed to Dewey to the end, had vacated the premises, leaving his vote with an alternate.

"It might have been worse," McCormick sighed as he departed. "It could have been Vandenberg."

18

"Shifty and somewhat slimy"

At 8:21 PM, in her Bellevue-Stratford sitting room, forty-year-old Frances Hutt Dewey perched nervously upon a rose-colored divan, intently watching television as Ohio's John Bricker reluctantly tossed the nomination to her husband.

She sighed.

Arising, she announced: "I guess I'd better put on my hat." As she reached her bedroom, her husband—trailed by a small army of reporters and photographers, their flashbulbs popping—entered their suite. Nominee and wife hugged silently. Within two minutes they were en route to the hall, where Tom Dewey would dent tradition by delivering his acceptance speech before the convention had designated a running mate. As the Deweys sped forward, a rainbow filled the previously sodden evening sky.

Congressman Walter Judd had jibed that Dewey had "promised so many cabinet jobs they'll have to operate in three shifts." Dewey, perhaps protesting too much, began his oration by strenuously denying any such tainted bargains. He told his delegates, "I am happy to be able to say to you that I come to you unfettered by a single obligation or promise to any living person"—a statement true only if he had qualified it with the five simple words, *that I meant to keep.* He continued, "I come free to join with you in selecting to serve our nation the finest men and women in the country."

The remainder of his message excelled only in vacuity. Nine times he invoked the words "unity" or "united," though it was difficult to determine what he might have sought unity for—or even against. Words such as "Soviet Union," "Communism," "Taft-Hartley," "the Marshall Plan," "selective service," "Czechoslovakia," "Palestine," "agriculture," "the cost of living," "taxes," "veterans," "housing," "civil rights," "the New Deal," or "states' rights" never appeared in his text. He referenced nothing specific, save that he favored harnessing the "unimaginable possibilities of atomic energy, to bring men and women a larger, fuller life."

Was Dewey's blandness—this fear of the specific—a mark of supreme overconfidence? A signal that, with November's race all but decided, he need never resort to ungainly details? Or was it the reverse? Was it the reaction of a man already once vanquished in America's highest-stakes competition—who had tasted defeat at the 1940 convention after leading in early balloting; who had received not a single delegate in the crucial Wisconsin contest against the hapless Stassen and the absent, aged MacArthur; who had once even lost in the race for governor? Were his empty words emblematic of the fabled Dewey arrogance—or born of the fear that greater specificity might only guide him down the path of defeat once more?

With his speech concluded and a Hawaiian lei draped incongruously around his neck, Dewey waved to his audience—in the hall, on TV, and later on the newsreels. Recalled California Republican J. Raymond Bell, "Dewey waved to the packed auditorium, ignoring the woman who stood at his side. On any great occasion in any man's life, it is instinctive for him to reach for, or embrace, the one female who shares his life. Not so with Dewey. That glaring omission seemed to be communicated to the gathered Republicans and, ostensibly, to those who watched the event on television."

But such questions seemed quite meaningless, for as the *Los Angeles Times* noted, Tom Dewey was quite definitively "The Next President."

Yet however much Dewey desired to eschew specificity, he now faced making one very specific, very crucial decision: the selection of a running mate.

It might, of course, have been Charlie Halleck.

Joe Martin departed the hall and chanced upon five-term congressman Forest A. Harness of Kokomo, Indiana. Harness exuded sheer joy that his fellow Hoosier, Halleck, would become their nominee's running mate.

"Isn't it great for Charlie!" chirped Harness.

"Charlie who?" Martin snapped, not betting at all on such a scenario.

"If they don't give it to him," Harness snapped back, "there's going to be hell to pay in Indiana."

"I'm afraid, Forest," Martin responded, "there's going to be hell to pay in Indiana."

At 11:00 PM, Dewey's brain trust gathered in his suite. Its numbers included not only Dewey insiders Brownell, Sprague, Jaeckle, Hall, foreign policy adviser John Foster Dulles, and press secretary James C. Hagerty, but also governors Bradford (Massachusetts), Driscoll (New Jersey), and Martin (Pennsylvania); former Washington State governor Arthur B. Langlie; senators Vandenberg, Baldwin, and Saltonstall; Pennsylvania committeeman G. Mason Owlett; roly-poly *Kansas City Star* editor Roy Roberts (formerly for Eisenhower); Arrangements Committee chair Walter S. Hallanan; and former national committeemen Lew Wentz (Oklahoma) and Barak Mattingly (Missouri).

Like the 1920 GOP convention's famous "smoke-filled room," this gathering ultimately wielded much less influence than it fancied itself possessing. In 1920, real power lay on the convention floor among the weary, frustrated delegates. It now resided with cold-blooded Tom Dewey.

The brain trust's first decision concerned Dwight Green. His selection would now only roil Col. McCormick, so he was out. "Let's not be mealymouthed about this," Dewey growled. "We can't take him."

The second ax fell nearly as quickly—and far more cruelly—upon Charlie Halleck.

For it wasn't just Joe Martin who disliked Halleck (and Martin did *not* like him); just about everyone seemed to dislike him, most prominently the editorial board of the *New York Times*.

"SURELY NOT MR. HALLECK!" the august *Times* practically shouted.

Herbert Brownell asked the gathering, "Well, how about Charlie?"

Arthur Vandenberg, echoing Joe Martin, asked, "Charlie who?"

"Charlie Halleck."

Vandenberg could not help but exclaim, "Oh, my God!" Massachusetts bluebloods Salstonstall and Bradford eagerly seconded Vandenberg's opposition. Long Island's Len Hall argued for honoring Sprague's commitment to Halleck. Sprague—and Herbert Brownell—remained conspicuously silent. Finally, Dewey himself matter-of-factly ruled, "Halleck won't do."

Charles Abraham Halleck was finished.

Dewey broke the news personally to the stunned Halleck. "I can work for you and talk for you," Halleck exclaimed, "but I can't run with you!" His words had no effect upon the "stony-faced" Dewey.

"You're running out on the Eightieth Congress," Halleck finally countered, "and you'll be sorry."

"I don't know how I can face Charlie Halleck again," Len Hall confided to Dewey after Halleck's departure. "Oh," Dewey responded blandly, "I don't see that you did anything."

Robert Taft and the Ohio delegation argued strenuously for John Bricker, hoping to reprise the ill-fated 1944 Dewey-Bricker ticket in its totality. "Arrangements for Senator Bricker to receive the vice-presidential nomination have already been worked out," grandly announced Taft strategist, former Ohio congressman Dudley A. White. "He will accept."

Taft and Bricker were ideological twins, diverging sharply, however, in terms of style and substance. Taft delivered the goods in terms of erudition and legislation. But it was the handsome, photogenic, distinctly less intellectual Bricker who excited and inspired from the stump. Bricker, observed Norman Thomas, was the "real hero" of the Right. "I don't belong to his political church," the Socialist leader admitted. "But if I did . . . I'd like him for my minister."

At 1:00 AM, Ohio governor Thomas J. Herbert visited the Dewey suite to pitch Bricker. He got nowhere. Shortly thereafter, Taft phoned with the same message—and received the same result. Few other Republicans outside Ohio's borders desired to so faithfully replicate a losing ticket.

Nor did Dewey's brain trust relish Taft's fallback suggestion: the already discarded Dwight Green. "Tom's whole concern seemed to be about carrying the Atlantic seaboard," Taft later informed Green, "and he seemed to be afraid of all midwestern candidates because they were too isolationistic!"

Rumors swirled that conservative California senator Bill Knowland possessed the inside track, furnishing not only geographic but ideological balance to the ticket. In the end, his candidacy boiled down to just that—rumors.

Some argued that neither ideological nor geographic balance should hold sway, suggesting New England liberals Henry Cabot Lodge Jr. or Raymond Baldwin.

By 2:30 AM, as Arthur Vandenberg departed, the choice boiled down to either Earl Warren or Harold Stassen. Vandenberg, amenable to

Warren, nonetheless preferred Stassen. And while Warren did nothing to encourage a second-place candidacy, the ever-ambitious Stassen feverishly angled for the nomination, modestly admitting that he would submit to "a real draft."

Real drafts, however, are hard to come by, and Stassen had committed a number of blunders that made his selection impossible. Blinded by hatred of Dewey, he had failed to throw his votes to an arguably inevitable winner and push him over the top (though, goodness knows, such a move had done little to finally assist Charlie Halleck). Beyond that, after conferring with Dewey in June 1947—and again after the Oregon primary—Stassen had publicly vowed never to accept a berth on a Dewey-Stassen ticket. "Dewey supporters regarded this as a gratuitous slap at their man," observed columnist Frank Kent, "and resented it."

As late as 7:00 AM, governors Luther Youngdahl and Alfred Driscoll argued for Stassen, but with little success. This left Earl Warren—Dewey's first choice four years previously. Save for the presidency, however, Warren possessed little desire to relocate to Washington.

At 4:30 AM, Dewey, working through *Los Angeles Times* political editor Kyle Palmer, had roused Earl Warren from bed and bathrobe to summon him to his Bellevue-Stratford suite and to a jawboning designed to lure him onto the ticket. Warren still possessed no interest in such a hollow ceremonial post. Merely presiding over the Senate was not for him. Dewey countered that the vice presidency would be beefed up, given more authority, that the two men would work together for a truly liberal agenda—"You'll sit with the Cabinet and be a real Assistant President."

Warren reminded Dewey that the vice presidency paid $5,000 less than his $25,000-a-year salary as governor—and would deprive him of his Sacramento executive mansion (the vice president as yet enjoyed no official residence). Dewey promised to lobby a Republican Congress for a raise.

Beyond that, Earl Warren simply did not care for Dewey. They had first met in 1939, and Warren's initial impression was scathing: "a vain and hollow fellow," he confided to his diary, "shifty and somewhat slimy . . . one of the most transparent frauds of all time."

At 1944's annual Governors' Conference in Hershey, Pennsylvania, Dewey further alienated Warren, this time through calculated sniping at western agricultural interests. The following year, at Gettysburg, Dewey angered Warren with his remark: "If there are any more of these Chamber of Commerce–type programs to take up the time of busy men, I will not return."

"He puts his foot in his mouth all the time," Warren growled to Ed Martin, "the little fool."

At 6:00 AM, Earl Warren trudged back to the Warwick through darkened streets. He had still not made up his mind.

Bill Knowland and much of the California delegation urged him to refuse. But *Washington Post* owner Eugene Meyer argued, "No man is too big to run for Vice President." Nina Warren agreed with Knowland. "You could never be happy in that job," she pleaded.

In the end, it was a matter of reluctant political calculation: If Earl Warren ever wanted the presidency (and he evidently *did*), he could not twice reject the vice presidency.

"What made him change his mind?" a reporter asked a Warren aide.

"They put a gun to his head."

"I had to take it this time," Warren explained to his aide—and physical look-alike—Merrell F. "Pop" Small, "else they never would have considered me for anything again."

At 11:30 AM, with the convention thirty minutes away from reconvening, Warren phoned Dewey. At 11:33, Russell Sprague burst forth from Dewey headquarters and exclaimed, "It is the unanimous opinion of all of us that Governor Warren should be the candidate."

It was none too soon. Recorded Arthur Vandenberg:

I went to the Convention Hall. . . . Governor Sigler told me that Governor Youngdahl of Minnesota had urgently requested him to nominate Stassen from the floor. There was a distinct spirit of rebellion in the air. I think the Convention feared the recommendation of an unacceptable nominee. I advised that no decision regarding a rival nomination should even be discussed until it was known who would be recommended because the Convention could not afford to repudiate its nominee for President twelve hours after naming him unless his V.P. choice was impossible. Then came the Warren news. The rebellion disintegrated. A good job was finished.

Almost finished.

Arizona delegates nominated Stassen. Charlie Halleck had warned them, "You're sticking your necks into a buzz saw," but they went ahead anyway. No voice seconded Stassen—not even from Minnesota.

Halleck, with precious little pride remaining, now attempted to second Warren. He failed even in that. As reporters jostled to get a glimpse of the new nominee, they rushed past the disconsolate Halleck, completely ignoring him.

Warren had prepared no speech for this unwanted circumstance. Extemporaneously, with his wife and three blonde daughters—Virginia, 19; Dorothy, 17; and Nina "Honey Bear," 14—looking on, he confided to the delegates:

> For the first time in my life I know what it feels like to get hit by a streetcar. You know, yesterday, I received something of a jolt. I had no idea, I am sure, that there was any such shock awaiting me as today. And before you change your mind I want to say—I accept the nomination.
>
> I accept the nomination for the vice presidency of the United States. Now the reason that I am so quick to say that is that I have not yet recovered my breath, much less my thoughts, and if I let it go any longer, I'm afraid I'll forget to say even that.

That night, Governor Warren called California to relay the news to his sons. Thirteen-year-old Bobby answered, and Earl Warren explained his nomination for vice president of the United States.

"Is that good?" Bobby Warren asked.

"Yes, I think so," his father answered.

But Earl Warren really did not know.

19

"What *do* these people want?"

The Dewey-Warren ticket was not good news for the Democrats.

Democratic defeat seemed assured. The Republican ticket had it all—thoroughly liberal, no tangible connection to the decidedly unpopular congressional wing of its party, geographic diversity, experience, and even relative youth.

The Democratic ticket had Harry Truman

Which was why so many Democrats wanted someone else, and why so many of those wanting someone else still desired Dwight David Eisenhower.

Eisenhower, however, remained aloof from the presidential fray. In anticipation of assuming leadership of Columbia University, he had authored his wartime memoirs, *Crusade in Europe*, for which Doubleday & Co. had advanced him $635,000. In a ruling without precedent, the Treasury Department decreed Ike's earnings to be exempt from then-sky-high personal tax rates, subject instead to the significantly lower capital gains rate. Since Ike, it reasoned, was not a professional writer, he was not so much writing as marketing a lifetime asset. Accordingly, Eisenhower paid only $158,750 in taxes—saving approximately $400,000. Not bad compensation for three months of work.

Thus, in mid-1948, buffeted by his new academic and literary ventures, Dwight Eisenhower remained stubbornly unfocused upon the White House, though the White House remained focused upon him. At a Thursday, July 1, press conference, reporters peppered Harry Truman with questions regarding vice-presidential possibilities. Any thought of a Truman-Eisenhower slate, HST responded, was "up to General Eisenhower."

With the Republican ticket selected and Democrats scheduled to convene in Philadelphia on Monday, July 12, Georgia and Virginia

Democrats instructed their delegates to support Ike on Friday, July 2. A day later, a group of nineteen prominent Democrats headed by James Roosevelt and Florida's Claude Pepper telegraphed all 1,592 Democratic delegates, requesting them to convene on Saturday, July 10 "to pick the ablest and strongest man available. . . . It is our belief that no man in these critical days can refuse the call to duty and leadership implicit in the nomination and virtual election to the Presidency of the United States." Roosevelt and Pepper named no names, but their implication was obvious. This was a draft-Eisenhower movement running at full tilt, and with more than a little of the element of personal grudge match now added to it. There had, in fact, been even more to the brutal Truman-Roosevelt encounter in Los Angeles than Truman's private tongue-lashing of his predecessor's son. Tom Scully (James's former rival for the chairmanship) had also arranged a private cocktail party for the president. Pointedly absent from the guest list: James Roosevelt.

Roosevelt and Pepper now spearheaded a diverse, ideologically incoherent coalition—committed liberals, big-city bosses, Southern segregationists—united only in their Democratic affiliation, their distaste for Truman, and, above all, an almost desperate desire to stave off humiliating defeat that November. Their ranks included four Southern governors—Strom Thurmond (South Carolina), William M. Tuck (Virginia), Ben Laney (Arkansas), and Beauford H. Jester (Texas)—as well as Connecticut gubernatorial candidate Chester Bowles; Alabama senator Lister Hill; Minneapolis mayor Hubert Humphrey; New York City's Irish-born mayor William O'Dwyer; Chicago Democratic chieftain Col. Jacob M. Arvey (a rare non-Irish—indeed, a Jewish—big-city boss); national committeemen from Michigan, Wisconsin, Kansas, and Arkansas; plus Nebraska's evidently still-irked state chairman, William Ritchic.

How desperate they were may be gauged from Chester Bowles's continuing pursuit of the Ike bandwagon. "No one knew Eisenhower's political views, and I felt it was quite possible that he did not have any," recalled Bowles. "I decided to find out. I called Columbia University and an appointment was arranged for the following day. After a two-hour discussion I was convinced: 1) that he wanted to become president; 2) that this desire was qualified by his reluctance to participate in the turmoil of political life; 3) that his ideas on domestic policy were almost wholly unformed; and 4) that he was incredibly naive politically."

Before their session concluded, Eisenhower inquired if it were possible for anyone to win both the Democratic and Republican nominations. "I came away," said Bowles, "badly shaken."

Ike wasn't naïve at all. He knew exactly where everyone was coming from. In his diary, he wrote: "All Republicans thought they'd win easily. So, no 'leaders' wanted me or bothered me. All the 'Republican' pressure on me was truly from the grass roots, because the bosses wanted the top man to be one they could control. The 'Democratic' pressures came from the bosses, all except Harry S. Truman and his personal crowd. They were desperate, and I was a possible port in a storm."

On Sunday, July 4, veteran Jersey City Democratic boss Frank "I am the Law" Hague jumped on board, hastily convening a meeting of the state's convention delegation to unanimously endorse "the people's choice," Eisenhower. On July 5, Tennessee governor Jim Nance McCord (a progressive product of Ed "Boss" Crump's notorious Memphis machine) pledged his state's twenty-eight delegates to Ike. From Washington radio station WINX, Alabama's John Sparkman (a "terribly concerned American citizen") urged Ike to "respond to the call of duty" and run, providing ten reasons why he should. "We are concerned," Sparkman chided Truman, "because we do not ourselves seem to have leaders in office or clamoring for office who are equal to the task of guiding us in this crucial and perilous era." In Vicksburg, Mississippi, conservative senator John C. Stennis informed a crowd of fifteen thousand that he too favored Ike.

But for all the thunder, the urge to stampede was hardly unanimous, for as former federal judge Thurman Arnold quipped, "Never have so few been led by so many."

From Charleroi, Pennsylvania, Ike's electrical engineer brother, Earl—who had once said, "Dwight would be considered a liberal by Republicans and a conservative by Democrats. He is slightly left of center, but close to center"—dashed cold water on any Eisenhower candidacy.

In Washington, liberal stalwart David Lilienthal, the former director of FDR's Tennessee Valley Authority, confided to his diary on July 5, 1948: "I am simply aghast at the unfair way in which President Truman is being 'judged,' if the current lynch law atmosphere can be called 'judging.' And the attitude of liberals and progressives, so whooping it up for Eisenhower or Douglas, is the hardest to understand or be other than damn mad about . . . my God! What *do* these people want?"

And to his own private journal the next day, Truman wrote: "Met with Democratic strategy board. Everything in order. Jim Roosevelt, Jake Arvey, A.D.A. and Frank Hague are for Eisenhower. Doublecrossers all. But they'll get nowhere—a doubledealer never does."

Secretary of State Marshall dispatched State Department counselor Chip Bohlen to ascertain Eleanor Roosevelt's thoughts on her sons' actions. Bohlen's prying only irritated her. She testily wrote to Marshall:

> Mr. Bohlen told me that you felt this move would so jeopardize President Truman's standing that it would hurt the position of our foreign policy in the world. I hardly think that is really true. In an election year all countries know that the man who is at the head of the government may not win. [Yes, the United States must] have an election at a crucial time in the nation's history just as it was in 1940 and 1944, but we managed to have elections in both of those years when the rest of the countries gave up holding elections temporarily. I rather think we will weather holding an election this year.

Marshall apologized for troubling her.

The din necessitated yet another Eisenhower denial. On Monday, July 5, Ike stated: "I will not at this time identify myself with any political party and could not accept nomination for any public office." Truman, busy dedicating a monument to Venezuelan hero Simón Bolívar in 104-degree ("hotter than hell") Bolivar, Missouri, immediately recognized the jeopardy residing in Ike's "at this time" caveat. White House assistant press secretary Eben A. Ayers recorded to his journal that "the president showed some disgust . . . indicating he felt it was weasel-worded, and he referred to the general as a [s——] ass."

Nor was the import of Ike's words lost upon his potential acolytes. From Chicago, Jake Arvey announced: "In view of the general's . . . concept of duty, I am still of the belief that despite his unwillingness to be a candidate . . . that if the convention means to draft him, he cannot and will not refuse to serve his country." On Tuesday, July 6, Claude Pepper and James Roosevelt even proposed junking the Democratic label, urging that Ike run as "a national candidate," above party. "The Democratic party's rewards would lie in the tribute it would gain for its magnanimity in a time of crisis," said Pepper. The following day, Queens Democratic leader James A. Roe announced that he would present a resolution to the convention urging Truman to step aside in favor of Eisenhower. "Despite Eisenhower's statement that he is not a candidate," Roe contended, "no man can honestly turn down the nomination . . . at a time of crisis." Frank Hague publicly urged Harry Truman to personally nominate Eisenhower.

Truman's forces rallied. Convention sergeant at arms Leslie L. Biffle flooded the galleries with eighty police and fifty private detectives to stifle any pro-Eisenhower demonstrations. Over drinks on the White House's South Portico, Truman's aides assured him that even should Eisenhower declare his candidacy, his nomination was by no means guaranteed. Army secretary Kenneth Royall dared dissent. When the session adjourned, Truman bade Royall, Clark Clifford, and Treasury Secretary Snyder to remain. "I agree with you about Ike," Truman confided to Royall. "What can we do to prevent this from happening?"

Royall phoned Eisenhower and secured his consent for a more definite refusal. With Clark Clifford, Royall then drafted a lengthy statement, which Ike telegraphed on Friday, July 9, to Pepper, who promptly released it the press. It read in part:

> Under no conditions will I be in the position of repudiating or even seeming to swerve from the letter or spirit of my prior announcements.
>
> I will not violate my own conception of my appropriate sphere of duty.
>
> No matter under what terms, conditions or premises a proposal might be couched, I would refuse to accept the nomination.

In Jersey City, Frank Hague crushed out his cigar. "Truman, Harry Truman," he cried. "Oh my God."

20

"The bright sunshine of human rights"

While James Roosevelt's anti-Truman plot fizzled, his ostensibly pro-Truman effort rolled forward.

From Minneapolis on Sunday, July 4, he—along with forty-nine other prominent Democratic liberals—had issued a call to "actively seek, at Philadelphia, to make [the Truman Civil Rights Commission's] program a part of our party's platform for 1948."

Joining him were pro-Eisenhower Democrats Chester Bowles, Col. Jacob Arvey, and Minneapolis mayor Hubert Humphrey, together with a wide variety of party liberals standing aloof from their pro-Ike efforts: Herbert Lehman, Henry Morgenthau, Bronx boss Edward J. Flynn, U.S. senators Robert F. Wagner and James E. Murray, former Southern California congressman Will Rogers Jr., attorney Thurman Arnold, Pittsburgh mayor and Pennsylvania party boss David L. Lawrence, and AFL president William Green.

But for all these glorious names—Roosevelt included—it was the relatively unknown Humphrey who had pulled the petition together, drafted its message, and corralled its signatories.

And he would be heard from in Philadelphia.

Yet Harry Truman's nomination was not quite assured. Not everyone took Dwight Eisenhower at his word, and not all who did wanted to surrender. From Jersey City, Frank Hague issued this statement:

[I]t is inconceivable that the President would enter a campaign as important as this one without conferring with the Democratic leaders . . . and ascertaining the true sentiment of the people rather than relying upon the advice of a few inexperienced advisors.

If the President knew the real conditions and knew the disastrous results that confront the Democratic Party . . . I am sure that he would hesitate to subject the party to such a disastrous defeat. It is the duty of the Democratic leaders throughout the country not to sit idly by . . . but to advise him truthfully as to the real conditions in their respective states.

. . . I can advise the President that New Jersey will go [Republican] by over 300,000 votes, but . . . will remain in the Democratic column by 200,000 votes if General Eisenhower is a candidate and a close survey of states surrounding New Jersey will reveal the same condition.

And from South Carolina, segregationist Olin Johnston announced he would present a resolution urging Chairman Howard McGrath to call upon Truman to withdraw in favor of Ike. Hague and Johnston fought on.

Other anti-Truman activists shifted to Supreme Court justice William O. Douglas.

Like Glen Taylor, Bill Douglas was the offspring of an itinerant minister, a product of the Pacific Northwest, a child of poverty, no stranger to manual labor, and an ardent liberal. But while Taylor opted for itinerant minstrelsy, Douglas attended college, taught high school, and finally graduated from Columbia Law School. After considering a partnership with Tom Dewey (they could not agree on which name would be listed first), Douglas joined a prestigious Wall Street firm before assuming teaching positions, first at Columbia and then at Yale. In 1935, he joined the fledgling Securities and Exchange Commission, soon ingratiating himself with FDR (Roosevelt relished his stock of "risqué" stories and the fact that Douglas "played an interesting game of poker"). The *Saturday Evening Post* characterized him as "one of the most brilliant minds enlisted by the New Deal, and perhaps the most deadly and efficient administrator it has produced." In 1939, FDR made Douglas a surprise pick to the U.S. Supreme Court. Douglas was just forty.

He was, to say the least, a free spirit. Ultimately he married four times, and in 1948 his first marriage was in poor shape. In 1944, FDR may have also ultimately preferred Truman to Douglas because of reports concerning Douglas's drinking. He remained, however, a wit and an intellect, a favorite in New Deal circles—though when, in 1944, FDR presented Douglas's name to party insiders Hannegan, Pauley, Ed Flynn, and Chicago mayor Ed Kelly, they, in the words of George Allen, quickly countered that he "had no visible followers, with the possible exception of Ickes, who also had no visible followers, with the possible exception of Ickes."

Nonetheless, Douglas was the sort of fellow Harry Truman needed to reach out to as his popularity receded among party liberals. In the summer of 1945, Truman stood ready to offer Douglas the post of secretary of war. If Douglas nursed presidential ambitions—and he certainly did—he needed to vacate the court and position himself on a more traditional launching pad. Still, he vacillated. As "Tommy the Cork" Corcoran confided to a friend, "Bill has to make up his mind to take his chances, and he is never going to do it sitting up there waiting. . . . The days for that to happen are gone."

In February 1946, when Harold Ickes bolted the administration, Truman again looked to Douglas to join his cabinet and assuage growing liberal angst. Pressuring Douglas to take the Interior position were House Speaker Sam Rayburn and Rayburn's bumptious protégé, Texas congressman Lyndon Baines Johnson. "I had about three or four hours last night," said Douglas, "with Sam Rayburn and Lyndon, and the heat is really on."

Again, Douglas refused.

For his part, Johnson considered Douglas "an awfully curious fellow." Playing the psychoanalyst, LBJ diagnosed Douglas as insecure, informing Corcoran that Douglas had confessed that he "had lived on the other side of the tracks. He didn't have any magic. So I asked him what folks on the other side of the tracks would think of him if [the country] went right straight to hell and he had a chance to save it and didn't do anything."

LBJ contended that he had told Douglas he "had his chance now to get the goddamn ball and run with it and we'd all run with him, and [that] he couldn't do much for the three-fourths of the people of the world that couldn't read the Atlantic Charter with his ass up there on that [Supreme] Court."

Douglas wouldn't budge, though he should have. "I had two classmates [at Columbia]," recalled federal judge Simon Rifkind, "who wanted to be President . . . , one [Dewey] who ran for the office, and one [Douglas] who didn't. [Douglas] just wanted the office handed to him, but he wanted it just as much as the other."

With an Eisenhower candidacy even less likely, some bitter-end Truman opponents scampered once more toward Douglas. Hubert Humphrey stood ready to nominate him. Walter Reuther and the ADA's Joe Rauh and Leon Henderson raised funds. Michael Straight, editor of Henry Wallace's old magazine, the *New Republic*, endorsed him. In Newark, a group of supporters, some attired in judicial robes, distributed Douglas literature to rush-hour commuters. "The Democratic party," argued the boisterous Henderson, "must choose Douglas or invite a disaster that will imperil the future of progressivism in America."

But huge portions of the disparate Eisenhower coalition wanted no part of Bill Douglas. Southerners feared his liberalism. Big-city bosses—Arvey, Flynn, and Hague—distrusted his electability.

"I am not a candidate," Douglas announced on Friday, July 9, from his remote Wallowa, Oregon, fishing cabin, "have never been a candidate and don't plan to be a candidate." But he still harbored some hopes that he might yet wear the crown without having to reach for it. When reporters asked if he would accept a draft, his resolution turned to vacillation. "I have no comment on that," he purred.

Douglas wouldn't run. Claude Pepper would.

Declaring that "this is no time for politics as usual," Pepper argued that his late-blooming candidacy was "no gesture but a fight." He established a headquarters at Philadelphia's Warwick Hotel, very recently home to the ill-fated Stassen and Warren candidacies. Joe Rauh quickly endorsed Pepper, but Leon Henderson had finally had enough. "We have already had two dark horses shot from under us," said Henderson. "Why the hell should we get up and ride on a red roan?"

Even in Claude Pepper's Florida they asked that question. Only 6.5 votes declared themselves for their senior senator; the rest remained committed to the state primary winner, segregationist Mississippi governor Fielding L. Wright. Pepper boasted no delegates elsewhere.

Scripps-Howard columnist Robert Ruark noted:

The almost ridiculous plight of the Democrats in '48 was capsuled on [Philadelphia's] Walnut Street, around the corner from headquarters. There . . . men were removing the name "Eisenhower" from vivid signs which said "Eisenhower—People's Choice for President." All day long you could see just "People's Choice for President" looking forlorn—a promise without a prophet. Then, in the dusk, there was activity again. Three Negro men, on stepladders, were busy painting a new name under "People's Choice for President." There it was, in small red letters: "Claude Pepper." In a way, it was more sad than funny.

Then came Saturday evening, July 10, the date scheduled for James Roosevelt and Jake Arvey's stop-Truman caucus. At 6:55 PM, reduced to Claude Pepper, they announced their meeting was cancelled.

"Tell those amateurs at the ADA," snapped Harry Truman, "that any shithead behind this desk can get re-nominated."

Unless, of course, Dwight Eisenhower wanted the nomination.

The Ike boom expired reluctantly, but it expired nonetheless. At Philadelphia, the Texas delegation posted a mock Ike-induction notice on its bulletin board, reading: "Order for induction. We couldn't refuse the draft. You can't refuse ours." But Ike could refuse, and he did. At the Bellevue-Stratford Hotel, a burly former Army mess sergeant named Monty Snyder pinned an Eisenhower-for-President button on Ike's friend George Allen's jacket. Allen waited for Snyder to trundle off before stuffing it into his pocket. "Four years from now," promised Allen, "you'll see a lot of these buttons at the convention. I'll save it for that day."

But if it were not Ike, it could be no one but Truman. In late June, Gallup had polled Democrats and revealed that, without Eisenhower, any ADA backed dump-Harry move inspired little confidence. The old adage proved true yet again—you can't beat somebody with nobody—and Gallup's numbers read:

Harry Truman	76%
Gen. George C. Marshall	10%
James F. Byrnes	3%
Harry F. Byrd	2%
James V. Forrestal	1%
James A. Farley	1%
William O. Douglas	1%
No Choice	6%

But while the nomination seemed settled, the platform—or, at least, one key portion of it—did not.

The battle that Harry Truman's Civil Rights Commission had ignited was about to erupt into a war to be fought on the convention floor. Southerners angled for a plank affirming the inviolability of states' rights. "What we must have," demanded Florida's Charles E. Sheppard, a member of the platform and resolutions committee, "is a plank setting forth, in unmistakable terms, that this is 'the United Sovereign States of America,' and in it the states may handle their own internal affairs."

Minimally, Southerners required—as Howard McGrath had promised Strom Thurmond—an almost verbatim repetition of 1944's innocuous plank, to read: "We believe that racial and religious minorities have the right to live, develop and vote equally with all citizens and share the rights that are guaranteed by our constitution. Congress should exert its full constitutional powers to protect those rights."

What satisfied minorities and party liberals in 1944, however, no longer sufficed four years later. As the NAACP's Walter White insisted, "The Democratic party can demonstrate its right to exist only by . . . adopting an unequivocal position on civil rights such as the President's committee recommended. If it does not have the courage to cleanse itself of the barnacles of bigotry its southern wing has affixed to it, it has no right to continue to exist. The day of reckoning has come." Reinforcing White's words were the National Negro Council's actions. In early July, it presented petitions bearing 1.2 million signatures to Truman, Dewey, Taft, and House Speaker Joe Martin, demanding complete implementation of the Truman civil rights program.

Democrats, caught in the cross fire of their own contrary internal elements, faced an unexpected threat from the 1948 GOP platform.

"Republicans . . . had adopted a relatively forward-looking civil rights plank," recalled Hubert Humphrey. "If we had been mild, the Republicans might have seized the issue by default. I felt that was ideologically absurd and politically stupid. So I came down hard on the side of a strong civil rights plank, both as a matter of conscience and . . . political pragmatism."

Humphrey did not exaggerate. The GOP platform was far more specific than any policy statement Democrats planned. The 1948 Democratic plank, with some embellishment, essentially reiterated its 1944 pronouncement:

> The Democratic party is responsible for the great civil rights gains made in recent years in eliminating unfair and illegal discrimination based on race, creed, or color.

> The Democratic Party commits itself to continuing its efforts to eradicate all racial, religious, and economic discrimination. We again state our belief that racial and religious minorities must have the right to live, the right to work, the right to vote, the full and equal protection of the law, on a basis of equality with all citizens as guaranteed by the Constitution. We again call upon the Congress to exert its full authority to the limit of its constitutional powers to assure and protect these rights.

The 1948 GOP plank read:

> Lynching or any other form of mob violence anywhere is a disgrace to any civilized state, and we favor the prompt enactment of legislation to end this infamy.

> One of the basic principles of this Republic is the equality of all individuals in their right to life, liberty, and the pursuit of happiness. This principle is enunciated in the Declaration of Independence and embodied in the Constitution of the United States; it was vindicated on the field of battle and became the cornerstone of this Republic. This right of equal opportunity to work and to advance in life should never be limited in any individual because of race, religion, color, or country of origin. We favor the enactment and just enforcement of such Federal

legislation as may be necessary to maintain this right at all times in every part of this Republic.

We favor the abolition of the poll tax as a requisite to voting.

We are opposed to the idea of racial segregation in the armed services of the United States.

The Democratic Party power structure, wary of increasing Southern alienation, believed that it had progressed as far as prudence dictated. "The words to which liberals objected," Clark Clifford noted in his memoirs, "were hardly a betrayal of the civil rights movement; they should have been sufficient to hold the party together through the convention."

Hubert Humphrey, of course, differed. Elected mayor of Minneapolis in 1945, he now stood poised for a run for Republican Joseph Ball's U.S. Senate seat. In 1944, progressive that he was, he had stood foursquare for Henry Wallace, shouting himself hoarse for the embattled Wallace at that year's convention. Recalled Drew Pearson, "Few will ever forget the sight of Humphrey and Barney Allen, a Red River Valley farmer, their clothes half torn off their back and their voices gone, racing through the Chicago Stadium carrying an American Flag and a Wallace banner, begging and pleading with the delegates to support their man."

By 1948, though no longer enamored of Wallace, Humphrey remained steadfastly disgusted by Truman. That March, he wrote to acting ADA chairman James Loeb:

How can we peacefully and effectively get rid of the present incumbent[?] There is no enthusiasm for Truman out here. Our right wing CIO and AFL boys are holding tough against the Third Party, but they keep asking me "Who are we for?" the tacit assumption being that we certainly aren't for Truman. . . .

If nothing happens soon we must act. Eisenhower, of course, would be a winning candidate. Douglas might not win. But at the margin we should take Douglas because we not only face defeat in November—we face the possible disintegration of the whole social-democratic bloc in this country. If we are going to lose, we ought to lose with a good candidate who can help us hold our forces together and, particularly, help us on the Congressional level.

"The reelection of the President," he argued to Chester Bowles, "is a political impossibility."

Humphrey was, in truth, galloping off in all directions—for Eisenhower one minute, for Douglas the next, running for the Senate, crusading for civil rights, and, most improbably and ambitiously of all, angling for the vice presidency.

On July 2, his South Dakota delegate–father wrote to him regarding how widely his ambitions were becoming known: "[Hubert Jr.'s assistant] Bill Simms informed me over the phone the other night that you contemplated having your name presented to the Convention as a candidate for vice president, that Mrs. Roosevelt would nominate you, and that you wanted me to give one of the seconding speeches."

Logically and traditionally, any change to the platform should have been accomplished within the 108-member Resolutions Committee, but despite Hubert's maneuvering (a slightly drunken Illinois Senator Scott Lucas accused him of double-dealing) his attempt to strenghten his party's tepid civil rights plank failed seventy to thirty, and not since 1932, when the party's Prohibition plank had been reversed via a floor fight, had the convention seriously amended its platform from the floor.

"Practically everybody thought there was nothing to lose by carrying the fight further," recalled Minnesota National Committeewoman Eugenie "Genie" Anderson. "But at the caucus the best count was about 150 [votes] sure and 100 probable for the Minority report, which we didn't think was too bad. We didn't have any idea we could really win."

As Humphrey attacked from the left, Southern Democrats counterpunched from the right. Satisfied with neither the 1944 plank nor the proposed 1948 version, and angered by Truman's initiatives (Georgia's Richard Russell considered HST's program "a vicious and unwarranted attack . . . on our Southern civilization"), they demanded an affirmation of states' rights principles. Former Texas governor Dan Moody ("I have never bolted a Convention, and I never intend to") and fourteen other delegates from eight Southern states proposed the following substitute plank:

The Democratic Party stands for the principles that the Constitution contemplated and established a union of indestructible sovereign states and that under the Constitution the general Federal Government and the separate States have their separate fields of power and permitted activities.

Traditionally it has been, and it remains a part of the faith of the Democratic Party that the Federal Government shall not encroach upon the reserved powers of the States by centralization of government or otherwise. Within the reserve powers of the States, to be exercised subject to the limitations imposed by the Fourteenth and Fifteenth Amendments to the Constitution on the manner of their exercise, is the power to regulate and control local affairs and act in the exercise of the police power.

Moody's states' rights plank failed ignominiously, 925 to 309, receiving only three votes from outside the South, all from the Far West—fractional votes from California, Wyoming, Oregon, Colorado, and Alaska.

Humphrey's moment had arrived. Proponents of the official plank excoriated him for rocking the boat, further disrupting unity in a party already dangerously rent by factionalism. If he lost, he would be anathema to the party establishment. Scott Lucas jeered, "Who does this pipsqueak think he is?" The Resolutions Committee chair, Pennsylvania senator Frances Myers, remained similarly unimpressed. White House minorities adviser David K. Niles warned the ADA's Joe Rauh, "Joe, you won't get fifty votes for your minority plank and all you'll do is ruin the chances of the best liberal product to come down the pike in years." If Humphrey triumphed—and the South bolted—he might very well be condemned for his party's ultimate defeat, perhaps, even, for its dissolution.

Norman Thomas warned the minority plank's cosponsor, former Milwaukee congressman and former Socialist and Progressive, Andrew J. Biemiller, "Oh, Andy, stop the nonsense, you can't get a civil rights plank into that platform." Muriel Humphrey worried for her husband's future. Still, she advised him to fight on. So did his father.

After first advising retreat, Hubert Sr. finally conceded, "This may tear the party apart, but if you feel strongly, then you've got to go with it. You can't run away from your conscience, son. You've got to go with it."

"What do you think will happen?" his son asked.

"I don't know," the senior Humphrey responded. "But you'll at least have the eight votes of the South Dakota delegation."

Humphrey wavered. For three hours, Biemiller, Genie Anderson, and Minnesota Democratic Farm Labor Party secretary Orville L. Freeman (Hubert's best friend) sat up with him to urge him forward. "All right," he finally concluded, "I'll do it."

Though the stakes were high for Humphrey—particularly with a Senate seat on the line—it would be an exaggeration to see him as standing alone, or even at the forefront of a small phalanx of hardy idealists. From the start he had enjoyed the tacit sympathy of bosses Flynn, Arvey, and Pennsylvania's David Lawrence, men whose liberalism had been tempered with practicality. Their hold on power often rested upon minority support. They could not risk black and Jewish votes jumping aboard the Dewey bandwagon—or into the Wallace camp.

Humphrey—now pretending rather transparently to be an administration loyalist, sporting a bright yellow Truman button—sat nervously on the platform, awaiting his turn to address the convention. "Look, here's what we're asking," he said, nearly apologetically, to Ed Flynn. "It isn't too much. We think we ought to make the fight. I'm sure we don't really have much chance to carry it, but we ought to make the fight. We surely would welcome your advice."

"You kids are right," Flynn reassured Humphrey; "you know what you're doing. This is the only way we can win this election. Stir up the minorities." Flynn summoned Arvey and Lawrence to the dais, begging, "Can't you fellows swing your delegations? I'll swing New York." They agreed, as did Connecticut state boss John Bailey.

Hubert Humphrey might not win, but he would not be humiliated by the vote to follow.

Andy Biemiller made the actual motion for the minority plank. Hubert Humphrey's address to the convention was technically merely a seconding motion—perhaps the most famous and significant seconding address in history.

It was, by Humphrey standards, an exceedingly succinct effort (Biemiller: "He knew he had to be shorter"), only eight minutes long, but he held the crowd and swept them along:

We are confronted by emotionalism on all sides, but there is no single religion, no single class, no single racial group. President Truman had the courage to issue a new emancipation proclamation. . . .

My friends, to those who say that we are rushing this issue of civil rights, I say to them we are 172 years late. To those who say that this civil rights program is an infringement on states' rights, I say this: The time has arrived in America for the Democratic Party to get out of the shadow of states' rights and to walk forthrightly into the bright sunshine of human rights. People—human beings—this is the issue of the 20th century. People of all kinds—all sorts of people—and these people are looking to America for leadership, and they're looking to America for precept and example.

My good friends, my fellow Democrats, I ask you for a calm consideration of our historic opportunity. Let us forget the evil passions and the blindness of the past. In these times of world economic, political, and spiritual— above all spiritual crisis, we cannot and we must not turn from the path so plainly before us. That path has already led us through many valleys of the shadow of death. And now is the time to recall those who were left on that path of American freedom.

For all of us here, for the millions who have sent us, for the whole two billion members of the human family, our land is now, more than ever before, the last best hope on earth. And I know that we can, and I know that we shall [begin] here the fuller and richer realization of that hope, that promise of a land where all men are truly free and equal, and each man uses his freedom and equality wisely well.

My good friends, I ask my Party, I ask the Democratic Party, to march down the high road of progressive democracy. I ask this convention to say in unmistakable terms that we proudly hail, and we courageously support, our President and leader Harry Truman in his great fight for civil rights in America!

"It was the President's name, spoken without quibble or apology, which seemed to lift the convention out of its lethargy," observed columnist Holmes Alexander. "The appeal sounded through the Convention Hall like a trumpet.

It proved to all who saw it happen that, regardless of weasel platform words and other failures, this was a liberty-minded convention, representing a party that will go down fighting."

Millions of Americans watched Humphrey on television; uncounted millions more heard him on radio. As the roll call commenced, however, his cause still seemed uncertain. Then came South Dakota—"I am Hubert H. Humphrey Sr.," announced its chairman. "I cast South Dakota's eight votes for the plank"—and his son's minority plank finally assumed its lead.

Hubert Humphrey Sr. was not the only delegate in support—so (though very grudgingly) were Scott Lucas and Frances Myers, dragooned into assent by their respective state bosses. Lucas, recalled Biemiller, "was willy-nilly voted . . . for our minority plank; because Arvey just voted everybody. Francis Myers was . . . willy-nilly voted for our plank, because Dave Lawrence just voted everybody. [Brooklyn congressman] Manny Celler made the speech defending the majority plank. He was willy-nilly voted for the minority plank by Ed Flynn. Very curious development."

It remained, however, a very closely run game, not pushed to completion until Biemiller's Wisconsin cast its votes. The final tally: 651.5 to 582.5.

From New York, Eleanor Roosevelt wrote in her daily column that "the Democratic party took one step toward greatness." In Washington, Harry Truman grimly watched on his $1,795 DuMont combination television-radio-phonograph. "Platform fight in dead earnest," he confided testily to his journal. "Crackpot Biemiller from Wisconsin offers a minority report on civil rights. . . . The Convention votes down States Rights and votes for the crackpot amendment to the Civil Rights Plank. The crackpots hope the South will bolt."

In Philadelphia, an outraged Bull Connor tried to obtain the floor after the full platform had passed. Sam Rayburn gaveled him down and ordered a recess. "We're not going to walk [out]," vowed Connor, "it's too slow. We are going to fly."

21

"Behold, the validity of Christian principles"

The Democratic Party had a platform. It still possessed little chance of victory.

When its temperament wasn't angry, it was dismal. "We got the wrong rigs for this convention," quipped one Philly cabdriver. "They shoulda given us hearses."

"The index to the mood of this slowly assembling party," noted *New York Times* reporter Meyer Berger, "was outstanding in the Texas headquarters in the Ben Franklin Hotel. Even Texans whispered, probably for the first time in history."

To assist in reigning-in opposition, convention organizers had retaliated against dissidents through a judicious allocation of accommodations. As columnist George Dixon observed:

> You can almost tell how a state delegation stands with Chairman McGrath and the Die-with-Truman forces by the kind of hotel accommodations they've been allotted. I do not wish to be too specific because many hotels are inclined to be touchy about being referred to as fleabags, but you ought to see what some of the southern delegates have drawn. To rub it in, the loudest dissenters against Truman and his civil rights program have been housed on the edge of the colored district.
>
> Mayor Hague, of Jersey City, and Jacob Arvey of Chicago, evaded punitive measures by McGrath. They made their own hotel arrangements a long time ago.

The opening sessions contained the usual hoopla: an invocation by Philadelphia's eighty-two-year-old Dennis Cardinal Dougherty; "The Star-Spangled Banner" sung by national anthem specialist Lucy Monroe (she would ultimately sing it more than five thousand times); Mrs. India Edwards, executive director of the party's Women's Division, waving a $1.10 piece of "top round steak" to illustrate high food prices and releasing a balloon out of a box to illustrate inflation; and a paean to FDR by Hollywood star Van Heflin. Supporting Bill Douglas, twenty-two-year-old New Yorker Winifred Galbraith Todd, "Miss Equestrienne of 1948," galloped her horse into arena confines. "Hey, lady!" yelled assistant sergeant at arms William Romano, "He can't come in here. He hasn't got a badge!"

And, of course, there was television. The *New York Times* reported not only that NBC's Dick Smith was applying brown lipstick to female speakers (it photographed better), but that all Democratic politicians present, male and female alike, would wear a makeup formula known as "clown white." In the commentary department, CBS took the lead, with its team of Edward R. Murrow, Quincy Howe, and Douglas Edwards "very much in a class by itself. Some of Mr. Murrow's ad-lib quips were far and away the most amusing words heard all week in Philadelphia, reflecting as they did a good-natured yet perceptive sense of detachment that was truly mature journalism."

But the big event was Senator Alben W. Barkley's Monday evening convention keynote speech.

Born in a Kentucky log cabin, Barkley (né Willie Alben Barkley) was elected to the House in 1912. He narrowly lost a hard-fought Kentucky gubernatorial primary in 1923, but that campaign enabled him to capture a U.S. Senate seat three years later. By 1933 he was assistant Senate majority leader, and four years after that he assumed the majority leader's post, having survived a tough 1936 primary against conservative Gov. (and later Commissioner of Baseball) A. B. "Happy" Chandler. Barkley might have been his party's vice-presidential nominee in 1944, but for a very public tussle that February concerning FDR's veto of tax legislation. Rather than support Roosevelt's inflammatory veto ("not a tax bill but a tax-relief bill, providing relief not for the needy but for the greedy"), the invariably tractable and pro–New Deal Barkley exploded that FDR's statement was "a calculated and deliberate assault upon the legislative integrity of every member of the Congress." He resigned his position, urging his colleagues to override Roosevelt. Unanimously reelected majority leader, he had dealt FDR a mighty embarrassment.

In spite of this, with Henry Wallace's fortunes in disarray, Barkley, having coveted the vice presidency since 1928, hoped finally to win his place on a national ticket. Like Jimmy Byrnes, he had even asked Truman to nominate him. Assigned, however, to nominate FDR in 1944, when Barkley discovered that Roosevelt would accept only Truman or Douglas as the vice-presidential nominee, he flew into a rage. A similarly miffed Jimmy Byrnes advised Barkley "not to say anything too complimentary" about FDR.

Jim Farley commiserated, "Alben, you have been double-crossed by the boss—just as I was," but he finally dissuaded the disgusted Barkley from literally tearing up his prepared text.

Barkley's relationship with FDR ran no smoother than it would run with Truman. The Missourian had supported the conservative Finance Committee chair, Pat Harrison of Mississippi, rather than the more liberal Barkley in 1937 (even crossing the White House to do so). Barkley triumphed by a single vote. "I have often wondered," Barkley mused, "how I would have felt about Harry Truman if I had lost . . . by one vote."

Relations were no more amicable when Truman hopscotched over Barkley to assume the presidency. Observed columnist Tris Coffin, "Senator Barkley had no cause for personal loyalty to Mr. Truman. In the Senate, Harry Truman was just another youngster Barkley had patiently guided along. Later, President Truman ignored his Senate leader in White House huddles.

"Many times, in private, the good nature of the courtly Kentuckian broke down in angry complaint at the President's indifference to party chiefs in Congress."

Everything Harry Truman lacked as an orator, Alben Barkley possessed. In fact, he was so marvelous that for years (due to the financial necessity of supporting his invalid wife, Dorothy) he augmented his congressional income with appearances as a professional speaker. "He frequently went to the Senate floor sleepless to face a killing day of debate and cloakroom wrangling," recalled George Allen. "I came to think of him in those times—and so did most of his friends—as a sort of modern-day saint."

Delivered from memory, Barkley's 1948 keynote address proved to be a stem-winder—electrifying a dispirited gathering, and providing the party with its first cause for hope in months.

Commencing with a program-by-program apologia for the New Deal, Barkley progressed to slashing attacks upon the GOP. "I am not an expert on cobwebs," he jibed, "but, if my memory does not betray me, when the Democratic Party took over the Government of the United States sixteen years ago, even the spiders were so weak from starvation that they could not weave a cobweb in any department of the government in Washington."

Unloading on aged former Pennsylvania GOP boss Joe Grundy, Barkley provided this parody of the eighteenth-century hymn, "All Hail the Power of Jesus' Name":

All Hail the Power of Grundy's Name,

Let candidates prostrate fall,

Bring forth the Republican diadem,

And crown him boss of all.

"A bureaucrat," he continued, "is a Democrat who holds an office that some Republican wants."

Drawing near to his conclusion, Barkley turned more serious:

Behold the gentle touch of tender hand upon millions and millions of children who long for life and bread and happiness and education and for a full life. They are heard knocking at our door.

Behold, destiny itself knocks at the door in behalf of all these things. Shall we hear the voice and open the door, or shall we slam it in the face of an appealing world; turn our backs upon a divine obligation and refuse to lead the children of men out of the boundaries of fear and slavery into a free world and a free life?

As one . . . who has stood by the side of Wilson and Roosevelt and Truman to make his humble contribution to rescue and preserve the things by which men wish to live, and for which they are willing to die, may I in reverence and deep sincerity utter this simple prayer: "God of our fathers, lead Thou us on. As a nation, as a people, and as an assembly of people, give us wisdom to see the path of our duty, and courage to keep our feet upon it. Amen."

Barkley had electrified the formerly listless crowd. For twenty-eight minutes it lustily shouted, applauded, marched, and cheered—and Barkley was in no mood to halt their frenzy. The band erupted into "My Old Kentucky Home" and FDR's old anthem, "Happy Days Are Here Again." The ever-flexible James Roosevelt bounded onto the podium to furiously pump Barkley's hand. "One of the greatest speeches I ever heard in my life," he gushed. A delegate quickly crossed out the "Vice" in his "Barkley for Vice President" placard.

A moment in history was taking shape. "This was the last chance to stop Harry Truman," Tris Coffin wrote. "If Alben Barkley had said, 'Yes,' or even just nodded his head and slipped out of town, he could have had the top spot in an uproar of acclamation."

"It was no secret," said the *St. Louis Post-Dispatch*, "that many of the delegates would have preferred . . . [Barkley] . . . in place of President Truman."

Yet Barkley drew back. Perhaps he, like Harry Truman, knew that the quiet power of incumbency easily overcomes the noise of crowds and bands. Perhaps a man who covets the *vice* presidency for twenty years suspects his own limitations more than others might realize. That evening, delegates from seventeen states trouped to Barkley's Bellevue-Stratford suite to inform him that his moment might finally be now. He declined, explaining, "I'd rather be loyal than President."

The supposedly opportunistic Biffle also drew back. In fact, he did more than that. The White House feared grievously that if, on the presidential roll call, Alabama yielded to Kentucky, and the Bluegrass State nominated its favorite son, all might still unravel for Truman. Accordingly, Biffle approached Alabama senators Lister Hill and John Sparkman to entreat them to hold their delegation in line. He succeeded. Alabama would not yield to Kentucky.

Only Harry Truman's segregationist opponents now stood between him and the nomination. They had planned to nominate Arkansas governor Ben Laney, but it now appeared Laney would receive only between a hundred and a hundred-and-fifty votes. Possessing little stomach for lost causes, Laney dropped out. Replacing him, however, was a far more formidable figure: Georgia's Richard B. Russell.

On Wednesday evening, July 16, Macon attorney Charles J. Bloch placed Russell in nomination, bluntly warning his fellow Democrats:

> I say to you delegates from all parts of the nation here assembled, you know, or if you do not know, you can learn here and now, you cannot longer take the south for granted. . . .

> I do not mean to suggest, even, secession from the Democratic Party, but I do mean to say to you Democrats of the north and west and the east, paraphrasing the language of the great commoner of a generation ago, "You shall not crucify the south on this cross of civil rights."

> The south has accomplished so much in the last eighty-three years; when Lee and Johnson and the other leaders of the Southern Confederacy were forced to surrender, and their war-weary soldiers tread their forlorn way homeward, they were left to fend for themselves. There was no treaty of peace. There was no Southern Recovery Program. There was no Marshall Plan for us. We had to use the force bill, bayonet rule, and the tragic era of reconstruction which ended only with the [Rutherford] Hayes-[Samuel] Tilden [presidential] election of 1880, and we do not propose to return to that tragic era of reconstruction in the vehicle of "civil rights."

Strom Thurmond seconded Russell. "We do not wish to take from any American his constitutional rights," Thurmond contended, "but we do not intend that our constitutional rights shall be sacrificed for the selfish and the sordid purpose of gaining minority votes in doubtful states."

Missouri governor Phil M. Donnelly had collapsed from the 104-degree heat in Bolivar a few days earlier, but he had recovered sufficiently to nominate Harry Truman. Truman, said Donnelly, was "a man of the people. He understands the problems and speaks the language of the average man and woman. . . . [He is] a soldier, patriot, and statesman, whose splendid courage has never faltered, in war or in peace, and who is today leading this nation to a new and greater destiny."

California's Will Rogers Jr. ("They say that Harry Truman is a man of small stature . . . ") seconded Donnelly's motion. A former Fielding Wright delegate from Florida quixotically rose to nominate handsome but hard-drinking former Indiana governor Paul V. McNutt. No second followed, and 1948's Democratic nominations were concluded.

It was not close. Harry Truman, given up for dead so many times in the preceding months, bested Russell 947.5 to 263. Paul McNutt secured half a vote, not from Florida, but from Vermont.

It was customary for the nomination to now be acclaimed unanimous—particularly for a sitting president. But convention chairman Sam Rayburn sensed that tempers still ran too high for such niceties. He never made that motion, and Russell's votes stood.

Harry S. Truman remained the champ—but only by a split decision.

22

"An interesting and instructive evening"

Willie Alben might have wowed them, but Harry Truman still wanted Bill—William O. Douglas—as his running mate.

Continuing to believe that the South had nowhere to go and the liberals did (or, at least, might inflict greater damage by staying home), Truman concentrated his fire on the ever-reluctant Supreme Court justice.

He had other choices, as well, of varying degrees of charm: the jug-eared ADA chairman and former Louisville mayor Wilson W. Wyatt (Ed Flynn's suggestion); House minority leader John W. McCormack of Massachusetts; New York City Planning Commission chairman (and son of a United States senator) Robert F. Wagner Jr.; governors Mon C. Wallgren (Washington) and William Preston Lane (Maryland); and senators Scott Lucas (Illinois), Millard E. Tydings (Maryland), and Joseph O'Mahoney (Wyoming). O'Mahoney coveted the job so overtly, he opened a headquarters on the mezzanine of the Bellevue-Stratford Hotel. Howard McGrath, however, warned against placing a fellow Catholic on the ticket. Tydings famously suffered from both conspicuous conservatism and unbridled vanity.

Also angling was the idealistic but intensely ambitious newcomer, Hubert Humphrey. "Mayor Humphrey asks your advice. In view of Franklin's experience in 1920," his ADA allies Jim Loeb, Joe Rauh, and Eugenie Anderson had inquired of Eleanor Roosevelt, "should Hubert accept the vice-presidential nomination with Truman if he can get it?"

"Of course," she advised, recalling her husband's experience in 1920. "You're going to get better known."

She too was being mentioned—though she wanted no part of any of it.

"She [Eleanor] is the only person in the party qualified to tear the Roosevelt mantle from Mr. Wallace," Republican Clare Boothe Luce publicly advised, "and by sharing it with Mr. Truman, partially restore it to him." Mrs. Luce further calculated that selecting a woman "would challenge the loyalty of women everywhere to their sex, [as] the defeat of the ticket meant the defeat for a hundred years of women's chance to be truly equal with men in politics."

Eleanor was not in the habit of taking advice from Clare—and didn't.

Which transported Harry Truman back, as always, to Bill Douglas.

As the convention neared, Douglas had remained holed up at his remote Oregon fishing cabin, though not so distant from civilization that he could not be reached via party-line phone at a nearby U.S. Forest Service station. Author—and former New Deal insider, former *Time* and *Fortune* factotum, *and* former British Communist Party member—Eliot Janeway recalled one attempt by administration forces, through him, to cajole Douglas:

> We did it as burlesque [expecting the results of the conversation to be quickly relayed to the White House], you see? . . . It was obviously an open line: "Hey, Bill, I'm sitting in the Warwick Hotel in Philadelphia and I'm a pretty important fellow." He said, "Well, I know that. Why are you bothering with me?" I said, "Bob Hannegan instructed me to. That's what proves I'm so important." He said, "What did he instruct you to do?" "To call you and tell you to go on the ticket and say if you did . . . you'd have the [presidential] nomination in 1952." He said, "Call Bob back and say he got there late. Stu Symington [then secretary of the Air Force and close to both Truman and Douglas] and [attorney] Abe Fortas have called and given me the same message.["] I said, "Well you've got the message from me. So that means the message is confirmed from them. I'll call Bob back and tell him I gave you the message." He said, "[Y]ou're a good reporter. I'm sure you'll get it straight."

On Friday afternoon, July 9, it fell to Harry Truman himself to grovel before the great Douglas. Douglas said he'd think about it, and requested that Truman phone him again on Monday morning—just as the convention was beginning.

In his journal, a furious Truman recorded:

McGrath calls me from Philadelphia and asks me to call Bill Douglas . . . and ask him to be candidate for Vice President. I call him, tell him I'm doing what FDR did to me. He owes it to the country to accept.

He belongs to that crowd of Tommy Corcoran, Harold Ickes, Claude Pepper crackpots whose word is worth less than Jimmy Roosevelt's. I hope he has a more honorable political outlook. No professional liberal is intellectually honest. That's a real indictment—but true as the Ten Commandments. Professional liberals aren't familiar with the Ten Commandments or the Sermon on the Mount.

Most Roosevelts aren't either! Jimmy, Elliott and the mother used the White House for personal promotions, most of which cost investors. Terrible.

Yet Clark Clifford had recruited Eleanor Roosevelt to assist Truman in recruiting Douglas. She telegraphed the recalcitrant prospective candidate: "I feel you are the best judge of where your services are most valuable, but you would be of great value and give some confidence in the party to liberals if you accept. My confidence in your good judgment prevents my urging you to do anything but I want you to know that your acceptance would give hope to many for the future of a liberal Democratic party."

It would take more than Mrs. Roosevelt to recruit the elusive Douglas.

Douglas, tired of having "probably a dozen people listening in," had decided to take the president's Monday morning call on a private line at downtown Portland's posh Benson Hotel. In the interim, he recalled, he "talked with friends in Portland and there were dozens and dozens of telephone calls from people, some of whom wanted me to do it, and some of whom thought it would be silly. I was tempted to accept because I thought perhaps . . . I could have a voice in foreign policy, an idea I later learned to be utterly foolish. In spite of the gloomy prediction of Truman's chances, I thought at the time he could and would win. But I finally decided against it because, on balance, I concluded that my place was on the Court."

So, his decision was still no

Truman confided to his diary: "Douglas says he can't quit the Supreme Court. Says the family are of the opinion that his lack of political experience would cause trouble in the campaign. Says no to my request that he take second place on the ticket with me. I'm inclined to give some credence to Tommy Corcoran's crack to Burt Wheeler that Douglas had said he could 'not' be a No. 2 man to a No. 2 man."

It now came down to Alben Barkley, neither the best nor the worst of choices. Barkley had not grown any younger since 1944, when a dying FDR rejected him as too old for the job. Now seventy, Barkley would, if elected, be the oldest vice president ever to assume that office. Hailing from a border state, he added little geographically to the ticket. But coming from Kentucky was not altogether bad, as he might significantly shore up Truman's sagging popularity in such wavering neighboring states as West Virginia, Virginia, and Tennessee. He was sufficiently Southern and adequately liberal. He would do.

He would do—but would he do it?

In the wake of his masterful keynote address, Alben Barkley was feeling his oats, and was now unwilling to supplicate for a position for which he would have more than gladly begged four years—or two decades—previously.

Truman might have secured Barkley at bargain-basement prices as late as that Monday, but he had not, and neither he nor Barkley was particularly satisfied with the result. In his diary, Truman wrote:

Call old man Barkley and soothe his feathers so he'll go ahead and make the keynote speech.

McGrath calls me and suggests I call Barkley again and say I am not against him. I don't do it.

Barkley makes a real keynote speech. Ends up at midnight. I can't get him by phone. My "good" friend Leslie Biffle spends all his time as sergeant at arms of the convention running Barkley for President. I watched the demonstration on television. Having been in on numerous demonstrations I'm not fooled. I can see everything taking place on the platform. The "actors" forget that.

Barkley in his good speech mentions me only casually by name.

"It was a good index of how demoralized the Democrats had become," noted Margaret Truman, "that someone as normally loyal and dependable as Mr. Biffle would try to double-cross the President."

And as paranoid as Harry Truman seemed, he was indeed correct. Barkley *had* slighted him. Only *once* in the entire 6,300-word speech had he mentioned Truman by name, and this he did only as he concluded, lumping him together with Woodrow Wilson and FDR (thus mentioning the long-dead Wilson as many times as the not-quite-dead Truman). Harry Truman, ever alert to slights, knew precisely what he was, and was *not*, hearing.

The rumors—and the games—continued the next day. Truman wrote: "I called Barkley and smoothed him down again. Tried to call him last night after his good speech but can't get him. . . . [Secretary of the Treasury John] Snyder calls and says Jimmy R., Leon Henderson and Wilson Wyatt are running Barkley for President. Maybe so, but Barkley is an honorable man. He won't give me the double cross, I'm sure."

Truman's options had boiled down to Barkley. "The convention," as Jim Farley noted, not without pleasure, "made up the President's mind for him." Yet Truman still drew back. For though he considered Barkley an agreeable sort of party workhorse, he nonetheless appraised him as distinctly mediocre. Moreover, having held the vice presidency himself—and watched Henry Wallace hold it—Truman possessed little respect for the position, or for its selection process.

"Talking about the vice presidency," Eben Ayers recorded in his diary, "the president said he never did care much who was nominated to run with him. 'I stuck my neck all the way out for Douglas, and he cut the limb out from under me,' the president said."

Truman's strongest reason for pulling back from Barkley may have also been the rawest. "Barkley, though Senate Minority Leader, had not been invited to the White House for months at a time," noted 1948 campaign historian Jules Abels. "The reason is ascribed to 'jealousy'—Truman could not abide a strong and popular figure in the party other than himself."

As Truman dawdled, Barkley fumed. "It will have to come quick," the Kentuckian loudly complained to his friends. "I don't want it passed around so long it is like a cold biscuit."

Beyond that, word had reached him of the rumors of his "double-crossing" the president, which only fueled his rising anger.

"Would you take the vice-presidential nomination?" asked Les Biffle.

Barkley now huffed that he would *not*. Biffle argued that the ticket's chances for success were slim (conspicuously, Barkley had never once mentioned victory in his keynote address). Barkley, Biffle pointed out, would not really have to *be* vice president, but merely to *run* for vice president. Such a move would not only prevent the party from fracturing, it would also cement his position as Senate leader—and de facto *party* leader when Truman went down in flames. "If the ticket loses, you will be the active leader of the party," argued Biffle. "You can determine policy in Congress. You are the only man who can keep peace in the party. All the boys respect you."

Barkley surrendered.

"Why didn't you tell me you wanted to be vice president, Alben?" Truman disingenuously asked. "It's all right with me."

Barkley remained testy. "Mr. President," he answered, "you do not know it yet."

"Well, if I had known you wanted it, I certainly would have been agreeable."

"Mr. President, I appreciate that, but I know that you have considered other men for the nomination, so I just did not calculate upon it at all.

"But now, from what I hear, it looks as if the convention wants to nominate me as your running mate. I am not going to lift a finger to get the nomination, but, if the convention does nominate me, I think I should accept."

"I think you should accept, and I hope you will."

Wilson Wyatt nominated his fellow Kentuckian. A former New Dealer cajoled by Jake Arvey into running against Illinois governor Dwight Green provided one of the seconding speeches. Forty-eight-year-old patrician Adlai E. Stevenson had wanted to run for the U.S. Senate that year, but reluctantly ("It's now or never") had allowed himself to be drafted by Arvey for a long-shot run at the governorship. The Choate-educated Illinoisan and the former janitor Kentuckian, it turned out, were distant relatives—Stevenson's grandfather was a second cousin to Barkley's mother. "I am proud," proclaimed Stevenson, "to be able to call him my kinsman."

Thanks to Lister Hill's beneficence, Alabama's George Wallace was now a full delegate. He rose to nominate ("the South will not be crucified upon the cross of so-called civil rights") the trim and capable Richard Russell, but Russell had no great desire to oppose the wildly popular Barkley. A convention that would not nominate a sitting president unanimously nominated Alben Barkley by acclamation.

In his acceptance speech, Barkley, "with great pride and with deep humility," laid it on thick. "If anybody had told me when I left my home for Philadelphia . . . that I would leave here tomorrow as the nominee . . . I would have pronounced such person as a prophet without honor," he informed the crowd. "I did not come here as a candidate; I did not become one after I got here, and I was not one."

Harry Truman had long since arrived from Washington. Carefully watching on television from the White House, he had received a call from Treasury Secretary Snyder, advising him that he must entrain now if he wished to deliver his own acceptance address that evening. The presidential party—the Trumans, Clark Clifford, appointments secretary Matt Connelly, et al.—departed Washington's Union Station. Truman recorded the trip in his diary:

> Take the train for Philadelphia at 7 p.m. Eastern Daylight Time, arrive in the rain at 9:15. Television sets [i.e., reception] at both ends of trip. No privacy sure enough now.

> Hear Alabama & Mississippi walk out of the convention. Hear Gov. Donnelly nominate me. Both on the radio. Hard to hear. My daughter & my staff try to keep me from listening. Think maybe I'll be upset. I won't be.

He *should* have been upset. The convention had deteriorated into near chaos. It should have quickly wrapped up its remaining business. It had not. The balloting and the speeches and the unease dragged on and on. Southern delegates stalked out. It was, as Clark Clifford remembered, "perhaps the strangest evening of politics I ever witnessed."

Convention officials advised Truman to await his cue at a nearby hotel room. He decided otherwise, instead holing up in a room within the hall, which Clifford dubbed, none too fondly, the "Black Hole of Calcutta." Truman finally retreated to a balcony overlooking the stifling streetscape.

"Have a pleasant time visiting with Barkley out on a balcony of the hall back of the stage," noted Truman. "It was an interesting and instructive evening."

Recalled Margaret Truman less diplomatically, "Never have I seen so much smoke without a fire as I saw that humid night in Philadelphia. I thought sure I was going to expire. Oxygen was my only thought."

Compounding Truman's troubles was what Clifford later termed "a gastrointestinal upset"—and, perhaps, a larger problem.

He had not really prepared a speech.

Sam Rosenman and thirty-nine-year-old Truman administrative assistant Charles S. Murphy had collaborated on one version. Clark Clifford and speechwriter George Elsey had patched together an outline, but only an outline. Harry S. Truman, his back to the wall, would now wing the single most crucial address of the campaign—and of his career.

But before he took the platform, *near* chaos erupted into *true* chaos.

In the course of this horridly long evening, Chairman Rayburn had yelled himself hoarse, unsuccessfully pleading for the delegates to hold applause and for the band ("I could control this convention if I could run that band") to keep music to a minimum. They ignored him. With the convention running three hours and forty-three minutes behind schedule, Rayburn nevertheless undertook one last chore before introducing the exceedingly patient Truman: "I want to introduce Mrs. Emma Guffey Miller, Pennsylvania delegate-at-large. She has a surprise for us which I hope the convention will enjoy."

The plump, white-frocked, seventy-three-year-old Mrs. Miller, younger sister of former Pennsylvania senator Joseph Guffey, had prepared an elaborate, six-foot-high floral display composed of red and white carnations, in the shape of the Liberty Bell. Imprisoned inside it for several hours were forty-eight caged white pigeons, officially and symbolically designated "doves of peace." In the horrible heat, a couple had already expired. The band stoked up "Hail to the Chief," and the surviving birds—crazed by the noise, the lights, and the heat—exploded out of the opened "Liberty Bell."

All hell broke loose.

Pigeons flew into the rafters. They dive-bombed delegates. Men and women shouted, "Watch your clothes!"

"Though the press delicately did not mention it," noted Clark Clifford (who did), the "doves of peace began, not surprisingly, to drop the inevitable product of their hours of imprisonment on any delegate who had the bad luck to be underneath them."

Some birds landed on the platform. Rayburn frantically shushed them away. One nearly landed on his glistening, bald head. Another headed straight for the blades of a thirty-six-inch electric fan, saved from filleting only by Rayburn's quick action. "Get those damned pigeons out of here!" he screamed over live radio and TV.

"As [Truman] spoke," *Time* reported, "pigeons teetered on the balconies, on folds in the draperies, on overhead lights, occasionally launched on a quick flight to a more pigeonly position."

Thus, Harry Truman's choice of a crisp, double-breasted white suit that evening may not have been the wisest choice of the campaign. Nonetheless, at 1:54 AM, he strode to the rostrum, adjusted his microphones so he might better see the black, loose-leaf notebook containing his triple-spaced talking points, and began his talk—not just to weary, assembled Democrats, but to whatever small portion of the nation remained awake.

Cannily, he began by referencing the most popular man in the hall—"my good friend and colleague, Senator Barkley . . . a great man, and a great public servant" with a line that electrified the crowd: "Senator Barkley and I will win this election and make these Republicans like it—don't you forget that!"

Similarly feisty was his quick, almost angry challenge to the nation's farmers and workers:

> Farm income has increased from less than two-and-a-quarter billion dollars in 1932 to more than eighteen billion dollars in 1947. Never in the world were the farmers of any republic or any kingdom or any other country as prosperous as the farmers of the United States; and if they don't do their duty by the Democratic Party, they are the most ungrateful people in the world!

> Wages and salaries in this country have increased from twenty-nine billion in 1933 to more than 128 billion dollars in 1947. That's labor, and labor never had but one friend in politics, and that is the Democratic Party and Franklin D. Roosevelt.

And I say to labor what I have said to the farmers: They are the most ungrateful people in the world if they pass the Democratic Party by this year.

Truman did not mention Dewey once. He did, however, take almost instant note of the newly minted Republican platform, harshly contrasting it with the actions of the Republican Eightieth Congress. Delving into class warfare ("the favored classes or the powerful few"), he largely glossed over foreign policy (neither the word "Communist" nor "Soviet" nor any reference—however oblique—to Henry Wallace appears in the speech), concentrating withering fire on a range of bread-and-butter domestic issues. One by one, he progressed through a list of the Eightieth Congress's supposed deficiencies, centering on inflation and housing, but passing on to civil rights, taxes, social security, health care, the minimum wage, federal aid to education, and a recently enacted displaced persons immigration act ("this anti-Semitic, anti-Catholic law"). His delivery, however, was unsure, fumbling, and halting. Again he went through the same laundry list of issues. Though momentarily roused from its torpor by mention of the hated Taft-Hartley Act, the bone-weary crowd responded listlessly . . .

Until Truman spat out this challenge:

> There is a long list of these promises in that Republican platform. If it weren't so late, I would tell you all about them. I have discussed a number of these failures of the Republican Eightieth Congress. Every one of them is important. Two of them are of major concern to nearly every American family. They failed to do anything about high prices, they failed to do anything about housing.

> My duty as President requires that I use every means within my power to get the laws the people need on matters of such importance and urgency.

> I am therefore calling this Congress back into session July 26th.

> On the twenty-sixth day of July, which out in Missouri we call "Turnip Day," I am going to call Congress back and ask them to pass laws to halt rising prices, to meet the housing crisis—which they are saying they are for in their platform.

Observers almost unanimously pronounced the performance a home run. "Nothing short of a stroke of magic could infuse the remnants of the party with enthusiasm," *Newsweek* reported. "But magic he had; in a speech bristling with marching words, Mr. Truman brought the convention to its highest peak of excitement."

"It was a great speech for a great occasion," marveled journalist Max Lerner, hitherto no fan of Truman, "and as I listened I found myself applauding."

"It was fun to see the scrappy little cuss come out of his corner fighting," observed the *New Republic*'s normally acerbic Richard Strout, "not trying to use big words any longer, but beyond himself and saying a lot of honest things." Elsewhere, the *New Republic* headlined: THE FUNERAL IS CALLED OFF.

The even more veteran, congenitally acerbic H. L. Mencken saw something else.

"It was the snarling and defiant harangue of a badly scared man," said Mencken. "The more he whooped and hollered the more manifest it was that he was fighting with his back to the wall."

Harry Truman's back *was* to the wall, but that didn't matter. He'd fought that way before, in 1934 and 1940. He'd fought that way before—and won.

23

"The wool hat woman of Byron, Georgia"

As Harry Truman's train steamed away toward Washington's Union Station, twenty-two Mississippi and thirteen Alabama delegates stormed angrily out of Philadelphia's Democratic Convention, vowing "never to cast their vote for a Republican, never to cast their vote for Harry Truman, and never to cast their vote for any candidate with a civil rights program such as that adopted by the convention."

"We bid you good-bye," said Alabama's delegation chair and former lieutenant governor, Leven Handy "Big Handy" Ellis.

Their action generated headlines, aggravating Truman's dire situation, threatening to separate Dixie from the national Democratic coalition as it had not been separated in nearly a hundred years.

However, more careful observation would have revealed this: Nobody else walked out.

In a convention in which every Southern state, save North Carolina, cast its votes for Richard Russell—and against Harry Truman—no one else, not even a solitary delegate from Strom Thurmond's South Carolina, followed. Half of Alabama's delegation refused to join the protesters. Lister Hill did not join them. Nor did George C. Wallace.

The states' rights movement was in trouble—and its difficulties were about to compound in spectacular fashion. In early May, its partisans had agreed that they would meet again immediately following the Democratic National Convention to chart their final course. They had never quite determined what that course might be. Many never believed in the Electoral College option or any third-party initiative. Nevertheless, in

Birmingham, on Saturday, July 17, they convened—to accomplish what, no one quite knew.

It was not even certain where they would gather. Originally scheduled to assemble in a three-hundred-seat hotel meeting room, the group switched gears on Thursday, July 15, announcing plans to convene instead in Birmingham's six-thousand-seat, redbrick City Auditorium, and thereby necessitating the rapid removal of reminders of the new venue's Monday evening wrestling card.

Dismantling a wrestling ring was one thing; deciding on their own décor was another. Organizers banned Confederate flags and similar souvenirs of the Lost Cause, vainly hoping to downplay an overt sectional image in favor of national constitutional principles. Nonetheless, individual attendees soon flooded the hall with their own Stars and Bars flags. The conference's official musical repertoire centered on such Southern hymns as "Swanee River," "My Old Kentucky Home," "Deep in the Heart of Texas," "Carry Me Back to Old Virginny," and, of course, most prominently of all, "Dixie."

Thirteen Southern states—Virginia, North and South Carolina, Oklahoma, Louisiana, Mississippi, Alabama, Tennessee, Texas, Georgia, Florida, Kentucky, and Arkansas—were officially represented. In reality, hardly anyone from outside Mississippi or Alabama bothered to attend. No one at all arrived from either Kentucky or North Carolina. The Virginia delegation was composed of four University of Virginia students plus a young woman returning home from New Orleans. Tennessee—represented by a strong delegation from "Boss" Crump's Memphis-based machine at May's conference—was now reduced to four students from the University of Tennessee, six from Cumberland University, and five "sympathizers."

Mississippi U.S. senator James Eastland attended, theorizing, "I don't think Truman will get any electoral votes, especially if we run a strong campaign in the border states. We will then become the minority party—the real Democratic Party. Then we would make the minority party assignments on committees in the Senate and the House." His Senate colleague John Stennis also graced the gathering, as did a quintet of Magnolia State congressmen: John Bell Williams, William M. Colmer, William A. Winstead, Jamie L. Whitten, and Thomas G. Abernethy. But not a single member of Congress beyond Mississippi—not Richard Russell, nor Olin Johnston, nor

Harry Byrd, nor a single Alabamian—bothered to attend. Even Mississippi's vociferously racist and anti-Semitic John Rankin skipped the session.

Gubernatorial ranks—Alabama's Folsom, Arkansas's Laney, South Carolina's Thurmond, Virginia's Tuck, and, of course, Mississippi's Wright—seemed better represented, but closer examination revealed similar weakness. Tuck snuck in and out, barely assuming even a minimal role in proceedings. Folsom arrived late. Thurmond, reviewing the 228th AAA Group of the South Carolina National Guard at Camp Stewart, Georgia, planned on absenting himself ("I would like to go to Birmingham, but I just don't see right now how I can"), until Laney and Wright phoned to change his mind. Thus, like Tuck and Folsom, he also arrived late. Laney—widely rumored to be the gathering's presidential nominee—arrived early but holed up in his hotel and avoided the hall, obviously embarrassed by the entire operation. Only Wright stood foursquare for action. "The chips are down," he proclaimed, "the die is cast."

A quartet of former governors also attended: Alabama's Frank M. Dixon, Louisiana's anti–Long family stalwart Sam Houston Jones, Mississippi's Hugh L. White, and Oklahoma's "Alfalfa Bill" Murray. No two Southern segregationists could have been more disparate than the patrician conservative Dixon and the hayseed populist Murray.

Fifty-six-year-old bachelor Dixon (a nephew of *The Clansman* author Thomas Dixon Jr.) had graduated from both Phillips Exeter Academy and Columbia University, and had lost his right leg serving in the Air Corps in July 1918. Opposed to Klan violence, he had privately wrestled with the moral issues of racial segregation. In November 1944, Dixon wrote to a friend:

> As a cosmopolitan and a church man I can justify, in theory, racial amalgamation. As a Southern man with the normal human dislike of foreigners both in space and in blood, I doubt my ability to put Christian charity into practice. . . . We are behind the times, I admit. The Huns have wrecked the theories of the master race with which we were so contented so long. Derbies are now being worn by Jackasses and silk purses being made out of sow's ears. Blood lines are out. The progeny of a cornfield ape blackened with the successive suns of Africa and Alabama, mated with a swamp gorilla from the Louisiana rice fields has developed promise as great as the sons of the great American families such as the Adams clan of New

England. Henry Wallace is right—anthropology so teaches. But I buy dogs of a certain breed to fight, and I know that the sons of Man-O'-War are going to win races against all comers. The man who is close to the land— who follows blood lines, knows the doctrines in which in my very human weakness, I prefer to keep my faith.

And so he kept his Southern faith, and as delegates converged on Birmingham, Dixon took to the airwaves to denounce a "national party [that] has put a knife into the heart of the South" and that now worked to "reduce us to a status of a mongrel, inferior race . . . to crush with imprisonment our leadership, and thereby kill our hopes, our aspirations, our future, and the future of our children."

If, however, William Henry Davis "Alfalfa Bill" Murray ever possessed qualms regarding white racial superiority, they were never recorded. Born in Toadsuck, Texas, Murray had been, in his prime, the very image of the stage Western villain—cigar-chomping and walrus-mustached. As chief of the territory's 1906 Constitutional Convention, Murray ("I appreciate the old-time ex-slave, the old darky, they are the salt of their race, who comes to me talking in that humble spirit which should characterize their actions and dealings with the white man") had written white supremacy and segregation provisions into his constitution, only to see them excised by Theodore Roosevelt.

In 1912, Murray proved instrumental in securing Woodrow Wilson's presidential nomination and won election to Congress. In the late 1920s, he migrated to Bolivia but returned to run for governor in 1930, vowing to oppose "The Three C's—Corporations, Carpetbaggers, and Coons." Elected by the largest margin in state history, Alfalfa Bill declared martial law dozens of times, shut off oil production to force up prices, and nearly went to war with Texas regarding a Red River toll bridge. In 1932, he sought the Democratic presidential nomination on a platform of "Bread, Butter, Bacon, and Beans." One Murray campaign ditty went:

He may eat flapjacks with a shovel or pick,

And be dubbed by the mob as a country hick,

But he can't be swayed by the glitter of gold.

He has stood the test with a courage bold.

In nineteen hundred and thirty-two

We'll hoist the old Red, White and Blue,

And swat the Republican plutocrat

And proceed to elect a Democrat—

For President vote for Bill Murray.

That was then. Now seventy-eight years old, half-deaf, and almost blind, tieless and clad in a dirty shirt, Murray had arrived via a two-day journey by bus—losing his luggage along the way. He had not, however, misplaced his copy of his own recent treatise, *The Negro's Place in Call of Race: The Last Word on Segregation of Races, Considered in Every Capable Light as Disclosed by Experience.* Excoriating black intelligence, the document contended, "Social or any intimacy, with a Negro and white woman, is too great a risk to tolerate or condone. His 'stronger' [passion] may overwhelm her." It praised Hitler as "right in his science," not an altogether surprising contention, considering that, a year earlier, he had penned a work entitled *Palestine: Shall Arabs or Jews Control It or America Admit 100,000 Communist Jews From Behind the Iron Curtain?*

Largely ignored, and occupying a small room without a private bath, he cut a pathetic figure. "A bell hop had to lead [Murray] to the elevator," reported the *Los Angeles Times.* "He made his way slowly to his room where he removed his coat, revealing long winter underwear, torn at the forearm."

"I'm the man," boasted Murray, "who introduced Jim Crow in Oklahoma."

Periodically, he read aloud from *The Negro's Place in Call of Race.* Otherwise, Murray added little to the proceedings save for advice on how to defeat Harry Truman in his home state. "It's agin the law," he warned, regarding efforts to displace Truman from the Democratic line in Oklahoma. "Won't work. There's only one way they can do it. There's a clause in the Constitution says no military or civil actions can interfere with the actions of voters.

"And everything is either civil or military, so the only thing they can do is write in the name of a candidate other than Truman. It'll work in Oklahoma. Has before."

Even bigger crackpots than Murray graced the convention. Anti-Semitic rabble-rousers Gerald L. K. Smith of the Christian Nationalist Crusade; Chattanooga's J. B. Stoner (head of the "Stoner Anti-Jewish Party" and a proponent of a constitutional amendment deeming it "illegal to be Jewish in the U.S., punishable by death"); Los Angeles's Rev. Jonathan E. Perkins (author of *The Jews Have Got the Atomic Bomb* and *Jesus Christ Was Not a Jew*); and Columbus, Georgia's National Patrick Henry Organization president, Mrs. Jessie Welch Jenkins ("Communism is Judaism, Internationalism is Judaism, Judaism is Bolshevism"), attended. The gathering, trumpeted Smith, who had previously unsuccessfully attempted to rally support at Philadelphia's Democratic Convention, "will go down in history as one of the most significant things that has ever happened. It challenges every white man to fulfill his destiny as it relates to the future of America." The Rev. Perkins, a close Smith aide, had helped organize the convention, even escorting speakers to the podium, but that didn't prevent wary conference authorities from denying Smith's far-too-controversial credentials as an Oklahoma delegate.

Also unwelcome was Emory O. Jackson, black editor of the *Birmingham World*. "You are in a good place to get killed," warned two burly police officers as they escorted the forty-year-old Jackson off the premises. "Get out of here as fast as you can and don't stop walking."

Preceding the opening gavel, placard-wielding Progressive Party supporters picketed. "Win with Wallace" and "Down with Lynching," their signs read. Bull Connor ordered them to march fifty feet apart to comply with local ordinances.

The convention opened an hour late—at 11:00 AM, July 17. Metropolitan Opera star Ruby Mercer, a "portly" registered Republican, in town for the summer opera season, opened the meeting with renditions of "The Star-Spangled Banner" and "Dixie." Pointedly referring to attendees of the recent national Democratic gathering, Bull Connor promised delegates, "You will not find a Negro lawyer [Missouri's George L. Vaughn, who opposed seating the Mississippi delegation] speaking on this platform, nor an ex-convict from Boston [Mayor James M. Curley]," convicted of fraud in 1904, and demanding "absolute and complete independence of Ireland as a republic" at the 1948 convention.

Frank Dixon delivered the keynote address—though no one had

bothered to inform him of his assignment until 7:00 AM that morning. Formulating a three-pronged strategy, Dixon advocated:

1. A ticket for President and Vice President.

2. Throwing the election into Congress, where "we could win control."

3. And, finally, after Truman had been annihilated in both the North and South, "we would be the Democratic party."

"All of us . . . ," Dixon reminded his audience, "heard the jeers when Alabama and Mississippi walked out at Philadelphia. Jeers from sections where not a single elective officer, not even a Justice of the Peace, is a Democrat." For twenty-five minutes the crowd roared approval, waving Confederate flags, and shouting "We want Dixon!" "Dixie wants Dixon!" and "To hell with Truman!" Ole Miss students countered with shouts of "Fielding L. Wright and States' Rights!"

But for all their bravado, both Dixon and his audience knew something was amiss: far too many Southern officeholders had absented themselves. "Some of the officeholders in the South," challenged Dixon, "are afraid of losing their jobs if they follow us, and if they think they can weasel their way through this and weather the storm we will soon retire them to private life."

"Where is Lister Hill?" came a shout from the crowd.

"Drive the quislings out," sounded another.

Lloyd E. Price, a greasy-haired former Texarkana-area state legislator, now a Fort Worth attorney, followed Dixon to the podium, attacking "so-called Northern and Eastern liberals," reserving special scorn for New Englanders, whom he blamed for having imported "howling, screaming savages" to American shores. Price concluded his address at 12:50 PM and ABC terminated its convention coverage at 1:00 PM, declaring Dixiecrat proceedings "too inflammatory."

Adjournment followed Price. What followed adjournment rattled the already shaky gathering to its core.

Its presumed presidential candidate—Arkansas governor Laney—dropped out.

Few should have been surprised. At Philadelphia, Laney refused to have his name placed in nomination, leaving delegates to cast their votes instead for Richard Russell. Southerners, said Laney in Birmingham, "should get together and get united opposition to this legislation, and they can't get it by forming a new organization. They should unite within the party all the leaders.

"[W]e in the south are outnumbered . . . but we are Americans. . . . Shall our nation be torn with unnecessary political strife, now when unity is vital, merely for the sake of politics or the personal satisfaction and ambition of any man?

"Whatever is done, must be done through and by the official Democratic organizations in each respective state."

Panic-stricken organizers needed a candidate—and quick. Fielding Wright was too dull. "Alfalfa Bill" Murray was clearly out of the question. Frank Dixon turned them down—which left Strom Thurmond, recently arrived via private plane from Camp Stewart, Georgia. Only an hour remained to convince the reluctant South Carolinian. "I knew that accepting the nomination would have future political repercussions," Thurmond recalled, "but I had little time to make up my mind, and I thought somebody ought to do something, so I finally decided to take the plunge. I didn't know then even if my own state would support me."

Before the convention anointed Thurmond, however, the Platform and Resolutions Committee chairman, Alabama judge Horace Cornelius Wilkinson, had work to do. In his time, the sixty-year-old Wilkinson had played many parts. Originally a staunch progressive, he graduated to Exalted Cyclops of the KKK's Woodlawn, Alabama, Klavern and bolted the party in August 1928 rather than support Catholic Al Smith ("Up North all negroes are for this alleged nominee of the Democratic party"). In the 1930s, however, Wilkinson had supported organized labor and the New Deal so loyally that FDR designated him to dispense administration patronage in Birmingham. But when Roosevelt instituted a wartime FEPC, that was too much for Wilkinson, and by 1948 he was irrevocably at war with any fellow Democrat even hinting at racial equality.

Negroes, he wrote, are "inferior, unreliable, irresponsible, and easily corrupted. There are not enough exceptions . . . to merit discussion. If it be said that I am influenced by racial prejudice, I admit it." One of his state's eleven presidential electors—and director of the White Supremacy League—

the teetotaling, devout Baptist, cigar-chomping Wilkinson now presented four resolutions to the convention:

1. To carry the campaign to Truman's Missouri and Barkley's Kentucky

2. To adopt an eight-point, anti-Truman, pro–states' rights platform

3. To appoint "a Southern States' Rights campaign chairman" who in turn would appoint a finance committee and chair

4. To hold another conference on October 1, or another date designated by the chairman, to which representatives from all states would be invited

All four proposals carried by loud voice vote. "Harry Truman won't be able to carry Independence, Missouri," Wilkinson practically shouted.

The platform that Wilkinson presented, and which the conference approved, dealt merely with states' rights—and protecting segregation—ignoring all other issues, such as the rapidly escalating Cold War, the Taft-Hartley Act, inflation, and a housing shortage. Their Declaration of Principles read in part:

> We affirm that a political party is an instrumentality for effectuating the principles upon which the party is founded. . . .

> We believe that the protection of the American people against the onward march of totalitarian government requires a faithful observance of article X of the American Bill of Rights which provides that: "The powers not delegated to the United States by the Constitution, nor prohibited by it to the States, are reserved to the States respectively, or to the people."

> **THE PRINCIPLES OF STATES' RIGHTS**

> We direct attention to the fact that the first platform of the Democratic Party, adopted in 1840, resolved that: "Congress has no power under the Constitution to interfere with or control the domestic institutions of the several States, and that such States are the sole and proper judges of everything appertaining to their own affairs not prohibited by the Constitution." Such pronouncement is the cornerstone of the Democratic Party.

The executive department of the Government is promoting the gradual but certain growth of a totalitarian state by domination and control of a politically minded Supreme Court. As examples of the threat to our form of government, the executive department, with the aid of the Supreme Court, has asserted national dominion and control of submerged oil-bearing lands in California, schools in Oklahoma and Missouri, primary elections in Texas, South Carolina, and Louisiana, restrictive covenants in New York and the District of Columbia, and other jurisdictions, as well as religious instruction in Illinois.

. . . The latest response to our entreaties was a Democratic convention in Philadelphia rigged to embarrass and humiliate the South. This alleged Democratic assembly called for a civil-rights law that would eliminate segregation of every kind from all American life, prohibit all forms of discrimination in private employment, in public and private instruction and administration and treatment of students; in the operation of public and private health facilities; in all transportation, and require equal access to all places of public accommodation for persons of all races, colors, creeds, and national origin. . . .

We call upon all Democrats and upon all other loyal Americans who are opposed to totalitarianism at home and abroad to unite with us in ignominiously defeating Harry S. Truman and Thomas E. Dewey, and every other candidate for public office who would establish a police state in the United States of America.

Now came time to nominate Thurmond and Wright. Seventy-five hundred voices roared their assent. Birmingham–Southern College students carried aloft a portrait of Robert E. Lee. Seventy-nine-year-old Beulah Waller ("the wool hat woman of Byron, Georgia") danced a jig.

A new candidate, however, suddenly materialized: Brig. Gen. Herbert C. Holdridge (U.S. Army, Ret.). That Holdridge was a crank there was no doubt; the surprise was that he was not a right-wing crank general—but an extreme left-wing crank general.

Holdridge had been the only active general to retire during World War II (he was just fifty-two), and upon departing the service had become instantly embroiled in politics, endorsing Socialist Norman Thomas for president in 1944. Dewey and FDR, Holdridge contended, were mere "jockeys of the same old capitalistic horse, both competing for the privilege of leading the country into Fascism."

In 1946, Holdridge sued Mississippi's John Rankin for libel. In April 1948, he threatened South Dakota Republican senator "Chad" Gurney that "if [your activities lead] to a favorable vote for universal conscription, which can only lead to World War III, I shall include your name on my personal purge list of those whom we think should be hanged for treason to the people."

In January 1948, Holdridge announced his candidacy for the Democratic presidential nomination. "No more depression," he promised, "no more war and no compromise with capitalism." Not surprisingly, Harry Truman fended off the Holdridge crusade, but now Holdridge materialized on Birmingham's Municipal Auditorium floor, shouting his objections to the Thurmond and Wright nominations, igniting an uproar from angry self-appointed "delegates." "Throw the Communist out!" they yelled. Police obliged, escorting "the peace general candidate" to the auditorium manager's office before releasing him without pressing charges.

Wright and Thurmond should now have assumed center stage—but Thurmond had disappeared. Governor Folsom stalled for time, delivering a short speech. Careful listeners might have noted that he failed to endorse any third-party scheme.

At 7:00 PM Thurmond and Wright took the rostrum. Wright protested:

This is not a bolt. This is not a fourth party. I say to you that we are the true Democrats of the Southland and these United States. . . .

Don't let anybody tell you the South is bolting the Democratic Party. Our people are going to vote for J. Strom Thurmond, a man of integrity—a man in whom you'll be proud to place your trust. . . .

This is the South's great opportunity. It is a chance to prove to the Nation that we are the Democratic Party. We have saved the Democratic Party in the past and we will save it in the future. But we will not save it for those who have crashed into the party, seized control and led it astray.

Thurmond had little time to draft an acceptance speech. One by one, he removed his scribbled notes from his pockets, throwing each piece of paper on the floor as he made his points to the assemblage. But lack of preparation did not blunt his ardor. Thurmond, father of a Negro daughter, thundered:

> I want to tell you the progress of the Negro race has not been due to these so-called emancipators—but to the kindness of the Southern people. . . . We believe that there are not enough troops in the Army to force the Southern people to admit the Negroes into our theaters, swimming pools, and homes. . . . If the South should vote for Truman this year, we might as well petition the Government for colonial status. . . . We are going back to the real bosses of the Democratic Party, the people.

> President Truman has betrayed the South and we Southerners are going to cast our votes for candidates who are true believers in states' rights principles. For our loyalty to the party we have been stabbed in the back by a President who has betrayed every principle of the Democratic Party in his desire to win at any cost.

> I can think of nothing worse than for the South to tuck its tail and vote for Truman. If we did, we would be nothing worse than cowards. We are not going to do it.

And now, he came to the heart of the matter: "If we throw the election into the House of Representatives we will hold the balance of power."

It was a strategy that still might work.

24

"I have been thinking of you holding the casket"

Dixiecrats had possessed the semblance of a strategy: Throw the election into the Electoral College, hold a gun firmly to the head of the national Democratic Party, cut a deal—and return to business as usual. How they would implement that grand strategy was, of course, another story.

Henry Wallace's strategy remained, as ever, open to question.

As Harry Truman's popularity plummeted each month, Wallace proved himself roundly incapable of capitalizing on his rival's discomfort—in fact his own poll numbers plunged even faster.

Now, with two conventions concluded in Philadelphia, and a third completed in Birmingham, a fourth—Henry Wallace's—stood ready to commence in Philadelphia.

Discussions regarding a party platform preceded the convention's official opening. Ostensibly conducted under the direction of left-wing but non-Communist Rexford Guy Tugwell ("We have to decide whether the Russians are playing poker or post office, and I don't think they are playing post office"), they were, in actuality, guided by the abrasive pro-Soviet Lee Pressman. "Either the United States and Russia have good relations and peace, or bad relations and war," Pressman had said, "and if you want good relations you don't have a draft or a Truman Doctrine."

"Pressman handled everything," said a Nebraska delegate, the retired Omaha Methodist minister Arthur F. Stearns, admiringly. "He's a smart man.

You couldn't tell he was there, he was so quiet. Yes sir, he was like a silken thread running through the whole thing."

The seventy-six-member Tugwell-Pressman platform committee eventually delivered a twenty-two-page, six-thousand-word manifesto, advocating all manner of things eventually adopted by the major parties—racial desegregation, abolition of HUAC, repeal of Taft-Hartley, national health insurance, a federal education department, the eighteen-year-old vote, statehood for Alaska and Hawaii, District of Columbia home rule, indemnification for Japanese-Americans. But the manifesto also advocated far more controversial items, such as the destruction of U.S. atomic weapons; a $100-a-month pension for those reaching age sixty; nationalization of large banks, railroads, the merchant marine, and manufacturers of aircraft and synthetic rubber; and full taxation of capital gains.

On foreign policy the document faithfully hewed to the Soviet line, reminding everyone of the new party's hard-left tilt. Nonetheless, the platform committee, vainly coveting support from more mainstream former New Dealers, invited ADA executive secretary James Loeb to testify at its pre-convention sessions. However, when Loeb released the text of what he would say, organizers flew into a panic, stalling the entire process for seven-and-a-half hours. Under pressure from deadline-conscious reporters, they finally agreed to let Loeb speak.

He blistered them. "The Communists and their collaborators guide the major policies and word the major pronouncements of this party," Loeb maintained, charging that the new party lent "itself to the support and extenuation of Soviet totalitarianism and Soviet aggression." It was, he said, "a dangerous adventure undertaken by cynical men in whose hands Henry A. Wallace placed his political fortunes. . . . [W]ere the Communists to withdraw from your party today, your organization would soon join that long list of discarded groups which testify eloquently to the inevitable failure of the so-called 'United Front'—which always becomes decreasingly united and increasingly 'front.'"

"The presence of Mr. Wallace," the seersucker-clad Loeb concluded, "does not alter the fact that the real authority in your party is vested in the hands of men and women, many of whom followed the dictates of totalitarianism in the period of the Nazi-Soviet pact.

"Mr. Wallace's candidacy does not obscure the fact that the Communists and their collaborators will guide the major policies and word the major pronouncements of this party."

Heckled throughout his address, Loeb exited under police protection.

As Loeb departed, Glen Taylor arrived.

"I think the pink Communists who believe in changes in our form of government by evolution rather than revolution will support our party," he had announced on Tuesday, June 22. "The red Communists will support Mr. Dewey, because they hope that the best way to get a revolution is to have another Hoover administration."

"I don't consider Communist support of our party a major issue," agreed fifty-one-year-old New Yorker Elinor Steiner Gimbel, a major Progressive financial angel. "If they support Mr. Wallace and our program, we're happy to have them."

Wallace was to have traveled from New York by train—in proletarian coach fashion. Instead, he and Mrs. Wallace traveled in an air-conditioned stateroom, the remainder of the entourage in a parlor car. "The coaches," a spokesman blandly explained, "were too crowded."

Taylor, Mrs. Gimbel, Beanie Baldwin, and between fifteen hundred and two thousand supporters greeted the Wallaces as they debarked at Philadelphia's Broad Street Station. "We want Wallace, we want Wallace," they chanted. "People Before Profits: Vote for Wallace," "Veterans Want Wallace," and "Had Enough Milk at 25 Cents a Quart? Vote for Wallace," read their placards. To the tune of "The Battle Hymn of the Republic," a group calling themselves "Youth of the Fourth Congressional District" sang their own "Battle Hymn of '48."

A light drizzle descended. "We've got to get out of here," Beanie Baldwin advised. "Let's turn to the left." Wallace laughed, and the assemblage began a half-mile procession to their Bellevue-Stratford headquarters.

Most Philadelphians ignored them.

The press did not.

Atop the Bellevue-Stratford, Wallace quickly convened a press conference. One controversy followed another, leaving what remained of his candidacy a tattered ruin.

Flanked by Taylor, Baldwin, and Wallace-for-President chairman Elmer A. Benson (the same Benson whom Harold Stassen had defeated for the Minnesota governorship), Wallace began by candidly admitting, "I am getting a lot [of Communist support] and there is no question that this is a liability." Refusing to renounce that support, however, he continued with a prepared statement:

> [T]he Communist leaders seem to think they have to endorse me every day or two. . . . The Communists oppose my advocacy of progressive capitalism. They support me because I say we can have peace with Russia.
>
> I will not repudiate any support which comes to me on the basis of interest in peace. The Communists are interested in peace because they want a successful Socialist experiment in Russia.
>
> I am interested in peace because I want our American system to demonstrate the enormous vitality of which it is capable, that vitality which is being wasted in preparations for war. If, during the war, we had accepted the idea that you can't work with Communists, we might not have succeeded in our joint efforts to stop Hitler.
>
> If you accept the idea that Communists have no right to express their opinions, then you don't believe in democracy. And if you accept the notion that it is impossible to live in a world with sharply differing ideas, then you accept the inevitability of war. I don't believe in the inevitability of war. I do believe in democracy.

"No matter how hard you try, I am not going to engage in Red baiting," said Wallace. "No matter how hard you try, you are not going to get me to admit that I am a Communist."

He followed with a rather mystifying presentation regarding the May 1948 murder of anti–Truman Doctrine CBS radio correspondent George Polk (Polk's younger brother, a Harvard undergraduate, sat beside the podium with Wallace) in war-torn Greece, with Wallace intimating that not enough was being done to solve the crime. Asked what might indeed be done, Wallace offered no answer. Mystified and hostile, reporters judged the presentation pointless.

"I have often thought the diplomats sent out by the state department and the foreign office maladroit," recorded a stunned Rebecca West, "but never have I seen them achieve such a miracle of tactlessness as this opening to the press conference. Mr. Wallace, however, made the beginning seem as nothing by his subsequent answers to questions, which in almost every case alienated the questioner in a deep way."

He artlessly dodged questions from a black reporter regarding the sending of federal troops into the South to enforce civil rights, and from Norman Thomas regarding why Wallace, though demanding to debate Truman, refused to debate him. He did, however, participate in an arcane debate with columnist Dorothy Thompson regarding what constituted "feudal" conditions in the Balkans.

All of which was bad enough. What followed transcended the merely bad.

"Have you ever," came a query, "repudiated the authenticity of the Guru letters?"

It was a question Henry Wallace would never answer.

The letters in question had been written in 1933 and 1934 to exiled Russian artist, mystic, and 1929 Nobel Prize nominee Nicholas Konstantinovich Roerich, whose plans for wartime cultural preservation had inspired the International "Roerich Pact"—to which the United States, with Henry Wallace as official signatory, adhered in 1935. Cultural preservation was not controversial, but the white-bearded Roerich's early-1930s mission to China was. Dispatched by Wallace to Asia, ostensibly to research drought-resistant grasses, Roerich soon embarrassed U.S. diplomats by flagrantly trafficking with Japan's puppet government in Manchuria. The once-promising Wallace-Roerich relationship fizzled.

But not before Wallace (sometimes terming himself "Galahad") had sent to Roerich the so-called Guru letters—mystical, altogether silly documents that could only trigger disquieting questions about the cabinet officer who had composed them.

On March 5, 1933—just three days after taking office as secretary of agriculture—Wallace wrote to Roerich:

Dear Guru,

I have been thinking of you holding the casket—the sacred most precious casket. And I have thought of the New Country going forth to meet the seven stars under the sign of the three stars. And I have thought of the admonition "Await the Stone."

We await the Stone and we welcome you again to this glorious land of destiny, clouded though it may be with strange fumbling fears. Who shall hold up the compelling vision to those who wander in darkness? In answer to this question we again welcome you. To drive out depression. To drive out fear. . . .

And so I await your convenience prepared to do what I am to do.

May Peace, Joy and Fire attend you as always,

G [Galahad]

In the great haste of this strange

maelstrom which is Washington.

And to this suspected Japanese sympathizer, Wallace wrote: "The rumor is the Monkeys [the British] are seeking friendship with the Rulers [the Japanese] so as to divide the land of the Masters [Manchuria] between them. The Wandering One [referred to as "FDR" when Wallace was better disposed to Roosevelt, or, alternately, as "The Flame"] thinks this and is very suspicious of Monkeys. . . . He does not like the Rulers and wants adequate preparation for two or three years hence."

On another occasion Wallace displayed even greater disloyalty to his presumed idol: "[FDR's] extraordinary sliminess makes even simple problems difficult at times. The One has a lovely, upward surging spirit with a certain appreciation of what he calls 'hunches.' Combined with this is a charming open mindedness which makes him the prey at times of designing people—for example the Tigers [Russians]. This past week I have talked . . . both to him and the sour one [Cordell Hull] in the most emphatic terms."

By 1940, the incriminating correspondence—presumably peddled by the Roerich clan—had fallen into the hands of two Republican newspaper publishers, Roy Howard and Paul Block. With Henry Wallace now Roosevelt's running mate, the letters' value had increased a thousandfold.

"Oh, God!" exclaimed administration official Anna Rosenberg, on hearing that Wallace's letters were in GOP hands. "Out of a hundred million Americans, we had to pick *him* for vice president."

Wallace could not be removed from the ticket, but Roosevelt ("We can handle sex, but we can't handle religion") had, as usual, an ace up his sleeve.

Blackmail.

Roosevelt's opponent in the 1940 presidential election, Wendell Willkie, had been conducting an extramarital affair with a forty-nine-year-old divorcée, *New York Herald Tribune* book review editor Irita Bradford Van Doren. Until now, the wily FDR (with at least one affair in his own history) had possessed no desire to exploit Willkie's predicament.

Now he did.

"[We can] spread it as a word-of-mouth thing," Roosevelt strategized to his aide, former *Washington Daily News* editor Lowell Mellett, "or by some people way, way down the line. We can't have any of our principal speakers refer to it, but the people down the line can get it out. I mean the Congress[ional] speakers, and state speakers, and so forth. They can use the raw material. . . . Now, now, if they want to play dirty politics in the end, we've got our own people. . . . Now you'd be amazed at how this story about the gal is spreading around the country. . . . Awful nice gal. Writes for the magazines and so forth and so on, a book reviewer. But nevertheless there is the fact."

And no more was ever heard regarding the Guru letters—until May 1947.

Westbrook Pegler may have been the angriest columnist in America.

Fairly early in his career he had even defended a San Jose lynching, albeit, it must be conceded, of two white men. Working for the Hearst press, he ceaselessly attacked all things Roosevelt and New Deal—particular Eleanor ("*la boca grande*"—"the big mouth"). He remained a force to be reckoned with. In 1941, he not only won the Pulitzer Prize for journalism, he finished third (behind FDR and Stalin) for *Time*'s Man of the Year.

The Guru letters had by now fallen into his hands. After verifying the handwriting as Wallace's, Pegler ("I believe the author of these letters was off-center mentally") launched a series of columns exposing every bizarre facet of the correspondence. "His open cordiality to Communists and his current partiality to Soviet Russia," concluded Pegler, "could be no more than a momentary political convenience in the aspiration of a messianic fumbler toward an idealistic brotherhood of man and the purification of the whole human race through suffering, philosophy and politics."

Before—and after—publishing the letters, Pegler had attempted to secure Wallace's comments. "To hell with your farm, your chickens and your strawberries," Pegler publicly railed against Wallace in August 1947. "For two months I have been calling at your office and telephoning to ask whether you ever were a disciple or pupil of Nicholas Roerich. . . . I have been trying to corner you to make you answer whether you wrote Roerich a lot of idiotic letters and whether you regarded him as a god or supernatural master of mankind as many of your associates in the cult did. . . . Wallace, you are nailed on most counts."

Wallace admitted nothing, denied nothing, commented on nothing.

And so, in Philadelphia, when queried regarding the Guru letters, Henry Wallace flushed. "I never engage in a discussion with a stooge of Westbrook Pegler," he answered.

A hush enveloped the gathering. From the back of Wallace's audience, a man arose, his hair slicked straight back, his hands juggling his glasses, a pen, his sheaf of notes. "He [was] a short man," wrote Rebecca West, "and Wallace is tall, but he seemed to be made of a more durable substance, and his very blue eyes looked hard as fact itself."

"My name is Westbrook Pegler, Mr. Wallace," he announced. "You twice referred to the subject of letters in your remarks and you have reminded us journalists of the important duty of getting all the available facts [of the George Polk incident]. Therefore, I ask you whether you did or did not write certain letters to Nicholas Roerich, addressing him as Dear Guru, and his wife as Modra?"

"I will never," answered Henry Wallace, "engage in any discussion with Westbrook Pegler."

The *Los Angeles Times*'s Warren Francis and the *Detroit News*'s Martin Hayden repeated Pegler's question—the same damnable question—and received the same rebuff. Henry Wallace would answer no Pegler "stooges." His supporters grumbled their assent. "If you stooges don't like this," shouted a man near the front row, a Wallace pin fastened to his chest, "why don't you get the hell out of here?"

Washington Post correspondent Mary Spargo sprang to her feet. "I am not a stooge for anybody, Mr. Wallace," she sputtered. "I don't even agree with his column. But you have been talking here about objectivity in reporting and you cited that point in your letter to Joseph Stalin. Therefore, I demand that you answer this question."

He wouldn't.

"Would you consider me a Pegler stooge?" demanded still another reporter. His colleagues laughed. So did Wallace.

"No, Mr. Mencken," Henry Wallace answered, "I would never consider you anybody's stooge."

"Well, then, it's a simple question. We've all written love letters in our youth that would bring a blush later on. There's no shame in it. This is a question that all of us here would like to have answered, so we can move on to weightier things."

"I will handle that in my own way and in my own time."

"But why? These things have no importance."

"Let's get on to something important."

"Why not now?" asked Mencken. "We are all here."

Still no answer.

The atmosphere approached chaos. "Some people defended you and your actions in 1940 and 1944," said columnist Doris Fleeson. "You owe it to them to clear up this matter."

Wallace said he would—but not here.

When it was finally over, Henry Louis Mencken snarled, "Everybody named Henry should be put to death. If somebody will do it for Henry Wallace, I promise to commit suicide."

Henry Wallace's campaign already had.

25

"Half of the gallery are FBI agents"

The Dixiecrat convention had fallen distinctly short on current elected officials. Progressives fell shorter still. Their contingent represented New York City and nowhere else—just two members of Congress (East Harlem's Vito Marcantonio and the Bronx's Leo Isacson) plus a Brooklyn assemblyman, a state senator, and a black Manhattan city councilman.

There was, however, no absence of other celebrities.

California provided a voice from the past: eighty-one-year-old Dr. Francis Townsend, founder of the Depression-era old-age pension campaign known as the Townsend Plan, and a veteran of Gerald L. K. Smith and Father Charles Coughlin's decidedly ill-fated 1936 Union Party. Townsend remained fixated on pensions. If the new party "pussyfoots" on the issue, he threatened, he would prove "as indifferent [to it] as I am to the Republicans and Democrats."

Younger—and more doctrinaire—leftists augmented Townsend. From the Dakotas came two future U.S. senators: twenty-six-year-old Northwestern graduate theology student George S. McGovern, son of a Wesleyan Methodist minister; and forty-year-old Quentin N. Burdick, son of former isolationist North Dakota Republican congressman Usher L. Burdick. Army Air Corps veteran and registered Republican McGovern, along with his wife, Eleanor, attended as Illinois delegates. "Wallace was attacked by his enemies as a 'pink' or a 'red,'" McGovern would recall. "He was, in fact, an old-fashioned free-enterprise capitalist and a practical internationalist."

Embattled Hollywood screenwriters and actors, leery of HUAC subpoenas and indictments and studio blacklists, largely steered clear of the proceedings. Other hard-core leftists in the arts did not. In attendance were sculptor Jo Davidson; singers Paul Robeson, Michael Loring, Laura Duncan, and folksinger Pete Seeger (Seeger's father had been a CPUSA member, even writing for the *Daily Worker*, but quit in 1938 following Stalin's purges); and authors Louis Adamic, Howard Fast, Rockwell Kent, Louis Untermeyer (later Consultant in Poetry to the Library of Congress—poet laureate), Dorothy Parker, Donald Ogden Stewart, Anna Louise Strong, Eslanda Goode Robeson (cultural anthropologist, Paul Robeson's wife, a relative of Benjamin Cardozo, and a candidate for secretary of state in Connecticut), and Shirley Graham (in 1951, Mrs. W.E.B. Du Bois). Also in attendance were Broadway actor Sam Wanamaker and the compulsively pro-Soviet Broadway producer Herman Shumlin (another of Lillian Hellman's former lovers).

For embattled thirty-three-year-old Communist Party activist Howard Fast (he faced three months' jail time after defying a HUAC summons to produce records from the Joint Anti-Fascist Refugee Committee), the convention's opening day brought an unexpected and joyous surprise. Fast heard that H. L. Mencken—a particular hero of his—had been seeking him out. The news startled Fast, and when Mencken finally found him, the event proved yet more startling: The rumpled, straw-boater-clad Mencken gushed to Fast that had he—Mencken—written Fast's recent historical novel, *The American*, "he would have put down his pen with pleasure."

But H. L. also provided words of caution. "Fast," he asked, "what in hell's name are you doing with this gang?"

Nervous at the thought of arguing with an old idol, Fast stammered that it was better than being among the Democrats or Republicans.

"There's a better place than that . . . with yourself," countered Mencken.

"But I can't put politics aside."

"Put it aside?" Mencken exclaimed. "Hell, no. Henry Louis Mencken is a party of one. Do you understand me? You're a party of one. You don't put politics aside; you taste it, listen to it, and write it. You don't join it. If you do, these clowns will destroy you as surely as the sun rises and sets."

Mencken offered good advice. Fast didn't want to hear it.

Not quite an artist, but a loyal Wallace attendee nonetheless, forty-five-year-old Virginia Foster Durr was a dogged anti–poll tax advocate, a candidate for the U.S. Senate from Virginia—and the sister-in-law of Supreme Court Justice Hugo Black. Virginia Durr would later recall:

> Henry was so sweet and so serious. He tried to help us in the poll tax fight. He was a horrible politician, but I just adored him. [My] Sister [Josephine, Hugo Black's wife] and Henry were very fond of each other. They loved to talk about mysticism. He believed in revelations and that people could have contact with the other world. . . . Sister could not support Henry because Hugo would have had a fit. . . . Hugo just gave it to me up and down. He thought I was a total idiot to leave the Democratic party and vote for Henry Wallace. Hugo was a yellow-dog Democrat. He thought you had to stick by the party, even though he didn't think much of Harry Truman.

Then there were the rank and file.

"The people that I'd met at that convention were just ordinary farmers, workers, small business people, doctors, and lawyers—just ordinary Americans from across the country," recalled George McGovern. "I thought it was wonderful. . . . These were church people and right out of the soil of America. I'd say that 95 percent of them were people that could have been attending a Democratic or a Republican convention almost as easily." The other 5 percent, however, were something else. "I also remember encountering a few hard-line Communists whose rigidity I found obnoxious," McGovern noted.

Observed Hearst columnist George Dixon:

> I am aware that it is not considered cricket to dwell upon the physical infirmities of people, but I have never seen so many obvious defectives gathered together before. The worst of it is they seem to flaunt their imperfections, rather than minimize them. Hotel dining rooms have been having a terrible time trying to enforce their rules that diners wear coats and neckties. This goes for cocktail lounges and private clubs where the weird crew tries to force entry. Their attitude gives them away. Obviously, it isn't a question of comfort in a hot and muggy city; they're trying to create situations.
>
> It'd be easy to laugh at these people—but, actually, they're frightening.

There's something sub-human about the looks of so many of them. Every time one of them shoves by you, jostles you deliberately in an elevator, or deliberately steps on your feet, you find yourself welling up with an urge to crush. This is a terrible thing that has been let loose in our America. We can't laugh it off much longer.

"Many of the men had their collars folded back over their lapels," observed the *Manchester Guardian*'s thirty-nine-year-old correspondent Alistair Cooke, "at that time a sign of an emancipated clerk at Atlantic City or a fledgling Los Angeleno. The women divided sharply between down-to-earth, no-nonsense types with sandals and off-the-shoulder Mexican blouses, and thin brunettes wearing earrings as long as icicles, meant to convey the piercing, on-stage elegance of Greenwich Village *femmes fatales*."

Their ways were not the old ways. Whether they hailed from Greenwich Village or Pocatello, these were the vanguard of a new age—and not merely politically. Noted columnist Tris Coffin:

> Those hardy sophisticates, the Philadelphia hotel bell-hops, were bug-eyed at the casual way the Wallace followers did their spooning. It was not romance in the conventional way—the bold, man-of the-world approach, the shy, "Well, I don't know what mother would think, Mr. Jones. We haven't been introduced," the jolly tinkle of ice; the struggle for a kiss. These moderns sat before the open doors, kissing with about as much enthusiasm as two old maids meeting at a tea party. It looked as much fun as riding blindfold along a scenic drive.

Resplendent in a white, double-breasted suit, Elmer Benson banged the convention to order at 5:30 PM, Friday, July 23, before introducing such speakers as Leo Isacson ("After the elections are over, Israel would commence the affair of making itself submit to Anglo-American tutelage"). A series of three-minute addresses followed. *New York Times* music critic Olin Downes (the *Times* studiously avoided reporting on Downes's presence) spoke on "The Arts." Shirley Graham spoke for "The Negro." Frank Danowski, a UAW local president and the secretary of "National Polish-Americans for Wallace," spoke on "Nationalities." Northern New Jersey congressional candidate Katherine Van Orden ("a mother, a housewife, and a very angry woman") spoke for "Women." Cornell University atomic physicist Philip Morrison, among the first to tour post-atomic Hiroshima and Nagasaki, spoke for "Science." "We must work for one world," Morrison warned, "or get none."

Wallace had wanted an African-American to deliver the keynote address, but both W.E.B. Du Bois (ostensibly because he was an academic, but in reality for fear of breaking the NAACP ban on electioneering) and Paul Robeson had declined, leaving that honor to Wallace's fifty-eight-year-old fellow Iowan Charles P. Howard Sr.

A longtime Republican, Howard was a former legal counsel for the Polk County Insanity Commission, a Des Moines city prosecutor, a prominent defense attorney (seventy-eight death penalty clients and none executed), and owner with his three sons of seven Midwestern weekly papers (the Howard Newspaper Syndicate). Howard had, however, misappropriated nine hundred dollars in client funds in 1940 and ultimately found his license suspended for six months.

Virtually all 3,240 delegates and alternates had assumed their places as the stocky, bespectacled Howard began his address. But the galleries remained half-empty—and the situation could well have been even worse than that: "Half of the gallery," cracked one Philadelphia police sergeant, "are FBI agents checking on the commies."

Howard bluntly informed his audience that their choice was "Wallace or war," charging that, regarding the newly imposed military draft, "the President's greetings" bear "postmarks of corruption in China and betrayal in Israel and murder in Greece. They bear the mark of every Nazi we have restored to power in Germany."

"Look across this hall," Howard continued, "and I see no one tonight to answer the roll call for du Pont or the House of Morgan. I see no delegate who will rise to speak for the Ku Klux Klan. I see no delegates from the Hague machine and the Kelly machine, the Pew machine or the Grundy machine.

"We are not the party of the mechanical smile or the Missouri [C]ompromise."

Keenly observing Howard's address was H. L. Mencken, who described the Iowan as "a tall, full-bodied barrister of the color of a good ten-cent cigar," with a shiny diamond ring upon his finger. Mencken noted that Howard possessed "an African roll in his voice that is far from unpleasant," and that his speech was "mainly devoted to excoriating Hitler, the du Ponts, the Rockefellers, Truman and other such malefactors."

In typical Menckenite fashion, he noted that "if the night's proceedings were actually maneuvered by goons of the Kremlin, there was certainly no overt sign of it"—but neither were there many "dark faces spotted in the hall. . . . [D]istinctly Jewish faces were decidedly scarce. . . . I saw no Indians, Chinese, Malays, Eskimos or Arabs."

Mencken's diagnosis outraged the Progressives. Maryland's delegation chairman, the youthful Baltimore attorney (and covert Communist) Harold Buchman, offered a resolution condemning Mencken's "contemptible rantings which pass for newspaper reporting" and his "Hitlerite references to the people of this convention. . . . The fighting spirit of equality and brotherhood is entirely lost to [Mencken]. . . . [H]e has resorted to un-American slander against the people of this convention, and . . . his obscenities against the American people mark him as unfit to report the proceedings of a people's convention. . . . [He] Red baits, Jew baits, and Negro baits."

Buchman's resolution got nowhere. "The cooler, more crafty brass hats who remained most of the time in seclusion in a room to the rear of the auditorium issued a stop-and-desist order," observed Pennsylvania's *Chester Times.* "Rumors spread that they decided that if there were to be any martyrs to come out of the convention they would be Wallace and Taylor. No mere reporter was to be wafted off to glory on the wings of martyrdom."

Buchman's counterblast initially rattled Mencken, who argued, "Nobody denounced me as a white-baiter when I wrote that Herbert Hoover had a complexion like unrisen dough." But ultimately the controversy pleased him, as controversy had always pleased him. "I'm only sorry," H. L. finally grinned, "the resolution was not passed."

On Saturday, the convention reopened at the unconventional hour of 6:30 AM—with a half hour of singing (and another half hour scheduled for four hours later).

At midday, delegates skipped lunch to nominate a ticket.

Iowa Farmers Union president Fred Stover placed Henry Wallace ("the most courageous crusader for peace") in nomination. "Instead of carrying out the peace hopes of World War II," said Stover, "our foreign policy is reversed and directed against democracy everywhere.

"A big business oligarchy rules both parties and [is] sending its monopolies on a world scale under the protection of an American military machine lubricated by Arabian oil and paid for by American taxpayers."

Seconding speeches included those by San Diego AFL activist Alfredo N. Salazar (his delivered in Spanish) and forty-two-year-old United Farm Equipment and Metal Workers of America (of the CIO) president Grant W. Oakes. "If anyone wanted a leader for a temperance crusade," proclaimed the burly, "rugged-faced" Oakes, the party's candidate for Illinois governor, regarding Truman, "he wouldn't pick the town drunk."

A thirty-two-minute demonstration followed, before Larkin Marshall, editor of the black *Macon Herald* and the party's U.S. Senate candidate in Georgia, nominated Glen Taylor. Taylor, said Marshall, who had accompanied him on his earlier trip to Birmingham, "believes that all men are created equal, and when men malign him because of that belief, and their torrent wrath in furious imprecations o'er him break[s], he keeps his counsel as he keeps his path."

Taylor's nominating process seemed a family affair; he was seconded by his sister, Annabelle Taylor Way, a Michigan delegate, and his railroad engineer brother Paul, now a Northern California congressional candidate for the Progressives. Idaho women, some wearing cowboy outfits, displayed large cardboard potatoes. "Idaho potatoes in every oven," promised one demonstrator's banner; "Wallace and Taylor."

"This nominating session was a dull and dreadful affair," fussed H. L. Mencken, "but certainly no worse than those staged by the Republican and Democratic conventions."

Wallace and Taylor had watched the proceedings unfold on television. Now they appeared at the hall. "Taylor came in first," noted the *Hartford Courant*, "accompanied by his wife, and two of their children. He carried their youngest child in his arms. There was a tremendous outburst. The youngster, baby-fashion, waved to the crowd [then] seemed to lose interest in the crowd and focused his attention on newspapermen, busy typing in the press section just below where his father was standing."

Yet there would be no speeches from either nominee—at least not then, at least not here.

Wallace's new party had received use of Philadelphia's convention hall rent-free—on condition that they waive any fee for admission. Invariably, any national convention agreed to this. Progressives, however, normally employed Wallace's public appearances as major fund-raising events. It seemed a shame to waste the opportunity presented by his acceptance speech.

So, they didn't.

For $30,000 they rented Shibe Park, home to the city's usually woeful Athletics and Phillies, hosting a rally as exciting and professionally stage-managed as the remainder of their convention had been repetitiously dull. Approximately thirty thousand Progressives paid from twenty-five cents for students in bleacher seats to two dollars sixty cents for prime seating. Admissions, however, provided only a segment of the evening's fund-raising. Former Upper West Side rabbi, auto thief, and WJZ radio commentator William S. Gailmor—supported, as H. L. Mencken approvingly noted, "by a troupe of cuties"—worked the crowd like a combination revivalist, carnival barker, and auctioneer. First, Gailmor solicited one-thousand-dollar donations, and received ten of them, including those from Elinor Gimbel, Lillian Hellman, and sixty-four-year-old *York Gazette and Daily* publisher Josiah "Jess" Gitt. Descending to the five-hundred-dollar level, he secured four more donors, before asking for two hundred dollars, then one hundred (thirty donors), and then ten dollars, eventually hectoring his audience for mere loose change—the entire process netting Wallace between sixty and seventy thousand dollars. "Never mind what they say about us starting in the red," Gailmor laughed, "we're finishing in the black."

Shibe Park remained half-empty at the event's scheduled 8:00 PM starting time. Outside, however, a massive stream of latecomers struggled to get in. Inside, a band and a choir struggled to be heard. "The convention banjo player (not Taylor himself, but Comrade [Pete] Seeger, a very superior artist) fared much better," judged Mencken. "Having had plenty of radio experience, he hugged the mike on the stand, and as a result his plucking of the strings had the effect of a series of blows with an ax."

At 8:40 PM actor Sam Wanamaker introduced Vito Marcantonio. It was Marcantonio's third speech of the convention, and it was not only fiery and frenetic (delivered, as *Time* noted, "with violent arm-flailings, like a drowning man"), but also, thanks to a combination of his own booming style and the park's reverberating sound system, largely unintelligible.

Paul Robeson ("Absentee ownership still rules supreme") provided renditions of "Ol' Man River," "The House I Live In," "Los Cuatros Generales" (a Spanish loyalist anthem), and a "Glory, Glory, Hallelujah" parody that started out "Marching on With Henry Wallace."

At 10:30 PM Glen Taylor, not in his best form, announced he was "proud to be associated with Henry Wallace in the founding of this new party." He promised a fight against the "forces that would bankrupt America by spending billions in a futile effort to bribe whole nations into becoming our mercenaries in a senseless struggle for world domination," recalled Norman Thomas, recoiling at Taylor's "repudiation of the Marshall Plan. . . . I have not heard such jingoistic indifference to the plight of the needy peoples of Europe since I debated the same issue with a small-time spokesman for the National Association of Manufacturers."

Before Taylor left the stage, his congressional candidate brother Paul, his wife, Dora, and their three sons—Arod ("Dora" spelled backward), age twelve; Paul Jon ("P. J."), six; and Gregory Alan, two—joined him in a performance of "When You Were Sweet Sixteen" that only seemed to illustrate why Taylor had forsaken show business. "Taylor's amazingly cheap speech and the excruciating barbershop family quartet which he inflicted upon millions of Americans listening in on the radio," summarized Norman Thomas, "were only two of the disquieting features of [the] night's demonstrations."

"A third-rate mountebank from the great open spaces," thought H. L. Mencken, reprising his assessment of Harold Stassen. "Soak a radio clown for ten days and ten nights in the rectified juices of all the cow-state Messiahs ever heard of, and you will have [Taylor] to the life."

With Taylor's harmonizing completed, Henry Wallace entered by auto, illuminated by roaming spotlights and a nearly full moon. He circled Shibe Park's base paths, enveloped by the cheers and chants of an adoring, ideological multitude. State standards in hand, they snake-danced round the infield, as Wallace begged them to cease "in justice to the radio companies and radio listeners."

Broadcast live to the nation by radio and to much of the East Coast by television, he commenced his speech by once more summoning a familiar specter:

> Franklin Roosevelt looked beyond the horizon and gave us a vision of peace, an economic bill of rights. The right to work, for every man willing. The right of every family to a decent home. The right to protection from the fears of old age and sickness. The right to a good education. All the rights which spell security for every man, woman, and child, from the cradle to the grave.
>
> It was the dream that all of us had, and Roosevelt put it into words, and we loved him for it.
>
> Two years later the war was over, and Franklin Roosevelt was dead.
>
> And what followed was the great betrayal.
>
> Instead of the dream, we have inherited disillusion.
>
> Instead of the promised years of harvest, the years of the locust are upon us.
>
> In Hyde Park they buried our president and in Washington they buried our dreams.
>
> One day after Roosevelt died, Harry Truman entered the White House.
>
> And forty-six days later, Herbert Hoover was there.
>
> It was a time of comings and goings.
>
> Into the Government came the ghosts of the great depression, the banking house boys and the oil-well diplomats.
>
> In marched the generals—and out went the men who had built the TVA and the Grand Coulee [Dam], the men who had planned social security and built Federal housing, the men who had dug the farmer out of the dust bowl and the workman out of the sweatshop.

A time of comings and goings . . . the shadows of the past coming in fast—and the lights going out, slowly—the exodus of the torchbearers of the New Deal.

He excoriated the parties that had survived Roosevelt:

The party Jefferson founded 150 years ago was buried here in Philadelphia last week. It could not survive the Pauleys, the Hagues, the Crumps, the racists and bigots, the generals, the admirals, the Wall Street alumni. A party founded by a Jefferson died in the arms of a Truman.

Lincoln, with the Emancipation Proclamation, fulfilled the promise of the new party which held to victory. He headed a government of the people, by the people, and for the people. In the generations which followed, his party became a party of the corporations, and for the corporations. The party of a Lincoln has been reduced to the party of a Dewey.

Wallace professed concern for the common man, but unlike Truman, he glossed over the bread-and-butter domestic issues of concern to common men, ultimately stumbling into generalities worthy of Dewey. Except, that is, regarding the Cold War, and particularly the case of Germany—"an American and British Puerto Rico." Wallace warned:

Germany will be the core of every world crisis until we have come to an agreement with the Soviet Union. We have been maneuvered into a policy whose specific purpose has been this, and only this: to revive the power of the industrialists and cartelists who heiled Hitler and financed his fascism, and who were the wellspring of his war chest. . . .

Berlin need not have happened. Berlin did not "happen." Berlin was caused.

When we were set on the road of "get tough" policy, I warned that its end was inevitable. Berlin is becoming that end.

There is no reason why the peace of a world should hang on the actions of a handful of military men stationed in Germany!

In all earnestness, I assure you that if I were president, there would be no crisis in Berlin today. I assure you that without sacrificing a single American principle or public interest, we would have found agreement long before now with the Soviet Government, and with our other wartime allies.

It was 12:06 AM when Wallace concluded his prepared text, but he still had some unused radio airtime. Unbeknown to his aides, he had prepared additional remarks. Reaching back to his agricultural roots and to the book of Micah, this is what he said:

> The American dream is the dream of the prophets of old, the dream of each man living in peace under his own vine and fig tree; then all the nations of the world shall flow up to the mountains of the Lord and man shall learn war no more. We are the generation blessed above all generations, because to us is given for the first time in all history the power to make the dream come true.

> To make that dream come true, we shall rise above the pettiness of those who preach hate and factionalism, of those who think of themselves rather than the great cause they serve. All you who are within the sound of my voice tonight have been called to serve mightily in fulfilling the dream of the prophets and the founders of the American system.

Henry Wallace's "Gideon's Army" fought in curious battle formation. Designating its nominee in the calendar year previous to its convention, and his running mate fully five months before the convention's opening, it had not formally converted from its original working title of the "New Party" to the "Progressive Party" until the convention's second day. Its candidates accepted their nominations, not in a hall but in a ballpark—and then adopted a platform, which the *New York Times* compared line by line to the Communist Party's, and discerned remarkable similarities.

That platform did not finally emerge until Sunday's concluding session, when attendees heard from a variety of dignitaries, who highlighted the document's various planks: journalist Anna Louise Strong (denouncing Nationalist China's Chiang Kai-shek), Paul Robeson (opposing the Marshall

Plan and "the entire fabric of imperialism"), former U.S. assistant attorney general O. John Rogge (damning the recent arrests for sedition of Communist Party leaders), Howard Fast (against HUAC—"the apostles of terror, reaction, and death"), and Rockwell Kent (advocating a cabinet-level Department of Culture).

Platform adoption moved along quite gracefully—until two very large flies plunged deep into its collective ointment. The first concerned the unlikely Balkan precincts of Macedonia. The original draft of the Progressive platform, in studious lockstep with long-standing Communist policy, supported Macedonian independence, but Moscow's relationship with Belgrade's Josip Tito had precipitously deteriorated and the Kremlin's sympathies for a Macedonian state consequently evaporated—as did the CPUSA's and, miraculously and instantly, the Progressive Party's. Paralleling previous Communist flexibility toward the Hitler-Stalin pact, the episode provided a powerful hint of the realities of Progressive Party leadership. "What in God's name are these people trying to do—hang themselves?" growled the *New York Times*'s Bill Lawrence to the *Post*'s Jim Wechsler. The second fly involved thirty-five-year-old West Burke, Vermont, delegate James Hayford—a teacher, published poet, and friend of Robert Frost's. Denying any intention to "Red bait," Hayford offered an amendment, reading: "While we are critical of the foreign policy of the United States, it is not our intention to give blanket endorsement to the foreign policy of any other nation."

Simple enough, but not simple at all for some—indeed, most—delegates.

Former Seattle congressman Hugh DeLacy (later identified by John Abt as a secret Communist) bolted to his feet to object: "If there is any merit in the platform at all, it is that it comes out fighting for a firm, solid positive basis of friendship between this country and the Soviet Union."

"Such words [as the Hayford plank]," protested one delegate, "would be interpreted as an insinuation against a foreign ally."

"From reading this platform studied here," countered Pennsylvania delegate Albert Hartunian, "one would be perfectly justified in drawing the conclusion that we endorse the Soviet Union's policies 100 percent. I do not support the Soviet Union's policies 100 percent. I favor this amendment that we make our position clear."

"I am in favor of peace and friendship with the Soviet Union," agreed a New York clergyman, "but not blind friendship. We are not Communists here."

Hayford's fellow Vermonter, former National Labor Relations Board (NLRB) member Edwin S. Smith of Putney (in May 1953, Smith would invoke the Fifth Amendment on CPUSA membership), condemned the amendment as "weaken[ing] our whole presentation of the subject of peace." Rexford Tugwell objected to Hayford's amendment as being merely "redundant," contending that the plank adopted by his committee—"Responsibility for ending the tragic prospect of war is a joint responsibility of the Soviet Union and the United States"—satisfied any objections.

Vermont delegation chairman Charles Zimmerman placed his arm around Hayford, whispered a few words, and led him from the auditorium. In their absence, the convention narrowly shouted down Hayford's motion.

"Well," said Hayford nervously, after returning to the convention floor, "I guess the majority should rule." But since the convention's chairman, the pudgy United Electrical, Radio and Machine Workers union president Albert J. Fitzgerald, had ruled that no roll call was necessary, no one would even know if it had—or not.

26

"Bases, bombs, Moscow, Leningrad, etc."

The politicians talked.

The B-29s flew.

Vanquished, devastated, divided Germany remained a four-power powder keg within the heart of Europe, a pivot point of ever-maddening tension. The Kremlin schemed to consolidate, and perhaps even expand, its hard-fought wartime gains. Its erstwhile Western partners scrambled not merely to resist them but to rebuild a devastated enemy people.

In January 1948, the United States and the United Kingdom economically merged their occupation zones. Perhaps the Soviets feared the revival of their old German adversaries. Perhaps they saw hopes dashed that they might soon rule all Germany—Stalin had, after all, commented in 1946: "All of Germany must be ours, that is, Soviet, Communist." Whatever its reasons, Moscow contended that the Anglo-American initiative violated the Potsdam Agreement and warned of abrogating Western access to divided Berlin. A month later, the Soviets installed their own puppet East German regime. "There is no room in Berlin for adherents of [German] partition," a Red Army newspaper threatened, adding that continued Western action would only "lead to a change" in Berlin's "occupation status." In March 1948, the Soviet Union stormed out of four-power Allied Control Council talks. It would never return.

On Friday, April 1, 1948, the Soviets terminated rail and highway trade and travel to West Berlin. Not yet a total blockade (military shipments were exempt), their action nonetheless presaged further harassment to come. "Any weakness on our part," U.S. Zone military governor Gen. Lucius D. Clay warned Kenneth Royall, "will lose us important prestige. . . . I do not believe this means war, but any failure to meet this squarely will cause great trouble."

On Thursday, April 22, Soviet authorities halted passenger train travel. On May 10, Kremlin foreign minister Vyacheslav Molotov issued peace feelers. By now, such Soviet gestures rang distressingly hollow.

Before nineteen-thousand supporters at Madison Square Garden, on Tuesday evening, May 11, Henry Wallace dispatched an "open letter" to Joseph Stalin, outlining a wide-ranging series of Cold-War initiatives, including creation "of a peace-loving German government" and the withdrawal of foreign troops from German soil within one year of a general German peace treaty.

Stalin dramatically replied via a May 17 radio broadcast:

> I do not know whether the United States Government approves of Mr. Wallace's program as a basis for agreement between the USSR and the United States. As far as . . . the USSR is concerned it considers that Mr. Wallace's program could serve as a good and fruitful basis [for] international cooperation, since the USSR government considers that, despite the differences in the economic systems and ideologies, the coexistence of these systems and a peaceful settlement of differences . . . are not only possible but also doubtlessly necessary to the interests of general peace.

Introduction of a new currency, the Deutschmark, for the allied zones, however, soon triggered increased Soviet hostility. On Tuesday, June 22—the second day of the Republican National Convention—Moscow severed all rail and highway traffic to Berlin. Two days later, it banned canal transport.

The Berlin Blockade had begun.

In response to earlier provocations, the West's Berlin command had, on March 25, initiated "Operation Counterpunch," stockpiling significant food and fuel reserves. Thus, when June's blockade struck, Allied authorities enjoyed thirty-six days' supply of foodstuffs (up from fifteen days) and thirty days' worth of coal. These augmented stockpiles prevented a general panic; they enabled municipal officials to continue pumping municipal water and sewer lines.

The situation, nonetheless, remained precarious. Food rationing remained at draconian levels, and unless massive supplies were transported into Berlin—and fast—the Western presence was doomed. A nervous populace tottered on the brink of rioting. Embattled, starving Berliners might beg for a Soviet takeover.

"No one was sure how the Russian move could be countered," recalled the State Department's head of Policy Planning Staff, George Kennan, "or whether it could be countered at all. The situation was dark and full of danger."

Surrender in Berlin might trigger a Soviet seizure of all Germany—perhaps of all Western Europe. Domestic Communist agitation buffeted both Italy and France. Moscow had pressured neighboring Finland into a non-aggression pact. Norway feared it might be next.

The Soviet-run *Tägliche Rundschau* ominously reminded readers that—as even Western observers admitted—should war erupt, Soviet advance units could reach the Rhine within days and the North Sea within mere weeks. "Even adventurous politicians of American imperialism would not now risk starting a war," it warned, "because they know they would then have against them the people of Europe who want peace. American imperialists would not venture it in the clear knowledge that the forces of democracy are stronger today than the forces of imperialism."

Yet the United States would not budge. Three days before the crisis, Truman recorded in his diary:

> Have quite a day. See some politicos. A meeting with General Marshall and Jim Forrestal on Berlin and the Russian situation. Marshall states the facts and the condition with which we are faced. I'd made the decision ten days ago to stay in Berlin.
>
> Jim wants to hedge—he always does. He's constantly sending me alibi memos, which I return with directions and the facts.
>
> We'll stay in Berlin—come what may
>
> [Kenneth] Royall, [undersecretary of the Army Gen. William H.] Draper & Jim Forrestal come in later. I have to listen to a rehash of what I know

already and reiterate my "stay in Berlin" decision. I don't pass the buck, nor do I alibi out of any decision I make.

Lieutenant General Arthur G. Trudeau, commander of the American constabulary force, advocated direct action: dispatching armed convoys on the Autobahn (with himself personally in the lead) across Soviet-occupied territory, to reinforce beleaguered Berliners, while decimating Soviet air forces before they might intervene.

"Naturally, we knew where [the Soviet planes] were," recalled the USAF commander in Europe, Lt. Gen. Curtis E. LeMay, architect of the air war against both Germany and Japan. "We had observed the Russian fighters lined up in a nice smooth line. . . . I think we could have cleaned them up pretty well, in no time at all."

Few supported LeMay. "The Russians could stop an armed convoy without opening fire on it," countered Joint Chiefs of Staff chairman, Gen. Omar Bradley. "Roads could be closed for repair or a bridge could go up just ahead of you and then another bridge behind you and you'd be in a hell of a fix."

The alternative was an airlift—a situation even more complex than loading, flying, and unloading planes, avoiding the Soviets, and feeding 920,000 German families. Such an operation would have to be based in Belgium and France, yet both nations barred foreign troops from their soil in peacetime. And both contained a significant and noisy domestic Communist presence.

"We decided to load up a bunch of [fuel and supply] trains right away and start shuttling them around in France and Belgium," recalled LeMay. "We had not only to elude enemy observation. We had to fool the civilian populations— our late allies . . . —because of the extra-legality of the whole procedure.

"We zig-zagged our trains from hell to breakfast. We wanted to lose them and we did. . . . Whole trainloads could be lost in the shuffle this way, and that was what we wanted."

America's Berlin commandant, Brig. Gen. Frank L. Howley, recalled: "On top of threatened starvation, frightening rumors were spread that the dreaded Mongolian troops, the soldiers who had sacked [Berlin] with . . . Asiatic savagery . . . were coming back. To [fuel] these rumors, Russian troops maneuvered . . . in plain sight of the Germans. . . . [T]error filled the hearts of the German women who had survived the first Mongol invasion."

On Thursday, July 15—within hours of Harry Truman's triumphant acceptance speech to the Democratic National Convention—James Forrestal confided to his diary:

> I informed the President this morning that I asked for a meeting with him for the next week to discuss . . . custody of atomic weapons. I said I did not propose to ask him for a decision on their use because I felt confident his decision would be the right one whenever the circumstances developed that required a decision. He then remarked he wanted to go into this matter very carefully and he proposed to keep, in his own hands, the decision as to the use of the bomb, and did not propose "to have some dashing lieutenant colonel decide when would be the proper time to drop one."

From Washington, Harry Truman (at British foreign secretary Bevin's suggestion) conspicuously dispatched two squadrons of B-29s to Germany— the same class of plane employed to deliver atomic weapons, and theoretically capable of bombing the Urals. These B-29s carried only conventional weapons—but Truman was not about to inform the Russians of this.

"In Berlin the war clouds were everywhere," noted Under Secretary of the Army Draper. "It was a question of what hour or day the war might break out."

Yet it all worked out—in part, because Truman enjoyed unusual domestic political cover on the issue, in spite of the fact that American diplomacy had failed in Berlin: Dwight Eisenhower had neglected to obtain written Russian guarantees for Allied access, and Truman had similarly failed to secure those rights for the Allies. Republicans might have capitalized on the issue, but Tom Dewey, still smarting from controversies ignited by his second-guessing on Pearl Harbor, kept silent. Standing alongside Vandenberg and Foster Dulles on July 24, Dewey noted that "our representatives at London, Yalta, and Potsdam unfortunately relied on assumptions rather than specific guarantees to define our rights in Berlin," but then hastened to affirm that Americans would not be "divided by past lapses but [would] unite to surmount present dangers. We shall not allow domestic partisan irritations to divert us from the indispensable unity."

Harry Truman would, at least, not have to wage the battle of Berlin on any Republican front.

Flour and coal were flown in virtually around the clock. Britain constructed a new landing strip at their Tempelhof airfield. The French hastily built an entirely new airfield at Tegel. Recalled Gen. Howley:

> I was down at Tempelhof . . . that first morning to see the planes arrive. They were wartime twin-engined C-47 transports . . . Old, tired, and patched, the planes had been hastily collected . . . and rushed into the Berlin service. Many . . . still wore their camouflage paint from North Africa. Each plane had brought in two-and-a-half tons of flour in a two-hour flight from Frankfurt.
>
> They wobbled into Tempelhof . . . through the bomb-shattered buildings around the field . . . but they were the most beautiful things I had ever seen. As the planes touched down, and bags of flour began to spill out of their bellies, I realized that this was the beginning of something wonderful—a way to crack the blockade. I went back to my office almost breathless with elation.

Powerful obstacles remained. In late August, as Army undersecretary Draper recalled:

> We weren't keeping even. We got down to three or four or five days' stock of food. . . . There was one way we could save this situation if we were willing to take the risk . . . to take all the DC-4s that we had around the world, Army planes and private airline planes, and substitute them for the DC-3s. The DC-4 will carry ten tons where the DC-3 carries two-and-a-half. But it meant stripping our Army in Japan, it meant stripping our Army in Europe, and the airlines in the United States, of the only really available and useful carriage for troops if we were going to war. . . .
>
> So immediately the level of food shipments by air went up. And by that time, the coal was also running out, and so some of these were then made

coal wagons, the most expensive coal wagons the world ever saw. We tried dropping the coal in chutes, or . . . into big nets, or on the ground. By the time it got near the ground it was powder and blew away and it didn't work at all, so we had to land the planes and unload them just like the food. . . . But it began to work.

If Moscow could not break Berliners one way, they would try another. On Monday, September 6—America's Labor Day—the four-sector city assembly convened at City Hall, within the Soviet zone. A pro-Communist mob stormed the building, and when forty-six Western gendarmes rushed to restore order, two hundred Communist police surrounded them. The Western police fled into the three Allied liaison offices within the building. Soviet police burst into the American liaison office and arrested twenty men. The Reds then promised that the twenty-six Western police sheltered in the British and French offices might depart unharmed, but broke their pledge, arresting every one.

At dusk on Thursday, September 9, nearly three hundred thousand Berliners assembled in the city's Platz der Republik, outside the former Reichstag building. A group of youths scaled the Brandenburg Gate. Soviet troops opened fire, killing a sixteen-year-old boy and wounding 222. Remarkably, the Soviet volley ended when a British officer calmly marched toward the Russians and motioned with his swagger stick for them to stop.

Four days later, with events rapidly deteriorating, the Atomic Energy Commission's David Lilienthal recorded in his diary: "The situation in Berlin is bad. . . . The Russians seem prepared to kick us in the teeth on every issue. Their planes are in the air corridor today, and anything could happen. Anything—they might walk in tomorrow and shoot Gen. Clay. The President is being pushed hard by Forrestal to decide that atomic bombs will be used."

And Harry Truman wrote to his diary: "Have a terrific day. Forrestal, Bradley, [Hoyt] Vandenberg (the Gen., not the Senator!), [Secretary of the Air Force W. Stuart] Symington brief me on bases, bombs, Moscow, Leningrad, etc. I have a terrible feeling afterward that we are very close to war.

"I hope not."

27

"A last hysterical gasp of an expiring administration"

Turnip Day approached.

Though Harry Truman was, more than anything, a product of the Pendergast machine, he was nearly as much a man of the Congress, having served longer in the Senate than with Jackson County government, far longer than he might ever serve as president.

However, from the very genesis of his presidency, he had suffered from poor relations with his former congressional colleagues. In November 1946, he had flayed the Democratic-controlled Seventy-ninth Congress as "the worst any President had since Andrew Johnson, and the new one couldn't be any more so."

He would soon revise that opinion.

The Republican Eightieth Congress would ultimately assent to any number of key Truman measures—most prominently the Marshall Plan, Greek-Turkish aid, reinstitution of a peacetime draft, and armed forces unification. But, on virtually every domestic issue, the generally conservative legislators and the generally liberal president stood at loggerheads. Truman proposed. The Congress balked. Congress acted. Truman vetoed.

The June 1947 Taft-Hartley Act provided a spectacular illustration of the latter category of contretemps, but Truman and congressional Republicans had also clashed on tax policy, as Robert Taft and his allies revived long-jettisoned Harding-Coolidge-Mellon tax-cut policies. The Democratic Seventy-ninth Congress had already trimmed historically high Depression- and wartime-era tax rates: The highest bracket dropped from 94 to 85.45 percent, the lowest from 23 to 19 percent. An estimated twelve million persons were lopped off the rolls entirely. Now, the Taft-led Congress proposed to do more.

With the war—and many New Deal programs—concluded, the federal budget had shriveled from $98 billion in fiscal year 1945 to $33 billion in 1948. By July 1948, Treasury Secretary Snyder could announce the largest surplus in history: $8,419,469,843.81—a full seven times larger than the previous record, $1,155,000,000, achieved in 1927.

In 1947, Snyder had recorded a $754-million surplus, and, that June, Congress enacted a $6-billion tax cut. Truman, damning the measure as inflationary, vetoed it, and the veto stuck. Taft modified the bill, but a second Truman veto still succeeded. In April 1948, Congress not only finally overrode Truman, it rolled over him—311 to 88 in the House and 77 to 10 in the Senate. A mere ten Democrats remained with him in the Senate, only eleven in the House.

Top marginal rates now stood at 82.13 percent, the lowest at 16.6 percent. Exemptions for both single persons and dependents rose from $500 to $600 per person. The legislation created deductions for home mortgage payments and the splitting of spousal income for tax purposes. Forty-seven million persons had their taxes reduced; 7.4 million were exempted from the income tax entirely.

As the Eightieth Congress rumbled to a close, it enacted such measures as term extensions for members of the Atomic Energy Commission, modest displaced-persons legislation, reciprocal trade agreements, and selective service. Yet numerous issues remained unsettled, among them Truman's proposals on housing, agriculture, the minimum wage, tidelands mineral rights, civil rights, and Social Security. "For a Congress under Republican leadership to adjourn with such a record in a presidential year would be political suicide," warned the *New York Herald Tribune*, bellwether of East Coast Republicanism, urging congressional leadership to return to work following June's national convention "to finish the job and finish it well. Any other course would mean abdication." Yet the Congress had not been entirely idle. As the 1948 Republican platform contended:

> In the past eighteen months, the Republican Congress, in the face of
> frequent obstruction from the Executive Branch, made a record of solid

Harry Truman takes the oath of office on April 12, 1945. To his left, Henry Wallace looks on warily as Chief Justice Harlan F. Stone administers the oath. Secretary of the Navy James V. Forrestal stands second to Wallace's right. Secretary of Labor Frances Perkins is at the far left, Bess Truman center, Speaker of the House Sam Rayburn fifth from right, and GOP House Leader Joe Martin third from right. (Courtesy of the Harry S. Truman Library & Museum)

Left: Outspoken Harlem congressman Adam Clayton Powell had little love for Harry S. Truman but, in the end, endorsed him anyway. (Collection of the Author)

Right: In 1948, Brotherhood of Sleeping Car Porters leader A. Philip Randolph threatened "mass civil disobedience" if Truman failed to integrate the armed services. (The Library of Congress)

Harry S. Truman and the famous desk where the buck stopped. (The Library of Congress)

Ardent New Dealer Harold Ickes angrily resigned from the Truman cabinet in 1946 but, like so many, eventually provided his support in 1948. (The Library of Congress)

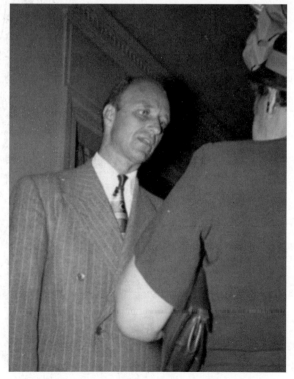

FDR and Eleanor's son James Roosevelt. There existed little affection between Truman and the Roosevelt clan. (Courtesy of the Harry S. Truman Library & Museum)

Former Connecticut congresswoman Clare Boothe Luce, wife of Time Inc. publisher Henry Luce. She roused the 1948 GOP convention by mocking Truman as a "gone goose." (Courtesy of the National Archives)

Stung by the Taft-Hartley Act, organized labor swallowed its misgivings about Harry Truman and poured its efforts into his campaign. (Collection of the Author)

Secretary of State George C. Marshall. His resignation over the recognition of the Jewish state in spring 1948 might have permanently sunk the foundering Truman candidacy. (Courtesy of the Harry S. Truman Library & Museum)

Democratic leaders pose under a banner depicting Truman and a decidedly youthful Alben Barkley at their Missouri headquarters. (Courtesy of the Harry S. Truman Library & Museum)

(Clockwise from the left) Harry Truman in transit to Winston Churchill's "Iron Curtain" speech at Fulton, Missouri, on March 5, 1946. Clark Clifford—still a naval aide—and Harry Hood Vaughan are to Truman's left. Truman's personal physician, Gen. Wallace H. Graham and press secretary Charles Ross are on his right. (Courtesy of the Harry S. Truman Library & Museum)

"Give 'em Hell" Harry Truman campaigning aboard the Ferdinand Magellan. (Courtesy of the Harry S. Truman Library & Museum)

Harry Truman campaigning with his beloved only child, Margaret. She proved to be a significant asset in the 1948 campaign. (Courtesy of the Harry S. Truman Library & Museum)

At Sun Valley, Idaho, during his spring 1948 whistle-stop tour, Harry Truman takes aim with a shotgun—and on election for a full term of his own. (Courtesy of the Harry S. Truman Library & Museum)

For acerbic journalist H. L. Mencken, the 1948 campaign was the last hurrah. (The Library of Congress)

Texas congressman Lyndon Baines Johnson, Lady Bird Johnson, and their two daughters. He wants a Senate seat in 1948, and as "Landslide Lyndon" he will get it. (The Lyndon Baines Johnson Library and Museum)

Dewey and Truman come face to face in
New York at Navy Day 1945. (Courtesy of
the Harry S. Truman Library & Museum)

The campaign's solitary meeting between
candidates Dewey and Truman, at the
dedication of New York's Idlewild Airport
on Saturday, July 31, 1948. (Courtesy of the
Harry S. Truman Library & Museum)

The hoopla and business of politics. A Chicago-based vendor advertises button and badges—for *both* sides. (Collection of the Author)

Victory! In Washington, in November 1948, Vice President–elect Alben Barkley greets Harry Truman following their historic triumph. (Courtesy of the Harry S. Truman Library & Museum) achievement. Here are some of the accomplishments of this Republican Congress:

The long trend of extravagant and ill-advised Executive action reversed;

the budget balanced;

taxes reduced;

limitation of Presidential tenure to two terms passed;

assistance to veterans, their widows and orphans provided;

assistance to agriculture and business enacted;

elimination of the poll tax as a requisite to soldier voting;

a sensible reform of the labor law, protecting all rights of Labor while safeguarding the entire community against those breakdowns in essential industries which endanger the health and livelihood of all;

a long-range farm program enacted;

unification of the armed services launched;

a military manpower law [the draft] enacted;

the United Nations fostered;

a haven for displaced persons provided;

the most far-reaching measures in history adopted to aid the recovery of the free world on a basis of self-help and with prudent regard for our own resources;

and, finally, the development of intelligent plans and party teamwork for the day when the American people entrust the Executive as well as the Legislative branch of our National Government to the Republican Party.

Congress suffered from abysmally low public-opinion ratings and loomed as the Achilles' heel for Republican chances that fall. The gap between the party's relatively liberal platform and presidential ticket and its substantially more conservative congressional Old Guard only increased that danger.

The idea of forcing a special session had long circulated. That June, Rep. Helen Gahagan Douglas had suggested that Truman threaten an extraordinary session if Congress failed to enact acceptable housing legislation. Truman aides such as George Batt and George Elsey opposed her idea, but others—Charles Murphy, Sam Rosenman, and Clark Clifford, most prominently—supported it. Elsey warned, perhaps recalling Truman's recent tax-cut fiasco, "The Democrats have splintered in all directions and at the moment I see little prospect of any early or happy family reunion."

The special-session advocates triumphed. At Philadelphia, Truman had famously flung down this gauntlet:

> On the twenty-sixth day of July, which out in Missouri we call "Turnip Day," I am going to call Congress back and ask them to pass laws to halt rising prices, to meet the housing crisis—which they are saying they are for in their platform.
>
> At the same time, I shall ask them to act upon other vitally needed measures. . . .
>
> Now, my friends, if there is any reality behind that Republican platform, we ought to get some action from a short session of the Eightieth Congress. They can do this job in fifteen days, it they want to do it. They will still have time to go out and run for office.

Truman's call echoed those of two major Republican adversaries. In mid-May, House Speaker Martin had proposed that Congress return following the Democratic convention. Taft himself had toyed with reconvening between the two conventions. The House Republican Steering Committee, however, vetoed such ideas on June 10.

Now, Republicans uniformly opposed reconvening. Dewey, already playing it far too safe, had no comment, though Herbert Brownell pronounced, "The Republican platform calls for the enactment of a program by a Republican Congress under the leadership of a Republican President. Obviously this cannot be done at a rump session called at a political convention for political purposes in the heat of a political campaign."

"The only kind of Congress that could possibly pass upon all the highly controversial measures he advocated in a few weeks or even months," fumed Minnesota senator Joseph Ball, "would be one of the Hitler Reichstag variety. The Eightieth Congress is not that kind."

"This sounds like a last hysterical gasp of an expiring administration," muttered Arthur Vandenberg.

A confident Truman confided to his diary:

> Editorials, columns and cartoons are gasping and wondering.
>
> None of the smart folks thought I would call the Congress. . . .
>
> Dewey synthetically milks cows and pitches hay for the cameras just as that other faker Teddy Roosevelt did—but he never heard of "turnip day."
>
> I don't believe the USA wants any more fakers—Teddy and Franklin are enough. So I'm going to make a common sense intellectually honest campaign. It will be a novelty—and it will win.

Truman's "Turnip Day" agenda contained a civil rights component, exacerbating already acrimonious relations with Southern Democrats. Senator Olin Johnston complained:

> never before has a President [summoned a] special session from a political platform.
>
> This special authority . . . was clearly intended to be used only in dire emergencies. . . .
>
> In the event no National emergency is proclaimed, a resolution adjourning Congress in honor of Turnip Day in Missouri might be appropriate.

Such fiction would spare the nation from the spectacle of political strife and bitter battling for partisan advantage that is certain to follow.

The Republican majority indicated its unwillingness to pass a comprehensive housing bill or to take effective legislative action against high prices during the last session. Does the President think that through such histrionics he can threaten them into submission to his will? I think not. . . .

We won't submit easily now when he seeks revenge—factional political revenue—by trying to pass FEPC, anti-lynch and other anti-Southern legislation.

We have made considerable progress with our Southern problems and with the help of God and lack of interference from the agitators of the north, we shall do more. We will not be clubbed into subservience to the will of a man who has defied his party and the will of the American people by kidnapping a nomination for the Presidency.

Taft, Martin, and their fellow Republican leaders, however, were now boxed in. If they enacted Truman's programs, he would receive the credit. If they rejected them, they would be damned as obstructionist, even, perhaps, as opposed to their own national ticket. "We do not," Charlie Halleck confided to a friend, "want to open the Pandora Box of legislation."

Dewey and Brownell strongly advised Taft et al. to accommodate Truman, particularly on the matter of liberalizing recently enacted displaced-persons legislation, a measure of particular interest to key Catholic and Jewish constituencies. Taft refused—on that and everything else. "No," he responded to the Party's new national chairman, moderate Philadelphia congressman Hugh Scott, "we're not going to give that fellow anything."

At 12:25 PM on Tuesday, July 27, Truman, natty in a blue suit and black-and-white shoes, and sporting a fresh haircut, strode into the House chamber to deliver his message to an immensely hostile Congress. No one applauded as he took the podium. No one shook his hand. At Philadelphia, he had been off-the-cuff and combative. In Washington, he stiffly read his prepared text. "His hand gestures were few," observed the *New York Times*. "He used the tones of pleading and persuasion, and his voice never rose too high when he sought emphasis."

He proposed an agenda of amazing complexity, bold in its vision, sweeping in its scope. Even the most tractable Congress would require a good six months to enact its provisions. He demanded action within the fortnight.

His salient issue was inflation. Prices had been rising all year. On July 1, New York City subway fares had doubled from five to ten cents—the first increase since the city's subways opened in 1904. Over the previous two years, food prices had skyrocketed 47 percent. In Washington, they had risen 2.7 percent in just the last month. In August, the cost-of-living index reached an all-time high of 173.

"The cost of living is now higher than ever," Truman informed his audience. "There are not many very rich men in the Congress. . . . You all—most of you—have to live on your salaries. All you need do is just go home and ask your wife how living costs are now, as compared to what they were January 1st, 1947.

"We cannot risk the danger, or suffer the hardship, of another eight months of doing nothing about high prices."

His anti-inflation program included the following:

An excess-profits tax

Consumer credit controls

Bank credit controls

Regulation of commodities speculation

Authority for allocations and inventory controls

Strengthened rent controls

Authority to ration

Authority for price controls

His other recommendations included:

Passage of the Taft-Ellender-Wagner housing program

Aid to education

Raising the minimum wage to seventy-five cents an hour

Increased Social Security benefits

Amending the recently passed Displaced Persons Act

A loan for the new United Nations headquarters

Ratifying the International Wheat Agreement

Restoring vital power appropriations and removing crippling restrictions

Reforming federal pay scales

Civil rights legislation

"Perhaps the most remarkable thing . . . is that foreign policy was entirely absent," observed Truman biographer Alonzo Hamby. "The President had defined the difference between Democrats and Republicans as almost exclusively about domestic policies; he was shrewd in perceiving that here he had a distinct edge."

Republicans instantly responded in a joint statement:

The President's quarrel with the Eightieth Congress is not its failure to enact legislation, but a fundamental difference in Government philosophy. . . . The President would fix wages, fix prices, expand Government spending, increase Federal taxes, socialize and nationalize medicine and generally regiment the life of every family, as well as agriculture, labor and industry, and his proposals would create an annual budget which could not be less than sixty billion dollars, which would make inflation inevitable and permanent. . . .

... the restoration of the OPA [Office of Price Administration], subsidies, price controls, wage control and rationing, the police state methods decried by President Truman himself, would only make the situation worse, create black markets and check the increase in production which is the only ultimate solution. . . .

Amending the Displaced Persons Act was high upon Truman's agenda. He had signed it that June 25—and Senate Democrats had supported it by a twenty-four to twelve margin. The measure allowed 205,000 European displaced persons (including two thousand recent Czech refugees) and three thousand non-quota orphans to enter the country. Deficient numerically, its provisions contained further landmines. To be eligible, immigrants needed to have entered Germany, Austria, or Italy by December 22, 1945, a requirement that barred many Jewish and non-German Catholic refugees who had fled westward after that date. Congress further reserved 40 percent of the quota for persons from areas "de facto annexed by a foreign power," thus skewing the numbers toward Protestant Germans and Balts. Moreover, these refugees would not be admitted to American shores in *addition* to existing quotas, but in *advance* of them. Every displaced person admitted in the next two years translated into one less in the years to come. "This is a most begrudging method of accepting useful and worthy people," said Truman, reluctantly signing the July 25 measure.

Pressure was building on Truman not just to propose, but to act. In June 1941, Brotherhood of Sleeping Car Porters president, A. Philip Randolph, had vowed that fifty thousand African-Americans would march on Washington unless Franklin Roosevelt established a Fair Employment Practices Commission. FDR acquiesced. In March 1948, with Truman moving to institute a peacetime draft, he conferred with Randolph, who bluntly threatened him with "mass civil disobedience" unless the armed forces were integrated. Truman quickly cut the meeting short.

Nine days later, Randolph went even further. "This time Negroes will not take the Jim Crow laws lying down," Randolph informed shocked members of the Senate Armed Services Committee. "The conscience of the world will be shaken as by nothing else when thousands and thousands of us second-class Americans choose imprisonment in preference to permanent military slavery. . . . I personally pledge myself to openly counsel, aid and abet youth, both white and Negro, to quarantine any Jim Crow conscription system." The Congress of Racial Equality (CORE), boasting such notables as Roger Baldwin, John Dewey, A. J. Muste, and Bayard Rustin, quickly voted its support. The NAACP polled black students and found that only 24 percent said they would register and serve.

Congress, however, refused to see any need for action. In mid-June, by a sixty-seven to seven margin, the Senate tabled legislation banning segregation in the armed services. With draft registration scheduled to commence on August 30—just ten weeks before Election Day—the administration was on an accelerated collision course with the nation's black minority. Seventeen years before Martin Luther King Jr.'s nonviolent civil rights march in Selma, Alabama, America was about to experience Mohandas Gandhi's tactic of nonviolent civil disobedience—not just in the Black Belt, but nationwide.

It was within such an explosive context that, on July 26, Truman responded with Executive Orders 9980 and 9981, desegregating federal employment, most particularly in the military. It was undeniably a bold move—Truman's boldest yet.

His timing revealed remarkable calculation. The Dixiecrat revolt had, by now, revealed itself to be less akin to a Democratic Party civil war than a localized civil disorder. At worst, a handful of states would depart Democratic ranks—and, at the present moment, nothing might be done to win them back. Henry Wallace, however, remained poised to seize substantial, crucial portions of the northern black vote. Wallace had not employed Paul Robeson, convention keynoter Charles P. Howard, and scores of black preachers at Progressive Party meetings nationwide without some premeditation. By desegregating the armed services, Truman had checkmated his rival once more.

Attention shifted from inflation and immigration to civil rights, specifically to a previously approved House measure to abolish the poll tax.

A key Truman civil rights proposal involved abolishing the poll tax. Twenty-one Democratic senators from eleven Southern states, led by Georgia's Richard Russell, reacted with an extremely low-key, but nonetheless effective filibuster, bringing Senate debate to a virtual halt. On August 4, twenty-four

Democrats (the majority of their caucus) joined forty-five Republicans in terminating debate on the poll tax repeal. In the end, however, terminating the filibuster made little difference. At 7:40 PM on Saturday, August 7—thirteen days into the special session—the House voted 236 to 56 to adjourn. Thirty-two minutes later the Senate (54 to 18) followed their lead. The Turnip Day session was over.

It had enacted a bare handful of items: consumer credit controls, the regulation of bank credit, a thirty-two-year, interest-free $65-million loan for United Nations construction (dear to New Yorker Tom Dewey's heart), and a "free enterprise" measure facilitating the private construction of small homes and apartments—but not the Taft-Ellender-Wagner Act.

Democrats guffawed at the results.

Charged Howard McGrath:

The Republican "new look" now stands revealed as camouflage for a tongue-tied candidate hiding behind the long skirts of a reactionary congressional leadership.

The Republican Presidential candidate did take a semi-public stand on the issue of amending the Displaced Persons Law. The Republican Congress rammed this request right back down their leader's throat. This gives him the opportunity to explain, during the campaign, how he proposes to force liberal legislation out of a reactionary Congress in the unlikely event that he is elected.

The Republican Presidential candidate refused to take a public stand against the transparent maneuver by which the Republican leadership tied both hands behind its back and announced—with a copious flow of crocodile tears—that it could not force the anti–poll tax bill to a vote. He thus has forfeited the right to discuss civil rights during the campaign.

In a similar fashion, Governor Dewey has let the International Wheat Agreement, Federal aid to schools, a higher minimum wage, broader Social Security, an expanded federal power program and fair pay for Federal workers go by default.

It is reported that the Governor is now preparing a campaign speech. It is difficult to see how it can honestly contain anything more than the silence which Governor Dewey has maintained during the special session of Congress.

"My special session has turned out to be a dud as I was sure it would," Harry Truman wrote to his sister, Mary Jane. "They are just fooling around doing nothing as I expected. It is a crying shame for them to act like that when the country so sorely needs action. . . . The Congress ran off and left everything just as I expected they would do and now they are trying to blame *me* because they did nothing. I just don't believe people can be fooled that easily."

"Would you say it was a do-nothing session, Mr. President?" asked a reporter at President Truman's Thursday, August 12, press conference.

"I would say it was entirely a 'do-nothing' session," Truman responded, seizing an opening when he saw one. "I think that's a good name for the Eightieth Congress."

"I have never laid eyes on him"

Harry Truman's summoning Congress back into session unleashed unintended consequences, for 1948, a year of elections, was also very much a year of Communism—in Prague, in Berlin airspace, on Chinese battlefields, in a radio studio in Portland, Oregon, in the councils of Henry Wallace's Progressive Party.

And, certainly, in Washington.

Republicans had enjoyed some success in raising the issue of Communist infiltration of federal agencies in both the 1944 and 1946 elections, and Truman knew more trouble was headed his way in 1948. "It was a *political* problem," recalled Clark Clifford to journalist Carl Bernstein in 1978. "Truman was going to run in '48 and that was it. . . . We never had a serious discussion about a real loyalty security problem. . . . The president did not attach fundamental importance to the so-called communist scare. He thought it was a lot of baloney."

Yet, despite his private doubts, Truman acted. He began cleansing the house Franklin Roosevelt had bequeathed to him, for Communists had indeed infiltrated the New Deal, sometimes as agents of espionage, more often as agents of influence. The Progressive Party's Edwin S. Smith, Lee Pressman (Soviet cover name: "Vig"), John Abt ("Bat"), and Charles Kramer ("Plumb" or "Mole") were among the Communist Party members employed in such agencies as the NLRB and the departments of State, Commerce, Agriculture, and the Treasury. Party supporters Martha Dodd Stern (daughter of FDR's first ambassador to Berlin; cover name: "Liza") and her millionaire husband, Alfred K. Stern, were similarly Soviet agents.

In spring 1947, the Truman administration acted to seize control of the situation—and the *political* issue—or, as Truman himself put it to Federal

Communications commissioner Clifford Durr, "to take the ball away from [HUAC chairman] Parnell Thomas."

In March 1947, the president issued Executive Order 9835, instituting the Federal Loyalty Review Board, ultimately leading to the resignation of approximately five thousand federal employees. The same month, U.S. Atty. Gen. Tom Clark released an "Attorney General's List of Subversive Organizations," following up on his predecessor Francis Biddle's similar, albeit secret, May 1942 compendium, the latter document primarily a guide for federal hiring. Biddle's forty-seven suspect organizations had included "12 Communist or Communist 'front' organizations; 2 American Fascist organizations; 8 Nazi organizations; 4 Italian fascist organizations; and 21 Japanese organizations." By 1948, the Justice Department's focus on subversion had shifted nearly completely away from targeting largely defunct native fascism to probing still-flourishing Communist activities.

Meanwhile, HUAC, now under Republican control, continued its own survey of Communist infiltration. Through much of 1947 and early 1948, it focused on high-profile Hollywood investigations, eventually jailing director Edward Dmytryk and nine equally uncooperative screenwriters (the "Hollywood Ten") for contempt of Congress.

Not involving HUAC, however, were events of Tuesday, July 20, 1948—three days prior to the opening of the Progressive Party's national convention—when federal officials arrested CPUSA chairman (and the party's three-time presidential candidate) William Z. Foster, two-term black New York City councilman Benjamin J. Davis, Ohio Communist Party chairman Gus Hall, and nine other party leaders for violating 1940's Smith Act, outlawing sedition.

"The defendant has been a member of said Communist Party of the United States of America," each indictment read, "the defendant well knowing . . . that said Communist Party . . . was and is a society, group and assembly of persons who teach and advocate the overthrow and destruction of the Government of the United States by force and violence."

CPUSA spokesmen denounced the "Truman effort to win the election, by hook or crook . . . , this American version of the Reichstag Fire," terming the arrests "the domestic counterpart of the criminal bipartisan attempts to turn the war in Berlin from cold to hot."

"Terrified of the growing support for the Wallace-Taylor ticket," they continued, "the Democratic high command is seeking to brand the new party as 'criminal' because among the opponents of Wall Street's two parties and their candidates are the Communists, who also join with all other progressives in supporting the new people's anti-war party."

"Defense of the civil rights of Communists," Henry Wallace would say at his convention, "is the first line of defense of the liberties of a democratic people. The history of Germany, Italy, Japan and Franco-Spain should teach us that the suppression of the Communists is but the first step in an assault on the democratic rights of labor, national, racial and political minorities, and all those who oppose the policies of the Government in power."

"It seems to me," added Glen Taylor, "that the indictments were timed strategically in respect to our convention. They are trying to brand us as a Red outfit on the eve of the convention.

"I am not disturbed by talk of Red infiltration so far as the Reds controlling our party. The only thing that disturbs me is the propaganda value to our opponents.

"If they want to vote for our program, I welcome the support of anybody."

The federal grand jury that indicted a dozen Communist Party leaders on July 20 had heard from those with first-hand knowledge regarding domestic communism's least idealistic aspects. Among its witnesses was self-confessed former Soviet espionage agent Elizabeth T. Bentley. Working alongside her Russian-born lover Jacob Golos (a conspirator in the assassination of Leon Trotsky), the forty-year-old Vassar and Columbia graduate had collected data from a network of between thirty and fifty agents and sympathizers covertly operating within Roosevelt administration confines.

Bentley's testimony might never have reached Congress—and never resulted in the chain of events that propelled one very junior HUAC committee member into the White House—were it not for Harry Truman's "Turnip Day" strategy. Save for Truman, congressmen would never have been in session. They would have been home, campaigning in Mississippi or

California or South Dakota. None would have been present to hear Elizabeth Bentley—or Whittaker Chambers, or Alger Hiss.

On Friday, July 30, Michigan senator Homer Ferguson's Senate Investigations Subcommittee received Miss Bentley's public testimony, regarding how thirty-nine-year-old Mary Watkins Price ("Kid," "Dir," or "Arena")—the North Carolina Progressive Party chairwoman, the state's first female gubernatorial candidate, and a former confidential and editorial secretary to columnist Walter Lippmann—had rifled through Lippmann's files to obtain information on United States–British relations.

That, however, was the least significant aspect of Elizabeth Bentley's testimony.

On Saturday, July 31, the *New York Times* headlined not Miss Price, but rather Miss Bentley's allegations concerning the President's Council of Economic Advisers functionary William W. Remington (cover name: "Fedya").

That, however, was the *second* least significant aspect of Elizabeth Bentley's testimony.

HUAC (thanks to the urging of South Dakota's balding, rotund Karl Mundt) had secretly also been interrogating Miss Bentley. Now "scooped," it rushed her into public testimony, where she quickly identified Henry Wallace's aide John Abt, former FDR economic adviser Lauchlin Currie (cover name: "Page"), and assistant secretary of the Treasury Harry Dexter White ("Lawyer" or "Jurist") as members of her ring. Mississippi's insanely anti-Semitic John Rankin said her testimony "smears Currie by remote control [coming] from two [Jewish] Communists [George Silverman and Nathan Silvermaster] who would just as soon lie."

White was the biggest fish Bentley named. Early in 1948, Henry Wallace had remarked that, if elected, he would designate White—a close friend of Lee Pressman—as his Treasury secretary. White's name might be better known to history but for the fact that within three days of his testifying before HUAC on Friday the 13th of August, 1948, he dropped quite permanently dead of a heart attack.

Nonetheless, while White lived, he was quite the catch, and to verify Bentley's charges against him and the others, HUAC summoned to its witness stand another former Communist spy courier—an exceedingly talented, exceedingly disheveled, forty-seven-year-old *Time* senior editor named Whittaker Chambers.

In a largely empty hearing room, struggling to make his testimony heard as the public address system failed, Chambers (cover name: "Karl") corroborated Bentley's testimony against both White and Abt, and fingered Lee Pressman and Charles Kramer. Maintaining an earnest, odd reluctance, a profound sadness, even an immense weariness, Chambers was clearly no publicity-seeking grandstander, but a man who softly informed his audience, "Yet so strong is the hold which the insidious evil of Communism secures upon its disciples that I could say to [my wife, Esther] at the time—'I know that I am leaving the winning side for the losing side but it is better to die on the losing side than to live under Communism.'"

Chambers then issued a new bombshell: forty-four-year-old former State Department rising star Alger Hiss (cover name: "Ales") was a Communist. Chambers's revelation captured the attention of the nation. Perhaps it was the obvious physical contrast between the two men: Hiss's confident, even arrogant, patrician bearing versus his accuser's short, rumpled, halting mien. "If Chambers might have been played by Sydney Greenstreet," observed Truman biographer Alonzo Hamby, "the role of Hiss would have required a stock Hollywood nice guy, possibly Ronald Reagan."

Or perhaps what caught everyone's notice was substantive: Hiss's palpable influence on the nation's foreign affairs—as FDR's adviser at the now-controversial Yalta Conference; as executive secretary of 1944's Dumbarton Oaks Conference; as secretary general of 1945's United Nations Conference in San Francisco; and now—thanks in part to the patronage of Tom Dewey's éminence grise John Foster Dulles—as the $20,000-a-year president of the prestigious Carnegie Endowment for International Peace. Hiss personified the silken workings of the nation's foreign policy establishment.

But more than that, the contretemps was palpably and obviously personal—as evidenced by Chambers's oddly pained accusation and the dismissive, even haughty manner of Hiss's denial not only of Communist sympathies, but of even knowing his accuser.

"I was very fond of Mr. Hiss," Chambers testified. "He was certainly the closest friend I ever had in the Communist Party. But in the moment of historic jeopardy in which this nation now stands, so help me God I cannot do otherwise."

"I am not and never have been a member of the Communist Party," Hiss countered. "I do not and never have adhered to the tenets of the Communist Party. . . . So far as I am aware, I have never laid eyes on him, and I would like the opportunity to do so."

The nation easily accepted Hiss's masterful public rebuttal. Chambers had laid an egg. HUAC, populated by men of an exceedingly political nature, who possessed no great stake in Chambers, were inclined to retreat. "We've been had," exclaimed Karl Mundt. "We've been ruined."

Wizened little John Rankin rushed to shake Alger Hiss's hand, fighting his way through a crowd of like-minded well-wishers. The *Washington Post* denounced "the entry of our society into a twilight zone between government by law and government by lawlessness."

"Smearing good people like Laughlin Currie, Alger Hiss and others is, I think, unforgivable . . . ," wrote Eleanor Roosevelt in her daily newspaper column. "Anyone knowing either Mr. Currie or Mr. Hiss, who . . . I happen to know fairly well, would not need any denial on their part to know they are not Communists. Their records prove it. But many people who do not know them would read of the accusations and never know that they were cleared."

At a Thursday, August 5, press conference, Harry Truman spoke out. He shouldn't have. In November 1945, J. Edgar Hoover had dispatched to Truman a memorandum warning that Harry Dexter White (among others) was, in all probability, a Communist agent, echoing an admonition columnist Drew Pearson had earlier provided to then–Treasury Secretary Fred Vinson. Ignoring such intelligence, in January 1946 Truman had nonetheless appointed White as executive director of the newly formed International Monetary Fund.

Normally, presidential press conferences were not at that time quoted directly. On August 5, Harry Truman angrily made an exception:

Q. Mr. President, do you think that the Capitol Hill spy scare is a "red herring" to divert public attention from inflation?

THE PRESIDENT. Yes, I do. . . . The public hearings [serve] no useful purpose. On the contrary, they are doing irreparable harm to certain people, seriously impairing the morale of Federal employees, and undermining public confidence in the Government. . . . They are simply a "red herring" to keep from doing what they ought to do.

At HUAC, everyone was inclined to shut the case down—save, that is, for thirty-five-year-old freshman Southern California congressman Richard Milhous Nixon. To the still unknown Nixon, Chambers's charges rang familiar. He had once consulted Father John F. Cronin, author of a November 1945 report for American Catholic bishops regarding domestic communism. Cronin strongly suspected Hiss of party membership. Beyond that, Eastern establishment liberal Hiss simply annoyed small-town California Republican Nixon. "Nixon had his hat set for Hiss," recalled HUAC lead investigator Robert Stripling. "It was a personal thing."

Unlike Karl Mundt and the other HUAC members, Nixon grasped an item of high significance: Alger Hiss had overplayed his hand. Most men accused of espionage or mere CPUSA membership simply denied the charges or invoked the Fifth Amendment. Alger Hiss baldly denied ever knowing Whittaker Chambers, by that name or any other, in any way, shape, or form, thus climbing to the very end of the longest limb in Washington.

Richard Nixon would saw it off.

"In most cases," pondered Nixon, "we were in an almost impossible position of having to prove whether or not an individual had actually been a Communist. This time, however, because of Hiss's categorical denials, we did not have to establish anything more complicated than whether the two men had known each other."

Pursuing that line of inquiry, the committee interviewed Chambers once more, eliciting a wealth of detail in support of his claim: Chambers had sublet a Washington apartment from Hiss; Hiss was deaf in one ear; Chambers had received a dark blue 1929 Ford Model A from Hiss; they had addressed each other in Quaker "plain speech"; Hiss's hobbies included tennis and bird-watching; and numbered among Hiss's boasts was that he had sighted a very rare bird indeed along the banks of the Potomac—a prothonotary warbler.

Interrogated in private session, point by point, Hiss confirmed the mass of detail provided by Chambers, most significantly when Nixon queried Hiss regarding his hobbies, and Congressman John McDowell of Wilkinsburg, Pennsylvania—himself a bird-watcher—interjected, "Did you ever see a prothonotary warbler?" In all innocence, and, yet, not quite all innocence, Hiss answered, "I have—right here on the Potomac. Do you know that place? . . . They come back and nest in those swamps. Beautiful yellow head, a gorgeous bird."

Shortly thereafter, the committee brought the two men together, and finally Alger Hiss grudgingly admitted that the man he had so categorically denied knowing was an individual he had indeed known as "George Crosley," to whom he had indeed rented an apartment and transferred an automobile—but whom he had not known to be a Communist. Hiss dared Chambers to repeat his allegations in a public, non-congressional venue—where he might be sued.

On NBC television's *Meet the Press*, on August 27, 1948, Chambers, interrogated by a hostile panel moderated by James Reston (who had recommended Hiss for his position at the Carnegie Endowment), did just that.

"Are you willing to say now that Alger Hiss is or ever was a Communist?" asked the *Washington Post*'s Edward T. Folliard.

"Alger Hiss was a Communist and may be now," answered Chambers.

One month later, on Monday, September 27, Hiss sued Chambers for libel, seeking $50,000 in damages.

"I welcome Mr. Hiss's daring suit," said Chambers. "I do not minimize the audacity or ferocity of the forces which work through him. But I do not believe Mr. Hiss or anybody else can use the means of justice to defeat the ends of justice."

And on Wednesday afternoon, October 20, 1948, fifty-three-year-old W. Marvin Smith, the Justice Department attorney who notarized the transfer of Hiss's Model A to Chambers, was found dead on the marble floor of a Justice Department Building circular stairwell, after a five-story plunge. Authorities ruled it a suicide.

His widow believed it was murder.

Overseeing the Hiss investigation, and indeed HUAC, was one of 1948's less admirable personalities: New Jersey congressman J. Parnell Thomas, an

Irish Catholic stockbroker originally named John Parnell Feeney, who, in the interests of career advancement, had legally changed his surname ("Your petitioner . . . believes that he can get more recognition under the name of Thomas that he could not get under . . . Feeney") to his mother's less Gaelic maiden name. He had also changed his faith to Baptist, and, on occasion, even to Episcopalian.

Thomas, noted Drew Pearson staffer Jack Anderson, was "an improbable archvillain who would never have been cast in that role. He was obese, ballooning over the arms of his chair like a cartoon caricature of glutted triumph. He had a bald head and a round face that glowed perpetually in a pink flush. The eyes were small, or perhaps they only seemed small, encroached as they were by fat cheeks."

Thomas's public unraveling began, oddly enough, on Wednesday, August 4, 1948, the day after Chambers's testimony implicating Hiss and White. On that date, Drew Pearson revealed details of a series of Thomas's no-show employee kickback schemes dating back to January 1940. The first involved a $1,200-a-year clerk named Myra Midkiff, whose salary was deposited directly into the congressman's own bank account—and for which Thomas did not even bother to pay $118.92 in income taxes. A similar $1,800-a-year scam involved Arnette Minor, in reality a housecleaner for Thomas's confidential secretary, Miss Helen Campbell. In January 1945, Thomas's aged aunt, Grace Wilson, replaced Minor on the payroll (at $2,900 a year), until she was ensconced on the Bergen County relief rolls, and Thomas's daughter-in-law Lillian assumed the perennially phantom position. In July 1947, the increasingly rapacious Thomas added yet another no-show, Allendale housewife Mrs. Jacqueline Voss Hill, to his payroll at $3,000 per annum.

Pearson's source for such information was Thomas's aforementioned secretary, Helen Campbell. Her motive: unrequited love for Thomas and jealousy of a much younger Thomas staffer, Vera Halyburton. Trailing Thomas to Halyburton's apartment, Campbell found that he had spent the night therein. Heartbroken and vengeful, she retaliated by assembling an incriminating dossier on Thomas and providing it to a "congressional insider," who in turn leaked it to Pearson's man, Jack Anderson.

Pearson soon followed up with details of Thomas's inappropriate lobbying to keep the sons of contributors and clients out of combat, and on

October 22, 1948, a Washington grand jury commenced an inquiry into one J. Parnell Thomas.

As the Hiss and Thomas dramas unfolded, so did another—perched ever so precariously and momentarily upon a third-story Manhattan ledge.

Fifty-two-year-old Oksana Stepanovna Kasenkina served as a natural science instructor at the USSR's New York City consulate, teaching the children of personnel assigned to that legation and to the nearby Soviet UN mission. Never a Communist, she hated the system, having lost her daughter in 1933 to Joseph Stalin's artificially contrived Great Famine, her husband to his purges in 1937, and her son to the world war that 1939's Moscow-Berlin nonaggression pact had helped facilitate. She believed an "insane worship" had enveloped her homeland, with "a vast sacrificial altar claiming believers and nonbelievers [i.e., noncommunists] alike."

Kasenkina had schemed for years to reach the West, but having been assigned to Moscow's New York legation at 7 East Sixty-first Street, she still hesitated to actually defect. That changed when authorities scheduled her passage home for July 31, 1948, aboard the steamship *Pobeda* ("Victory"). "To go back to the dreariness and terror of Soviet reality," she recalled, "when a free and abundant existence lay within reach, was an unbearable thought." She took refuge with Count Leo Tolstoy's aged anticommunist daughter, Alexandra, at her Tolstoy Foundation farm near Nyack, New York.

On Saturday, August 7, 1948, Soviet agents led by Consul General Yakov M. Lomakin seized Kasenkina and forcibly returned her to East Sixty-first Street. News of the kidnapping outraged a young Connecticut housewife named Louise McKeon, who reached out to her neophyte attorney brother, Peter W. Hoguet, for assistance. Hoguet first dismissed the case as hopeless, then devised a stratagem hinging upon the principle of habeas corpus, demanding that Lomakin produce "the body of Oksana Stepanovna Kasenkina by you detained and imprisoned, as it is said."

New York State Supreme Court justice Samuel Dickstein granted Hoguet's motion, outraging the Soviets, who argued that this was a violation of diplomatic protocol. They, however, possessed an even greater reason for anger: the Russian-born Dickstein, when a member of Congress (where he'd helped initiate what eventually became HUAC), had been on the Soviet payroll, ultimately pocketing twelve thousand dollars. By June 1939, the Soviets had concluded that Dickstein (cover name: "Crook") was "a complete racketeer and a blackmailer" and terminated his payments. Congressman Dickstein, now Judge Dickstein, ruled against his former clients.

Hoguet personally served Dickstein's writ upon Lomakin, running into him by chance on East Sixty-first Street. The generally jovial Lomakin angrily tossed the unwanted document onto the pavement and failed to appear for a scheduled hearing on the morning of Thursday, August 12. The State Department urged Dickstein and Governor Dewey to delay action in the case. For his part, Lomakin determined to spirit Kasenkina onto a waiting Soviet vessel that evening, and he might have done so, except that at roughly 4:00 PM Oksana Kasenkina, now a captive on the legation's third floor, overheard a local radio broadcast regarding her plight. Knowing that her case was before American courts—and still before the public—gave her hope. She would leap from the third floor, hoping to slow her fall by falling onto an adjacent telephone wire.

She leapt ("I jumped to escape. Not to kill myself"). She fell. She landed—on the legation's concrete-paved grounds. Soviet personnel rushed out to retrieve her, but two 17th Precinct police officers, Sgt. Lester Abrahamson and Patrolman Frank Candelas, sprung over an eight-foot-high fence. Fending off the Soviets, they carried the severely injured woman (she had sustained fractures of the right ankle and the right kneecap, a fractured femur, and possible back and pelvis fractures) to freedom. At Roosevelt Hospital, two policewomen remained with Kasenkina in her $18-a-day, third-floor private room. Six detectives stood watch upon her floor. Six patrolmen and a sergeant guarded its two entrances. The Kremlin fumed. Radio Moscow broadcast: "Fascist White Guard gangsters operate in the streets of New York with impunity. Political banditism is flourishing alongside of conventional gangsterism in an atmosphere typical of present-day America, an atmosphere of reaction and suppression of elementary democratic liberties."

"They call it paradise," Kasenkina said of Russia. "I call it jail."

29

"The unseemly spectacle we are now witnessing"

Strom Thurmond's forces convened once more.

They had met in Jackson in February, walked out in Philadelphia in July, and assembled again in Birmingham just three days later.

Now, in Houston, on Wednesday, August 11, they assembled again. In Birmingham—tentative as they were about nearly every aspect of their crusade, even whether they comprised a separate party or not—they had not quite decided whether they had designated Thurmond and Wright as actual candidates or as mere placeholders. But now, in Houston, they would formally and irrevocably designate them as their candidates.

There were between six and ten thousand attendees and delegates from thirteen states—Mississippi, Louisiana, Kentucky, South Carolina, North Carolina, Oklahoma, Tennessee, Virginia, Florida, Texas, Alabama, Arkansas, and Georgia. It was the largest political gathering in Houston since Democrats had nominated Al Smith in that city in June 1928. Gathered at the Sam Houston Coliseum, the Dixiecrat convention would finally jolt this quixotic enterprise off the ground.

One hundred and seventy-five police guarded them from four Progressive Party members who picketed slowly and gravely outside the coliseum. "Boy, those boys really took a beating from the people going in," observed one Houston police officer. "They called 'em everything in the books and those guys just kept on walking, like they didn't hear 'em. About the only printable ones are 'comrade' and 'dirty Commie.'"

Nonetheless, when one Dixiecrat supporter snatched a placard from one of the demonstrators, ran down half a block, and then proceeded to rip it to pieces with news photographers' flashbulbs popping, none of the 175 police took action.

Inside, the band tootled "Deep in the Heart of Texas," "The Eyes of Texas," and "Dixie." Frank Dixon reminded attendees that Strom Thurmond's Edgefield County had produced not only their own prospective nominee, but also the Alamo's Col. William B. Travis and James Butler Bonham—namesake of Bonham, Texas, Sam Rayburn's hometown.

Houston's mayor, Mobile, Alabama–born Oscar F. Holcombe, attended. Other Texas officeholders proved disquietingly absent. Thurmond, "gesticulating so freely that several times he nearly upset the numerous microphones banked before him," began his address. He claimed that Harry Truman's FEPC had been "patterned after a Russian law written by Joseph Stalin about 1920" and "was made-to-order for Communist use in their designs upon national security." He contended that the clamor for integration "comes from agitators and socially maladjusted persons who do not care about or understand the conditions existing in the many communities of the United States where people of different races work and live together.

"Even in states where there are anti-segregation laws, the people voluntarily establish segregation; otherwise, there would be no Harlem in New York City, no Chinatown in San Francisco, no South Side in Chicago."

Reported the *Houston Post*: "With a band blaring, rebel yells sounding through the big convention hall and scores of banners of all kinds waving—including Confederate flags—the steaming delegates snake-danced, churned, and paraded through the jam-packed aisles for more than five minutes after the conclusion of Governor Thurmond's address."

Fielding Wright, attired in what one reporter dubbed a "Robert E. Lee" gray suit, accused "the present Democratic and Republican parties" of being "philosophically bankrupt":

They are mere vehicles for getting into and holding office.

They veer from point to point without regard to principle, but only with an insensate desire to pander to any minority for votes.

Government by bloc, by vociferous minorities, is a cowardly thing. It is a disgrace to America. It paves the way for ultimate dictatorship or socialism.

Only a return to American principles, to local self-government, can halt the unseemly spectacle we are now witnessing.

Following the convention, one Dixiecrat wired Thurmond: "I cried as I listened to your compelling voice. . . . You saturated the sensibilities of us . . . in the South who take off our hats and shed tears when we see a Confederate flag. The Lord willing I'll vote for you with every fibre of my being and every drop of blood in my body."

No longer so enthusiastic was veteran racist Gerald L. K. Smith. Following Birmingham, Smith had pledged the support of "our 3,000,000 enrolled followers [who] believe that the Negro and the Jew are exerting too much control in American politics." Thurmond recoiled and instantly protested, "We do not invite and we do not need the support of Gerald L. K. Smith or any other rabble-rousers who use race prejudice and class hatred to inflame the emotions of the people."

"We're not going to fool with a bird like Gerald L. K. Smith," concurred even the White Supremacy League's Horace Wilkinson.

Thurmond's South Carolina, Wright's Mississippi, and Frank Dixon's Alabama remained rock-solid for the Dixiecrat rebellion, but that wasn't enough. The Solid South had to rebel very solidly against Truman to toss the contest into the House of Representatives, where Southerners might broker the election and, perhaps more importantly, compel other Democrats to reflect twice about trifling with trip-wire Southern racial sensibilities. "We expect to carry most if not all of the Southern states," predicted Thurmond, "and expect to receive more than 100 electoral votes."

One by one, however, most Southern states defected from defection.

North Carolina had never held much promise for Dixiecrats. Fear of a Dewey victory in the state if Democrats splintered only dampened North Carolina's lukewarm-at-best interest in Thurmond's adventure. As Jonathan Daniels, now editor of the family-owned *Raleigh News & Observer*, pointedly reminded his readers, it was Yankee Tom Dewey who had made it illegal for "a white hotel, theater or restaurant" to exclude Negroes. In early August, Tar Heel Dixiecrats filed eighteen thousand signatures to secure ballot position. State election officials ruled that they had, in fact, fallen short of submitting the necessary ten thousand valid signatures. Only an appeal to the state's highest court garnered North Carolina Dixiecrats even third-party ballot access.

Georgia and Virginia seemed more likely additions to the Dixiecrat map, but neither hope was meant to be. In Virginia, the Jeffersonian Harry Flood Byrd machine quickly distanced itself, leaving Thurmond high and dry. "The course to follow," advised Attorney General J. Lindsay Almond, "is to hold to the anchor of our fundamental faith and remain in the home of our fathers even though there are bats in the belfry, rats in the pantry, a cockroach waltz in the kitchen, and skunks in the parlor."

Georgia Dixiecrats faced indifference, primarily from senators Russell and George, or outright opposition, primarily from moderate—and generally pro-Truman—acting governor Melvin E. Thompson. Their luck seemed ready to change, however, when thirty-five-year-old Dixiecrat-favorite Herman Talmadge—son of the late race-baiting populist, Governor Eugene Talmadge, and Thurmond's remote cousin—narrowly defeated Thompson in the September 8 gubernatorial primary. But the cagey Talamadge possessed no desire to alienate his national party for the sake of a protest vote. Though Talmadge himself publicly claimed to be voting for the Thurmond-Wright ticket, the official Georgia Democratic slate ran as unpledged electors. Georgia Dixiecrats ultimately fielded their own slate, hoping against hope to capture a majority of votes, but if that failed, to replicate their national strategy, as Georgia law provided that if no presidential candidate won a majority, state legislators would designate the state's twelve electors.

Texas's twenty-three electoral votes made the Lone Star State the largest prize below the Mason-Dixon Line and the fifth largest nationwide. Dixiecrats argued that Texas Democrats should be allowed to vote in the July 2 primary or the August 28 runoff on whether to nominate either Truman or Thurmond. In the spring, Texas governor Beauford Jester, a budding Dixiecrat, had absented himself from Birmingham. Facing intense pressure from Texans Sam Rayburn and Lyndon Johnson, he now worked to hold his state for Truman. "We ought to tell Lord Beauford, the Duke of Jester," threatened Houston Bar Association president, Nowlin Randolph, "that there is no need for him to bear any further the responsibilities of his high office and that he can leave the people's path and follow the dim path [to] oblivion."

But no longer did Jester, or very many other Southern politicians, fear such bluster. Texas Dixiecrats were left to scramble for mere third-party status.

In Arkansas, thirty-six-year-old anti-Dixiecrat Hot Springs prosecuting attorney Sid McMath captured the gubernatorial nomination. In Tennessee, Memphis's "Boss" Ed Crump ("Truman has sold the South down the river for Negro votes in large northern cities") had tumbled into the Dixiecrat camp, railing against anti-Dixiecrat former governor Gordon Browning in that state's gubernatorial primary. "Browning, as governor for one term," fumed the seventy-four-year-old Crump, "converted the proud capital of Tennessee into a regular Sodom and Gomorrah, a wicked capital, reeking with sordid, vicious infamy." For good measure he railed against Chattanooga anti-Dixiecrat congressman Estes Kefauver in the Volunteer State's Senate primary. "Kefauver reminds me of the pet coon that puts its foot in an open drawer in your room, but invariably turns its head while its foot is feeling around in the drawer," jeered Crump in a series of huge newspaper ads. The Yale-educated Kefauver responded by donning what would become his trademark coonskin cap and won easily. So did Browning.

Louisiana's governor Earl Long, the late Huey's highly unstable younger brother, possessed sufficient stability to steer as clear as he could of the Dixiecrat cause. He feared alienating the national Democratic establishment. He feared jeopardizing the influence of his twenty-nine-year-old nephew, Russell Long (Huey's son), recently and narrowly nominated for the U.S. Senate. He also feared a looming Justice Department probe of his income tax returns, and he feared local opinion, particularly that of Plaquemines parish boss Leander Perez. "Now a Trumancrat is a political hydrat [*sic*]," the multimillionaire Perez, concerned as much about tidelands oil rights as about race, would fulminate, "a cross between a Jeffersonian Democrat and a Socialist or Communist or a homo, of whom there have been thousands exposed in Washington lately, which can only produce an illegitimate offspring called a Bastocrat."

Earl Long and Leander Perez cut a deal. Russell Long would appear on both the Truman and Thurmond "Democratic" lines, but the Truman-Barkley ticket would achieve Louisiana ballot position not only minus the official Democratic line, but also stripped of the traditional Southern Democratic Party "rooster" symbol, both of which were ceded to the Thurmond slate. In the Pelican State, the Dixiecrats would have the edge.

On Sunday, August 1, Thurmond garnered a rare—and quite unlikely—endorsement. Baltimore's H. L. Mencken had fashioned a career from tossing verbal barbs at Southern backwardness, excoriating everyone from fire-breathing anti-evolutionists to bone-dry prohibitionists, to pitchfork-toting populists, to the region's unlikely collaborators with FDR's New Deal. But now, nauseated by Dewey (a "limber trimmer"), Truman (a "shabby mountebank"), and Barkley (whom he dismissed as merely feeble-minded), and petrified of Henry Wallace's parlor pinks and outright reds, he turned to what in 1948 passed for Jeffersonian Democracy: the Thurmond-Wright ticket. Mencken announced to startled readers:

> Certainly it would be absurd to dismiss such men as [Thurmond] . . . as windbags of common sort. They are men of intelligence and . . . have a genuine grievance.

> The colored brother, it seems to me, is hardly more than a bystander in the combat, though he will be injured, no matter what the issue. . . . [H]e will be the chief victim of the ensuing revival of Reconstruction.

> It is this threat of another dismal dose of Reconstruction that chiefly alarms the intelligent Southerners. . . . They believe that they have some civil rights, too, and they are resolved not only to protest those that remain but to regain those that have been already lost to New Deal totalitarianism. They hope to do it peacefully by an appeal to Article X of the Bill of Rights, but if that appeal fails they are willing to try stronger medicines.

> . . . It must be manifest that if the whole program of the Yankee messiahs[,] by the Force Bill of 1890 out of the Communist Manifesto, is put through with any vigor, life will become almost impossible in large areas of the South, and a third Bull Run will begin casting its shadows before.

In Alabama, senators Lister Hill and John Sparkman had promised Horace Wilkinson that they would vote the Thurmond-Wright ticket. In spite of this, in mid-August, Sparkman pointedly refused to appear at a Dixiecrat rally. In actuality, both senators worked behind the scenes for Truman, and Governor "Big Jim" Folsom (a former Wilkinson ally) did more than that, formally endorsing Truman on Thursday, October 7.

Former governor Chauncey Sparks (antiwalkout at the Philadelphia convention), on the other hand, now announced he would vote to rid the Democratic Party of "such aliens as Truman and his satellites." Horace Wilkinson tapped into his still-widespread labor connections to organize a massive Dixiecrat rally in steel-producing Fairfield, Alabama. Twenty-five thousand persons, mostly steelworkers and their fellow unionists, attended. In August, Wilkinson composed an article for the anti-Dixiecrat *Richmond Times-Dispatch*, defending his course:

> Neither of us . . . Frank Dixon . . . and the writer . . . ever expect[s] to hold another political job . . . and both of us [believe] that Harry S. Truman has done more than any living American towards destroying the Democratic party. . . . If Dewey is elected, he should make Truman Post-Master General in recognition of his great service in wrecking the National [party]. . . . You tell us we must be politically emancipated but you also say we must vote for whichever of the two parties offers us a candidate . . . to our liking. Aren't you telling your readers that they may go out to swim but they must not go near the water? . . . [Segregation is] indispensable to good racial relations. . . . Wallace, Truman, and Dewey are all pledged to destroy segregation and impose a worse fate on us than we have imposed on the Germans and the Japs.

Yet, for all his protestations of selflessness, Wilkinson had hopes of a political job, and it was not a negligible position. If Strom Thurmond did indeed capture the presidency, Horace Wilkinson would be his nominee for attorney general.

Thurmond had officially kicked off his campaign on Saturday, July 31, at the Cherryville, North Carolina, Watermelon Festival, warning listeners that "the President has directed that a nationwide federal police system be set up . . . to police elections, to meddle in private business affairs, to spy into their private records, to intervene in private law suits, [and] to keep people in a state of fear and intimidation." He declared:

> Is there anyone left who does not know that the South has almost wiped out lynching without outside assistance? Lynching is murder. We all know that. And murder is a violation of state laws, punishable by state laws. We do not intend to let the federal government come in and take over our state courts.

Lambasting the Truman agenda, Thurmond continued:

> They have named this program "civil rights." . . . If the segregation program of the president is enforced, the results of civil strife may be horrible beyond imagination. Lawlessness will be rampant. Chaos will prevail. Our streets will be unsafe. And there will be the greatest breakdown of law enforcement in the history of the nation. Let us also tell them, that in the South, the intermingling of the races in our homes, in our schools, and in our theaters is impractical and impossible. . . .
>
> Unless a man is willing to hire the kind of people the FEPC tells him to, he must go to jail.
>
> Dewey has already set up the FEPC in New York State.
>
> Harry Truman is demanding that the so-called civil rights be forced upon every state.
>
> And Henry Wallace is the daddy of them all.

As Thurmond excoriated integration in Cherryville, his staff, however, was inadvertently committing him to it in Columbia, dispatching the following letter to the governor of the U.S. Virgin Islands, William H. Hastie:

> Dear Governor Hastie:
>
> It was indeed a disappointment to me that you were unable to attend the

Governors' Conference. . . . It is my earnest hope that during my term of office, you and your family will honor South Carolina with a visit to Columbia and be our guests at the mansion.

Unfortunately for Thurmond, Governor Hastie, former dean of Howard University Law School, was black. Hastie discreetly declined Thurmond's invitation on August 15, and on October 24, Drew Pearson reported the incident in his nationally syndicated column.

Thurmond explained that, after attending the annual governors' conference in Salt Lake City, he had instructed his staff to issue form invitations to his fellow chief executives and that the clerk "did not know that Harry Truman, in his all-out bid for Negro votes, had gone so far as to take the unprecedented action of appointing a Negro governor of the Virgin Islands. . . .

"I would not have written him if I knew he was a Negro," Thurmond continued. "Of course, it would have been ridiculous to invite him. . . .

"Governor Hastie knows that neither he nor any other Negro will ever be a guest at the governor's house in Columbia as long as I am governor or as long as the Democratic Party . . . continues to elect the Governors in my state."

South Carolina NAACP president James M. Hinton wrote to Thurmond:

The Mansion does not belong to you, but the taxpayers of the state, and though you are the host (while Governor) and the right to invite is your personal privilege, you have no mortgage on the Mansion.

Negroes will be happy when the campaign is over and you settle down to your position of Governor of South Carolina, and to make [an] attempt to heal the wounds opened in this hectic year.

Essie Washington, Strom Thurmond's Negro daughter, remained in Orangeburg at South Carolina State College. By now she was married to a handsome, black law student named Julius Williams, who remained unaware of his bride's ancestry.

Nonetheless, Thurmond's visits to the Orangeburg campus had provoked widespread rumors that the governor had a daughter at the school—though speculation centered not always on Essie Mae, but rather occasionally on her extremely light-skinned sorority sister, Lizzie Mae Thompson.

Listening to a Thurmond speech on the radio, Julius Williams would exclaim, "I fought Hitler to end up with *that!* What's the difference?"

One evening, Essie dared reveal her secret, or, at least, that is how she recounted events decades later. The truth may have been less dramatic, and far less hidden.

Years later, college staff remembered seeing Thurmond requesting that Essie Mae be summoned to the South Carolina State president's office to meet with him. He would send his black chauffeur to Edgefield to take her shopping at the finest department store in Columbia.

"As long as she was enrolled in State, we'd see the [governor's] limo come down from time to time," recalled Julius Williams's fellow law student, Frank Cain. "The story was that he helped her out whenever she had troubles down at the college. She never talked about it. Everybody just assumed she was his daughter."

"Nobody needed to talk about it," remembered Julius's cousin, Robert Bellinger. "I used to tease my cousin that he had married the governor's daughter. He'd just laugh and say, 'Well, I wish I could get some of that money.'"

"At the time," recalled another ex-student, Dr. M. Maceo Nance Jr., "it was accepted belief on campus that the top assistant to the president of the college was the son of a white trustee. For her to be the daughter of the governor was not viewed as any big deal."

In any case, Essie Mae would later joke to her husband that she doubted that her father would ever invite them to the White House.

"That's why they call it that," Julius Williams answered bitterly.

30

"You simply can't make a politician out of him"

In late August, Henry Wallace invaded Strom's Southland.

In electoral terms, it made little sense for him—or for any candidate at all in the previous century—to head south in search of votes. Dixie remained solidly Democratic, and neither Democrat nor Republican standard-bearers had expended much effort, time, oratory, or treasure below the Mason-Dixon line. In 1948, Henry Wallace dared to do just that.

Morality drove him forward—to drive home Jim Crow's inequities, to show that segregation might, and should, be directly challenged by men of national stature and within the South's very borders.

Beyond morality, however, lay the inevitable calculation. He would harvest no votes in the South—but he would reinvigorate his northern African-American support, perhaps appropriating even more black votes from the embattled Truman. "It was probably the only occasion in American presidential history when a candidate traveled so many miles in the South in order to win votes in the North," noted James Wechsler.

Wallace's journey commenced on Sunday, August 29. By September 3, he had addressed a modest thirty-five thousand persons, in thirty integrated audiences, in twenty-eight cities, in seven Southern states, and delivered, into the bargain, twelve radio broadcasts. He alternately stirred up untold hatred and admiration, and, of course, generated much-needed publicity for his faltering effort.

At the City Armory in Durham, North Carolina, that first evening, National Guard Sgt. Calvin Hackney—his .45-caliber revolver drawn and at the ready—escorted Wallace to the podium. Protesters wielded placards—

"Send Wallace Back to Russia"; "We Don't Have Race Relations Here"; "Wallace Alligator Bait"—and shouted, "Hey, Communist! Nigger lover!"

Twenty-four-year-old war veteran James D. Harris, a University of North Carolina student and Wallace "bodyguard," tried to prevent a crowd of twenty protesters from stampeding into the building. A knife was pulled, and Harris was cut eight times—two flesh wounds to his left wrist and six in the back. Police threatened to arrest Harris.

That was the last of the knife-work, but hardly the end of the violence. Throughout North Carolina—at Burlington, Greensboro, Winston-Salem, High Point, Hickory, and Charlotte—demonstrators pelted Wallace and his forty-six-year-old campaign treasurer Clark Howell Foreman, a grandson of the founder of the *Atlanta Constitution*, with eggs, tomatoes, peach pits, and green peppers.

At Burlington, a father held an eight-year-old upon his shoulders, so the boy might fling tomatoes—and his ice-cream cone—at FDR's former vice president. "Am I in the United States of America?" Wallace shouted thrice to an elderly resident of the city, placing his hands firmly upon the man. "Take your damn hands off of me!" the man answered, backing furiously away.

Wallace's "face was livid," recalled national director of the Southern Negro Youth Congress and Communist Party member, Louis E. Burnham, a black Wallace supporter, "and he was obviously angry. Then, as suddenly as that emotion had been aroused, something miraculous happened. His grip relaxed. The anger went off his face, which took on the most gentle look I've ever seen. And with a composed gesture that seemed almost messianic, he waved to the crowd. . . . 'Goodbye, my friends, I'll see you again.'"

In Greensboro, an egg hit Wallace in the head. Police took the youthful assailant into custody. Wallace urged his release "because he really didn't know what he was doing."

Protest provoked counter-protest, even sympathy for Wallace. Harry Truman pronounced the outbursts a "highly un-American business," violating national standards of "fair play." "Police tried to quiet the crowds," noted *Life* magazine. "Almost all the newspapers along the Wallace route published strong editorials deploring the heckling."

It was all very bad, and yet it was all very good. At the cost of dry-cleaning a few suits, and several days of very frayed nerves—rumors even flew that the Wallace train might be dynamited in Alabama—his campaign reaped a remarkable quotient of positive press coverage. Wallace aides crowed that the turmoil was "the best thing that could have happened for us."

Threats and canceled meetings greeted Wallace in Alabama and Louisiana. Little Rock's all-black Arkansas Baptist College denied him use of its facilities, and when he petitioned Arkansas secretary of state C. G. "Crip" Hall for ballot access, Hall countered that Wallace must file an affidavit that he was not communist-affiliated. As Wallace departed Memphis's Bellevue Park, an angry crowd rocked his car and smashed his windshield.

At Birmingham, Bull Connor advised that "Wallace has a right to speak and we are not going to let anyone disturb his meeting," but Connor was not about to countenance any violation of his city's segregation ordinances. Nor was Wallace about to speak to a segregated crowd. Approximately 2,750 whites and 250 blacks gathered at the Jefferson County courthouse to hear Wallace. Some of the blacks carried signs reading:

> "Mr. Wallace, your program has set the Negro back 50 years. We are tired of being made a political football."

> "The Negro has accomplished more in the past 100 years than Russia has in the past 1,000 years."

> "We, the colored people, want education, not agitation."

> "I'd rather live in the south and know where I stand than live elsewhere and have no standing."

Before Wallace appeared, Connor urged the crowd to "help me see that he [Wallace] has a respectful and full hearing of whatever he has to say. Birmingham must not injure her good name by being unkind to any visitor within her gates." When Wallace arrived, however, he saw a pair of sawhorse-borne, inch-thick ropes drawn down the courthouse's steps and stretching all the way to the fountain on its lawn. A five-foot neutral zone lay between the two ropes, separating the races: whites to their south side, blacks to their north. Wallace might still have spoken. He might have stridden down those steps and into the black section of his audience, thus daring Bull Connor to arrest him, as Glen Taylor—being pelted with eggs and peaches that very night in Rexburg, Idaho—had been arrested in Birmingham just four months to the day previously. Wallace did neither. Instead, he instructed state party chairman J. P. Mooney, a Mine, Mill, and Smelter Workers union organizer, to announce that the appearance was canceled. A half-dozen eggs sailed Mooney's way.

Following North Carolina, however, Wallace's pronouncements significantly improved. In the South, Wallace "threw away the scripts which others had prepared for him," wrote James Wechsler. "Most of the time he appeared to be preaching the Sermon on the Mount rather than the gospel according to William Z. Foster; he said a good many things that needed to be said about the brotherhood of man. He may even have jolted the complacency of a few citizens who had never doubted that the Lord preferred them to those born with darker skins. He established in at least a dozen places that unsegregated meetings could be held without civil war."

"Wallace has marched into the Southland and given hope to Negroes all over the land," noted Paul Robeson.

The journey south had been the moral high point of a campaign piled high—if such things are possible—with nadirs. True, there remained the huzzahs of the intellectuals. Dimitri Mitropoulos, principal conductor of the Minneapolis Symphony Orchestra, displeased the orchestra's management by plugging Wallace on stage. Ben Shahn composed campaign artwork, including a send-up of the famous Truman-Bacall episode, featuring Dewey in lieu of the piano-sprawled actress. Chicago radio commentator Louis "Studs" Terkel often emceed at Wallace and Paul Robeson events. Frank Lloyd Wright pledged, "We shall vote for you here at Taliesin and we hope you are supported by millions." Walter Huston, Judy Holliday, S. J. Perelman, Arthur Miller, Thomas Mann, Artie Shaw, I. F. Stone, Clifford Odets, Linus Pauling, Artur Schnabel, Aaron Copland (publicly for the Earl Browder-James Ford Communist Party ticket in 1936), Marc Blitzstein, and young Leonard Bernstein all remained on board. But the spotlights designed to add drama to the candidate's stadium and arena entrances only reminded critics of all-too-recent totalitarian pomp. Verbal gaffes proliferated. "Wallace either would be dreaming while you talked to him," recalled his chief speechwriter Lewis Frank Jr., "or when the time came, he'd forget. He never learned you had to be careful."

Wallace learned that it was not only in the South that he was despised. On Monday night, October 19, at Pittsburgh's Duquesne Gardens, protesters launched several eggs his way. Scheduled to speak one mid-September evening at the Boston Garden, he seized advantage of a rare break in the schedule to attend that afternoon's Braves-Pirates contest. Following the final out, he strolled unannounced across the Braves Field diamond. The crowd recognized him and roared disapproval. "G'wan back to Moscow!" people shouted. "Give our regards to Stalin!"

He reached the street and climbed into his car. Hecklers followed, booing and yelling still more insults. Afterward, Henry Wallace muttered, "I don't understand it. I can't understand it. The American people. Young people."

The Communist issue would not go away—however hard the new party tried to make it go away.

Progressive Party Field Service director Lillian H. Traugott (Beanie Baldwin's future wife and yet another CPUSA member—as was her brother) instructed local members to answer critics that "hurling the word 'Communist' is a verbal device used by political propagandists of the Right to discredit the progressive movement in general and to divide progressives into rival camps. It succeeded in Germany. . . . To fall into their trap is merely to become dupes of their propaganda."

"If the ADA 'rejects any association with Communists or sympathizers with Communism' how will it determine who falls into these categories?" argued another party missive. "Will it adopt a screening technique? Will it call in the FBI or the Un-American Activities Committee to serve as its private Gestapo?"

Wallace himself often fell back upon his very real, if often very strange, spirituality to safeguard him from charges of Communist sympathies. "My first objection to Russian communism," he would write, "is the emphasis which it places on dialectical materialism as a complete explanation of the universe. I disagree. . . . I believe the final explanation of the universe lies in our faith in God who created it. And the tolerance I expect from the communists is a healthy respect for my right to believe this, without attempts on their part to prohibit or undermine my faith."

Such protestations were easily overshadowed by other Progressives' pronouncements—particularly those now issued with disturbing regularity by Wallace's Communist allies. At Madison Square Garden in early August, at the fourteenth annual Communist Party conference, for example, CPUSA chairman William Z. Foster announced:

> The new Progressive Party offers the opportunity for the forces fighting for peace and against inflation and fascism to organize and express their strength.

> Its national ticket, Wallace and Taylor, will rally hosts of workers, Negroes, farmers, veterans, women, youth, intellectuals and other patriotic Americans who are determined that our people shall not be butchered for the profit and glory of Wall Street.

August was a bad month for Wallace regarding the issue of Communist infiltration of his crusade. Lee Pressman and John Abt invoked the Fifth Amendment before HUAC on their own CPUSA membership. In mid-month, the *Baltimore Sun* reported that key Wallace aide Rexford Guy Tugwell was quite "uneasy" about Communists within the Progressive Party.

Now Republican-dominated, HUAC, however, focused its anti-communism not so much on the Wallace effort, but rather on Truman's failure to houseclean the New Deal. The Dewey campaign, when it bothered to deal with domestic anti-communism at all, did so not only in the vaguest of terms, but also, like HUAC, focused tepidly on the Truman administration's actions—or lack thereof.

It continued to fall, therefore, to anticommunist liberals to skewer their Progressive rivals. "In my opinion," said Hubert Humphrey, "if you ask someone if he follows the Communist party line, that is not red-baiting. It is merely a matter of identification."

FDR's former National Youth Administration (NYA) executive director, Aubrey Williams, was a New Dealer sufficiently left-wing for his nomination to the Rural Electrification Administration to have been rejected fifty-two to thirty-six in March 1945 by the Democratic-controlled Senate. In late September, he too joined the anti-Progressive chorus. In a front-page editorial in his newspaper, *Southern Farmer*, Williams pointedly warned Wallace that his new party "was hatched up by the Communist Party. It was the brain child of Lee Pressman and John Abt. It has been dominated and controlled by communists throughout its existence."

With regret, the Alabama-born Williams urged his old friend "to repudiate the whole thing and come home. He is the last man in America who should have gotten mixed up with that New York crowd of sharpers."

"I tried to spell out the obvious facts about the men behind Wallace's campaign," recalled James Wechsler, "but, as the months passed, Wallace grew increasingly irritable at any reference to facts. . . . The communists have taken a lot of credulous men for a ride; Wallace seemed anxious to step on the accelerator himself."

Publicly, Lillian Hellman thought a great deal of Henry Wallace. She had, after all, proclaimed, "There is no difference between the two major parties, and Henry Wallace is the greatest political progressive in the field."

Her onetime lover, Dashiell Hammett, like her a Communist, thought differently. He had never cared much for Wallace. "I love him as much as you do," Hammett advised Hellman, after Henry had been dumped as vice president, "but you simply can't make a politician out of him." Wallace, Hammett concluded, would "be better off leaving things alone and crossbreeding himself." He warned Hellman, without success, to "stop playing around with that Iowa yogi and his fringe impracticals." Ultimately, Hellman privately concluded Hammett was right.

From China, another erstwhile Hellman lover, John F. Melby—now the second secretary of the United States' Nanjing embassy, and at one time favorably disposed to Wallace—wrote to Lillian in disillusion: "But of course the best show [is] Br'er Wallace. What he and his lack in good sense and realism they make up in noise. Wallace himself makes less and less sense to me, though there are plenty of the followers who know exactly what they are after, I am afraid there is altogether too much of the whole rabble-rousing business which is strangely and uncomfortably reminiscent of the early days of the Nazi party."

One afternoon during the campaign, Hellman and Wallace lunched, and the almost obsessively parsimonious Wallace left his customary five-cent tip—a trait that distressed not merely Hellman, but nearly all of the candidate's associates. Later, they strolled alone together. Wallace inquired if it were true that much of his party's central core was indeed Communist. She laughingly responded that of course it was so.

"Then it is true," he responded.

"Yes," Hellman continued, "I thought you must have known that. The hard, dirty work in the office is done by them, and a good deal of the bad advice you're getting is given by the higher-ups. I don't think they mean any harm; they're stubborn men."

"I see," muttered Wallace.

The conversation ended. The campaign progressed. Wallace's poll numbers regressed. Hellman concluded that progressive energies might be better expended on efforts less Progressive, urging both Wallace himself and the CPUSA to "turn attention and money away from the presidential campaign and . . . into building small chapters around the country in the hope of a solid, modest future, not into a flashy [hopeless] national campaign."

Hellman complained to three CPUSA "high officials" regarding six Communist Party members within the Wallace party—"two of them intelligent and flexible, four of them stubborn and unwise."

"I think I understand Henry Wallace," she said in that same session. "He does not oppose your people, because what they want fits at the minute what he wants. But when he loses, he will turn on all of you, and you will deserve it. You have a political party of your own. Why do you want to interfere with another political party? It's plain willful meddling and should stop, because it is going to fail. Please think about what I am saying."

Lillian's role now was to chaperone Wallace's wife, Ilo—a woman with little use for Communists, Jews, or even her husband's campaign. After once sharing a ride with Paul Robeson and Zero Mostel, Ilo had snapped at Wallace, "Where do they get those people!" For a month, Hellman hosted Ilo at her rented Martha's Vineyard home. Her mission: to prevent Ilo from saying "stupid things." It was not an assignment she relished.

Disgusted with the whole operation, Hellman hastened that October to—of all places—the Balkans, to attend the Belgrade premiere of her 1939 play, *The Little Foxes*, and to interview Stalin's most recent nemesis, Yugoslavia's Marshall Tito. She wanted to ask him about his break with Moscow, though she was too shy to ask. He wanted to ask her about Henry Wallace.

He was not yet the Norman Mailer he would become—but by 1948 he had already written *The Naked and the Dead*, and he was for Henry Wallace. Mailer's postwar politics had quickly moved from anarchism to what he informed the left-wing *New York Star* might be termed "collective action," in his case the Progressive Party. Mailer discerned little that he liked in American foreign policy and a great deal to be excused in the Soviet version:

> Italy is pretty bad right now, a pretty ugly country. The Marshall Plan definitely is keeping in power the smartest, dirtiest, old-time politicians, the broken-down aristocracy that would normally have been kicked out. Italy would be better off under communism than under the kind of very bad capitalism they have there. You don't have to be a Communist to see that.
>
> About France and England, I don't know. As far as the countries of eastern Europe go—like Poland, where they had one fascist dictator after another—they're better off. Czechoslovakia—I don't know what the score is there.

Though hardly a great speaker, or even much of a platform appearance (actor Mickey Knox, his future brother-in-law, had to keep hectoring him to pull his socks up), Mailer was soon barnstorming for Wallace, delivering speeches for the cause and contributing a piece, "A Credo for Living," to the premier issue of the party house organ, the *National Guardian*.

Mailer's pro-Soviet myopia soon passed, and by campaign's end he had shocked listeners at a Los Angeles rally by faulting Russian, as well as American, imperialism.

In New York, the NAACP fired eighty-year-old W.E.B. Du Bois for supporting Henry Wallace. The ostensible reason was that Du Bois had criticized NAACP executive director Walter White for accepting a "political" post as consultant to the United States delegation to the United Nations. That was a fiction. Du Bois, increasingly the fellow traveler, particularly with regard to the Southern Negro Youth Council, had proven obstreperously insubordinate, even haggling with White over office furniture. His burgeoning detachment concerning desegregation ("I think that a deliberately segregated economy would eventually be the best way toward attacking economic injustice") puzzled many. He had decried the Marshall Plan as "the most stupid and dangerous proposal ever made by the leader of a great modern nation" and endorsed Wallace. The NAACP board decided that Wallace was a dangerous detour and that it was finally time for Du Bois to depart when his contract expired at year's end.

Back in 1944, after Atlanta University had shown Du Bois the door, Walter White had surprised many by bringing the increasingly left-wing Du Bois back into the organization that he had helped found in 1909 and had left on similarly strained terms in 1934. "Knowing you as I did," White now wrote to Du Bois, "I expected no gratitude nor did I want any. . . . It is a matter of profound regret to me that, having attempted to give you freedom from worry and the opportunity to be of service and to utilize your knowledge and experience, you have chosen instead to wreck or, more accurately, to attempt to wreck the Association which came to your rescue in time of need."

The Wallace campaign continued to pit progressive against progressive, liberal against liberal, editor against publisher—and man against wife.

There was no doubt that in New York, the *Chicago Tribune*–owned tabloid, the *Daily News*, was a conservative Republican paper; Whitelaw Reid's *Herald Tribune* was a liberal Republican paper; and Arthur Hays Sulzberger's *Times* was the preeminent Democratic paper. But the flagship liberal daily was Dorothy Schiff's humble tabloid, the *New York Post*.

The *Post* was a family affair, but not in the traditional manner. In October 1932, much to the surprise of her friends, recently divorced twenty-nine-year-old Dolly Schiff, heiress to Wall Street's prominent Kuhn, Loeb & Co.

fortune, married thirty-year-old real estate executive George Backer. By 1936, the formerly Republican Schiff was a New Deal Democrat, and by 1938, her husband was an ALP city councilman. In June 1939, at Backer's behest—he had formerly been a reporter for the old *New York Globe*—Dolly acquired the money-hemorrhaging *Post*, and installed him as editor.

But their marriage soon foundered. When Backer resigned in April 1942, she replaced him with features editor Theodore O. Thackrey. A week after the Backers' July 1943 Reno divorce, the now forty-year-old Dolly Schiff married forty-one-year-old and also recently divorced Thackrey, in a ceremony presided over by Judge Samuel Rosenman.

By 1948, the Schiff-Thackrey honeymoon was also *finis*. Dolly Schiff, though thoroughly disappointed with the floundering Truman presidency, remained wary of the Wallace effort. Thackrey, on the other hand, jumped in feet-first for Wallace. Mr. and Mrs. Thackrey battled privately—and very publicly. In the Sunday, August 15, 1948, *Post*, for example, Ted Thackrey issued "An Appeal to Reason":

Mr. Wallace . . . is deeply devoted to political freedom, to a system of private profit, to capitalism freed of monopoly, to production for peace, to an economically free world, and to action through the United Nations to bring it into life as a substitute for national economic and military rivalries. . . .

It is possible to oppose Mr. Wallace's candidacy on sincere and reasoned grounds: believers in the theory of boom and bust cycle is inevitable and desirable can make a case; those who prefer sovereignty enforced by military means at home and abroad can find reason to deplore his program.

Thus far, however, the outcry against him has been confined to the chant that he is a fool (which his canny business successes alone would tend to belie) or a traitor—a charge as readily sustained against Lincoln or Roosevelt.

It is time for us to emerge from the simulated red fog into the pure air of reason.

Mrs. Thackrey, still the *Post*'s publisher, found her editor's call to reason far from reasonable. The following Sunday she issued the missive, "A Further Appeal to Reason," in answer to her husband:

> I, a sincere liberal, take issue with Mr. Thackrey's reasoning. First of all I do not believe that the grounds stated above for opposing Mr. Wallace's candidacy are either "sincere" or "reasoned"; in the second place and which is more important, I do believe there ARE grounds on which a sincere and reasoned person can and does oppose his candidacy.
>
> Wallace's own position is not always clear and he, himself, does not always give the impression of being a sincere and reasoned person. . . . How can a man believe so strongly that civil liberties are essential for the progress of his own country, and at the same time believe that the same ideals can be achieved by another country without them?

Dolly and Ted quickly escalated their acrimonious running public battle. In the end, the paper, in a sense, issued three endorsements. Thackrey endorsed Wallace. Schiff, contending that "Truman . . . has proved himself to be the weakest, worst informed, most opportunistic president ever to hold the highest office in the land," endorsed Dewey. "I feel," she argued, "that a competent and fairly liberal Republican will make a better president than an incompetent and inconsistent Democrat." Sixty-five *Post* staffers, led by James Wechsler and city editor Paul Sann, fearing that their superiors had gone quite mad, publicly issued their own endorsement of Harry Truman.

In a campaign based upon equality, a few players quickly discovered that some were more equal than others. Illinois U.S. senatorial candidate Curtis MacDougall, for example, complained of the campaign's "top down" and "cold fish" attitudes. "The Wallace party," recalled MacDougall, "swept into town and you were expected to consider it a great privilege to be associated with the movement."

"In some places," he continued, it was Beanie Baldwin's "long cigarette holder that gave offense. Almost everywhere, there was suspicion that the national office had too much of a New Yorker's attitude toward the hinterland. I personally got awfully tired of hearing the Easterners talk about 'Middle Western prejudices,' and I know the others did too."

But one didn't have to hail from Peoria or Muskegon to resent such attitudes. In the Coney Island section of Brooklyn, Lee Pressman, jettisoned by the CIO, followed his own path back to redemption, hoping to emulate Vito Marcantonio and Leo Isacson as ALP members of Congress. Running against freshman Democratic congressman Abraham J. Multer, Pressman's career only spiraled further downward, his hubris overshadowing his brilliance. His campaign manager—and fellow Communist Party member— Victor Rabinowitz recalled:

> I wasn't very fond of Pressman. . . . [H]is arrogance came across strongly. He had been accustomed to associating with the most influential figures in the Truman administration, and the task of touring the six or eight ALP clubs in the congressional district or addressing anything less than a mass meeting did not appeal to him; he carried out such chores seldom and reluctantly. But a remote campaign, consisting of speeches at Madison Square Garden meetings, did not go over with the electorate, who were interested in someone they could relate to on a more personal level.

Never far removed from the Progressive consciousness was a question that was never easily answered: Of what value was it to punish offending Democrats, if one merely replaced them with infinitely more retrograde Republicans?

Mysteriously, the question rarely proved particularly troubling with regard to Harry Truman; but regarding local and state candidates, it festered continually. For all their faults, anti-Wallace liberals such as Chet Holifield, Helen Gahagan Douglas, and Minnesota Senate hopeful Hubert Humphrey, might prove useful, even inspiring, in Congress. Former New Dealers Chester Bowles and Adlai Stevenson might work wonders as state governors. Yet official Progressive Party candidates opposed them all, as well as many other liberal Democratic nominees.

The debate reached a very public climax, in unlikely circumstances, on Tuesday evening, September 21, 1948.

Beanie Baldwin had just finished informing four hundred $100-a-plate Progressive Party supporters at Manhattan's Commodore Hotel that the party would now be backing Bowles in Connecticut, and might possibly back Holifield and Douglas in California. Following Baldwin on the platform, Henry Wallace looked immensely uncomfortable. "We've got to build a party, Beanie," said Wallace, with more sorrow than anger; "we've got to build a party."

Wallace lectured: "Beanie, what do you do with our party, with all the talk here, supporting Chester Bowles? Maybe it's the thing to do. Maybe you want to get these scared liberals off our backs. Maybe that's all right. But when guys go two directions so determinedly at the same time, I wonder where you will end up?"

Within twenty-four hours, Wallace apologized. In a prepared statement, he said:

> Today, I read, much to my amazement, that I have "split" with my old friend and associate, C. B. Baldwin. I don't understand why such a story should ever have been written. The last time I spoke about Beanie . . . was last night. And I thought—and still believe—that I spoke of him most affectionately and sincerely.
>
> I have had complete confidence in Beanie for years. I still have. As I said last night, "We have been together since 1933 and I don't think we have ever had any real disagreement." He's running this campaign just the way it should be run.
>
> Perhaps some reporters thought that Beanie and I had split because I discussed some of the undertones of his remarks.

On Thursday, September 30, came further confusion—and surrender—as the party announced the withdrawal of thirteen candidates from key congressional races, including those involving Holifield and Gahagan Douglas, as well as those siphoning off votes from Bowles and Humphrey.

More than a month before Election Day, the new party was already rushing to haul up the white flag of defeat.

The campaign no longer smiled. But it sang. Paul Robeson was by far the most prominent musician on board, although he was not alone. Keeping third-party efforts in tune, pioneer folk musicologist Alan Lomax headed an impressive staff of performers and composers that included Pete Seeger, Ronnie Gilbert, Woody Guthrie, Cisco Houston, Michael Loring (Wallace particularly favored his version of the folk song, "Acres of Clams"), and Lee Hays, as well as composer E. Y. "Yip" Harburg. "President Truman has proved to me that he don't like my trade unions," sniped Guthrie, "don't like organized labor, don't like the Communist Party, don't like the human race."

"My most vivid memory of that [Progressive Party] convention," recalled George McGovern, "was the group singing led by Pete Seeger." The Harvard-educated Seeger (JFK was a classmate) toured with Wallace, even on Wallace's perilous journey to the South. In North Carolina, a heckler demanded of Seeger, "Bet you can't sing 'Dixie.'" Seeger responded, "Sure. Bet you can't sing it with me," and proceeded to plow through any number of obscure verses unknown even to his Tar Heel audience.

The candidates themselves also got into the act—for former traveling entertainer Glen Taylor, it was hardly a great stretch. Very late in October, the campaign issued a fifteen-minute recording, commencing with a quartet singing "We've Got a Ballot" (new lyrics by Yip Harburg to the tune of "I've Got Sixpence"). Wallace then announced that "more tunes" rather than more "pompous phrases is what we need these days." Some black spirituals (Wallace: "bigotry goes back a long time") followed, as did the by-now almost obligatory Taylor Family rendition of "When You Were Sweet Sixteen." Senator Taylor apologized that, in the current atmosphere, the group dared not attempt "Red River Valley."

It would be easy to romanticize the party's musical efforts. "The alliance between People's Songs [in effect the party's songwriting arm] and Henry Wallace was an inspired mating of innocents," summarized Woody Guthrie biographer Joe Klein. "It produced a great many enthusiastic rallies and a staggering amount of bad music."

"How a man with such a long road of sensible travels behind him, Alan Lomax, could expect such a shallow jingly and insincere number as 'I've Got a Ballot' to touch the heartstrings and conscience of the hard-hit masses, is a problem beyond me," Guthrie groused. "I never did hear a living human being call his vote a 'magic little ballot.' People I have seen call their vote a number of things, none of which are nearly as cutiepie, as highly polite, as flippant, as sissy nor effeminate as this song."

If Glen Taylor now served a purpose in this campaign, it was to make Henry Wallace appear moderate.

At Madison, Wisconsin, on Monday, September 20, Taylor charged that "Nazis are running our government," including Defense Secretary Forrestal, John Foster Dulles, and Under Secretary of the Army William Draper Jr.— Wall Street monopolists, the lot of them, he claimed, who had helped Hitler to power. "So why should Russia make peace with them?" he continued. "If I was a Russian at the Moscow conference, I wouldn't agree to anything."

In New Jersey, he exclaimed: "I tell you this here, but if that committee in Washington [HUAC] called me down there and asked me if I am a Communist, I'd tell them it was none of their damn business."

The party's great last hurrah arrived far too early, on Friday evening, September 10, 1948, when Henry Wallace and Glen Taylor addressed what they hoped would be a jam-packed Yankee Stadium, in their electoral heartland of New York City.

Forty-eight thousand attended—an impressive number, but nowhere approaching what organizers had counted on. Present was the usual supporting cast—Paul Robeson; congressmen Marcantonio and Isacson; congressional hopefuls Lee Pressman, the black former Republican Ada B. Jackson from Brooklyn's tenth district, and former Hadassah president and Palestinian kibbutznik Irma Levy Lindheim from the sixth district in Queens; radical former assistant attorney general O. John Rogge; and, of course, the most utilitarian Progressive of all, fundraiser par excellence, William S. Gailmor.

Norman Mailer, already "quite full of himself," boasted privately before taking the stage: "When they put the spotlight on me, I'm going to stand up and say that I'm joining the Communist Party tomorrow."

Rain had washed out the event's original scheduled date the previous evening. Sixty thousand tickets had been sold, and twenty thousand Progressives had gathered, before rain swept away the night. Still, observers hailed Friday's gathering as the largest mass political assemblage in New York political history. The evening's crowd paid $78,000 in admissions and donated $51,657.75 more.

A correspondent from the tony *New Yorker* graced the night with his presence, traveling by plebeian subway to the yet more plebeian Bronx: "Many Wallacites boarded my car. Half of them pretty girls with shining straight hair cut pageboy style, ballet slippers, and a look of unalterable conviction (Barnard? Hunter?)."

At second base, a platform had been erected for speakers. "Ushers passed among [the] crowd," observed the *New Yorker*, "offering blank checks and pens. Gailmor called out the names of the benefactors. 'Check for a thousand from Mrs. Elinor Gimbel.' 'Check for a thousand from E. Y. Harburg.' 'Check for five hundred from Norman Mailer.' Etc. Then Gailmor asked for hundred-dollar checks. Made everybody feel cheap. Finally, everyone asked to hold up dollar bills while ushers gathered them. Practically everybody did. Gailmor said, 'We want you to leave here with nothing but carfare.'"

In the heavy night air, banners festooned stadium ramparts: "No Israel Embargo"—"Fight Jim Crow"—"Young Progressives, Repeal the Draft"— "Safeguard Freedom"—"Keep America Free." Police, standing twenty feet apart, ringed the field, facing the overwhelmingly young crowd—an estimated two-thirds of which was teenaged. Paul Robeson sang "Let My People Go" and "Ol' Man River." "The crowd's emotional reaction to music—all music— was extraordinary," noted the *New York Times*. "Peter Seeger, a slender youth . . . stood at the microphone with a five-string banjo. Head thrown back, face bathed in strong light. . . . The words and the rhythm got the crowd swaying. It clapped the beat[;] when the song ended, the youthful singer raised his hand. The hand-clapping fell away into silence."

"I can tell you a lot of things the newspapers don't tell you," Seeger fairly shouted. "They were wonderful things. In Memphis, in Birmingham, in Durham, where white men and Negroes had never sat side by side before, they sat together and they sang and cheered Wallace—but the newspapers didn't tell you that."

"Boy, were they enthusiastic!" Seeger would recall. "This was New York City. And Wallace is going to carry New York, we thought."

"'Let them eat cake,' a foolish French queen said long ago," roared John Rogge, now running for Manhattan surrogate judge. "And when the cake grows stale and the bread too dear, let them eat stones. Let mothers tune in to the [Parnell] Thomas committee; let spy scares make them forget the hungry wails of their children."

Vito Marcantonio admonished Mayor Bill O'Dwyer, excoriating him as "Whirling Willie" and "Flip-Flop Willie." He wasn't merely referring to O'Dwyer's gyrating preferences for president, but to backroom deals cut and uncut regarding Rogge's judicial race and Marcantonio's own reelection bid. Complicating matters further were circumstances surrounding O'Dwyer's younger brother Paul (president of the New York chapter of the National Lawyers Guild), who was seeking to unseat Manhattan Republican congressman Jacob K. Javits. The bushy-browed, forty-one-year-old Paul O'Dwyer was running with the support of his brother, the Democratic Party, and the Marcantonio-run ALP.

Marcantonio introduced Wallace at 11:30 PM. Inspired perhaps by Marcantonio's fulminations, Wallace warned that "Fascism has become an ugly reality—a reality which I have tested."

"Big ovation," observed the New Yorker of Wallace's entrance. "Paper floating down onto infield. Wallace in blue suit, natty. Hair carefully brushed."

Yet, for all the hoopla and buildup, stiff, otherworldly Henry Wallace could not hold a crowd—not even his own crowd. Even before he ended, clumps of supporters started drifting away, out of their seats and down the beer-soaked ramps of Yankee Stadium, into the Bronx streets.

Back into Harry Truman's America and Tom Dewey's New York.

31

"Fifty million pounds of lard"

F ew, if any, presidential efforts began with more genuinely justified optimism than Thomas Edmund Dewey's, as his Victory Special campaign train rolled westward from Albany's granite Beaux Arts Union Station on Sunday, September 19, 1948.

His putative rival, Socialist Norman Thomas, pronounced that a Truman victory would be nothing short of "a near miracle." Mississippi Dixiecrat congressman Jamie Whitten similarly predicted Dewey's triumph. Endorsements flowed in from sources as diverse as the *Chicago Tribune* and New York State Liberal Party founder (and Dewey's ALP opponent for governor in 1942) Dean Alfange, even former Wallace supporter and world heavyweight champion Joe "The Brown Bomber" Louis.

Yet this most popular of presidential challengers remained among the least popular of men. "Truman makes friends without influencing people," noted Arthur Schlesinger Jr. "Dewey influences people without making friends."

"I had the impression," summarized columnist Dorothy Thompson, "by no means unique to myself that the man who so quickly rolled up a majority of votes [at Philadelphia] had fewer real friends than any other leading candidate and that if he had been defeated more people would have been pleased with themselves."

One by one, Dewey had drawn his defeated rivals near to him. Warren, he designated his running mate. Taft, he dispatched on a fruitless, halfhearted effort to win over the South. Vandenberg, he secured to deliver a radio address on his behalf in early October. It was, however, Harold Stassen for whom Dewey had very special plans.

No moss had grown under Master Harold's ambitious feet. By late July 1948, emulating Dwight Eisenhower's new command at Columbia, Stassen had already secured the presidency of the similarly Ivy League University of Pennsylvania. Academia, though, would prove no bar to Stassen's partisanship. Within two minutes of Dewey's naming Earl Warren as his running mate, Stassen had narrated to reporters an amazing tale, painfully reflecting upon his own stunted but never vanquished ambition. "If the convention drafts me, I will accept," Stassen said, contending that he had informed Dewey that "I would not instruct my friends to withdraw my name if someone puts it in." Stassen's dream-world shamelessness dumbfounded GOP leaders.

Dewey, calculating that anyone so crassly bold might make an effective battering ram in the coming campaign, invited Stassen to Dapplemere, his Dutchess County estate (as he had Eisenhower, but not Taft), to confer regarding matters political. Again, Dewey's prickliness took center stage. When Dewey announced to reporters later that afternoon that the two Republicans planned a swim in nearby Quaker Lake, photographers requested a few shots.

"This is for our benefit," Dewey sneered, "not yours."

Inflation continued to reign as the campaign's preeminent domestic issue. As 1948 commenced, 72 percent of respondents informed pollster Elmer Roper that they considered the problem among the nation's greatest challenges—the highest of all their responses. Dewey deputized Stassen to carry the inflation fight to Truman. But while Truman personalized the issue for consumers, Stassen entangled himself in a heavy-handed and largely pointless broadside on government bureaucracy, attacking Washington for purchasing twenty-five million pounds of lard during July 1947. "This purchase," Stassen contended at Dapplemere, "compared with fifty million pounds of lard for all the preceding year, has caused lard and all other fats, including oils, to skyrocket."

A foray to the Midwest to discuss farm prices proved even less salutary. At Detroit's Masonic Temple on Tuesday, September 7, Stassen rebutted Truman's Labor Day address—and merely alienated labor. Some suspected Dewey of sabotaging his onetime rival. "Stassen is the first casualty of the campaign. . . . In two times at bat, Stassen appeared to have lost . . . his greatest source of political strength before—agriculture and labor," pronounced columnist Tris Coffin—and no one argued with him.

★

For Earl Warren, the vice-presidential nomination remained a most uncomfortable honor.

Within California's perfect First Family, it had triggered an immediate domestic crisis. Swedish-born Nina Warren's first husband, the classically trained jazz pianist Grover Cleveland "Grove" Meyers, had died of tuberculosis in 1919. The Warrens' eldest offspring, James, was, in reality, Meyers's boy—a fact unknown even to Nina's other children. None even knew of their mother's first marriage. "Nina finally decided [to] let it be said," recalled Warren family friend and campaign biographer, the novelist Irving Stone. "We called [daughter] Virginia in, and told her first. She asked Virginia to tell the other children."

More turmoil followed. Dewey and Warren possessed precious little philosophical harmony—with Warren ranging far to the left of either Dewey or his party. "Your governor pursues forward-looking, liberal policies," Harry Truman said to a California crowd that June. "He's a man of sense and ability. The facts of the case are he is a real Democrat and doesn't know it."

Beyond that, the easygoing Warren and the perennially off-putting Dewey were a match made in hell. "They struck fire every time they got close together," recalled *Los Angeles Times* political editor Kyle Palmer.

Privately, Dewey derided Warren as "that big dumb Swede," a judgment shared by some skeptical members of the press corps. Recalled NBC's David Brinkley: "We all thought if Warren was dumb enough to believe [Dewey would share power with him], he was too dumb to hold office. Every presidential nominee says his vice president will be given a serious, important role in the new administration, but [it] almost never materializes. A strong, totally self-centered politician like Tom Dewey sharing his hard-won power with a vice president? Don't count on it."

Compelled to echo Dewey's bland platitudes, even the notoriously non-partisan Warren rebelled. "I wish I could call somebody an SOB," he muttered to Herbert Brownell.

"But Tom," Warren begged Dewey, "we gotta say somethin' about somethin' some of the time!"

Warren maintained a heavy speaking schedule, drafting most of his own speeches, but he found his words held hostage to heavy editing from Dewey's Albany high command. "There was always a feeling," recalled chief

Warren aide William T. Sweigert, "that you were not to say something unless it meshed with what Dewey was saying."

"The press referred to the Dewey campaign as being 'tailor-made,'" Warren would eventually write. "It was, indeed, tailor-made, but tailored to fit people of any age, any size, any place, under any circumstances. Naturally, it didn't fit snugly for most."

Warren opened a thirteen-state eastern tour on Saturday evening, September 25, 1948, addressing 3,500 persons at Buffalo's Kleinhans Music Hall. "Really provoked" by his treatment at the hands of Dewey operatives, Warren phoned Dewey in California. "That is a hell of a way to run a railroad," he fumed. Dewey apologized, but stonewalled Warren's plea that he address federal irrigation and public power issues—concerns crucial to westerners.

"Maybe they know what they're doing," Warren complained to a family friend, "but I can tell you I never won any of *my* campaigns this way."

"Honey, do you really think you will win this election?" Nina Warren asked her husband, as they returned from their railway campaign tour.

"Oh, I think so," he replied. "Why do you ask?"

"I don't want to see you hurt, but I don't believe you will win this one," she answered.

Despite the setbacks, Warren found himself drawing support, often from the most unlikely locales. *Time* magazine's October 25, 1948, issue, for example, ran this missive from author Green Peyton (formerly its southwestern bureau chief) of San Antonio, Texas:

> Sir: [L]et me tell you how this thing looks to me. Tom Dewey is running for President of Rotary International. Harry Truman is running for Mayor of Independence. Mr. Strom Thurmond is running for President of the Confederate States of America. Henry Wallace is running for President of the Soviet Union. The only man who seems to be running for national office is Earl Warren. He's running for Vice President of the United States. We've had a Vice President for the last three years. I'm running for cover.

As both Harry Truman and Henry Wallace eyed the increasingly significant African-American vote, so did Thomas E. Dewey. Dewey, playing it safe and wary of taking a chance on much of anything, did little more than eye it.

Wallace and Truman talked a good game on civil rights. Dewey had acted. New York State's Quinn-Ives Act had outlawed hiring based on religious, racial, or national grounds. He had established the State Commission against Discrimination. Racial and religious bias had been banned in Dewey's newly established state university system. Prominent, and even lucrative, appointments had been tendered to black New Yorkers. Such achievements garnered presidential candidate Dewey a slew of endorsements—from *Vanguard* magazine (he "has displayed more than all of his predecessors put together a concrete interest in the wholesome aspirations of Negroes"), the *Richmond Afro-American,* the *New York Amsterdam News* ("forthright, courageous, informed, and wise"), the *New York Afro-American* (disturbed by the "ineptness" of Truman's administration), and the *Los Angeles Sentinel* ("New York had the first FEPC and the nation has none"). Dewey, added *Sentinel* founder and columnist Leon Washington Jr., possessed "an admirable record. If you've ever been [to New York] you know that you'll find less prejudice than any place in the 48 states."

Though the Dewey message reached segments of the black elite, it failed to connect with that community's masses. "A majority of voters . . . know where Mr. Truman stands on the poll tax and FEPC," Elmo Roper noted in October 1948. "The same is not true of Dewey. Supporters of the Republican nominee by more than a two-to-one count say they think Mr. Truman would work harder than Mr. Dewey in trying to get the poll tax repealed and [establishing] a Fair Employment Practices Commission. The voters are not at all sure where Dewey stands on civil rights legislation."

Fueling the confusion—as well as black suspicion—was Dewey's strategy toward the suddenly unsolid South. Relatively moderate Southern states such as Virginia, North Carolina, Florida, and Tennessee (all for Hoover in 1928) again seemed within GOP reach. The Dixiecrat split placed even Texas (another GOP state in 1928) in play. The Dewey-Warren ticket gathered endorsement after endorsement from newspapers across Dixie—the *Memphis Commercial Appeal, Houston Post, Miami Herald, Roanoke Times, Dothan*

Eagle, Charlotte News, St. Petersburg Independent, the *Norfolk Virginian-Pilot,* and more. Such endorsements merely reinforced Negro reluctance to support the GOP.

Dewey himself never ventured southward, instead dispatching Robert Taft and Carroll Reece to the region in his behalf. Reece was noted for his spirited opposition to antidiscrimination legislation. The flinty Taft, famous for comfortable working relationships with both Southern GOP delegates and Southern Democratic senators, had rarely expressed great sympathy toward Negro rights. Taft, argued the black *Chicago Defender,* is:

> a known opponent of federal FEPC legislation, and is reported to have minimized Dewey's . . . FEPC law record in his appeal for support in the South. He has inferred that discrimination in employment is a "purely local matter," which Dewey will leave to the discretion of the various states if a Republican administration comes to power.

> Southern Republicans are reported to have a complete "understanding" with Senator Taft whom they supported at [Philadelphia]. His appearance in Dixie . . . is taken to mean that . . . Taft will be [Dewey's] chief advisor on "things Southern" in building up a Republican party in that section. . . .

Tom Dewey, without gaining anything of value in the South, was tossing away carloads of crucial black votes in the North.

In a profession noted for its unpleasantries, Dewey seemed intent on making his campaign an exception—"proud of the fact," noted one columnist, "that he has gone through the entire 1948 campaign without saying a bad word."

His speeches were—if they had a point—to the point, never extending beyond a half hour. "No souls are saved after twenty minutes," the candidate himself had observed.

To Dewey, if brevity was the soul of wit, stagecraft was the very center of politics. He was not merely a successful executive and prosecutor—marvelously skilled in how one might best sway a skeptical jury—but also a former aspiring vocalist, blessed with the most mellifluous and pleasing of baritone vocal cords, and he was married to a former professional stage performer.

Thomas E. Dewey knew how to work a crowd.
Observed the *New Yorker*'s Richard Rovere:

> [H]is effects are more dramatic and electrifying. . . . The instant his name
> is spoken, he comes onstage, seemingly from nowhere, arms outstretched
> to embrace the crowd and gather in the applause that breaks the hush. It
> is an uncannily effective piece of business. Dewey doesn't seem to walk;
> he coasts out like a man who has been mounted on casters and given a
> tremendous shove from behind. However it is done, he rouses the crowd to
> a peak of excitement and enthusiasm, and he has to wait an agreeably long
> while for the racket to die down.

In late September, columnist Thomas L. Stokes wrote that Dewey's
campaign was akin to:

> . . . a slick New York musical whose leading man knows the script
> meticulously with mechanical inevitability and wears a china doll smile
> that never wears off. Or, to change the simile . . . Truman is like that easy-
> going grandpappy, of whom he loves to speak, who sold knick-knacks to
> Indians and early settlers as he roved the early West, as contrasted with
> the more modern city feller who deals glibly and lavishly in land he never
> has seen, which, according to the crowd of the moment, might do for
> farms—if it would grow anything—or might possibly bear oil or gold—
> just possibly. . . .
>
> . . . [T]he Dewey show . . . has been polished up no end, almost too much,
> in fact. It is almost too mechanically perfect. . . . Dewey can do things with
> his eyes and hands that no one ever suspected four years ago, and also has
> discovered new tricks with his deep and melodious voice which has been
> pronounced by radio engineers as perhaps the best on any circuit today.

But even a wonderful soloist needs a song. Even a pitch-perfect voice needs
a message. Dewey had determined his message to be of efficiency and unity.
That he was wondrously efficient there was no doubt. Even his harshest critics

conceded him that, and even Harry Truman's few ardent supporters dared not argue his virtues in that regard. Regarding unity, Dewey had proved himself adept at bullying an overwhelmingly Republican New York state legislature into submission, and he argued that he might work correspondent wonders with the doubtlessly Republican-controlled Eighty-first Congress.

Here, however, Dewey's logic began to fail spectacularly. Congressional Republicans faltered well behind him in popularity. On their worst days, they faltered even behind the pratfalling Truman. Dewey might have defended their record, arguing their effectiveness, pointing to the GOP's crucial role in implementing America's newfound bipartisan foreign policy, recent tax-cutting initiatives, or the highly controversial yet still efficacious Taft-Hartley Act. Instead, he did nothing—and sometimes worse than nothing.

Recalled House Speaker Joe Martin:

> I telephoned [Dewey] from North Attleboro and told him . . . that the best defense was a good offense . . . that he [should] talk about the constructive aspects of the Eightieth Congress and not let Truman get away, unanswered. . . . Before Labor Day I lunched with Dewey at the Executive Mansion in Albany. . . . While we had taken certain actions that he did not approve, the impression I got . . . was that he considered the whole record a good one. Yet . . . he remained generally aloof from this issue, believing he had the election won without it, while Truman . . . tore into the record all the harder when he saw that it was not being defended.

Dewey, Robert Taft privately informed the *New York Times's* William S. White, campaigned on the premise, "We Republicans can do everything the Democrats want to do and do it better."

In Minnesota, Dewey wasted his efforts on bolstering terminally endangered U.S. senator Joe Ball. He entreated Kentucky voters to reelect moderate senator John Sherman Cooper, "even if you don't vote for me." But elsewhere he remained studiously distanced from individual Republican hopefuls. In West Virginia, he pointedly snubbed Senator Chapman Revercomb, author of Congress's controversial Displaced Persons Act. Touring Chicago, his attitude toward Governor Green and Senator Brooks was little better. Dewey, fumed the *Tribune's* Robert McCormick, comported himself "as though he was not in his right mind. The Governor and Senator met him at the station and he put them in the fourth and fifth cars in the procession behind some New York state policemen. At the meeting, he came on the stage just as he was introduced and left immediately afterwards without speaking to anybody."

Only rarely did Dewey allow any emotion to seep past his icy, confident façade. In Beaucoup, Illinois, on Wednesday evening, October 13, Victory Special engineer Lee Tindle suddenly and inexplicably backed up his train fifteen feet ("nobody told me there was supposed to be a speech"), nearly injuring, or even killing, a portion of the crowd of one thousand—including Dewey's diminuitive special assistant, Lillian Rosse. Dewey exploded: "That's the first lunatic I've had for an engineer. He should probably be shot at sunrise, but we'll let him off this time since no one was hurt."

Democrats rushed to portray Dewey not as a man concerned about the safety of his audience, but rather as a patrician cavalierly attacking a workingman. "I've been doing a lot of traveling," jibed Missouri Democratic chairman John Hendren, "and I haven't found a single railroad man for Dewey."

The GOP might have explained that Frances Dewey was herself the daughter of Orla Thomas Hutt, a retired railroad trainman.

It didn't bother.

On September 13, 1948, Maine voters went to the polls, providing Dewey operatives with reasons for optimism by electing Republicans— including the white-tressed, liberal congresswoman Margaret Chase Smith into the retiring Wallace White's Senate seat—to every statewide office.

Everything seemed to be proceeding quite according to plan.

It wasn't.

The warnings had come early—and been brushed off quickly. On August 11, newly installed RNC chairman Hugh Scott conferred with Dewey, urging an "indictment" of the Truman administration. Dewey ignored him. Within Dewey's camp a battle raged. The bulk of his staff, his wife, and his high-toned Dutchess County neighbors urged caution—and, above all, quiet Republican dignity. There would be no descending into the gutter occupied by Harry Truman. Almost alone, the savvy Herbert Brownell advocated tougher measures, including greater emphasis on a midwestern-centered farm strategy. In mid-September, the Nebraska-born Brownell, smarting from his loss of influence to Dewey's executive secretary, Paul Lockwood, angrily tendered his resignation—but then quickly withdrew it.

Joe Martin recalled:

> As the campaign wore on, certain doubts were planted in my mind that should have assumed greater proportions. . . . I was forever hearing from our state leaders such comments as, "Dewey will carry Illinois, but Stevenson will be elected governor," and "Oh, Dewey is going to take Ohio, but we are going to lose this, this, and this House seat," and "Dewey's a cinch to take Iowa but [Democrat Guy] Gillette will be elected to the Senate." I remember thinking how curious it was that we were going to lose so much and still win the presidency. Something was in the air that fall that kept us from following evidence through to the logical conclusion.

At Worcester, Massachusetts, on October 28, Boston industrialist Frederick Ayer Jr. (his older sister Beatrice was Gen. George Patton's widow) boarded the Victory Special with disquieting news. "We can't find that there's any interest at all in Dewey," warned Ayer. "He's not stirring the people with the kind of campaign you're running." Wiser, calmer heads advised Ayer not to worry.

"There is gloom on the [Dewey] train at the reports of the crowds that come out to hear Truman," reported Gannett columnist May Craig in late October. "'Oh, well, crowds don't mean anything,' they console themselves. In St. Paul, Dewey faced an auditorium with all the back gallery seats empty, a vast blank wall. 'Looks like Omaha, the place where advance arrangements had fallen down and Truman faced an almost empty hall.'"

The *Philadelphia Bulletin*'s Carl McCardle, having covered both major national campaigns, informed his editor that sure-thing Dewey faced defeat. The editor exploded in response, "Don't write that! Don't talk to me about it. Don't even think about it. You're wrong!"

By mid-October, George Gallup's sampling reported that Dewey's once insurmountable lead had shrunk to a modest 5 percent.

Nobody seemed to notice.

★

Confident of victory, the Dewey campaign—and the press—expended inordinate time and energy pondering what shape his new administration might take. Arthur Vandenberg and Robert Taft would most certainly remain in the Senate, but men like Harold Stassen might join the cabinet. Dewey's Albany crew—secretary to the governor Paul Lockwood, press secretary Jim Hagerty, banking superintendent Elliot Bell, legal adviser Charles Brietel, state budget director John Burton, and Erie County GOP boss Ed Jaeckle— would all transplant themselves from the Hudson to the Potomac.

Albany contained no division of foreign affairs, but Dewey possessed men more than ready to assume control of his State Department. The Dulles brothers, John Foster and Allen, were two high-powered Wall Street lawyers with the most personal of connections to the nation's foreign policy establishment. Their maternal grandfather, John W. Foster, had served as Benjamin Harrison's secretary of state; their uncle, Robert Lansing, as Woodrow Wilson's. Both boys had served in Wilson's diplomatic corps, with Foster Dulles acting as Wilson's counsel at Versailles. Their sister Eleanor now functioned as a highly respected State Department economist.

Dewey had long relied on the Dulles brothers for foreign policy advice, but both—particularly Foster—generated intense opposition. On the left, many remained wary of Foster Dulles's prewar commerce with Nazi Germany and his involvement with German postwar reconstruction. "He who had never risen to plead for the victims," jeered left-wing journalist I. F. Stone, regarding Foster, "asked mercy in defeat for the oppressors."

From the right, New Hampshire senator Styles Bridges, an internationalist like the Dulleses, was suspicious of Foster, reminding Dewey how Dulles had pressured the reluctant Carnegie Foundation to hire the now very suspect Alger Hiss. Dewey admitted Foster's "mistake on that one," but still expressed confidence in his adviser. Bridges warned that Dulles would face difficulties in winning Senate confirmation.

"He's the only man in America who can get along with Molotov," Dewey countered.

"And I suppose," Bridges snapped, "that Molotov is a good Republican and wants us to win in November."

Foster—like Eleanor Roosevelt, a delegate to the UN General Assembly—

toiled in Paris from mid-September forward. Allen Dulles, increasingly beset by painful gout, remained stateside. At Dewey's Roosevelt Hotel headquarters, Allen assembled a high-toned campaign team that included Paris-born Massachusetts congressman Christian A. Herter; the thirty-seven-year-old, Geneva-born chairman of Dillon, Read & Co., C. Douglas Dillon; and twenty-nine-year-old "Frankfurter Republican" McGeorge Bundy.

Boston Brahmin and Yale graduate Bundy described himself as "one of those Republicans who wanted to rescue Theodore Roosevelt's party," and stood ready to jump on Dewey's winning horse to bolster GOP support for such internationalist-tinged initiatives as the Marshall Plan. Bundy found Allen Dulles amiable ("he was always looking for tennis partners") and speechwriting for Dewey not particularly taxing. "Dewey's view was that if he made no mistakes he would win," Bundy recalled. "So we sat around making sure he would make no mistakes. And I think we succeeded, but in fact that wasn't the way it went. We wrote a lot of drafts and sometimes they were used and sometimes not. Then we spent an unconscionable time, I am afraid, interviewing lots of people whom we thought would make good ambassadors."

At a July 1 Albany press conference, Dewey gingerly attempted to move foreign policy to campaign center stage, but soon reverted to his June pledge to follow Arthur Vandenberg's brand of innocuous bipartisanship. "The subjects the Republicans chose to side-track," noted Foster Dulles biographer Ronald Pruessen, "included the Soviet 'satellites,' Palestine, China, and the internal subversion, or 'spy,' question that was already becoming so prominent. Almost incredibly, the Republicans made no systematic effort to cultivate ethnic groups generally seen as politically potent."

"The next Republican Secretary of State is going to need Democratic votes in the Senate just as badly as the present Administration has needed Republican votes," Vandenberg had warned Foster Dulles early in the campaign. "It is peculiarly *our* job—yours and mine—to see that bipartisan liaison in the next Congress does not become impossible. Otherwise, November will represent a Pyrrhic victory."

Vandenberg, Dulles recalled, proved "particularly anxious to avoid anything in the nature of attack." He thought Vandenberg "a little too dispassionate," but insisted "there must not be any 'break' between [Vandenberg] and Dewey."

On Wednesday, July 28, Walter Lippmann chided Foster Dulles: "Putting the matter on the lowest ground, there is no important body of vote to be gotten, I think, by the attempt to prove that Dewey would have been a better war president than Roosevelt. It is much easier for him to prove that he will be a better peace president than Truman, and if he sticks to that issue, I am confident he will win without involving himself in controversies that must disturb and may alienate many who are determined to support him."

Dewey heeded Vandenberg and Lippmann, and, thus, while his campaign may have been profoundly dull—particularly for such a momentous time in American foreign affairs—it was also exceedingly cozy. Anticipating a Dewey accession, and having no great fear of its presumed policies, Truman's foreign policy establishment proceeded not only to confer regularly with their presumed successors, but to feed them as much classified data as they might comfortably digest. Under Secretary of State Robert Lovett (an enrolled Republican) proved particularly adept at such back-channel communication.

Whittaker Chambers's pumpkins had nothing on what migrated from George Marshall's State Department to the Dulles brothers and their assistants.

As early as June 29, Dean Acheson had informed Lovett that Lovett might succeed Marshall as secretary of state.

In late October, Marshall, fearing the "emergency character" of the times, suggested to Foster Dulles that Dulles should replace him immediately following the election.

Beyond that, there was always the chance of the adept and particularly agile bridging of the two administrations. Many suspected Defense Secretary Forrestal, for example, of coveting a slot in the new regime.

"Bipartisanship was seen as a jewel, achieved against odds, that must be preserved," recalled McGeorge Bundy.

For Thomas E. Dewey this jewel would prove to be a pearl of too great a price.

32

"Daddy, you shouldn't say 'hell'"

Harry Truman coveted but one pearl—reelection—and knew exactly how to pry it loose.

He would hammer the Republican Party at every turn, targeting its dignified, non-ideological standard-bearer, as well as its decidedly less sightly, less sonorous, and less liberal representatives in the Eightieth Congress. He would move left to pound Henry Wallace, pilfer his domestic issues, and woo back millions of his voters. He would, when necessary, swerve right to decry Wallace as a dupe of the Pinks and the Reds. He would studiously ignore his erstwhile Southern allies.

And, above all, he would ride the rails.

His June pilgrimage to Berkeley provided the blueprint. He had rolled his campaign out for its test drive, visiting the hustings as he had so desperately done in 1940. He would buttonhole voters at every inglorious whistle-stop, trot out the missus and Miss Margaret—and, above all, attack, attack, attack.

"It looks like another four years of slavery," he wrote to his sister, Mary Jane, on Thursday, September 2. "I'd be better off personally if we lose the election but I fear that the country would go to hell and I have to try and prevent that." How sincerely he believed in his slim chances remained open to question. Certainly, few other Democrats possessed such confidence.

His first great general-election swing would not commence until mid-September. Before that, standing alongside the UAW's Walter Reuther, he had formally initiated his campaign on Labor Day afternoon, September 6, before a crowd of 175,000 at downtown Detroit's Cadillac Square. Earlier that day he had attracted 25,000 in the rain at Grand Rapids, but two mornings previously, the radio networks had bluntly informed his advance man Oscar Chapman that, unless their campaign ponied up $50,000 in advance, their broadcasts would be ingloriously canceled. Chapman approached his old friend, Oklahoma governor Roy Turner, a successful oilman and Hereford breeder. Turner, with the help of wealthy fellow–Sooner State Democrats, mercifully came through.

"We were operating," as press secretary Charlie Ross put it, "as if we were just one jump ahead of the sheriff." Not helping matters was longtime Democrat fiscal powerhouse Bernard Baruch's refusal to officially assist in party fundraising—and Truman's testy response: "A great many honors have passed your way, both to you and your family, and it seems when the going is rough it is a one-way street." Financier Joe Kennedy—a key FDR moneyman in 1932—refused to contribute a cent.

On Friday morning, September 17, the campaign began in earnest— and bestowed upon its protagonist a nickname.

"Good luck—and mow 'em down," Alben Barkley advised Truman as the Ferdinand Magellan prepared to depart Washington's Union Station.

"I'm going to fight hard," Harry responded, "and I'm going to give 'em hell!"

"Daddy," Margaret Truman cautioned, "you shouldn't say 'hell.'"

That first day, Truman progressed through Baltimore, Harrisburg, Altoona, and Pittsburgh. At Pittsburgh, only two hundred actually saw him speak, but another twelve thousand heard him via loudspeaker outside the train station. He awoke at 3:00 AM CST to address a waiting crowd at Chicago's Englewood Station. At 6:50 AM, he greeted well-wishers at Rock Island.

At noon, he addressed the National Plowing Contest at Mrs. Lois Agg's farm, outside Dexter, Iowa. Normally, fifty thousand would have attended. Instead, sixty to eighty thousand persons greeted Truman, heard him blast Republican "gluttons of privilege," and saw him laugh as he charged that "the Republican Congress has already stuck a pitchfork in the farmer's back."

"If they should get both Congress and the presidency," Truman poured it on, "what they have taken away from you thus far would be only an appetizer for the economic tapeworm of big business."

Truman would blast Dewey—though rarely by name. He would blast Congress with pleasure. And he would skewer the Republican administrations of the past. Truman informed North Carolina fairgoers:

Nowhere in the United States this year have I seen a single exhibit of that famous North Carolina farm invention—that product of ingenuity and hard times of personal despair and political mockery—the Hoover cart.

You remember the Hoover cart—the remains of the old Tin Lizzie being pulled by a mule because you couldn't afford to buy a new car or gas for the old one. You remember. First you had the Hoovercrats and then you had the Hoover carts. One always follows the other.

His unremitting harshness, this descent into prairie-populist demagoguery—so unprecedented for a presidential candidate, let alone a sitting president—revealed, for all Truman's brave words, his innate desperation. "This was a strategy born out of weakness . . . because he felt like he had very little to lose," contended campaign historian Zachary Karabell. "[Losers] break the rules. There's no point in obeying them because if you obey the unwritten rules of civility, you're going to lose anyway. So why not just do what you can?"

"It was class warfare with a verbal ferocity [not] seen certainly since the populist days of the 1890s," noted presidential historian Richard Norton Smith. "Truman talked about Republican bloodsuckers on Wall Street who are going to stick a pitchfork in the back of every farmer. At one point he even cleverly likened Dewey with his little mustache to Hitler and the forces of fascism. It wouldn't happen today. . . . [I]f you look at Truman's campaign, it was a steady progression to the left."

"We were on our own 20-yard line," recalled Clark Clifford. "We had to throw long passes—anything to stir up labor and the other mass voters."

"Anything" included a touch of the demagogic. Once, in the course of the campaign, Truman listened to a recording of one of his own speeches. "What demagoguery!" he exclaimed to speechwriter David Lloyd. "Why did I say that?" Then he laughed, "Demagoguery—that's part of the game."

No one knew if Truman's strategy was succeeding. Stony silence greeted Truman's "gluttons of privilege" line in Dexter, Iowa. Clark Clifford and White House physician Wallace Graham often found it necessary to wade into crowds to spur applause for their boss's best lines. Yet the crowds Harry Truman attracted were immense—far larger than Dewey's—and seemingly growing larger with each stop along the route.

Where Dewey projected sonorous dignity, Truman projected being "just folks." He chatted about local history. He shared his audiences' dreams and, above all, their resentments—and, last but not least, he introduced the rest of the family, winking as he presented Bess as "the boss" and his twenty-four-year-old daughter as "Miss Margaret." "It involves no disrespect for Mrs. Truman to say that her daughter gets a bigger hand than she does," observed Richard Rovere; "this country may be run by and for mothers, but its goddesses are daughters. Margaret's entrance comes closer than anything else to bringing down the house."

And the crowds grew bigger. Wisconsin's Andrew Biemiller recalled riding the Truman train from Madison to Milwaukee:

> [H]uge crowds appeared everyplace. One . . . was the little jerkwater stop of Wyeville. I think the town's population is about 300 people. . . . Three thousand people had assembled without any attempt being made to bring them there. The word had simply spread that that train would have to stop.
>
> [In] Waukesha, . . . the station was just so crowded that you couldn't get anybody else into it. . . .
>
> In Milwaukee [Democratic leaders] had done something that everybody told us [was] crazy. . . . [W]e rented the American Association ball park, simply because we couldn't find an indoors hall worth a presidential visit. Now, this was [October 15]. . . . I spoke in a topcoat, it was that cold. But . . . we had that ball park filled to capacity. There were about 15,000 people. Nothing like that had ever been seen before in Milwaukee. The street from the train to the ball park was just lined with people, and the enthusiasm for Harry Truman was very obvious.

Much of the press corps covering Truman saw—but did not see—the crowds before them that they chronicled. An unimpressed James Reston of the *New York Times* pondered:

> Mr. Truman started out with the promise to "give 'em hell," and he has tried hard. He is not, however, the warrior type. . . . Mr. Truman is a mild

man. He has the words but he doesn't get the melody. He says he is mad at everybody, but he doesn't really look as if he's mad at anybody.

And the curious thing about it is that, the crowds who listen to the President and the Governor react in very much the same way. They don't act as if they really feel as divided as Mr. Dewey says they are: they don't look scared when Mr. Truman tells them what's going to happen if Mr. Dewey and "the interests" take over. And much to the surprise of Mr. Truman's colleagues on the train, Herbert Hoover is not the bogy he used to be, and to most of the young people along the railroad track, the "great depression" is an ancient event without personal meaning.

"There was something sad about the respective campaign debuts here in Iowa," noted Joe Alsop, ignoring the altogether significant fact that Truman consistently drew far greater audiences than his challenger. "The Truman show was visibly unsuccessful—the Dewey show was opulent. . . . The contest was really too uneven."

Yet others perceived something quite different. "Now and then a particularly large crowd or a noisy ovation starts a mighty surge of hope in the rear staff car," wrote veteran *Washington Post* political reporter Robert C. Albright in mid-October. "Some of it filters forward to the press car, and hard-bitten reporters ask themselves, 'Could we be wrong?'"

Truman aide Eben Ayers confided to his diary: "Were it not for all these predictions and the unanimity of the pollsters and experts, I would say the president has an excellent chance. All of the signs that I see indicate it. The crowds . . . have grown steadily. Those I saw last week were remarkable. Many of them were enthusiastic though others were not so much so. Yet I cannot believe they came out of curiosity alone. Other conditions are favorable to the president, the general prosperity in the country. It is contrary to political precedent for the voters to kick out an administration in times of prosperity."

Harry Truman possessed little use for polls—save for one.

Secretary to the Senate Democratic minority Leslie Biffle had developed an idea. To ascertain popular opinion, in fall 1947, he had hitchhiked incognito through Wisconsin, western New York, and Rhode Island. On

Sunday, August 1, 1948, the fifty-nine-year-old Biffle, now at the wheel of an old pickup and posing as a poultry dealer, would commence a new fact-finding tour, this time through West Virginia, Kentucky, southern Ohio, and Illinois. Later, he would travel across Minnesota, eastern Idaho, western Montana, and Washington State.

On Capitol Hill, the diminutive, curly-haired Biffle lived far beyond his official means and sported tailor-made suits. On the road, he donned an old shirt and a worn, blue sweater. What he now heard failed to substantiate anything the professional pollsters had recorded. Biffle recalled: "I was hunched on the porch of a country store in northern West Virginia. A farmer drove up and soon, he was in an argument with a miner about John L. Lewis. And then the storekeeper joined us. They almost got into a fistfight—but I found out what I wanted to know. All three of them were going to vote for President Truman. . . . What the people were saying just didn't support the polls and the political predictions. I came back convinced the President would win—and I told him what I had found."

While Harry Truman jabbed at the unpalatable mushiness of Tom Dewey's campaign and periodically lashed out at Henry Wallace's left flank, he could not altogether ignore the now muted, but nonetheless continuing, menace along his Southern, right flank.

Four states—Mississippi, South Carolina, Alabama, and Louisiana— remained unalterably for Thurmond and Wright. The remainder of the South seemed safely and normally Democratic, with one very large exception— Texas.

Sam Rayburn and Governor Beauford Jester had skillfully shoved the Dixiecrats off the Democratic ballot line, but not off the ballot itself. Not a few observers foresaw a three-way Truman-Thurmond-Dewey contest for Texas's twenty-three electoral votes. Accordingly, in late September, Truman spent four days whistle-stopping through Texas. At Uvalde, he breakfasted on "chicken and white-wing dove . . . ham and bacon and scrambled eggs and hot biscuits" with seventy-nine-year-old former vice president, John Nance "Cactus Jack" Garner. Huge crowds appeared at each of his twenty-four Texas stops. In Dallas, with little uproar, he addressed an integrated capacity crowd of twenty thousand at Rebel Stadium. At the Waco train station, scattered booing greeted his shaking hands with Mrs. E. L. Harrison, a local Negro woman and representative of the Interracial Council. At Bonham he drew twenty-five thousand; at San Antonio, two hundred thousand.

Truman welcomed scores upon scores of hitherto-standoffish Texas politicians onto the Ferdinand Magellan. Some, like Mrs. Harrison, came for a presidential handshake. Some came to sample Missouri bourbon and branch water. In San Antonio, on Monday, September 27, Lyndon Baines Johnson scurried aboard, needing a whole lot more than handshakes or spirits.

Intense ambition had always gripped the now forty-year-old Austin-area congressman. In 1941, running as an unabashed New Deal liberal, he had sought a U.S. Senate seat—and ever so narrowly lost. In 1948, he tried again, reinventing himself as a more conservative candidate, voting against Taft-Hartley ("Labor's not much stronger in Texas than a popcorn fart . . . ") and railing against Truman's FEPC legislation. "The civil rights program is a farce and a sham—an effort to set up a police state in the guise of liberty," LBJ warned. "I am opposed to that program. I have voted *against* the so-called poll tax repeal bill; the poll tax should be repealed by those states which enacted them. I have voted AGAINST the FEPC; if a man can tell you whom you must hire, he can tell you whom you can't hire."

In the Democratic primary's first round, Johnson trailed his genuinely more conservative rival, sixty-year-old former governor Coke R. Stevenson. The August 28 runoff saw LBJ triumph by a mere eighty-seven votes. Among the more questionable of the votes recorded were the 203 ballots discovered by local Democratic boss George Parr's henchmen a week following the runoff. In the heavily Mexican-American border town of Alice, they recorded one new vote for Coke Stevenson, and 202—in perfect alphabetical order—for Lyndon Baines Johnson.

Stevenson petitioned U.S. district judge T. Whitfield Davidson to prevent Johnson's certification as the official Democratic nominee. Davidson, contending that the nomination was by now so tainted that the winner would travel to Washington only "under a cloud," offered to place both men on the November ballot. LBJ angrily refused. But any further delay might sink his ultimate chances. He needed closure—and now.

As Lyndon Johnson boarded the Truman campaign train, the strain showed. He looked "like the damnedest tramp I ever saw in my life," recalled Jonathan Daniels. "He couldn't have shaved in at least two days and he looked sick as hell. At that point he was going to be just another Texan or a great guy. And he didn't know and nobody else knew which it was going to be. . . . If he lost at that point, he was pretty well licked for the rest of his life." Someone offered Lyndon a scotch. His hands shook.

Fate took LBJ's side. The Truman camp wanted no part of the conservative Stevenson, much preferring erstwhile New Dealer Johnson in the Senate. Beyond that, it recoiled from any thought of Stevenson's candidacy complicating Truman's already problematic Texas chances. George Parr—no stranger to spectacularly suspect senatorial primary victories—may have already personally lobbied Truman to intervene with the Justice Department and the federal courts. LBJ's attorney, the savvy thirty-eight-year-old Washington insider Abe Fortas, had most certainly already conferred with Clark Clifford.

The alignment of interests between old New Dealers Truman and Johnson only increased. On Saturday, September 25, an all-star LBJ legal team assembled, not in Texas, but in Washington. In addition to Fortas, it included his law partners Paul Porter and Thurman Arnold, as well as Washington legal heavyweights Ben Cohen, Tommy Corcoran, Francis Biddle, and Joe Rauh. Fortas conceived a strategy to expeditiously terminate Stevenson's complaint—and his candidacy. Fortas would end-run Judge Davidson by bringing an appeal before reliably liberal Democratic Supreme Court justice Hugo Black. Black, however, had to agree to hear Fortas, and that was by no means a certainty. If certain highly placed Democrats interceded, however . . .

Johnson boarded the Ferdinand Magellan bedraggled. He detrained exhilarated. "Something happened [to LBJ] between Fort Worth and Bonham," recalled one member of the Democratic state committee, and it may not have been simply Harry Truman's exhortations to the crowds to "send Lyndon Johnson to the Senate."

Two days later, Hugo Black heard Abe Fortas's arguments. He suspended Judge Davidson's temporary injunction, thus placing Johnson—not Coke Stevenson—on the Democratic line. "Davidson definitely believed that Truman or somebody spoke to Black and suggested he do it," recalled Houston oilman Wright Morrow, a Texas Democratic national committeeman.

While Lyndon Johnson rode the Magellan with Harry Truman, as skittish as he remained regarding his own senatorial chances, he calculated them far superior to those still enjoyed by his host. At Garland, Texas, Lyndon surveyed the great crowd that had come to greet Harry. "Just goes to show you the great respect people have for the presidency of the United States," he mused. "Isn't it a shame they won't vote for Harry Truman!"

Early October witnessed not merely the strangest and least seemly episodes of the entire reelection effort, but, perhaps, one of the oddest, least deft, and least considered efforts of Truman's entire presidency—the proposed Vinson Mission.

On Sunday, October 3, Truman summoned Supreme Court chief justice Fred M. Vinson to the White House. Truman proposed to Vinson, his former Treasury secretary, that Vinson embark upon an unprecedented personal mission to Stalin to discuss the emerging topic of the control of atomic power—there would be no Soviet atomic bomb until August 1949—and to convince the Russian leader of "our nation's peaceful aspirations for the whole world." Vinson listened in stunned silence, before protesting that the assignment would be most inappropriate for a sitting Supreme Court justice. He had, in fact, warned his court to beware of anything smacking of politics in an election year. Nonetheless, he soon yielded to Truman's wishes.

Political considerations indeed lay at the heart of Truman's plan. The Wallace camp—incessantly harping that Truman was a warmonger, and greeting Truman in Detroit with placards reading "Wallace or War"— had to be silenced. At least a segment of Wallace voters would have to be enticed back into Democratic ranks. This, Truman hoped, might be accomplished by dispatching the reluctant Vinson to Moscow.

The idea had originated with speechwriters David M. Noyes and Albert Z. "Bob" Carr, both desperate to catapult their faltering boss back into the race. Short-circuiting normal channels, appointments secretary Matt Connelly funneled the idea to Truman. Normally aggressive aides Clark Clifford, Charles Murphy, and George Elsey derided the move as an obvious political stunt. Truman approved it anyway, instructing press secretary Charlie Ross to quietly secure a half hour of free airtime on the four major radio networks, so the president might announce his bombshell to the world—and to the electorate.

Ross did as ordered. No one had yet consulted Secretary of State Marshall, then in Paris to conduct four-power talks. When Assistant Secretary of State Robert Lovett caught wind of the scheme, he sped with sirens blaring to the White House, entreating Truman to inform Marshall immediately.

On Tuesday, October 5, Truman finally reached Marshall via Teletype. Marshall considered Truman's idea abysmal. The State Department had just secured British and French promises to forego any direct bilateral negotiations with Moscow as long as the Berlin crisis continued. Vinson's mission undercut Marshall, the entire State Department, and even the fledgling United Nations.

Marshall drafted a reply, commencing, "Never in the history of diplomatic bungling . . ." But hearing his words read back to him, he concluded, "I cannot send a message like that. I am talking to my President." What he sent, however, was tough enough.

Truman returned to his advisers. Recalled Jonathan Daniels, "His magnified eyes seemed almost slate gray. Then he said very quietly, 'I have heard enough. We won't do it.'" With that, he exited and walked back to the White House through the rose garden, silently and very alone.

Yet he had not entirely abandoned his scheme. That evening, he invited Arthur Vandenberg and Vandenberg's Democratic counterpart on the Foreign Relations Committee, Texas senator Tom Connally, to the White House. The archaically attired seventy-one-year-old Connally ("he looks like a faded and yellowed newspaper clipping") arrived first, and Truman ran the Vinson plan past him. Connally thought it was terrible. When Vandenberg arrived, the president asked their opinion of his personally phoning Stalin. Both proved skeptical. Truman continued lobbying them for another hour before surrendering. Truman "must be feeling desperate about the campaign," said Vandenberg to Connally following their departure.

Meanwhile, Charlie Ross's surreptitious request for radio time had leaked from Truman's old friend Burton K. Wheeler to *Chicago Tribune* correspondent Walter Trohan. As Truman whistle-stopped through upstate New York on Friday morning, October 8, news of Vinson's abortive mission exploded onto the *Tribune* front page.

"This was the worst mistake of the Truman campaign," recalled Clifford. The *Washington Post* ("a tragic exhibition of lack of judgment"), the *New York Times* ("Mr. Truman's Blunder"), and *Life* ("Truman's Last Stand") blasted the move. "What Next?" asked an incredulous Walter Lippmann.

Privately, Tom Dewey fumed that Truman's bumbling could bring America closer to—not further from—war. "If Harry Truman would just keep his hands off things for another few weeks—," he groused, "particularly . . . foreign policy, about which he knows considerably less than nothing!"

"The President," concluded Clark Clifford, "made a mistake which could have cost him the election—had Dewey exploited it."

Tom Dewey—obsessed by "unity," transfixed by "bipartisanship," and, above all, blinded by the incandescent gleam of his own inevitability—did not.

Harold Ickes had remained Harold Ickes.

Excusing himself from that July's Democratic National Convention (his first absence since 1932), Ickes was convinced that Truman had "practically no chance of winning. . . . Whether the Democrats can make a respectable showing is not clear at this date."

Though he had reregistered as a "nonpartisan" the previous year, he could not quite remain absent from his adopted party. Nor could he remain aloof from the fray—*any* fray.

Accordingly, on Monday, October 4, Ickes, fresh from his annual Maine vacation, traveled to the White House. "When I was shown into the President's office," he recorded, "I walked to his desk and he stood up to shake my hand. He expressed pleasure at seeing me and said, in effect, 'You never should have left me. I did not want you to go and I have never been critical of you.'"

"Of course, this was not true," thought Ickes, but after making a few face-saving gestures ("I gave as my reason, Dewey's side-stepping of all the conservation issues"), he enlisted as the newest, though not exactly the most optimistic, of Truman partisans. "I had no illusions," he privately noted, "as to who would be elected."

At a Willard Hotel press conference the following Monday, Ickes revealed his conversion in a prepared statement: "As between Thomas 'Elusive'

Dewey, the candidate in sneakers, I prefer to support Mr. Truman, who is straightforward and sincere, if at times more unpredictable than I would wish." Three evenings later, from Washington's radio station WMAL, he trumpeted his dislike of Dewey to a nationwide audience. At month's end he stood beside Harry Truman and the rail workers' union's A. F. Whitney and skewered Dewey ("he is on the make for Wall Street interests") at Madison Square Garden.

"It was all pro forma," noted Ickes's primary biographer, T. H. Watkins, but Harry Truman would take every vote he could get, whether Ickes's or Whitney's, enthusiastic or not, sincere or not. Every vote counted the same in November.

Unlike Harold Ickes, Eleanor Roosevelt had never publicly trashed Harry Truman—but neither had she quite publicly endorsed him.

Not aiding matters were her sons' unending machinations. Truman's nomination had ultimately made James's position as California Democratic chairman untenable. In early August, he declined to seek reelection.

In late September, Drew Pearson reported that Eleanor would not be publicly speaking out on behalf of her husband's successor. Such news greatly upset former labor secretary Frances Perkins, who phoned Eleanor in Paris (where she now served on the American United Nations delegation), urgently soliciting not only her support, but that of another erstwhile Democrat, financier Bernard Baruch.

Mrs. Roosevelt responded:

> I haven't actually endorsed Mr. Truman because he has been such a weak and vacillating person and made such poor appointments in his Cabinet and entourage, such as [former Secretary of Treasury John] Snyder and [Harry] Vaughan. That unless we are successful in electing a very strong group of liberals in Congress, in spite of my feeling about the Republican Party and Governor Dewey, I cannot have much enthusiasm for Mr. Truman. Though there are many people in government that I would hate to feel would not be allowed to continue their work, I still find it very difficult to give any good reasons for being for Mr. Truman. . . .

Nevertheless, since you asked me to send you the enclosed letter, I am doing so because you are quite right, if we are going down to defeat, we probably should go down having done what we could for the candidate and we should try for a good vote. I have addressed my letter to the President as being the most effective way.

To Truman, Eleanor dutifully and unenthusiastically wrote:

Paris October 4, 1948

Dear Mr. President:

I understand that there is some comment in the newspapers in the United States that I have not come out for you as the Democratic candidate and prefer the election of the Republican candidate. I am unqualifiedly for you as the Democratic candidate for the presidency.

This year I hope every Democrat and independent voter is concentrating on the election of as many liberal Democrats to Congress as possible. I hope for this particularly from the labor and farm groups who have perhaps the greatest stake in the preservation of liberal leadership.

Liberal policies during these next few years are of vast importance on domestic issues. A Democratic administration, backed by a liberal Democratic Congress, could really achieve the policies for which you have stood.

As delegate to the United Nations I have become very much aware of the fact that stability in our own government and in its policies is essential to help the Western democracies on their road to rehabilitation.

It was hardly much of an endorsement, but it was enough to make her wince. To Baruch, she apologetically explained:

I am enclosing to you a copy of a letter which I sent to the President today. I am sending it to Frances Perkins because she telephoned me last night pointing out that Drew Pearson was saying that I had never come out for the President as the Democratic candidate and was supposedly in favor of Governor Dewey. That, of course, is untrue and I do agree with Frances Perkins that we should try to get as good a Democratic vote as possible. I told her there was no chance of a Democratic victory except that we might keep some of the liberals in Congress and even increase the number if we acted wisely. I hope you will approve of this letter even though I was, as you know, loath to do more than state in general my support of the Democratic Party and its policies.

That was good enough for a desperate Harry Truman. "I am deeply grateful to you for your generous letter," he wrote to her on Thursday, October 7. "Have I your permission to release it for publication?"

"Glad have you use letter any way you wish," she tersely responded.

And that was that.

The Ickes and Roosevelt endorsements, perfunctory as they might have been, opened the liberal floodgates. On Friday, October 22, three dozen former New Deal officials ("all the prominent men and women associated with the Roosevelt administration") tilted their cigarette holders upward and held their pince-nezed noses to endorse a man so many had found so deficient for so long. Among them were not only cashiered cabinet members Ickes, Attorney General Frances Biddle, and Postmaster General Frank Walker, but also ADAers Leon Henderson and Elmer Davis; FDR's personal secretary, Grace Tully; stellar Roosevelt speechwriters Sam Rosenman and Robert Sherwood; Librarian of Congress Archibald MacLeish (an old friend of Alben Barkley); FDR insiders such as "Tommy the Cork" Corcoran and James Rowe; Herbert Lehman; Senator Robert F. Wagner Sr.; and high-powered Washington attorneys Paul A. Porter, Abe Fortas, and Thurman Arnold.

A coalition was coming together.

Henry Wallace retained his folksingers, and Tom Dewey enjoyed a respectable coterie of Hollywood stars, including Gary Cooper, Cary Grant, Ginger

Rogers, Jeanette MacDonald, Frank Morgan, Charles Coburn, and twenty-year-old Vic Damone.

Harry Truman featured his own collection of show business supporters.

In 1940, actress Tallulah Bankhead's father—Speaker of the House of Representatives William B. Bankhead—had lost the vice-presidential nomination to Wallace. In late October 1948, she juggled her performance schedule at Broadway's Plymouth Theatre to take to the radio waves in behalf of David Dubinsky's International Ladies' Garment Workers for Truman—and against Dewey. "Mr. Dewey is neat," the still spectacularly hedonistic forty-six-year-old Tallulah sneered. "Oh so neat. And Mr. Dewey is tidy. Oh, so tidy. . . . It seems a great pity to risk exposing Mr. Dewey to the smells and noises and ills of humanity."

"I want you to vote for Harry Truman," she continued, "because he is a *true* man."

At the White House, the Trumans and about a dozen staffers listened. "She's implying that Tom Dewey is not a real man," Truman interjected. "I don't like that." But he grinned as he said it, and her words seemed to invigorate him. When it was over and speechwriter Frank Kelly expressed guarded optimism, Jonathan Daniels bluntly warned, "Don't get your hopes up too far. . . . If you completely identify with him, you will be torn apart when he loses."

At an only partially filled Gilmore Stadium in Los Angeles on Thursday evening, September 23, Truman fumed that "Communists are using and guiding the third [Progressive] party." He shared the flag-draped podium with the now twenty-four-year-old Lauren Bacall and the bespectacled thirty-seven-year-old president of the Screen Actors Guild (SAG), Ronald Reagan. Previous to the event, Truman had dined with the very pregnant Bacall and placed a twenty-dollar bet with her forty-nine-year-old husband, Humphrey Bogart, that the child would be a boy. Later in the campaign, Reagan himself took to the airwaves, not only for Truman, but also for Minnesota's Hubert Humphrey. His ideology was distinctly un-Reagan, but his oratory clearly bore the Reagan stamp:

The profits of corporations have doubled while workers' wages have increased by only one quarter. In other words, profits have gone up four times as much as wages. And the small increase workers did receive was more than eaten up by rising prices, which have also bored into their savings.

For example, here's an Associated Press dispatch I read the other day about Mr. Smith L. Carpenter, a craftsman in Union Springs, New York. Seems that Mr. Carpenter retired some years ago thinking he had enough money saved so that he could live out his last years without having to worry. But he didn't figure on this Republican inflation which ate up all his savings and so he's gone back to work. The reason this is news is Mr. Carpenter is 91 years old.

Now, take as a contrast the Standard Oil Company of New Jersey, which reported a net profit of $210 million after taxes in the first half of 1948. An increase of 70 percent in one year. In other words, high prices have not been caused by higher wages, but by bigger and bigger profits.

Early October brought evidence that Truman's bare-knuckle populist effort might finally have become a little *too* populist, abandoning presidential gravitas altogether. The DNC announced that three million of its projected total of nine million pieces of campaign literature would consist of the first-ever presidential campaign comic book—the sixteen-page, four-color *The Story of Harry S. Truman*. Thirty-three-year-old Navy veteran Malcolm Ater, whose previous comic enterprise had been *The History of Gas* for the American Gas Association (featuring "Miss Flame") had originally approached Republicans with his idea for a candidate comic bio. "I thought that if anybody needed comic books—and could afford them—it was the Republicans," recalled Ater. The GOP, for its part, thought the concept "too undignified." Watching the Democratic Convention on television, Ater spied an old friend, Illinois newspaper publisher Vincent Y. Dallman, in the crowd and hustled by overnight train to Philadelphia to pitch his concept. The DNC—and Truman personally—authorized what the publication's front page termed "THE THRILLING STORY OF OUR THIRTY-THIRD PRESIDENT OF THE UNITED STATES."

"FARM BOY, SOLDIER, STATESMAN, PRESIDENT!" it trumpeted. "SUCCEEDING TO THE HIGHEST OFFICE IN AMERICA DURING A CRUCIAL PHASE OF WORLD WAR II, HE MADE THE AWESOME DECISION TO USE THE ATOM BOMB AND THUS SAVED UNTOLD THOUSANDS OF AMERICAN LIVES." The comic, noted the *New York Times*, had devoted two-and-a-half pages to Truman's World War I service ("Captain Truman, thrown from his horse, immediately leaped to his feet") but not a syllable to the equally significant Tom Pendergast. *Time* magazine, however, pronounced *The Story of Harry S. Truman* to be "something new in 'campaign literature.'"

But October 1948 was also a time when the sixty-million-copy-per-month comic book industry was being roundly damned as too violent or suggestive, and for fostering postwar juvenile delinquency. To protect impressionable youth, fifty cities—including Los Angeles, Detroit, Terre Haute, and Indianapolis—now regulated their sales. "The Demos didn't have enough money to put President Truman on the air," groused Drew Pearson, "but they have invested $50,000 for a comic book."

Comic books had their purposes, but the campaign really hinged on winning support in the place where it had commenced, in the cornfields of the Midwest. And who better to exploit the issues upon which such support turned—far more effectively than the gentleman farmer of Dutchess County or the Edgefield plantation-owner's son, or even the Iowa scientific farmer—than turnip-planting, hell-raising, Missouri dirt farmer Harry S. Truman?

Everything centered on prices—high food prices in the city and low grain prices on the farm. Postwar city dwellers may not have relished paying historically high prices for beefsteak and other commodities, but they were in some sense growing used to it. As European markets adjusted, however, and American fields produced bumper crops, American agriculture found itself skidding toward a sudden, economically crippling jolt. Corn had fetched growers $2.46 per bushel in January and $2.25 in July. By September 15, it was down to $1.78. By late October, it had tumbled to a mere $1.26. Wheat had crashed from $2.81 in January to $1.97 by September.

Truman—himself the son of a failed grain speculator—saw it coming. He smelled the fear on the prairies. At Dexter, Iowa, he charged:

> When the Republicans rewrote the charter of the Commodity Credit Corporation this year, there were certain lobbyists in Washington representing the speculative grain trade. These big-business lobbyists and speculators persuaded the Congress not to provide storage bins for the farmer. . . . They don't want the farmer to be prosperous. . . . What they have taken away from you thus far will be only an appetizer for the economic tapeworm of big business. . . . . Republican spokesmen are now complaining that my Administration is trying to keep food prices up. They have given themselves away. . . . They are ready to let the bottom drop out of farm prices.

Alben Barkley echoed Truman's accusations. From Mankato, Minnesota, on Saturday, October 2, he told a nationwide radio audience:

> On the one hand the governor of California has been quoted as saying that farm policy, like foreign policy, ought to be removed from the realm of political discussion. . . . The governor of New York . . . couched his discussion in such vague and general terms that I am unable to determine just what his views are. . . . I do not believe that the farmers of the United States are willing to allow themselves to be taken in by doses of New York soothing syrup, accompanied by the faint odor of California orange blossoms. . . . It has been reliably reported that the Republican leadership of the state of Minnesota is deeply disturbed about what the next Congress, if it is a Republican Congress, will do in the field of farm legislation. . . . They have watched the dead hand of the Republican leadership in the Eightieth Congress do its work on . . . the Democratic farm program. . . . Thousands of farmers have had to sell their grain at distress prices. . . . Right here in Minnesota, your corn crop is seventy-five million bushels larger than it was before the war . . . but the Republicans have seen to it that storage capacity will stay small.

In a January 1948 survey, 54 percent of farmers believed another depression was on the way. Only 13 percent said they did not. Fifty-eight percent of those who responded yes said the depression would arrive in the next forty-eight months. "What would be swept out with the [Dewey] house cleaning?" Truman asked nervous farmers. "Price supports and other agricultural aids? If another depression comes, what will the farmer do?"

In early September, even before Harry Truman hit Dexter, even before corn and wheat prices hit rock bottom, Republican congressman August H. Andresen, chairman of the Select Committee on Commodity Exchanges, had warned Dewey: "I have been to Minnesota for the past two weeks, and I regret to state that many farmers do not intend to vote the Republican ticket in the coming election. . . . We cannot win without the farm vote."

Congressman Andresen knew it. Harry Truman and Alben Barkley knew it. Tom Dewey did not.

33

"Ain't he coming?"

Nnational public opinion surveys continued to forecast an easy Dewey
triumph.

The *Nation* pronounced his chances "overwhelming." "Dewey is in,
of course," *Business Week* breezily assured its readers. The *Wall Street Journal*
prognosticated that only "a major miracle" might rescue Truman.

Nonetheless, the *Journal* highlighted some troublesome signs for the
GOP: For the first time since 1924, "the winner will get less than 430 electoral
votes," and GOP control of the Senate rested precariously on Dewey's coattails.
Two Republican seats—in Minnesota and Oklahoma—were almost certainly
headed for oblivion. "G.O.P. strategists," the *Journal* granted, "confess that
Truman's strength, at its low ebb when he was nominated, has been rising and
that Dewey, riding his crest at Philadelphia, has slipped slightly."

Colonel McCormick's *Chicago Tribune* forecast a 400-vote Electoral
College blowout, with Dewey breaking into the Solid South in Virginia,
Florida, and Tennessee, and with even Missouri and Texas within his reach.
Time magazine anticipated Dewey would win in twenty-nine states with
350 electoral votes. Fifty "experts" unanimously informed *Newsweek* ("The
Magazine of News Significance") that it was Dewey all the way, with 366
electoral votes to 126. The *New York Times*, while conceding that the Senate
might narrowly go Democratic, reported that Dewey "appears certain to
defeat" Truman. On his Sunday-night radio program, Walter Winchell
reported that gambling odds ran 15 to 1 against Truman. Rival gossip
columnist Ed Sullivan made it 18 to 1.

Elmo Roper's *Fortune* poll of September 29 seemed so conclusive—Dewey
led 44 to 31 percent with 16 percent undecided—that Roper suspended polling,
barring "some development of outstanding importance." None occurred.

In the campaign's last fortnight, Roper did, however, sample public opinion, not regarding whom it favored, but who might win. In July, respondents had theorized Dewey by a 64 to 27 percent margin. They now bet on Dewey 3 to 1. Gallup reported that 79 percent believed Dewey would triumph; only 9 percent predicted Truman.

Archibald M. Crossley's poll reported a 49.9 to 44.8 percent Dewey lead. Even Democratic activist Louis H. Bean, once confident of Truman's ultimate rebound, now predicted a 44 to 31 percent Dewey lead. Said Bean:

> President Truman will need an all-time turnout of nearly 60,000,000 voters to win the election. That is what he is fighting for . . . to get out the vote. . . . The president may succeed to the extent of winning a Democratic Senate and—as a long shot—a Democratic House of Representatives.

> There are some interesting new trends. . . . Many voters who seem to be Democrats when thinking about the congressional elections are Republicans when thinking about the presidential race. Ordinarily that would mean a close race for Senate and House control, with the Democrats coming out ahead by slight margins.

Truman lost all nine post-convention Gallup surveys. In his final sampling, Gallup conceded only Arizona, Arkansas, Florida, Georgia, North Carolina, Oklahoma, Rhode Island, Tennessee, and Texas to the Democrats. In Cleveland, an infuriated Truman ripped into Gallup's "sleeping polls"— designed, he contended, to "lull the voters into sleeping on Election Day." In New York City, he vowed to "throw the Gallup polls right into the ashcan."

Yet even a cursory reading of Gallup's results revealed significant Dewey slippage. From a formidable 17 percent advantage in late September, he had tumbled to 9 percent in mid-October, and to just 5 percent from October 15 to 25. With Dewey fading and a Gallup margin of error of 3.9 percent, if anyone cared to look, a runaway had turned into a horse race.

In Michigan, Battle Creek congressman Paul W. Shafer toured his district and concluded Truman would carry it. "If that is going on in my district," the isolationist Republican concluded, "it's going on all over the Midwest, and that means Truman is going to win." Shafer advised a Democratic friend,

Washington liquor wholesaler Milton S. Kronheim Sr., whose son Milton Jr. coveted a District of Columbia judgeship, that he should funnel as much money as possible, through as many friends and relatives as possible, into HST's threadbare coffers—and fast. Harry would appreciate those who were with him *before* Election Day.

Wisconsin's Andrew Biemiller recalled getting a call from the DNC, saying, "Do you fellows still stand by your claim that you're going to carry Wisconsin?"

"Absolutely," Biemiller responded. "Fifty thousand votes is what it will be."

Silence followed.

"What's the matter?" Biemiller asked. "Nothing else going well?"

"Well, if you fellows are right," came the DNC response, "and if everybody else is right that we've talked to, we carry the White House in '48."

Les Biffle had returned from his fact-finding tour. On Tuesday, October 26, he conferred with James Forrestal, who confided to his diary:

> Biffle told me that he thought the President had made very substantial gains in the last two weeks. He thought he would carry Massachusetts, Rhode Island and possibly Connecticut. The Senate, he thinks, will be Democratic by a majority of five, and thinks there is a possibility of the House also being Democratic.
>
> On the contrary, I asked Arthur Krock his view this morning and he saw no change. So far as the Senate and House are concerned, he thinks that "the hair will go with the hide"; in other words, Dewey's strength will counterbalance local tendencies.

Arthur Krock was not alone. *Life* trumpeted Dewey as "The Next President" as it published a glossy full-page photo of him traversing San Francisco Bay by ferry. Drew Pearson wrote:

> Dewey had conducted one of the most astute and skillful campaigns in recent years. . . . He made nobody mad. He called no names; he answered no challenges. He ignored many of the issues. He knew that he was certain

to win if he made no mistakes and aroused no tempers. So his whole campaign was carefully geared to that end. . . .

Harry Truman has put up a courageous and magnificent fight. If he had fought as hard and as effectively during all his three years he would not be in the trouble he is today. But thanks to the . . . Dixiecrats and Wallaceites he cannot possibly win this election. He will roll up a bigger popular vote than previously expected, which will be good. It is always bad for one party to be too cocksure and overconfident.

"Mr. Truman is by now worse than unimpressive," Alistair Cooke wrote in the *Manchester Guardian*, twenty-four hours before the election. "He has committed the unwritten, un-American crime of being outsmarted."

Commanding 150 Klansmen in a seventy-car cavalcade, the state Ku Klux Klan's grand titan, W. H. Brough, a Wildwood metalworker, rode forty miles through seven communities in central Florida—Plymouth, Zellwood, Mount Dora, Tavares, Lisbon, Leesburg, and Wildwood—near to Orlando. They set five-foot-high crosses ablaze outside Negro roadhouses and warned "both black and white" alike that they were "out to stop the Communist movement in Florida." *Orlando Morning Sentinel* "girl reporter" Leigh Tucker claimed that they had smashed her camera and advised her "not to make trouble." Klansmen denied her charges, saying they merely objected to close-ups.

"At the head of the cavalcade and at its end was a vehicle bearing a huge cross, lighted by red electric bulbs," noted the Associated Press. "Hundreds of spectators lined the streets to watch, but Negroes remained close to their homes."

A barbecue concluded their sojourn. "We have no quarrel with Negroes," Brough announced, "unless they [are] tied up with the Communist party. We want our Negroes to vote tomorrow but we are out to stop the Communist movement and that applies to white and black."

From Paris, over ABC's radio network, Eleanor Roosevelt's words crossed the Atlantic via shortwave. She had bestirred herself from indifference and outright hostility to Harry Truman to broadcast an endorsement of sorts for him (though, in reality, again more for congressional Democrats). In tandem with a brace of seventy-year-olds—Alben Barkley and former New York governor Herbert Lehman—she announced that Harry Truman "has made his record clear. . . . He has shown courage, but he needs the people's mandate to help him if he is going to be our president. He must know that they want progressive Democrats in the Senate and in the Congress. I think that many people may feel an anxiety as they look at the record of the last Congress, as to what might happen if the people do not go out and vote for progressive liberals."

Nineteen forty-eight may have been the year of television's entrance onto the national stage, but it was a highly tentative debut. Radio, and, yes, even the newsreels, still dominated debate.

To reach the nation's estimated sixty-five million weekly filmgoers, the well-heeled Dewey operation commissioned Louis de Rochemont, producer of the popular *March of Time* newsreel series, to develop *The Dewey Story,* a short film to be distributed in the campaign's final two weeks to the nation's twenty thousand theaters. The production cost thirty-five thousand dollars, plus another thirty-five dollars per print to duplicate nine hundred prints for theater distribution.

Democrats never got around to producing their own film. Hearing of Dewey's effort, they worked through former DNC executive director Gael E. Sullivan, now executive vice president of the Theater Owners of America, to threaten picketing of the nation's theaters unless accorded "equal time" for a similar Truman mini biopic. Recalled DNC communications operative Sam Brightman:

> The movie people said "You make the film; we'll distribute it." We said, "We don't have money to make a film. We thought the newsreel industry would want to do a nice film about Truman." They seemed reluctant. Jack [Redding, Democratic director of publicity] remarked that . . . the

Democrats were sure to control the Senate and he knew some Senators who sure would want to hold hearings. They would be very curious to know how the arrangements were made to show the Dewey film. So the newsreel companies drew lots. The loser handled the hunt for footage and the other handled putting it together.

Brightman helped craft the screenplay. Short-straw loser Universal Studios cobbled together *The Truman Story*—largely out of stock newsreel footage. The Dewey short used professional actors and looked slick, even artificial. The crudely made *Truman Story* had the look of authenticity—of a documentary.

To this ragbag, Universal added existing cutting-room-floor footage of Truman ("Soldier . . . statesman . . . farmer . . . humanitarian . . . Harry S. Truman . . . President of the United States!") greeting an awkward March of Dimes poster child. "The child was looking stilted throughout the picture-taking. . . . Truman smiles at her. She smiles at him and just reaches out and hugs him. You couldn't have actors do that. You couldn't get that kind of reality," recalled Brightman.

"During the last six days of the campaign," said Jack Redding, "no one could go to the movies anywhere without seeing [*The Truman Story*]. It was probably the most important, most successful publicity break in the entire campaign."

In Connecticut, Chester Bowles remained markedly dubious about his chances. In early September, Bowles had commissioned a poll; it revealed not only that he would lose to liberal Republican acting governor James C. Shannon by 220,000 votes—twice the largest margin in state history—but, even more distressingly, that there was nothing he might do to recoup more than a small portion of that immense difference. The Sunday after receiving this dismal news, Bowles traveled to the outskirts of Hartford to campaign. Dining on lamb and gravy, with vanilla ice cream and butterscotch sauce for dessert, he was so dispirited that he ladled the gravy over his ice cream. "For many months," he recalled, "I was unable to eat either lamb or ice cream."

In Michigan, things were not quite so settled. State election law required the filing of elector slates with Republican secretary of state Fred M. Alger Jr. twenty-five days before Election Day. Michigan Democratic Chairman John R. Franco had neglected to do so. Barely four days before the polls opened, a panic-stricken Franco flew in from Hartford to formally and finally place Harry Truman on the ballot for Michigan's nineteen electoral votes. Alger, perhaps displaying Republican overconfidence, kept the office open late for Franco.

Editor & Publisher reported that 65.17 percent of the nation's 771 daily newspapers, accounting for 78.55 percent of total circulation, had endorsed Dewey. No more than 182 papers—15.38 percent, with a mere 10.03 percent of total circulation—supported Truman. Even in Democratic New York, only Bartley Crum's faltering morning tabloid, the 90,000-circulation *New York Star*, endorsed the president. In so acting, Bartley had ignored personal entreaties from Henry Wallace, Paul Robeson, and Lillian Hellman. The normally Democratic *Times* endorsed Dewey, announcing: "Mr. Dewey is now running for the Presidency on a platform that takes for granted the survival and continuation of all the major reforms and innovations of the First Roosevelt Administration. There is no good reason to question the sincerity of this position."

When the DNC's Jack Redding demanded space for a rebuttal, *Times* publisher Arthur Hays Sulzberger responded incredulously: "Do I understand that you were threatening the *Times*?"—but Redding got his way.

In Chicago, the *Tribune* reluctantly endorsed Dewey "because, borrowing one of Westbrook Pegler's better phrases, we consider him the least worse of the candidates. . . . We are for him in part, of course, because of the character of his opponent. Mr. Truman is not only the worst President this country has had; but he has the least capacity for the office. While he is incapable of great betrayals, he is possessed of an invincible stupidity and a political morality that has never risen above the ghost voting and the draft of the Pendergast machine."

Meanwhile, disquieting signs were multiplying for Tom Dewey.

In Massachusetts, as he visited House Speaker Joe Martin and Martin's eighty-seven-year-old mother, the Martin family–owned newspaper, the North Attleborough *Daily Chronicle*, editorialized:

> Dewey's speeches have been designed for tonal effect. They must sound good. He does not scold, but exhorts. His addresses are filled with maxims old and new, such as "We need a rudder to our ship of state, and a firm hand on the tiller." Sounds good, and brings the applause. But promises nothing. "Our country is at the crossroads of its history," is another Dewey phrase, old and a bit trite. Dewey also still uses "profound" and "profoundly" although he wore both words threadbare in 1944.

The editorial, alibied an embarrassed Martin, "certainly does not reflect my views. . . . It has no political significance at all." Democrats committed dwindling resources to getting the story out to their precinct workers.

At a New York City dinner party, Herbert Hoover was heard muttering that voters resented Dewey's lackluster, distant style—and that this flaw would soon be the cause of "his everlasting regret."

On Monday, October 25, 1948, seventy-three-year-old stockbroker E. F. Hutton telegraphed Dewey, warning him he would lose unless he "starts to slug."

Watching newsreels of Truman's huge, enthusiastic crowds, Dewey worried. As his Victory Special departed Buffalo for its final campaign swing, he asked the equally uneasy John Burton, his state budget director, "We're in trouble, aren't we, John?"

Tom Dewey grew more nervous. Harry Truman grew nastier.

On Monday, October 25, at Gary, Indiana's Memorial Auditorium, after his normal skewering of Republicans as the "special privilege boys," Truman went further. "If anybody in this country is friendly to the Communists," he alleged, "it is the Republicans."

Having smeared the GOP as Reds by day, by night he proceeded to condemn its leadership as Nazi and fascistic. At 9:00 PM CST, he addressed a capacity Chicago Stadium crowd of twenty-three thousand. By now, Jake Arvey had forgotten every objection he had ever presented against the Man from Missouri. Noted the *New York Times*, "Everywhere was evidence that the Cook County Democratic machine had exerted the utmost effort to bring out members of unions, veterans organizations and ward political groups. The parade route blazed and echoed to the crash of fireworks."

Truman's address—largely drafted by aides David Noyes and Bob Carr—was designed to incite Dewey into an emotional counterattack. So emotional himself, Truman stumbled over his words. Gripping his text with his right hand, he gestured "excessively" with his left. He ran roughshod over Dewey's reputation, pillorying his opponent as no president ever had or ever would:

> When a few men get control of the economy of a nation, they find a "front man" to run the country for them. Before Hitler came to power, control over the German economy had passed into the hands of a small group of rich manufacturers, bankers, and landowners. These men decided that Germany had to have a tough, ruthless dictator who would play their game and crush the strong German labor unions. So they put money and influence behind Adolf Hitler. We know the rest of the story.

> We also know that in Italy, in the 1920s, powerful Italian businessmen backed Mussolini, and that in the 1930s, Japanese financiers helped Tojo's military clique take over Japan. . . .

> To preserve freedom and democracy in this country, we must put control of the Congress back in the hands of the American people. This means we must have a Democratic Congress and a Democratic President.

> Now, I must speak of the third evil force which works secretly to destroy freedom: racial and religious prejudice.

> The tragic story of what happened in Germany is all too fresh. We know how Hitler used anti-Semitic propaganda as a way of stupefying the German people with false ideas while he reached out for power.

This was not the first time such a thing has happened. The persecution of minorities goes hand in hand with the destruction of liberty.

This country has been mercifully spared extreme racial and religious strife. But in recent years there has been a new outcropping of demagogues among us. Dangerous men, who are trying to win followers for their war on democracy, are attacking Catholics, and Jews, and Negroes, and other minority races and religions.

Some of these demagogues have even dared to raise their voice of religious prejudice in the Eightieth Congress. We need only remember the shocking Displaced Persons Bill passed in the second session of the Eightieth Congress, which cruelly discriminated against Catholics and Jews.

The *New York Times* headlined PRESIDENT LIKENS DEWEY TO HITLER AS FASCISTS' TOOL. Aboard his Victory Special, Dewey listened to Truman's words. Incensed, he seemed finally ready to take the gloves off.

He didn't.

He had threatened to shred his usual lackluster prepared speech and respond in kind to Truman. His wife begged him not to. "If I have to stay up all night to see that you don't tear up that speech, I will," she pleaded. Hagerty, Lockwood, and Jaeckle—his coterie of insiders, plus a consensus of state party leaders—backed her up. "They responded ninety to one," recalled Herbert Brownell, "that no change was needed to win."

Dewey surrendered. "I can't go against the entire Republican party," he mourned. The next evening, he delivered his first live Midwest telecast; it was an amazingly bland response. Democrats, he charged, "are openly sneering at the ancient American ideal of a free and united people. They have attempted to promote antagonism and prejudice. They have scattered reckless abuse along the entire right of way from coast to coast and now, I am sorry to say, reached a new low of mudslinging. . . . That is the kind of campaign I refuse to wage."

Someone in the cowbell-ringing crowd shouted, "You're an American, that's why!"

Dewey answered, "That's right, sir."

It was not exactly "Give 'em Hell, Tommy."

He went downhill from there. Near Cleveland the following day, thousands of well-wishers gathered outside his train. He refused to greet them. John Bricker was aghast. That evening, Dewey addressed an audience of thirteen thousand at Cleveland Municipal Auditorium, and Robert Taft joined him onstage. Dewey ignored him.

"I don't understand," Taft mourned privately, "why he hates me so."

On Thursday, October 28, Dewey rode across Massachusetts. In town after town, local Republicans warned Dewey insiders of slippage in their communities. GOP national committeewoman Katherine Howard asked Frances Dewey aide Mrs. Rebecca McNabb why Dewey allowed Truman to "get away with murder." McNabb responded that Dewey wanted to counterpunch "desperately. You should hear them, night after night, arguing with the policy group. Everything in his nature longs to attack, and every night, the policy group tells him the same thing: 'Don't get nasty, keep cool, don't make any mistakes and you've got it won.'"

In Manhattan, on Saturday evening, October 30, Republicans—led by Senator Irving Ives, the 69th Regiment band (plus two other bands), two rows of marchers, sixty cars, and forty mounted policemen—processed sixteen blocks from the Dewey-Warren Citizens Committee headquarters on East Fortieth Street to Madison Square Garden. An estimated thirty thousand onlookers watched. Overhead, two skywriting planes spelled out "D-E-W-E-Y." The only thing missing *was* Dewey.

"Ain't he coming?" asked one mystified police officer.

At Madison Square Garden that night, in his final campaign address, Dewey came close to taking the gloves off. He told nineteen thousand supporters:

> Since this campaign began, some people . . . give the impression that every night is Halloween. Grown men have been going around the country threatening, "Vote our way, or the goblins will get you!" We have been hearing bloodcurdling stories about "mossbacks," "bloodsuckers," "men with calculating machines where their hearts ought to be," and one shadowy ogre after another. Members of Congress, elected by the people, have had special Halloween treatment by these tellers of tall tales. They are described as "predatory animals." . . . They do their dreadful work with

"meat axes, butcher knives and sabers," and what do these monsters eat? Why, "red herring" of course.

That was as tough as he got.

All roads led to Manhattan—even for Strom Thurmond. He had visited the city in early October and addressed the National Press Club. Staying at the Roosevelt Hotel, he dodged an interview invitation from black society columnist Lillian Scott. "The Governor sounded like many another small-town, middle-aged Southerner does when he gets to New York—sort of quiet and intimidated," Scott noted.

In Boston and New York, Harry Truman pitched for minority votes. As the campaign rounded third, heading for home, he seemed marvelously composed, playing a waltz on his hotel-suite piano before heading out through Boston streets for Mechanics Hall, breezily finishing his number with a flourish and a broad grin. "Let's go, boys," he announced, "we can't keep a crowd of good Democrats waiting. It won't be long now before we are finished with this traveling."

The crowds he rode through were immense. Police shoved people back onto the curb. "Roosevelt never had a crowd this size," a Boston-Irish cop informed Truman speechwriter Frank Kelly. "I've been on the force twelve years and I've never seen a mob this big. We like Harry better than Roosevelt. He's a grand man."

"I hate Communism," Truman told his overflow Mechanics Hall crowd. "I have fought it at home. I have fought it abroad. . . . A vile whispering campaign was spearheaded by the Ku Klux Klan and by Klan-minded people to discredit Al Smith. The Republican appeal was based on religious prejudice because of Al Smith's Catholic faith. The leaders of the Republican Party served notice on America then and there that they would stop at nothing in order to gain power. Don't think that the elephant has changed his habits in the last twenty years. This Republican elephant is not that kind of elephant."

From there, it was on to an open-air, sixty-five-thousand-person Harlem rally, to deliver his only civil rights speech of the campaign, and to Madison Square Garden, where he announced, "I have never changed my position on Palestine or Israel."

During his twenty-six-mile Gotham motorcade, 1.2 million persons saw—and largely cheered—Truman. That did not keep him from feeling the effects of months of travel and pressure. At the Brooklyn Academy of Music, traditionally the last stop in Democratic presidential campaigns, he received a twelve-minute standing ovation, but he looked and sounded haggard—still giving his opponents hell, but noticeably stumbling over his words.

At his Greenwich Village apartment, Truman speechwriter Frank Kelly entertained warmly positive thoughts regarding the campaign's progress—but not entirely positive. He had already accepted a position at Boston University rather than hope for the best in an administration that might never win a term of its own. Still, he thought back to 1940, when he had won $600 on the FDR-Willkie race, and considered borrowing $500 to place on the president now. He had seen the confidence in Truman's manner. He had seen the great crowds in Boston.

But, in the end, Frank Kelly didn't bet—and he kept his bags packed for Boston University.

Hard on Truman's heels, in New York City on Friday, October 29, was Henry Wallace—quite literally, as he had to make three left turns in midtown to avoid merging into HST's motorcade. Wallace campaigned furiously in the city, his last stronghold, perhaps the only one he had ever possessed. At noon, he addressed twelve thousand people at Twenty-ninth Street and Seventh Avenue, before heading to Columbia University and then to West 125th Street's Hotel Theresa. There, alongside Paul Robeson, he spoke over the Mutual radio network. That evening, at Harlem's packed Golden Gate Ballroom, he accused Truman of making "shallow, hollow, worthless promises" on civil rights and having "invited the Dixiecrats, the race-haters, the lynch boys, the poll-taxers back into his camp."

Strom Thurmond was not back in Truman's camp. At Longview, Texas, on October 30, the Dixiecrat charged that Truman's "campaign talks were tinted with red in Harlem and his actions were yellow when he stumped the South. President Truman in his Harlem address of last Friday came out squarely for his Red-inspired civil rights program. But President Truman refused my challenge to discuss his vicious Red measures when he campaigned through the South."

Not long before Strom Thurmond uttered those words, his daughter Essie Mae had received a phone call from her Aunt Mary in Coatesville, Pennsylvania—telling her to return north because her mother was seriously ill.

She rode north by train, alone, leaving her husband in Orangeburg, because she possessed secrets not only about her mother and father, but also about her husband. She had told none of her family that she had married. Telling them now, she thought, would only further complicate a painful situation.

Reaching home, she learned that her mother lay in a Philadelphia hospital, in a "poverty ward," abandoned by her latest lover, suffering from recurrent kidney failure.

Carrie "Tunch" Butler, just thirty-nine years of age, was dying.

Essie revealed her secret marriage to her aunt, then to her mother. When she brought Tunch a bouquet a flowers, a nurse callously informed Essie Mae that her mother would not live long enough to enjoy them.

Essie Mae took the train back to Coatesville, meaning to return the next morning. That nurse may have been callous, but she was right. A phone call reached Essie Mae before she departed her aunt's home. Her mother was dead.

Though Tunch Butler had suffered much, her casket was open. Hymns filled the Baptist church where they buried her.

And though J. Strom Thurmond was running for president and knew many things, when he entered the polling booth to cast his ballot for himself, he did not know that the woman whom he had loved—and who had borne his daughter—was dead.

34

"The campaign is ending and you still don't know"

From Brooklyn, Harry Truman—joined by his former haberdashery partner Eddie Jacobson at Manhattan's Penn Station—traveled home to Independence, pausing at St. Louis for one last stem-winding public appearance. At 9:30 on Saturday night, October 30, he addressed a screaming, stomping crowd of over 12,500 Democrats jammed into 9,300-seat Kiel Auditorium. Missourians John Snyder, Stuart Symington, and Bob Hannegan—and, of course, his daughter, Margaret—stood beside him. The huge crowd shouted, applauded, rang bells, and waved placards, interrupting him with applause after nearly every sentence. "Pour it on, Harry!" they yelled, as he largely discarded his prepared remarks to once more flay his opponents. Ratcheting up his rhetoric to reference the "do-nothing idiot Congress," he was only beginning:

> Hearst character assassins, McCormick-Patterson saboteurs, all began firing at me as did the conservative columnists and the radio commentators. Not because they believed anything that they said or wrote, but because they were paid to do it. . . .

> Now I have an old-fashioned notion that a candidate for public office has a duty to tell the voters where he stands on the issues in a campaign. I have traveled twenty-two thousand miles, made about 270 speeches and taken a positive position on every issue. But the Republican candidate refuses to tell the American people where he stands on any issue. The campaign is ending and you still don't know. All you have got is platitudes and double-talk.

It was indeed Truman's 270th address. Tom Dewey had delivered precisely 101 fewer talks in his decidedly less frenetic effort. Truman, however, still had one more speech to deliver. On election eve, he addressed a nationwide radio audience from his white-frame Independence home. In the interim, he slogged through Kansas City in the rain, campaigning retail-style, attending several Masonic ceremonies. Downtown at Eleventh and Central's Arafat Shrine Temple, his home fraternal temple, the fez-clad president accepted a life membership in a Shrine veterans unit.

From the living room of his fourteen-room North Delaware Street home, with Margaret beside him, at 9:37 PM, he took to the radio waves:

> I believe that the Democratic Party is the party of the people. I believe that through the Democratic Party, all classes of our citizens will receive fairer treatment and more security.

> I believe, in particular, in the industrial workers, the farmers, and the small businessmen of this country. I believe they can best protect themselves against reaction and against inflation through the Democratic Party.

> I believe that a Democratic administration, pledged to continue the present policies of our country, is our best insurance against going back to the dark days of 1932.

> I believe with all my heart and soul that Almighty God has intended the United States of America to lead the world to peace. We were in that position thirty years ago. We failed to meet our obligation then, and World War II was the result.

> This time we must live up to our opportunity to establish a permanent peace for the greatest age in human history.

> We have two great goals: one, to build a secure life for ourselves here at home, and the other, to build a lasting peace for the world.

At 9:55 the next morning, the Trumans drove the short distance to the Independence Memorial Building, voting place for Blue Township's 7th Precinct. Within a cramped, six-foot-high, plywood voting booth in the gymnasium, he marked Ballot 101. Bess and Margaret, both clad in fox stoles, voted alongside him in similar booths. For Margaret, it was her first vote.

"How does it look to you?" a reporter asked the president.

"I can't see anything but victory," he answered. "What do you think?" Then he added, not surprisingly, that he had voted the Democratic ticket "top to bottom."

Departing down the gymnasium steps, he shook hands with neighbors. Reporters asked, "Are you going to stay up tonight and listen to the returns?"

"I doubt it," he responded, a hint of a smile upon his lips. "I think I'll go to bed early. You won't know anything until tomorrow."

Harry Truman had, as was his habit, risen early that Election Day. Before he went to vote, photographers and a raincoated Secret Service man followed him as he briskly trod familiar neighborhood streets, walking stick in hand. At the Roosevelt Hotel in New York, Tom Dewey slept in, not rising until 9:30. In their fifteenth-floor, three-bedroom suite, the Deweys breakfasted on orange juice, eggs, toast, and coffee. Sirens and cheering workers at the nearby General Electric Building greeted their motorcycle-escorted limousine (New York State license plate "1") as it processed to 121 East Fifty-first Street, the polling place for the largely Republican First Assembly District's 63rd Precinct—in the basement of Public School 18. Well-wishers, many waiting for an hour, greeted the Deweys as they entered at 12:07 PM. Tom Dewey sported a blue-gray, pin-striped suit and his trademark gray homburg. His wife appeared oddly solemn in a black two-piece suit trimmed with black Persian lamb, a black feathered hat, black suede pumps, and even black accessories—with only a two-strand pearl choker and pearl earrings to relieve her sartorial severity.

Dewey signed the election registry, "I'd like to tear that page out and save it," an election worker whispered. Clearly, history was being made on East Fifty-first Street.

Further downtown, within the confines of a carpet-cleaning establishment near his Gramercy Park home, Socialist nominee Norman Thomas voted at 9:05 AM. At Princeton, the previous evening, Thomas had predicted a Republican victory and wished Dewey "well for the sake of the United States and for the sake of mankind." Thomas refused to speculate upon his own prospects—but professed he wouldn't "be surprised at a considerable vote."

In Chicago, eighty-five-year-old Vegetarian Party candidate Dr. John Maxwell wrote in his own name. In Los Angeles, Prohibition candidate Dr. Claude A. Watson and his wife, Maude, attempted to cast their ballots. Election officials demanded the couple first surrender the unused absentee ballots mailed to them at their Winona Lake, Indiana, vacation home. Failing to produce those ballots, Claude and Maude were turned away.

At the Edgefield County Courthouse, shortly before noon, Strom Thurmond, his seventy-eight-year-old mother, and his twenty-year-old wife (it was her first vote) motored to the polling place, then returned to his mother's home for lunch.

Farmer that he was, like Harry Truman, Henry Wallace had also risen early in New York's Westchester County. By 8:00 AM, he, his wife, their son-in-law, and campaign press secretary Steve Fisher had motored from his 124-acre Farvue Farm to the 2nd Precinct voting station in the town of Lewisboro to cast votes. Lewisboro was Republican turf, with Dewey besting FDR there in 1944 by 201 to 68. Within old South Salem's ancient public library, flashbulbs popped, and Wallace promised to pick up "more votes than the pollsters say," then departed to tend to his chrysanthemums and his twelve hundred hens.

At Hart's Location in New Hampshire's White Mountains, the polls opened at 7:00 AM, in the modest dining room of Mr. and Mrs. Joseph Burke, specifically on their old-fashioned dining-room table.

By the flickering, smoky light of kerosene lamps, town clerk Douglas Macomber opened a cardboard box and distributed the paper ballots to the ten voters present. One local voter remained absent: railroad engineer John P. McCann said he wasn't going to vote—he didn't want "all that publicity."

Gray-haired Mrs. Florence P. Morey, a Dewey supporter and the owner of the local Willey House hostelry, went first. By 7:06 AM the votes were counted. With the help of two absentee ballots, Dewey had defeated Truman eleven to one. Four years earlier, Hart's Location had favored FDR six to four.

Haywood County, North Carolina's Cataloochee precinct, reported next: Truman seven, Dewey zero. Four years previously, Dewey had garnered two votes to Roosevelt's eight.

Voting in Bourbon County, Kentucky—home to Democratic U.S. Senate candidate Rep. Virgil Chapman—proceeded less smoothly. As the polls opened at Clintonville's Precinct 3, Deputy Sheriff John Neal inspected its ballot box—and found it stuffed with seventeen Democratic ballots.

In rural Godfrey, Illinois, that morning, Mrs. Frank Page and Mrs. Ray Hendricks arrived at the 15th Precinct polls via ambulance. Attendants wheeled them into the booth on stretchers. In nearby Alton, George Bean arrived at Precinct 1 in a full body cast. In Atkinson, Nebraska, however, eighty-two-year-old Frank O. Hammerberg did them one better. In ill health for weeks, he survived long enough to cast his absentee ballot for the Dewey-Warren ticket. Soon after Atkinson's polls opened, Hammerberg died. Authorities ruled that his vote counted.

In the western Pennsylvania coal-mining town of Donora (population: 14,000), the sun broke through the clouds for the first time in ten days and people voted. For six days during that period, a poisonous, pollution-fueled smog had enveloped the city, killing twenty persons and sickening approximately six thousand more. Doctors observed that, had the haze not lifted, a thousand more would have perished. In the weeks to come, fifty more would die from exposure to the deadly air inversion, including fifty-nine-year-old Lukasz Musial, father of St. Louis Cardinals star "Stan the Man" Musial.

In Nashville, Mayor Thomas L. Cummings reported that his city's Negro neighborhoods were "flooded" with anonymous letters warning blacks not to vote. Two of the letters contained the following message, scrawled in red pencil:

Keep away from the polls November 2.

KKK

The Klan knows you.

In Atlanta, Klan imperial wizard Samuel Green protested that he had no organization "within a hundred miles of Nashville" and offered his "full cooperation" in "tracking down and apprehending the perpetrators of this hoax."

In Oklahoma, Nebraska, and Illinois, if you wished to vote for Henry Wallace, you simply couldn't. In Ohio, you could—sort of. His name didn't appear on the ballot, and neither did his party. But if you could discern the identity of the twenty-five Progressive Party electors on the state ballots, and if you marked an "X" alongside each of those twenty-five names, then—and only then—could you vote the Wallace-Taylor ticket.

In New York's 18th District, Wallace-supporting congressman Vito Marcantonio faced competition from thirty-five-year-old stockbroker John Ellis on the GOP and Liberal tickets ("[Marcantonio] is constantly in favor of Russia's communistic policies") and sixty-three-year-old Tammany assemblyman and district leader John P. Morrissey. Marcantonio derided the inarticulate Morrissey as a *testa di cappuccio* or "cabbage head."

Nonetheless, Marcantonio took no chances. The American Labor Party dispatched approximately 1,750 poll watchers to guard against Tammany fraud (and provided breakfasts for five hundred of them). When Tammany operatives shooed one ALP watcher away from the polls, Marcantonio protested. Special Deputy Harold Glasser threatened the congressman with arrest.

Not far south of Marcantonio's district, at some time between 2:00 and 6:00 AM, thieves lifted $35,000 in jewels—including a $25,000 diamond ring—from Clare Boothe Luce's Waldorf-Astoria apartment. Police did not reveal if she had been present.

In Baltimore, H. L. Mencken hankered to vote for Strom Thurmond, particularly after hearing him speak (and finding him "dignified and intelligent . . . suave and gentle") on Friday evening, October 1, at the local Lyric Theatre. But Thurmond had failed to make the Maryland ballot. Earlier in the year, never trusting much in the intelligence of his fellow Americans, Mencken had predicted a Truman victory; by now, barely more trusting in the electorate, he had resigned himself to a Dewey triumph and cast his vote for the New Yorker.

In Paris, Eleanor Roosevelt announced that she had cast her absentee ballot for Truman. Asked if she might continue at the United Nations under Dewey, she merely responded, "I've got to finish my work here."

At 10:00 AM at Half Day, Illinois, Adlai and Ellen Stevenson (he nervous and worn, rumpled in his dark suit; she in much more festive plaid) voted at a local school, too late for a photo of the event to make even the afternoon papers.

Stevenson's campaign against Dwight Green, the first Illinois governor to seek a third term, had taken on certain interesting aspects, not necessarily of Stevenson's design. In March, *Harper's Magazine's* John Barlow Martin had exposed massive corruption regarding Illinois mining inspections in the wake of the March 1947 Centralia No. 5 mining disaster that took 111 lives. In April, the *Chicago Daily News* and the *St. Louis Post-Dispatch* revealed that Green had secretly retained at least thirty-two downstate Illinois editors and reporters or their relatives on the public payroll from 1940 through 1948. The number eventually grew to fifty-one, with payments in excess of $475,000. In mid-campaign, the *Post-Dispatch's* Theodore C. Link uncovered another Green-related scandal, involving gambling in Peoria: "Gamblers, slot machine operators and punch-board distributors in at least six counties were 'shaken down' for nearly $100,000 for Gov. Dwight Green's 1944 political campaign."

Yet Stevenson's chances against Green remained so gossamer that gamblers offered three-to-one odds against his election. Jake Arvey plunked down $3,000 on Stevenson anyway.

In New York, Penny Olson, wife of ABC-radio *Whiz Quiz* host Johnny Olson, pondered the possibilities of having her waist-length hair cut, not having done so since Herbert Hoover's defeat in 1932. At that time, her father, Fred W. Powers of Wisconsin Rapids, Wisconsin, had told her, "You can't get it cut again, until a Republican is elected President."

In Westbrook Pegler's column that morning, Democrat Bernard Baruch blasted Harry Truman as "a rude, ignorant, uncouth man." At 5:45 AM, the seventy-eight-year-old financier arrived at his Manhattan voting precinct— fifteen minutes before it opened. A woman who had arrived ahead of Baruch let him vote first.

Robert Taft, preparing with Martha for a postelection European vacation, wired Dewey and Warren his congratulations.

Clark Clifford had traveled west with Harry Truman, detraining at St. Louis. Early Tuesday morning, he voted with his mother, then caught a flight for Washington. At the White House, he received a call from Under Secretary of State Robert Lovett. Lovett, inveterate leaker of information to Dewey's foreign-policy brain trust, suggested a meeting to prepare transition documents for the new administration. Some thought Lovett might be part of that team, perhaps even secretary of state or defense.

At Washington's Mayflower Hotel, the DNC's Howard McGrath and Jack Redding displayed their bravest faces. But in planning for Election Night, they had revealingly neglected to engage the Mayflower ballroom for any prospective victory celebrations. At the party's New York headquarters, in the Biltmore Hotel's Music Room—a short two blocks from Dewey's Roosevelt Hotel digs—pessimistic Democrats had failed to erect a scoreboard.

The White House, for two hours each weekday, opened its doors to the public. On the preceding Tuesday, 1,858 tourists had trooped through its East Gate; on Election Day, just eighty-eight visited, the lowest total in eight months.

In newspapers nationwide, Drew Pearson reported that during the previous spring "a little group of military men discussed the idea of taking advantage of Russian tension a couple of weeks before election day in such a way as to justify dropping the atomic bomb" to "(1) get inevitable war over with in a hurry, and (2) re-elect President Truman." Pearson remained unsure whether the matter was ever reported to Truman.

In Moscow, *Pravda*, *Izvestia*, and *Trud* each reported on Harry Truman's pre–Election Day activities, but seemed far more interested in what Henry Wallace and Glen Taylor had to say. The three papers noted: "Police said at least a half million people greeted Wallace, who rode about eighty miles through the Brooklyn district in an automobile, accompanied by fifty machines decorated with banners and posters appealing for support of the Progressive Party. Several times groups of people pushed through the police and rushed up to Wallace in order to shake his hand." None carried a word about Dewey.

It rained in Paducah, keeping Alben Barkley indoors until noon. He voted at the home of his neighbor R. L. Lang—Number 233, just ahead of one of his own farmhands. In Pocatello ("nominally his home town," as a wire service put it), Glen Taylor voted for himself and for Henry Wallace, then boarded a plane for Salt Lake City, and then another to San Jose. There, his brother Paul was an even longer shot than himself, running for Republican John Z. "Jack" Anderson's Eighth District congressional seat. They would await returns together.

It drizzled in Oakland. At 8:00 AM, in a residential garage at the rear of 193 Montecito Avenue, a block from their home, Earl and Nina Warren, accompanied by their twenty-year-old daughter, Virginia, voted. As Warren marked his ballot, twenty-seven-year-old *Life* photographer John Dominis raised his camera above the booth's canvas curtain.

Flash!

Warren's face reddened. "Don't you know it is an invasion of privacy and illegal to photograph a person while he is voting?" he stormed. "I want you to destroy that film."

No one had ever seen Earl Warren so angry. Dominis's fellow photographers echoed Warren's rage, repeating his demand. Dominis protested that he thought Warren was merely posing for the cameras. He destroyed his negative anyway.

Before Warren had voted, however, purple-suit-clad Nina Warren had cast her own ballot. "Well, Mother," her husband advised her, as she entered the booth, "you'd better sign on the dotted line." Nina smiled. Wanting no part of Tom Dewey or of being a vice president's wife, she very calmly and privately marked her ballot—for Harry Truman.

35

"Don't bother me anymore; I'm going to bed"

adio and television marshaled as many commentators as they could to fill the hours to come.

Mutual Broadcasting's radio staff included Gabriel Heatter, Fulton Lewis Jr., William L. Shirer, and pollster Dr. Louis H. Bean. Abroad, the Canadian Broadcasting Corporation (CBC), the British Broadcasting Corporation (BBC), the French Broadcasting System (FBS), and Argentina's Radio Belgrano all piggybacked onto Mutual's coverage. From "a special vote tabulating center" in New York City's Ritz-Carlton hotel, ABC trotted out a seemingly unending stream of commentators: Paul Harvey, Tris Coffin, George Sokolsky, Elmo Davis, Dr. George Gallup, Martin Agronsky, Walter Kiernan, Pauline Frederick, Walter Winchell, and Drew Pearson—the latter two making their television debuts and enlivening matters with some faux on-air sparring.

CBS's star-studded crew included Eric Sevareid, Robert Trout, Lowell Thomas, John Daly, Quincy Howe, Richard C. Hottelet, Elmo Roper, Joseph C. Harsch, and—from Times Square—Norman Brokenshire. The news service of the newly formed Voice of America relied on CBS to transmit returns worldwide.

NBC's coverage—operated in tandem with Henry Luce's *Life* magazine and "brought to you by Chevrolet and Chevrolet dealers across the entire NBC network"—emanated from Radio City's Studio 8-H and featured H. V. Kaltenborn (*Billboard*: "easily the standout"), Morgan Beatty, Ben Grauer (*Billboard*: "still 90 per cent hambone and 10 per cent sound newspaperman"), and Richard Harkness. Anticipating a Dewey victory, NBC and *Life* (the DuMont TV network similarly tied its coverage into *Newsweek*'s) constructed a huge model of the White House, from which treadmills would propel two cardboard pachyderms at history's appropriate juncture.

A potential ten million television viewers resided along the Boston–Richmond broadcast corridor. In late September, AT&T had linked live coverage from Cleveland to stations in Buffalo, Toledo, Detroit, Chicago, Minneapolis, and St. Louis. Los Angeles boasted three stations. Harry Truman, however, would not see a second of coverage. Kansas City still lacked even a single station.

In Munich, the *Münchner Merkur* confidently headlined, "*Thomas E. Dewey Amerikas neuer Präsident.*" In Chicago, Col. McCormick's *Tribune* found itself beset by labor problems and needed at least two hours' lead time to publish stories. Its longtime Washington correspondent, the seventy-one-year-old Arthur Sears Henning, reassured his editors there was no reason to fear delay: Dewey's election was in the bag, and so DEWEY DEFEATS TRUMAN ran eight columns wide across the *Tribune*'s front page.

Voting ran heavy in Baltimore, Boston, Akron, Newark, Green Bay, Milwaukee, and Philadelphia. Chicago forecast a record vote. History's largest presidential turnout had occurred in 1940—when 49,820,312 voted. Analysts predicted that tonight's turnout might far exceed that.

In the East, polls closed as early as 4:00 PM EST in parts of South Carolina and Tennessee, and as late as 9:00 PM EST in both New York and Rhode Island. Depending on where you resided in California, polls remained open to 9:00 PM or 10:00 PM PST; in Oregon and Washington until 11:00 PM PST. Always-crucial Ohio closed at 6:30 PM EST; Harry Truman's Missouri at 8:00 PM CST. Eight states voted on the sale of alcohol, twelve on veterans' benefits. Massachusetts balloted on a Catholic-opposed constitutional amendment relaxing regulations on birth control. Baltimoreans voted on $2.5 million in improvements to their Municipal Stadium.

In Independence, Harry Truman . . . vanished.

At 4:30 that afternoon, Truman completed a leisurely late lunch with about thirty friends and supporters at Independence's Rockwood Country Club. Suddenly, Independence police officer Mike Westwood roared away on his motorcycle, followed closely by a limousine. Reporters, assuming the president had also left, piled into their cars to give chase. As they careened through Independence streets, a black four-door Ford sedan pulled up on Maple Avenue, a block behind the clubhouse. Truman scurried out the Rockwood Country Club's back exit, through a neighboring backyard, and onto Maple Avenue, where he entered the rear door of his sedan, squeezing between Secret Service agents Henry Nicholson and Gerald McCann.

Soon enough reporters caught wind of the chief executive's disappearance.

"The President is entitled to a night to himself," announced Truman press secretary Charlie Ross, without further explanation, from Kansas City's Muehlebach Hotel.

Truman had fled thirty miles to the northwest of Independence, to the resort community of Excelsior Springs. He took refuge in Room 200 of that city's major hostelry, the stone-and-masonry Elms Hotel, long a favorite of statesmen—and of gangsters.

"We drove down to Excelsior Springs," Truman would recall, "and I had a bath in the hot springs and a little something to eat [a ham-and-cheese sandwich, a glass of buttermilk] and went to bed, about six o'clock in the evening." With bottles of scotch and bourbon atop his dresser, he ordered Agent Rowley not to awaken him unless something "important" happened.

He had fled so precipitously that he had neglected to bring either nightclothes or toiletries. From hotel management he borrowed slippers and a bathrobe, for bed and for the rubdown and the Turkish bath he enjoyed prior to his sandwich supper.

Truman turned in. At New York's Roosevelt Hotel, a thousand jubilant party faithful gathered at Dewey headquarters. The polls had now closed in more than a dozen states, all outside the South. With the exception of Ohio and Illinois, however, few were particularly significant. Herbert Brownell crowed:

> This is definitely a Republican year. . . . I am confident that the Dewey-Warren ticket has already carried ten [Illinois, Indiana, Ohio, Connecticut, Delaware, Maine, Maryland, New Hampshire, Vermont, and South Dakota] of these twelve states, with a total of 101 of the 120 electoral votes.

In . . . Kentucky and West Virginia—returns are not yet conclusive enough to indicate definite results, but the trend to the Dewey-Warren ticket is heartening.

In 1944, our party carried only five of these ten states.

At precisely 6:07 PM EST, Governor Dewey, his wife, and his seventy-year-old mother climbed into the family limousine and headed for an election-night dinner at the 6 East Ninety-third Street apartment of R. H. Macy's department-store magnate, Roger Williams Straus. It was a good-luck election-night custom (albeit with decidedly spotty results) that had commenced when Dewey had first run for district attorney. Rendezvousing with the Deweys were two of their sons, thirteen-year-old John and sixteen-year-old Tom Jr., chauffeured from the Albany Academy by New York State police corporal Joseph Micklas.

Frances Dewey wore a black dinner dress and a hat trimmed with gold sequins. Dewey, tossing formalities to the wind, went hatless.

Polls closed at 6:00 PM EST in Illinois. Adlai Stevenson had motored into Chicago, dined with his mother-in-law, and arrived at Democratic headquarters at 7 South Dearborn. Early Chicago totals gave him a lead, but nervous party leaders fretted that it would be insufficient to overcome returns from Republican strongholds. Stevenson thought differently. "I think I've won," he said, barely raising his voice.

Around 8:00 PM EST, as the Deweys returned to the Roosevelt, Dr. George Gallup noticed something. Henry Wallace had tanked in Connecticut working-class areas. Massachusetts returns told the same story. Wallace was drawing nowhere near the number of votes that Gallup and other pollsters had forecast he would steal from Harry Truman. Wallace and George Gallup were in trouble—and so was Tom Dewey.

Herbert Brownell knew something too, but he wasn't telling. "Dewey's statisticians had analyzed the early returns from key districts throughout the country," he remembered, "and told us confidentially that the outcome would be decided by a hair's breadth."

In Dewey's suite, newsreel cameramen demanded footage of the family's reactions. To increase authenticity, the Deweys switched on the radio, only to hear the ominous words, "Truman is leading by—"

"Holy gee, Dad!" exclaimed thirteen-year-old John.

"That doesn't mean anything," Dewey smiled. "It doesn't count. That's just the South."

In Washington, at 9:00 PM EST, Robert Taft rang up *Chicago Tribune* reporter Walter Trohan, soliciting his prognosis. Trohan predicted a Republican rout. Taft wasn't shocked.

At the same time, precisely 9:00 PM EST, the DuMont network switched off its coverage to join announcer Dennis James and its regularly scheduled Tuesday-night prizefights at the Park Arena, at Park Avenue and East 169th Street in the Bronx. It would not resume supplying returns until nearly 11:00 PM.

Turmoil reigned on Delaware Street in Independence. Margaret Truman would recall:

> Reporters were practically storming the house. Again and again I was forced to go out on the porch in my best black dress and ballet slippers (great for weary feet) to assure them that my father was not in the house. When they finally believed me, they began trying to wheedle out of me exactly where he was. That was one night when I was grateful for my native Missouri stubbornness. I sometimes wonder if I could have resisted the terrific pressure those reporters put on me, without it.

Truman led in the popular vote. But those votes seemed to be city votes, and when rural totals arrived, Truman's lead—like Truman himself—would necessarily vanish. In any case, as Herbert Brownell had calculated, the popular total didn't matter: Dewey led in the electoral vote. At 9:30 PM EST, Brownell proclaimed Republican victory. "As of this moment," he announced, "the Dewey-Warren ticket is assured, in my opinion, of the votes of at least twenty-four states with a total of 295 electoral votes. That is twenty-nine electoral votes more than is required to win."

By 10:00 PM EST, Adlai Stevenson no longer looked like a mere possibility in Illinois. He looked solid. Sequestered in a tiny corner office, he furiously reworked his acceptance speech. Stevenson would always be rewriting his speeches.

In Washington, at 10:30 PM EST, Republican national chairman Hugh Scott, sharing Brownell's expressed optimism, proclaimed: "Now we have come to the Republican half of the evening."

Some disagreed. Forty-three-year-old *New York Times* Washington correspondent Cabell Phillips had traveled to Manhattan to be available, if necessary, at the *Times*'s West Forty-third Street offices. His editors, however, deemed his presence unnecessary in such a lopsided contest, and Phillips instead took in a play on West Forty-seventh Street. At intermission, between sips of scotch at a nearby bar, he heard over the radio, "Truman's lead now looks almost unassailable. If he can hold his edge in Ohio." The news stunned him. Abandoning his topcoat (an expensive one) at the theater, he scampered to the *Times* building.

History was being made. Cabell Phillips coveted a role in reporting it.

At the Biltmore, listless Democrats gathered, their forlorn ballroom bereft of even the most basic of campaign decorations. Former DNC chairman Jim Farley arrived early. Truman loyalists such as Bob Hannegan and Ed Pauley—and even disloyalists such as FDR Jr. and Mayor O'Dwyer—followed, but most Democratic celebrities proved more notable by their absence. "No cabinet member, no diplomat, no angel eager for one reason or another to identify himself with a victor, no socialite, no Hollywood star, no ambitious brain truster—none of these ornaments of four Roosevelt victories showed," noted columnist Doris Fleeson.

Newsweek's Walter Fitzmaurice, unable to secure an interview with Howard McGrath for ABC radio, buttonholed Farley. "But this is only an early lead," Farley said, dismissing Truman's popular-vote totals. "He cannot win, for when the reports come in from the country—the Dewey strongholds—his early lead will fold up." DNC publicity chief Jack Redding, listening to him nearby on the radio, wanted to strangle him.

In Westminster, Maryland, Whittaker Chambers, also hearing the returns on his radio, despondently turned to his wife, Esther Shemitz Chambers, and said, "I think President Truman has won." Like Harry Truman—who had vowed to help abolish HUAC if reelected—Whittaker Chambers went to bed.

Elsewhere in Maryland, H. L. Mencken dropped into the *Sun*'s offices to catch the returns. He did not like what he saw. "I think Dewey is in trouble," he snorted. "Truman is running better than expected in Baltimore."

In the south-central Kentucky town of Eighty Eight, Truman and Dewey had battled to a flat-footed tie—88 to 88.

In Washington, Clark Clifford, his wife, Margery, and their three daughters went to the nearby home of his friend, veteran *Detroit News* Washington correspondent—and television set owner—sixty-four-year-old Jay Hayden. Clifford, unwilling to prolong his misery, planned to stay but an hour. In a state of nerves, he remained there through the night.

In Cambridge, Massachusetts, Arthur and Marian Schlesinger gathered together a small group of friends—John Kenneth and Catherine "Kitty" Galbraith and *Boston Traveler* editorial writer Barbara Wendell Kerr among them—to await the inevitable. Hearing the first results trickle in, Kerr grabbed her coat and rushed for the door. Anticipating a Dewey victory (she was a Democrat, but the *Traveler* was Republican), she had already composed an appropriate commentary for Wednesday's edition. "That editorial on 'Return to Sanity' isn't going to run," Mrs. Kerr hastily explained as she exited. "I've got to substitute my alternative editorial, 'No Mandate for Socialism.'"

By 11:00 PM EST, Adlai Stevenson knew that he had improbably crushed Dwight Green, and that fifty-five-year-old University of Chicago economist (and former Chicago alderman) Paul H. Douglas had similarly dispatched U.S. senator "Curly" Brooks. At 7 South Dearborn, jubilant Democrats jeered at the *Tribune's* "DEWEY DEFEATS TRUMAN" headline.

At 11:08 EST, reports placed Truman ahead not merely in popular votes, but also in the Electoral College, leading in twenty-one states with 284 electoral votes, compared to Dewey's 191 electoral votes from twenty states. The tide had turned. Herbert Brownell declined comment.

By 11:15 EST, Brownell had recovered his composure enough to issue the following statement:

> The pattern is beginning to develop. As in all elections the big cities in which the Democrats normally have majorities are reported during the early hours after the polls close.
>
> That has been happening tonight, but the Democratic majorities in practically every instance have been substantially smaller than would be necessary for the Democratic candidates to win.
>
> We are now getting into the state of the election returns which permit a definite appraisal . . . and I am convinced, as I stated earlier, the election of the Dewey-Warren ticket is assured. . . .

A case in point is the city of Philadelphia. In 1944 Republicans lost the city by about 150,000. The complete returns are just in for Philadelphia and the Dewey-Warren ticket carried the city by 2,800.

So we conclude here at Republican headquarters that Dewey and Warren are elected.

"Herb, do you really think Dewey still has a chance?" asked New York *Daily News* Washington correspondent Ruth Montgomery.

"I hope so," Brownell answered without conviction.

New York, a seesaw all night, now looked like a win for Dewey. He swept Michigan, Maryland, Connecticut, Pennsylvania, and New Jersey. Truman counterpunched with solid victories in Massachusetts and Rhode Island. He quite naturally captured Missouri, but also took Minnesota, Iowa, and Wisconsin— as well as the great bulk of the West. In the South, the Thurmond-Wright ticket prevailed only in Mississippi, Alabama, South Carolina, and Louisiana. Otherwise, Dixie held firmly Democratic. California, Ohio, and Illinois wobbled in the balance, but all three seemed within reach for the resurgent Truman.

Truman now led by at least a million popular votes. Even Howard McGrath exuded a genuine optimism. "We pitched the campaign on getting out a big vote," he announced just after midnight, "and it is paying off. I think that the vote will be in excess of fifty-four million, and I think that will be enough to put President Truman over."

At the Roosevelt Hotel, a humble elevator operator knew how to read the tea leaves. "The cops are spreading nets outside the windows of the upper floors," he told a reporter.

They might have been looking for Allen Dulles. Recalled his son-in-law, the former Austrian resistance fighter Fritz Molden:

It's the only time I ever saw Papa (that's what I came to call Allen) drunk. We were in a special family box at the Hotel Roosevelt, up in the balcony. And someone said that if Dewey carried Philadelphia he would win, because Philadelphia, for some reason, had always voted for the winning president. And Dewey carried Philadelphia early in the evening, so we all began to celebrate. But around midnight, someone came into the box and said something was going wrong; we were still ahead, but the reports from the Middle West were bad. So we stayed up nearly all night drinking and watching, and it got worse and worse.

Earl Warren received returns at San Francisco's St. Francis Hotel. At 9:00 PM California time, he advised his son Earl Jr. to drive his younger brother Bobby back to the governor's mansion in Sacramento. Earl Jr. took this as an ominous sign.

Warren displayed equanimity, in large part because he simply didn't care. "He didn't seem upset at all," recalled his daughter-in-law Margaret. Nina Warren expressed relief. "Thank God," she sighed.

Warren's friend Irving Stone phoned the St. Francis to ask how the candidate felt. "As though," Warren responded, "a hundred-pound sack of potatoes has been lifted off my back."

From the Muehlebach Hotel, Harry Truman's old friend and campaign treasurer, Tom Evans, periodically phoned him with returns. Having his sleep interrupted by fragmentary data merely annoyed Truman. "He said not to call him until he called me—I don't know what time it was," Evans recalled. "I imagine it was somewhere around 10:30 or 11 o'clock that I talked to him. He had carried a couple of states that I didn't expect him to, and he laughed. 'Well, we're going to win.' Then it got fairly late, and . . . I remember talking to him. I said: 'Well. Mr. President, you're just about in this position that you've got to carry either Ohio, Illinois, or California.'"

"That's good," Truman responded. "Don't bother me anymore; I'm going to bed; don't call me anymore."

"What the hell do you mean you're going to bed!" Evans exclaimed. "You can't go to bed until you carry one of those states!"

"Oh, you know, [I was] just screaming," Evans recalled, "I was worn out and excited, naturally."

"Why," Truman answered ever so calmly, "I'm going to carry all three."

"Oh, boy," was all Evans could respond, "I'll settle for one."

Just before midnight, Kansas City time, Harry Truman's Secret Service men also received a call from the Muehlebach, informing them that their boss had carried Massachusetts. Agent Nicholson saw that Truman was asleep— and that an inch of bourbon was now gone from Truman's nightstand bottle. He woke him anyway.

"Nick, stop worrying," Truman answered. "It's all over. You all go to sleep, and we'll get up early in the morning."

And as long as he was up . . .

"Oh, yes," Truman would recollect, "and about midnight I tuned in the little radio there, and old H. V. Kaltenborn was carrying on about how, while I was ahead, he didn't see how I could win."

But he still went back to sleep.

Thirty miles away, Bess Truman finally went to bed. Buoyed by the increasing good news, her spirits had significant improved. With an odd smile upon her face, she remarked to her daughter, "I wonder if Clare Boothe Luce will think I'm real now."

In Washington, former under secretary of state Dean Acheson stayed up listening to the returns at the home of his Covington & Burling law partner and friend, Gerhard Gesell, a former staff attorney for Bill Douglas at the SEC. Acheson was fortified not only by the good news, but also by a steady stream of alcohol. By early morning he would be thoroughly drunk.

On Chicago's WGN, owned by the *Chicago Tribune*, Washington correspondent Arthur Sears Henning remained on the air, prattling on about the inevitability of a Dewey victory. As Henning spoke, *Tribune* editor Don Maxwell nervously withdrew the DEWEY DEFEATS TRUMAN headline from his paper's front page.

Henry Wallace fared not well at all. Originally forecast to receive as many as ten million votes, he secured 1,156,103—just 2.38 percent of the vote—and proved to be almost as regional a standard-bearer as Strom Thurmond, with 501,167 of those votes coming in New York State (422,000 in New York City's five boroughs) and 101,085 in Los Angeles County.

Wallace exceeded 4 percent in only New York (8.12 percent in the state; 13.4 percent in the city) and California (4.73 percent). While 4.5 percent of

Independents voted for Wallace, only 0.5 percent of those identifying with an existing party voted for him. Union households proved no more supportive than non-union households. Ruled off the ballot in Illinois, he faltered in both Pennsylvania (1.47 percent) and Ohio (1.28 percent). His third-highest finish was an inconsequential 3.82 percent in inconsequential North Dakota. In Missouri, 53,000 voters had signed designating petitions for Wallace, but he received only 3,998 votes; in Georgia, 80,000 had signed for him, 1,636 voted for him; in Massachusetts, 135,000 signed for him, 38,157 voted for him; and in California, 482,781 signed for him, 190,281 voted for him. Nationwide, Wallace carried a mere thirty precincts—eighteen in New York (eight in East Harlem, two in the East Bronx), five in Los Angeles, plus seven Cuban-American Tampa districts.

"Once you find yourself in the voting booth," recalled Pete Seeger, "you still vote for the lesser evil. I had a sister-in-law that said, 'Pete, I know Wallace is a wonderful man but I didn't want to see Dewey get to be President, so I voted for Truman.' And she apologized to me. . . . Wallace got a far smaller vote than even his most cynical supporters thought."

Seeger's sister-in-law was not alone. George Gallup estimated that in the campaign's final ten days, a full third of Wallace's supporters shifted to Truman.

In only three states—New York, Michigan, and Maryland—did Wallace's totals prove meaningful to the general outcome: All three states went for Dewey.

The Wallace vote was an ethnic vote. Three-quarters of his total came from blacks and Jews, with 15 to 20 percent of all Jews voting Progressive.

Of Wallace's congressional allies, only the uniquely resilient Vito Marcantonio survived—and he only by virtue of a tight three-way split in the vote—Marcantonio, 36,278; Democrat John P. Morrissey, 31,211; Republican and Liberal parties candidate John Ellis, 30,899. In the Bronx, the Democratic, Republican, and Liberal nominee, state senator Isidore Dollinger, swamped Leo Isacson 74,971 to 43,933. Lee Pressman fared even worse—103,676 to 29,502—in Brooklyn.

In Manhattan, O. John Rogge garnered 96,000 votes for New York County surrogate judge—good enough for a third-place finish, and to elect a Republican to the $28,000-a-year post for the first time in more than a half century.

In Brooklyn, ALP and Communist Party candidate Simon W. Gerson—former confidential examiner to Republican Manhattan Borough president Stanley M. Isaacs and a *Daily Worker* correspondent—received 150,369 votes to replace the late three-term Communist, Peter V. Cacchione.

But most Progressive candidates never had a chance. In Detroit, thirty-year-old Tuskegee Airmen veteran and CIO official Coleman Young ("the biggest political mistake of my life") ran for state senate. The future mayor of Detroit lost. Hugo Black's sister-in-law, Virginia Foster Durr, garnered but six thousand votes for the U.S. Senate in Virginia. Eslanda Goode Robeson lost for Connecticut secretary of state.

The Wallace-Taylor ticket itself ultimately tanked so badly that it ran behind its congressional candidates not just in Marcantonio- and Isacson-dominated New York, but also in California, Maryland, Oregon, Tennessee, and Virginia.

At 5:00 PM, the Wallaces departed Farvue for Park Avenue's Hotel Russell, where they dined, all the while fixed on the television for any news that might hearten them. Instead, they heard ABC's Drew Pearson predict that within six months Wallace would disown Communist support.

"I couldn't do it if I wanted to," fussed Wallace.

By 8:30, Henry and Ilo Wallace had reached his nearby headquarters to await news with Paul Robeson, Beanie Baldwin, and other supporters. Returns provided little cause for cheer. Baldwin, nonetheless, thought Wallace "to be in very good spirits." "I don't think I detected how hurt he was," he recalled.

While watching images of Harry Truman on television, Wallace privately muttered to his wife that Truman was "a lying SOB." At this, Ilo Wallace broke down. Sobbing heavily, she screamed repeatedly that she'd told him so. "I told him so all the time. He should never have done it [run for president]," she recalled. Caring not at all for the race—and even less for the Communists who infested her husband's entourage—she *had* warned him.

And he had ignored her.

On certain obvious levels, Strom Thurmond had also failed abysmally. He had not forced the election into the House of Representatives. He came nowhere near his initial goal of over a hundred electoral votes. Even in the

South, he won few votes outside the four states he carried—Mississippi, South Carolina, Alabama, and Louisiana. In the South as a whole, he received but 22.6 percent of the vote.

Beyond Dixie, Thurmond enjoyed no support at all—98.8 percent of his vote came from eleven Southern states. In only nine other states did he receive any votes whatsoever. In those states, his greatest success was hardly any success at all: 1.3 percent in Alben Barkley's Kentucky.

And though Thurmond protested mightily that his campaign had not been about race, the election returns demonstrated that it undoubtedly was, with clear correlations between his vote and the percentage of the black population—87.2 percent of the vote in Mississippi, the state with the highest percentage of blacks; 72 percent in second-ranking South Carolina; 50 percent in third-ranking Louisiana; and 79.8 percent in fourth-ranking Alabama. In Texas, he received his highest percentages in overwhelmingly black counties. In Georgia's heavily African-American McDuffie County, he garnered 84 percent of the vote.

Others ran besides Truman, Dewey, Wallace, and Thurmond.

The Senate shifted from 51–45 Republican to 54–42 Democratic. Republicans Karl Mundt and Margaret Chase Smith bucked the tide in South Dakota and Maine, respectively, to advance from the lower to the upper house. Otherwise, GOP carnage was widespread. Former RNC chairman B. Carroll Reece flopped badly in trying to capture Tennessee's open Senate seat, falling to anti-Crump congressman Estes Kefauver. West Virginia's Chapman Revercomb (a pariah to Dewey for his work on the Displaced Persons Act) fell to former governor and senator Matthew M. Neely. In Oklahoma, wealthy oilman and former Democratic governor Robert S. Kerr replaced retiring Republican Edward Moore. Iowa Republican George Wilson, his campaign hampered by the loss of his lower row of teeth, found himself upset by the silver-haired Democratic underdog and former senator, Guy Gillette. Illinois's "Curly" Brooks lost by a stunning 407,728 votes to Paul Douglas. Brooks's fellow isolationist, Henry Dworshak, lost his seat to seventy-year-old Idaho Supreme Court justice Bert Miller. Kentucky's John Sherman Cooper also lost. And in Minnesota, ebullient Hubert Humphrey swamped Joe Ball 729,494 to 485,801, becoming his state's first Democratic senator.

To the south, Russell Long resumed his family's interrupted senatorial tradition—both of his parents, Huey and Rose, had served in "the world's greatest deliberative body." In Texas, Lyndon Johnson ran behind Harry Truman, and far, far behind Beauford Jester. Nevertheless, he defied widespread forecasts of a close race and demolished Houston oilman Jack Porter with 65 percent of the vote.

The Senate had seemed in doubt. The House had not. No one really expected Republicans to lose it—but they did. The lower house swung from 243–185 Republican to 263–171 Democratic.

Republican congressmen Joe Martin, John Taber, Clarence Brown, Walter Judd, Leonard Hall, and August Andresen retained their seats. Charlie Halleck did too, though his normally healthy victory margin was slashed severely. Parnell Thomas also survived—though not for long, scheduled as he was to face a federal grand jury convening in Newark to examine his office kickbacks. Elsewhere in northern New Jersey, Democratic attorney and veteran Peter W. Rodino Jr. picked up the seat of retiring Taft-Hartley Act sponsor Fred A. Hartley.

Richard Nixon, having captured both the Republican and Democratic nominations, won reelection. His Republican HUAC colleagues—Illinois's Richard B. Vail and Pennsylvania's John McDowell (he of prothonotary warbler fame)—did not. Neither did Minnesota's Norwegian-born Harold Knutson, the grumpy, balding, sixteen-term, tax-cutting chair of the Ways and Means committee. In the state's fourth district, thirty-seven-year-old freshman Edward J. Devitt fell easily to thirty-two-year-old St. Paul economics professor Eugene J. McCarthy.

In Grand Rapids, isolationist Bartel J. Jonkman had already lost the Republican primary to thirty-five-year-old attorney Gerald R. Ford. In Texas's Rio Grande Valley, the future vice-presidential candidate and former Army Air Corps bomber pilot, Lloyd Bentsen, captured the first of his three House terms. In Connecticut, Hartford Police Court judge Abraham A. Ribicoff vanquished incumbent William J. Miller. (It was the third time the resilient— but ever-vulnerable—Miller had been ousted from his seat.) In Boston, thirty-one-year-old freshman congressman Jack Kennedy ran unopposed. Wisconsin's Andrew Biemiller recaptured his former seat.

Democrats swept into governors' mansions nationwide. A handful of Republicans—including Sherman Adams in New Hampshire—hung on. In Ohio, decidedly conservative Democrat Frank Lausche triumphed. But the day's most significant news on gubernatorial fronts was the election of a quartet of liberal Democratic hopefuls. Michigan's Kim Sigler fell to thirty-seven-year-old Mennen soap heir G. Mennen Williams. In Connecticut, a "flabbergasted" Chester Bowles narrowly defeated Acting Governor James C. Shannon. Adlai E. Stevenson rolled past Dwight Green by 572,067 votes— the largest margin in Illinois history.

In Massachusetts, young Jack Kennedy, tempted by ambition and promises of Progressive Party support, had pondered a gubernatorial run, but, daunted by a June 1948 poll showing him losing to incumbent Robert F. Bradford 43.3 to 39.8 percent, declined to make the race. Attorney General Paul Dever ran instead and bested Bradford by two hundred thousand votes.

Howard Brownell's initial statements notwithstanding, early returns from Cook County provided Harry Truman with a huge—but steadily shrinking— Illinois lead. Jake Arvey phoned U.S. District Attorney Otto Kerner to watch for downstate Republican fraud. "Kerner has deputized . . . enough men to cover every downstate county," Arvey informed Howard McGrath. "Each man has a subpoena for the ballot boxes and the officials, to go *duces tecum* to the United States District Court, in case they refuse to count the votes tonight and try to take the ballots home with them."

At midnight, at his upper Manhattan headquarters, Republican-Liberal congressman Jacob K. Javits, who had captured his seat in 1946 thanks to a Democratic-ALP split, listened to radio reports indicating that he had lost to his Democratic-ALP challenger, Paul O'Dwyer. He switched off the lights, locked the door behind him, and headed home.

At the Biltmore, a Democratic campaign worker belatedly rushed upstairs to the nineteenth floor to secure Truman and Barkley posters, to hastily adorn the Music Room's hitherto forlorn walls. A wake had finally turned into a party.

At 1:30 AM EST, Herbert Brownell reappeared. Mobbed by reporters, he balanced himself on a chair to make himself seen and heard. "We now know," Brownell shouted, "that Governor Dewey will carry New York State by at least 50,000 votes and is the next president of the United States."

"All the figures that I have had which I have managed to compare with four years ago," said NBC's H. V. Kaltenborn, "indicate a gain of from 2, 3, 4, 5, up to 10 percent for Dewey. I am inclined to think that while it is a very close race, on the basis of the figures as they now stand on our board, Dewey has the best chance."

At 2:00 AM EST, however, Mutual's Fulton Lewis Jr., echoing an earlier Jim Farley comment on CBS, informed weary listeners that the election might very well—as Strom Thurmond had planned all along—be tossed into the House of Representatives. There, said Lewis, its members might proceed to elect anyone they damned well pleased—even, if they so deigned, Vito Marcantonio.

"The South always supported the Democratic Party in its darkest hour," said Jim Farley hopefully at 2:20 AM, regarding the unfolding House of Representatives scenario. "It would do so again if the proper approach were made."

From the *New York Post*, editor Ted Thackrey and reporter James Wechsler had reached Wallace's Park Avenue headquarters, but had quickly become separated, with the pro-Wallace Thackrey gaining entrance to the candidate's inner sanctum. Pro-Truman Wechsler, despite his protests that he too was from the *Post*, found himself barred from the room by a beefy young Progressive. Wechsler fumed that it was about time for some non-Communists to secure access to Wallace, earning him a punch in the nose.

Wallace emerged, apologized, and invited Wechsler inside. There, Wechsler found Wallace and Thackrey sitting "amid the ruins, heroes to the clamorous youngsters outside the door but strangely removed from the real political currents of America, two tired men after a long night out with the communists."

At 2:00 AM EST, Henry Wallace exited Park Avenue for East Harlem, to convey personal congratulations to the victorious Vito Marcantonio. Before he departed, a concession statement seemed appropriate. John Abt approved one, but it pointedly contained not a scintilla of congratulation. Convention keynoter Charles Howard and other key aides urged Wallace to include such a gesture.

"Under no circumstances," Wallace snapped, "will I congratulate that son of a bitch."

Jacob Javits had not gone to bed. His wife Marion, his brother Ben, his sister-in-law Lily, and a handful of supporters had remained with him. But nothing much had changed and, save for Marion, all had drifted away. At 2:00 AM, however, new returns were being reported. Paul O'Dwyer's lead had evaporated. Javits had pulled into a slim lead. He rushed onto Riverside Drive to call his friends back—and to have Ben run out for more food. It was going to be a very long night, but Jake Javits was going back to Congress.

"What a night," Margaret Truman confided to her diary. "I haven't been to bed at all. I've been running up and down the stairs all night answering the phone on the direct-line telephone [to the Muehlebach] to [longtime Truman crony] Bill Boyle, who gave me the returns. We are ahead, but at about 1:30 am we hit a slump—then gradually came up again. Dad has slipped away to Excelsior Springs and the reporters are going crazy trying to find him. They have offered me anything if I'll just tell them in which direction he went."

Just before midnight California time, Earl Warren, his invariably neat hair badly mussed from a night of pondering disconcerting returns, emerged from his eleventh-floor suite. Going through the motions, he advised reporters that the election remained "too close to make any estimate."

"As I read the vote," he continued, with photographers' flashbulbs popping, "still less than one-half of the total has been reported. I don't know from whose strongholds the vote up to now has come, if it does represent anybody's strongholds.

"I am inclined to think, however, that most of the votes in are from the industrial centers, but I don't know."

Senator William Knowland remained even more optimistic, forecasting the Golden State would remain "in the Republican column by approximately 250,000 votes."

In New York, Tallulah Bankhead had a matinee scheduled for Wednesday afternoon, but she remained at her hotel, glued to her radio. Her friends thought her mad, but she was determined to see this campaign through to the end.

In France, John Foster Dulles's fifty-three-year-old sister, Eleanor Lansing Dulles, drove toward Paris as French radio kept repeating that Harry Truman led Thomas E. Dewey. Their obvious error first amused, then angered her. "How clumsy the French are!" she finally exploded. "They don't know the difference between Truman and Dewey. Don't they realize that *Dewey* is the man who's going to win?"

Eleanor drove and fussed. In Paris, her brother, John Foster Dulles, sat beside a stony-faced man he hoped to replace as secretary of state, George C. Marshall, listening to returns broadcast by the Voice of America. Dulles issued a guarded statement pledging "unity and vigor" in any event. Reporters queried Marshall regarding his own position. Marshall grinned, "I am an Episcopalian."

At 4:20 AM, Dewey press secretary Jim Hagerty—not Herbert Brownell—appeared at the Roosevelt Hotel podium. A mere two hundred Dewey supporters remained. "We're in there fighting," Hagerty argued. "The returns are still coming in but it looks as if we won't know definitely until mid-morning."

At the Schlesingers', the party broke up. Arthur Schlesinger, disappointed that New York, thanks to Henry Wallace's Progressives, had fallen to Dewey, had nonetheless convinced himself that the Congress might now be Democratic. "I still had no expectation that Truman himself could make it," he recalled.

At 4:55 AM, Jim Hagerty reappeared once more. "We are not making any predictions or claims," he said. "We are simply waiting out the returns." He warned reporters that his candidate would not, in any case, personally appear until 7:00 AM at the earliest.

As Hagerty spoke, reporters in Kansas City still clamored to know the president's whereabouts. Charlie Ross merely responded that his boss had retired for the evening and would not be available until the afternoon.

Clark Clifford, exhausted and ready to sleep, finally departed neighbor Jay Hayden's home, still unsure of his—and Harry Truman's—fate. As Clifford turned in, Truman's Secret Service agents had received a call from the Muehlebach: Illinois had gone for Truman. "And all of a sudden," Agent Rowley recalled, "about four in the morning . . . the tide has changed. And so I figured, '*This* is important!' And so I went in and told him, 'We've won!'"

Truman heard Secret Service agents enter his room. Without his glasses, he barely recognized them, but he grasped the import of their news. "That's it," he exclaimed, but still remained fixated upon his rest. "Now let's go back to sleep, and we'll go downtown tomorrow early and wait for the telegram from the other fellow."

Suddenly, he changed his mind and reached for the bottle of bourbon atop his dresser. "Well, boys, we'll have one and then we'll all go to sleep. I'll pour the first one."

He turned on his radio and heard H. V. Kaltenborn. Truman, said Kaltenborn, now led by two million votes, but ultimately, armies of rural Dewey voters would reverse the Truman tide.

"We've got 'em beat," snapped Truman, ordering his men to get his car. "We're going to Kansas City."

An hour later, Clark Clifford arose, switched on his radio, and began making phone calls. It was starting to look good.

At the Roosevelt Hotel, it looked bad. "By dawn, we went out into the street with Dewey still ahead by the slimmest of margins," Allen Dulles's son-in-law Fritz Molden recalled. "Allen was staggering but trying to cheer up everyone else. But by then they knew it was over and they had lost. It was awful."

At 6:00 AM CST, breakfasted but unshaven, Truman arrived at his press headquarters on the seventh floor of the Muehlebach. He found Charlie Ross sprawled facedown on a bed, completely exhausted. Truman, with nearly ten hours of sleep under his belt, may have been the most refreshed politician in America.

Two states remained undecided—California and Ohio. Both soon fell into Truman's lap. In California's agricultural Central Valley, Truman led Dewey by 180,000 votes, dooming the Dewey-Warren ticket to lose the state's twenty-five electoral votes by 17,865 votes—1,913,134 to 1,895,269—a margin of less than half a vote per precinct.

In New York, Howard McGrath received news from Ohio. Its secretary of state, he informed the press, reported that "9,360 precincts of 9,710 show Truman 1,403,000, Dewey 1,390,000. The precincts still to come are from Democratic districts in Cuyahoga County—Cleveland." An immense cheer erupted. McGrath pled for silence. "We got it," he explained. "We have at least 270 electoral votes. Maybe it will be more."

At 8:00 AM, Dean Acheson and Gerhard Gesell were at Union Station heading for New York. The news that Truman had won left the still-tipsy Acheson nearly giddy. "I'm going to do something I've never done," he informed Gesell, "I'm going to have a highball for breakfast." And with that, he toasted Harry Truman's victory.

In San Francisco, reporters asked Earl Warren if he possessed an explanation for what had transpired. "Yes, I have," Warren answered, smiling broadly. "The President got too many votes for us."

And then he went to have breakfast.

In Baltimore, H. L. Mencken returned to the *Sun*'s offices, in time to receive the official word. "This is it," Mencken said, as he sprang to his feet, too disgusted to remain any longer. "This is the end of everything."

With typical efficiency, Thomas E. Dewey already knew that. "What do you know?" he had concluded privately at 5:30 AM. "The son of a bitch won."

36

"One for the books"

It came down to so many factors: an underdog who refused to surrender, a presumed victor who refused to fight, disgruntled Democrats—on the left and right—who, by deserting their party, merely strengthened it, and fearful Republican farmers who, in the end, proved more farmer than Republican.

Dewey, in many ways, proved a victim of his 1944 campaign. Sharply criticized by the Eastern power structure for his attacks on Sidney Hillman and domestic Communists in 1944, in 1948—even with the Hiss and Harry Dexter White cases about to engulf the Truman administration—he studiously refrained from exploiting a potentially far more explosive issue.

Having largely carried the Midwest in 1944, and lost the Northeast, this time he concentrated on carrying the latter region, rich in electoral votes. Doing so, he dangerously and pointedly ignored every other part of the country, particularly their interests regarding vital agriculture issues.

In 1948, Dewey flipped New York, New Hampshire, New Jersey, Connecticut, Pennsylvania, and Maryland into the GOP column. Republican gains in the Midwest, achieved in 1944, simply collapsed. Dewey's vote totals declined 7 percent in Missouri, Minnesota, and Oklahoma; 6 percent in Kansas; 4 percent in Wisconsin; and 1 percent in Ohio. He lost each of those states save for Kansas, thus forfeiting seventy-five electoral votes that he had captured in 1944. In ten midwestern states—Ohio, Illinois, Indiana, Michigan, Minnesota, Nebraska, Kansas, Missouri, Iowa, and Minnesota—his vote declined by 585,300.

"The farm vote switched in the last ten days," Dewey later wrote to Henry Luce. "You can analyze figures from now to kingdom come," he would admit, "and all they will show is that we lost the farm vote which we had in 1944, and that lost the election."

Dewey's aggregate national total had actually *declined* since the low-turnout war year of 1944—from 22,017,929 in 1944 to 21,991,292 in 1948. It needn't have. By campaign's end, his numbers had slid dramatically. By Election Day, 14 percent of Dewey's prospective vote had switched to Truman, and 13 percent stayed home.

Some, however, believed the opposite, that it was apathetic northeastern Democrats who had remained homebound. "Far from costing Dewey the election," contended election analyst Samuel Lubell, "stay-at-homes may have saved him as crushing a defeat as Landon in 1936."

Whoever stayed home, people stayed home. In 1952, thirteen million more Americans would vote than four years previously. In 1952, 61.6 percent of the electorate would vote; in 1948, just 51.1 percent did, the lowest presidential turnout since 48.9 percent in 1924.

In terms of complacency, it was Republican overconfidence that showed up—or rather didn't show up—in party coffers. As the campaign wore on, RNC chairman Hugh Scott publicly warned confident party faithful that their contributions were lagging, while unions and Democrats poured funds into Harry Truman's efforts. At campaign's end, Democrats had expended $2,736,334 to the Republicans' $2,176,296, though a good $700,000 in Democratic contributions arrived following Election Day—including a check from Henry Morgenthau Jr.

Strom Thurmond had failed, though, thanks to Tom Dewey's immensely greater failings, he had come amazingly close to his goal. Truman had carried Ohio by a mere 7,107 votes, Illinois by 33,612, and California by 17,865. Losing those three states and their seventy-eight electoral votes would have reduced Truman's Electoral College total to 225, increased Dewey's to 267, and deprived either of a majority. Thurmond's quixotic crusade had come within a switch of 29,292 votes of becoming a solid political reality.

The ethnic vote had come through for Truman. While a fair percentage of Jews deserted him for Wallace, the majority remained Democratic. And, conversely, now that Wallace had lured the pro-Communists and strident left-wingers from the party, Catholics felt safer voting Democratic—and for Truman. In many areas, he garnered a higher share of the Catholic vote than either FDR or Al Smith had ever done. It was no accident that, while Tom Dewey captured the bulk of northeastern states, he failed to capture either Massachusetts or Rhode Island, the nation's most Catholic states. In 1944, Roosevelt carried Providence's Italian wards with 64.3 percent of the votes. Four years later, Truman received 80 percent. In 1944, FDR carried Suffolk County—Boston—by 95,000 votes. Grand Master of Missouri Masons Harry Truman carried it by 159,000.

African-Americans had also proven key to Truman's victory, with an estimated four out of five voting Truman-Barkley. Dewey lost Harlem by 75,000 votes—a greater margin than his loss there four years earlier. Newark's 80 percent black Third Ward, Republican in 1946, went for Truman three to one. In Philadelphia—narrowly for Truman despite Herbert Brownell's brave words at 11:15 PM—blacks provided the difference, going for Truman three to two.

It was, however, in Ohio, Illinois, and California where African-Americans really counted. In Ohio, 130,000 blacks voted for Truman; he carried the state by just 7,000 votes. He carried Illinois by only 33,000 votes—thanks to winning the black vote, 85,000 to 35,000. In California, his 70,000 black votes proved essential to his 18,000-vote margin.

"You may not believe Truman," a black Arkansas minister had informed Progressive Party keynoter Charles Howard late in the campaign, "but the Dixiecrats believe him, and that's enough for me."

A multitude of reasons brought a single result. Blacks proved pivotal in three crucial states, as did farmers. So did the blocking of Progressives from the ballot in crucial Illinois and Ohio. And in both states, reverse coattails had worked wonders for Truman, as Dewey's slumping popularity hurt his local candidates.

Conservative Democrat Frank J. Lausche captured Ohio by 222,261 votes. Liberals Adlai Stevenson and Paul Douglas carried Illinois by 572,067 and 407,728 votes, respectively. They proved essential in hauling the embattled Truman across the finish line in their respective states.

And, of course, there was Dewey's insufferably confident, bland tone. "No presidential candidate in the future," opined the *Louisville Courier-Journal*, only marginally exaggerating, "will be so inept that four of his major speeches can be boiled down to these historic four sentences: Agriculture is important. Our rivers are full of fish. You cannot have freedom without liberty. Our future lies ahead."

Aside from the general, overwhelming vapidity of his campaign, Tom Dewey had committed a series of smaller, but still pivotal, blunders. It was just as well that he failed to select the star-crossed Dwight Green as his running mate, but Indiana's double-crossed Charlie Halleck might have proven just the trick—not only in neighboring Ohio and Illinois, but also throughout the Midwest. Earl Warren, selected to swing his own California as well as largely Scandinavian Minnesota, failed to deliver either.

And there was simple, unspeakable, blundering arrogance. Harry Truman crisscrossed Ohio. Tom Dewey spoke there but once (whereas in Oklahoma he spoke thirteen times), refusing even to emerge from his Victory Special to address waiting crowds. In California, Dewey-Warren operatives shuttered their San Francisco office in mid-October. They lost the city by thirty thousand votes.

At Henry Wallace's giddy peak, analysts had projected his total at ten million votes. At campaign's end, barely a million Americans stood with him. Neither Wallace nor his backers had ever dared dream of victory. Unlike Thurmond and Wright and Jim Eastland, they had never formulated a strategy even as basic as the South's Electoral College scheme. Progressives merely coveted Harry Truman's defeat and not only failed to accomplish that, but also lost their once considerable influence in Democratic and labor ranks. They dismantled the Popular Front era, and as they goaded Harry Truman to counterattack with loyalty-security programs, attorney general's lists, and Smith Act prosecutions, they had, in fact, initiated the McCarthy era.

In the end, it was conservative columnist David Lawrence who—on December 30, 1947, the day after Wallace announced his candidacy—had gotten it most right regarding Wallace and his doomed endeavor. Wallace, Lawrence presciently warned readers, might "make a lot of noise," but the mechanics of ballot access—and here Lawrence referred specifically to Illinois—made any third-party effort problematic. His effort would ultimately prove "relatively inconsequential in a political sense." Beyond that, Wallace's absence from Democratic ranks could only "deprive the Republicans of their apparent plan to try to pin the Communist label on the Democratic Party." Lawrence concluded "The Wallace movement will help the Democrats more than it will hurt them. . . . [It] will peter out by the time election time rolls around."

With so much riding on Electoral College scenarios, it was easy to lose sight of the race's popular-vote totals. Truman defeated Dewey 24,179,345 (49.51 percent) to 21,991,291 (45.12 percent). Thurmond garnered 1,176,125, (2.4 percent). Henry Wallace, who had once dreamt of a tenth of the vote, received just 2.38 percent—1,157,326 votes.

In was a gray Wednesday morning in New York. Tom Dewey finally went to bed at 8:30 AM, and as he slept, Roosevelt Hotel workers downstairs removed all his campaign posters and banners. Arising two hours later, he phoned Earl Warren to coordinate their concession statements. Arriving from his East Sixty-first Street townhouse, Allen Dulles found the defeated, bathrobe-clad Dewey standing silently, pondering his fate. "He took it like a man," Allen confided to his brother.

At 11:10 AM, two blocks away, Howard McGrath declared victory. Four minutes later, Dewey confirmed McGrath's verdict. At 1:00 PM, tired and glum, he faced the press. "I am just as surprised as you are," he informed reporters, his voice quiet and even in tone, "and I gather that is shared by everybody in the room, as I read your stories before the election." Even now, however, he played it safe. Queried regarding any proposed repeal of Taft-Hartley, he guardedly responded, "No comment."

Toward the end of this unpleasant exercise, however, he grew impatient, several times asking his interrogators if they had had enough, but when it came time to exit, he forced a smile. "It's been grand fun, boys and girls," he said as he exited, just forty-six years old, to run for president no more. "Good luck!"

In the Muehlebach Hotel, as Harry Truman shook Charlie Ross awake, the first words out of his mouth were: "Labor did it." A few hours later, the CIO's Philip Murray called to congratulate him, and Truman burst into tears.

Harry Truman received a shave and a haircut, changed into a clean shirt and a new suit, and prepared to face the world, finally, as an elected president. Independence had prepared no celebration for him, but forty thousand people nonetheless spontaneously assembled in Courthouse Square. Every factory whistle in town sounded in unison. He nearly wept. Within the next twenty-four hours, well-wishers would wire him fifteen thousand congratulatory cables, many running between five hundred and a thousand words.

In New York, Tallulah Bankhead wired Harry Truman her congratulations. "The people have put you in your place," it read.

"You can send the same telegram to Dewey," advised a friend.

In Washington, the ax fell on the *Chicago Tribune*'s Arthur Sears Henning. Robert McCormick phoned to inform Henning that, effective Inauguration Day 1949, he would no longer serve as the paper's chief Washington correspondent—or as anything else. He was finished.

Unable to break a successful habit, Truman whistle-stopped back to Washington, departing Independence that Wednesday morning at 7:45 AM sharp. The combative "Give 'em Hell" Harry now gave way to the humble Harry Truman who had once begged reporters to pray for the man who "felt like the moon, the stars, and all the planets had fallen" upon him.

At Jefferson City, Missouri, a "Negro quartet" known as The Cavaliers—Willy Smith, Book Mason, and brothers Zeek and Herb Bagby—serenaded him with their rendition of "Happy Days Are Here Again." When they finished, he read a telegram from the *Washington Post,* inviting him to a dinner of turkey for him and "breast of tough old crow *en glace*" for embarrassed *Post* staffers.

Truman eschewed gloating. "After an election is over," he explained, "I don't bear any malice, or feel badly towards anyone, because the fellow who lost feels badly enough without being crowed over."

A screaming, shouting crowd of ten thousand awaited him at St. Louis's

Union Station. Penned behind huge glass gates, they clamored to draw closer. "Open the gates," they demanded, "or we'll break them down."

"Let the people behind the bar come in," Truman's voice boomed out from the Ferdinand Magellan loudspeakers.

Here, Treasury Secretary Snyder and his family joined Truman, as did campaign advance man Don Dawson. The beefy, invariably cheerful Dawson brought with him a historic artifact, one possessing the power to forever transform a failed Kansas City haberdasher into an enduring political icon: a copy of the early edition of the November 3 *Chicago Tribune*, its headline blaring, DEWEY DEFEATS TRUMAN.

"That's one for the books," Truman grinned, as he waved it to the ten thousand admirers before him.

Margaret Truman, bereft of sleep for thirty-six hours, slept through this moment. She was awake, however, at 10:55 AM EST, as the Ferdinand Magellan reached Washington's Union Station. There, a redheaded woman in a fur coat tried to kiss her father. He ducked once, pulling seventy-nine-year-old Washington Senators baseball team owner Clark Griffith before him as a shield. She missed and tried again—unsuccessfully. Displaying barely more dignity was South Carolina senator Olin Johnston, there with his eleven-year-old daughter Sally Lee, protesting that, despite everything, he had indeed voted for Truman. Johnston had pressed desperately through the crowd to reach Truman. As he did, Truman's usually exceedingly guarded chief of staff, Adm. William D. Leahy, called to him: "I don't think you'll make it, Senator."

A huge banner hung from the headquarters of the *Washington Post*, confirming their previous invitation. Ten bands—the forty-two-piece Metropolitan Police Boys Band, the Navy Band, the Quantico Marine Band, the Marine Band Orchestra, the Army Band, the Metropolitan Police Boys Club Band, the St. John's College High School Band, the National Guard Band, the Negro Elks Band, and the Howard University Band— provided accompaniment, most, it seemed, blaring "I'm Just Wild About Harry." Twenty-nine persons along the Pennsylvania Avenue parade route collapsed—three from heart conditions. Three-quarters of a million people, two-thirds of the city's population—among the largest of crowds in district history—lined the route ten and twenty persons deep, as Truman and his running mate Alben Barkley climbed onto the jump seat of their immense, open Lincoln. Howard McGrath was tucked beneath, with Margaret, Bess, and Barkley's daughter Marian ("Sis") in the seat before them, all to embark on what not long previously would have seemed the most improbable of processions.

Though it was now Friday, November 5, many of those greeting them were, no doubt, what the Trumans themselves would disdainfully term "Wednesday morning Democrats." "Remember," Bess Truman asked her daughter, "how many came to see us off last month?"

And at thirty minutes past noon, her husband entered the White House to meet with his cabinet.

For the first time in his life, Harry S. Truman entered as president in his own right.

Acknowledgments

As always, I extend sincere thanks to the many wonderful institutions that have in some sense assisted in the compilation of my work, in this case, the New York State Library; the New York State Legislative Library; the Mid-Continent Public Library of Independence, Missouri; the Albany (NY) Public Library; the Begley Library at Schenectady County Community College; the Clifton Park-Halfmoon (NY) Public Library; the Saratoga Springs (NY) Public Library; the Schenectady County Public Library; the Williams College Libraries; the Harry S. Truman Library and Museum (particularly archivist David Clark); the Franklin D. Roosevelt Presidential Library and Museum; the Schaffer Library of Union College; the Capital District Library Council; and the New York Public Library.

Sincere thanks are also extended to the incredibly knowledgeable John Rothmann, who very kindly supplied me with research materials from his extensive private collection; to my friends Douglas R. Burgey, John Thorn, Catherine Karp, Robert N. Going, and Mary Katherine Masterson Ilowiecki for their assistance in completing *1948*; to my editors at Union Square Press, Iris Blasi, Anna Bliss, Joe Rhatigan, and Rick Ball; to Philip Turner, my original editor at Union Square Press (and before that at Carroll & Graf); and to my agent, Carol Mann, at the Carol Mann Agency.

And, of course, to my beloved wife, Patty.

Notes

CHAPTER 1

1 "Go to hell." Brinkley, *Memoir*, p. 48.

1 "tall, white . . . dressed." Ibid., p. 50.

1–2 "It was a shock . . . large." Brinkley, *Washington*, p. 252.

CHAPTER 2

3 "blind as a mole." David McCullough, *Truman*, 41.

3 Did not start school. Miller, *Truman*, p. 18.

3 Paderewski and Chopin. McCullough, p. 61.

3 Meeting Paderewski, Hamby, *People*, p. 14.

3 "To tell the truth . . . ran." Miller, *Plain*, pp. 34–35.

3 "I don't know . . . did." Miller, *Truman*, p. 32.

3 "on the farm . . . military." Ibid., p. 33.

3–4 "get a man . . . lust]." Ibid., pp. 33–34.

4 "the kind . . . readers." Daniels Interview, Truman Library, 4 October 1963.

4 "He had a remarkable . . . Harvard." Neal, *HST*, pp. 36–37; McNay, p. 75.

4 "the happiest days of my life." *Newsweek*, 26 June 1942, pp. 47–48.

4 "I thought . . . earth." Truman, *Bess*, p. 10.

4 Bess's father's alcoholism. Ibid., pp. 16–19.

4 "You know . . . anyway." Ibid., pp. 39–40.

5 "Just think . . . souls." Ibid., p. 254.

5 "Sometimes . . . here." Ibid., p. 59.

5 "short sight." McCullough, p. 67.

5 "It really doesn't . . . drive." Pemberton, p. 15.

5 Independence with her mother. *Agricultural History*, October 1974, pp. 481–82; Truman, *Bess*, p. 82; Miller, *Plain*, p. 107.

5 Extended inventory. Truman, *Decisions*, pp. 133–34; Miller, *Plain*, pp. 112, 116.

5 James M. Pendergast. Ibid., p. 136; Miller, *Plain*, p. 125; Truman, *Bess*, p. 34; Miller, *Truman*, p. 110.

5 $3,465-a-year post. McCullough, p. 160.

5 Active Mason. *Columbus Telegram*, 27 December 1972, p. 9; Miller, *Truman*, pp. 68–72. Truman, who claimed he memorized Masonic rituals by reciting them to his plow horses, ascended to grand master of the Missouri Lodge in the key campaign year of 1940. In 1949, he remarkably claimed

that being elected grand master was "the highest honor that has ever come to me." Truman, *Decisions*, p. 162. Earl Warren similarly became grand master, of California's seven hundred lodges, in October 1935.

5 *Oakland Tribune*, 11 October 1935, p. 1.

5 Ku Klux Klan. Ferrell, *Life*, pp. 96–97; Burnes & Martin, p. 106; Chalmers, p. 136; Larsen & Hulston, p. 64.

6 279 votes and triumphed. Miller, *Truman*, p. 174; Ferrell, *Pendergast*, p. 7; Gullan, p. 15. The Klan turned. McCullough, pp. 170–71; Miller, *Plain*, pp. 130–31; Burnes & Martin, p. 94. The NAACP also opposed him that year. Leuchtenburg, p. 156.

6 8,791 to 7,932. Hamby, *People*, p. 130; Truman, *Decisions*, p. 138; Larsen & Hulston, pp. 64–65; Burnes & Martin, p. 94.

6 "It gave me a substantial income." Truman, *Decisions*, p. 138.

6 winning election as presiding judge. *Current Biography*, 1947, p. 646.

6 "a sound . . . administration." Jenkins, p. 23.

6 58,000 votes. Hamby, *People*, p. 158.

6 "The real seat . . . Street." *NY Times*, 14 September 1947, p. BR6.

6 Bluff and corrupt. Larsen & Hulston, pp. 61, 72, 165.

6 "If you want . . . world." Milligan, p. 12.

6 "Am I a fool? . . . know." Truman, *Presidency*, p. 74; Truman, *Bess*, p. 106.

6 Tire-stealing. Ferrell, *Pendergast*, p. 13.

7 "I had to . . . know." Burnes & Martin, p. 99.

7 "At the same . . . issue]." Ibid., p. 99; Poen, p. 87; Ferrell, *Pendergast*, p. 18.

7 "Am I an administrator . . . can't." *Political Science Quarterly*, Spring 1991, p. 43.

7 "I am obligated . . . Lord?" Truman, *Presidency*, p. 74.

7–8 "Truman adored . . . Harry." Douglas, *East*, p. 418.

8 Two-term limit. Miller, *Truman*, p. 248; Powell, *Tom's Boy*, p. 61.

8 Support for governor. Truman, *Presidency*, pp. 79–81; McCullough, pp. 192, 194; Miller, *Truman*, pp. 248–50.

8 "I have . . . Congressman." Truman, *Decisions*, p. 141; Miller, *Truman*, p. 251.

8 Lazia. *Moberly Monitor-Index*, 10 July 1934, p. 1; *NY Times*, 11 July 1934, p. 3; Hartmann, *Pendergast*, pp. 17–24; Steinberg, *Bosses*, pp. 338–45, 347; Larsen & Hulston, pp. 108–16.

8 "I just told . . . facts." Miller, *Plain*, p. 145.

8 Truman swept. Allen & Shannon, p. 8; Ferrell, *Life*, p. 130. Truman carried Jackson County 137,000 to 9,000 for Senator Champ Clark–backed congressman Jacob "Tuck" Milligan and 1,525 for St. Louis-machine–backed congressman John J. Cochran. Powell, *Tom's Boy*, p. 71; Steinberg, *Bosses*, p. 348.

8 Supreme Court. Allen & Shannon, p. 11.

8 Not a single Senate colleague. *Washington Post*, 16 February 1938, p. X2; *NY Times*, 16 February 1938, p. 8; Hamby, *People*, pp. 230–31; Miller, *Truman*, pp. 301–03; Ferrell, *Pendergast*, pp. 44–45; Larsen & Hulston, pp. 128–29.

8 Indicted 278—and convicted 259. *Wisconsin State Journal*, 24 March 1948, p. 6; Hamby, *People*, p. 230. The scope of Kansas City vote fraud may perhaps be judged from the following numbers. Despite a stable population, 285,000 voted in Jackson County in 1936; after the fall of the machine, 239,000 voted in 1940. Powell, *Tom's Boy*, p. 72; Barone, p. 183. In one election, Kansas City's second ward (total population: 18,478) delivered 19,201 votes for its judicial candidate. Steinberg, *Bosses*, p. 355.

8 "He needed. . . . race." Burnes & Martin, p. 83.

8–9   Good Friday 1939. *NY Times*, 8 April 1939, pp. 1, 13; Hartmann, *Pendergast*, pp. 73, 105.

9   "Tell them . . . Senate." Ferrell, *Pendergast*, p. 83.

9   "a no-good son of a bitch." Miller, *Plain*, p. 158.

9   "pleasant enough . . . office." Pepper, pp. 127–28.

9   Workhorse. *Christian Science Monitor*, 20 March 1939, p. 17; *Current Biography*, 1942, p. 846.

9   Administration viewed it warily. Fleming, *New Dealers'*, p. 100.

9    $15,000. *NY Times*, 2 March 1941, p. 14.

9   "needless waste." *NY Times*, 15 August 1941, p. 18; Truman, *Presidency*, p. 140.

9–10   "Republican [commitee members . . . scandals." *Washington Post*, 22 January 1945, p. 9.

10   Patterson. Truman, *Presidency*, p. 145; Fleming, *New Dealers'*, p. 101.

10   "the ten . . . war." Daniels, *Independence*, p. 228; Harwood, p. 188.

10   "We [FDR and I] . . . least." Flynn, p. 195.

10   "You are not nominating . . . President." Eaton, p. 402.

10   Hannegan DNC chairman. Daniels, *Witness*, pp. 233–34.

11   "Of course . . . Wallace." Ibid., p. 231.

11   "Dear Bob . . . ticket." *NY Times*, 21 July 1944, p. 1; *Chicago Tribune*, 25 July 1944, p. 6; Tully, p. 276. For decades the rumor held that Douglas had been named first in the FDR-Hannegan note. Recent scholarship has cast doubt upon that contention. Walch, p. 68.

11   "I'm not going . . . to me." Eaton, p. 405.

12   "Well, tell . . . responsibility." Miller, *Plain*, p. 182.

12   "second Missouri Compromise." *NY Times*, 14 April 1945, p. 14.

12   "Hello, fellows . . . Truman." Murphy, p. 226.

12   He was drunk. Miller, *Plain*, p. 182. It was basically the end of the line for Clark, who was not even able to win renomination that year. Truman, who never forgot a slight, never forgot a favor either. In 1945, he appointed Clark associate justice of the District of Columbia Court of Appeals. *Chicago Tribune*, 26 September 1945, p. 8.

12   Douglas fainted. Ferrell, *Choosing*, pp. 89–90.

12   "watched the . . . swell." Coffin, pp. 13–14.

12   "I missed . . . Truman." Daniels, *Witness*, p. 239. As Truman's close friend Harry Easley once reflected, "I never did hear him say that he didn't want the nomination." Ferrell, *Choosing*, p. 94.

12   Eating a sandwich. *Harper's*, July 1948, p. 27.

13   "You don't know . . . thank you." Truman, *Presidency*, p. 182. He returned to the sandwich—or, as some noted, a hot dog—when finished.

13   "met the requirements . . . presidency." Gosnell, p. 192.

13   "the grinning . . . gangsters." *Chicago Tribune*, 17 October, 1944, p. 14.

13   Klan. *Lowell Sun*, 28 October 1944, p. 17; Hamby, *People*, pp. 284–85; Truman, *Presidency*, pp. 187–88; Daniels, *Independence*, p. 256; Chalmers, p. 313; Gabler, pp. 449–50.

13   Part Jewish. Hamby, *People*, p. 286; Miller, *Plain*, p. 186; Truman, *Presidency*, p. 187.

13    $4,500. *Chicago Tribune*, 27 July 1944, p. 6.

13   "Payroll Bess." *NY Times*, 19 October 1982, p. B8. In retribution, neither Luce nor her husband, publisher Henry Luce, were ever to be invited to the Truman White House. *Political Science Quarterly*, Spring 1991, p. 45.

13   "every cent . . . on them." *Abilene Reporter-News*, 29 April 1945, p. 49. He had also placed his sister Mary Jane on the Senate payroll in September 1943 at $1,800 a year. A no-show, she never visited the District of Columbia, living in Missouri and taking care of their aged mother. In Jackson County, he had

placed several relatives on the public payroll. Ferrell, *Choosing*, pp. 73, 75; Hamby, *People*, p. 262; Burnes & Martin, p. 231.

13 "the meanest . . . remember." Miller, *Plain*, p. 185.

14 "Eddie . . . of me." Daniels, *Independence*, p. 255; Radosh & Radosh, *Haven*, p. 37.

14 Pendergast funeral. *LA Times*, 29 January 1945, p. 1; *NY Times*, 30 January 1945, p. 20; Powell, *Tom's Boy*, p. 133; Miller, *Plain*, pp. 196, 385; Larsen & Hulston, p. 187.

14 "He was always . . . been his." Hamby, *People*, p. 287; Steinberg, *Bosses*, p. 366.

14 Bacall. *Jefferson City Daily Capital News*, 28 February 1945, p. 4; McCullough, pp. 336–37.

14 "quickly and quietly . . . trouble now." Truman, *Decisions*, p. 5; Truman, *Harry S. Truman*, pp. 208–09; Bishop, pp. 597–98. One account has Truman not evading the Secret Service (they simply weren't there) and suspecting that it was not FDR who had died but former Arizona Episcopal bishop Julius Atwood and that FDR wished to discuss with him Atwood's funeral arrangements. As FDR was not in Washington at the time, that is unlikely. Besides, Atwood died in 1925. Hardeman & Bacon, pp. 308–09.

CHAPTER 3

15 "Good Farming . . . Living." *Life*, 2 September 1940, p. 84.

15 George Washington Carver. Ibid.

16 $4 million. Kingdon, pp. 6–7.

16 Al Smith. *Life*, 2 September 1940, p. 86.

16 "He is open-minded . . . cold." Schapsmeier & Schapsmeier, *Agrarian*, p. 158.

16 "make the world safe for corn breeders." *Current Biography*, 1947, p. 660. Mysteriously, Wallace donated $25 to Socialist Norman Thomas's 1932 campaign. *NY Times*, 8 February 1948, p. SM14.

16 "He seems to . . . ideas." MacDonald, p. 45.

16 "Roosevelt . . . ally." Galbraith Interview, Iowa PBS, 22 May 2003.

16 Limited farm production. Kingdon, p. 61.

16 "The Greatest Butcher in Christendom." Lord, p. 448. Wallace argued that his acts "were not acts of idealism in any sane society. They were emergency acts made necessary by an almost insane lack of world statesmanship during the period 1920 to 1932." *Harper's*, February 1943, p. 285.

16 "There was a medium . . . corn." Douglas, *East*, pp. 338–39.

17 Not even an enrolled Democrat. *Current Biography*, 1940, p. 836. His hobbies. *Harper's*, February 1943, p. 288; *Current Biography*, 1947, p. 663; *Time*, 9 August 1948, p. 17, MacDougall, p. 84.

17 "He remained out . . . giggle." Schlesinger, *New Deal*, p. 34; *NY Times*, 19 November 1965, p. 35.

17 "Henry Wallace . . . thrilled." *Current Biography*, 1940, p. 837.

17 "How wonderful . . . race." MacDougall, p. 84. At Salem, Oregon, in May 1948, he would say, in a similar eugenic vein, "The government should buy up substandard lands which can't be served by electricity. If people insist on living on such lands then the government shouldn't let them have children." He soon denied that is what he meant. MacDougall, p. 376.

17 "Old Man Common Sense." *Frederick Post*, 24 February 1986, p. 14.

17 Unprecedented third term. *Washington Post*, 9 January 1940, pp. 1–2. Harry Truman was far less supportive. Asked in 1938 how he felt regarding the subject, HST declined to comment until he saw if FDR would reappoint Maurice Milligan. When FDR did, Truman answered, "I am not for anyone for a third term." *Chicago Tribune*, 25 July 1944, p. 6. Elliott Roosevelt, however, viewed Wallace's timing as "inexcusable." At the 1940 convention, Elliott planned to second Jesse Jones's nomination for VP, but Eleanor sternly ordered her wandering son to support Wallace. MacDougall, p. 181.

17 "A good many . . . apparent." *Current Biography*, 1940, p. 836.

17   Hull declined. Daniels, *Witness*, p. 232.

18   "you must know . . . fellow." Farley, p. 254.

18   "Exhibiting the weakness . . . affairs." Black, *Roosevelt*, p. 567.

18   "The conservative . . . for him." Goodwin Interview, Iowa PBS, 15 November 2003.

18   "Just because . . . Republican." Sherwood, p. 179.

18   "Henry's my. . . nomination." Miller, *FDR*, p. 451.

18   "Well, damn it . . . nominate." McCullough, p. 279. William O. Douglas reported that at one point in 1940 even FDR wished to abort Wallace's candidacy. Douglas, *East*, pp. 338–39.

18–19   "Something close . . . hisses." Culver & Hyde, p. 221.

19   "I shall never . . . show." Goodwin, p. 130.

19   "You cannot treat . . . time." *NY Times*, 19 July 1940, p. 5; Goodwin, p. 133.

19   Dared not mention Wallace. Ibid.

19   Harry Hopkins. Sherwood, p. 179.

19   "Don't do it, . . . you do." Smith, *FDR*, p. 463.

19   No acceptance speech. Sherwood, p. 179.

19   Iowa results. Kieran, p. 137.

19   "cheerful and loyal." Barone, p. 158.

19–20   "The march of . . . Lord." Lord, pp. 492–93.

20   "half in fun . . . day." *Washington Post*, 31 May 1942, p. B7.

20   "to give . . . Hottentot." *NY Times*, 3 December 1942, p. 14.

20   "We shall decide . . . inevitable." MacDougall, pp. 92–93; Romerstein, p. 11.

20   China and Siberia. Lord, p. 519. "I don't think you ought to go out of the country," Frances Perkins had warned Wallace; "somebody will sell you down the river while your back's turned." Downey, p. 335.

20–21   "a combination . . . Company." Hollander, *Pilgrims*, p. 156. His traveling companion, the Far Eastern scholar Owen Lattimore, employed the same TVA–Hudson's Bay comparison in a *National Geographic* article. Fleming, *Manifesto*, p. 252.

21   Nikishov. Lipper, p. 112; Hollander, *Survival*, p. 179.

21   "an extraordinary . . . needlework." Lipper, p. 113. The women, mostly former nuns, were, of course, prisoners. Lipper, p. 113.

21   "In traveling . . . Cheremisenov." Wallace & Steiger, p. 84.

21   "He [Roosevelt] . . . votes." Daniels, *Witness*, p. 231. When FDR confided to Harold Ickes that Wallace would cost him a million votes, Ickes countered that it could be three million. Wallace, *Diary*, p. 362.

21   "who divides . . . government." *Paris News*, 16 July 1944, p. 10; Steel, p. 412. Lippmann, close friends with Wallace's sister Mary, seriously doubted the vice president's mental stability. Lippmann may have been on to something. On July 18, 1944, as Wallace's chances disintegrated, he assaulted a photographer at the Wardman Park Hotel. *Amarillo Daily News*, 18 July 1944, p. 11.

21   "Wallace had . . . twice." Eaton, p. 405.

21   "I hope it's . . . affairs." Wallace, *Diary*, pp. 367, 371–72.

21–22   "I have been . . . deciding." Ibid., pp. 366–67.

22   "coup de grace." Barkley, p. 189.

22   64 percent. *El Paso Herald-Post*, 16 July 1948, p. 1.

22   "You can talk . . . again." Ferrell, *Choosing*, p. 76.

22   "A Dewey . . . Japan." MacDonald, p. 79.

22–23   "campaigned for . . . hotel." Lader, p. 36. Perhaps he was also loyal to himself. Drew Pearson reported that Wallace's frenzied schedule was part of his plan to capture the 1948 presidential nomination. *Washington Post*, 6 October 1944, p. 16.

23 In the course of their first awkward, post-convention meeting, Wallace, smiling "very sweetly," reassured Truman, "Harry, we are both Masons." Wallace ended his involvement with Masonry as he began his 1948 presidential campaign. Wallace, *Diary*, p. 373.

23 Rosenman. Rosenman & Rosenman, p. 439.

23 "poetic justice." Culver & Hyde, pp. 373, 376.

23 Nearly torpedoed Wallace's nomination. *NY Times*, 19 November 1965, p. 35.

23 "Henry was not . . . did it." Miller, *Plain*, p. 196.

23 "The century of . . . own." Culver & Hyde, p. 387.

24 "was the only . . . policy." Smith Interview, Iowa PBS, 10 September 2003.

24 "That's right . . . I believe." Wallace, *Diary*, p. 612.

24 "And just two . . . administration." *NY Times*, 13 September 1946, p. 4.

24 "With conservative . . . Dulles?" Ibid., p. 1.

24–25 "To prevent . . . will get." Ibid., p. 1; Wallace, *Diary*, p. 664; Lord, p. 577.

25 "Henry A. Wallace . . . States." *Washington Post*, 13 September 1946, p. 1. On the other hand, the following day, the *Daily Worker* also blasted Wallace's address. Eugene Dennis later disavowed that editorial, however. Steinberg, *Menace*, p. 69.

25–26 Press conference. *Washington Post*, 13 September 1946, p. 3.

26 "we can only . . . time." *NY Times*, 15 September 1946, p. 1; Markowitz, p. 187; Culver & Hyde, p. 422; Schapsmeier & Schapsmeier, *Prophet*, p. 157.

26 "You and I . . . day." Markowitz, p. 190; McCullough, p. 517.

26 "natural . . . speech." *NY Times*, 15 September 1946, p. 15.

26 "He [Wallace] is   Stalin." *Nation*, 20 January 1966, p. 42.

26 Letter from Wallace. *Washington Post*, 18 September 1946, p. 1; Wallace, *Diary*, pp. 601*fn.*, 615.

26 "Henry . . . resignation." *Chicago Tribune*, 21 September 1946, p. 1.

26 "He was so . . . backed out." Donovan, p. 228.

27 Reading about chickens. Culver & Hyde, p. 426.

CHAPTER 4

28 1902, the last year. Cohodas, p. 26.

28 "Edgefield . . . heaven." Sherrill, p. 260.

28 Tillman's eyepatch. Logan, p. 207.

28–29 "carry pistols . . . fingers." Ayers, *Promise*, p. 227.

29 "We have . . . ashamed of it." Logan, p. 91.

29 Campaign manager. Thurmond Interview, Southern Oral History Program Collection, July 1978.

29 Sharecropper-employing. Cohodas, p. 28.

29 Federal attorney. *Aiken Standard*, 20 January 1993, p. 12.

29 Shot and killed a man. *Aiken Journal & Review*, 31 March 1897, p. 1. Thurmond claimed self-defense, that the drunken and abusive ("You are a low, dirty scoundrel") drug salesman reached toward his pocket as if to draw a pistol.

29 "He was my idol . . . could." Bass & Thompson, *Strom*, p. 25. "Big Mister Will," recalled Carrie Butler, "he was the nicest man you ever met. Always took an interest in me, always 'please' and 'thank you.' Sometimes he'd pick flowers and give them to me. Bought clothes for our whole family. Sweet as sugar, so that other stuff was just politics. He was no Simon Legree." Washington-Williams, p. 42.

29   "I want to shake . . . since." Thurmond Interview, Southern Oral History Program Collection, July 1978.

29   "Stint them . . . competitors." Cohodas, pp. 26–27.

29–30   "You people . . . Jones." Ibid., p. 31.

30   "They put up . . . day." Bass & Thompson, *Ol' Strom*, p. 31.

30   Graduated high school. Cohodas, p. 32.

30   "This handsome . . . sex." Ibid., p. 33.

30   "Love . . . just politics." Washington-Williams, p. 42.

30   "Mister Will . . . jealous." Ibid.

30–31   "He knew . . . way." Ibid.

31   Board of Education. *Current Biography*, 1948, p. 622.

31   Superintendent of education. Dorn, p. 56.

31   Zachariah Walker. *NY Times*, 14 August 1911, pp. 1, 4; *NY Times*, 15 August 1911, p. 1.

31   "With all . . . Caucasian." Washington-Williams Interview, *Tavis Smiley Show*, 28 December 2003.

31   "Well . . . family." Washington-Williams Interview, CBS News, 17 December 2003.

32   Thurmond's decorations. *Current Biography*, 1948, p. 622.

33   "Don't come in . . . kill you." Bass & Thompson, *Ol' Strom*, p. 68.

33   "a cross-eyed fellow." Dorn, p. 127.

33   They escorted Mrs. Logue. Ibid., passim; Lachicotte, pp. 6–8.

33   "Now that takes guts." Bass & Thompson, *Ol' Strom*, p. 68. An increasingly widespread story holds that Thurmond escorted Sue Logue to her January 1943 death, "a-huggin' and a-kissin' the whole way," and even having sex with her. As Thurmond entered the service on December 11, 1941, and was stationed in New York City from April 17, 1942, until being transferred to England in October 1943, this tale seems, to say the least, logistically unlikely. In any case, Sue Logue wasn't that attractive. Frederickson, p. 101.

33   "a progressive . . . leadership." Bass & Thompson, *Ol' Strom*, p. 80.

33   "As a member . . . accept it." *Aiken Standard and Review*, 9 August 1946, p. 2.

34   "was known as . . . believe." *Washington Post*, 25 July 1948, p. B3. Or as *Greenville News* editor Wayne Freeman put it: "Strom may not be all that smart. But he's a rarity in South Carolina politics. He's honest. He won't steal." Bass & Thompson, *Strom*, p. 113.

34   Democratic primary. Bass & Thompson, *Ol' Strom*, pp. 81–82.

34   "A half-century . . . decades." Ibid.

34   "more attention given to Negro education." Ibid., p. 83.

34   "The low standing . . . state." Ibid.

34   Willie Earle. *Jefferson City Daily Capital News*, 18 February 1947, p. 2; *Life*, 2 June 1947, pp. 28–31; *The Gleaner*, 6 May 1947, p. 9; *New Yorker*, 14 June 1947, p. 31; Huff & Huff, pp. 399–400; Moore & Burton, pp. 93–94.

34–35   "Using one . . . shotgun." *Pittsburgh Courier*, 1 March 1947, p. 4.

35   "never order . . . women." Hietala, p. 69.

35   Defend lynchers pro bono. Moore & Burton, p. 84.

35   "prove their . . . world." *Florence Morning News*, 11 January 1946, p. 3.

35   "every facility . . . solved." Cohodas, p. 100.

35   "decency law . . . living." Ibid., p. 99.

35   "unhesitating vigor." Ibid., p. 100.

35   "There seems . . . contest." *NY Times*, 14 August 1947, p. E7.

35   "was nice to know . . . Thurmond." *Life*, 23 June 1947, pp. 5, 7.

35   "I believe . . . lynchings." Cohodas, p. 112.

35　Last lynching. Bass & Thompson, *Ol' Strom*, pp. 84–85. This was the nation's sole lynching in 1947. Previous totals read: 1940 (5), 1941 (5), 1942 (6), 1943 (3), 1944 (0), 1945 (1), and 1946 (6). *New Republic*, 16 February 1948, p. 7.

35　Regional convention. *Christian Science Monitor*, 17 September 1947, p. 7.

36　Thurmond marries his secretary. *Florence Morning News*, 8 November 1947, p. 1.

36　"Virile Governor . . . fool." *Life*, 17 November 1947, pp. 44–46.

36　"To most people . . . cameras." Frederickson, p. 102. When Dorn's sister considered taking employment with Thurmond, he counseled her, "[U]se your own judgment. Personally, I had rather you stay out of Strom Thurmond's office, for your own good if for no other reason. His reputation and fastness concerning women is nation-wide." Dailey, Gilmore, & Simon, p. 266.

36　"Among the black . . . people." Washington-Williams Interview, CBS News, 17 December 2003.

36　"He knows . . . that." Sherrill, p. 264; Bass & Thompson, *Strom*, p. 46.

36–37　"Though apparently . . . fatal." Sherrill, pp. 264–65. Sherrill later stated he believed the rumors were true but had been censored by his publisher.

37　Home rule. *Washington Post*, 25 July 1948, p. B3.

37　Poll tax. *Current Biography*, 1948, p. 622.

7　Voting was not secret. *Washington Post*, 25 July 1948, p. B3.

CHAPTER 5

38　Dewey's father. *Current Biography*, 1940, p. 238.

39　Basshorn. *Life*, 9 October 1944, pp. 97, 99, 106.

39　Harvard Law. Stone, *Also Ran*, p. 372.

39　William O. Douglas and Paul Robeson. Douglas, *East*, pp. 152–53.

39　Laryngitis. *New Yorker*, 29 October 1938, p. 13.

39　Jefferson Davis. Walker, *Dewey*, p. 187.

39　George White's *Scandals*. *Time*, 3 July 1944, p. 17.

39　Moustache. *Current Biography*, 1940, p. 239. The mustache was always a political liability. Even Herbert Hoover mused, "A man couldn't wear a mustache like that without it affecting his mind." Reinhard, p. 40.

39　Tramping streets for GOP candidates. *New Republic*, 21 June 1948, p. 13. Among those candidates was his future associate, Herbert Brownell.

39–40　"I dropped . . . field." Walker, *Dewey*, p. 36.

40　Medalie resigned. *Current Biography*, 1940, p. 239.

40　Medalie's interim successor. *NY Times*, 23 November 1933, p. 2.

40　Gordon. *NY Times*, 2 December 1933, pp. 1, 6; Dewey, pp. 117–38; Walker, *Dewey*, pp. 40–43.

40　"Gentlemen . . . case." Smith, *Dewey*, p. 135.

40　$10.76. Rockaway, p. 121.

40　Medalie and Charles Evans Hughes. *Current Biography*, 1940, p. 239.

40　Douglas. Smith, *Dewey*, p. 149.

41　"If you want . . . Jersey." Ibid.

41　"Your businesses . . . murder." *NY Times*, 31 July 1935, p. 6.

41　109,019 votes. Mearns, *1949*, p. 15.

41　Louis "Lepke" Buchalter. Winchell, pp. 134–48, 185; Rockaway, pp. 137–38; Gabler, pp. 274–80.

41　"Dutch Schultz." Smith, *Dewey*, pp. 170–71.

42　"Tom Dewey broke . . . doing." Stone, *Also Ran*, p. 377.

42　64,394. Mearns, *1948*, p. 14.

42 "Don't worry . . . win it." Stone, *Also Ran*, p. 378.

42–43 "If a young . . . fifty." *Current Biography*, 1940, p. 240.

43 "In public . . . both." Brinkley, *Washington*, p. 259.

43 "You really . . . dislike him." *Current Biography*, 1940, p. 240.

43 "Only one person . . . week." Douglas, *East*, p. 153.

43 Sterling Morton. Reinhard, p. 40.

43 "You make me . . . beat?" Smith, *Dewey*, p. 397.

43 "I . . . think . . . together." Farley, p. 188.

43 Dewey announced his candidacy. *NY Times*, 2 December 1939, p. 1.

43 "thrown his diaper . . . ring." *Hayward Daily Review*, 22 April 1940, p. 2. Once asked if he had heard a Dewey speech, Ickes answered, "No, I did not listen because I have a baby of my own." *NY Times*, 17 September 1961, p. SM16.

43 Nationwide tour. Stone, *Also Ran*, p. 370.

43–44 George Gallup's results. *Current Biography*, 1940, p. 240.

44 "Sir Galahad . . . victory." *Lowell Sun*, 22 January 1940, p. 1.

44 "N'ya, N'ya, . . . needs me." Joyner, p. 24.

44 "a simple . . . lawyer." *Washington Post*, 20 August 1940, p. 2. The phrase was not originally Ickes's; it was coined by columnist John Franklin Carter (aka Jay Franklin). Rovere, p. 198.

44 3 percent. *Appleton Post-Crescent*, 18 May 1940, p. 4.

45 "This department . . . win." *New Yorker*, 22 June 1940, p. 50.

45 Twenty percentage points. Eaton, p. 375.

45 "they were the wrong three." Stone, *Also Ran*, p. 381.

45 647,628. Mearns, *1945*, p. 549.

44–45 "For my part . . . York." *NY Times*, 25 August 1942, p. 1.

45 How can . . . wedding cake?" Smith, *Dewey*, p. 496. Many observers credit the quip to Teddy Roosevelt's acerbic daughter, Alice Roosevelt Longworth. She denied posing the question, but nonetheless added, "I wish I had." Brownell, p. xi. David McCullough attributes it to Ethel Barrymore. McCullough, p. 672.

45 "I regard . . . dangerous." Watkins, p. 808.

45 "calm, neat . . . efficient." Eaton, p. 369.

45 "Dewey and his . . . Platt." *NY Times*, 18 June 1942, p. 42.

45 51 to 30 percent. Fleming, *New Dealers'*, p. 325.

45 "New Deal Republican." *Harper's*, May 1944, p. 483.

45 "If there is . . . Europe." *Washington Post*, 21 January 1940, p. 2.

45 Internationalist camp. *NY Times*, 28 April 1944, pp. 1, 12.

45 Dulles. Ibid., 19 August 1944, pp. 1, 24; *Harper's*, May 1944, pp. 481–82; *Harper's*, October 1948, pp. 42–44; *Life*, 4 October 1948, pp. 130–42; Divine, pp. 122–25.

45 "So far as . . . clear." *Time*, 3 July 1944, p. 18.

46 "We refuse . . . them." Beyer, p. 33.

46 Pearl Harbor. *Life*, 24 September 1945, pp. 110–11; Divine, pp. 145–47; Brownell, pp. 60–61.

46 "traitor . . . ought to be impeached." Morgan, *FDR*, p. 738.

46 Polish-Soviet boundaries. Divine, pp. 140–41.

46 "turned green . . . head." Bohlen, pp. 143–44.

46 Harry Hopkins. Lomazow & Fettman, p. 91.

46 "I don't know . . . pains." Roosevelt & Libby, p. 278; McCullough, pp. 323–33.

46   *Life* magazine photograph. *Life*, 31 July 1944, p. 13.

46   "a sitting ghost." Lomazow & Fettman, p. 133.

46   "The President's . . . at all." *NY Times*, 13 October 1944, p. 20. Prior to FDR's announcing for a fourth term, McIntire warned him that he could survive for four years only if he halved his workload and avoided all stress. Black, *Roosevelt*, p. 1093. Another FDR physician, Dr. Frank Lahey, founder of Boston's Lahey Clinic, warned point-blank that Roosevelt would "again have heart failure and be unable to complete" another term. Lomazow & Fettmann, p. 120.

46–47   "a wicked . . . campaign." *Wisconsin State Journal*, 28 October 1944, p. 8; Brands, p. 782.

47   Dewey again kept silent. Boller, p. 266.

47   Hanigan quit. Brownell, p. 59.

47   "had not learned . . . campaign." Ibid., p. 54.

47   "Clear it with Sidney." *NY Times*, 25 July 1944, p. 18.

47   "Every worker a voter." Morgan, *FDR*, p. 738.

47   "Sidney Hillman . . . Committee." Ibid.

47   "the slickest . . . generation." *Time*, 24 July 1944, p. 20.

47   "It's your country . . . run it?" *Tipton Daily Tribune*, 4 September 1944, p. 1.

47   "Now . . . States." *NY Times*, 2 November 1944, pp. 1, 12. Dewey had run with Hillman's support (and a $5,000 donation) in 1937. *Washington Post*, 8 September 1944, p. 14. Editorialists recoiled. Smith, *Dewey*, pp. 433–34.

48   Oklahoma City. *Joplin Globe*, 19 June 1948, p. 4.

48   "I've done . . . eight." *Washington Post*, 18 June 1944, p. B5. Dewey's eventual choice, John Bricker, was 6 feet 2 inches—Stassen and Joseph Ball 6 feet 3 inches; Leverett Saltonstall, 6 feet 1 inch; Earl Warren 6 feet 0¾ inches; Taft 6 feet even.

48   Rumors circulated. Smith, *Dewey*, p. 421. Fala never received special treatment, but following the election, FDR's son Elliott's 135-pound mastiff, Blaze, did bump three sailors from an army transport plane headed to the West Coast. *LA Times*, 20 January 1945, p. 2; *NY Times*, 21 January 1945, p. 64; Roosevelt & Libby, p. 269.

48   "These Republican . . . since." *Washington Post*, 24 September 1944, p. M3.

48–49   "Dewey . . . job." Abels, *Victory*, p. 147.

49   "Now, I had not . . . oath." *Washington Post*, 26 September 1944, p. 5.

49   Polls all projected. *Daily Capital News*, 3 November 1944, p. 8.

49   Roosevelt feared a close race. Fleming, *New Dealers*, p. 459.

49   53.8 percent. Mearns, *1948*, p. 611.

49   "I still think he is a son of a bitch." Hassett, p. 294.

49   $350,000 surplus. *Current Biography*, 1944, p. 168.

49   687,151 votes. *NY Times*, 17 March 1971, p. 50; Mearns, *1948*, pp. 14, 665. Though FDR and Lehman had achieved larger pluralities.

50   "I'll be different . . . nominee." *NY Times*, 21 March 1948, p. 50.

CHAPTER 6

51   "Boys, if you . . . on me." *Washington Post*, 14 April 1945, p. 1. It was, however, noted Alonzo Hamby, "a sincere, heartfelt, and unwise request that did nothing to establish him as a leader." Hamby, *People*, p. 295.

51   "The buck stops here." *Phylon Quarterly*, 2nd Quarter 1958, p. 163; Ferrell. *Life*, p. 181.

51   "It was a terrible . . . War." Truman, *Presidency*, pp. 7–8. Did Truman have to drop the bomb on Hiroshima? Would Japan have surrendered anyway? The answer is simply this: Even after Hiroshima, if

he wished to end the war quickly, he still had to bomb Nagasaki. And with both Hiroshima and Nagasaki incinerated and the Soviets now in the war, Tokyo still required six additional days to finally capitulate.

51   87 percent. *Harper's*, May 1948, p. 28.

51   Wages dropped by 8.5 percent. Mooney, p. 36.

52   "Food prices rose . . . prices." *Middletown Times-Herald*, 23 August 1946, p. 8.

52   Price controls on meat. Kieran, p. 339; Ferrell, *Presidency*, pp. 87–89; Allen & Shannon, pp. 28–29; Coffin, pp. 142–85; Horowitz, pp. 215–16.

53   Strikes engulfed the economy. Coffin, pp. 186–203; Phillips, pp. 113–25; Donovan, pp. 209–17; Mooney, pp. 34–35; Ferrell, *Presidency*, pp. 90–92; Atleson, pp. 210–13.

53   "Draft men . . . or Germany." McCullough, p. 506; Atleson, pp. 132, 203.

53   "I am not willing . . . established." Mooney, p. 34.

53   Seventy to thirteen. Donovan, p. 217.

53   "the worst I ever saw." *PBS, American Experience.*

53–54   "I am tired . . . job." Donovan, pp. 212–13.

54   "of the warp and woof of fascism." Saposs, pp. 120–21.

54   "You can't make . . . clerk." Redding, p. 94.

54   $47 million. Redding, p. 95. Whitney never did commit the entire $47 million, but did initiate a special $2.5-million anti-Truman fund. MacDonald, p. 171.

54   In September 1945. *NY Times*, 22 December 1945, p. 22.

54   Health insurance. Ibid., 20 November 1945, pp. 1, 13.

54   "We cannot . . . here." *Journal of American History*, March 1970, p. 859.

54   "Liberal rhetoric . . . alienation." Ibid., p. 866.

55   Endorsing Wheeler. Hamby, *Beyond*, p. 80.

55   Pat Harrison for majority leader. Allen & Shannon, p. 11; Neal, *Harry*, p. 32.

55   "If we see . . . possible." *NY Times*, 24 June 1941, p. 7.

55   "Those labor . . . leaders." *Washington Post*, 8 March 1948. p. B17.

55   "What line . . . spot." Dallek, *Lone Star*, p. 268.

55–56   "believe Roosevelt . . . died." Smith, *Hostages*, p. 612. In May 1945, Kennedy wrote to his twenty-three-year-old daughter, Kathleen, approving of Truman's "advocating Americanism as the Mid West knows it and not as the elements in New York want it."

56   "If you say . . . window." Miller, *Plain*, p. 186.

56   "I have been . . . have it.'" Hechler, p. 53.

56   "Dennison . . . book." *Political Science Quarterly*, Spring 1991, p. 48.

57   "Truman would give me . . . world." Douglas, *Court*, p. 291.

57   "What got Truman's . . . did." *Nation*, 8 February 1986, p. 144.

57   "What else can the little guy do? . . . joint." *Middletown Times-Herald*, 26 November 1948, p. 4.

57   "the lowest form of politician." Ferrell, *Record*, p. 35.

57   Wiretap. *Nation*, 8 February 1986, pp. 129–45. At one point, Truman, unimpressed by the level of intelligence gathered ("I don't give a goddam whether Mrs. Corcoran gets her hair fixed or doesn't get her hair fixed. What the hell is that crap?"), ordered Vaughan: "Cut them all off. Tell the FBI we haven't got any time for that kind of shit." But the taps continued until May 1948,

57   Preferred Douglas. Janeway, pp. 58–59, 73.

58   "surround . . . world." *Nation*, 8 February 1986, p. 142.

58   "Missourians . . . move in." McCullough, p. 365.

58   "Truman's midgets." *Current Biography*, 1945, p. 623.

58 "You get . . . positions." *Journal of American History*, March 1970, p. 860. "When Mr. Roosevelt was here, every day was Christmas," complained one aide. "Now it's Tuesday." *Harper's*, December 1945, p. 482.

58 McKim. *NY Times*, 13 June 1945, p. 17; Hamby, *People*, p. 302.

58 "The Great White Chief." *Washington Post*, 2 October 1945, p. 5.

58 Like McKim, soon exited. *NY Times*, 22 January 1946, p. 21. Vardaman personally attributed his appointment to a $300 Truman campaign contribution in 1940. Trohan, p. 214.

58 "a bull in . . . china shop." Hamby, *People*, p. 302. Vaughan once inquired of Truman's adviser on minorities, David Niles: "Don't you ever let any white folks in your office?" Coffin, p. 36.

58 "I was very . . . advice." Douglas, *Court*, p. 291. Snyder was, however, as David McCullough noted, a hardworking "plugger," often toiling seven days a week. McCullough, pp. 507–08.

59 "block head, nut." Ferrell, *Presidency*, p. 167.

59 "did not want any woman in the cabinet." Ayers, p. 78.

59 "Democratic leaders . . . reappointed." *Washington Post*, 8 February 1948, p. B5.

59 "When I became . . . times." Hamby, *People*, p. 436.

59–60 Press Conference. Truman, *Messages*, p. 113.

60 Ickes contended. Abels, *Scandals*, p. 38.

60 "This is the rawest . . . game." *Washington Post*, 6 February 1946, p. 2. Former assistant attorney general Norman Littell testified that Pauley had revealed to him: "These men have contributed to the campaign and they expect something for their money." *NY Times*, 2 February 1946, p. 28.

60 "the unsavory . . . Harding." Watkins, p. 835. Pauley once admitted to Jonathan Daniels attempting to "shake down" war contractor Henry J. Kaiser for campaign contributions. Daniels, *Witness*, p. 233.

60 "Mr. Truman . . . form." *Washington Post*, 16 February 1946, p. 7.

60 "I don't care . . . party." Ibid., 14 February 1946, p. 3.

61 Thieves blasted open. *NY Times*, 4 August 1946, pp. 1, 30; Abels, *Scandals*, pp. 24–29; Dunar, pp. 34–36; Powell, *Tom's Boy*, pp. 160–66. On becoming president in 1945, Truman had pardoned fifteen members of the Pendergast ring previously convicted of vote fraud. *Harper's*, January 1952, p. 33.

61 "He was not . . . terrible." Neal, *HST*, p. 97.

61 "She looks . . . years." *Abilene Reporter-News*, 29 April 1945, p. 49. Bess hated Washington, and her discomfort manifested itself, as David McCullough noted, in "an expression that looked as if her feet hurt." *PBS, American Experience*.

61 Axtell's first name. *Political Science Quarterly*, Spring 1991, p. 47.

61–62 "have you . . . [Continued laughter.]" Truman, *Messages*, p. 352.

62 "intellectual nonentity." Kurth, p. 396.

62 "He won't get . . . shotgun." Abels, *Victory*, p. 22.

62 "What are they . . . wait?" Neal, *HST*, p. 211.

62 "I'm just mild about Harry." Mooney, p. 57.

62 "To err is Truman." Abels, *Victory*, p. 19.

62 "I wonder . . . alive." Mooney, p. 57.

62 "Don't shoot . . . he can." Allen & Shannon, p. 35.

62 "Who is . . . drone?" Diggins, p. 102.

62 43 percent. Spragens, p. 392.

62 32 percent. *NY Times*, 23 October 1947, p. 51.

62 Not to campaign in 1946. Barone, p. 187.

63 Liberal forces in disarray. Mooney, p. 39.

63 Fulbright's demands. *NY Times*, 7 November 1946, p. 3.

63 "The *Constitution* . . . days." *Northwest Arkansas Times*, 7 November 1946, p. 1.

63–64 "How are . . . dignity." *Paris News*, 15 November, p. 10.

CHAPTER 7

65 Slaveholders. Miller, *Plain*, p. 59.

65 "Most were wedding presents." Ibid.

65 "concentration camps." Leuchtenburg, p. 149.

65 "I thought . . . shot." Ibid.

65 "The South . . . mother." Berman, *Civil Rights*, p. 21.

65 "I think one . . . Chinaman." Everson, p. 101.

65 The word "nigger." Leuchtenburg, p. 152.

65 "army of coons." Ferrell, *Life,* p. 292.

65 "Nigger picnic day." Truman, *Dear Bess*, p. 417; Independence's African-American neighborhood was popularly known as "Nigger Neck." *PBS, American Experience.*

66 "I wish to . . . relations." Miller, *Truman*, p. 329. In 1944, on being asked if he might be photographed with a group of Minnesota black leaders, Truman informed former governor Elmer Benson, "Well, now, I have no objection to having my picture taken with a nigger, but you know, I was put on this ticket to sort of offset Roosevelt in some ways." Leuchtenburg, p. 464. At the Lincoln Memorial, in June 1947, he, nonetheless, became the first president to address the NAACP. *NY Times*, 30 June 1947, pp. 1, 3.

66 "Harry isn't . . . I am." Hamby, *People*, p. 433. Mary Jane Truman made that statement in 1949. In 1955, Truman's memoirs contained this passage: "My appeal for equal economic and political rights for every American citizen had nothing at all to do with the personal or social relationships of individuals or the right of every person to choose his own associates. The basic constitutional privilege which I advocated was deliberately misconstrued to include or imply racial miscegenation and intermarriage. My only goal was equal opportunity and security under the law for all classes of Americans." Truman, *Trial and Hope*, p. 183.

66 "I believe . . . this." Daniels, *Independence*, p. 340.

66 New Deal sympathy. FDR even refused to allow black and white White House servants to dine together. Bartlett, p. xi.

66 "I call upon . . . before." Goulden, *Best*, p. 355.

66 Poll taxes. *Pittsburgh Courier*, 1 May 1948, p. 5. In 1948 seven Southern states—Alabama, Arkansas, Mississippi, South Carolina, Tennessee, Texas, and Virginia—plus New Hampshire possessed poll taxes. "Of course there are exceptions," noted one Texas wire service report, "but for the ordinary . . . citizen, it is pay your poll tax or lose your vote. . . . For years there have been movements to abolish the poll tax but they never have gained great popularity. . . . One of the reasons is that the state poll tax of $1 is dedicated to schools and no one seems to want to take that money away from the schools." *Lubbock Evening Journal*, 4 January 1948, p. 9.

66 *Grovey v. Townsend. Grovey v. Townsend*, 295 U.S. 45 (1935).

67 *Smith v. Allwright. Smith v. Allwright*, 321 U.S. 649 (1944).

67 South Carolina's blacks voted. *Atlanta World*, 3 January 1948, p. 5.

67 *Sipuel v. Board of Regents. Sipuel v. Board of Regents of University of Oklahoma*, 332 U.S. 631 (1948).

67 African-American population grew. Leuchtenburg, p. 168.

67 Jimmy Byrnes. Byrnes, p. 230, Morgan, *FDR*, p. 729.

67 Fifty thousand black votes. Moon, pp. 35–36.

68 Fifteen northern states. Ibid., p. 198.

68 Harlem. Ibid., pp. 167, 209. Dewey, nonetheless, lost Harlem in 1944 and 1946.

68 Ives-Quinn Act. *Atlanta Daily World*, 27 March 1946, p. 1.

68 "I have . . . liberals." Neal, *Eleanor*, p. 149. Or, as Drew Pearson wrote, "Biggest wearers of Wallace buttons are the colored people. . . . Democratic leaders privately have virtually given up New York State as lost, especially if Dewey runs. Wallace, they figure, will swing all the Harlem vote, and Dewey would take most of the New York Jewish vote." *Amsterdam Recorder*, 14 February 1948, p. 4.

68 "From now on . . . last." *NY Times*, 13 October 1945, p. 16; Powell, *Adam*, pp. 79–80. Compounding Truman's predicament was the fact that his perennial nemesis, Clare Boothe Luce, almost instantly resigned from the DAR in protest. Truman himself, in January 1947, courted controversy when he attended a performance at Washington's segregated National Theater. *Atlanta Daily World*, 19 October 1945, p. 1.

68 Truman banned Powell. *Political Science Quarterly*, Spring 1991, p. 43. In November 1946, Powell introduced Henry Wallace as "our next President." MacDougall, p. 663.

68 "That damn nigger preacher." Haygood, p. 45; Leuchtenburg, p. 152; Ferrell, *Life*, p. 293; McCullough, p. 576. Truman stormed that he "wanted to kick [Powell] around."

68–69 Missouri boasted an unusually large. Leuchtenburg, p. 158.

69 1940 victory. Miller, *Truman*, p. 325.

69 "Unless . . . Republican." Gullan, p. 35.

69 "Negroes . . . Negro." Tidwell, p. 151. Davis's *Star* "wholeheartedly" backed Wallace in 1948, so much so that the Progressive Party "apparatus" purchased the paper from him (converting it to the *Illinois Standard*) in summer 1948, enabling Davis's December 7, 1948, relocation (on Paul Robeson's advice) to Hawaii. There, Davis eventually befriended the young Barack Obama. Davis, *Blues*, pp. xiv, 298–99. Davis, said noted literary historian James Smethurst, "was almost certainly a CPUSA member." Smethurst, p. 48.

69 "Mr. Wallace's . . . come." Moon, p. 204.

69 91 to 3 percent. *Atlanta Daily World*, 19 May 1946, p. 1.

69 54 to 22 percent. *LA Sentinel*, 12 February 1948, p. 9; MacDougall, pp. 653, 663.

70 75 percent. Hamby, *Beyond*, p. 214.

70 SNYC poll. *Atlanta Daily World*, 18 March 1948, p. 2. Attorney General Tom Clark had already designated SNYC as a Communist front organization.

70 "My God . . . do something!" White, *White*, pp. 330–331.

70 After consulting White. Ibid., pp. 331–32.

70 *To Secure These Rights*. *Washington Post*, 30 October 1947, pp. 1, 10; Moon, pp. 221–36.

70 "the most . . . bigotry." Moon, p. 200.

70 End antilynching filibusters. *Chicago Defender*, 5 August 1944, p. 3; Leuchtenburg, p. 157. In 1936, however, Truman informed one friend, "You know I am against this bill. . . . All my sympathies are with you but the Negro vote in Kansas City and St. Louis is too important." Ferrell, *Life*, p. 293.

70 Supporting a permanent FEPC. *NY Times*, 6 June 1945, p. 23.

70–71 "Be a Southernor [sic] . . . Be one." Frederickson, p. 77.

71 "My forebears. . . this." Truman, *Presidency*, p. 392.

71–72 "I am going. . . cause." Ferrell, *Centenary*, pp. 191–92.

72 Already retreated once. Leuchtenburg, p. 165.

72 "the White . . . House." Clifford, p. 206.

72–73 Gallup Poll. *Oakland Tribune*, 26 July 1948, p. 4D. A *Fortune* magazine poll produced similar findings. *Fortune*, October 1948, p. 32.

73 February 2, 1948. *Washington Post*, 7 February 1948, pp. 1–2.

74 "We hail . . . leadership." *Chicago Defender*, 14 February 1948, p. 14.

74 "Truman talks . . . Hitler." Horne, *Davis*, p. 198.

74 "No president . . . gesture." *Chicago Defender*, 7 February 1948, p. 15.

CHAPTER 8

75 "President Truman . . . ignored." Leuchtenburg, p. 177.

75 Gallup forecast. *Lubbock Evening Journal*, 25 January 1948, p. 38.

76 George Washington. Frederickson, p. 74.

76 "wasn't what . . . discussions." Ibid.

76 49.2 percent black. Garson, p. 243.

76 "Vital . . . taken." Drake & Nelson, p. 184.

76 "The Little Man's Big Friend." Grantham, p. 120.

76 "worships . . . Wallace." *Dothan Eagle*, 23 January 1948, p. 4.

76 "Who's running . . . Belt?" *New Republic*, 15 March 1948, p. 7.

76 "He's been . . . enough." Karabell, p. 48.

76 "The South's . . . Party." *Florence Morning News*, 30 January 1948, p. 1.

76 Richard Russell. Abels, *Victory*, p. 10.

77 "consider . . . about." *Mexico Evening Ledger*, 3 February 1948, p. 1; Cohodas, p. 130.

77 "Harlem . . . South." Abels, *Victory*, p. 10.

77 "Give . . . President." *Washington Post*, 10 February 1948, pp. 1–2.

77 Fielding Wright, feverish. Frederickson, p. 78.

77 Thompson prepared a resolution. *Chillicothe Constitution-Tribune*, 7 February 1948, p. 1.

77 "I am a Democrat . . . nominee." Ibid.

77 "dignity . . . people." Schlesinger, *Parties*, pp. 190–92.

77 Wright resented Thurmond's call. Frederickson, p. 79.

77 "blood . . . Democracy." Cohodas, p. 134.

77 "all true white Jeffersonian Democrats." Ibid.

77 Truman's "un-American" program. Bass & Thompson, *Strom*, p. 107.

78 "a keen . . . Carolina." Frederickson, p. 79.

78 "Please . . . opportunity." Bass & Thompson, *Strom*, p. 107.

78 "the majority . . . Presidency." Karabell, p. 53.

78 Second best when drunk. Walser, p. 150.

78 In Little Rock. *Life*, 1 March 1948, p. 27.

78 Bob Hannegan. Talented Gael Sullivan, a classmate and close friend of McGrath, had been in line to succeed Hannegan as DNC chairman, but found his ambition derailed after an incident that looked suspiciously like drunk driving. *NY Times*, 30 July 1947, p. 22; Redding, pp. 89–92.

79 "because she . . . Negro." *NY Times*, 7 March 1948, p. E3.

79 Engaged a professional boxer. Frederickson, p. 81.

79 Governor and Mrs. Thurmond. *Florence Morning News*, 23 February 1948, p. 1. Had they been present, however, they might have heard the gaffe-prone Truman refer to Franklin Roosevelt as Theodore Roosevelt and witnessed key Senate functionary Les Biffle at the head table fall asleep during Truman's talk. *Washington Post*, 21 February 1948, p. 6.

79 Also absent. *Washington Post*, 20 February 1948, p. 8. McGrath, wrote Robert Allen and William Shannon, "has all the charm and personal warmth of cold tea, the magnetism of a lead dime, and the intellectual interests of a deputy sheriff." Allen & Shannon, p. 98.

79 "to the finish." *Washington Post*, 21 February 1948, p. 1; Barber, p. 49.

79 "Do you . . . Constitution?" *Atlanta Daily World*, 29 February 1948, p. 1.

79 1944 plank. *Tucson Daily Citizen*, 24 February 1948, p. 9.

79 "the farthest . . . mind." Ibid.

79 "hoodlumism." *Florence Morning News*, 24 February 1948, p. 1.

79 "Will you now . . . Congress?" Redding, pp. 136–37.

80 "The Southern states are . . . states." *Florence Morning News*, 24 February 1948, p. 1.

80 On April 19, the Supreme Court. *LA Sentinel*, 9 September 1948, pp. 7, 12.

80 Deed covenants banned. *NY Times*, 11 May 1948, p. 22.

80 "It wasn't . . . after." *Florence Morning News*, 24 February 1948, p. 1.

80–81 "It is fitting . . . Mississippi." *NY Times*, 10 May, 1947, p. 5.

81 "Let's Send Harry Back to the Farm." *Billboard*, 29 May 1948, p. 39. Thurmond executive assistant William Lowndes Daniel had penned the ditty.

81 Crump and Jester. *Logansport Pharos-Tribune*, 11 May 1948, p. 5.

81 Governor Thompson. *Dothan Eagle*, 11 May 1948, p. 2.

81 Folsom. *Washington Post*, 9 May 1948, p. M6.

81 "suffered. . . people." Cohodas, pp. 144–45.

82 "These big . . . amusement." *Dothan Eagle*, 11 May 1948, p. 2.

82 "There's not enough . . . homes." Frederickson, p. 140.

82 Now christened "Dixiecrats." *Moberly Monitor-Index*, 11 May 1948, p. 4. The term appears to have been coined by *Charlotte* (NC) *News* telegraph editor William Weismer. "We decided to name them ourselves," said managing editor Pete McKnight. "They ought to adopt it."

82 Saturday, July 17. *NY Times*, 11 May 1948, pp. 1, 22.

82 "all necessary . . . actions." *Chicago Tribune*, 11 May 1948, p. 1.

82 "Harry Truman . . . will be." Karabell, p. 113.

CHAPTER 9

83 Bulkley. *Zanesville Signal*, 6 August 1938, p. 10.

83 In 1944, however. Wunderlin et al., p. 468.

84 "dull, . . . magnetism." *Time*, 29 January 1940, p. 22.

84 "Dagwood . . . Politics." Ibid., 15 April 1940, p. 20.

84 "all blue . . . door." Brinkley, *Memoir*, p. 78.

84 "Impatient . . . establishment." Mooney, p. 43.

84 "There is . . . become." White, *Taft*, p. 59.

84 "informed . . . granite." Patterson, p. 396.

84 "To my surprise . . . him." Schlesinger, *Life*, p. 426.

85 Local black church. *Current Biography*, 1940, p. 788.

85 "My husband . . . you?" Ibid.

85 Taft-Ellender-Wagner Bill. *New Republic*, 1 March 1948, pp. 11–14.

85 "Probably . . . control." Reinhard, p. 40. In October 1947, rumors even floated of a Harold Ickes endorsement of Taft and of a Taft-Walter Reuther ticket. The UAW's Reuther was aghast. *Nation*, 25 October 1947, p. 435.

85 "Taft . . . views." Gannon, Frank, "Minnesota's Boy Wonder Was RN's Pick for POTUS," 2 September 2008. http://thenewnixon.org/2008/09/02/minnesotas-boy-wonder-was-rns-pick-for-potus/.

85 "Everybody . . . him." Gunther, p. 470.

86 "Don't make . . . represents." Patterson, p. 377.

86 "They think . . . Dewey." Donovan, p. 402.

86 July 1947 announcement. Harnsberger, p. 177.

86 CIO pickets. *LA Times*, 28 June 1947, p. 1.

86   Taft tested the waters. *NY Times*, 6 September 1947, p. 2.

86   In San Francisco . . . Angeles. Patterson, p. 380. The Hitlerian references may have been responses to Taft's opposition to the Nuremberg war crimes trials ("a blot on the American record which we shall long regret"). *Life*, 9 February 1948, p. 56; *Harper's*, April 1948, p. 292.

86   "an egg . . . something." *NY Times*, 24 September 1948, p. 14. Later in the campaign, a basket of eggs was presented to Truman with the suggestion that he throw them at Taft. "I wouldn't throw *fresh* eggs at Taft," said the president of the United States. Hamby, *People*, p. 443; Ross, p. 88; Barber, p. 58.

86   Car door. *NY Times*, 24 September 1948, p. 14.

86   "You goddamned son of a bitch!" Patterson, p. 380.

86   "self-control . . . 1940s." *Chicago Tribune*, 24 September 1948, p. 1.

86   "Eat less . . . extravagantly." *LA Times*, 13 September 1947, pp. 5–6. Dwight Eisenhower concurred, writing his brother Milton, "I agree with Taft one hundred percent." Ambrose, p. 466.

86   "That didn't . . . before." *NY Times*, 25 September 1947, p. 25.

87   "gassy and pompous." Rovere, p. 184.

87   "could strut sitting down." *Current Biography*, 1940, p. 823.

87   "with the largest . . . candidate." Ibid.

87   Death of Ferris. *Life*, 24 May 1948, p. 111.

87   Large-state Republican elected. *Harper's*, May 1948, p. 402; Gunther, p. 394.

87   "by the simple . . . in it." *Current Biography*, 1940, p. 823.

87   "His head . . . point." Douglas, *East*, pp. 418–19.

87   "Vandenberg . . . years." *Current Biography*, 1940, p. 821.

87   "You can't . . . cancels out." Gunther, pp. 391–92.

87   1936. *Harper's*, May 1946, p. 402.

87   Vice-presidential nod. *Brownsville Herald*, 17 June 1948, p. 6.

87   "Let me ask . . . anything?" Ibid.

87   "Senator Vandenberg . . . defeat." *Current Biography*, 1940, p. 823.

88   "I'll make . . . take." *New Yorker*, 24 March 1962, p. 158. Taft had similarly tendered the VP nod to Vandenberg—with identical results. Peters, p. 85.

88   Ambassador to Moscow. *NY Times*, 12 January 1934, p. 2. Yet, typically, Vandenberg waffled when the nomination reached the Senate floor. Oddly enough, Henry Wallace, horrified by Soviet farm collectivization, then opposed recognition. Saposs, p. 169.

88   "something precious . . . conscription." *NY Times*, 13 August 1940, p. 10.

88   "It certainly . . . corner." Jeansonne, Smith, p. 87.

88   Gerald L. K. Smith. *Brownsville Herald*, 17 June 1948, p. 6; Jeansonne, *Smith*, pp. 87–88.

88   "a statesman . . . elected." *NY Times*, 26 May 1948, p. 19.

88   "Vandenberg contributed . . . him." *New Yorker*, 24 March 1962, p. 165.

88   Supported Douglas MacArthur. *Brownsville Herald*, 17 June 1948, p. 6.

88   Walter Lippmann. Steel, p. 455.

89   "the most . . . affairs." Douglas, *East*, pp. 418–19.

89   Heart ailment. *Chicago Tribune*, 13 June 1948, p. 2.

89   "At least   guts." Krock, p. 244.

89   "cow country messiah." *LA Times*, 18 June 1948, p. A4.

89   "Stassen was . . . won." Gannon, Frank, "Minnesota's Boy Wonder Was RN's Pick for POTUS," 2 September 2008. http://thenewnixon.org/2008/09/02/minnesotas-boy-wonder-was-rns-pick-for-potus/.

90   "truculence and impatience." Risjord, pp. 199–200.

90   Between each voter and the exit. Gunther, p. 300.

90   "not a man afflicted with self-doubt." Mooney, p. 55.

90   "he replaced . . . leaders." *Life*, 1 March 1948, p. 45.

90   Despite vowing. *Harper's*, January 1946, p. 11.

90   San Francisco Conference. *NY Times*, 18 February 1945, p. E3.

90   December 1946. *Washington Post*, 17 December 1946. pp. 1, 6.

90   Forty thousand miles. Ross, p. 38.

90   "If Mr. Stassen . . . seriously." *NY Times*, 16 November 1947, p. BR7.

90–91   "revolutionizing campaign . . . corps." *Jefferson City News & Tribune*, 11 January 1948, p. 6.

91   "If I traveled . . . solution." Ibid.

91   Reborn Republicanism. *Harper's*, January 1946, pp. 17–18.

91   "I may do . . . internationalist." Patterson, p. 377.

91   "sophomoric." *Harper's*, January 1946, pp. 17–18.

91   "we are willing . . . organization." Ibid., p. 18.

91   "Certain of . . . nomination." *Brownsville Herald*, 18 June 1948, p. 6.

91   "Among the rank . . . Stassen." *Time*, 25 August 1947, pp. 20, 73.

CHAPTER 10

92   Version of Tom Pendergast. PBS, *American Experience.*

92   "I can deal . . . hell." Ferrell, *Record*, p. 53.

92   "I'm tired of babying the Soviets." Acheson, p. 190. HST's comment, typically, came in a never-sent letter to Byrnes.

92   Through outright landgrabs. McCoy, p. 134. Moscow had also annexed Czechoslovakia's easternmost province.

93   "From Stettin . . . Moscow." *Washington Post*, 6 March 1946, p. 2.

93   "The very . . . Communists." Truman, *Messages*, p. 177.

93–94   "I believe . . . processes." *Washington Post*, 13 March 1947, p. 1.

94   "chose a line . . . thrashing." Tugwell, p. 74.

94   "Our policy . . . exist." *NY Times*, 6 June 1947, p. 2.

95   "for many . . . advisable." Forrestal, p. 387.

95   "Papers this morning . . . war." Ibid., p. 394.

95   "to, say, the Mediterranean." Lilienthal, p. 302.

95   "The atmosphere . . . atmosphere." *Washington Post*, 17 March 1948, p. 13.

95   General Marshall persuaded. Forrestal, p. 394.

95   Green carnation. *NY Times*, 18 March 1948, p. 3.

96   "It is [their] . . . to hesitate." *Current History*, July 1947, p. 301.

96   "prompt passage." Ibid., p. 4

96   "temporary . . . legislation." Forrestal, p. 397.

96   "no extension . . . time." *NY Times*, 4 March 1947, p. 15.

96   "prompt enactment of universal training." Kofsky, p. 135.

96   St. Patrick's Day marchers. *NY Times*, 18 March 1948, p. 32.

96   Fifty motorcycle police. *Washington Post*, 18 March 1948, p. 3.

96   "I do not want . . . now." *NY Times*, 18 March 1948, p. 4.

96–97   "If [they] want . . . feels." Ibid., pp. 1, 7.

97   October 1947 poll. Walker, p. 177.

97   73 percent. Horowitz, p. 227.

97   Michael Straight. Perry, passim.

97   The *New Republic*. *New Republic*, 21 October 1946, pp. 497–98.

97   "the most hated nation in the world." Clifford, pp. 138–39. Wallace wasn't alone in attacking Truman's foreign policy. From various perspectives, so did Taft, Joseph P. Kennedy, and Bernard Baruch.

97   "Greek children . . . democracy." Abels, *Victory*, p. 33.

97   "toward . . . along." Walker, p. 168.

97   When Moscow opposed it. Abels, *Victory*, p. 33.

98   In Britain. *Christian Science Monitor*, 9 April 1947, p. 8; Newman, p. 111.

98   In Paris. *Washington Post*, 25 April 1947, p. 8; MacDougall, pp. 135, 412; Steinberg, *Menace*, pp. 62–66. A 1945 incident involving Duclos illuminates the intertwining of international Communist parties. When Duclos (recently returned from Moscow) denounced CPUSA leader Earl Browder, American Communists interpreted that as a signal from the Kremlin and ultimately jettisoned Browder in favor of veteran Communist Eugene Dennis. Saposs, pp. 114–16, 121–23, 243; MacDougall, pp. 272–74.

98   Logan Act. *Washington Post*, 15 April 1947, pp. 1, 4; *Harper's*, March 1948, p. 245; MacDougall, pp. 136–37.

98   "I inquired . . . States." Forrestal, pp. 261–62.

98   "scroll of greeting." *NY Times*, 7 April 1947, p. 40; MacDougall, pp. 132–33; Douglas, *Life*, p. 264. Conversely, seventy intellectuals (including Arthur Garfield Hays, A. Philip Randolph, Oswald Garrison Villard, Norman Thomas, Max Eastman, and Dorothy Thompson) had earlier wired Ernest Bevin disavowing Wallace. *NY Times*, 23 January 1947, p. 14.

98   Ann Arbor. *NY Times*, 16 May 1947, p. 4.

98   Crowds in Minneapolis and Detroit. MacDougall, p. 156.

98   Chicago Stadium. *NY Times*, 18 May 1947, p. E10; MacDougall, pp. 154–55. Tickets ranged from sixty cents to $2.40.

98   Berkeley. Walker, p. 173.

98   "I am not . . . fear." *NY Times*, 20 May 1947, p. 3; MacDougall, pp. 157–58.

99   "Take up the fight . . . peace." Pugliese, pp. 53–54. Appearing alongside Wallace were former California attorney general Robert W. Kenny, Dr. Linus Pauling (his wife eventually voted for Truman), and Katharine Hepburn. Event donors included Charlie and Oona O'Neill Chaplin, Edward G. Robinson, John Garfield, Hedy Lamarr, Paul Henreid, and screenwriter Budd Schulberg.

99   "I am not a Communist." *NY Times*, 19 May 1947, p. 1.

99   Primary in Olympia. Ibid., p. 15.

99   Carey. *Chicago Tribune*, 6 November 1947, p. 4; *New Republic*, 19 January 1948, p. 10; MacDougall, pp. 193–95, 284. Carey was endorsed by both the Chicago Bar Association and Hearst's *Chicago Herald-American*; 113,000 persons voted the straight Progressive ticket. *Nevada State Journal*, 30 November 1947, p. 28.

99   Missouri. Hamby, *Beyond*, p. 219. In Cleveland, Ohio, Communist Party leader Anton Krchmarek garnered 64,213 votes for the city's school board. *Nevada State Journal*, 30 November 1947, p. 28.

99   Sullivan. *Journal of American History*, June 1972, p. 92; White & Maze, p. 250; Markowitz, p. 242. The liberal Sullivan was stridently anti-Wallace. In March 1947, he publicly virtually read Wallace and Claude Pepper out of the party. When Truman and Alben Barkley objected, Sullivan had to privately apologize to Pepper. *Washington Post*, 6 April 1948, p. B5; *Washington Post*, 11 April 1948, p. 4; Redding, pp. 38–40; MacDougall, p. 186; Goldman, *Party*, p. 423.

99   Wallace announced candidacy. *Washington Post*, 30 December 1947, p. 2; *NY Times*, 30 December 1947, p. 15; *Vital Speeches*, 1 January 1948, pp. 172–74.

100   Cosmos Club. Douglas, *Life*, pp. 263–64.

100   Some said her lover. Caro, *Master*, pp. 144–45; Unger & Unger, p. 82.

100   LBJ. Douglas, *Life*, p. 273.

100   National headquarters. *NY Times*, 25 February 1948, p. 14; MacDougall, p. 301.

100   Corn planted. *Washington Post*, 2 April 1948, p. 16; *New Yorker*, 10 April 1948, p. 21.

100   Popularity estimates. Culver & Hyde, p. 461; Schapsmeier & Schapsmeier, *Prophet*, p. 189; MacDougall, pp. 291–92.

101   "the new party . . . million." Abels, *Victory*, p. 21.

101   11.5 percent. Taylor, p. 360.

101   15 and 18 percent. *Washington Post*, 11 January 1948, p. M1; *Nebraska State Journal*, 11 January 1948, p. 5.

101   California. MacDougall, p. 291.

101   Leo Isacson. *NY Times*, 18 February 1948, pp. 1, 17; *Nation*, 28 February 1948, p. 229; *Life*, 1 March 1948, pp. 24–25; *Journal of American History*, June 1972, p. 94; MacDougall, pp. 323–25; Hamby, *People*, p. 411; Hamby, *Belief*, pp. 218–19; Saposs, pp. 81–84; Yarnell, pp. 52–57; Jonnes, pp. 108–09. Public opinion expert Samuel Lubell visited Isacson's district and judged it to be a "dying Jewish neighborhood where the chill of being trapped penetrates everywhere." Jonnes, p. 109.

101   "The Communist . . . thought." *NY Times*, 18 February 1948, p. 1; *Washington Post*, 18 February 1948, p. 2. As improbable as it seems today, in 1946 Isacson lost his left-wing Bronx 13th assembly district to a Republican. *Amsterdam Recorder*, 6 November 1946, p. 1; Mearns, *1947*, p. 173.

101   "The people . . . program." *NY Times*, 18 February 1948, p. 17.

101–02   "Who asked Henry . . . membership." *Washington Post*, 25 July 1948, p. B6; Schmidt, p. 271; MacDougall, p. 243; Saposs, pp. 141–42; Culver & Hyde, p. 458. Kingdon, A. F. Whitney, and San Francisco attorney Bartley Crum immediately resigned from the PCA board of directors upon Wallace's announcement. *Nation*, 27 December 1947, p. 693; Saposs, p. 126.

102   Counterweight. *NY Times*, 5 January 1947, p. 1; *Journal of American History*, June 1972, p. 94; Wechsler, pp. 211–17; MacDougall, pp. 121–22; Schlesinger, *Life*, p. 412. At the ADA's founding meeting, chairman Elmer Davis commented, "This looks very much like the United States Government in exile." Loeb Interview, Truman Library, 26 June 1970; Wechsler, p. 216.

102   Hundred dollars. Wechsler, p. 215.

102   "Within the   great." *NY Times*, 5 January 1947, p. 1.

102   East Ninety-second Street. Kimball, pp. 167, 170, 236. Due to the severe postwar housing shortage, Kimball spent his honeymoon with Wallace.

102   "From everything . . . liberals." Schlesinger, *Life*, p. 414.

102   "We believe . . . the U.S." Ibid.

103   "'enigma' who 'couldn't write.'" Kimball, pp. 168–69.

103   "madhouse." Ibid., p. 171.

103   "Wallace was susceptible . . . politics." White, pp. 256–57.

103   "was seeing more . . . people." Hamby, *Beyond*, p. 201.

103   "I originally . . . campaign." *Hartford Courant*, 21 March 1948, p. 17.

104   Steinhardt. *NY Times*, 16 March 1948, pp. 1, 10; *Journal of American History*, June 1972, p. 96; MacDougall, pp. 334–35; White & Maze, pp. 259–60; Clifford, pp. 224–25.

104   "I live . . . knows?" *NY Times*, 16 March 1948, p. 10; *Journal of American History*, June 1972, p. 96; MacDougall, p. 334; Abels, *Victory*, p. 33; Wechsler, pp. 222–23; Culver & Hyde, p. 474. Four days earlier, the *Daily Worker*'s Joe Starobin had written, "Let Americans remember another suicide—that of

John Winant, who found that post-war America was not what he hoped and expected it to be, and could not endure the strain of it." Wechsler, p. 223.

104 "It is a shameful . . . respects." *LA Times*, 18 March 1948, p. 10.

104 "Yesterday . . . abroad." *Lowell Sun*, 19 March 1948, p. 32.

104 "[T]he men . . . everywhere." *Chicago Tribune*, 19 March 1948, p. 4.

CHAPTER 11

105 "establishment . . . people." Lacey, p. 318; Radosh & Radosh, *Haven*, p. 4.

105 September 1922. Wunderlin et al., p. 22.

105 5.6 million Jews. Evensen, p. 53.

105 Jewish vote in 1944. Bass, p. 19; Beschloss, *Courage*, p. 230.

105 Jews resided in New York. McCullough, p. 596.

105 Polls gave Wallace. *Washington Post*, 11 January 1948, p. M1.

106 110 electoral votes. Benson, p. 177.

106 Fifty-five percent. *Time*, 1 March 1948, p. 12. David Saposs estimates the district's Jewish population at 35 percent. And with the black population at 18 percent, the results hardly augured well for Truman on that front either. Saposs, p. 82.

106 Eleanor Roosevelt's campaigning. *NY Amsterdam News*, 14 February 1948, p. 7.

106 "Truman talks . . . Arab." Abels, *Victory*, p. 12.

106 "Both moves . . . way." *Hartford Courant*, 24 March 1948, p. 10.

107 "the Jews have no place to go." Beschloss, *Presidential*, p. 200.

107 Like FDR before him. Divine, pp. 105–08. In 1945, en route home from Yalta, FDR had promised Saudi Arabia's King Ibn Saud that no alteration in Palestine's status would transpire "without full consultation with both Arabs and Jews." He also provided the similarly lame Saud with his spare wheelchair. Saud, unfamiliar with the technology, was much impressed. *American Heritage*, December 1976, p. 13; Morgan, *FDR*, p. 757; Radosh & Radosh, *Haven*, p. 18.

107 British government terminated it. Divine, p. 105.

107 "Regarding . . . New York." *NY Times*, 13 June 1946, pp. 1, 4; Benson, p. 68; Dinnerstein, pp. 97–98; Schoenbaum, p. 43; Druks, *Friendship*, p. 88. In the course of the same speech, Bevin advocated that all Palestinian land be publicly owned. "The most revealing feature of the debate," noted the *New York Times*, "was the surprising amount of antagonism toward the United States as a capitalist country. . . . Mr. Bevin . . . made no defense of the United States, except to point to its genuine liberals and to voice the hope that capitalism there would not last forever." While, at that point, Truman considered Bevin's immigration remarks to be "pretty raw [and] ignominious," to Zionist rabbi Arthur J. Lelyveld, HST excused Bevin's rant "because he is often tempted 'to blow up' himself because of the pressure and the agitation from New York." Gannin, pp. 74–75.

107 "I am sorry . . . constituents." Donovan, p. 322. Truman made an almost identical comment in 1948, when asked by old friend and newspaper publisher John A. Kennedy if he planned on recognizing the new Jewish state: "Well, how many Arabs are there as registered voters in the United States?" Benson, p. 175. 100,000 letters. McCullough, p. 598.

107 "Of course . . . friends." Spiegel, p. 20.

108 "Jesus Christ . . . luck?" Wallace, *Diary*, p. 607. Wallace recalled that "Truman said he had no use for them and didn't care what happened to them." Donovan, p. 319; Benson, p. 93; Spiegel, p. 20; Radosh & Radosh, *Haven*, p. 178.

108 "Those New York . . . Disloyal." *Chester Times*, 8 March 1948, p. 6. Beschloss, *Courage*, p. 215.

108 March 1948 press conference. http://www.trumanlibrary.org/publicpapers/index.php?pid= 1414&st=&st1=; Truman *Presidency*, p. 386. Truman once threatened Pearson: "Over in that desk I've got a gold plated automatic pistol that was given to me for a present. And, you son of a bitch, if you write one more derogatory line about my women, I'm going to take that pistol and use it on you!" Mitchell, pp. 194–95.

109 Snyder believed Truman unelectable. *Washington Post*, 6 July 1948, p. B13.

109 "Truman made . . . beginning." Gabler, pp. 345–46. Neal Gabler, in his otherwise excellent biography of Winchell, dates the incident as occurring in 1946 and indicates that Hannegan was not supporting Truman's renomination. A review of Pearson's columns casts doubt upon this.

109 "He's not a President." Gabler, p. 346.

109 Mere holiday greeting. Truman, *Trial and Hope*, p. 154; Hamby, *People*, p. 407; Spiegel, p. 24. Truman also represented the letter as being merely about the refugee question, omitting any reference in his memoirs to the more explosive question of statehood.

109 "the Jewish Agency . . . States." *NY Times*, 5 October 1946, pp. 1–2; *Washington Post*, 5 October 1946, p. 4; Truman, *Messages*, p. 443.

109 Bevin had begged. Donovan, p. 320; Druks, *Friendship*, p. 90.

110 "If [Truman] . . . policy." *Washington Post*, 5 October 1948, p. 1.

110 "A few days . . . only." Truman, *Memoirs*, p. 154. In fact, Truman had been urged by his minorities adviser David K. Niles to upstage Dewey. Ganin, p. 105.

110–11 "Had ten . . . comes." *NY Times*, 11 July 2003, p. A14; *Washington Post*, 11 July 2003, pp. A01, A10; *NY Times*, 14 July 2003, p. A17; Druks, *Kennedy*, p. 13. Morgenthau seemed to particularly annoy Truman. After a Morgenthau visit in June 1945, Truman confided to his diary, "The Jews claim God Almighty picked 'em out for special privilege. Well, I'm sure he had better judgment." Beschloss, *Conquerors*, p. 240.

111 "[T]hese ships . . . side." *NY Times*, 14 July 2003, p. A17.

111 "preferring fascist . . . Palestine." Donovan, p. 325.

111 "It is such . . . him." Snetsinger, p. 54.

112 "I don't know . . . country." Abels, *Victory*, p. 17.

112 "I don't care . . . right." Spiegel, p. 20.

112 Resolution 181. *NY Times*, 30 November 1948, pp. 1, 63; Gosnell, p. 362; Spiegel, pp. 29–30; Lash, p. 124; Druks, *Friendship*, 96.

112 Silver. Spiegel, p. 30; Radosh & Radosh, *Haven*, pp. 8–9; McCullough, pp. 598–99. Silver, observed historians Ronald and Allis Radosh, was "not only confrontational and unyielding, but . . . not charming."

112 High-level State Department personnel. Isaacson & Thomas, p. 251; Clifford, p. 5; Spiegel, pp. 27, 32; Druks, *Friendship*, p. 99.

112 Gridiron Club dinner. Forrestal, p. 347; Abels, *Victory*, p. 16.

113 "My dear friend . . . be." Truman, *Memoirs*, pp. 160–61; Truman, *Presidency*, pp. 387–88; Donovan, pp. 374–75; McCullough, pp. 606–07; Snetsinger, pp. 76–77; Bass, p. 29; Gosnell, p. 362; Druks, Friendship, p. 98.

114 Weizmann secretly passed through. Truman, *Trial and Hope*, pp. 161–62; Donovan, p. 375; McCullough, pp. 608–09; Daniels, *Independence*, p. 318. Jacobson may have felt more at home at the White House than he ever did visiting Truman's Independence home, always, as it were, under the sway of Harry's anti-Semitic (and generally snobbish) mother-in-law. "Under the circumstances," recalled Eddie's wife, Bluma, "the Trumans couldn't afford to have Jews in their house." Miller, *Plain*, p. 104; Beschloss, *Conquerors*, p. *229fn*.

114 "informed Weizmann . . . Palestine." Ganin, pp. 167–68.

114 "my government . . . delay." *NY Times*, 20 March 1948, p. 2; *Chicago Tribune*, 20 March 1948, p. 5; Hamby, *People*, pp. 412–13; Daniels, *Independence*, p. 318; Snetsinger, pp. 87, 89.

114   "Shift . . . 'Sellout.'" *NY Times*, 20 March 1948, p. 3.

114   "land of milk . . . considerations." *NY Times*, 21 March 1948, p. E8; Benson, pp. 137–38.

114   "double cross." *Washington Post*, 23 March 1948, p. B3.

114–15   "the most terrible . . . blood." *NY Times*, 20 March 1948, p. 3; Evensen, p. 153.

115   "With sorrow . . . again." *NY Times*, 28 March 1948, p. 11.

115   "The UN . . . trusteeship." *Chicago Tribune*, 21 March 1948, p. 16. Taft, as well as Truman, came under fire for his pro-Zionist views. "Senator Taft," a Mrs. K. K. Cottingham wrote to Strom Thurmond, "must be a Jew because people who are white want the Arabs as friends and they do not want the Jews going into Palestine and pushing up and joining the Russians." Karabell, p. 106.

115   Nearly resigned. *Hartford Courant*, 27 March 1948, p. 2; Black, *Shadow*, p. 80; Neal, *Eleanor*, p. 120.

115   "The Jews . . . wounded." Hamby, *Beyond*, p. 221.

115   "There wasn't . . . States." Donovan, p. 376.

115   "The State . . . doing so." Ferrell, *Record*, p. 127; Truman, *Harry S. Truman*, p. 388; McCullough, pp. 610–11.

115   On March 6, 1948. Benson, p. 136.

116   "There is absolutely . . . there." Benson, p. 136; Spiegel, p. 33.

116   "As I quickly . . . help." Elsey, p. 161.

116   March 25, 1948. Levantrosser, p. 46.

116   "It has become . . . mandate." *NY Times*, 26 March 1948, p. 11; Divine, pp. 1, 11.

116   "The choice . . . law." Levantrosser, p. 61; Druks, *Friendship*, p. 103.

116   "You just . . . be on." Clifford, p. 4; Isaacson & Thomas, p. 452; Benson, p. 112. America imported only 6 percent of its oil in 1948, and only 6.3 percent of that originated in Saudi Arabia. Washington's concern was for Europe's supply and for fueling—quite literally—European recovery. The continent's traditional fuel source, coal, remained labor intensive and in France, Britain, and western Germany, miners' unions were largely Communist-controlled. Oil, political scientist Benjamin Schwadran would write, was "the decisive factor in the recovery of Europe and the backbone of NATO structure." Bass, pp. 28, 33; *American Heritage*, December 1976, pp. 79–81.

116   "the President knows . . . state." Clifford, p. 4.

117   "a limited number of police." *NY Times*, 21 April 1948, p. 20.

117   Rosenman. Levantrosser, p. 62.

117   May 12, 1948. Divine, pp. 197–98. Most White House staffers anticipated the new state would be named "Judea." Clifford, p. 5.

117   "Marshall did not like me." Clifford, p. 6.

117   "Mr. President . . . poke." Clifford, p. 12; Gosnell, p. 363. An aide's notes read: "CMC [Clifford] was enraged. Marshall glared at CMC." Spiegel, p. 37.

117   "If you follow . . . you." Bass, p. 31; Clifford, p. 14. Marshall, like many career military men of his time, had never voted. *Current Biography*, 1947, p. 427.

117   "Be careful . . . Marshall." Clifford, p. 15.

118   "I'm afraid . . . resign." Ibid.

118   "One did not . . . one." Bass, p. 32.

118   This new nation: Israel. Clifford, p. 20.

118   Eleven minutes. Hamby, *People*, pp. 416–17.

118   "indecent haste." Clifford, p. 20.

118   "THIS GOVERNMENT . . . Israel." *NY Times*, 15 May 1948, pp. 1, 3. That, however, was mere de

facto recognition (a suggestion made by Lovett. Clifford, p. 18.). De jure recognition did not arrive until following Israel's January 1949 elections. Benson, p. 178.

118 "Blessed . . . day." *NY Times*, 15 May 1948, p. 3.

118 The U.S. delegation. Gosnell, p. 363.

118 Eleanor Roosevelt. Lash, pp. 133–34; Neal, *Eleanor*, p. 120.

118 "get up . . . mass." Ferrell, *Presidency*, p. 311.

118 "The hour for jihad has struck." *NY Times*, 15 May 1948, p. 2.

118 "I want . . . him!" Truman, *Messages*, p. 814.

CHAPTER 12

119 Comfortable lead in the polls. *Washington Post*, 18 July 1947, p. 19.

119 "The family . . . performance." Hamby, *People*, p. 437.

119 55 percent. *Washington Post*, 11 June 1948, p. 15.

119 1947 *Fortune* magazine poll. *Fortune*, February 1948, p. 5.

119 *Look* magazine. *Amarillo Globe*, 23 December 1947, p. 1.

119 47 to 39 percent. Spragens, p. 398.

119 Every Republican but Taft. *Washington Post*, 29 April 1948, p. 4.

119 36 percent. *Washington Post*, 11 June 1948, p. 15; *Harper's*, July 1948, p. 30.

119 June 1948 Roper poll. *Fortune*, June 1948, p. 5.

119 Pearson forecast. *Washington Post*, 14 October 1948, p. B15.

120 Hannegan's blood pressure. Ibid., 28 September 1947, p. M1.

120 Forrestal. Clifford, p. 48; Elsey, p. 139.

120 "He was like . . . handsome." Schlesinger, *Ghosts*, p. 34.

120 "He was energetic . . . appointees." Ibid.

120 "be controversial . . . presents." Hechler, p. 61.

121 "prominent liberals . . . wanted." Leuchtenburg, p. 177; Frederickson, p. 68; Donaldson, p. 27; Dallek, p. 69; Delton, p. 130; Ross, p. 22.

121 "volatile." Leuchtenburg, p. 177.

121 "It is inconceivable . . . ignored." Ibid.

122 "In the land . . . duties." Clifford, p. 194; Barber, pp. 56–57; Schlesinger, *Ghosts*, p. 34.

123 State of the Union address. *NY Times*, 8 January 1948, pp. 1–2, 4; Abels, *Victory*, pp. 3–4; Clifford, p. 195.

123 Gen. Marshall's entrance. *NY Times*, 8 January 1948, p. 3; Clifford, p. 195.

123 Hoffman didn't bother standing. *NY Times*, 8 January 1948, p. 3.

123 Stony silence. Abels, *Victory*, p. 3.

123 "The extraordinary . . . together." Wallace, 8 January 1948, p. 2.

123 "performance . . . calf." *Charleston Gazette*, 15 January 1948, p. 20.

123 "The Wallace . . . room." Abels, *Victory*, pp. 4–5.

123–24 "Success in '48!" Elsey, p. 159.

124 "I was astounded . . . nature." Ibid.

124 "flat, emotionless manner." Ibid.

124 "so bad that . . . head." Hechler, p. 66.

124 "He began . . . all." Daniels, *Independence*, pp. 348–49; Hechler, p. 67.

124 *New Republic*. *New Republic*, 3 May 1948, p. 4.

124–25 "It [created] . . . conviction." *Uniontown Morning Herald*, 4 April 1948, p. 4; Hamby, *Beyond*, p. 234.

125 "Seemed to . . . into it." Hechler, p. 67.

125   Laughed or applauded eight times. Ibid.

125   "There is only . . . withdraw." *Washington Post*, 20 March 1948, pp. 1, 4; MacDougall, p. 472.

125   "President Truman is out . . . unrest." *Alabama Historical Quarterly*, Spring and Summer 1970, p. 23.

125   Truman Democrats. *NY Times*, 17 March 1948, pp. 1, 17.

125   36 percent. *Harper's*, July 1948, p. 30.

125   When he vetoed. *NY Times*, 3 April 1948, pp. 1, 2; Phillips, p. 200. The measure removed 7.4 million low-income taxpayers from the rolls and cut rates for the remaining 47 million. HST derided the measure as inflationary.

126   "The Democratic . . . history." *NY Times*, 4 April 1948, p. E3.

126   Democratic support soared. *Washington Post*, 11 December 1946, p. 11; *Washington Post*, 4 June 1948, p. 10.

126   Thirteenth honorary degree. Ibid., 13 June 1948, p. 5.

126   Banners mocked him. Ibid., 5 June 1948, p. 1.

126   "If I felt . . . stand it." *NY Times*, 4 June 1948, p. 1.

126   9,505-mile journey. Hechler, p. 70.

127   "the next Governor of Ohio." *Washington Post*, 5 June 1948, p. 3.

127   "On this nonpartisan . . . too." *NY Times*, 5 June 1948, p. 2.

127   Chicago Stadium. *Chicago Tribune*, 5 June 1948, pp. 1, 8. This was the first presidential speech televised from Chicago.

127   Carl Sandburg. Abels, *Victory*, p. 42.

127   "was rousing . . . Chopin." Strout, pp. 64–65.

127   "Nebraska . . . Democrats." *Brownsville Herald*, 3 June 1948, p. 6.

127   "acres of empty seats." *Life*, 21 June 1948, p. 43; *LA Times*, 7 June 1948, p. 1.

127   William Ritchie. *NY Times*, 6 June 1948, p. 12.

128   "I am making . . . talk to." Donovan, p. 397.

128   160,000 Omaha residents. *Washington Post*, 6 June 1948, p. M1. The *New Republic*'s TRB still found the Chicago rush-hour crowd "apathetic." Illinois Democrat boss Jacob Arvey remained noticeably absent. Strout, p. 65.

128   "I understand . . . clothes." Ross, pp. 86–87.

128   "treatment . . . receiving." *Washington Post*, 8 June 1948, p. 9.

128   Charlie Ross. Nelson, pp. 104–05.

128   "one of the great . . . war." *Long Beach Press-Telegram*, 9 June 1948, p. 1.

128   "more honored . . . country." *Life*, 21 May 1948, p. 43.

128   "No, our Wilma . . . here." Ibid.

128   "I have been . . . me." *NY Times*, 8 June 1948, p. 19; Hamby, *People*, p. 442.

129   "in the chatty . . . store." *Frederick News*, 12 June 1948, p. 1.

129   "I like old Joe . . . them." *Christian Science Monitor*, 12 June 1948, p. 1.

129   "Isn't there . . . Union?" Elsey, p. 163.

129   "Well, I guess I goofed." Hamby, *People*, p. 443.

129   "I am going . . . degree." *Washington Post*, 13 June 1948, p. 5.

129   "They can't . . . degree." Abels, *Victory*, p. 41.

129   "one of the finest . . . presidency." McCullough, p. 627.

129   Two-and-a-half to three million. *Chicago Tribune*, 19 June 1948, p. 5; Goldzwig, pp. 34–35.

130   "We won't be peddling . . . them." Kelly, p. 31.

130   "We [provided] . . . alike." Batt Jr. Interview, Truman Library, 26 July 1966.

130　"You know . . . Webster did." Truman, *Messages*, p. 353.

131　22 percent. Smith, *Dewey*, p. 478.

131　"Two-thirds . . . funeral." Truman, *Messages*, p. 353.

131　"Your dollar . . . about it." Ibid., p. 286.

131　"[T]his Congress . . . done." *Christian Science Monitor*, 9 June 1948, p. 12.

131　"I guess . . . know." Truman, *Messages*, p. 305.

131　"about two acres of people." McCullough, p. 627.

131　"They're going . . . you are." Abels, *Victory*, p. 43.

131　"The *Chicago* . . . for it." *Hartford Courant*, 10 June 1948, p. 1. It was Felknor's very first byline. "Nothing personal to you, young man," HST smiled, as his train departed the station.

131–32　Cliff Clevenger. *Washington Post*, 11 June 1948, p. 14.

132　"blackguarding . . . country." *Washington Post*, 12 June 1948, p. 1.

132　"Very poor taste." Redding, p. 179.

132　"Must have the wrong city." Ibid.

132　"The term hardly applies." Ibid., pp. 179–80.

132　"His easy air . . . critics." Oil City *Blizzard*, 16 June 1948, p. 6.

132　"the best . . . show." Ibid.

CHAPTER 13

133　Tom Dewey in 1940. Thomas, *Pursuit*, p. 141. Three primaries resulted in unpledged slates.

133　Only five true primaries. www.mnhs.org/market/mhspress/MinnesotaHistory/FeaturedArticles /5504150-165. Accessed 2009.

133　Willkie stumbled in Wisconsin. Eaton, pp. 397–99.

134　Warren E. Burger. *Life*, 26 April 1948, p. 36. *Life* found Burger "handsome, high-strung."

134　"but not on . . . principles." *NY Times*, 9 October 1947, p. 3; *Nation*, 25 October 1947, p. 436.

134　"integrity, sincerity, and ability." Eaton, p. 412.

134　"grave mistake." *NY Times*, 27 January 1948, p. 10. The bumptious Stassen even considered challenging Dewey in New York. Smith, *Dewey*, p. 485

134　"Old cemeteries fascinate me." Smith, *Dewey*, p. 482.

134　Vapid Dewey tabloid. *NY Times*, 8 March 1948, p. 11; *Nation*, 8 May 1948, p. 498.

134　"an uphill . . . Party." *NY Times*, 5 March 1948, p. 14.

134　five of eight delegates. Ibid., 11 March 1948, p. 22.

134　The switch. Ibid.

134　MacArthur touted for presidency (1944). Manchester, *Caesar*, pp. 353–63; Horowitz, p. 212; Eaton, p. 395. MacArthur received 74 percent in the 1944 Illinois GOP primary.

135　Gallup poll. *Lubbock Evening Journal*, 9 March 1947, p. 9.

135　"I think . . . flying." Nasaw, p. 591.

135　Hearst endorsement. *Washington Post*, 9 March 1948, p. 1; Eaton, p. 412.

135　"We must . . . HOUR." Manchester, p. 521.

135　Wisconsin supporters filed petitions. *NY Times*, 4 March 1948, p. 28.

135　New England Democrats. *Lowell Sun*, 4 March 1948, p. 34.

135　"The man . . . recall." Ibid.

135　MacArthur-for-President offices. *Washington Post*, 6 March 1948, p. 3.

135　"extraordinary occurrence." *NY Times*, 10 March 1948, p. 14.

136　"I have been . . . people." Ibid., 9 March 1948, p. 1.

136   "We Japanese . . . President." Manchester, p. 522.

136   "Pray for . . . Election." Ibid., p. 523.

136   March 15 Gallup poll. *Nevada State Journal*, 28 March 1948, p. 11.

136   Paternal grandfather. *Current Biography*, 1948, p. 388.

137   "wholesome . . . progressive." Steinke, p. 61.

137   Coleman's organization. *Nation*, 20 March 1954, p. 236. Personally, Coleman preferred Taft, but, pessimistic regarding the Ohioan's chances and wishing to derail Dewey, threw in with Stassen. Reeves, p. 146.

137   "refusal to discuss the issues." Reeves, p. 146.

137   "The Governor . . . practice." *NY Times*, 14 November 1947, p. 19.

137–38   "Dear Folks . . . McCarthy." Andersen & May, pp. 235–36.

138   Grain speculation. *NY Times*, 10 January 1948, pp. 1, 9; Smith, *Dewey*, p. 484.

138   Ten visits to state. Eaton, p. 413.

138   "Paul Revere Riders." Smith, *Dewey*, p. 485.

138   "I will probably . . . Stassen." *NY Times*, 8 April 1948, p. 24.

139   Dewey received none. *Chicago Tribune*, 9 April 1948, p. 2.

139   "Now we have . . . acquired." Eaton, p. 414.

139   Overall lead. *NY Times*, 8 April 1948, p. 18.

139   "Mr. Stassen . . . giant killer." *NY Times*, 8 April 1948, p. 24.

139   "should follow . . . Wisconsin." *Chicago Tribune*, 8 April 1948, p. 2. Minnesota congressman August Andreson said Stassen's victory in dairy-rich Wisconsin was "due to the fact that he recognized that oleo margarine has no place in the agricultural picture in America." *Nation*, 24 April 1948, p. 429.

139   "My statement . . . die." *NY Times*, 10 April 1948, p. 8.

139   McConnell. Ibid., 9 April 1948, p. 2; Ross, pp. 45–46.

140   "dramatic . . . carpetbaggers." *Washington Post*, 12 April 1948, p. 7; Abels, *Victory*, p. 51.

140   Critique of farm supports. *Council Bluffs Nonpareil*, 14 February 1948, p. 1.

140   Nebraska's final results. Eaton, p. 415.

140   April 25, 1948, George Gallup. *Washington Post*, 25 April 1948, p. B1.

140   New Jersey's GOP primary. *NY Times*, 2 May 1948, p. 38.

140   Pennsylvania write-in. *Washington Post*, 29 April 1948, p. 5.

140   Four years previously. *NY Times*, 29 April 1948, p. 22.

141   Ohio's battlefield. *New Republic*, 17 April 1948, p. 9; Paterson, p. 407.

141   "Your Next President . . . that." *Nation*, 8 May 1948, p. 494.

141   May 9, George Gallup. *La Crosse Tribune*, 9 May 1948, p. 1.

141   Stop-Stassen coalition. *Washington Post*, 7 April 1948, p. 7; *NY Times*, 18 April 1948, p. E3; *Nation*, 8 May 1948, p. 494.

141   "Although . . . friends." *Nation*, 8 May 1948, p. 498.

141   "win or else." Smith, *Dewey*, p. 489.

142   "some good . . . love." *NY Times*, 2 May 1948, p. 65.

142   Ninety-two speeches. *Life*, 31 May 1948, p. 33.

142   "Senator McCarthy . . . promises." *NY Times*, 21 May 1947, p. 16.

142    $250,000. Ross, p. 49.

142   2,465 miles. Ibid.

142   Dewey's campaign bus. *Waukesha Daily Freeman*, 17 May 1948, p. 2.

143   "one of . . . War III." *Joplin Globe*, 9 May 1948, p. 31.

143   "The Communist . . . freedom." *NY Times*, 3 April 1948, p. 13.

143 "DEWEY . . . STASSEN." Ibid., 2 May 1948, p. 1. Robert Taft similarly disagreed with Stassen: "it is somewhat doubtful whether we gain much by outlawing communism and driving the organization underground." *Joplin Globe*, 9 May 1948, p. 31. Harry Truman also stood in opposition.

143 "The proper . . . command." *NY Times*, 2 May 1948, p. 1.

143 "Staring . . . unequivocally." Karabell, p. 97.

143 "the little son of a bitch." *American Heritage*, February–March 1986, p. 68.

144 "With Stassen . . . do it!" Ibid.

144 "Governor, if . . . voters?" Ibid., p. 69.

144 Between forty and eighty million. Karabell, p. 105.

144 Mutual, NBC, and ABC. *Lowell Sun*, 18 May 1948, p. 1.

144–45 "It does not . . . necessary." Dewey, *Papers*, p. 624.

145 "my distinguished confrere." Ibid.

145 "In rebuttal . . . confidence." *American Heritage*, February–March 1986, p. 71.

145 "Now, if Governor . . . nation." Dewey, *Papers*, p. 630. Four days earlier the House had passed the Mundt-Nixon Bill, 319 to 58. White, *Cold War*, p. 58.

145 "Why is it . . . America." Dewey, *Papers*, p. 629.

145–46 "I gather . . . other." Ibid., p. 630. An earlier measure by California congressman Gordon McDonough would have made CPUSA membership akin to treason. A particularly slipshod bill introduced previously by Mississippi congressman John Rankin made teachers potentially liable to $10,000 in fines and ten years of imprisonment for merely conveying "the impression of sympathy with . . . Communist ideology." Parmet, p. 151.

146 "I am unalterably . . . believe in." Dewey, *Papers*, p. 627.

146 "Now, we have . . . States." Ibid., pp. 631–32; *Vital Speeches*, 1 June 1948, p. 489.

146 7,500-vote victory. Smith, *Dewey*, p. 494.

147 Twelve Oregon delegates. *NY Times*, 24 May 1948, p. 10.

147 "Dewey's substantial . . . himself." Lorant, p. 691.

147 "You can't make a soufflé rise twice." *NY Times*, 17 March 1971, p. 50.

CHAPTER 14

148 24 percent. *Washington Post*, 23 April 1947, p. 1; *American Heritage*, December 1976, p. 46.

148 13 percent. *Fortune*, February 1947, p. 5; *Fortune*, June 1948, p. 5; *Washington Post*, 12 July 1947, p. 5; *Benton Harbor News-Palladium*, 22 October 1948, p. 9; MacDougall, pp. 229, 291; White, *Cold War*, pp. 56–57. Fifty-seven percent of Democrats agreed with the proposition of Communist domination.

148 "lay the foundation . . . 1947." Dennis, pp. 37–38.

148 "the building . . . movement." *NY Times*, 19 September 1948, p. 3.

148 "the Wallace . . . war." Ibid., 15 January 1948, p. 15. Foster also took time to decry the anti-Wallace Eleanor Roosevelt as "one of the principal spokesmen of American imperialism."

149 "What will . . . growers?" Abt, p. 33; Culver & Hyde, p. 121.

149 "a symbol of the Communist influence." Kempton, p. 39. It is generally recorded that Pressman was "forced out" of the CIO because of his ties to Wallace, but John Abt has revealed that the CIO's Philip Murray provided Pressman with a $20,000 severance check upon his departure—"an enormous sum in those days." Abt, p. 148. Murray replaced Pressman with future Supreme Court justice Arthur J. Goldberg. Hamby, *Beyond*, pp. 216–17.

149 Pressman denied his membership. Abels, *Victory*, p. 117; Rabinowitz, p. 99.

149   Abt rarely bothered. Markowitz, pp. 96–97; Gall, pp. 37–38, 121, 192.

149   "I told him . . . counsel." Abt, p. 144; MacDougall, p. 279.

149   Charles Kramer. *Christian Science Monitor*, 12 August 1948, p. 1; *NY Times*, 13 August 1948, p. 3; *LA Times*, 29 August 1950, p. 14; Abt, p. 155; Romerstein & Breindel, pp. 160, 162–64; Weinstein & Vassiliev, pp. 232–35; Latham, p. 107; Trahair, p. 259; Romerstein, p. 16.

149   Carl Marzani. *Washington Post*, 8 October 1948, p. C8; Marzani, p. 252; Cannistraro & Meyer, p. 217. The OSS was the forerunner of the CIA.

149   Arnold Johnson. Morgan, *Reds*, p. 308.

150   Martin Popper. Gall, p. 240; Rabinowitz, p. 171; O'Dwyer, p. 122.

150   American Labor Party. MacDougall, pp. 195–97; Rabinowitz, p. 69; Jackson, p. 29; Stedman & Stedman, pp. 117–20. In each year but one from 1937 through 1949, the ALP secured at least 11 percent of the New York City vote. In 1946, 252,313 city residents enrolled as ALP members. Mearnes, *1947*, p. 593; Saposs, p. 101.

150   "Beanie" Baldwin. *NY Times*, 11 June 1949, pp. 1, 6; Romerstein, pp. 11–15; Morgan, *Reds*, p. 309. Baldwin refused to state under oath in 1949 if he had ever held CPUSA membership.

150   "the chief . . . Wallace." Romerstein, pp. 11–12.

150   "Our efforts . . . something." Billingsley, p. 178. In 1944, FDR joked to Davidson, "Jo, have they called you a Communist yet?" Davidson, p. 342.

150   Entertainment industry support. MacDougall, pp. 151–52, 200; Billingsley, p. 178.

150   Celebrity ranks narrowed. MacDougall, pp. 201, 230; Walker, p. 173; Morgan, *Reds*, p. 307; Abt, p. 162; Dunaway, pp. 144–47.

150   Lillian Hellman enlisted. Rollyson, *Hellman*, p. 265; Newman, pp. 111–12, 120.

150   "If someone . . . would go." Newman, p. 111.

150   "I love . . . him." Mellen, p. 222.

150   "He'd be better . . . himself." Hellman, *Scoundrel Time*, p. 124.

150–51 "I'm very upset . . . Party?" Radosh & Radosh, *Hollywood*, pp. 180–81.

151   "He was naïve . . . baiter, too." Markowitz, p. 258.

151   "Wallace was . . . totalitarianism." Schlesinger, *Vital Center*, p. 115.

151   "Harry Truman . . . bitch." MacDougall, p. 82.

151   "If there . . . wailing." Ibid., p. 634.

151–52 "We are not . . . Comintern." Donaldson, p. 193.

152   "will appeal . . . souls." *Cumberland Evening Times*, 7 January 1948, p. 4.

152   Rockwell Kent. *Canandaigua Daily Messenger*, 27 March 1948, p. 1.

152   Evansville. *NY Times*, 7 April 1948, p. 18; MacDougall, pp. 362–63, 410. Wallace remained in his hotel until things quieted down.

152   George Parker. MacDougall, pp. 363–64, 400.

152   Protesters egged Wallace. *NY Times*, 29 April 1948, p. 5; MacDougall, pp. 366–67.

152   Indianapolis. *NY Times*, 20 April 1948, p. 24.

152   Madison Square Garden. Ibid., 14 May 1948, p. 28; MacDougall, pp. 370–71. The film was Twentieth Century-Fox's *The Iron Curtain* at the Roxy, which subsequently received a bomb threat. *NY Times*, 13 May 1948, p. 21.

152   Wallace petition signatories. MacDougall, pp. 444–45.

152   Robert W. New Jr. *NY Times*, 8 May 1948, p. 3; Fariello, p. 415; MacDougall, p. 407; Schmidt, p. 86; Horne, *Black and Red*, p. 87.

152   "At the trial . . . waterfront." MacDougall, p. 407.

153 "Help me! . . . arm." *NY Times*, 21 April 1948, p. 4.

153 "Those dirty . . . fight." Schlesinger, *Life*, p. 460.

153 "management, Communists, or a screwball." *NY Times*, 21 April 1948, pp. 4, 22; Reuther had earlier received two threatening letters, the writer of one upset because "even Communists have rights," the other angry over Reuther's efforts to integrate the American Bowling Congress.

153 "that many . . . despair." *NY Times*, 12 November 1946, p. 3.

153 Yet Pepper drew back. Pepper, p. 157.

153 "I have felt . . . particular." Schlesinger, *Life*, p. 412.

153 "the poorest . . . world." Lait & Mortimer, p. 102.

153 "His voting record is perfect." Luthin, p. 218.

154 Robert W. Kenny. *New Republic*, 19 January 1948, p. 11.

154 Rev. John Taylor. *Current Biography*, 1948, p. 628.

154 "I began . . . wrong." Gunther, pp. 108–09.

154 "We were so broke . . . cookies." *Washington Post*, 25 July 1948, p. S1.

154 "We have needlessly . . . Pacific." Taylor, p. 258.

155 "not a relief . . . grab." *NY Times*, 5 April 1947, p. 5.

155 "get rid of the militarists." *Current Biography*, 1948, p. 629.

155 "It isn't . . . Hitler." *Washington Post*, 13 May 1948, p. 2.

155 "rhetorically self-intoxicated." Allen & Shannon, p. 275.

155 "the least . . . Senate." *Current Biography*, 1948, p. 628.

155 "a third-rate . . . life." Goulden, *Mencken*, p. 87.

155 "Taylor's . . . charm." Gunther, p. 111.

155 His first speech. Gunther, p. 111. Among Taylor's first actions was a move to bar Mississippi bigot Theodore Bilbo from the body. It stole Republican thunder on that front.

155 "pleaded . . . wept." Taylor, p. 339.

156 Shabby firing of Landis. *Cumberland Evening Times*, 10 March 1948, p. 4; MacDougall, p. 308.

156 "What's this . . . nut?" Taylor, p. 338.

156 "All the Russians . . . is force." Ibid.

156 "He repeated . . . parrot." Ibid.

156 "This is the most . . . ignorance." *Chicago Tribune*, 24 February 1948, p. 12.

156 "I am not . . . over." *NY Times*, 24 February 1948, p. 15.

156 SNYC. Nunnelley, p. 32; Klehr, p. 275. Previous attendees of SNYC conferences included the Rev. Martin Luther King Sr. and W.E.B. Du Bois. Author Nina Mjagkij notes that "The 1948 meeting proved to be the 'last hurrah' for the SNYC," presumably because of its subversive designation. Mjagkij, pp. 635–36; *Phylon Quarterly*, First Quarter 1987, pp. 38–50.

156 "There's not . . . Commies." *NY Times*, 2 May 1948, p. 37.

156 "really a huge . . . pound." Taylor, p. 344.

156 "This is the colored . . . side." *NY Times*, 2 May 1948, p. 37; Taylor, p. 344. Taylor contended that Casey had said, "I'm sorry, buddy, but this door is for niggers. The door for white folks is around there."

156 "I'll go in here anyway." *NY Times*, 2 May 1948, p. 37.

157 Taken to the local jail. Ibid.; MacDougall, pp. 390–91. Taylor's autobiography provides a lengthy version of events at some variance with press accounts, even providing the wrong date (April 13 instead of May). He also incorrectly contends he addressed the Senate regarding the incident on the following day—which would have been a Sunday. Taylor, pp. 341–56.

157 "It was obvious . . . something." *NY Times*, 4 May 1948, p. 5. Connor denied all, saying the

most direct route was taken. "The only talk I know about," said Connor, "was that [Patrolman James] Hale told Mr. Taylor to throw away his cigar because it made him sick."

157 "not sure . . . States Senator." Taylor, p. 355.

157 "I expected . . . mouth." Ibid. Liberal Alabama senator John Sparkman praised Connor and derided Taylor as having traveled to Birmingham "in order to get the publicity out of it." Frederickson, p. 92.

157 Taylor was convicted. *Anniston Star*, 5 May 1948, p. 1.

157 "Please accept . . . color." *Nation*, 15 May 1948, p. 560.

CHAPTER 15

158 "I studied . . . years!" Karnow, p. 275.

158 "the best clerk I ever had." Neal, *Ike*, p. 209.

159 Harry Truman's fellow boarder. Ferrell, *Presidency*, p. 34. Another of Ike's six brothers, Milton, served as an aide in Henry Wallace's Agriculture Department. Neal, *Ike*, p. 109.

159 Truman's recommendation. Eisenhower, *Mrs. Ike*, p. 212.

159 Capper. Ibid.

159 "Baloney! . . . orders?" *Life*, 19 July 1948, p. 30.

159 Cheer him in New York. *Washington Post*, 20 June 1945, p. 1.

159 "General. . . 1948." Keech & Matthews, p. 40.

159–60 "At 3:30 . . . quote him." *NY Times*, 11 July 2003, p. A14. In January 1955, Ike informed Frank Lausche that Truman had twice "personally asked me to run on the Democratic ticket. . . . I told him no both times." Neal, *Ike*, p. 111.

160 Royall. Phillips, p. 196.

160 "Was Truman . . . date?" Hamby, *People*, p. 437. Hamby once observed that "at that time his . . . public opinion polls [were] high. Perhaps he wanted to maneuver Eisenhower into an early refusal before a group of ambitious president-makers could surround the general." Hamby, *Beyond*, pp. 228–29.

160 "said I offered . . . was." Miller, *Plain*, pp. 338–39; Donaldson, p. 140.

160 Rosenman. Goulden, *Best*, p. 261.

160 Robert G. Nixon. Nixon Interview, Truman Library, 16 October 1970; Neal, *Ike*, p. 106.

161 58 percent were unsure. *Washington Post*, 27 August 1947, p. 1.

161 55 to 45 percent. Ibid., 4 January 1948, p. B1. At St. Paul on September 1, 1947, Ike had commented, "I am neither a Republican nor a Democrat. I have not ambition of any kind which lies along the lines of politics." *NY Times*, 24 January 1948, p. 2.

161 40 to 47 percent. *Washington Post*, 21 January 1948, pp. 1, 8.

161 "He gave . . . heard." Smith, *Dewey*, p. 481.

161 "He is obviously . . . apparent." Forrestal, p. 326.

161 "every sound and cogent reason." Smith, *Dewey*, p. 482.

161 "We had . . . hatches." Ibid., p. 483.

161 "Not only . . . loyalty." Eisenhower, *Papers*, p. 1986.

162 "Wallace's third . . . them." McCann, p. 111.

162 "some shelter . . . friends." Eisenhower, *Papers*, p. 1890.

162 "I do not . . . commander." Ibid., p. 1933.

162 Lichtenwalter. *Washington Post*, 10 December 1947, pp. 1, 6; *Life*, 29 December 1947, p. 20; Vandenberg, p. 423. Lichtenwalter was elected in a September 1947 special election.

163 "General . . . government." *Lowell Sun*, 10 December 1947, p. 1.

163 "Political . . . true." *Washington Post*, 10 December, 1947, p. 6.

163 "I would advise . . . story." Vandenberg, pp. 423–24.

163 "There is only . . . general." *Lowell Sun*, 10 December 1947, p. 1.

163 "get into that." Ibid.

163 "On such . . . spiral." Neal, *Ike*, p. 114.

164 Jack Warner. *NY Times*, 20 December 1947, p. 20.

164 "I Like Ike" buttons. Ibid., 9 October 1947, p. 3.

164 "My partner . . . interference." *New Yorker*, 8 May 1948, p. 26.

164 "While we . . . convention." *Brooklyn Daily Eagle*, 23 January 1948, pp. 1–2.

164 "The tossing . . . votes." Ferrell, *Eisenhower Diaries*, p. 147. In mid-October 1947, Eisenhower had traveled to New Hampshire to deliver a speech, spending the night at Finder's home. Accordingly, he felt a special obligation to publicly answer the Manchester publisher.

164 Fort Myer, Virginia. *Life*, 12 April 1948, p. 49.

164–65 "[R]emarked . . . himself." Forrestal, pp. 465–66.

165 "my failure . . . office." *NY Times*, 24 January 1948, pp. 1–2; *Chicago Tribune*, 24 January 1948, pp. 1, 7; *Life*, 19 July 1948, p. 30. "That's grand," joyously exclaimed Senator Joe McCarthy, campaigning for Stassen in New Hampshire, upon hearing of Ike's demurral.

165–66 "Several . . . stand.'" Eisenhower, *Papers*, p. 2197.

166 "If General . . . Washington." Gabler, p. 380.

166 Twelve million responses. Goulden, *Best*, p. 360; Gabler, p. 380.

166 Tossed his support to Dewey. *NY Times*, 4 February 1948, p. 3.

166 "I believe . . . won." *Long Beach Independent*, 27 March 1948, p. 1. Elliott had earlier flirted with Wallace. "An agreeable fellow," noted Arthur Schlesinger of Elliott, "not too bright or quick, who wanted very much for people to like him"—which was far more than Schlesinger thought of Elliott's brother James ("a charmer, but shallow, opportunistic and unprincipled"). Schlesinger, *Life*, p. 436. Forrestal caught wind. Forrestal, pp. 404–05.

166 "brings things . . . South." *Hartford Courant*, 27 March 1948, p. 2.

166 Eleanor Roosevelt declined. *Long Beach Independent*, 27 March 1948, p. 1.

166–67 "There is without . . . activities." Hechler, pp. 64–65.

167 "Here was . . . party." Clifford Interview, Truman Library, Washington, D.C., May 10, 1971. 329,235 votes. Mearns, *1948*, p. 662.

167 "a candidate . . . time." *NY Times*, 30 March 1948, p. 18.

167 Pointedly failed to endorse. *Lowell Sun*, 6 May 1948, p. 13. Met in Pittsburgh and endorsed. Ibid.; Hamby, *Beyond*, p. 226.

167 "We are sunk . . . rule." Goulden, *Best*, pp. 361–62.

168 "Eisenhower . . . ticket." Loeb Interview, Truman Library, 26 June 1970. Such speculation was not merely private in 1948. In April 1948, columnist Marquis Childs recorded, "Should the Republicans nominate Harold Stassen, . . . Vandenberg or . . . Dewey, the general would not feel any compulsion to run. He could then follow his inclination . . . to stay [at] Columbia University and keep out of politics." *Washington Post*, 10 April 1948, p. 9.

168 "the kind . . . locally." *NY Times*, 4 April 1948, p. E6.

168 "AS A CANDIDATE . . . QUIT." *New Republic*, 5 April 1948, p. 1.

168 Hollander. *NY Times*, 28 March 1948, p. E1.

168 "The Eisenhower thing . . . organization." Loeb Interview, Truman Library, 26 June 1970. The first favorable mention of an Eisenhower candidacy by a high-ranking public labor figure occurred in December 1946, when Morris S. Potofsky, president of the Amalgamated Clothing Workers of America

(John Abt's union) plumped for either Ike, Henry Wallace, Claude Pepper, or liberal Georgia governor Ellis Arnall as desirable progressive alternatives to HST. *NY Times*, 15 December 1946, p. 53.

168–69 "You have . . . spontaneously." *Connellsville Daily Courier*, 29 March 1948, p. 6.

169 Lister Hill and John Sparkman. *Washington Post*, 20 March 1948, pp. 1, 4.

169 "There cannot . . . nominee." *NY Times*, 28 March 1948, p. E1.

169 "be happy . . . either." Ibid., 20 March 1948, p. 11.

169 "Unalterably . . . program." *Dothan Eagle*, 17 July 1948, p. 1.

169 "speculation . . . nomination." *NY Times*, 28 March 1948, p. E1.

169 "the Democrats . . . on it." Neal, *Ike*, p. 126.

169 Eleanor for vice president. According to James Roosevelt, she refused "because she was afraid of it." (Neal, *Eleanor*, p. 119.) In any case, her reply to North Dakota Democrats appears by today's lights distinctly unprogressive and un-Eleanor: "Nothing could induce me to run for any public office. I seriously doubt any woman could be nominated, but in that eventuality, I could not even permit my name to be entered." *Joplin Globe*, 13 June 1947, p. 2

169 Whispers of her assuming the presidency. Neal, *Eleanor*, p. 137.

169 Elliott predicted. *New Yorker*, 8 May 1948, p. 26.

170 "sticking with Mr. Truman." *Long Beach Independent*, 27 March 1948, p. 1.

170 Jackson Day. Hamby, *Beyond*, p. 226.

170 He abruptly resigned. *Auburn Citizen-Advertiser*, 11 March 1946, p. 1. Harold Ickes enlisted as ICCASP executive chairman (also at $25,000) in March 1946. He angrily resigned that November.

170 "Your father . . . Good day." Donovan, pp. 400–01. This version of Truman's comments comes from Secret Service agent Henry Nicholson. Truman later provided Jonathan Daniels with an even more vigorous "[I] told him that he ought to have his head punched" version, but as Truman's accounts of his conversations often provide a tad more drama than originally transpired, it is perhaps wiser to rely on Nicholson's account.

170 "No smoke." *New Republic*, 28 June 1948, p. 10.

CHAPTER 16

171 Gold standard. Mooney, p. 44.

171 "Martin, Barton, and Fish." *NY Times*, 7 March 1968, p. 43. The other two being New York congressmen Bruce Barton and Hamilton Fish.

171 Never attended church. Kenneally, pp. 3–4, 37–38, 154. Nonetheless, persistent reports of Martin being Catholic only further damaged his long-shot presidential ambitions.

171 "a friend . . . heart." Mooney, p. 44.

172 "a great . . . kind." Kenneally, p. 152.

172 "We are not . . . wonderful." *NY Times*, 7 March 1968, p. 43.

172 Like a presidential campaign. *Reno Gazette*, 20 August 1947, p. 1; *Life*, 1 September 1947, p. 34; Kenneally, pp. 152–53.

172 "was insistent . . . about." Eaton, p. 419.

172 Saltonstall. Kenneally, p. 155. The cagy Martin may not have wanted to appear too strong on the first ballot.

172 Vice-presidential possibility. *NY Times*, 20 June, 1948, p. E5.

172 Lodge. Ibid., 22 June, 1948, p. 1.

172 "by long . . . stature." *LA Times*, 26 June, 1948, p. 4.

172 "I was a . . . state." White, *Warren*, p. 131.

172   1912. Katcher, p. 42; Ibid., p. 132.

173   Death by bludgeoning. *Life*, 10 May 1948, p. 144; Stone, *Warren*, p. 103. The crime remains unsolved.

173   Mormon-turned-atheist. Mathews, p. 402. Olson ran with CPUSA support in 1938, even conferring with party functionaries in his home. He broke with them by 1940 and signed a bill outlawing the party. It was alleged that Olson's lieutenant governor, Ellis E. Patterson, was a covert CPUSA member. Saposs, pp. 47–48, 51–52.

173   "political eunuch . . . governor." Pollack, *Warren*, p. 78.

173   "Leadership, not politics." Cray, *Warren*, p. 128; Pollack, *Warren*, p. 82.

173   Carrillo. Stone, *Warren*, pp. 116–17; Cray, *Warren*, p. 128.

173   "is the slickest . . . met." Pollack, *Warren*, p. 83.

173   "Warren has . . . radical." *Cumberland Evening Times*, 9 September 1948, p. 4.

173   "Warren's dominant . . . distinction." Gunther, pp. 20–21.

173   "socialized medicine." *Life*, 10 May 1948, pp. 148, 150; Stone, *Warren*, pp. 142–44; White, *Warren*, pp. 107–12; Warren, *Memoirs*, p. 187.

173   Nisei population. Cray, *Warren*, p. 51. Early in his career, Warren had enjoyed membership in the anti-Oriental Native Sons of the Golden West.

173   "there's no such . . . ourselves." Katcher, p. 146.

173–74   "Earl Warren embodied . . . values." Starr, p. 242.

174   Warren keynoted. *NY Times*, 26 June 1948, p. 1.

174   "I wouldn't . . . money." Stone, *Warren*, p. 150.

174   Delegate breakthroughs. *LA Times*, 25 June 1948, p. 2.

174   *U.S. News & World Report. NY Times*, 16 June 1948, p. 3.

174   "unselfish . . . demand." *NY Times*, 20 June 1948, p. 1.

175   "I wouldn't . . . doing." Ibid., *Washington Post*, 20 June 1948, p. M1.

175   Averred to Marquis Childs. *NY Post*, 14 June 1948, p. 33.

175   "Several pamphlets . . . line." *NY Times*, 24 June 1948, p. 5. What these pamphlets alleged is lost to history (at least to this history), but Richard Rovere once noted that the previously "bone dry" Prohibitionist Vandenberg had "become a conspicuous friend of the highball and a busy and quite charming ladies' man." Walter Trohan noted that the senator's philandering had been the subject of Office of Naval Intelligence and British intelligence reports. Beyond that, Vanderberg's bachelor son, Arthur Jr., was a reputed homosexual—and was ultimately forced out of the Eisenhower administration as a result. Rovere, p. 186; Trohan, pp. 141–42; Beschloss, *Glory*, pp. 98–99.

175   Stassen reduced to predicting. *NY Times*, 20 June 1948, p. E3.

175   "I have never . . . now." *Washington Post*, 21 June 1948, p. 1.

175   MacArthur to Wainwright. *NY Times*, 20 June 1948, p. E3.

175   "It may . . . ballot." *Washington Post*, 21 June 1948, p. 7.

175   "make . . . smoke-filled room." Ibid., p. 1.

175   "Do you mean . . . make a deal?" Ibid.

175   "usually reserved for weddings." *LA Times*, 21 June 1948, p. 2.

"working headquarters." *NY Times*, 15 June 1948, pp. 1, 6. Warren and Vandenberg stayed at the Warwick; Martin at the Bellevue-Stratford.

175   Stassen's Bellevue-Stratford digs. *NY Times*, 20 June 1948, p. 3; *Chicago Tribune*, 21 June 1948, p. 3.

175   Cheese mistakenly delivered. *NY Times*, 20 June 1948, p. 3.

176   "Cheese at Stassen's very good." *New Yorker*, 3 July 1948, p. 16.

176   "We thought . . . barflies." *Chicago Tribune*, 21 June 1948, p. 3.

176 Elaborate giveaways. *NY Times*, 20 June 1948, p. 20; *LA Times*, 20 June 1948, p. 1; *NY Times*, 22 June 1948, p. 8; Dewey. *Smith*, p. 495.

176 "It's such outrageous sport, really." *NY Times*, 22 June 1948, p. 8.

176 Warren's ill-fated Bellevue-Stratford suite. *Fresno Bee*, 23 June 1948, p. 12.

176 Largest campaign buttons. *Chicago Tribune*, 21 June 1948, p. 3.

176 *This Week in Philadelphia*. *NY Times*, 19 June 1948, p. 7.

176 Actual elephant. Ibid., 20 June 1948, p. 3.

176 "Renounce . . . Truth." Patterson, p. 410.

176 Organ music and television sets. *LA Times*, 20 June 1948, p. 1. With the Benjamin Franklin Hotel's Crystal Ballroom, Taft made available to delegates a set with a 6-by-9-foot screen. (http://www.lunacommons.org/luna/servlet/view/all/what/Taft,+Robert+A./when/1948/)

176 "Taft Victory Song." *Chicago Tribune*, 20 June 1948, p. 5.

177 350-pound campaign manager. *Life*, 21 June 1948, p. 32.

177 158 miles. *Washington Post*, 21 June 1948, p. 7.

177 "Shake his trunk." Ibid.

177 "The elephant was . . . prophetic." *LA Times*, 21 June 1948, p. 4.

178 "There is more . . . action." Patterson, p. 410.

178 "All bla-a-ah." *Frederick News-Post*, 22 June 1948, p. 7.

178 "Shortly . . . 1908." Manchester, *Mencken*, p. 307.

178 "tight . . . thighs." *Billboard*, 3 July 1949, p. 4.

178 "[w]as escorted . . . Harrisburg." *New Yorker*, 3 July 1948, pp. 16–17. The *New Yorker* correspondent also recorded, "Met a senator, and a senator's dog. Very nice dog."

178 In April 1939, NBC inaugurated. *McKean County Democrat*, 4 May 1939, p. 2; Von Schilling, pp. 7–8; Jamieson, p. 34. FDR owned a set at Hyde Park.

178 In 1940, viewers witnessed. *NY Times*, 22 June 1940, p. 10; *Billboard*, 15 January 1949, p. 12; Kraus, p. 35.

179 Stratovision. *Billboard*, 3 July 1948, pp. 1, 12.

179 Commercial television broadcasting. *Washington Post*, 23 June 1948, p. 6; Kraus, pp. 38–39.

179 Two shows. *NY Times*, 20 June 1948, p. X8; *NY Times*, 19 September 1948, p. X11; Trager, p. 566.

179 Tele-Tone model. *New Republic*, 7 June 1948, p. 17.

179 $51.89 per week. Kieran, pp. 335, 337.

179 Thirty-seven stations. *NY Times*, 30 June 1948, p. E5.

179 Philadelphia seemed inundated. *Billboard*, 3 July 1948, p. 5.

179 "Thanks to TV . . . happened." *Time*, 5 July 1948, p. 34. Radio still greatly outdistanced TV. CBS radio, for example, estimated it had sixty-two million listeners for the convention. *Billboard*, 3 July 1949, pp. 1, 6.

179 *Camel Newsreel Theatre*. *Billboard*, 13 November 1948, p. 15.

179 Coverage with NBC. *NY Times*, 29 June 1948, p. 16; *Life*, 21 June 1948, p. 31.

179 At CBS. Murray, pp. 49, 68.

180 "I hate . . . newspapers." Rodgers, p. 518.

180 Nearly as many networks. Von Schilling, p. 104.

180 The old newsreel cameras. Goulden, *Mencken*, pp. 32–33.

180 10,000-watt bulbs. *Washington Post*, 20 June 1948, p. M8.

180 "In a few . . . bottle." *Time*, 5 July 1948, p. 34.

180 115-degree heat. *Billboard*, 3 July 1949, p. 6.

180 "keep your clothes neat." *NY Times*, 27 June 1948, p. E8.

180 Ultraviolet sunlamps. Ibid.

180 "I look just awful." *NY Times*, 12 July 1948, p. 3.

180 "No politician . . . generation." Ibid.

CHAPTER 17

181 "bosses, boodle . . . Europe." *NY Times*, 22 June 1948, pp. 10, 24.

181 For a full five minutes. Ibid., p. 12.

181 Dewey's "Chicago edition." *Time*, 17 April 1939, p. 20.

181 In 1940, McCormick. Smith, *Colonel*, pp. 380–81.

181 Flirted with MacArthur. Eaton, p. 412.

182 "I am for . . . reasons." *NY Times*, 27 June 1948, p. E1.

182 Dewey supporter in 1944. Smith, *Colonel*, p. 444.

182 "I was convinced . . . delegation." Brownell, p. 78.

182 237,000-vote victory margin. *NY Times*, 21 February 1958, p. 23.

182 Stassen and Brooks. *Washington Post*, 22 June 1948, p. 11.

182 "wholly . . . proud of it." *Washington Post*, 21 October 1948, p. B15.

183 "What in the . . . up to?" Trohan, p. 233.

183 "Green's chances . . . quickly." Brownell, p. 79.

183 "a sight . . . flatties." Swanberg, *Luce*, p. 269.

183 "a brilliantly vicious speech." Eaton, p. 400.

183 "the unheroic . . . war." Ibid.

183 "launched . . . hers." *NY Times*, 22 June 1948, p. 3. *New York Journal-American* columnist Bob Considine, however, argued that she "wore the wrong kind of outfit and war paint and showed up on the [television] screen looking like a stand-in for the ghostly Leonora Corbett in *Blithe Spirit*." Shadegg, p. 221.

183 "Democratic Presidents . . . abroad." Lorant, p. 697.

183 "Let us . . . goose." *NY Times*, 22 June 1948, p. 5. Luce was, in fact, echoing Klan Grand Dragon Samuel Green, who in March had labeled Truman a "gone goslin." *Washington Post*, 5 March 1948, p. 7.

184 "Reporters . . . Michigan." *Hagerstown Daily Mail*, 29 June 1949, p. 8.

184 "Vandenberg . . . limp hand." Allen & Shannon, p. 252.

184 "Probably . . . sincere." Vandenberg, p. 442.

184 "It was said, . . . time." White, *Taft*, p. 119.

184 Credentials committee. *LA Times*, 19 June 1940, p. 1, *NY Times*, 27 June 1940, p. E1.

184 Taft- and Stassen-controlled states. Patterson, p. 411.

185 "Don't worry . . . chairman." *Chillicothe Constitution-Tribune*, 23 June 1948, p. 6.

185 Federal judgeships. Abels, *Victory*, p. 63.

185 Perry Howard. *Nevada State Journal*, 16 June 1948, p. 4. Since 1928, a "lily white" faction had been unsuccessfully challenging the "black and tans," who had controlled the state party since 1874.

185 Defecting Mississippi delegate. Abels, *Victory*, p. 63. The "lily whites"—the Independent Republican Party of Mississippi—sued for recognition, contending Perry Howard's group existed "to cater to and inveigle the votes of the colored race throughout the United States." *NY Times*, 20 June 1948, p. 5.

185 "Well, . . . all of us is for sale." Lodge, p. 76*fn*.

185 "If I was . . . attention." Reinhard, p. 45.

185 "one of . . . life." Smith, *Dewey*, p. 496.

185 Jay Cooke IV. Eaton, p. 416.

185 1912 election. *Current Biography*, 1948, p. 164.

185 "a strapping . . . evangelist." *Time*, 8 March 1948, p. 23.

186   Duff despised Dewey. Brownell, p. 77.

186   Favored Eisenhower. *Time*, 8 March 1948, p. 24.

186   Pro-Vandenberg Henry Luce. Swanberg, *Luce*, p. 269. Coincidentally, Duff graced *Time*'s June 21 cover.

186   He backed Vandenberg. *NY Times*, 27 June 1948, p. E1.

186   Pronounced Taft a "socialist." Eaton, p. 420.

186   An early-1948 attempt. Reinhard, p. 45.

186   Threw his support to Taft. Ibid.

186   Clare Boothe Luce. Swanberg, *Luce*, p. 269.

186   Ed Martin as a favorite son. *NY Times*, 27 June 1948, p. E1.

186   "a story that big." *NY Times*, 23 June 1948, p. 13.

186   Ed Martin stunned everyone. Ibid., p. 1.

186   "There has been . . . clear?" Ibid., p. 13.

186   "Grundy-Dewey." Ibid., p. 3; *Washington Post*, 23 June 1948, p. 1.

186   "a desperate . . . weakness." *NY Times*, 23 June 1948, p. 3.

186–87 "must now . . . all." *Washington Post*, 23 June 1948, p. 1.

187   "a great break." Ibid.

187   "a deal in a smoke-filled room." Ibid.

187   "the force . . . bomb." *NY Times*, 23 June 1948, p. 3.

187   "Two Cadillac Charlie." Abel, p. 500.

187   Considered a Dewey man. Allen & Shannon, pp. 190–91.

187   "a familiar . . . aleck." Coffin, p. 78.

187   "one of . . . Washington." Allen & Shannon, p. 190.

187   "Charlie . . . be all." Abels, *Victory*, p. 65.

187   Stuck in the elevator. *Life*, 5 July 1948, p. 24.

187   Taft bluntly suggested. *NY Times*, 24 June 1948, p. 2.

187   "give Illinois to Dewey." *Harper's*, October 1948, p. 42.

187   At 2:00 AM, all departed. *NY Times*, 23 June 1948, p. 1.

187–88 "Neither . . . did." Patterson, p. 412.

188   Conferred twice more. *NY Times*, 24 June 1948, pp. 1–2.

188   "to be . . . at all." Ibid.

188   "There is no . . . one." *Oakland Tribune*, 24 June 1948, p. 2.

188   Dwight Green committed. *NY Times*, 24 June 1948, p. 8.

188   Governors Driscoll and Bradford. Ibid., pp. 4, 7.

188   "He is too socialistic." *Hagerstown Daily Mail*, 29 June 1949, p. 8.

188   Burger. *NY Times*, 25 June 1948, p. 4.

188   "I am particularly . . . stands." *El Paso Herald-Post*, 16 June 1948, p. 8.

188   "The stage . . . Republicans." *Hartford Courant*, 21 June 1948, p. 7.

189   Dulles. *Journal of American History*, June 1972, pp. 100–01.

189   Mushily worded plank. Ibid.

189   "within . . . welfare." *Washington Post*, 23 June 1948, p. 4.

189   "*My* platform . . . consolations." Vandenberg, p. 429.

189   Adopted it without opposition. *NY Times*, 27 June 1948, p. E1.

189   "towers above all others." *Washington Post*, 25 June 1948, p. A4.

189   "We have . . . places." Smith, *Dewey*, p. 498.

189   "calm, logical and judicial." *NY Times*, 24 June 1948, pp. 1, 4. Warren had unsuccessfully tried to convince Sproul to run for governor in 1942. *LA Times*, 25 June 1948, p. 7.

189 "on the sucker . . . unwary." *San Mateo Times*, 24 June 1948, p. 2.

190 "that of . . . Robert E. Lee." *Oakland Tribune*, 24 June 1948, p. 16.

190 Twenty-two-minute floor demonstration. *Fresno Bee*, 23 June 1948, p. 12.

190 "the millions . . . November." *LA Times*, 24 June 1948, p. 2.

190 "unprecedented . . . matched." *NY Times*, 24 June 1948, p. 7.

190 Remaining nominations. *NY Times*, 24 June 1948, pp. 1, 4.

190 "It was the only . . . call." Brownell, p. 77.

190 Joe McCarthy and Tom Coleman. *Washington Post*, 23 June 1948, p. 11.

190 Monitored events via television. *NY Times*, 25 June 1948, p. 3; Patterson, p. 414.

191 "I decided . . . convention?" Brownell, p. 77.

191 First-ballot tally. *NY Times*, 25 June 1948, p. 2; Eaton, p. 422; Patterson, p. 413.

191–92 Second-ballot tally. Ibid.

192 Brownell decided against. Ibid., pp. 2, 22.

192 "The New York . . . recess." Ibid., p. 2.

192 Vandenberg wasn't interested. Vandenberg, pp. 437–38.

192 Tried phoning Dwight Eisenhower. Eaton, p. 423.

192 "I believe the General . . . *anybody*." Vandenberg, p. 434.

192–93 "Harold . . . Republican Party." *Hagerstown Daily Mail*, 29 June 1948, p. 8.

193 Earl Warren's sixteenth-floor suite. Cray, *Warren*, p. 187.

193 "I think . . . wrong." Patterson, p. 414.

193 "I don't know . . . know." Ibid.

193 Warren released. *NY Times*, 25 June 1948, p. 3.

193 "I have a statement . . . enthusiasm." Ibid.

193 "I saw [Joe McCarthy] . . . Dewey." http://thenewnixon.org/2008/09/02/minncsotas-boy-wonder-was-rns-pick-for-potus/

193 Thunderstorms. *LA Times*, 25 June 1948, p. 4.

193 "It might . . . Vandenberg." *NY Times*, 25 June 1948, p. 3.

CHAPTER 18

194 "I guess I'd better put on my hat." *LA Times*, 23 June 1948, p. A4.

194 Dent tradition. *LA Times*, 25 June 1948, p. 3.

194 Rainbow filled. Ibid., p. 6; *Washington Post*, 26 June 1948, p. 3.

194 "promised . . . shifts." *Chicago Tribune*, 26 June 1948, p. 2.

194 "I am happy . . . country." *NY Times*, 25 June 1948, p. 2. Presumably to increase his height, he delivered his address perched upon a box hidden behind the podium. *PBS, American Experience*.

194 "unimaginable . . . life." *LA Times*, 25 June 1948, p. 6.

195 "Dewey waved . . . television." Pollack, *Warren*, p. 112.

195 "The Next President." *LA Times*, 25 June 1948, p. A4.

195 "Isn't it great for Charlie!" Martin, p. 167.

196 Dewey's brain trust. *NY Times*, 25 June 1948, p. 4.

196 Dwight Green. Martin, p. 167.

196 "SURELY NOT MR. HALLECK!" *NY Times*, 25 June 1948, p. 22.

196 "Halleck won't do." Martin, pp. 167–68.

196–97 "I can work . . . sorry." Abels, *Victory*, pp. 66–67.

197 "I don't know . . . anything." Abels, *Victory*, pp. 67.

197   "Arrangements . . . accept." *Chicago Tribune*, 25 June 1948, p. 4.

197   "real hero." *LA Times*, 25 June 1948, p. 7.

197   "I don't . . . my minister." Ibid.

197   Thomas J. Herbert. *Marion Star*, 25 June 1948, p. 1.

197   "Tom's whole . . . isolationistic!" Patterson, p. 421; Reinhard, p. 48. Perhaps Dewey posited that his Michigan origins might suffice to entice midwestern votes, and a "second" midwesterner on the slate might prove superfluous.

197   Rumors swirled. *NY Times*, 25 June 1948, p. 4.

197   Lodge or Raymond Baldwin. Ibid.

197–98   Vandenberg, amenable to Warren. *Washington Post*, 26 June 1948, p. 1.

198   "a real draft." *NY Times*, 25 June 1948, pp. 1, 4.

198   "Dewey supporters . . . resented it." *LA Times*, 23 June 1948, p. A4.

198   Youngdahl and Alfred Driscoll. *NY Times*, 25 June 1948, p. 4.

198   "You'll sit . . . President." Katcher, p. 226.

198   Warren reminded Dewey. Katcher, p. 225. Warren had earlier complained publicly regarding similar financial considerations, in denying any interest in being Dewey's $15,000-a-year attorney general. *LA Times*, 25 June 1948, p. 2.

198   "a vain . . . time." Hobson, p. 499.

199   "If there are . . . little fool." *Cumberland Evening Times*, 18 August 1944, p. 4.

199   The California delegation. Katcher, p. 226.

199   "No man . . . President." Newton, p. 210.

199   "You could . . . job." Cray, *Warren*, p. 188.

199   "They put a gun to his head." Ibid., p. 189.

199   "I had to . . . again." Ibid., p. 189.

199   Warren phoned Dewey. Cray, *Warren*, p. 188; Smith, *Dewey*, p. 500.

199   "It is the unanimous . . . candidate." *Washington Post*, 26 June 1948, p. 1.

199   "I went to the Convention . . . finished." Vandenberg, p. 441.

200   Arizona delegates. *Washington Post*, 26 June 1948, p. 1.

200   "You're sticking . . . buzz saw." Smith, *Dewey*, p. 500.

200   The disconsolate Halleck. *Harper's*, September 1948, p. 29.

200   "For the first . . . that." *LA Times*, 26 June 1948, p. 2.

200   "Is that good?" Stone, *Warren*, p. 133.

CHAPTER 19

201   *Crusade in Europe*. Eisenhower, *Crusade*, passim; Childs, pp. 107–08; Ambrose, pp. 474–75. "up to General Eisenhower." *NY Times*, 2 July 1948, p. 1; http://www.trumanlibrary.org/publicpapers/index.php?pid=1696&st=&st1=.

201–02   Georgia and Virginia Democrats. *NY Times*, 3 July 1948, pp. 1, 6.

202   "to pick . . . States." *NY Times*, 4 July 1948, p. 14.

202   Tom Scully. *New Republic*, 28 June 1948, p. 10.

202   Their ranks included. *NY Times*, 4 July 1948, p. 14; Eaton, p. 427. O'Dwyer, however, did not favor Ike; he preferred Douglas. *NY Times*, 4 July 1948, p. 16. Historian Ralph Goldman indicates the idea for an Eisenhower draft actually emanated from Richard Russell, who was much surprised that liberals followed his lead. Goldman, *Party*, p. 423.

202–03   "No one knew . . . politically." Bowles, p. 173; Neal, *Ike*, pp. 129–30.

203   "I came . . . shaken." Neal, *Ike*, p. 130.

203   "All Republicans . . . storm." Ibid.

203   Hague jumped on board. *NY Times*, 5 July 1948, pp. 1, 26.

203   McCord. Eaton, p. 428.

203   "terribly concerned American citizen." *Salt Lake Tribune*, 5 July 1948, p. 3.

203   "respond to the call of duty." *NY Times*, 5 July 1948, p. 26.

203   "We are concerned . . . era." *Salt Lake Tribune*, 5 July 1948, p. 3.

203   John C. Stennis. *Greenville Delta Democrat-Times*, 5 July 1948, p. 2.

203   "Never have so few . . . many." *Cumberland Evening Times*, 27 July 1948, p. 4.

203   "Dwight would be . . . center." *NY Times*, 6 July 1948, p. 21. Brother Milton once described Earl as "a real left-winger." *Life*, 9 November 1942, p. 116.

203–04   "I am simply . . . want?" McCullough, p. 634.

204   "Met with Democratic . . . does." Ferrell, *Record*, p. 141.

204   "Mr. Bohlen . . . year." Lash, p. 148.

204   "I will not . . . office." *NY Times*, 6 July 1948, p. 1. Assisting Eisenhower in drafting his July 5 statement was his close friend, former DNC treasurer and secretary George E. Allen. Contemporary news reports and historians Cabell Phillips and Steve Neal contend that Allen was sent by Truman "on a do-or-die assignment" to pry a definitive denial from Ike. Allen countered that was "wrong, completely wrong." Allen Interview, HST Library, 15 May 1969.

204   "hotter than hell." Ferrell, *Record*, p. 141.

204   "the president . . . ass." Ayers, p. 264.

204–05   "In view of . . . country." *NY Times*, 7 July 1948, p. 1.

205   "a national candidate." *Lowell Sun*, 7 July 1948, p. 5. Olin Johnston suggested an Ike–James Roosevelt ticket.

205   "The Democratic party's . . . crisis." Truman, *Presidency*, p. 7.

205   "Despite . . . crisis." *Jefferson City Daily Capital News*, 8 July 1948, p. 6.

205   Frank Hague publicly urged. Ibid.

205   Biffle flooded the galleries. Ibid. Like Harry S. Truman's S, Biffle's middle initial stood for nothing. Allen & Shannon, p. 238.

205   "I agree . . . happening?" Krock, p. 243.

205   "Under no . . . nomination." *NY Times*, 10 July 1948, p. 1. Royall had assured Ike that he would not need to release the document himself: "Five minutes after Pepper receives it, it will be public property." Krock, p. 244.

205   "Truman, . . . my God." McCullough, p. 635.

CHAPTER 20

206   "actively seek . . . 1948." *NY Times*, 5 July 1948, p. 26.

206   Joining him. Ibid.; Hamby, *Beyond*, p. 243.

207   "[I]t is inconceivable . . . condition." *NY Times*, 7 July 1948, p. 1. Johnston announced. Ibid. Johnston never did dare offer his resolution. *Washington Post*, 11 July 1948, p. M1.

207   After considering a partnership. Douglas, *Go East*, pp. 152–53.

207   "'risqué' stories." Ibid., p. 333.

207   "played . . . poker." Allen, p. 127. Douglas shared something else with FDR—polio, which he contracted at age four, recovering through intense exercise. Kirkendall, p. 99; Allen & Shannon, pp. 377–78.

207   "one of the most . . . produced." *Washington Post*, 11 July 1948, p. 8.

208   Douglas's drinking. Walch, pp. 66–67.

208   "had no visible . . . Ickes." Allen, p. 128.

208   "Bill . . . gone." Janeway, pp. 60–61. This conversation was among those J. Edgar Hoover wiretapped for Truman.

208   "I had about . . . on." Janeway, p. 61.

208   "an awfully curious fellow." Ibid.

208   "had lived . . . do anything." Ibid.

208   "had his chance . . . Court." Ibid.

209   "I had two . . . other." Murphy, p. 212.

209   Humphrey stood ready. Hamby, *Beyond*, p. 242.

209   Reuther and Rauh. *NY Times*, 6 July 1948, p. 21.

209   Michael Straight. *Washington Post*, 10 July 1948, p. 9.

209   Rush-hour commuters. *NY Times*, 9 July 1948, p. 7.

209   "The Democratic Party . . . America." Truman, *Presidency*, p. 7.

209   Bill Douglas unwanted. *NY Times*, 6 July 1948, pp. 1, 21.

209   "I am not . . . a candidate." *NY Times*, 10 July 1948, p. 1.

209   "no time for politics as usual." Donovan, p. 404.

209   "no gesture but a fight." *Hartford Courant*, 12 July 1948, p. 10.

209   "We have already . . . roan?" Hamby, *Beyond*, p. 243.

209   Claude Pepper's Florida. *Hartford Courant*, 12 July 1948, p. 10.

210   "The almost ridiculous . . . funny." *Tucson Daily Citizen*, 13 July 1948, p. 8.

210   6:55 PM. *Washington Post*, 11 July 1948, p. 3.

210   "Tell those amateurs . . . re-nominated." Simon, p. 272; Janeway, p. 63.

210   "Order . . . ours." *NY Times*, 12 July 1948, p. 3.

210   "Four years . . . day." *Cumberland Evening Times*, 16 July 1948, p. 4.

210   Gallup's numbers. *Washington Post*, 4 June 1948, p. 10.

211   "What we must . . . affairs." *NY Times*, 8 July 1948, p. 1.

211   "We believe . . . rights." *Tucson Daily Citizen*, 24 February 1948, p. 9.

211   "The Democratic . . . come." *Mansfield News-Journal*, 11 July 1948, p. 14.

211   1.2 million signatures. *Chicago Defender*, 26 June 1948, p. 1.

212   "Republicans . . . pragmatism." Humphrey, p. 76.

212   "The Democratic party . . . rights." *NY Times*, 15 July 1948, p. 7.

212–13   "Lynching . . . States." Ibid., 23 June 1948. p. 6.

213   "The words . . . convention." Clifford, p. 118. "Although I had supported the President vigorously in his civil rights program," Clifford later said, "I felt that there was no need to mortify the South by pressing for an extreme civil rights plank at the convention." Clifford Interview, Truman Library, 26 July 1971.

213   "Few will . . . man." *Washington Post*, 6 November 1948, p. B13.

213–14   "How can we . . . level." Hamby, *People*, p. 446.

214   "The reelection . . . impossibility." Solberg, p. 124.

214   "Bill Simms . . . speeches." Ibid., p. 125.

214   Slightly drunken. Biemiller Interview, Truman Library, 29 July 1977; Solberg, p. 14.

214   1932. *NY Times*, 15 July 1948, p. 8.

214   "Practically . . . win." Solberg, p. 15.

214   "a vicious . . . civilization." Karabell, p. 52.

214–15   "I have never . . . intend to." Brown, p. 182.

215   "The Democratic . . . power." *NY Times*, 15 July 1948, p. 8.

215   States' rights plank failed. Ibid., pp. 1, 8.

215   "Who does this pipsqueak think he is?" Solberg, p. 14.

215   "Joe, you . . . years." Ibid., p. 16.

215   "Oh, Andy . . . platform." Biemiller Interview, Truman Library, 29 July 1977.

215   "This may tear . . . with it." Humphrey, p. 77.

216   "All right, I'll do it." Biemiller Interview, Truman Library, 29 July 1977.

216   "Look, here's what . . . your advice." Ibid.

216   "You kids . . . minorities." Ibid.

216   Biemiller made the actual motion. Brown, pp. 181–82.

217   "He knew he had to be shorter." Biemiller Interview, Truman Library, 29 July 1977.

217   "We are confronted . . . America!" *Washington Post*, 15 July 1948, p. 6. Though Humphrey read his address, his famous "bright sunshine of human rights" passage appears to have been entirely spontaneous.

218   "It was the President's . . . fighting." *Titusville Herald*, 17 July 1948, p. 8.

218   "I am Hubert . . . plank." Humphrey, p. 78.

218   "was willy-nilly . . . development." Biemiller Interview, Truman Library, 29 July 1977.

218   651.5 to 582.5. Brown, pp. 202–10.

218   "the Democratic . . . greatness." *Laredo Times*, 19 July 1948, p. 3.

218   $1,795 DuMont. *Washington Post*, 15 July 1947, p. 6.

218   "Platform fight . . . bolt." Ferrell, *Record*, p. 143. Further hints of Truman's actual views on the subject are found in this July 15 entry from James Forrestal's diary: "At [a] brief meeting with Secretary Royall and myself [HST] made the observation that he had not, himself, wanted to go as far as the Democratic platform went on the Civil Rights issue. He said he had no animus toward the delegates from the Southern states who had voted against the Civil Rights plank and against his nomination. 'I would have done the same thing myself if I were in their place and came from their states.'" He also informed Mobile, Alabama, congressman Frank W. Boykin: "Frank, I don't believe in this civil rights program any more than you do, but we've got to have it to win." Forrestal, p. 458.

218   "We're not going . . . fly." *Washington Post*, 15 July 1948, p. 1.

CHAPTER 21

219   "We got the wrong . . . hearses." *NY Times*, 12 July 1948, p. 3.

219   "The index . . . history." Ibid.

219   "You can almost . . . ago." *Tucson Daily Citizen*, 13 July 1948, p. 8.

220   The opening sessions. *Huntingdon Times*, 17 July 1948, p. 6. Van Heflin's older brother, Martin H. "Marty" Heflin, a former publicist for Oklahoma Democratic senator Elmer Thomas's Agriculture Committee, was among those recently accused of egg speculation. *Tucson Daily Citizen*, 13 August 1947, p. 6. India Edwards. *Bridgeport Telegram*, 14 July 1948, p. 57.

220   "Hey Lady! . . . a badge." Ibid.

220   "clown white." *NY Times*, 12 July 1948, p. 3.

220   "very much . . . journalism." *NY Times*, 18 July 1948, p. X7.

220   Né Willie Alben Barkley. Barkley, p. 27.

220   "not a tax . . . greedy." Morgan, *FDR*, p. 708.

221   "a calculated . . . Congress." Ibid.

221   Vice presidency since 1928. *Hartford Courant*, 30 June 1928, p. 4.

221   Like Jimmy Byrnes. Barkley, p. 189.

221   "not to say . . . complimentary." Ibid., p. 190.

221   "Alben, . . . was." Wyatt, p. 39.

221   Tearing up his prepared text. Farley, p. 367. Barkley denied ever being on the verge of ripping up the speech. Barkley, pp. 190–91.

221   Pat Harrison. McCullough, pp. 227–29.

221   "I have often . . . vote." Kirkendall, p. 22.

221   "Senator Barkley . . . Congress." *Cumberland Evening Times*, 22 October 1948, p. 4. In the wake of the Truman-Bacall piano flap, Barkley delivered an address, "Advice to Newly Elected Senators," warning that if any among them played the piano they would be wise to avoid employing any actresses to hold down its lid, as that "would hew their destinies to an end." Kirkendall, p. 22.

221   "He frequently . . . saint." Allen, p. 187.

222   "I am not . . . Washington." *NY Times*, 13 July 1948, p. 10.

222   "All Hail . . . Name." Ibid.

222   "A bureaucrat . . . wants." Brown, p. 42.

222–23   "Behold . . . Amen." Ibid., p. 47.

223   The band erupted. *Hartford Courant*, 13 July 1948, p. 1.

223   "One of the greatest . . . life." *Moberly Monitor-Index*, 13 July 1948, p. 2.

223   "Barkley for Vice President." *Hartford Courant*, 13 July 1948, p. 1.

223   "This was the last . . . acclamation." *Cumberland Evening Times*, 22 October 1948, p. 4.

223   "It was no secret . . . Truman." Barkley, p. 201.

223   "I'd rather . . . President." Allen, p. 189.

224   Alabama would not yield. *Charleston Gazette*, 1 August 1948, p. 6.

224   Ben Laney. *Washington Post*, 14 July 1948, pp. 1, 2.

224   "I say to you . . . rights.'" Brown, p. 233.

224   "We do not wish . . . states." Ibid., p. 263.

224   Donnelly had collapsed. *NY Times*, 6 July 1948, p.19.

224–25   "a man of . . . destiny." Brown, p. 238.

225   "They say . . . stature." Ibid., p. 240.

225   McNutt. Ibid., pp. 247–48.

225   947.5 to 263. *NY Times*, 15 July 1948, p. 1. New York originally cast eighteen votes for Queens party leader James A. Roe—then thought better of it.

225   Rayburn never made that motion. Ibid., p. 3.

CHAPTER 22

226   He had other choices. *New Republic*, 28 June 1948, p. 10.

226   Tydings. Allen & Shannon, pp. 257–58.

226   "Mayor Humphrey . . . get it?" Solberg, p. 125.

227   "She [Eleanor] is . . . in politics." Lash, p. 149. Helen Gahagan Douglas reported a small VP boomlet for herself as well that year. Douglas, *Life*, pp. 273–74.

227   "We did it as burlesque . . . straight." Janeway, p. 64.

228   McGrath . . . Terrible." Donovan, p. 405. HST may have been referring to Elliott's spectacularly ill-fated 1939 effort, the Transcontinental Radio Network. *Tucson Daily Citizen*, 2 July 1945, p. 10; *St. Petersburg Times*, 27 August 1945, p. 2; Morgan, *FDR*, pp. 460–61.

228   "I feel . . . party." Lash, p. 150.

228   "probably . . . in." Douglas, *Court*, p. 289.

228 "talked . . . Court." Ibid., pp. 289–90. Clark Clifford, a close Douglas friend and an advocate of his for the vice-presidential nomination, writes that he believed Douglas's real motivation stemmed from fear of a November defeat. Clifford, p. 216.

228–29 "Douglas says . . . man." Truman, *Presidency*, p. 9.

229 "Call old . . . name." Ibid., p. 10.

230 "It was a good . . . President." Ibid.

230 "I called . . . sure." Ibid.

230 "The convention . . . for him." Barkley, p. 199.

230 Barkley distinctly mediocre. Hamby, *People*, p. 449.

230 "Talking . . . under me." Ayers, p. 265. Ayers's next paragraph reads: "The president in commenting on the Barkley talk, said you have to be cold-blooded about these things and added that now they can nominate Barkley and turn things over to him. He indicated he did not feel Barkley was the best candidate but that if the delegates wanted him, let them have him." Whether Truman meant Barkley as the presidential or vice-presidential candidate is thus unclear.

230 "Barkley, though . . . himself." Abels, *Victory*, p. 93.

230 "It will have . . . biscuit." *Wall Street Journal*, 13 July 1948, p. 4.

231 Never mentioned victory. Gullan, p. 98.

231 "If the ticket loses . . . you." *Cumberland Evening Times*, 22 October 1948, p. 4.

231 "Why didn't you . . . Alben?" Barkley, p. 202.

231 "It's now or never." Davis, *Stevenson*, p. 291.

231 Distant relatives. Ibid., p. 299.

231 "I am proud . . . kinsman." Brown, p. 286. Stevenson had prepared a five-minute address. Sam Rayburn warned him to keep it under a minute.

231–32 "the South . . . rights." *Portland Press Herald*, 15 July 1948, p. 19. Wallace was so impecunious, friends had to raise money for his hotel room and meals. He reached Philadelphia by providing gas money for a delegate driving there. Carter, p. 87.

232 Barkley by acclamation. Abels, *Victory*, p. 93; Wyatt, p. 55.

232 "If anybody . . . not one." Brown, p. 300; Williams, p. 229.

232 "Take the train . . . won't be." Truman, *Presidency*, p. 11.

232 "perhaps the strangest . . . witnessed." Clifford, p. 220.

233 "Have a pleasant . . . evening." Ferrell, *Record*, p. 143.

233 "Never . . . thought." Truman, *Presidency*, p. 11.

233 "a gastrointestinal upset." Clifford, p. 220.

233 Rosenman and Murphy. Murphy Interview, Truman Library, 21 May 1969; Schlesinger, *Ghosts*, p. 51.

233 "I could control . . . band." *Anniston Star*, 15 July 1948, p. 13.

233 "I want to introduce . . . enjoy." *Anniston Star*, 15 July 1948, p. 13.

233 "doves of peace." Schlesinger, *Ghosts*, p. 52.

234 "Watch your clothes!" Clifford, p. 231. Philadelphia florists had provided a similarly ill-starred display to Dewey—a floral map of the United States. It proved too large to fit on the platform. *Portland Press Herald*, 15 July 1948, p. 19.

233–34 "Though the press . . . them." Clifford, p. 221.

234 Rayburn's glistening, bald head. Truman, *Presidency*, p. 13. When Truman recounted this story, Rayburn fumed, "Harry Truman is a goddamn liar. No pigeon ever lit on my head." Hardeman & Bacon, p. 338.

234 "Get those damned . . . here!" Hamby, *People*, p. 450.

234 "As [Truman] . . . position." *Time*, 26 July 1948, p. 15.

234–35 "my good friend. . . . platform." Brown, pp. 300–01, 305–06.

236 "Nothing short . . . excitement." Lorant, p. 705.

236 "It was a great . . . applauding." Truman *Presidency*, p. 13.

236 "It was fun . . . things." *New Republic*, 26 July 1948, p. 3.

236 THE FUNERAL IS CALLED OFF. Ibid., p. 10.

236 "It was the snarling . . . wall." Rodgers, p. 520.

CHAPTER 23

237 Delegates stormed angrily out. *NY Times*, 15 July 1948, p. 8.

237 "never to cast . . . convention."Clifford, p. 220.

237 "We bid you good-bye." *Portland Press Herald*, 15 July 1948, p. 19.

237 Hill did not join them. *Dothan Eagle*, 12 July 1948, p. 1.

238 Wrestling card. *Alabama Historical Quarterly*, Spring and Summer 1970, p. 30.

238 Southern hymns. Ibid., p. 31.

238 Thirteen Southern states. *NY Times*, 18 July 1948, p. 3.

238 Hardly anyone from outside. Ibid.

238 Tennessee delegation. Ibid.

238 "I don't think Truman . . . House." *Charleston Daily Mail*, 17 July 1948, p. 1.

238 Magnolia State congressmen. *NY Times*, 18 July 1948, p. 3.

238 Not a single member. Barnard, *Dixiecrats*, p. 113.

239 "I would like . . . can." Karabell, p. 165.

239 He also arrived late. Lachicotte, p. 42.

239 Laney rumors. Cohodas, p. 175.

239 "The chips . . . cast." *Harlingen Valley Morning Star*, 17 July 1948, p. 2.

239 A quartet of former governors. *LA Times*, 18 July 1948, p. 2.

239 Thomas Dixon Jr. *Dothan Eagle*, 11 December 1932, p. 1.

239 Lost his right leg. Ibid. The CIO's *Alabama News Digest*, in February 1943, derided the anti–organized labor Dixon as "a peg-legged bigot." Feldman, *Demagogue*, pp. 106, 245.

239 Opposed to Klan violence. *Washington Post*, 3 June 1934, p. 5; Feldman, *Alabama*, p. 234.

240 "As a cosmopolitan . . . faith." Barnard, *Dixiecrats*, pp. 98–99.

240 "national party . . . South." *NY Times*, 16 July 1948, p. 3.

240 "reduce us . . . children." *San Antonio Light*, 17 July 1948, p. 3.

240 Toadsuck, Texas. *NY Times*, 21 February 1932, p. E5.

240 "I appreciate . . . man." Egan, p. 109. The anti-Semitic, anti-immigrant ("low grade races") Murray practiced a selective white supremacy, boasting of his descent from Pocahontas and being married to a part-Chickasaw bride. Luthin, pp. 102–04.

240 In 1912, Murray proved instrumental. Eaton, p. 239.

240 Migrated to Bolivia. *NY Times*, 1 February 1925, p. E1.

240 "The Three C's . . . Coons." Egan, p. 108.

240 Martial law. Egan, p. 109.

240 "Bread, Butter, Bacon, and Beans." *NY Times*, 6 March 1932, p. 6.

240–41 "He may eat flapjacks . . . Murray." Luthin, p. 118. Three weeks before the convention, Murray alleged that FDR's paralysis stemmed not from polio but rather from syphilis. On the convention's second ballot, Alfalfa Bill's twenty-two Oklahoma votes went to Will Rogers. Eaton, p. 350.

241 Journey by bus. *LA Times*, 17 July 1948, p. 6.

241 "Social . . . her." Hirsch, p. 34. Decades later, a researcher discovered a copy in which Murray had inscribed, "I hate Indians too."

241 "right in his science." Murray, *Negro's*, passim; Hirsch, pp. 34–35.

241 *Palestine: Shall Arabs or Jews Control It.* Murray, *Palestine*, passim.

241 "A bellhop . . . forearm." *LA Times*, 17 July 1948, p. 6.

241 "I'm the man . . . Oklahoma." *San Antonio Light*, 17 July 1948, p. 3.

241–42 "It's agin the law . . . before." *LA Times*, 17 July 1948, p. 6.

242 "illegal . . . death." *Cedar Rapids Tribune*, 29 July 1948, p. 4.

242 "Communism is . . . Bolshevism." Weintraub, p. 100.

242 Philadelphia's Democratic Convention. Fine, p. 111.

242 "will go down . . . America." *Alabama Historical Quarterly*, Spring and Summer 1970, p. 34.

242 Rev. Perkins. Fine, p. 110; Jeansonne, *Smith*, pp. 157, 159.

242 Controversial credentials. Barnard, *Dixiecrats*, p. 114.

242 "You are in a good . . . walking." *Pittsburgh Courier*, 24 July 1948, p. 4.

242 Progressive Party supporters picketed. *Moberly Monitor-Index*, 17 July 1948, p. 1.

242 Ruby Mercer. *Portland Sunday Telegram and Sunday Press Herald*, 18 July 1948, p. 8.

242 "portly." *Portland Sunday Telegram and Sunday Press Herald*, 18 July 1948, p. 8.

242 "You will not find . . . Boston." *Alabama Historical Quarterly*, Spring and Summer 1970, p. 36*fn*. Adlai Stevenson and Hubert Humphrey Sr. cosponsored Vaughn's resolution.

242 "absolute . . . republic." Brown, p. 195.

242 "we could win control." *Charleston Daily Mail*, 18 July 1948, p. 2.

243 "we would be the Democratic party." Ibid.

243 "All of us . . . Democrat." *LA Times*, 18 July 1948, p. 2.

243 The crowd roared approval. Feldman, *Demagogue*, p. 141.

243 "Some of the . . . life." *NY Times*, 18 July 1948, p. 3.

243 "Where is Lister Hill?" *Washington Post*, 18 July 1948, p. 2.

243 "Drive the quislings out." Ibid. Quislings (named after the World War II Norwegian minister-president, Vidkun Quisling) were originally Norwegian collaborators with the Nazi occupiers. To this convention, they were Southerners collaborating with Truman.

243 "so-called Northern and Eastern liberals." *Alabama Historical Quarterly*, Spring and Summer 1970, p. 38.

243 "howling, screaming savages." Feldman, *Demagogue*, p. 141.

243 "too inflammatory." Frederickson, p. 137.

244 "should get together . . . leaders." *Charleston Daily Mail*, 18 July 1948, p. 2.

244 "[W]e in the south . . . man?" *Maryville Daily Forum*, 19 July 1948, p. 1.

244 "Whatever . . . state." Abels, *Victory*, p. 99.

244 "I knew that . . . support me." Lachicotte, p. 43.

244 Cornelius Wilkinson. *NY Times*, 17 July 1948, p. 6; Barnard, *Dixiecrats*, p. 100; Feldman, *Demagogue*, passim; Feldman, *Alabama*, pp. 66, 293, 295.

244 "Up North . . . party." Feldman, *Demagogue*, p. 89.

244 "inferior . . . admit it." Ibid., p. 127. In the 1930s, Wilkinson similarly sparred with Bull Connor, charging Connor with favoring blacks for public employment. "In due time," Wilkinson's *Alabama Herald* charged, "the NAACP will doubtless recognize [Connor's] distinguished service . . . to render the negroes of Jefferson County [masters], and if intelligence tests are not too high [Connor] . . . will be able to qualify for the Senegambian Service medal and the Caucasian Double Cross." Feldman, *Demagogue*, p. 110.

245 White Supremacy League. *Chicago Defender*, 26 December 1942, p. 4.

245 Four resolutions. *Washington Post*, 18 July 1948, p. 2.

245 "Harry Truman . . . Missouri." Ibid.

245 Declaration of Principles. *NY Times*, 18 July 1948, p. 2.

246 Portrait of Robert E. Lee. *Hartford Courant*, 15 July 1948, p. 1.

246 Beulah Waller. *Washington Post*, 18 July 1948, p. 1.

246 "the wool hat woman . . . Georgia." Frederickson, p. 139.

247 "jockeys . . . Fascism." *NY Times*, 21 October 1944, p. 9.

247 Holdridge sued. *Salt Lake Tribune*, 27 June 1946, p. 5.

247 "If [your activities lead] . . . people." *NY Times*, 2 April 1948, p. 3.

247 "No more . . . capitalism." *Joplin Globe*, 16 July 1948, p. 9.

247 "Throw the Communist out!" *Pittsburgh Courier*, 24 July 1948, p. 4.

247 Folsom stalled for time. Barnard. *Dixiecrats*, p. 115.

247 "This is not a bolt . . . States." *Washington Post*, 18 July 1948, p. 1.

247 "Don't let . . . trust." *LA Times*, 18 July 1948, p. 1.

248 "This is the South's . . . astray." *Oakland Tribune*, 18 July 1948, p. 1.

248 Removed his scribbled notes. Cohodas, p. 177.

248 "I want to tell . . . cost." *Chicago Tribune*, 18 July 1948, p. 2.

248 "I can think . . . do it." *NY Times*, 18 July 1948, p. 3.

248 "If we throw . . . power." *Washington Post*, 18 July 1948, p. 1.

CHAPTER 24

249 "We have to decide . . . office." Gall, p. 241.

249 "Either . . . Doctrine." Ibid.

249–50 "Pressman handled . . . thing." *Time*, 2 August 1948, p. 13.

250 Tugwell-Pressman platform. *NY Times*, 23 July 1948, p. 10.

250 "The Communists . . . 'front.'" Ibid.

250–51 "The presence . . . party." Ibid., p. 1.

251 Loeb exited under police protection. Donaldson, p. 194.

251 "I think the pink . . . administration." *Moberly Monitor-Index*, 22 July 1949, p. 2.

251 "I don't consider . . . them." *NY Times*, 23 July 1948, p. 10. Mrs. Gimbel's fortune stemmed not merely from Gimbel Brothers department stores (her late husband was a son of one of the founders), but also from ownership of Liebmann Breweries, brewers of New York's Rheingold Beer. MacDougall, pp. 245–46.

251 "The coaches . . . crowded." *Waterloo Daily Courier*, 23 July 1948, p. 1.

251 "We want Wallace." *NY Times*, 24 July 1948, p. 6.

251 "We've got to . . . left." Ibid.

252 "I am getting . . . liability." Ibid., p. 1.

252 "[The] Communist leaders . . . democracy." Ibid., p. 6.

252 "No matter . . . Communist." Ibid.

253 "I have often . . . way." *Winnipeg Free Press*, 24 July 1948, p. 15.

253 "Have you ever . . . letters?" Abels, *Victory*, p. 115.

254 "Dear Guru . . . Washington." *Dixon Daily Telegraph*, 10 March 1948, p. 4.

254 "The rumor . . . hence." Morgan, *FDR*, pp. 531–32.

254–55 "extraordinary sliminess . . . terms." *Dixon Daily Telegraph*, 10 March 1948, p. 4;

255   "out of a hundred . . . president." *Hope Star*, 20 March 1948, p. 2.

255   "We can handle . . . religion." Daniels, *Witness*, p. 184.

255   Irita Bradford Van Doren. Shlaes, pp. 327–29.

255   "spread it as . . . fact." Persico, pp. 40–41.

256   "I believe . . . mentally." *Dixon Daily Telegraph*, 10 March 1948, p. 4.

256   "His open . . . politics." Ibid.

256   "To hell . . . counts." *Tucson Daily Citizen*, 27 August 1947, p. 6.

256   Wallace flushed. *Chicago Tribune*, 24 July 1948, p. 4.

256   "I never . . . Pegler." *NY Times*, 24 July 1948, p. 6.

256   "He [was] a short . . . itself." *Winnipeg Free Press*, 24 July 1948, p. 15.

256   "My name is . . . Modra?" *Hartford Courant*, 24 July 1948, p. 3; *LA Times*, 24 July 1928, p. 2; *Time*, 2 August 1948, p. 35; MacDougall, p. 497; Farr, p. 189.

257   "I will never . . . Pegler." *Chicago Tribune*, 24 July 1948, p. 4; *Oakland Tribune*, 24 July 1948, p. 2; Farr, p. 189.

257   "If you . . . here?" *Chicago Tribune*, 24 July 1948, p. 4; *Oakland Tribune*, 24 July 1948, p. 2; Farr, p. 190.

257   "No, Mr. Mencken . . . all here." *NY Times*, 24 July 1948, p. 6. Though Mencken spoke exceedingly civilly to Wallace, to his diary he admitted "he nettled me." Fecher, p. 454.

257   "Some people . . . matter." *Oakland Tribune*, 24 July 1948, p. 2.

257   "Everybody . . . suicide." *Cumberland Evening Times*, 27 July 1948, p. 4.

CHAPTER 25

258   Two members of Congress. *NY Times*, 23 July 1948, p. 10.

258   "as indifferent . . . Democrats." *Washington Post*, 23 July 1948, p. 15.

258   Two future U.S. senators. McGovern Interview, Iowa PBS, 3 May 2003; Culver & Hyde, p. 485. Usher Burdick supported the Union Party in 1936 and accordingly forfeited his congressional seniority.

258   "Wallace was attacked . . . internationalist." McGovern, p. 43.

258   Other hard-core leftists. *NY Times*, 23 July 1948, p. 10; *Washington Post*, 26 July 1948, p. 7; Kurth, pp. 397–98; MacDougall, p. 586; Goulden, *Mencken*, p. 84; Davidson, p. 347; Strom, p. 215. Laura Duncan, wife of Abel Meeropol and future stepmother of the Rosenberg orphans, in 1952 was the first to record "We Shall Overcome."

259   Pete Seeger's father. Wilkinson, pp. 52–54; Weisman, pp. 43–45, 62; Pescatello, pp. 124–25, 131–32. On the other hand, Charles Seeger's biographer, Ann M. Pescatello, contends he "never held [CPUSA] membership." p. 209.

259   Howard Fast. *NY Times*, 15 June 1948, pp. 1, 12; *Daily Worker*, 15 June 1948, pp. 1–2.

259   Lillian Hellman's former lover. Mellen, pp. 150–51.

259   "he would . . . pleasure." Fast, pp. 192–93.

259   "Fast, . . . rises and sets." Ibid.

260   "Henry was so sweet . . . Truman." Barnard, *Outside*, p. 196. Her husband, Clifford J. Durr, resigned from the FCC in April 1948, rather than acquiesce in an administration implementing a loyalty program. Oddly enough, among those urging Durr to remain was Wisconsin's Joe McCarthy. Salmond, p. 121. Others, however, suggest Durr was pressured out because of his wife's activities. *Billboard*, 1 May 1948, p. 6; MacDougall, p. 399.

260   "The people that . . . easily." McGovern Interview, Iowa PBS, 3 May 2003.

260   "I also remember . . . obnoxious." McGovern, p. 43.

260–61   "I am aware . . . longer." *Cumberland Evening Times*, 27 July 1948, p. 4.

261 "Many of the men . . . *fatales.*" Cooke, *Six Men*, p. 111. Cooke possessed a keen sense of fashion. A photo taken of six indicted national Communist leaders being released on bail on July 20, 1948, reveals two with the open-shirt-collar-over-coat-lapel look he describes. *NY Times*, 21 July 1948, p. 3.

261 "Those hardy . . . drive." *Cumberland Evening Times*, 27 July 1948, p. 4.

261 Benson banged. *Oakland Tribune*, 23 July 1948, p. 7.

261 "After the elections . . . tutelage." *NY Times*, 24 July 1948, p. 6.

262 "a mother . . . woman." Ibid.

262 "We must work . . . none." Ibid.

262 W.E.B. Du Bois and Paul Robeson. Lewis, pp. 536–37.

262 Howard Newspaper Syndicate. *Washington Post*, 27 January 1969, p. C2.

262 Howard's license suspended. *Time*, 2 August 1948, p. 12.

262 "Half of the gallery . . . commies." *Chicago Tribune*, 24 July 1948, p. 1.

262 "Wallace or war." *NY Times*, 24 July 1948, p. 1.

262 "the President's greetings . . . Germany." *Washington Post*, 24 July 1948, p. 14.

262 "Look across . . . [C]ompromise." *Chicago Tribune*, 24 July 1948, p. 4. Howard's keynote address was drafted in part—as was Wallace's acceptance speech—by onetime Communist Party member Allan E. Sloane. MacDougall, p. 513; Saposs, p. 249.

262 "a tall, full-bodied . . . cigar." Goulden, *Mencken*, p. 77.

262 "an African roll. . . . such malefactors." Ibid.

263 "if the night's . . . of it." *LA Times*, 25 July 1948, p. 2. Norman Thomas thought Mencken displayed "touching innocence in suggesting American Communists and fellow travelers look like goons. They look like the rest of us. And, to an extent even greater than I had anticipated, they are running the show."

263 Covert Communist. Pederson, pp. 156, 158, 218.

263 "contemptible . . . reporting." Rodgers, p. 524.

263 "Hitlerite . . . convention." *Chicago Tribune*, 26 July 1948, p. 2.

263 "The fighting . . . baits." Ibid.

263 "The cooler . . . martyrdom." *Chester Times*, 26 July 1948, p. 1. It was during this convention that Wallace informed *Time* magazine, "I would say that the Communists are the closest things to the early Christian martyrs we have today." *Time*, 9 August 1948, p. 19.

263 "Nobody denounced . . . dough." Rodgers, p. 524.

263 "I'm only sorry . . . passed." *Chicago Tribune*, 26 July 1948, p. 2.

263 Half hour of singing. *Oakland Tribune*, 23 July 1948, p. 7.

264 "the most courageous . . . peace." *Hartford Courant*, 25 July 1948, p. 5.

264 "Instead of . . . taxpayers." *NY Times*, 25 July 1948, p. 36.

264 Grant W. Oakes. *Chicago Tribune*, 2 November 1948, p. 3.

264 "If anyone. . . drunk." *Hartford Courant*, 25 July 1948, p. 5. In 1944, HUAC identified Oakes as a Communist. In 1952, he declined to testify regarding whether he had ever been a CPUSA member. HUAC, *CIO*, pp. 34, 178; HUAC, *Chicago*, p. 3719.

264 "rugged-faced." *Current Biography*, 1952, p. 426.

264 "believes . . . path." *Hartford Courant*, 25 July 1948, p. 5.

264 "Idaho . . . Taylor." Ibid.

264 "This nominating. . . convention." Goulden, *Mencken*, p. 81.

264 "Taylor came . . . standing." *Hartford Courant*, 25 July 1948, p. 5.

265 $30,000. *NY Times*, 26 July 1948, p. 10.

265 Progressives paid. *Chicago Tribune*, 24 July 1948, p. 4.

265 Auto thief. *NY Times*, 28 March 1939, p. 3; *Time*, 2 August 1948, p. 13; Bernays & Kaplan, pp. 58–59; MacDougall, pp. 380-81, 529. Gailmor was a truncated anagram of his pre–auto theft name of Margolies. Curtis MacDougall described Gailmor's criminal activities as "a compulsive neurosis. It caused him to borrow others' automobiles, which he drove at breakneck speed before returning them to their owners."

265 "by a troupe of cuties." Goulden, *Mencken*, p. 85.

265 The entire process netting Wallace. *NY Times*, 26 July 1948, p. 10. Gailmor's "voice is sharp and incisive," noted the *New York Times*'s Cabell Phillips. "His delivery modulates easily from an infectious chuckle to an arrogant challenge, to shouted, impassioned invective. Twenty minutes of this usually induces a state of ecstasy in his audience." *NY Times*, 23 May 1948, p. SM24.

265 "Never mind . . . black." *Chester Times*, 26 July 1948, p. 2. "The Wallace 'cause' always has its hand out," complained *Chicago Sun-Times* political editor John Dreiske. MacDougall, p. 384.

265 "The convention . . . ax." Goulden, *Mencken*, p. 83.

266 "with violent . . . man." *Time*, 2 August 1948, p. 13.

266 "Absentee . . . supreme." MacDougall, p. 530.

266 Robeson provided renditions. Schmidt, p. 186. "The House I Live In," composed by Abel Meeropol (adoptive father of Julius and Ethel Rosenberg's two sons), was originally sung by Frank Sinatra in the Albert Maltz–written 1946 Oscar–winning antidiscrimination film of the same name.

266 "proud . . . party." Schmidt, p. 186.

266 "forces that . . . Manufacturers." *LA Times*, 26 July 1948, p. 2.

266 "Taylor's amazingly . . . demonstrations." Ibid.

266 "A third-rate . . . life." Rodgers, p. 522.

267 "in justice to . . . listeners." *Hartford Courant*, 25 July 1948, p. 6.

267–68 "Franklin Roosevelt . . . Deal." *Washington Post*, 26 July 1948, p. 7.

268 "The party . . . Dewey." *Washington Post*, 26 July 1948, p. 7.

268–69 "Germany . . . allies." *NY Times*, 25 July 1948, p. 28.

269 "The American . . . system." Ibid.

270 *New York Times* compared. *NY Times*, 28 July 1948, p. 2. Among planks not included, however, was one for "sexual privacy," advocated by CPUSA member Harry Hay, who also developed the idea of establishing "Bachelors for Wallace." Two years later, the latter idea gave birth to Hay's Mattachine Society. The sexually prim CPUSA expelled Hay. Miller, *Out*, p. 333; Bullough, pp. 76–79; Gross, p. 51*fn*.

270 A variety of dignitaries. *Washington Post*, 26 July 1948, p. 7. In October 1946, Attorney General Tom Clark fired Rogge following the latter's leaking of documents alleging that the CIO's John L. Lewis had conspired with Nazi agents to defeat FDR in 1940—and that John Nance Garner, Herbert Hoover, Jim Farley, and Burton K. Wheeler could, in the Nazis' opinion, "be organized against United States participation in the war." Rogge later charged that Truman was planning a virtual "Reichstag fire" move against the CPUSA. *NY Times*, 23 October 1946, p. 8.

270 "the apostles . . . death." MacDougall, p. 583.

270 "What in God's . . . themselves." Wechsler, p. 231.

270 Published poet. *Bennington Banner*, 1 October 1966, p. 6.

270 "While we . . . nation." *Washington Post*, 26 July 1948, p. 7.

Identified by John Abt. Abt, p. 117; Saposs, pp. 37–38, 138. Abt also identified Minnesota's former Farmer-Labor Party congressman John Bernard as another covert CPUSA member. Abt's sister Marion Bachrach served on the Corsican-born Bernard's staff. In 1952, Bernard invoked the Fifth Amendment regarding CPUSA membership. *Chicago Tribune*, 4 September 1952, pp. 1, 4.

271   "If there is any . . . Union." *NY Times*, 25 July 1948, p. 28.

271   "Such words . . . ally." Brock, p. 78.

271   "From reading . . . clear." *NY Times*, 25 July 1948, p. 28.

271   "I am in favor . . . here." *Washington Post*, 26 July 1948, p. 7. Or as Reinhold Niebuhr once commented, "I don't believe in the slogan, 'My country, right or wrong'—particularly when it isn't even my country." Wechsler, p. 232.

271   Smith would invoke. *Troy Times Record*, 22 May 1952, p. 3.

271   "weaken[ing] . . . peace." MacDougall, p. 572.

271   "Responsibility . . . States." Lader, p. 50.

271   Shouted down Hayford's motion. Divine, p. 220.

271   "I guess . . . rule." *Time*, 2 August 1948, p. 13.

CHAPTER 26

272   "All of Germany . . . Communist." Gaddis, p. 22.

272   "There is no room . . . partition." Coffey, p. 262.

272–73   "Any weakness . . . trouble." Donovan, p. 364.

273   "of a peace-loving German government." *NY Times*, 12 May 1948, p. 14.

273   "I do not know . . . peace." Ibid., 18 May 1948, p. 4.

274   "No one was sure . . . danger." Large, p. 403.

274   Norway feared. *New Republic*, 12 January 1948, pp. 22–23. Queried by the *Christian Science Monitor*'s Nate White regarding Henry Wallace's convention boast that if "I were President there would be no crisis in Berlin," Howard Fast responded, "there would be no crisis because we would get out of Berlin." "And afterward?" asked White. "Afterward," explained Fast, "out of western Germany and out of Europe and Asia." *Portland Press Herald*, 7 August 1948, p. 7.

274   "Even adventurous . . . imperialism." *Moberly Monitor-Index*, 17 July 1948, p. 1.

274–75   "Have quite . . . make." Hamby, *People*, p. 444.

275   "Naturally . . . at all." Large, p. 397.

275   "The Russians . . . fix." Ibid., pp. 402–03.

275   "We decided . . . wanted." Coffey, p. 567.

275–76   "On top of . . . invasion." Howley, pp. 198–99. Soviet soldiers raped an estimated two million German women between 1945 and 1947. Gaddis, p. 14.

276   "I informed . . . one." Forrestal, p. 458.

276   Two squadrons of B-29s. Ibid., p. 456.

276   "In Berlin . . . out." Draper Interview, Truman Library, 11 January 1972.

276–77   "our representatives . . . unity." *NY Times*, 25 July 1948, p. 1.

277   "I was down . . . elation." Howley, pp. 204–05.

277–78   "We weren't . . . work." Draper Interview, Truman Library, 11 January 1972.

278   Arresting every one. *NY Times*, 7 September 1948, pp. 1, 52.

278   Thursday, September 9. Ibid., 10 September 1948.

278   "The situation . . . used." Lilienthal, p. 406.

278   "Have a terrific . . . not." Truman, *Life*, p. 258.

CHAPTER 27

279   "the worst . . . more so." *NY Times*, 29 June 1947, p. E3. "Between you and me," Truman also

wrote to Indiana senator Sherman Minton just after the 1946 election, "I don't expect this Congress to be any worse than the one I had to deal with for the last two years." Reichard, p. 19.

279 Seventy-ninth Congress. *NY Times*, 2 November 1945, pp. 1, 34.

280 Federal budget had shriveled. Patterson, p. 374.

280 Largest surplus in history. Ibid.

280 Finally overrode Truman. *NY Times*, 3 April 1948, pp. 1–2.

280 Top marginal rates. Ibid.; Wanniski, p. 185. The personal exemption was not raised until 1970—when the dependent exemption was lowered to $525.

280 Enacted such measures as. Lorant, p. 697.

280 "For a Congress. . . . abdication." Abels, *Victory*, p. 134.

280–82 1948 Republican platform. *Vital Speeches*, 1 July 1948, p. 574.

282 Douglas had suggested. Hartmann, *80th Congress*, p. 193.

282 "The Democrats have splintered . . . reunion." Ibid.

282 "On the twenty-sixth . . . office." Truman, *Presidency*, p. 13.

282 Two major Republican adversaries. Abels, *Victory*, p. 47.

283 "The Republican platform . . . campaign." Hartmann, *80th Congress*, p. 196. For his part, Dewey wrote to an aunt: "Mr. Truman's special session is a nuisance but I do not believe it will have much effect on the election." Donovan, p. 412.

283 "The only . . . kind." *NY Times*, 28 July 1948, p. 3.

283 "This sounds . . . administration." *NY Times*, 16 July 1948, p. 2.

283 "Editorials . . . win." Truman, *Presidency*, pp. 14–15.

283–84 "never before . . . Presidency." *Florence Morning News*, 17 July 1948, p. 1.

284 "want to open . . . legislation." Reinhard, p. 51.

284 "we're not . . . anything." Ross, p. 137.

285 blue suit and black-and-white shoes. *Washington Post*, 28 July 1948, p. B5.

285 "His hand . . . emphasis." *NY Times*, 28 July 1948, p. 3.

285 Subway fares. *Chicago Tribune*, 21 April 1948, p. 3.

285 47 percent. *Washington Post*, 24 July 1948, pp. 1, 5.

285 Cost-of-living index all-time high. Trager, p. 563.

285 "The cost of living . . . ever." *NY Times*, 28 July 1948, p. 3.

285–86 Anti-inflation program. Ibid., p. 4.

286 "Perhaps . . . absent." Hamby, *People*, p. 453.

286–87 "The President's quarrel . . . solution." *NY Times*, 28 July 1948, p. 4.

287 "de facto . . . power." *Berkshire Eagle*, 8 July 1948, p. 14.

287 "This is a most . . . people." Truman, *Messages*, p. 384. Dewey also objected to the bill's provisions. *Logansport Press*, 30 October 1948, p. 1. Not one non-Southern Democrat voted against the bill's passage. *NY Times*, 3 June 1948, p. 2.

288 "mass civil disobedience." Cochran, p. 230.

288 "This time Negroes . . . down." *Washington Post*, 1 April 1948, pp. 1–2.

288 Congress of Racial Equality. *Chicago Defender*, 3 July 1948, p. 5.

288 NAACP. *NY Times*, 5 June 1948, p. 16.

288 Sixty-seven to seven. *NY Times*, 14 June 1948, p. 14. By a sixty-one to seven margin it also tabled a measure making lynching a serviceman a federal offense.

288 Executive Orders 9980 and 9981. *NY Times*, 27 July 1948, pp. 1, 4. The wary Randolph publicly damned Truman's moves as "misleading" and vowed to continue his opposition to the draft.

Walter White's NAACP quickly distanced itself from Randolph; the group's Harlem branch, however, supported Randolph. Not until August 18 did Randolph relent. *Washington Post*, 19 August 1948, p. B2.

289 Effective filibuster. *NY Times*, 5 August 1948, pp. 1, 6. Southerners generally contended that they had no animus to poll tax repeal, but that it should be implemented not by mere legislation but by constitutional amendment. Kansas Republican senator Clyde Reed reminded his GOP colleagues that the 1944 Republican platform had advocated just such an amendment. Taft ignored him. *Washington Post*, 9 August 1948, p. B15.

289 Terminating debate. *Washington Post*, 6 August 1948, pp. 1, 6.

289 236 to 56. *Washington Post*, 8 August 1948, pp. M1–M2.

289 Bare handful of items. *NY Times*, 8 August 1948, p. 1.

289–90 "The Republican 'new look' . . . Congress." Ibid., p. 9. Though few noticed, and Republicans, as usual, never bothered to point it out, Democrats possessed a similar schizophrenia. "It is a topsy-turvy situation," wrote the *New Republic*'s Richard Strout that August. "Truman is the candidate on a Democratic platform that makes it practically a labor party, but a majority of his party in Congress are conservative." Strout, p. 67.

290 "My special . . . easily." Truman, *Presidency*, p. 19.

290 "I would say . . . a 'do-nothing' session . . . Congress." *NY Times*, 13 August 1948, p. 1. The term "do-nothing Congress" had already been employed by Howard McGrath on August 7. *NY Times*, 8 August 1948, p. 9.

CHAPTER 28

291 "It was a *political* . . . baloney." Bernstein, pp. 195–98.

291 "Soviet cover name." Klehr, Haynes, and Vassiliev, pp. 27, 425, 433; Romerstein & Breindel, p. 163; http://www.johnearlhaynes.org/page66.html.

291 Martha Dodd Stern. *NY Times*, 20 October 1948, p. 32; Trahair, pp. 304-05.

292 "to take the ball . . . Thomas." Kovel, p. 146.

292 Federal Loyalty Review Board. Bontecue, passim.

292 Francis Biddle's compendium. Ibid., p. 170*fn*; Navasky, p. 22.

292 Biddle's forty-seven. Bontecue, pp. 361–63.

292 "Hollywood Ten" The nine screenwriters were Alvah Bessie, Herbert Biberman, Lester Cole, Ring Lardner Jr., John Howard Lawson, Albert Maltz, Samuel Ornitz, Adrian Scott, and Dalton Trumbo. All of the "Hollywood Ten" eventually admitted to CPUSA membership. Morgan, *Reds*, pp. 518–525.

292 "The defendant . . . violence." *NY Times*, 21 July 1948, p. 3. O. John Rogge had unsuccessfully overseen Smith Act prosecutions of various profascist and isolationist individuals in 1944.

292 "Truman effort . . . Fire." Ibid.

292 "the domestic . . . hot." Ibid.

292–93 "Terrified of the . . . party." Ibid.

293 "Defense of the civil . . . power." *NY Times*, 22 July 1948, p. 2.

293 "It seems to me . . . anybody." Ross, pp. 158–59.

294 Mary Watkins Price. HUAC, *Espionage*, p. 725. Price never denied Communist Party membership and, following the campaign, moved to Washington and took employment with the Czech embassy.

294 Remington ("Fedya"). http://www.johnearlhaynes.org/page66.html. Convicted of perjury in 1953, Remington was murdered in Lewisburg Federal Penitentiary in November 1954.

294 Mundt. Parmet, p. 165.

294 Cover name: "Page." Haynes & Klehr, pp. 146–47, 346.

294 "Lawyer." Romerstein & Breindel, p. 45.

294 "smears . . . lie." *NY Times*, 1 August 1948, p. 3.

294 Wallace had remarked. Janeway, p. 135. HUAC, Wallace charged, "killed White with poisonous slander, with venomous rumor, with the vicious gossip of self-confessed spies." *NY Times*, 22 August 1948, p. 47.

294 Friend of Lee Pressman. Morgan, *Reds*, p. 261.

295 Cover name: "Karl." Klehr, Haynes, and Vassiliev, pp. 18, 27.

295 "Yet so strong . . . Communism.'" Chambers, p. 541.

295 Cover name: "Ales." Morgan, *Reds*, p. 269.

295 "If Chambers . . . Reagan." Hamby, *People*, p. 522.

295 United Nations Conference. *San Antonio Light*, 18 December 1947, p. 1. It appears likely that Hiss recruited future Hollywood Ten screenwriter Dalton Trumbo to help draft Secretary of State Stettinius's address to the San Francisco conference.

295 Dulles. White, *Cold War*, pp. 52, 59. Dulles's involvement with Hiss helped sidetrack any Dewey pronouncement on the Communists-in-government issue, as did Dulles's sister Eleanor's involvement with a heavily Communist-infiltrated group in the late 1930s.

295–96 "I was very fond . . . otherwise." HUAC, *Espionage*, p. 572. From 1933 or 1934 through 1938, Chambers was a practicing homosexual ("I never had a prolonged affair with any one man"). There is no evidence, however, that the Hiss-Chambers relationship was of that nature. Though the Hiss forces were tempted to exploit Chambers's situation, they did not, as Hiss's stepson, Timothy Hobson, had been dishonorably discharged from the Navy for his own homosexuality. Tanenhaus, pp. 344–45, 579.

296 "I am not . . . do so." HUAC, *Espionage*, p. 643.

296 "We've been . . . ruined." Tanenhaus, p. 228.

296 Rankin rushed. Chambers, p. 545. Thomas, though HUAC chairman, did not preside over much of the Hiss-Chambers testimony, bedridden as he was with bleeding ulcers. Tanenhaus, p. 219.

296 "the entry . . . lawlessness." *Washington Post*, 6 August 1948, p. 20.

296 "Smearing . . . cleared." *El Paso Herald-Post*, 16 August 1948, p. 6.

296 Hoover had dispatched. Brownell, pp. 236–41; Thomas, pp. 369–72; Latham, pp. 177-79; Neal, *Ike*, pp. 292–93. Hoover sent Truman a similar warning in late January 1946, which Harry Hood Vaughan neglected to forward to Truman until White was confirmed by the Senate. Publicly confronted in November 1953 with information regarding these communications, Truman initially and inaccurately denied receiving them.

296 "red herring." *Washington Post*, 6 August 1948, pp. 1, 3. It was John Abt who first used the term ("an old and malodorous red herring") regarding the proceedings. *New Yorker*, 4 September 1948, p. 50; Tanenhaus, p. 223. In September 1956, Truman denied ever terming the investigation a "red herring." Queried on Milwaukee television station WXIX ("Mr. President, is it true that you characterized Richard Nixon's investigation into the Alger Hiss case as a 'red herring'?") he answered, "No, but it was. I never characterized it that way, but that's exactly what it was." *NY Times*, 4 September 1956, pp. 1, 18.

297 Father John F. Cronin. Morris, pp. 391–92; Parmet, pp. 166–68, 174–75; White, *Looking Glass*, pp. 56, 263; Smith, *Hiss*, pp. 144–45; Romerstein & Breindel, p. 126. Historian Herbert Parmet, however, casts significant doubt on the influence Cronin's information may have had upon Nixon.

297 "Nixon . . . thing." White, *Looking Glass*, p. 56. Radical journalist I. F. Stone (himself a paid Soviet agent) for once shared Richard Nixon's opinion on something, considering Hiss "a climber and a snob." Guttenplan, p. 252.

297 "In most cases . . . other." Nixon, *Memoirs*, p. 55. William Remington, for example, never denied meeting Bentley or Golos.

298 "Did you ever . . . warbler?" *Time*, 30 August 1948, p. 14.

298   James Reston. Chambers, p. 648.

298   "Are you willing . . . Communist?" Ibid., p. 711.

298   "Alger Hiss . . . be now." Ibid.

298   Hiss sued. Tanenhaus, p. 283.

298   "I welcome Mr. Hiss's . . . justice." Ibid.

298   W. Marvin Smith. *Washington Post*, 22 October 1948, pp. 1, 21. On Friday evening, December 20, 1948, accused Communist Laurence Duggan, like Hiss a former State Department official now heading a foundation, plunged sixteen floors to his death into a West Forty-fifth Street snowbank. *NY Times*, 21 December 1948, pp. 1–2.

299   "Your petitioner . . . Feeney." Friedrich, p. 299.

299   "an improbable . . . cheeks." Anderson & Gibson, p. 67.

299   Kickback schemes. *Washington Post*, 4 August 1948, p. B13.

299   She retaliated by assembling. Anderson & Gibson, pp. 67–68.

299   Out of combat. *Washington Post*, 5 November 1948, p. C9.

300   Washington grand jury. Ibid., 23 October 1948, pp. 1, 11.

300   Lost her daughter. Ibid., 13 August 1948, p. 2. The surname is alternately spelled in the Latin alphabet "Kosenkina."

300   "insane worship . . . alike." Krasnov, p. 22.

300   "To go back . . . thought." *Northwest Arkansas Times*, 16 October 1948, p. 7.

300   "the body . . . said." Doe, p. 11.

300   Hoguet's motion. *Emmett v. Lomakin*, 84 N.Y.S.2d 562; *NY Times*, 12 August 1948, p. 1.

301   "a complete . . . blackmailer." Weinstein & Vassiliev, p. 149.

301   Lomakin angrily tossed. *New Yorker*, 4 September 1948, p. 46.

301   State Department urged. *NY Times*, 13 August 1948, p. 3.

301   "I jumped . . . myself." *Fredericksburg Free Lance-Star*, 25 August 1948, p. 1.

301   Carried the severely injured woman. *NY Times*, 13 August 1948, p. 3.

301   Roosevelt Hospital. *Brooklyn Eagle*, 22 August 1948, p. 2.

301   "Fascist . . . liberties." *NY Times*, 13 August 1948, p. 3.

301   "They call it . . . jail." *NY Daily News*, 26 July 1998, p. 43.

CHAPTER 29

302   "Boy, those boys . . . Commie.'" *Mexia Daily News*, 12 August 1948, p. 1.

303   "gesticulating . . . him." *Delta Democrat-Times*, 12 August 1948, p. 1.

303   "patterned . . . 1920." *San Antonio Express*, 12 August 1948, p. 1.

303   "was made-to-order . . . security." *NY Times*, 12 August 1948, p. 44.

303   "comes from agitators . . . Chicago." *San Antonio Express*, 12 August 1948, p. 1.

303   "With a band . . . address." Frederickson, p. 148.

303   "The present . . . parties." *NY Times*, 12 August 1948, p. 44.

303   "philosophically bankrupt." Ibid.

303–04   "They are mere vehicles . . . witnessing." Ibid.

304   "I cried . . . body." Garson, p. 285.

304   "our 3,000,000 . . . politics." *Washington Post*, 20 July 1948, p. 2.

304   "We do not invite . . . people." Ibid.

304   "We're not going . . . Smith." *Cedar Rapids Tribune*, 29 July 1948, p. 4.

304   "We expect . . . votes." *Amarillo Daily News*, 12 August 1948, p. 1.

304 "a white hotel, theater or restaurant." *Washington Post*, 8 August 1948, p. B3.

304 Tar Heel Dixiecrats. Ibid.

305 "The course . . . parlor." *Middletown Times-Herald*, 23 October 1948, p. 4.

305 Thurmond's remote cousin. Bass & Thompson, *Ol' Strom*, p. 113.

305 Georgia Dixiecrats. Sherrill, pp. 51–52.

305 Texas Democrats. *El Paso Herald-Post*, 10 August 1948, p. 1.

305 "We ought to tell . . . oblivion." *Abilene Reporter-News*, 12 August 1948, p. 1.

306 Third-party status. Frederickson, p. 158.

306 "Truman has sold . . . cities." *Anniston Star*, 7 October 1948, p. 1.

306 "Browning . . . infamy." Steinberg, *Bosses*, p. 129.

306 "Kefauver remains . . . the drawer." Ibid.

306 "Now a Trumancrat . . . hydrat." Garson, p. 298.

306 "a cross between . . . Bastocrat." Jeansonne, *Perez*, p. 174.

306 Earl Long and Leander Perez. *Chicago Defender*, 2 October 1948, p. 3; Frederickson, pp. 114–16, 158–62; Garson, pp. 258–59, 297–98; Jeansonne, *Perez*, pp. 178–83.

307 "limber trimmer." *Time*, 10 October 1948, p. 22.

307 "shabby mountebank." Ibid.

307 Merely feeble-minded. Manchester, *Mencken*, p. 310.

307 "Certainly . . . before." *Chicago Defender*, 28 August 1948, p. 15.

308 Lister Hill and John Sparkman. *Dothan Eagle*, 30 July 1948, p. 1.

308 A former Wilkinson ally. Feldman, *Demagogue*, p. 154.

308 Folsom. *Anniston Star*, 7 October 1948, p. 1.

308 Antiwalkout. *Dothan Eagle*, 12 July 1948, p. 1.

308 "such aliens . . . satellites." *Anniston Star*, 10 October 1948, p. 1.

308 Massive Dixiecrat rally. Feldman, *Demagogue*, p. 147.

308 "Neither of us . . . Japs." Ibid., p. 148.

308 Nominee for attorney general. Ibid., p. 143.

309 "the President has directed . . . intimidation." Frederickson, p. 146.

309 "Is there anyone . . . courts." *Charleston Daily Mail*, 1 August 1948, p. 1.

309 "They have named . . . impossible." Ibid.; Cohodas, p. 183.

309 "Unless a man . . . all." *Lawton Constitution*, 1 August 1948, p. 1.

310 "Dear Governor . . . mansion. " *Washington Post*, 24 October 1948, p. B5.

310 Hastie discreetly declined. *Florence Morning News*, 24 October 1948, p. 4.

310 "did not know that Harry . . . Islands." *Amarillo Daily News*, 26 October 1948, p. 1.

310 "I would not have written . . . him." *LA Times*, 26 October 1948, p. 11.

310 "Governor Hastie . . . state." *Florence Morning News*, 27 October 1948, p. 2.

310 "The Mansion does not . . . year." Ibid.

311 "I fought . . . difference?" Washington-Williams, p. 137. In her memoirs, Essie Mae records that she and her husband had watched Thurmond on television, but South Carolina's first station, Columbia's WOLO, did not sign on until 1953. It is worth noting a distinct difference in tone between her memoirs and interviews later granted to Dan Rather and Tavis Smiley, with profoundly greater sympathy granted to her father in the latter. http://www.cbsnews.com/stories/2003/12/17/60II/main589107.shtml; http://www.pbs.org/kcet/tavissmiley/archive/200501/20050128_washingtonwilliams.html.

311 "As long as she was . . . daughter." *Washington Post*, 4 August 1992, p. E2.

311 "Nobody needed . . . money." Ibid.; Bass & Thompson, *Ol' Strom*, p. 278.

311 "At the time . . . deal." Bass & Thompson, *Ol' Strom*, p. 279.

311 "That's why they call it that." Washington-Williams, pp. 140–41.

CHAPTER 30

312 "It was probably . . . North." Wechsler, pp. 225–26.

312 Durham. *NY Times*, 31 August 1949, pp. 1, 12.

312 Calvin Hackney. *Time*, 6 September 1948, p. 19; MacDougall, p. 709.

313 "Am I in the United States of America?" *Time*, 6 September 1948, p. 19.

313 "face was livid . . . again." MacDougall, p. 712.

313 Louis E. Burnham. *People's Weekly World*, 2 March 2002, page unknown.

313 "because he really . . . doing." *NY Times*, 31 August 1949, pp. 1, 12.

313 "highly un-American business." *LA Sentinel*, 2 September 1948, p. 9.

313 "Police tried . . . heckling." *Life*, 13 September 1948, p. 33.

314 Might be dynamited. Wechsler, p. 226.

314 "the best thing . . . us." Ibid.

314 Arkansas Baptist College. *NY Amsterdam News*, 11 September 1948, p. 15.

314 C. G. Hall. *Washington Post*, 4 September 1948, p. 1.

314 "Wallace has a right . . . meeting." *Lowell Sun*, 1 September 1948, p. 27.

314 Blacks carried signs. *Chicago Tribune*, 2 September 1948, p. 8. Hosea Hudson, a local Progressive Party activist and CPUSA member who stood on the northern side of the rope that afternoon, recalled: "Connor had went and got some Negro prisoners out of the city prisons—they got city prisons in Birmingham, they work the streets—and they went and got these Negro city prisoners and put on [them] some nice suit of clothes." Black & Reed, p. 130.

314 "help me . . . gates." *Statesville Landmark*, 2 September 1948, p. 3.

315 Rexburg, Idaho. *Anniston Star*, 2 September 1948, p. 2.

315 J. P. Mooney. *Washington Post*, 2 September 1948, p. 1; Black & Reed, pp. 130, 139–40. "I always did think that Wallace should have spoke," contended Hosea Hudson. "Everybody went home. It was a complete defeat, a letdown among the people. . . . I imagine a whole lot of people felt like I did."

315 "threw away . . . war." Wechsler, p. 227. Wallace's visit also posed a dilemma for rivals contemplating similar southern jaunts. "Southerners," noted the *Chicago Tribune,* "awaited word about arrangements for meetings by Gov. Dewey and President Truman in the south. Since Wallace made a point of holding unsegregated meetings, with Negroes and whites sitting or standing together, it is assumed that the same procedure must be followed by any candidate hoping to get Negro support in northern cities. Wallace slept in the homes of Negroes or on a private Pullman because southern hotels would not accommodate Negro members of his staff." *Chicago Tribune*, 6 September 1948, p. B2.

315 "Wallace has marched . . . land." *Time*, 20 September 1948, p. 27.

315 Dimitri Mitropoulos. *New Republic*, 19 January 1948, p. 10; *NY Times*, 26 March 1948, p. 16; Trotter, pp. 242–44. Management finally bid Mitropoulos *finis* after he pointedly snubbed an official after-concert reception in Atlanta to attend a Wallace fundraiser.

315 Ben Shahn. *NY Times*, 20 October 1948, p. 32.

315 "Studs" Terkel. *Chicago Tribune*, 15 May 1947, p. 9.

315 "We shall vote . . . millions." MacDougall, p. 303.

315 Aaron Copland. *NY Times*, 20 October 1948, p. 32; Pollack, *Copland*, pp. 280–83.

315 Leonard Bernstein. *NY Times*, 26 March 1948, p. 16; Seldes, pp. 43–47. Sculptor Jo Davidson ("I wanted to spend more time in my studio"), though still supporting Wallace, largely called it a day

regarding active involvement. Davidson, p. 347.

315   Spotlights reminded critics. Redding, p. 144.

316   "Wallace either . . . careful." MacDougall, p. 494.

316   Duquesne Gardens. *New Castle News*, 19 October 1948, p. 19. They missed. "This feels familiar, folks," grinned the nonplussed Wallace.

316   "G'wan back to Moscow!" *NY Times*, 19 October, 1948, p. 10.

316   "I don't understand . . . people." MacDougall, p. 813.

316   Baldwin's future wife. Ibid., p. 832.

316   "hurling . . . propaganda." Schapsmeier & Schapsmeier, *Prophet*, p. 190.

316   "If the ADA. . . . Gestapo?" Ibid.

316–17   "My first . . . faith." Ibid., p. 192.

317   "The new Progressive . . . Street." *Washington Post*, 3 August 1948, p. 1.

317   Lee Pressman and John Abt. Lader, p. 51.

317   "uneasy" about Communists. *Time*, 30 August 1948, p. 15; MacDougall, pp. 632–34.

317   "In my opinion . . . identification." Schapsmeier & Schapsmeier, *Prophet*, p. 190.

318   "was hatched . . . existence." *Chicago Defender*, 16 October 1948, p. 5.

318   "to repudiate . . . sharpers." Ibid.

318   "I tried to spell . . . himself." Wechsler, p. 221. Wechsler is not alone in that analysis. "If the Reds who managed to get close to him performed any function," Curtis MacDougall would write, "it was to tone-down [Wallace's] utterances, rather than the opposite. Experts in leftist clichés, they were able to spot and delete them from Wallace's own manuscripts." MacDougall, p. 430.

318   "There is no difference . . . field." *Albuquerque Journal*, 19 January 1948, p. 7.

318   "I love him . . . of him." Mellen, p. 222.

318   "be better . . . himself. " Hellman, *Scoundrel Time*, p. 124.

318   "stop playing . . . impracticals." Martinson, p. 231.

318   Favorably disposed. Newman, pp. 101–02.

318–19   "But of course . . . party." Ibid., p. 126.

319   "Then it is true. . . . I see." Hellman, *Scoundrel Time*, p. 121. "The only person toward whom I ever saw Wallace show a glimmer of generosity was Lillian Hellman," recalled John Abt. "Wallace's South Salem farm was quite near Lillian's, and at one of the meetings held in her home, Wallace brought her a present—a huge sack of cow dung for her garden." Abt, p. 155.

319   "turn attention . . . campaign." Hellman, *Three*, p. 688.

319   "two of them intelligent . . . unwise." Ibid.

319   "I think I understand . . . saying." Hellman, *Scoundrel Time*, pp. 122–23. Hellman, evidently, was not the only CPUSA member to walk away from Wallace in disgust. FBI undercover agent Herbert A. Philbrick reported similar disenchantment among his Boston-area party contacts. Philbrick, pp. 218–19.

319   "Where do they get those people!" *American Heritage*, December 1948, p. 44.

319   Ilo Wallace. Mellen, p. 261.

320   "stupid things." Ibid.

320   Marshall Tito. Ibid., pp. 261–63.

320   "collective action." Rollyson, *Mailer*, p. 56.

320   "Italy is pretty . . . there." Ibid., p. 57.

320   *National Guardian*. MacDougall, p. 505. Facing blacklisting, Knox emigrated to Italy in 1951.

320   Los Angeles rally. Rollyson, *Mailer*, p. 58.

321   Southern Negro Youth Council. Aptheker, pp. 169, 241.

321   Obstreperously insubordinate. Balaji, pp. 237–41; Janken, p. 297; Aptheker, pp. 95–101, 162.

321   "I think that a deliberately . . . injustice." Balaji, pp. 133–35; 243.

321   "the most stupid . . . nation." Lewis, p. 532; Wolters, p. 247.

321   Du Bois to depart. *Brooklyn Eagle*, 14 September 1948, p. 10; Record, p. 264*fn*; Wolters, p. 247. They did offer him a $12,000-a-year pension.

321   "Knowing you . . . need." Janken, p. 318.

322   Dolly Schiff married. *NY Times*, 30 July 1943, p. B2.

322   "An Appeal to Reason." *NY Post*, 15 August 1948, p. 2.

323   "A Further Appeal to Reason." Ibid., 22 August 1948, p. 2.

323   "Truman . . . land." Nissenson, pp. 93–94.

323   "I feel . . . Democrat." Ibid.

323   Sixty-five *Post* staffers. *Counterattack*, 5 November 1948, pp. 1–2. Schiff and Thackrey, nonetheless, both endorsed Wallace allies Marcantonio, Isacson, and Pressman, as well as Brooklyn city council candidate and CPUSA member Simon Gerson.

323–324   "top down. . . . did too." MacDougall, p. 383–84. MacDougall, a Northwestern journalism professor, faced threats and stoning during his campaign. *Binghamton Press*, 3 September 1948, p. 16; *Auburn Citizen-Advertiser*, 13 October 1948, p. 8.

324   "I wasn't very fond . . . level." Rabinowitz, pp. 66–67.

325   "We've got to build . . . a party." *NY Times*, 22 September 1948, p. 1. Textile Workers Union of America president Emil Rieve may have gotten the party's motivation most correct: "I think some people want a Third Party in this country in 1948, not for the purpose of electing anybody, but for the purpose of defeating someone, in order that they can show the world that anyone who has opposed them cannot be elected." McAuliffe, p. 41.

325   "Beanie, what do . . . up?" MacDougall, p. 748. Wallace, Douglas would later claim, had once personally offered her the Progressive nod, but she had refused it "firmly." Douglas, *Life*, p. 273.

325   "Today, I read . . . remarks." *NY Times*, 23 September 1948, p. 19; MacDougall, pp. 748–49.

325   Withdrawal of thirteen candidates. *NY Times*, 1 October 1948, pp. 1, 22. Remaining in the field against similarly liberal incumbent congressmen were Lee Pressman and Paul O'Dwyer.

326   Ronnie Gilbert. Fariello, p. 371.

326   "Acres of Clams." *New Republic*, 28 June 1948, p. 11.

326   "President Truman . . . race." Cray, *Ramblin' Man*, p. 327.

326   "My most vivid . . . Seeger." McGovern, p. 43.

326   JFK. Wilkinson, pp. 51–52.

326   "Bet you can't sing 'Dixie.'" Seeger Interview, Iowa PBS, 26 June 2003.

326   Fifteen-minute recording. *Billboard*, 6 November 1948, p. 42.

326   "The alliance . . . bad music." Klein, p. 377.

327   "How a man . . . song." Ibid.; Lieberman, p. 135.

327   "Nazis are. . . . anything." *NY Times*, 21 September 1948, p. 16.

327   "I tell you this . . . business." MacDougall, p. 829.

328   "quite full of himself." Rollyson, *Mailer*, p. 57.

328   "When they put the spotlight . . . tomorrow." Ibid.

328   Largest mass political assemblage. *Brooklyn Eagle*, 11 September 1948, p. 1.

328   "Many Wallacites . . . Hunter?)" *New Yorker*, 18 September 1948, p. 21.

328   "Ushers passed . . . carfare.'" Ibid., p. 22.

328   "The crowd's . . . silence." *NY Times*, 11 September 1948, p. 5.

329   "I can tell you . . . that." Ibid.

329 "Boy, were they enthusiastic! . . . thought." Seeger Interview, Iowa PBS, 26 June 2003.

329 "'Let them eat cake' . . . children." *NY Times*, 11 September 1948, p. 5.

329 Mayor Bill O'Dwyer. O'Dwyer, pp. 133–41.

329 "Fascism . . . tested." *Brooklyn Eagle*, 11 September 1948, p. 1.

329 "Big ovation . . . brushed." *New Yorker*, 18 September 1948, p. 22.

CHAPTER 31

330 "a near miracle." *NY Times*, 13 August 1948, p. 9.

330 Jamie Whitten. *NY Times*, 17 September 1948, p. 22.

330 Dean Alfange. Ibid.

330 Joe "The Brown Bomber" Louis. *Time*, 1 March 1948, p. 13; *Time*, 1 November 1948, p. 24.

330 "Truman makes . . . friends." Schlesinger, *Life*, p. 479.

330 "I had the impression . . . themselves." Abels, *Victory*, p. 71.

330 Vandenberg, he secured. *Vital Speeches*, 15 October 1948, pp. 11–12.

331 "If the convention. . . . leaders." *Chicago Tribune*, 26 June 1948, p. 1.

331 "This is for . . . yours." *NY Times*, 22 July 1948, p. 6.

331 72 percent. *Fortune*, February 1948, p. 6.

331 "This purchase . . . skyrocket." *NY Times*, 3 September 1948, p. 27.

331 "Stassen is the first . . . labor." *Amarillo News-Globe*, 3 October 1948, p. 48.

332 "We called [daughter] Virginia . . . children." Stone Interview, University of California at Berkeley, 18 February 1976.

332 "Your governor . . . know it." Cray, *Warren*, p. 183. Warren did not seem displeased.

332 "They struck . . . together." Ibid., p. 189.

332 "that big dumb Swede," Smith, *Colonel*, p. 479.

332 "We all thought . . . on it." Brinkley, *Memoir*, pp. 79–80.

332 "I wish . . . SOB." Smith, *Dewey*, p. 531.

332 "But Tom . . . time!" Cray, *Warren*, p. 190.

332–33 "There was always . . . saying." White, *Warren*, p. 135.

333 "The press . . . most." Warren, p. 243. It fit Robert Taft not at all. Following Warren's ultra-bland comments in Salt Lake City, he was heard to say, "You know, that is exactly contrary to everything I stand for." *Time*, 4 October 1948, p. 21.

333 "That is a hell . . . railroad." Warren, p. 242.

333 "Maybe they know . . . way." Mooney, p. 80.

333 "'Honey, do you. . . . this one?" Warren, pp. 243–44.

333 "Sir: [L]et me . . . cover." *Time*, 25 October 1948, p. 6.

334 Dewey had acted. *Atlanta Daily World*, 11 April 1948, pp. 1, 4. Controversy, however, dogged Dewey regarding his often sluggish efforts to integrate the New York State National Guard.

334 "has displayed . . . Negroes." *NY Amsterdam News*, 9 October 1948, p. 14.

334 *Richmond Afro-American*. Leuchtenburg, p. 206.

334 "forthright . . . wise." *NY Amsterdam News*, 9 October 1948, p. 10.

334 Disturbed by the "ineptness." Ibid., p. 14.

334 "New York . . . none." *LA Sentinel*, 28 October 1948, p. 1.

334 "an admirable . . . states." Ibid., p. 9.

334 "A majority . . . legislation." *Chicago Defender*, 16 October 1948, p. 6.

335 "a known . . . section." Ibid., 23 October 1948, p. 2.

335   "proud . . . word." Karabell, p. 144.

335   "No souls . . . minutes." Beyer, p. 208.

336   "[H]is effects . . . down." *New Yorker*, 16 October 1948, p. 75.

336   ". . . a slick . . . circuit today." *Hagerstown Daily Mail*, 29 September 1948, p. 4.

337   "I telephoned . . . defended." Martin, *50 Years*, pp. 195–96.

337   "We Republicans . . . better." Mooney, p. 80.

337   Joe Ball. *La Crosse Tribune*, 15 October 1948, p. 1.

337   "even if . . . me." Smith, *Dewey*, p. 521.

337–38   "as though . . . anybody." Smith, *Colonel*, p. 482.

338   "nobody . . . speech." *Logansport Pharos-Tribune*, 13 October 1948, p. 14.

338   "That's the first . . . hurt." Ibid. "I wasn't going to vote for Dewey in the first place," said the unrepentant Tindle.

338   "I've been doing . . . Dewey." *Chillicothe Constitution-Tribune*, 20 October 1948, p. 1.

338   Frances Dewey. Walker, *Dewey*, p. 186.

338   Hugh Scott. Smith, *Dewey*, p. 515.

339   Brownell. Ibid., p. 512.

339   "As the campaign . . . conclusion." Martin, p. 196.

339   George Patton's widow. *NY Times*, 22 April 1969, p. 47.

339   "We can't find . . . running." Mooney, p. 80.

339   "There is gloom . . . hall." *Portland Press Herald*, 20 October 1948, p. 14.

339   "Don't write that! . . . wrong!" Mooney, p. 81.

339   5 percent. Smith, *Dewey*, p. 533.

340   "He who had never . . . oppressors." Stone, *Truman Era*, p. 124.

340   "mistake on that one." *Washington Post*, 15 September 1948, p. B13.

340   "He's the only one . . . in November." Ibid.

341   Painful gout. Grose, pp. 288–89.

341   High-toned campaign team. Bird, pp. 103, 105.

341   "one of those . . . party." Ibid., p. 104.

341   "he was always . . . partners." Goldstein, p. 11.

341   "Dewey's view . . . ambassadors." Bird, p. 104.

341   Albany press conference. *NY Times*, 2 July 1948, pp. 1, 10.

341   Vandenberg's brand. Reinhard, p. 51.

341   "The subjects . . . potent." Pruessen, p. 366.

341   "The next Republican . . . victory." Ibid., p. 363.

341   "particularly anxious . . . and Dewey." Guhin, p. 160.

342   "Putting the matter . . . him." Steel, p. 456.

342   Lovett. Lovett Interview, Truman Library, 7 July 1971.

342   Whittaker Chambers's pumpkins. Chambers hid a microfilm of the papers Hiss stole from the State Department in a pumpkin on his Maryland farm—the so-called "Pumpkin Papers."

342   Forrestal. Grose, p. 289*fn*.

342   Acheson had informed Lovett. Isaacson & Thomas, p. 462.

342   "emergency character." Ibid.

342   "Bipartisanship . . . preserved." Ibid.

CHAPTER 32

343 "It looks like. . . . prevent that." Donovan, p. 416.

343 Cadillac Square. *Washington Post*, 7 September 1948, pp.1, 3.

343–44 $50,000. Phillips, p. 233.

344 "We were operating . . . sheriff." Farrar, p. 199.

344 "A great many . . . street." Donovan, p. 418.

344 Joe Kennedy. Ibid., p. 419.

344 "Good luck. . . . 'hell.'" *NY Times*, 18 September 1948, p. 1.

344 That first day. Ibid.

344 "gluttons of privilege." *Chicago Tribune*, 19 September 1948, p. 1.

344 "the Republican Congress . . . back." *NY Times*, 19 September 1948, pp. 1, 3. Speechwriter Albert Carr provided the actual phrase.

344 "If they should . . . business." *Moberly Monitor-Index*, 18 September 1948, p. 1.

345 "Nowhere . . . other." Ferrell, *Centenary*, p. 194.

345 "This was a strategy . . . can?" Lamb, p. 309.

345 "It was class . . . left." Smith Interview, Iowa PBS, 10 September 2003.

345 "We were on our . . . voters." Gosnell, p. 392.

345 "What demagoguery! . . . games." Kelly, p. 71.

345 Stony silence. *Chicago Tribune*, 19 September 1948, p. 1.

345 To spur applause. *New Yorker*, 9 October 1948, p. 69. "I rather enjoyed it," admitted Clifford.

346 "It involves . . . house." *New Yorker*, 9 October 1948, p. 70; Rovere, p. 69.

346 "[H]uge crowds . . . obvious." Biemiller Interview, Truman Library, 29 July 1977.

347 "Mr. Truman started . . . meaning." *NY Times*, 27 October 1948, p. 15.

347 "There was something. . . . uneven." Mooney, p. 76.

347 "Now and then . . . wrong?'" *Washington Post*, 17 October 1948, p. B1.

347 "Were it not . . . prosperity." Ayers, p. 280.

348 New fact-finding tour. *Washington Post*, 31 July 1948, p. 5.

348 Later, he would. *Titusville Herald*, 10 November 1948, p. 6.

348 Beyond his official means. Allen & Shannon, p. 239.

348 "I was hunched . . . found." *Titusville Herald*, 10 November 1948, p. 6. Biffle also predicted to Forrestal that not only would Democrats take the Senate by five seats, they might also possibly capture the House. Forrestal, pp. 511–12.

348–49 "chicken and . . . biscuits." McCullough, p. 675.

349 Rebel Stadium. *NY Times*, 28 September 1948, p. 20.

349 Scattered booing. Ibid.

349 Bonham. Hardeman & Bacon, p. 340.

349 September 27, Lyndon Baines Johnson. Clifford, p. 229.

349 "Labor's . . . fart." Baker & King, p. 40.

349 "The civil rights . . . hire." Miller, *Lyndon*, p. 118. Theodore White provided a slightly different version of this statement. White, *America*, p. 109.

349 "under a cloud." Dugger, p. 25. Subsequent historians have often accused Stevenson of also stealing votes. LBJ biographer Robert Caro regards such allegations as canards, largely devised by the Johnson camp. *NY Times*, 3 February 1991, p. BR26.

350 "like the damnedest . . . his life." Miller, *Lyndon*, p. 134.

350   His hands shook. Caro, *Ascent*, p. 373.

350   George Parr. Dugger, p. 335.

350   Abe Fortas. Dallek, *Lone Star Rising*, p. 339.

350   LBJ legal team. Ibid.

350   "Something happened . . . Bonham." Dugger, p. 336.

350   "send Lyndon . . . Senate." Caro, *Ascent*, p. 373.

350–51   "Davidson . . . it." Dugger, p. 335. Joe Rauh, for his part, "always thought that Tom Corcoran had spoken with Black before the hearing." Dallek, *Lone Star Rising*, p. 341.

351   "Just goes to show . . . Truman!" Miller, *Lyndon*, p. 134. In early October, with Truman requiring funds for radio airtime, LBJ cajoled Wright Morrow into contributing ten thousand of the thirty-nine thousand dollars required. In mid-October, Johnson again solicited Texas moneymen for badly needed campaign cash. Dallek, *Lone Star Rising*, p. 343.

351   "our nation's . . . world." Clifford, p. 233.

351   "Wallace or War." *Washington Post*, 7 September 1948, p. 3.

352   Lovett. Divine, p. 255.

352   "Never . . . my President." Ferrell, *Life*, p. 262.

352   "His magnified . . . do it." Daniels, *Independence*, pp. 28–29.

352   "he looks like . . . clipping." Coffin, p. 112.

352   "must be feeling . . . campaign." Connally, p. 331.

352   Walter Trohan. *Chicago Tribune*, 9 October 1948, p. 1.

353   "This was the worst . . . campaign." Clifford, p. 233.

353   "a tragic . . . judgment." *Washington Post*, 12 October 1948, p. 10.

353   "Mr. Truman's Blunder." *NY Times*, 11 October 1948, p. 22.

353   "Truman's Last Stand." *Life*, 18 October 1948, p. 42.

353   "What Next?" Gullan, p. 138.

353   "If Harry . . . nothing!" Donovan, p. 425.

353   "made a mistake . . . exploited it." Clifford, p. 232.

353   "practically . . . date." Watkins, p. 848.

353   Reregistered as a "nonpartisan." *Moberly Monitor-Index*, 12 October 1948, p. 3.

353   "When I was shown . . . you.'" Watkins, pp. 849–50.

353   "Of couse, . . . elected." Ibid., p. 850.

354   "As between . . . wish." *NY Times*, 12 October 1948, p. 22.

354   "he is on the make . . . interests." *NY Times*, 29 October 1948, p. 3.

354   "It was all pro forma." Watkins, p. 850.

354   Made James's position. *Christian Science Monitor*, 9 August 1948, p. 2.

354   Drew Pearson. *Charleston Gazette*, 30 September 1948, p. 6.

354–55   "I haven't actually . . . way." Lash, pp. 152–53.

355   "Paris, October 4 . . . rehabilitation." Lash, p. 153. In June 1948, Eleanor had written to Perkins that she had never forgiven Truman for not replacing her with another woman, adding that Truman had made "no suggestion so far of any woman or women in comparably important positions."

356   "I am enclosing . . . politics." Lash, p. 152.

356   "I am deeply . . . publication?" Neal, *Eleanor*, p. 32.

356   "Glad have . . . wish." Ibid. Her endorsement rated a mere thirty words in the *New York Times*, those thirty words including the headline, place, date, and the name of the wire service. *NY Times*, 14 October 1948, p. 24.

356 "all the prominent . . . administration." Divine, p. 260.

356 Former New Deal officials. *NY Times*, 23 October 1948, p. 6. Rosenman had been one of the few top New Dealers never seriously at odds with HST. For his part, however, HST rather correctly regarded Rosenman as a flatterer and a soft-soaper. Trohan, p. 212.

357 Hollywood stars. *Billboard*, 30 October 1948, p. 1.

357 Lost the vice-presidential nomination. Lobenthal, p. 321.

357 "Mr. Dewey is neat . . . humanity." Bankhead, p. 277.

357 "I want . . . *true* man." Kelly, p. 72.

357 "She's implying . . . that." Ibid., pp. 72–73.

357 "Don't get . . . he loses." Ibid., p. 73.

357 Gilmore Stadium. *LA Times*, 24 September 1948, p. 10.

357 "Communists are using . . . party." Ibid.

357 Twenty-dollar bet. Sperber & Lax, pp. 422–23. It was indeed a boy, and Bogart quickly dispatched a check to the White House. Truman returned the check, suggesting to Bogie that he deposit it in Stephen Bogart's "educational fund."

358 "The profits . . . profits." *Billboard*, 30 October 1948, p. 1.

358 Campaign comic book. *Washington Post*, 10 October 1948, p. M4; *Chicago Tribune*, 10 October 1948,p.3; *NY Times*, 10 October 1948,p.50; *Life*, 25 September 1950, p. 164; *Washington Post*, 6 September 1971, pp. B1–B2; Democratic National Committee, passim; http://www.tomchristopher.com/?op=home/ Comic%20History/Malcom%20Ater%20and%20the%20Commercial%20Comics%20Company. Democrats employed an Ater effort against Robert Taft in 1950. It blew up in their face. Klan-supported John Patterson used an Ater-drawn comic to defeat George Wallace for Alabama governor in 1958. Ater himself later produced a pro-segregation tract, *The Little Judge*, for Wallace and an effort on AIDS for Madonna.

358 "I thought that . . . Republicans." http://www.tomchristopher.com/?op=home/Comic%20 History/Malcom%20Ater%20and%20the%20Commercial%20Comics%20Company

358 "too undignified." Ibid.

359 "THE THRILLING . . . STATES." Democratic National Committee, p. 1.

359 "FARM BOY, . . . LIVES." Ibid.

359 "Captain Truman . . . feet." Ibid., p. 5.

359 Not a syllable. *NY Times*, 10 October 1948,p.50.

359 "something new in 'campaign literature.'" *Time*, 18 October 1948, p. 25.

359 Fifty cities. *Charleston Mail*, 23 October 1948, p. 4.

359 "The Demos . . . book." *Washington Post*, 16 October 1948, p. B13. Actually, at a half-cent apiece, the effort cost only $15,000. *Washington Post*, 6 September 1971, p. B2.

359 Corn had fetched. Abels, *Victory*, p. 176.

360 "When the Republicans . . . prices." Donovan, p. 421. "Unfortunately for this partisan thesis," noted the *New York Times*'s Arthur Krock, carefully dissecting Senate votes on the legislation, "it is impossible to sustain that charge against the Republicans in Congress as a group or to present [Democrats] in the opposite position." *NY Times*, 21 September 1948, p. 26.

360 "On the one hand . . . small." *NY Times*, 3 October 1948, p. 39.

361 54 percent. Abels, *Victory*, p. 292.

361 "What would be swept . . . do?" Ross, p. 260.

361 "I have been . . . vote." Donovan, p. 420.

CHAPTER 33

362 Chances "overwhelming." *Nation*, 6 November 1948, p. 515.

362 "Dewey is in, of course." *Business Week*, 30 October 1948, p. 16.

362 "a major miracle." *Wall Street Journal*, 29 October 1948, p. 1.

362 "G.O.P. strategists . . . slightly." Ibid.

362 *Chicago Tribune* forecast. *Chicago Tribune*, 1 November 1948, pp. 1–2.

362 *Time* magazine. *Time*, 18 October 1948, p. 24.

362 Fifty "experts." *Christian Science Monitor*, 28 October 1948, p. 1.

362 "appears certain to defeat." *NY Times*, 25 October 1948, p. 1.

362 Walter Winchell. Redding, p. 281.

362 Ed Sullivan. Ernst & Loth, p. 91.

362 "some development . . . importance." *Fortune*, October 1948, pp. 29–30, 32.

363 Sample public opinion. Smith, *Dewey*, p. 539.

363 79 percent. O'Neill, *High*, p. 93.

363 Crossley's poll. *Oakland Tribune*, 3 November 1948, p. 2.

363 "President Truman will . . . margins." *Lowell Sun*, 1 November 1948, p. 6.

363 "sleeping polls." *NY Times*, 27 October 1948, p. 20.

363 "throw the Gallup . . . ashcan." *NY Times*, 28 October 1948, p. 22.

363 Gallup's results. Ernst & Loth, pp. 123–31.

363 "If that is going . . . win." Trohan, p. 241.

364 "Do you fellows. . . . in '48?" Biemiller Interview, Harry S. Truman Library, 29 July 1977; Redding, p. 291. Truman once revealed to Biemiller: "I had put Indiana in. I did not think I was going to carry Wisconsin. I lost Indiana, but Wisconsin held up, and you've only got one less vote than Indiana in the electoral college, so I was absolutely on the head with what I was going to do."

364 "Biffle told me . . . tendencies." Forrestal, pp. 511–12.

364 "The Next President." *Life*, 1 November 1948, p. 38.

364–65 "Dewey had conducted . . . overconfident." *Waterloo Daily Courier*, 1 November 1948, p. 5.

365 "Mr. Truman is . . . outsmarted." Cooke, *Reporting America*, p. 41.

365 "both black . . . not to make trouble." *Waterloo Daily Courier*, 2 November 1948, p. 3.

365 "At the head . . . homes." *Oakland Tribune*, 2 November 1948, p. 4.

365 "We have . . . black." Ibid.

366 "has made his record . . . liberals." *Kingston Daily Freeman*, 1 November 1948, p. 3.

366–67 "The movie . . . together." Jamieson, p. 33.

367 "Soldier . . . States!" Ibid., p. 32.

367 "The child . . . reality." Ibid.

367 "During the last . . . campaign." Redding, p. 254.

367 "For many months . . . ice cream." Bowles, pp. 179–80.

368 In Michigan. *Benton Harbor News-Palladium*, 30 October 1948, p. 1.

368 *Editor & Publisher*. *NY Times*, 30 October 1948, p. 9.

368 "Mr. Dewey is now . . . position." *NY Times*, 3 October 1948, p. E6.

368 "Do I understand . . . *Times?*" Redding, p. 245.

368 "because, borrowing . . . machine." *Chicago Tribune*, 6 October 1948, p. 24.

369 "Dewey's speeches . . . 1944." *Lowell Sun*, 30 October 1948, p. 22.

369 "certainly . . . at all." Redding, p. 286.

369 To their precinct workers. Ibid.

369 "his everlasting regret." *NY Times*, 11 November 1948, p. 22. Hoover later denied the remark.

369 "starts to slug." Karabell, p. 250.

369 "We're in trouble . . . John?" Brownell, p. 84.

369 "special privilege boys." Smith, *Dewey*, p. 535.

369 "If anybody . . . Republicans." Ibid.

370 "Everywhere . . . fireworks." *NY Times*, 26 October 1948, p. 1.

370 David Noyes and Bob Carr. McCullough, p. 700.

370 Designed to incite Dewey. Ibid.

370–71 "When a few . . . Jews." *NY Times*, 26 October 1948, p. 18. Truman campaign aide Jay Franklin later termed the speech the campaign's one "blunder" and contended that "most of us were opposed" to it. *Life*, 15 November 1948, p. 48.

371 "PRESIDENT LIKENS . . . TOOL." *NY Times*, 26 October 1948, p. 1.

371 "If I have . . . will." Smith, *Dewey*, p. 535.

371 "They responded . . . win." Brownell, p. 83.

371 "I can't go against . . . party." Smith, *Dewey*, p. 535.

371 First live Midwest telecast. *Chicago Tribune*, 28 October 1948, p. 3.

371 "are openly sneering . . . wage." Smith, *Dewey*, p. 535.

371 "You're an. . . . right, sir." Ibid. Ole Olsen of the comedy team Olsen & Johnson served as master of ceremonies. *Chicago Tribune*, 26 October 1948, p. 1.

372 Cleveland Municipal Auditorium. Ibid., pp. 536–37.

372 "I don't understand . . . so." Patterson, p. 422.

372 "get away with murder." Smith, *Dewey*, p. 537.

372 "desperately . . . got it won." Ibid.

372 "Ain't he coming?" *NY Times*, 31 October 1948, p. 43.

372–73 "Since this campaign . . . course." Ibid.

373 "The Governor . . . intimidated." *Chicago Defender*, 16 October 1948, p. 9.

373 "Let's go, boys . . . traveling." Kelly, p. 74.

373 "Roosevelt never . . . man." Ibid., p. 76.

373 "I hate Communism . . . elephant. *NY Times*, 28 October 1948, p. 26.

374 "I have never . . . Israel." Donovan, p. 430.

374 1.2 million persons. McCullough, p. 702.

374 Twelve-minute standing ovation. Ibid.

374 Looked and sounded haggard. *NY Times*, 31 October 1948, p. 1.

374 Merging into HST's motorcade. Ibid., 29 October 1948, p. 10. Their schedules had coincided once previously, at a Dallas airfield. "Wallace got out of a rented DC-3 and saw the giant Presidential plane taxiing for a takeoff," a Wallace aide recalled. "He looked away quickly. You could see the pain on his face." *American Heritage*, December, 1976, p. 45.

374 "shallow. . . . camp." *NY Times*, 30 October 1948, p. 9.

375 "campaign talks . . . South." Ibid., 31 October 1948, p. 53.

375 Carrie "Tunch" Butler. Washington-Williams, pp. 141–43.

CHAPTER 34

376 "pour it on, Harry!" *Galveston Daily News*, 31 October 1948, p. 1.

376 "do-nothing idiot Congress." Ibid.

376 "Hearst character . . . double-talk." Ibid.

377 Truman's 270th address. Ibid.

377 Masonic ceremonies. *Nebraska State Journal*, 2 November 1948, p. 1.

377 "I believe . . . world." *NY Times*, 2 November 1948, p. 10.

378 "How does it . . . until tomorrow." *LA Times*, 3 November 1948, p. A.

378 "I'd like to tear . . . save it." *NY Times*, 3 November 1948, p. 3. Herbert Hoover, James A. Farley, and Francis Cardinal Spellman also voted at P.S. 18. *Oakland Tribune*, 2 November 1948, p. 11.

379 "well for the sake . . . mankind." *Oakland Tribune*, 2 November 1948, p. 6.

379 "be surprised . . . vote." *Washington Post*, 3 November 1948, p. 6.

379 Claude and Maude. Ibid.

379 Edgefield County Courthouse. *LA Times*, 3 November 1948, p. 6.

379 124-acre Farvue Farm. MacDonald, p. 124.

379 "more votes than the pollsters say." *NY Times*, 3 November 1948, p. 15.

379 Hart's Location. *Chillicothe Constitution-Tribune*, 2 November 1948, p. 14.

380 Haywood County. Ibid., p. 1.

380 Clintonville's 3rd Precinct. Ibid., p. 14.

380 In rural Godfrey. *Alton Evening Telegraph*, 2 November 1948, p. 1.

380 Frank O. Hammerberg. *NY Times*, 1 November 1948, p. 14.

380 Donora. *Charleroi Mail*, 2 November 1948, pp. 1, 6.

380 "Keep away . . . you." *Nebraska State Journal*, 2 November 1948, p. 1.

381 Oklahoma, Nebraska, and Illinois. *New Republic*, 9 August 1948, p. 10; MacDougall, pp. 441–42; Stedman & Stedman, pp. 125*fn*, 126–27. Though Progressives failed to qualify for the Illinois ballot, Prohibitionists and Socialists did.

381 Marcantonio. Schaffer, pp. 187–90; Meyer, p. 98.

381 Thieves lifted $35,000. *Syracuse Post-Standard*, 2 November 1948, p. 1.

381 Baltimore, H. L. Mencken. Goulden, *Mencken*, pp. 114–16; Hobson, p. 499.

381 "dignified . . . gentle." Ibid.

381 Eleanor Roosevelt. *Washington Post*, 3 November 1948, p. 6.

382 "I've got to finish . . . here." *NY Times*, 3 November 1948, p. 2.

382 Centralia No. 5. *Harper's*, March 1948, pp. 193–220.

382 Downstate Illinois editors. *Harrisburg Daily Register*, 14 May 1949, p. 1. One was the full-time director of agriculture. "They earned their money," argued Green in May 1949.

382 "Gamblers . . . campaign." McKeever, p. 121.

382 Stevenson's chances. *Chicago Tribune*, 3 November 1948, p. 6; McKeever, p. 126.

382 "You can't get it cut . . . President." *LA Times*, 3 November 1948, p. 3.

382 "a rude, ignorant, uncouth man." Donovan, p. 418.

382 Bernard Baruch. *Kingston Daily Freeman*, 2 November 1948, p. 12. Three days later, Baruch commented that he was "gratified" by the election results. *NY Times*, 5 November 1948, p. 3.

382 Taft. Patterson, p. 424. Following the election, however, Taft confided to William S. White that he had foreseen Dewey's demise. "I knew it for certain," said Taft, "when Martha told me she could no longer listen to Dewey's speeches or listen to him on the television."

383 Lovett. Clifford, pp. 237–38.

383 Mayflower ballroom. Ibid., p. 238.

383 Biltmore Hotel's Music Room. *Christian Science Monitor*, 3 November 1948, p. 11.

383 Lowest total in eight months. *Washington Post*, 3 November 1948, p. 6.

383 "a little group. . . . Truman." *Waterloo Daily Courier*, 2 November 1948, p. 6. On 5 May

1948, Truman had indeed been briefed regarding dropping forty atomic weapons on twenty Soviet cities ("Operation Halfmoon"). He ordered the plan scrapped, preferring conventional to nuclear weapons. On July 28, acting on his own initiative, James Forrestal overruled that policy and ordered planning for nuclear war. Ferrell, *Revisionists*, p. 68; Bogle, pp. 52–53.

383   "Police said . . . hand." *NY Times*, 3 November 1948, p. 17.

383   Alben Barkley. Ibid., 3 November 1948, p. 12.

384   Glen Taylor. *Washington Post*, 3 August 1948, p. 16.

384   "Don't you know. . . . film." *La Crosse Tribune*, 2 November 1948, p. 12.

384   "Well, Mother . . . line." *Oakland Tribune*, 2 November 1948, p. 1.

384   Nina Warren. Cray, *Warren*, p. 193.

CHAPTER 35

385   Mutual. *Billboard*, 13 November 1948, pp. 8–10.

385   NBC's coverage. Ibid., pp. 8, 16.

385   "Easily the standout." Ibid., p. 16.

385   "still 90 per cent . . . newspaperman." Ibid.

385   DuMont. *Billboard*, 13 November 1948, p. 9.

386   Model of the White House. Swanberg, *Luce*, p. 272.

386   Boston–Richmond broadcast. Von Schilling, p. 110.

386   *Münchner Merkur*. Lorant, p. 730.

386   Two hours' lead time. Smith, *Colonel*, p. 483.

386   "DEWEY DEFEATS TRUMAN." *Chicago Tribune*, 2 November 1948, p. 1.

386   Voting ran heavy. *Dixon Telegraph*, 2 November 1948, p. 1.

386   Closing times. *Joplin Globe*, 2 November 1948, p. 1.

386   Eight states voted on alcohol. Ibid.

386   Mike Westwood. *Kansas City Star*, 2 November 1998, p. 1.

387   "The President is entitled . . . himself." *LA Times*, 3 November 1948, p. A. Truman had similarly sequestered himself at the hotel in 1934, after learning he would not receive the gubernatorial nomination. *Kansas City Star*, 2 November 1998, p. 1.

387   "We drove down . . . evening." Miller, *Plain*, p. 283.

387   Not to awaken him. McCullough, p. 705.

387–88   "This is definitely . . . states." Lorant, p. 729.

388   Election-night dinner. *NY Times*, 8 November 1948, p. 3.

388   6:00 PM EST in Illinois. *Dixon Telegraph*, 2 November 1948, p. 1.

388   "I think I've won." Davis, *Stevenson*, p. 303.

388   Gallup in trouble. Smith Interview, Iowa PBS, 10 September 2003.

388   "Dewey's statisticians . . . breadth." Brownell, pp. 84–85.

388   "Truman is leading . . . the South." *Oakland Tribune*, 5 November 1948, p. 2.

389   Taft. Trohan, p. 243.

389   DuMont network. *Billboard*, 13 November 1948, p. 18.

389   "Reporters were . . . without it." Truman, *Presidency*, pp. 40–41.

389   "As of this moment . . . win." *LA Times*, 3 November 1948, p. A.

389   Reworked his acceptance speech. Davis, *Stevenson*, p. 303.

389   "Now we have come . . . evening." Donovan, p. 432.

390   "Truman's lead . . . Ohio." Phillips, p. 246.

390 Truman loyalists. *LA Times*, 3 November 1948, p. A.

390 "No cabinet . . . showed." *Chester Times*, 5 November 1948, p. 6.

390 "But this is . . . fold up." Redding, p. 17.

390 "I think President Truman has won." Morris, p. 452.

390 "I think Dewey . . . Baltimore." Rodgers, p. 525.

390 88 to 88. *NY Times*, 5 November 1948, p. 2.

391 Remained through the night. Clifford, p. 239.

391 "That editorial . . . Socialism.'" Schlesinger, *Life*, p. 481.

391 At 7 South Dearborn. Davis, *Stevenson*, p. 303.

391 At 11:08 EST. *LA Times*, 3 November 1948, p. A.

391–92 "The pattern . . . elected." Ibid.

392 "Herb, do. . . . hope so." Montgomery, p. 66.

392 "We pitched . . . over." *LA Times*, 3 November 1948, p. A.

392 "The cops are spreading . . . floors." Gould, *Best*, p. 419.

392–93 "It's the only time . . . worse." Srodes, p. 390.

393 "He didn't seem upset at all." Cray, *Warren*, p. 193.

393 "Thank God." Ibid.

393 "hundred-pound sack . . . back." Stone Interview, University of California at Berkeley, 18 February 1976.

393 "He said not to call . . . for one." Evans Interview, Truman Library, 18 September 1963; Neal, *HST*, p. 141.

394 "Nick, stop worrying . . . morning." Donovan, p. 433.

394 "Oh, yes . . . win." Miller, *Plain*, p. 264.

394 "I wonder if Clare . . . now." Truman, *Bess*, p. 333.

394 Acheson. Isaacson & Thomas, p. 462; Beisner, pp. 82, 675.

394 Don Maxwell. Trohan, pp. 243–44.

394 501,167. Caute, p. 34; Saposs, p. 93.

394 422,000. Rabinowitz, p. 69.

395 Wallace exceeded 4 percent. MacDougall, pp. 770, 838. In New York City, FDR had secured 390,171 votes on the ALP line in 1944. *NY Times*, 4 November 1948, p. 20.

395 Missouri, 53,000 voters. Lader, p. 55.

395 Thirty precincts. Lubell, pp.96,197.

395 "Once you find . . . thought." Seeger Interview, Iowa PBS, 26 June 2003.

395 Full third of Wallace's supporters. Culver & Hyde, pp. 500–01.

395 New York, Michigan, and Maryland. Gullan, p. 176.

395 From blacks and Jews. MacDougall, p. 858. Yet one should not overstate minority support for Wallace. Even in Harlem, where he drew 15 percent of the vote, he still ran behind not only Truman (65 percent) but also Dewey (20 percent). In Chicago, black congressman William Dawson's ward went 93 percent for Truman. *Hutchinson News-Herald*, 9 November 1948, p. 4.

395 Jews voting Progressive. Snetsinger, p. 190.

395 Marcantonio. Mearns, 1949, p. 722. Even in Marcantonio's district, Wallace drew only 21 percent of the vote. Meyer, p. 117. Six other Progressive-endorsed congressional candidates triumphed that evening. Former OSS agent John A. Blatnik (technically a Democratic-Farmer-Labor candidate) won in Minnesota's eighth district. In New York City, the Wallace-supporting ALP endorsed five successful Democratic congressmen, including Emanuel Celler and Adam Clayton Powell Jr. Mearns, *1949*, pp. 720, 722, 725.

395   Dollinger. Mearns, *1949*, p. 726.

395   Pressman. *Brooklyn Eagle*, 3 November 1948, pp. 1, 15.

395   Rogge. MacDougall, p. 841.

396   Gerson. Ibid., pp. 842–43. Running a poor third in Brooklyn's fifth state assembly district was ALP candidate Alfred A. Duckett, who would later assist on Jackie Robinson's autobiography and Martin Luther King Jr.'s "I Have a Dream" speech. *Atlanta Daily World*, 28 July 1948, p. 6; *Brooklyn Eagle*, 14 September 1948, p. 10; *NY Times*, 8 October 1964, p. D10.

396   Young. Young & Wheeler, p. 96. Young, purged by Walter Reuther from the CIO, worked full-time as Wallace's Michigan campaign director. Rich, p. 67.

396   "the biggest . . . life." Young & Wheeler, p. 96.

396   Durr. *Hartford Courant*, 3 November 1948, p. 12.

396   Robeson. MacDougall, pp. 664, 825; Record, p. 281. In Los Angeles, Progressives backed black assemblyman (and later congressman) Augustus F. Hawkins, but Hawkins ultimately supported Truman rather than Wallace.

396   Ran behind its congressional candidates. Schmidt, p. 240.

396   "I couldn't . . . wanted to." MacDougall, p. 881.

396   "to be in very good spirits." Culver & Hyde, p. 501.

396   "I don't think . . . he was." Ibid.

396   "a lying SOB." MacDougall, p. 883.

396   "I told him so . . . done it." MacDougall, p. 603. Wallace considered his wife "very violently anticommunist." According to Wallace biographers Culver and Hyde, she was "uncomfortable around blacks and Jews." Culver & Hyde, p. 496.

397   22.6 percent. Rosenstone, Behr, & Lazarus, p. 109.

397   Beyond Dixie. Cohodas, p. 190.

397   Percentage of the black population. Ibid., p. 189. These landslide percentages reflected purely white constituencies—blacks remained essentially disenfranchised.

397   McDuffie County. http://www.georgiaencyclopedia.org/nge/Article.jsp?id=h-1372.

397   Mundt and Margaret Chase Smith. *NY Times*, 7 November 1948, p. 56.

397   A pariah to Dewey. Reinhard, pp. 51–52.

397   Kerr. Gullan, p. 169.

397   Wilson. *Life*, 18 October 1948, p. 36.

397   Brooks. Reinhard, p. 51.

398   Ball. Ibid. Ball proved so endangered that Dewey had reputedly dangled a judgeship before Governor Luther Youngdahl if he would shoehorn Ball off the ticket. *Nation*, 28 August 1948, p. 222.

398   Long. *NY Times*, 7 November 1948, p. 56.

398   Johnson. *Amarillo Daily News*, 3 November 1948, p. 1.

398   Jester. Ibid.

398   Thomas. *NY Times*, 4 November 1948, p. 14.

398   Rodino Jr. Ibid.

398   Vail and McDowell. Morris, p. 452.

398   Knutson. Reinhard, p. 51.

398   Grand Rapids. *NY Times*, 7 November 1948, p. 56.

399   Kennedy. Dallek, *Kennedy*, p. 157.

399   Biemiller. *NY Times*, 7 November 1948, p. 56.

399   Democrats swept. Ibid.

399 Bowles. Abels, *Victory*, p. 267.

399 Largest margin in Illinois history. McKeever, p. 126.

399 Declined to make the race. *North Adams Transcript*, 21 July 1948, p. 1; Dallek, *Kennedy*, pp. 156–57; O'Brien, pp. 220, 229.

399 Dever. *NY Times*, 3 November 1948, p. 2.

399 "Kerner has deputized . . . them." Redding, p. 14. Arvey's pre-election canvas had forecast a Dewey Illinois win by "fifty to sixty thousand votes." Martin, *Stevenson*, p. 345.

399 Javits. Javits, p. 113; O'Dwyer, p. 141.

400 At the Biltmore. *LA Times*, 3 November 1948, p. A.

400 "We now know . . . States." Donovan, p. 433.

400 "All the figures . . . chance." Ibid., p. 434.

400 Fulton Lewis Jr. Lorant, p. 729.

400 "The South always . . . made." Abels, *Victory*, p. 268.

400–01 "amid the ruins . . . communists." Wechsler, p. 238.

401 "Under no circumstances . . . bitch." Abt, p. 164.

401 Javits had not gone to bed. Javits, p. 113.

401 "What a night . . . went." Truman, *Bess*, pp. 40–41.

401 "too close . . . estimate." *NY Times*, 3 November 1948, p. 8.

401–02 "As I read the vote . . . know." Ibid.

402 "in the Republican . . . votes." Ibid.

402 Bankhead. Bankhead, p. 280.

402 "How clumsy . . . win?" Mosley, p. 213.

402 "unity and vigor." *Washington Post*, 4 November 1948, p. 5.

402 "I am an Episcopalian." Ibid.

402 "We're in there . . . mid-morning." *NY Times*, 3 November 1948, p. 3.

403 "I still had no . . . make it." Schlesinger, *Life*, p. 481.

403 "We are not making . . . returns." *NY Times*, 3 November 1948, p. 3.

403 Ross. Ibid., p. 10.

403 Clifford. Clifford, p. 239.

403 Illinois had gone for Truman. Donovan, p. 435.

403 "And all of a sudden . . . We've won!'" McCullough, p. 707.

403 "That's it . . . first one." Donovan, p. 435.

403 "We've got 'em beat . . . City." McCullough, p. 707.

403 Clifford arose. Clifford, p. 239.

403 "By dawn . . . awful." Srodes, p. 390.

404 180,000. Smith, *Dewey*, p. 510.

404 "We got it . . . more." Redding, p. 22.

404 "I'm going to . . . breakfast." Chace, p. 189.

404 "Yes, I have . . . for us." Katcher, p. 236.

404 "This is it . . . everything." Manchester, *Mencken*, p. 311.

404 "The son of a bitch won." Cray, *Warren*, p. 193.

CHAPTER 36

405 Dewey's vote totals declined. Abels, *Victory*, p. 290; Barone, p. 219.

405 "The farm vote switched. . . . election." McCullough, p. 712. Both Gallup and Roper found

that 74 percent of the 14 percent of voters who made up their minds in the final two weeks voted for Truman. Roper also found that 1 percent of the entire vote shifted from Wallace to Truman in that fortnight. Mosteller et al., pp. 252–55.

406   slid dramatically. Ross, p. 251.

406   "Far from costing . . . 1936." McCullough, p. 714. Dewey himself spoke of "two or three million Republicans who had stayed home." Archibald Crossley disagreed, contending that it was Truman voters who in the end essentially abstained.

406   In 1952, thirteen million more. Gullan, p. 181.

406   48.9 percent. McCoy, p. 162.

406   Scott. *NY Times*, 14 October 1948, p. 1.

406    $2,736,334. McCullough, p. 712.

406   Morgenthau. Abels, *Victory*, p, 272. Organized labor expended $1 million against the GOP.

406   Electoral College total to 225. Ibid., p. 290. In more normal times, Truman might well have triumphed even if Thurmond had hijacked the entire South. In achieving his four national victories, FDR had not, in fact, required a single Southern electoral vote. Hamby, *People*, p. 465.

407   The Catholic vote. *New Republic*, 15 November 1948, p. 7. Rexford Tugwell's account of these years, for example, betrays a distinct anti-Catholicism, with references to "war-minded Catholics" and the "most vindictive among the prelates," of an "open alliance" of "Big business and the military" with "the Vatican," and the assertion that "certain higher levels in the Catholic hierarchy" indeed "wanted war." Tugwell, pp. 77, 78, 123.

407   Where African-Americans really counted. *Pittsburgh Courier*, 5 February 1949, p. 3.

407   "You may not believe . . . for me." MacDougall, p. 680.

408   "No presidential . . . ahead." Donaldson, p. 173.

408   Oklahoma. Smith, *Dewey*, p. 521.

408   San Francisco. Cray, *Warren*, p. 192.

409   "make a lot of noise." *Kingston Freeman*, 30 December 1947, p. 4; MacDougall, p. 286. Journalist David Lawrence is not to be confused with Pittsburgh mayor David Lawrence.

409   Popular-vote totals. Mosteller et al., pp. 316–17. Norman Thomas gathered barely more votes than Prohibitionist Claude Watson (139,569 to 103,708).

409   "He took it like a man." Grose, p. 290.

409   "I am just as surprised . . . election." *NY Times*, 3 November 1948, p. 3.

409   "No comment." Ibid.

409–10   "It's been grand . . . Good luck!" Ibid.

410   "Labor did it." Ferrell, *Presidency*, p. 262.

410   He nearly wept. *Chicago Tribune*, 4 November 1948, p. 1.

410   Congratulatory cables. *NY Times*, 6 November 1948, p. 2.

410   "The people have put you . . . place." Bankhead, p. 280.

410   "You can . . . Dewey." Ibid.

410   Henning. Trohan, pp. 244–45. McCormick pensioned Henning off at his full $35,000 salary, however.

410   "breast of tough . . . *glace*." *Washington Post*, 5 November 1948, p. 1.

410   "After an election . . . over." *NY Times*, 6 November 1948, p. 3.

411   "Open the gates . . . down." Ibid.

411   "Let the people . . . in." Ibid.

411   Dawson. Redding, p. 281.

411   "That's one for the books." *Washington Post*, 5 November 1948, p. 1. Slept through this moment. Truman, *Presidency*, p. 42.

411   Johnston. *Washington Post*, 6 November 1948, p. 3.

411   "I don't think . . . Senator." Ayers, p. 282.

411   Ten bands. *Washington Post*, 6 November 1948, p. 2.

412   "Wednesday morning Democrats." Truman, *Presidency*, p. 43. Eisenhower and Adm. Nimitz had both drawn larger crowds, but Truman's greatly exceeded those for every other event, including FDR's funeral. *Washington Post*, 6 November 1948, p. 2.

412   "Remember . . . last month?" Truman, *Bess*, p. 335.

412   Meet his cabinet. Truman, *Trial*, p. 222; Forrestal, p. 519.

Sources

BOOKS

Abell, Tyler, ed. *The Drew Pearson Diaries 1949–1959.* New York: Holt, Rinehart and Winston, 1974.

Abels, Jules. *Out of the Jaws of Victory: The Astounding Election of 1948.* New York: Henry Holt, 1959.

———. *The Truman Scandals.* Chicago: Regnery, 1956.

Abramson, Rudy. *Spanning the Century: The Life of W. Averell Harriman 1891–1986.* New York: William Morrow, 1992.

Abt, John J., and Michael Myerson. *Advocate and Activist: Memoirs of an American Communist Lawyer.* Urbana: University of Illinois Press, 1993.

Acheson, Dean. *Present at the Creation: My Years in the State Department.* New York: W. W. Norton, 1987.

Allen, George E. *Presidents Who Have Known Me.* New York: Simon & Schuster, 1960.

Allen, Robert S., and William V. Shannon. *The Truman Merry-Go-Round.* New York: Vanguard, 1950.

Ambrose, Stephen E. *Eisenhower: Soldier, General of the Army, President-Elect; 1890–1952. Vol. 1.* New York: Simon & Schuster, 1983.

Anderson, Jack, with Daryl Gibson. *Peace, War, and Politics: An Eyewitness Account.* New York: Macmillan, 2000.

Anderson, Jack, and Ronald May. *McCarthy: The Man, The Senator, The Ism.* Boston: Beacon Press, 1952.

Andrew, Christopher, and Vasili Mitrokhin. *The Sword and the Shield: The Mitrokhin Archive and the Secret History of the KGB.* New York: Basic Books, 2000.

Aptheker, Herbert, ed. *The Correspondence of W. E. B. Du Bois. Vol. 3, Selections, 1944–1963.* Amherst: University of Massachusetts Press, 1978.

Atleson, James B. *Labor and the Wartime State: Labor Relations and Law During World War II.* Urbana: University of Illinois Press, 1998.

Ayers, Edward L. *The Promise of the New South: Life after Reconstruction.* New York: Oxford University Press, 1993.

Bacall, Lauren. *By Myself and Then Some.* New York: Harper Paperbacks, 2006.

Baker, Bobby, and Larry L. King. *Wheeling and Dealing: Confessions of a Capitol Hill Operator.* New York: W. W. Norton, 1978.

Bankhead, Tallulah. *Tallulah: My Autobiography.* Jackson: University Press of Mississippi, 2004.

Barber, James David. *The Pulse of Politics: Electing Presidents in the Media Age.* San Francisco: Transaction Publishers, 1992.

Barkley, Alben W. *That Reminds Me.* Garden City (NY): Doubleday, 1954.

Barnard, Hollinger, ed. *Outside the Magic Circle: The Autobiography of Virginia Foster Durr.* Tuscaloosa: University of Alabama Press, 1990.

Barnard, William D. *Dixiecrats and Democrats: Alabama Politics 1942–1950*. Tuscaloosa: University of Alabama Press, 1985.

Barone, Michael. *Our Country: The Shaping of America from Roosevelt to Reagan*. New York: Free Press, 1990.

Bart, Philip Abraham. *Highlights of a Fighting History: 60 Years of the Communist Party, USA*. New York: International Publishers, 1979.

Bartlett, Bruce. *Wrong on Race: The Democratic Party's Buried Past*. New York: Palgrave Macmillan, 2008.

Bass, Jack, and Marilyn W. Thompson. *Ol' Strom: An Unauthorized Biography of Strom Thurmond*. Atlanta: Longstreet, 1998.

———. *Strom: The Complicated Personal and Political Life of Strom Thurmond*. New York: Public Affairs, 2006.

Bass, Warren. *Support Any Friend: Kennedy's Middle East and the Making of the U.S.-Israel Alliance*. New York: Oxford University Press, 2004.

Beasley, Maurine H., Holly C. Shulman, and Henry R. Beasley, eds. *The Eleanor Roosevelt Encyclopedia*. Westport (CT): Greenwood Press, 2001.

Belfrage, Cedric. *The American Inquisition 1945–1960*. Indianapolis: Bobbs-Merrill, 1973.

Benjamin, Gerald, ed. *Memories of Thomas E. Dewey: September 8, 1988*. Albany: Nelson A. Rockefeller Institute of Government, 1991.

Benson, Michael T. *Harry S. Truman and the Founding of Israel*. Westport (CT): Praeger, 1997.

Berman, Edgar. *Hubert: The Triumph and Tragedy of the Humphrey I Knew*. New York: G. P. Putnam's Sons, 1979.

Berman, William C. *The Politics of Civil Rights in the Truman Administration*. Columbus: University of Ohio Press, 1970.

Bernays, Anne, and Justin Kaplan. *Back Then: Two Literary Lives in 1950s New York*. New York: HarperCollins, 2003.

Bernstein, Carl. *Loyalties: A Son's Memoir*. New York: Simon & Schuster, 1989.

Beschloss, Michael. *Presidential Courage: Brave Leaders and How They Changed America, 1789–1989*. New York: Simon & Schuster, 2007.

——— (ed.). *Reaching for Glory: Lyndon Johnson's Secret White House Tapes, 1964–1965*. New York: Simon & Schuster, 2002.

———. *The Conquerors: Roosevelt, Truman and the Destruction of Hitler's Germany, 1941–1945*. New York: Simon & Schuster, 2002.

Beyer, Barry K. *Thomas E. Dewey, 1937–1947: A Study in Political Leadership*. New York: Garland, 1979.

Biesner, Robert L. *Dean Acheson: A Life in the Cold War*. New York: Oxford University Press, 2009.

Billingsley, Kenneth Lloyd. *Hollywood Party: How Communism Seduced the American Film Industry in the 1930s and 1940s*. Roseville (CA): Forum, 2000.

Bird, Kai. *The Color of Truth: McGeorge Bundy and William Bundy; Brothers in Arms*. New York: Touchstone, 1998.

Bishop, Jim. *FDR's Last Year: April 1944–April 1945*. New York: William Morrow, 1974.

Black, Allida M. *Casting Her Own Shadow: Eleanor Roosevelt and the Shaping of Postwar Liberalism*. New York: Columbia University Press, 1996.

Black, Conrad. *Franklin Delano Roosevelt: Champion of Freedom*. New York: PublicAffairs, 2003.

———. *Richard M. Nixon: A Life in Full*. New York: PublicAffairs, 2007.

Black, Merle, and John Shelton Reed. *Perspectives on the American South*. New York: Routledge, 1981.

Bogle, Lori Lyn. *The Cold War: National Security Policy Planning From Truman to Reagan and From Stalin to Gorbachev*. New York: Routledge, 2001.

Bohlen Charles E. *Witness to History: 1929–1969*. New York: W. W. Norton, 1973.

Boller, Paul F., Jr. *Presidential Campaigns*. New York: Oxford University Press, 1984.

Bontecue, Eleanor. *The Federal-Loyalty Security Program*. Ithaca: Cornell University Press, 1953.

Bosworth, Patricia. *Anything Your Little Heart Desires: An American Family Story*. New York: Touchstone, 1998.

Bowles, Chester. *Promises to Keep: My Years in Public Life*. New York: Harper & Row, 1971.

Boyle, Kevin. *The UAW and the Heyday of American Liberalism, 1945–1968*. Ithaca (NY): Cornell University Press, 1995.

Brands, H. W. *Traitor to His Class: The Privileged Life and Radical Presidency of Franklin Delano Roosevelt*. New York: Doubleday, 2008.

Brendon, Piers. *Ike: His Life & Times*. New York: Harper & Row, 1986.

Brinkley, David. *David Brinkley: A Memoir*. New York: Alfred A. Knopf, 1995.

———. *Washington Goes to War*. New York: Alfred A. Knopf, 1988.

Brock, Clifton. *Americans for Democratic Action: Its Role in National Politics*. Washington: Public Affairs Press, 1962.

Brough, James. *Princess Alice: A Biography of Alice Roosevelt Longworth*. Boston: Little, Brown, 1975.

Brown, C. Edgar, ed. *Democracy at Work: Being The Official Report of the Democratic National Convention Philadelphia, Pennsylvania July 12 to July 14, inclusive 1948 Resulting in the Nomination of Harry S. Truman of Missouri for President and Alben W. Barkley of Kentucky for Vice-President*. Philadelphia: Local Democratic Political Committee of 1949, 1949.

Brownell, Herbert, with John P. Burke. *Advising Ike: The Memoirs of Attorney General Herbert Brownell*. Lawrence: The University Press of Kansas, 1993.

Bulaji, Murali. *The Professor and the Pupil: The Politics of W. E. B. Du Bois and Paul Robeson*. New York: Nation Books, 2007.

Bullough, Vern L. *Before Stonewall: Activists for Gay and Lesbian Rights in Historical Context*. New York: Routledge, 2002.

Burnes, Brian, and Donna Martin. *Harry S. Truman: His Life and Times*. Kansas City: Kansas City Star Books, 2003.

Butcher, Harry C. *My Three Years with Eisenhower: The Personal Diary of Captain Harry C. Butcher, USNR, Naval Aide to General Eisenhower, 1942 to 1945*. New York: Simon & Schuster, 1946.

Byrnes, James F. *All in One Lifetime*. New York: Harper, 1958.

Cannistraro, Philip V., and Gerald Meyer, eds. *The Lost World of Italian American Radicalism: Politics, Labor, and Culture*. Westport (CT): Praeger, 2003.

Cannon, Lou. *Reagan*. New York: G. P. Putnam's Sons, 1982.

Caro, Robert A. *Master of the Senate: The Years of Lyndon Johnson*. New York: Alfred A. Knopf, 2002.

———. *Means of Ascent: The Years of Lyndon Johnson*. New York: Vintage Books, 1991.

Carter, Dan T. *The Politics of Rage: George Wallace, the Origins of the New Conservatism, and the Transformation of American Politics*. Baton Rouge: Louisiana State University Press, 2000.

Caute, David. *The Great Fear: The Anti-Communist Purge Under Truman and Eisenhower*. New York: Simon & Schuster, 1978.

Chace, James. *Acheson: The Secretary of State Who Created the American World*. New York: Simon & Schuster, 1998.

Chalmers, David M. *Hooded Americanism: The History of the Ku Klux Klan.* Chicago: Quadrangle Books, 1965.

Cherny, Andrei. *The Candy Bombers: The Untold Story of the Berlin Airlift and America's Finest Hour.* New York: Penguin Group, 2008.

Childs, Marquis. *Eisenhower: Captive Hero.* New York: Harcourt, Brace, 1958.

Christensen, Rob. *The Paradox of Tar Heel Politics: The Personalities, Elections, and Events that Shaped Modern North Carolina.* Chapel Hill: University of North Carolina Press, 2008.

Clifford, Clark. *Counsel to the President: A Memoir.* New York: Random House, 1991.

Cochran, Bert. *Harry Truman and the Crisis Presidency.* New York: Funk & Wagnalls, 1973.

Coffey, Thomas M. *Iron Eagle: The Turbulent Life of General Curtis LeMay.* New York: Crown, 1986.

Coffin, Tristan. *Missouri Compromise.* Boston: Little, Brown, 1947.

Cohen, Dan. *Undefeated: The Life of Hubert H. Humphrey.* Minneapolis: Lerner Publications, 1978.

Cohodas, Nadine. *Strom Thurmond & the Politics of Southern Change.* Macon (GA): Mercer University Press, 1995.

Collins, Charles Wallace. *Whither Solid South? A Study in Politics and Race Relations.* New Orleans: Pelican Publishing Group, 1947.

Conlin, Joseph R. *The Morrow Book of Quotations in American History.* New York: William Morrow, 1984.

Connally, Senator Tom, as told to Alfred Steinberg. *My Name is Tom Connally.* New York: Crowell, 1954.

Cook, Fred J. *The Unfinished Story of Alger Hiss.* New York: William Morrow, 1958.

Cooke, Alistair. *Six Men.* New York: Arcade Publishing, 1995.

———. *The Vintage Mencken.* New York: Vintage Books, 1955.

Cordery, Stacy A. *Alice: Alice Roosevelt Longworth, from White House Princess to Washington Power Broker.* New York: Viking, 2007.

Cray, Ed. *Chief Justice: A Biography of Earl Warren.* New York: Simon & Schuster, 1997.

———. *Ramblin' Man: The Life and Times of Woody Guthrie.* New York: W. W. Norton, 2004.

Crespi, Irving, and Harold Mendelsohn. *Polls, Television and the New Politics.* Scranton (PA): Chandler Publishing, 1970.

Culver, John C., and John Hyde. *American Dreamer: A Life of Henry A. Wallace.* New York: W. W. Norton, 2000.

Dailey, Jane Elizabeth, Glenda Elizabeth Gilmore, and Bryant Simon, eds. *Jumpin' Jim Crow: Southern Politics from Civil War to Civil Rights.* Princeton: Princeton University Press, 2000.

Dallek, Robert. *An Unfinished Life: John F. Kennedy, 1917–1963.* Boston: Little, Brown, 2003.

———. *Harry S. Truman.* New York: Times Books, 2008.

———. *Lone Star Rising: Lyndon Johnson and His Times, 1908–1960.* New York: Oxford University Press, 1991.

Daniels, Jonathan. *Man of Independence.* Philadelphia: J. B. Lippincott, 1950.

———. *White House Witness, 1942–1945.* Garden City (NY): Doubleday, 1975.

Davidson, Jo. *Between Sittings: An Informal Autobiography.* New York: Dial Press, 1951.

Davis, Frank Marshall, and John Edgar Tidwell, ed. *Livin' the Blues: Memoirs of a Black Journalist and Poet.* Madison: University of Wisconsin Press, 2003.

Davis, Kenneth S. *A Prophet in His Own Country: The Triumphs and Defeats of Adlai E. Stevenson.* Garden City (NY): Doubleday, 1957.

De Toledano, Ralph. *One Man Alone: Richard Nixon.* New York: Funk & Wagnalls, 1969.

Delton, Jennifer Alice. *Making Minnesota Liberal: Civil Rights and the Transformation of the Democratic Party.* Minneapolis: University of Minnesota Press, 2002.

Democratic National Committee. *The Story of Harry S. Truman.* Washington: Democratic National Committee, 1948.

Dennis, Eugene. *What America Faces: The New War Danger and the Struggle for Peace, Democracy and Economic Security.* New York: New Century Publishers, 1946.

Denton, Sally. *The Pink Lady: The Many Lives of Helen Gahagan Douglas.* New York: Bloomsbury Press, 2009.

Dewey, Thomas E. *Public Papers of Thomas E. Dewey, Fifty-first Governor of the State of New York.* Albany: Williams Press, 1949.

———. *Twenty Against the Underworld.* Garden City (NY): Doubleday, 1974.

Diggins, John Patrick. *The Proud Decades: America in War and Peace, 1941–1960.* New York: W. W. Norton, 1989.

Dinnerstein, Leonard. *America and the Survivors of the Holocaust.* New York: Columbia University Press, 1982.

Divine, Robert A. *Foreign Policy and U.S. Presidential Elections: 1940–1948.* New York: New Viewpoints, 1974.

Doe, Father John (Father Ralph Phau). *The Golden Book of Action.* Center City (MN): Hazelden, 1950.

Donaldson, Gary A. *Truman Defeats Dewey.* Lexington: University Press of Kentucky, 1999.

Donovan, Robert J. *Conflict & Crisis: The Presidency of Harry S. Truman, 1945–1948.* Columbia: University of Missouri Press, 1977.

Dorn, T. Felder. *The Guns of Meeting Street: A Southern Tragedy.* Columbia: University of South Carolina Press, 2001.

Dorn, William Jennings Bryan, and Scot Derks. *Dorn: Of the People, a Political Way of Life.* Orangeburg (SC): Sandlapper, 1988.

Douglas, Helen Gahagan. *A Full Life.* Garden City (NY): Doubleday, 1992.

Douglas, William O. *Go East, Young Man: The Early Years; The Autobiography of William O. Douglas.* New York: Random House, 1974.

———. *The Court Years: 1939–1975; The Autobiography of William O. Douglas.* New York: Random House, 1980.

Downey, Kirstin. *The Woman Behind the New Deal: The Life of Frances Perkins, FDR's Secretary of Labor and His Moral Conscience.* New York: Nan A. Talese, 2009.

Drake, Frederick D., and Lynn R. Nelson. *States Rights and American Federalism: A Documentary History.* Westport (CT): Greenwood Press, 1999.

Druks, Herbert M. *John F. Kennedy and Israel.* Westport (CT): Praeger , 2005.

———. *The Uncertain Friendship: The U.S. and Israel from Roosevelt to Kennedy.* Westport: Greenwood Press, 2000.

Duberman, Martin Bauml. *Paul Robeson.* New York: Alfred A. Knopf, 1988.

Du Bois, W. E. B. *Against Racism: Unpublished Essays, Papers, Addresses, 1887–1961.* Amherst: University of Massachusetts Press, 1988.

Dugger, Ronnie. *The Politician: The Life and Times of Lyndon Johnson, The Drive for Power, from the Frontier to Master of the Senate.* New York: W. W. Norton, 1982.

Dunar, Andrew J. *The Truman Scandals and the Politics of Morality.* Columbia: University of Missouri Press, 1997.

Dunaway, David King. *How Can I Keep from Singing? The Ballad of Pete Seeger.* New York: Villard, 2008.

Eaton, Herbert. *Presidential Timber: A History of Nominating Conventions, 1868–1960.* New York: Free Press of Glencoe, 1964.

Egan, Timothy. *The Worst Hard Time: The Untold Story of Those Who Survived the Great American Dust Bowl.* New York: Houghton Mifflin Harcourt, 2006.

Eisele, Albert. *Almost to the Presidency: A Biography of Two American Politicians.* Blue Earth (MN): Piper, 1972.

Eisenhower, Dwight D. *Crusade in Europe.* Garden City (NY): Doubleday, 1948.

———. *The White House Years: Mandate for Change; 1953–1956.* Garden City (NY): Doubleday, 1963.

Eisenhower, Susan. *Mrs. Ike: Memories and Reflections on the Life of Mamie Eisenhower.* Sterling (VA): Capital Books, 2002.

Ekirch, Arthur A., Jr. *Ideologies and Utopias: The Impact of the New Deal on American Thought.* New York: Quadrangle Books, 1971.

Elsey, George McKee. *An Unplanned Life: A Memoir.* Columbia: University of Missouri Press, 2005.

Ernst, Morris L., and David Loth. *The People Know Best: The Ballots vs. the Polls.* Washington: Public Affairs Press, 1949.

Evans, M. Stanton. *Blacklisted by History: The Untold Story of Joe McCarthy and His Fight Against America's Enemies.* New York: Crown, 2007.

Evensen, Bruce J. *Truman, Palestine, and the Press: Shaping Conventional Wisdom at the Beginning of the Cold War.* Westport (CT): Greenwood Press, 1992.

Fariello, Griffin. *Red Scare: Memories of the American Inquisition, An Oral History.* New York: W. W. Norton, 1995.

Farley, James A. *Jim Farley's Story.* New York: Whittlesey House, 1948.

Farr, Finis. *Fair Enough: The Life of Westbrook Pegler.* New Rochelle (NY): Arlington House, 1975.

Farrar, Ronald T. *Reluctant Servant: The Story of Charles G. Ross.* Columbia: University of Missouri Press, 1969.

Fast, Howard. *Being Red: A Memoir.* Armonk (NY): M.E. Sharpe, 1994.

Feldman, Glenn. *From Demagogue to Dixiecrat: Horace Wilkinson and the Politics of Race.* Lanham (MD): University Press of America, 1995.

———. *Politics, Society and the Klan in Alabama, 1915–1949.* Tuscaloosa: University of Alabama Press, 1999.

Ferrell, Robert H. *Choosing Truman: The Democratic Convention of 1944.* Columbia: University of Missouri Press, 1994.

———. *Harry S. Truman and the Cold War Revisionists.* Columbia: University of Missouri Press, 2006.

———. *Harry S. Truman and the Modern American Presidency.* Boston: Little, Brown, 1983.

———. *Harry Truman: A Life.* New York: Viking Adult, 1994.

———. *Off the Record: The Private Papers of Harry S. Truman.* Columbia: University of Missouri Press, 1997.

———. *Truman: A Centenary Remembrance.* New York: Viking, 1984.

———. *Truman and Pendergast.* Columbia: University of Missouri Press, 1999.

———, ed. *The Eisenhower Diaries.* New York: W. W. Norton, 1981.

———, ed. *Truman in the White House: The Diary of Eben A. Ayers.* University of Missouri Press, 1991.

Filler, Louis, ed. *The President Speaks: From McKinley to Lyndon Johnson.* New York: G. P. Putnam's Sons, 1964.

Fine, Morris, ed. *American Jewish Yearbook. Vol. 51.* New York: American Jewish Committee, 1950.

Fite, Gilbert C. Richard B. *Russell, Jr.: Senator from Georgia.* Chapel Hill: University of North Carolina Press, 1991.

Fleming, John V. *The Anti-Communist Manifestos: Four Books that Shaped the Cold War.* New York: W. W. Norton, 2009.

Fleming, Thomas. *The New Dealers' War: Franklin D. Roosevelt and the War within World War II.* New York: Basic Books, 2001.

Flynn, John T. *The Roosevelt Myth.* New York: Devin-Adair, 1948.

Foner, Philip S., ed. *Paul Robeson Speaks: Writings, Speeches, and Interviews, a Centennial Celebration.* New York: Citadel, 1998.

Forrestal, James, and Walter Millis, ed. *The Forrestal Diaries.* New York: Viking, 1951.

Franklin, John Hope. *From Slavery to Freedom: A History of Negro Americans.* New York: Vintage Books, 1969.

Fraser, Steve. *Labor Will Rule: Sidney Hillman and the Rise of American Labor.* Cornell (NY): Cornell University Press, 1993.

Frederickson, Kari. *The Dixiecrat Revolt and the End of the Solid South, 1932–1968.* Chapel Hill: University of North Carolina Press, 2001.

Freedomways, The editors of. *Paul Robeson, the Great Forerunner.* New York: International Publishers, 1998.

Friedenberg, Robert V. *Notable Speeches in Contemporary Presidential Campaigns.* Westport (CT): Praeger, 2002.

Friedrich, Otto. *City of Nets: A Portrait of Hollywood in the 1940's.* Berkeley: University of California Press, 1997.

Gabler, Neal. *Winchell: Gossip, Power and the Culture of Celebrity.* New York: Alfred A. Knopf, 1994.

Gall, Gilbert J. *Pursuing Justice: Lee Pressman, the New Deal, and the CIO.* Albany: State University of New York Press, 1999.

Ganin, Zvi. *Truman, American Jewry, and Israel, 1945–1948.* Teaneck (NJ): Holmes & Meier, 1979.

Gardner, Michael R. *Harry Truman and Civil Rights: Moral Courage and Political Risks.* Carbondale: Southern Illinois University Press, 2002.

Garson, Robert A. *The Democratic Party and the Politics of Sectionalism, 1941–1948.* Baton Rouge: Louisiana State University Press, 1974.

Gellman, Irwin. *The Contender: Richard Nixon; The Congress Years, 1946 to 1952.* New York: Free Press, 1999.

Giangreco, D. M., and Kathryn Moore. *Dear Harry . . . : Truman's Mailroom, 1945–1953.* Mechanicsburg (PA): Stackpole Books, 1999.

Goldman, Eric F. *The Crucial Decade—and After: America, 1945–1960.* New York: Vintage Books, 1960.

Goldman, Ralph M. *The Party Chairmen and Committees: Factionalism at the Top.* Armonk (NY): M.E. Sharpe,, 1990.

Goldstein, Gordon M. *Lessons in Disaster: McGeorge Bundy and the Path to War in Vietnam.* New York: Times Books, 2008.

Goldzwig, Steven R. *Truman's Whistle-Stop Campaign.* College Station: Texas A&M University Press, 2008.

Goodwin, Doris Kearns. *No Ordinary Time: Franklin and Eleanor Roosevelt; The Home Front in World War II.* New York: Simon & Schuster, 1994.

Gosnell, Harold F. *Truman's Crises: A Political Biography of Harry S. Truman.* Westport (CT): Greenwood Press, 1980.

Goulden, Joseph C., ed. *Mencken's Last Campaign: H. L. Mencken on the 1948 Election.* Washington: New Republic Book Co., 1976.

———. *The Best Years 1945–1950.* New York: Atheneum, 1976.

Graham, Katherine. *Personal History.* New York: Alfred A. Knopf, 1997.

Grantham, Dewey W. *The Life and Death of the Solid South: A Political History.* Lexington: University Press of Kentucky, 1988.

Griffith, Robert W. *Ike's Letters to a Friend, 1941–1958.* Lawrence: University Press of Kansas, 1984.

Griffith, Winthrop. *Humphrey: A Candid Biography.* New York: William Morrow, 1965.

Grose, Peter. *Gentleman Spy: The Life of Allen Dulles.* Amherst: University of Massachusetts Press, 1996.

Gross, Larry P. *Contested Closets: The Politics and Ethics of Outing.* Minneapolis: University of Minnesota, 1993.

Guhin, Michael A. *John Foster Dulles: A Statesman and His Times.* New York: Columbia University Press, 1972.

Gullan, Harold I. *The Upset That Wasn't: Harry S. Truman and the Crucial Election of 1948.* Chicago: Ivan R. Dee, 1998.

Gunther, John. *Inside USA.* New York: Harper & Bros., 1947.

Guttenplan, D. D. *American Radical: The Life and Times of I. F. Stone.* New York: Farrar, Straus and Giroux, 2009.

Hamby, Alonzo L. *Beyond the New Deal: Harry S. Truman and American Liberalism.* New York: Columbia University Press, 1973.

———. *Man of the People: A Life of Harry S. Truman.* New York: Oxford University Press, 1995.

Hardeman, D. B., and Donald C. Bacon. *Rayburn: A Biography.* Austin: Texas Monthly Press, 1987.

Harnsberger, Caroline. *A Man of Courage: Robert A. Taft.* Chicago: Wilcox and Follett, 1952.

Hartmann, Rudolph H. *The Kansas City Investigation: Pendergast's Downfall, 1938–1939.* Columbia: University of Missouri Press, 1999.

Hartmann, Susan M. *Truman and the 80th Congress.* Columbia: University of Missouri Press, 1971.

Harwood, Michael. *In the Shadow of Presidents: The American Vice-Presidency and Succession System.* Philadelphia: J. B. Lippincott, 1966.

Haskell, Harry. *Boss-Busters & Sin Hounds: Kansas City and Its Star.* Columbia: University of Missouri Press, 2007.

Hassett, William D. *Off the Record with F.D.R., 1942–1945.* New Brunswick (NJ): Rutgers University Press, 1958.

Haygood, Will. *King of the Cats: The Life and Times of Adam Clayton Powell, Jr.* New York: Harper Paperbacks, 2006.

Haynes, John Earl, and Harvey Klehr. *Venona: Decoding Soviet Espionage in America.* New Haven: Yale University Press, 2000.

Hechler, Kenneth. *Working with Truman: A Personal Memoir of the White House Years.* New York: G. P. Putnam's Sons, 1982.

Hellman, Lillian. *Scoundrel Time.* Boston: Little, Brown, 1976.

———. *Three: An Unfinished Woman, Pentimento, Scoundrel Time.* Boston: Little, Brown & Co., 1979.

Hietala, Thomas R. *The Fight of the Century: Jack Johnson, Joe Louis, and the Struggle for Racial Equality.* Armonk (NY): M.E. Sharpe, 2002.

Hillman, William. *Mr. President: The First Publication of the Personal Dairies, Private Letters, Papers and Revealing Interviews of Harry S. Truman, Thirty-Second President of the United States of America.* New York: Farrar, Straus and Young, 1952.

Hirsch, James S. *Riot and Remembrance: The Tulsa Race War and Its Legacy.* New York: Houghton Mifflin Harcourt, 2002.

Hobson, Fred. *Mencken: A Life.* New York: Random House, 1994.

Hollander, Paul. *Political Pilgrims: Western Intellectuals in Search of the Good Society.* New York: Oxford University Press, 1981.

———. *The Survival of the Adversary Culture: Social Criticism and Political Escapism in American Society.* San Francisco: Transaction Publishers, 1988.

Horne, Gerald. *Black and Red: W.E.B. Du Bois and the Afro-American Response to the Cold War, 1944–1963.* Albany: State University of New York Press, 1986.

———. *Black Liberation/Red Scare: Ben Davis and the Communist Party.* Newark: University of Delaware Press, 1994.

———. *Class Struggle in Hollywood, 1930–1950: Moguls, Mobsters, Stars, Reds, & Trade Unionists.* Austin: University of Texas Press, 2001.

Horowitz, David A. *Beyond Left & Right: Insurgency and the Establishment.* Urbana: University of Illinois Press, 1996.

Hourtoule, Gilbert O. *The Development of Arthur H. Vandenberg's Views on Foreign Policy.* Stanford: Stanford University, 1948.

Howard, Gene L. *Patterson for Alabama: The Life and Career of John Patterson.* Tuscaloosa: University of Alabama Press, 2008.

Howley, Frank. *Berlin Command.* New York: Putnam, 1950.

Huff, Archie, Vernon Huff, and Archie V. Huff, Jr. *Greenville: The History of the City and County in the South Carolina Piedmont.* Columbia: University of South Carolina Press, 1995.

Humphrey, Hubert H. *The Education of a Public Man: My Life and Politics.* Garden City (NY): Doubleday, 1976.

Ickes, Harold L. *The Secret Diary of Harold L. Ickes. 3 vols.* New York: Simon & Schuster, 1954.

Isaacson, Walter, and Evan Thomas. *The Wise Men: Six Friends and the World They Made.* New York: Simon & Schuster, 1988.

Jackson, Kenneth T., ed. *The Encyclopedia of New York City.* New Haven: Yale University Press, 1995.

Jamieson, Kathleen Hall. *Packaging the Presidency: A History of Presidential Campaign Advertising.* New York: Oxford University Press, 1996.

Janeway, Michael. *The Fall of the House of Roosevelt: Brokers of Ideas and Power from FDR to LBJ.* New York: Columbia University Press, 2004.

Janken, Kenneth. *Walter White: The Biography of Walter White, Mr. NAACP.* New York: New Press, 2003.

Javits, Jacob K. *Javits: The Autobiography of a Public Man.* New York: Houghton Mifflin, 1981.

Jeansonne, Glen. *Gerald L. K. Smith: Minister of Hate.* New Haven: Yale University Press, 1988.

———. *Leander Perez: Boss of the Delta.* Baton Rouge: Louisiana State University Press, 1977.

Jenkins, Roy. *Truman.* New York: Harper & Row, 1986.

Johnson, Paul. *A History of the American People.* New York: Harper Perennial, 1999.

Jonnes, Jill. *South Bronx Rising: The Rise, Fall, and Resurrection of an American City.* Bronx: Fordham University Press, 2002.

Joyner, Conrad. *The Republican Dilemma: Conservatism or Progressivism.* Tucson: University of Arizona Press, 1963.

Kabaservice, Geoffrey M. *The Guardians: Kingman Brewster, His Circle, and the Rise of the Liberal Establishment.* New York: Macmillan, 2004.

Karabell, Zachary. *The Last Campaign: How Harry Truman Won the 1948 Campaign.* New York: Alfred A. Knopf, 2000.

Karnow, Stanley. *In Our Image: America's Empire in the Philippines.* New York: Random House, 1989.

Katcher, Leo. *Earl Warren: A Political Biography.* New York: McGraw-Hill, 1967.

Keech, William R., and Donald R. Matthews. *The Party's Choice.* Washington: Brookings Institution, 1976.

Keller, Werner. *East Minus West: Russia's Debt to the Western World 862–1962.* New York: Putnam, 1962.

Kelly, Frank K. *Harry Truman and the Human Family.* Santa Barbara: Capra Press, 1998.

Kelter, Bill, and Wayne Shellabarger. *Veeps: Profiles in Insignificance.* Atlanta: Top Shelf Productions, 2008.

Kempton, Murray. *Part of Our Time: Some Ruins and Monuments of the Thirties.* New York: Simon & Schuster, 1955.

Kenneally, James Joseph. *A Compassionate Conservative: A Political Biography of Joseph W. Martin, Jr., Speaker of the U.S. House of Representatives.* Lanham (MD): Lexington Books, 2003.

Kessler, Lauren. *Clever Girl: Elizabeth Bentley; The Spy Who Ushered in the McCarthy Era.* New York: Harper Perennial, 2004.

Kieran. John, ed. *The New Information Please Almanac: 1949.* New York: Farrar, Straus, 1949.

Kimball, Penn. *The File.* New York: Harcourt Brace Jovanovich, 1983.

Kingdon, Frank. *An Uncommon Man: Henry Wallace and 60 Million Jobs.* New York: Readers Press, 1945.

Kirkendall, Richard S. *The Harry S. Truman Encyclopedia.* Boston: G.K. Hall, 1989

Klehr, Harvey. *The Heyday of American Communism: The Depression Decade.* New York: Basic Books, 1984.

———, John Earl Haynes, and Fridrikh Igorevich Firsov. *The Secret World of American Communism.* New Haven: Yale University Press, 1996.

———, John Earl Haynes, and Alexander Vassiliev. *Spies: The Rise and Fall of the KGB in America.* New Haven: Yale University Press, 2009.

Klein, Joe. *Woody Guthrie: A Life.* New York: Dell Publishing, 1999.

Kleinman, Mark L. *A World of Hope, a World of Fear: Henry A. Wallace, Reinhold Niebuhr, and American Liberalism.* Columbus: Ohio State University Press, 2000.

Kofsky, Frank. *Harry S. Truman and the War Scare of 1948: A Successful Campaign to Deceive the Nation.* New York: St. Martin's Press, 1995.

Kovel, Joel. *Red Hunting in the Promised Land: Anticommunism and the Making of America.* New York: Basic Books, 1994.

Krasnov, Vladislav. *Soviet Defectors: The KGB Wanted List.* Stanford: Hoover Press, 1985.

Kraus, Sidney. *The Great Debates: Kennedy vs. Nixon, 1960.* Bloomington: Indiana University Press, 1977.

Krock, Arthur. *Memoirs: Sixty Years on the Firing Line.* New York: Funk & Wagnalls, 1968.

Kurth, Peter. *American Cassandra: The Life of Dorothy Thompson.* Boston: Little, Brown, 1990.

Lacey, Michael James, ed. *The Truman Presidency.* New York: Cambridge University Press, 1991.

Lachicotte, Alberta Morel. *Rebel Senator: Strom Thurmond of South Carolina.* New York: Devin-Adair, 1967.

Lader, Lawrence. *Power on the Left: American Radical Movements Since 1946.* New York: W. W. Norton, 1979.

Lait, Jack, and Lee Mortimer. *New York: Confidential!* Chicago: Ziff-Davis Publishing, 1948.

Lamb, Brian, ed. *Booknotes: Stories from American History.* New York: PublicAffairs, 2001.

Large, David Clay. *Berlin.* New York: Basic Books, 2000.

Larsen, Lawrence Harold, and Nancy J. Hulston. *Pendergast!* Columbia: University of Missouri Press, 1997.

Lash, Joseph P. *Eleanor: The Years Alone.* New York: W. W. Norton, 1972.

Lasky, Victor. *It Didn't Start with Watergate.* New York: Dial Press, 1977.

Latham, Earl. *The Communist Controversy in Washington: From the New Deal to McCarthy.* New York: Atheneum, 1969.

Laurents, Arthur. *Original Story by Arthur Laurents: A Memoir of Broadway and Hollywood.* New York: Alfred A. Knopf, 2000.

Lesher, Stephan. *George Wallace: American Populist.* New York: Da Capo Press, 1995.

Leuchtenburg, William. *The White House Looks South: Franklin D. Roosevelt, Harry S. Truman, Lyndon B. Johnson.* Baton Rouge: Louisiana State University Press, 2007.

Levantrosser, William F., ed. *Harry S. Truman: The Man from Independence.* New York: Greenwood Press, 1986.

Levering, Ralph B. *The Cold War: A Post–Cold War History.* Wheeling (IL): Harlan Davidson, 2004.

Lewis, David Levering. *W. E. B. Du Bois: The Fight for Equality and the American Century, 1919–1963.* New York: Macmillan, 2001.

Lichtenstein, Nelson. *The Most Dangerous Man in Detroit: Walter Reuther and the Fate of American Labor.* New York: Basic Books, 1995.

Lieberman, Robbie. *My Song Is My Weapon: People's Songs, American Communism, and the Politics of Culture, 1930–50.* Urbana: University of Illinois Press, 1995.

Lilienthal, David E. *The Journals of David E. Lilienthal: The Atomic Energy Years, 1945–1950.* New York: Harper & Row, 1964.

Lipper, Elinor. *Eleven Years in Soviet Prison Camps.* Chicago: Regnery, 1951.

Lobenthal, Joel. *Tallulah!: The Life and Times of a Leading Lady.* New York: ReganBooks, 2004.

Lodge, Henry Cabot. *The Storm Has Many Eyes: A Personal Narrative.* New York: W. W. Norton, 1973.

Lomazow, Steven, and Eric Fettmann. *FDR's Deadly Secret.* New York: PublicAffairs, 2009.

Lorant, Stefan. *The Glorious Burden: The History of the Presidency and Presidential Elections from George Washington to James Earl Carter, Jr.* Lenox (MA): Author's Edition, Inc., 1977.

Lord, Russell. *The Wallaces of Iowa.* Boston: Houghton Mifflin, 1947.

Lubell, Samuel. *The Future of American Politics.* New York: Harper & Row, 1965.

Luconi, Stefano. *The Italian-American Vote in Providence, Rhode Island 1916–1948.* Madison (NJ): Fairleigh Dickinson University Press, 2004.

Luthin, Reinhard H. *American Demagogues: Twentieth Century.* Boston: Beacon Press, 1954.

Macdonald, Dwight. *Henry Wallace: The Man and the Myth.* New York: Vanguard Press, 1948.

MacDonogh, Giles. *After the Reich: The Brutal History of the Allied Occupation.* New York: Basic Books, 2007.

MacDougall, Curtis. *Gideon's Army. 3 vols.* New York: Marzani & Munsell, 1965.

Madison, Charles A. *Critics and Crusaders: A Century of American Protest.* New York: Frederick Ungar, 1959.

Malsberger, John William. *From Obstruction to Moderation: The Transformation of Senate Conservatism, 1938–1952.* Selinsgrove (PA): Susquehanna University Press, 2000.

Manchester, William. *American Caesar: Douglas MacArthur, 1880–1964.* Boston: Little, Brown, 1978.

———. *Disturber of the Peace: The Life of H. L. Mencken.* New York: Harper, 1951.

Markowitz, Norman. *The Rise and Fall of the People's Century: Henry A. Wallace and American Liberalism, 1941–1948*. New York: Free Press, 1973.

Martinson, Deborah. *Lillian Hellman: A Life with Foxes and Scoundrels*. New York: Counterpoint, 2005.

Marzani, Carl. *The Education of a Reluctant Radical: Reconstruction*. New York: Monthly Review Press, 2001.

Martin, Joe, and Robert J. Donovan. *My First Fifty Years in Politics*. New York: McGraw-Hill, 1960.

Martin, John Bartlow. *Adlai Stevenson of Illinois*. Garden City (NY): Doubleday, 1976.

Martin, Ralph G. *Henry & Clare: An Intimate Portrait of the Luces*. New York: G. P. Putnam's Sons, 1991.

Mathews, Joe. *The People's Machine: Arnold Schwarzenegger and the Rise of Blockbuster Democracy*. New York: PublicAffairs, 2006.

Mazo, Earl. *Richard Nixon: A Political and Personal Portrait*. New York: Harper & Bros., 1959.

McAuliffe, Mary Sperling. *Crisis on the Left: Cold War Politics and American Liberals, 1947–1954*. Amherst: The University of Massachusetts Press, 1978.

McCann, Kevin. *Man from Abilene*. Garden City (NY): Doubleday, 1952.

McCoy, Donald R. *The Presidency of Harry S. Truman*. Lawrence: University Press of Kansas, 1984.

McCoy, Donald R., and Richard T. Reutten. *Quest and Response: Minority Rights and the Truman Administration*. Lawrence: University Press of Kansas, 1973.

McCullough, David. *Truman*. New York: Simon & Schuster, 1992.

McGovern, George S. *Grassroots: The Autobiography of George McGovern*. New York: Random House, 1977.

McKeever, Porter. *Adlai Stevenson: His Life and Legacy*. New York: William Morrow, 1989.

McNay, John T. *Acheson and Empire: The British Accent in American Foreign Policy*. Columbia: University of Missouri Press, 2001.

Mearns, John S., ed. *The New York Red Book: 1945*. Albany: Williams Press, 1945.

———. *The New York Red Book: 1948*. Albany: Williams Press, 1948.

———. *The New York Red Book: 1949*. Albany: Williams Press, 1949.

Mellen, Joan. *Hellman and Hammett: The Legendary Passion of Lillian Hellman and Dashiell Hammett*. New York: HarperCollins, 1997.

Mencken, H. L., and Charles A. Fecher, ed. *The Diary of H. L. Mencken*. New York: Random House Value Publishing, 1991.

Meyer, Gerald. *Vito Marcantonio: Radical Politician, 1902–1954*. Albany: State University of New York Press, 1989.

Miller, Merle. *Lyndon: An Oral Biography*. New York: G. P. Putnam's Sons, 1980.

———. *Plain Speaking: An Oral Biography of Harry S. Truman*. New York: Berkley, 1973.

Miller, Nathan. *F.D.R.: An Intimate History*. Garden City (NY): Doubleday, 1983.

Miller, Neil. *Out of the Past: Gay and Lesbian History from 1869 to the Present*. New York: Vintage Books, 1995.

Miller, Richard Lawrence. *Truman: The Rise to Power*. New York: McGraw-Hill, 1986.

Milligan, Maurice M. *Missouri Waltz: The Inside Story of the Pendergast Machine by the Man Who Smashed It*. New York: Scribner's, 1948.

Mitchell, Franklin D. *Harry S. Truman and the News Media: Contentious Relations, Belated Respect*. Columbia: University of Missouri Press, 1998.

Mjagkij, Nina. *Organizing Black America: An Encyclopedia of African American Associations*. New York: Garland, 2001.

Montgomery, Ruth. *Hail to the Chiefs: My Life and Times with Six Presidents.* New York: Coward-McCann. 1970.

Moon, Henry Lee. *Balance of Power: The Negro Vote.* Garden City (NY): Doubleday, 1948.

Mooney, Booth. *The Politicians: 1945–1960.* Philadelphia: J. P. Lippincott, 1970.

Moore, John Hammond. *Carnival of Blood: Dueling, Lynching and Murder in South Carolina, 1880–1920.* Columbia: University of South Carolina Press, 2006.

Moore, Winfred B., and Orville Vernon Burton. *Toward the Meeting of the Waters: Currents in the Civil Rights Movement of South Carolina During the Twentieth Century.* Columbia: University of South Carolina Press, 2008.

Morgan, Ted. *FDR: A Biography.* New York: Simon & Schuster, 1985.

———. *Reds: McCarthyism in Twentieth Century America.* New York: Random House, 2003.

Morreale, Joanne. *The Presidential Campaign Film: A Critical History.* Westport (CT): Praeger, 1993.

Morris, Roger. *Richard Milhous Nixon: The Rise of an American Politician.* New York: Henry Holt, 1990.

Morrow, Lance. *The Best Year of Their Lives: Kennedy, Johnson and Nixon in 1948; Learning the Secrets of Power.* New York: Basic Books, 2003.

Mosley, Leonard. *Dulles: A Biography of Eleanor, Allen, and John Foster Dulles and Their Family Network.* New York: Dial Press, 1978.

Mosteller, Frederick, Herbert Hyman, Philip J. McCarthy, Eli S. Marks, and David B. Truman. *The Pre-Election Polls of 1948: Report to the Committee on Analysis of Pre-Election Polls and Forecasts.* New York: Social Science Research Council, 1949.

Murphy, Bruce Allen. *Wild Bill: The Legend and Life of William O. Douglas.* New York: Random House, 2003.

Murray, William H. *Palestine: Shall Arabs or Jews Control It or America Admit 100,000 Communist Jews from Behind the Iron Curtain?* Tishomingo (OK): William H. Murray, 1947.

———. *The Negro's Place in Call of Race: The Last Work on Segregation of Races, Considered in Every Capable Light as Disclosed Experience.* Tishomingo (OK): William H. Murray, 1948.

Nasaw, David. *The Chief: The Life of William Randolph Hearst.* New York: Houghton Mifflin, 2000.

Nash, Howard P., Jr., and M. B. Schnapper. *Third Parties in American Politics.* Washington: Public Affairs Press, 1959.

Navasky, Victor S. *Naming Names.* New York: Macmillan, 2003.

Neal, Steve. *Eleanor and Harry: The Correspondence of Eleanor Roosevelt and Harry S. Truman.* New York: Citadel Press, 2004.

———. *Happy Days Are Here Again: The 1932 Democratic Convention, the Emergence of FDR—And How America Was Changed Forever.* New York: William Morrow, 2004.

———. *Harry and Ike: The Partnership That Remade the Postwar World.* New York: Touchstone, 2001.

———. *HST: Memories of the Truman Years.* Carbondale: Southern Illinois University Press, 2003.

———. *Miracle of '48: Harry Truman's Major Campaign Speeches & Selected Whistle-Stops.* Carbondale: Southern Illinois University Press, 2003.

———. *The Eisenhowers: Reluctant Dynasty.* Garden City (NY): Doubleday, 1978.

Nelson, W. Dale. *Who Speaks for the President?: The White House Press Secretary from Cleveland to Clinton.* Syracuse (NY): Syracuse University Press, 2000.

Newman, Robert P. *The Cold War Romance of Lillian Hellman and John Melby.* Chapel Hill: University of North Carolina Press, 1989.

Newton, Jim. *Justice for All: Earl Warren and the Nation He Made.* New York: Riverhead Books, 2006.

Nixon, Richard M. *RN: The Memoirs of Richard Nixon.* New York: Grosset & Dunlap, 1978.

———. *Six Crises*. Garden City (NY): Doubleday, 1962.

Nunnelley, William A. *Bull Connor*. Tuscaloosa: University of Alabama Press, 1991.

O'Brien, Michael. *John F. Kennedy: A Biography*. New York: St. Martin's Press, Thomas Dunne Books, 2005.

O'Dwyer, Paul. *Counsel for the Defense: The Autobiography of Paul O'Dwyer*. New York: Simon & Schuster, 1979.

Offner, Arnold A. *Another Such Victory: President Truman and the Cold War, 1945–1953*. Stanford: Stanford University Press, 2002.

Olmsted, Kathryn S. *Red Spy Queen: A Biography of Elizabeth Bentley*. Chapel Hill: University of North Carolina Press, 2002.

O'Neill, William L. *A Better World: The Great Schism; Stalinism and the American Intellectuals*. New York: Simon & Schuster, 1983.

———. *American High: The Years of Confidence, 1945–1960*. New York: Simon & Schuster, 1989.

Packer, Herbert L. *Ex-Communist Witnesses: Four Studies in Fact Finding*. Stanford: Stanford University Press, 1962.

Parmet, Herbert S. *Richard M. Nixon and His America*. Boston: Little, Brown & Co., 1990.

———, and Marie B. Hecht. *Never Again: A President Runs for a Third Term*. New York: Macmillan, 1968.

Patterson, James T. *Mr. Republican: A Biography of Robert A. Taft*. Boston: Houghton Mifflin, 1972.

Pedersen, Vernon L. *The Communist Party in Maryland, 1919–57*. Urbana: University of Illinois Press, 2000.

Pemberton, William E. *Harry S. Truman: Fair Dealer and Cold Warrior*. Boston: Twayne Publishers, 1989.

Pepper, Claude, with Hays Gorey. *Pepper: Eyewitness to a Century*. New York: Harcourt, Brace Jovanovich, 1987.

Perret, Geoffrey. *Eisenhower*. New York: Random House, 1999.

Perry, Roland. *Last of the Cold War Spies: The Life of Michael Straight—The Only American in Britain's Cambridge Spy Ring*. New York: Da Capo Press, 2006.

Persico, Joseph E. *Roosevelt's Secret War: FDR and World War II Espionage*. New York: Random House, 2002.

Pescatello, Ann M. *Charles Seeger: A Life in American Music*. Pittsburgh: University of Pittsburgh Press, 1992.

Peters, Charles. *Five Days in Philadelphia: The Amazing "We Want Willkie!" Convention of 1940 and How It Freed FDR to Save the Western World*. New York: Public Affairs, 2005.

Philbrick, Herbert A. *I Led Three Lives: Citizen, "Communist," Counterspy*. New York: McGraw-Hill: 1952.

Phillips, Cabell. *The Truman Presidency: The History of a Triumphant Succession*. New York: Penguin Books, 1969.

Pickett, William B. *Eisenhower Decides to Run: Presidential Politics and Cold War Strategy*. Chicago: Ivan R. Dee, 2000.

Pilat, Oliver. *Pegler: Angry Man of the Press*. Westport (CT): Greenwood Press, 1973.

Poen, Monte M., ed. *Letters Home*. Columbia: University of Missouri Press, 2003.

Pogue, Forrest C. *George C. Marshall: Education of a General 1880–1939*. New York. Viking, 1963.

Pohl, Frances. K. *Ben Shahn*. San Francisco: Pomegranate Artbooks, 1993.

Pollack, Howard. *Aaron Copland: The Life and Work of an Uncommon Man*. Urbana: University of Illinois Press, 2000.

Pollack, Jack Harrison. *Earl Warren: The Judge Who Changed America*. Englewood Cliffs (NJ): PrenticeHall, 1979.

Powell, Adam Clayton, Jr. *Adam by Adam: The Autobiography of Adam Clayton Powell, Jr.* New York: Kensington Books, 2002.

Powell, Gene. *Tom's Boy Harry*. Jefferson City (MO): Hawthorn Publishing, 1948.

Pruessen, Ronald W. *John Foster Dulles: The Road to Power*. New York: Free Press, 1982.

Pugliese, Stanislao G. *Frank Sinatra: History, Identity, and Italian American Culture*. New York: Palgrave Macmillan, 1994.

Rabinowitz, Victor. *Unrepentant Leftist: A Lawyer's Memoir*. Urbana: University of Illinois Press, 1996.

Radosh, Ronald, and Allis Radosh. *A Safe Haven: Harry S. Truman and the Founding of Israel*. New York: Harper, 2009.

———. *Red Star Over Hollywood: The Film Colony's Long Romance with the Left*. San Francisco: Encounter Books, 2005.

Ramdin, Ron. *Paul Robeson: The Man and His Mission*. London: Peter Owen, 1987.

Record, Wilson. *The Negro and the Communist Party*. Chapel Hill: University of North Carolina Press, 1951.

Redding, Jack. *Inside the Democratic Party*. Indianapolis (IN): Bobbs-Merrill, 1958.

Reeves, Thomas C. *The Life and Times of Joe McCarthy: A Biography*. New York: Stein & Day, 1982.

Reinhard, David W. *The Republican Right Since 1945*. Lexington: University Press of Kentucky, 1983.

Rich, Wilbur. *Coleman Young and Detroit Politics: From Social Activist to Power Broker*. Detroit: Wayne State University Press, 1999.

Risjord, Norman H. *A Popular History of Minnesota*. St. Paul: Minnesota Historical Society Press, 2005.

Ritchie, Donald. *Reporting from Washington: The History of the Washington Press Corps*. New York: Oxford University Press, 2005.

Robbins, Charles. *Last of His Kind: An Informal Portrait of Harry S. Truman*. New York: William Morrow, 1979.

Robbins, Jhan. *Bess & Harry: An American Love Story*. New York: G. P. Putnam's Sons, 1980.

Robertson, David. *Sly and Able: A Political Biography of James F. Byrnes*. New York: W. W. Norton, 1994.

Rockaway, Robert A. *But He Was Good to His Mother: The Lives and Crimes of Jewish Gangsters*. Jerusalem: Gefen Publishing House, 1993.

Rodgers, Marion Elizabeth. *Mencken: The American Iconoclast*. New York: Oxford University Press, 2005.

Rollyson, Carl E. *Lillian Hellman: Her Legend and Her Legacy*. St. Martin's Press, 1988.

———. *The Lives of Norman Mailer: A Biography*. New York: Paragon House, 1991.

Romerstein, Herbert, and Eric Breindel. *The Venona Secrets: Exposing Soviet Espionage and America's Traitors*. Washington: Regnery, 2001.

Roosevelt, Eleanor, and David Emblidge, ed. *My Day: The Best of Eleanor Roosevelt's Acclaimed Newspaper Columns, 1936–1962*. New York: DaCapo Press, 2001.

Roosevelt, Elliott, and James Brough. *A Rendezvous with Destiny: The Roosevelts of the White House*. New York: G. P. Putnam's Sons, 1975.

Roosevelt, James, with Bill Libby. *My Parents: A Differing View*. Chicago: Playboy Press, 1976.

Rosenman, Samuel I., and Dorothy Rosenman. *Presidential Style: Some Giants and a Pygmy in the White House*. New York: Harper & Row, 1976.

Rosenstone, Steven J., Roy L. Behr, and Edward H. Lazarus. *Third Parties in America*. Princeton: Princeton University Press, 1984.

Ross, Irwin. *The Loneliest Campaign: The Truman Victory of 1948.* New York: New American Library, 1968.

Rovere, Richard H. *The American Establishment: And Other Reports, Opinions, and Speculations.* New York: Harcourt, Bruce & World, Inc., 1962.

Roy, Ralph Lord. *Apostles of Discord: A Study of Organized Bigotry and Disruption on the Fringes of Protestantism.* Boston: Beacon Press, 1953.

Safire, William. *Safire's Political Dictionary.* New York: Oxford University Press, 2008.

Salmond, John A. *The Conscience of a Lawyer: Clifford J. Durr and American Civil Liberties, 1899–1975.* Tuscaloosa: University of Alabama Press, 1990.

Saposs, David Joseph. *Communism in American Politics.* Washington: Public Affairs Press, 1960.

Schaffer, Alan. *Vito Marcantonio: Radical in Congress.* Syracuse (NY): Syracuse University Press, 1966.

Schapsmeier, Edward L., and Frederick H. Schapsmeier. *Henry A. Wallace of Iowa: The Agrarian Years, 1910–1940.* Ames: Iowa State University Press, 1968.

———. *Prophet in Politics: Henry A. Wallace and the War Years, 1940–1965.* Ames: Iowa State University Press, 1970.

Schlesinger, Arthur M., Jr. *A Life in the Twentieth Century: Innocent Beginnings, 1917–1950.* Boston: Houghton Mifflin, 2000.

———. *The Vital Center, the Politics of Freedom.* Edison (NJ): Transaction, 1997.

Schlesinger, Robert. *White House Ghosts: Presidents and Their Speechwriters.* New York: Simon & Schuster, 2008.

Schmidt, Karl M. *Henry A. Wallace: Quixotic Crusade 1948.* Syracuse (NY): Syracuse University Press, 1960.

Schoenbaum, David. *The United States and the State of Israel.* New York: Oxford University Press, 1993.

Scroop, Daniel. *Mr. Democrat: Jim Farley, The New Deal & The Making of Modern American Politics.* Ann Arbor: University of Michigan Press, 2006.

Seldes, Barry. *Leonard Bernstein: The Political Life of an American Musician.* Berkeley: University of California Press, 2009.

Shadegg, Stephen. *Clare Boothe Luce.* New York: Simon & Schuster, 1970.

Sherrill, Robert. *Gothic Politics in the Deep South.* New York: Ballantine Books, 1969.

Sherwood, Robert E. *Roosevelt and Hopkins, an Intimate History.* New York: Harper, 1948.

Shlaes, Amity. *The Forgotten Man: A New History of the Great Depression.* New York: Harper Perennial, 2008.

Simon, James F. *Independent Journey: The Life of William O. Douglas.* New York: Harper & Row, 1980.

Skidmore, Max J. *Presidential Performance: A Comprehensive Review.* Jefferson (NC): McFarland, 2004.

Smethurst, James Edward. *The New Red Negro: The Literary Left and African American Poetry, 1930–1946.* New York: Oxford University Press, 1999.

Smith, Amanda, ed. *Hostages to Fortune: The Letters of Joseph P. Kennedy.* New York: Viking, 2001.

Smith, Jean Edward. *FDR.* New York: Random House, 2007.

Smith, John Chabot. *Alger Hiss: The True Story.* New York: Holt, Rinehart and Winston, 1976.

Smith, Richard Norton. *Thomas E. Dewey and His Times.* New York: Simon & Schuster, 1982.

———. *The Colonel: The Life and Legend of Robert R. McCormick, 1880–1955.* Chicago: Northwestern University Press, 2003.

Snetsinger, John. *Truman, the Jewish Vote, and the Creation of Israel.* Stanford: Hoover Institution Press, 1974.

Solberg, Carl. *Hubert Humphrey: A Biography.* New York: W. W. Norton, 1984.

Songs for Wallace. New York: People's Songs for the National Office of the Progressive Party, 1948.

Sperber, A. M., and Eric Lax. *Bogart*. New York: William Morrow, 1997.

Spiegel, Steven L. *The Other Arab-Israeli Conflict: Making America's Middle East Policy, from Truman to Reagan*. Chicago: University of Chicago Press, 1986.

Spragens, William C. *Popular Images of American Presidents*. New York: Greenwood Press, 1988.

Srodes, James. *Allen Dulles: Master of Spies*. Washington: Regnery, 1999.

Starr, Kevin. *Embattled Dreams: California in War and Peace, 1940–1950*. New York: Oxford University Press, 2002.

Stedman, Susan W., and Murray Salisbury Stedman. *Discontent at the Polls: A Study of Farmer and Labor Parties, 1827–1948*. New York: Columbia University Press, 1950.

Steel, Ronald. *Walter Lippmann and the American Century*. Boston: Little, Brown, 1980.

Steinberg, Alfred. *Sam Johnson's Boy: A Close-Up of the President from Texas*. New York: Macmillan, 1968.

———. *The Bosses*. New York: Macmillan, 1972.

———. *The Man from Missouri: The Life and Times of Harry S. Truman*. New York: Putnam, 1962.

Steinberg, Peter L. *The Great "Red Menace": United States Prosecution of American Communists, 1947–1952*. Westport (CT): Greenwood Press, 1984.

Steinke, John P. "The Rise of McCarthyism." Master's thesis. University of Wisconsin, 1960.

Stolberg, Mary M. *Fighting Organized Crime: Politics, Justice, and the Legacy of Thomas E. Dewey*. Boston: Northeastern University Press, 1995.

Stone, I. F. *The Truman Era: 1945–1952*. Boston: Little, Brown, 1972.

Stone, Irving. *Earl Warren: A Great American Story*. Englewood Cliffs (NJ): Prentice Hall, 1948.

———. *They Also Ran*. Garden City (NY): Doubleday, 1966.

Strom, Sharon Hartman. *Political Woman: Florence Luscomb and the Legacy of Radical Reform*. Philadelphia: Temple University Press, 2001.

Strout, Richard L. *TRB: Views and Perspectives on the Presidency*. New York: Macmillan, 1979.

Swanberg, W. A. *Luce and His Empire*. New York: Scribner, 1972.

———. *Norman Thomas: The Last Idealist*. New York: Scribner, 1976.

Tanenhaus, Sam. *Whittaker Chambers: A Biography*. New York: Random House, 1997.

Taylor, Glen Hearst. *The Way It Was With Me*. New York: Lyle Stuart, 1979.

Terkel, Studs. *Talking to Myself: A Memoir of My Times*. New York, Pantheon Books, 1977.

Thomas, Lately. *When Even Angels Wept: The Senator Joseph McCarthy Affair—A Story Without a Hero*. New York: William Morrow, 1973.

Thurber, Timothy N. *The Politics of Equality: Hubert H. Humphrey and the African American Freedom Struggle*. New York: Columbia University Press, 1999.

Tidwell, John Edgar, ed. *Writings of Frank Marshall Davis: A Voice of the Black Press*. Jackson: University Press of Mississippi, 2006.

Timmons, Bascom N. *Jesse H. Jones: The Man and the Statesman*. New York: Holt, 1956.

Trager, James. *The New York Chronology: The Ultimate Compendium of Events, People, and Anecdotes from the Dutch to the Present*. New York: HarperResource, 2003.

Trahair, Richard C. S. *Encyclopedia of Cold War Espionage, Spies and Secret Operations*. Westport (CT): Greenwood Press, 2004.

Trohan, Walter. *Political Animals: Memoirs of a Sentimental Cynic*. Garden City (NY): Doubleday, 1975.

Trotter, William R. *Priest of Music: The Life of Dimitri Mitropoulos*. Portland (OR): Amadeus Press, 1995.

Truman, Harry S. *Memoirs. Vol. 1: Year of Decisions*. Garden City (NY): Doubleday, 1955.

————. *Memoirs. Vol. 2: Years of Trial and Hope.* Garden City (NY): Doubleday, 1956.

————. *Public Papers of Harry S. Truman: Containing the Public Messages, Speeches, and Statements of the President, 1945–53.* Washington: U.S. Government Printing Office, 1962.

Truman, Margaret. *Bess W. Truman.* New York: Macmillan, 1986.

————. *Harry S. Truman.* New York: William Morrow, 1973.

————. *Where the Buck Stops: The Personal and Private Writings of Harry S. Truman.* New York: Grand Central Publishing, 1990.

Tuck, Jim. *The Liberal Civil War: Fraternity and Fratricide on the Left.* Lanham (MD): University Press of America, 1998.

Tugwell, Rexford Guy. *A Chronicle of Jeopardy.* Chicago: University of Chicago Press, 1955.

Tully, Grace. *F.D.R.: My Boss.* Scribner, 1949.

Underhill, Robert. *FDR and Harry: Unparalleled Lives.* Westport (CT): Praeger, 1996.

Unger, Irwin, and Debi Unger. *LBJ: A Life.* New York: John Wiley, 1999.

Vandenberg, Arthur, Jr., with Joe Alex Morris, ed. *The Private Papers of Senator Vandenberg.* Boston: Houghton Mifflin, 1952.

Von Schilling, James Arthur. *The Magic Window: American Television, 1939–1953.* Philadelphia: Haworth Press, 2002.

Walch, Timothy, ed. *At the President's Side: The Vice Presidency in the Twentieth Century.* Columbia: University of Missouri Press, 1997.

Walker, Stanley. *Dewey: An American of This Century.* New York: Whittlesey House, 1944.

Wallace, Henry A. *The Price of Vision: The Diary of Henry A. Wallace, 1942–1946.* New York: Houghton Mifflin, 1973.

————. *Toward World Peace.* New York: Reynal& Hitchcock, 1948.

————, and Andrew Jacob Steiger. *Soviet Asia Mission.* New York: Reynal & Hitchcock, 1946.

Walser, Richard. *Tar Heel Laughter.* Chapel Hill: University of North Carolina Press, 1983.

Walsh, Michael F., ed. *Manual for the Use of the Legislature of the State of New York 1941.* Albany: Williams Press, 1941.

Walton, Richard J. *Henry Wallace, Harry Truman and the Cold War.* New York: Viking Press, 1976.

Wanniski, Jude. *The Way the World Works 1978.* New York: Simon & Schuster, 1978.

Washington-Williams, Essie Mae, and William Stadiem. *Dear Senator: A Memoir by the Daughter of Strom Thurmond.* New York: Harper, 2005.

Watkins, T. H. *Righteous Pilgrim: The Life and Times of Harold L. Ickes, 1874–1952.* New York: Henry Holt, 1990.

Weber, Ralph Edward. *Talking with Harry: Candid Conversations with President Harry S. Truman.* Wilmington (DE): Rowman & Littlefield, 2001.

Wechsler, James. *The Age of Suspicion.* New York: Random House, 1953.

Weill, Susan. *In a Madhouse's Din: Civil Rights Coverage by Mississippi's Daily Press, 1948–1968.* Westport (CT): Praeger, 2002.

Weinstein, Allen. *Perjury: The Hiss-Chambers Case.* New York: Vintage Books, 1979.

————, and Alexander Vassiliev. *The Haunted Wood: Soviet Espionage in America—The Stalin Era.* New York: Random House, 2000.

Weintraub, Ruth G. *How Secure These Rights? Anti-Semitism in the United States in 1948: An Anti-Defamation League Survey.* Garden City (NY): Doubleday, 1949.

Weissman, Dick. *Which Side Are You On?: An Inside History of the Folk Music Revival in America*. London: Continuum, 2006.

White, G. Edward. *Alger Hiss's Looking-Glass Wars: The Covert Life of a Soviet Spy*. New York: Oxford University Press, 2004.

———. *Earl Warren: A Public Life*. New York: Oxford University Press, 1987.

White, Graham, and John Maze. *Henry A. Wallace: His Search for a New World Order*. Chapel Hill (NC): University of North Carolina Press, 1995.

White, John Kenneth. *Still Seeing Red: How the Cold War Shapes the New American Politics*. Boulder (CO): Westview Press, 1998.

White, Theodore. *America in Search of Itself*. New York: Harper & Row, 1978.

White, Walter. *A Man Called White: The Autobiography of Walter White*. Athens: University of Georgia Press, 1995.

White, William S. *The Taft Story*. New York: Harper & Brothers, 1954.

Wilkinson, Alec. *The Protest Singer: An Intimate Portrait of Pete Seeger*. New York: Alfred A. Knopf, 2009.

Williams, Irving G. *The Rise of the Vice Presidency*. Washington: Public Affairs Press, 1956.

Winchell, Walter. *Winchell Exclusive: "Things That Happened to Me—And Me to Them."* Englewood Cliffs (NJ): Prentice Hall, 1975.

Wise, James Waterman. *Meet Henry Wallace*. New York: Boni & Gaer, 1948.

Witcover, Jules. *Crapshoot: Rolling the Dice on the Vice Presidency*. New York: Crown, 1991.

Wolters, Raymond. *Du Bois and His Rivals*. Columbia: University of Missouri Press, 2002.

Woods, Randall. *LBJ: Architect of American Ambition*. New York: Free Press, 2006.

Wunderlin, Clarence E., David E. Settje, Robin L. Bowden, Bette J. Sawicki, and Ellen Denning, eds. *The Papers of Robert A. Taft. Vol. 3, 1945–1948*. Kent (OH): Kent State University Press, 2003.

Wyatt, Wilson Sr. *Whistle Stops: Adventures in Public Life*. Lexington: University Press of Kentucky, 1985.

Yarnell, Allen. *Democrats and Progressives: The 1948 Presidential Election as a Test of Postwar Liberalism*. Berkeley: University of California Press, 1974.

Young, Coleman, and Lonnie Wheeler. *Hard Stuff: The Autobiography of Coleman Young*. New York: Viking, 1994.

NEWSPAPERS

Abilene (TX) *Reporter-News*
Aiken (SC) *Journal*
Aiken (SC) *Standard and Review*
Albuquerque (NM) *Journal*
Alton (IL) *Evening Telegraph*
Amarillo (TX) *Daily News*
Amarillo (TX) *News-Globe*
Amsterdam (NY) *Evening Recorder*
Anniston (AL) *Star*
Appleton (WI) *Post-Crescent*
Atchison (KS) *Daily Globe*
Atlanta (GA) *Daily World*

Auburn (NY) *Citizen-Advertiser*
Benton Harbor (MI) *News-Palladium*
Berkshire (MA) *Eagle*
Billings (MT) *Gazette*
Binghamton (NY) *Press*
Bluefield (WV) *Telegraph*
Bridgeport (CT) *Post*
Brooklyn Eagle
Brownsville (TX) *Herald*
Canandaigua (NY) *Daily Messenger*
Cedar Rapids (IA) *Tribune*
Charleroi (PA) *Mail*

Charleston (WV) *Daily Mail*
Chester (PA) *Times*
Chicago *Daily Defender*
Chicago *Daily Tribune*
Chillicothe (MO) *Constitution-Tribune*
Christian Science Monitor
Columbus (NE) *Telegram*
Connellsville (PA) *Daily Courier*
Coshocton (OH) *Tribune*
Council Bluffs (IA) *Nonpareil*
Cumberland (MD) *Evening Times*
Daily Capital (MO) *News*
Daily Worker
Delta (MS) *Democrat-Times*
Dixon (IL) *Telegraph*
Dothan (AL) *Eagle*
Dunkirk (NY) *Evening Observer*
El Paso (TX) *Herald-Post*
Emporia (KS) *Gazette*
Florence (SC) *Morning News*
Frederick (MD) *Post*
Fredericksburg (VA) *Free Lance-Star*
Fresno (CA) *Bee*
Galveston (TX) *Daily News*
Greenburg (IN) *News*
Greenville (MS) *Delta Democrat Times*
Hagerstown (MD) *Daily Mail*
Harlingen (TX) *Valley Morning Star*
Harrisburg (IL) *Daily Register*
Hayward (CA) *Daily Review*
Hope (AK) *Star*
Huntingdon (PA) *Daily News*
Hutchinson (KS) *News-Herald*
Florence (SC) *Morning News*
Frederick (MD) *Post*
Galveston (TX) *Daily News*
Hutchinson (KS) *News-Herald*
Jefferson City (MO) *Daily Capital News*
Jefferson City (MO) *News & Tribune*
Joplin (MO) *Globe*
Kansas City (MO) *Star*
Kingsport (TN) *Times*
Kingston (Jamaica) *The Gleaner*
Kingston (NY) *Daily Freeman*

Kokomo (IN) *Tribune*
La Crosse (WI) *Tribune*
Laredo (TX) *Times*
Lawton (OK) *Constitution*
Las Cruces (NM) *Sun-News*
Logansport (IN) *Pharos-Tribune*
Logansport (IN) *Press*
Long Beach (CA) *Independent*
Long Beach (CA) *Press-Telegram*
Los Angeles (CA) *Sentinel*
Los Angeles (CA) *Times*
Lowell (MA) *Sun*
Lubbock (TX) *Evening Journal*
Mansfield (OH) *News-Journal*
Marion (OH) *Star*
Maryville (MO) *Daily Forum*
Mexia (TX) *News*
Mexico (MO) *Evening Ledger*
Middletown (NY) *Times-Herald*
Moberly (MO) *Monitor-Index*
Modesto (CA) *Bee and News-Herald*
Nebraska (Lincoln) *State Journal*
New Castle (PA) *News*
New York Amsterdam News
New York Daily News
New York Journal-American
New York Post
New York Times
North Adams (MA) *Transcript*
Northwest Arkansas Times
Oakland (CA) *Tribune*
Ogden (UT) *Standard-Examiner*
Oil City (PA) *Blizzard*
Oneonta (NY) *Star*
Paris (TX) *News*
People's Weekly World
Pittsburgh (PA) *Courier*
Portland (ME) *Press Herald*
Portland (ME) *Sunday Telegram and Sunday Press Herald*
Reno (NE) *Evening Gazette*
Richmond (VA) *Afro-American*
St. Louis (MO) *Post-Dispatch*
St. Petersburg (FL) *Times*

Salt Lake (UT) *Tribune*
San Antonio (TX) *Express*
San Antonio (TX) *Light*
San Mateo (CA) *Times*
Spokane (WA) *Statesman-Review*
Statesville (NC) *Landmark*
Stevens Point (WI) *Daily Journal*
Sumner (IA) *Gazette*
Syracuse (NY) *Herald-Journal*
Syracuse (NY) *Post-Standard*
Tipton (IN) *Daily Tribune*
Titusville (PA) *Herald*

Troy (NY) *Times Record*
Tucson (AZ) *Daily Citizen*
Uniontown (PA) *Morning Herald*
Utica (NY) *Observer-Dispatch*
Wall Street Journal
Washington (DC) *Post*
Waterloo (IA) *Daily Courier*
Waukesha (WI) *Daily Freeman*
Winnipeg (MB) *Free Press*
Wisconsin State Journal
Zanesville (OH) *Signal*
Zanesville (OH) *Times Recorder*

PERIODICALS

Agricultural History
Alabama Historical Quarterly
American Heritage
American Political Science Review
Billboard
Business Week
Commonweal
Congressional Record
Counterattack
Current Biography
Fortune
Harper's Magazine
Journal of American History

Journal of Negro History
Life
The Nation
The New Republic
The New Yorker
Newsweek
Phylon Quarterly
Political Science Quarterly
Saturday Evening Post
Time
Vital Speeches of the Day

INTERVIEWS

Bancroft Library, University of California, Berkeley, Regional Oral History Office

Stone, Irving. Interview by Amelia R. Fry, 18 February 1976.

Harry S. Truman Library

Allen, George E. Interview by Jerry N. Hess, Washington, D.C., May 15, 1969.

Batt, William L., Jr. Interview by Jerry N. Hess, Washington D.C., July 26, 1966.

Biemiller, Andrew J. Interview by James R. Fuchs, Washington, D.C., July 29, 1977.

Clifford, Clark M. Interview by Jerry N. Hess, Washington, D.C., April 13, 1971; May 10, 1971.

Daniels, Jonathan. Interview by James R. Fuchs, Raleigh, North Carolina, October 4, 1963.

Draper, Gen. William H., Jr. Interview by Jerry N. Hess, Washington, D.C., January 11, 1972.

Evans, Tom L. Interview by James R. Fuchs, Kansas City, Missouri, September 18, 1963.

Loeb, James I. Interview by Jerry N. Hess, Washington, D.C., June 26, 1970.

Lovett, Robert A. Interview by Richard D. McKinzie and Theodore A. Wilson, New York, 7 July 1971.

Murphy, Charles S. Interview by Jerry N. Hess, Washington, D.C., May 21, 1969.

Nixon, Robert G. Interview by Jerry N. Hess, Bethesda, Maryland, October 16, 1970.

Iowa PBS

Galbraith, John Kenneth. Interview by Jack Shepard, May 22, 2003.

McGovern, George. Interview by John Hyde, Washington, D.C., May 3, 2003.

Seeger, Pete. Interview by Chip Duncan, June 26, 2003.

Smith, Richard Norton. Interview by Chip Duncan, September 10, 2003.

Southern Oral History Program Collection

Thurmond, Senator J. Strom. Interview by James G. Banks, July 1978.

Miscellaneous

Washington-Williams, Essie Mae. Interview by Dan Rather, *60 Minutes*, CBS News, 17 December 2003.

———. Interview by Tavis Smiley, *Tavis Smiley Show*, PBS, 28 January 2005.

CONGRESSIONAL REPORTS AND HEARINGS

U.S. Congress. House. *Report on the C.I.O. Political Action Committee.*78th Cong., 2nd sess. Washington: United States Government Printing Office, 1944.

United States. Congress. House. Committee on Un-American Activities. *Hearings regarding Communist Espionage in the United States Government.* 80th Cong., 2nd sess. Washington: United States Government Printing Office, 1948.

United States. Congress. House. Committee on Un-American Activities. *Communist Activities in the Chicago Area.* 82nd Cong., 2nd sess. Washington: United States Government Printing Office, 1952.

MONOGRAPHS

Romerstein, Herbert. *From Henry Wallace to William Ayers—The Communist and "Progressive" Movements.* Owings (MD): America's Survival, 2008. http://www.usasurvival.org/docs/Wallace_to_Ayers_Communist_Progressive.pdf

DOCUMENTARIES

"The Presidents: Truman."*American Experience*, PBS, 1997.

Index

Note: Page references P1 to P8 denote photographs.